Lecture Notes in Computer Science 10278

Commenced Publication in 1973
Founding and Former Series Editors:
Gerhard Goos, Juris Hartmanis, and Jan van Leeuwen

More information about this series at http://www.springer.com/series/7409

Margherita Antona · Constantine Stephanidis (Eds.)

Universal Access in Human–Computer Interaction

Designing Novel Interactions

11th International Conference, UAHCI 2017
Held as Part of HCI International 2017
Vancouver, BC, Canada, July 9–14, 2017
Proceedings, Part II

 Springer

Editors
Margherita Antona
Foundation for Research
  and Technology – Hellas (FORTH)
Heraklion, Crete
Greece

Constantine Stephanidis
University of Crete and Foundation
  for Research & Technology – Hellas
  (FORTH)
Heraklion, Crete
Greece

ISSN 0302-9743   ISSN 1611-3349 (electronic)
Lecture Notes in Computer Science
ISBN 978-3-319-58702-8   ISBN 978-3-319-58703-5 (eBook)
DOI 10.1007/978-3-319-58703-5

Library of Congress Control Number: 2017940384

LNCS Sublibrary: SL3 – Information Systems and Applications, incl. Internet/Web, and HCI

Printed on acid-free paper

This Springer imprint is published by Springer Nature
The registered company is Springer International Publishing AG
The registered company address is: Gewerbestrasse 11, 6330 Cham, Switzerland

Foreword

The 19th International Conference on Human–Computer Interaction, HCI International 2017, was held in Vancouver, Canada, during July 9–14, 2017. The event incorporated the 15 conferences/thematic areas listed on the following page.

A total of 4,340 individuals from academia, research institutes, industry, and governmental agencies from 70 countries submitted contributions, and 1,228 papers have been included in the proceedings. These papers address the latest research and development efforts and highlight the human aspects of design and use of computing systems. The papers thoroughly cover the entire field of human–computer interaction, addressing major advances in knowledge and effective use of computers in a variety of application areas. The volumes constituting the full set of the conference proceedings are listed on the following pages.

I would like to thank the program board chairs and the members of the program boards of all thematic areas and affiliated conferences for their contribution to the highest scientific quality and the overall success of the HCI International 2017 conference.

This conference would not have been possible without the continuous and unwavering support and advice of the founder, Conference General Chair Emeritus and Conference Scientific Advisor Prof. Gavriel Salvendy. For his outstanding efforts, I would like to express my appreciation to the communications chair and editor of *HCI International News*, Dr. Abbas Moallem.

April 2017   Constantine Stephanidis

HCI International 2017 Thematic Areas and Affiliated Conferences

Thematic areas:

- Human–Computer Interaction (HCI 2017)
- Human Interface and the Management of Information (HIMI 2017)

Affiliated conferences:

- 17th International Conference on Engineering Psychology and Cognitive Ergonomics (EPCE 2017)
- 11th International Conference on Universal Access in Human–Computer Interaction (UAHCI 2017)
- 9th International Conference on Virtual, Augmented and Mixed Reality (VAMR 2017)
- 9th International Conference on Cross-Cultural Design (CCD 2017)
- 9th International Conference on Social Computing and Social Media (SCSM 2017)
- 11th International Conference on Augmented Cognition (AC 2017)
- 8th International Conference on Digital Human Modeling and Applications in Health, Safety, Ergonomics and Risk Management (DHM 2017)
- 6th International Conference on Design, User Experience and Usability (DUXU 2017)
- 5th International Conference on Distributed, Ambient and Pervasive Interactions (DAPI 2017)
- 5th International Conference on Human Aspects of Information Security, Privacy and Trust (HAS 2017)
- 4th International Conference on HCI in Business, Government and Organizations (HCIBGO 2017)
- 4th International Conference on Learning and Collaboration Technologies (LCT 2017)
- Third International Conference on Human Aspects of IT for the Aged Population (ITAP 2017)

Conference Proceedings Volumes Full List

Universal Access in Human–Computer Interaction

Program Board Chair(s): **Margherita Antona
and Constantine Stephanidis, Greece**

- Gisela Susanne Bahr, USA
- João Barroso, Portugal
- Rodrigo Bonacin, Brazil
- Ingo K. Bosse, Germany
- Anthony Lewis Brooks, Denmark
- Christian Bühler, Germany
- Stefan Carmien, Spain
- Carlos Duarte, Portugal
- Pier Luigi Emiliani, Italy
- Qin Gao, P.R. China
- Andrina Granić, Croatia
- Simeon Keates, UK
- Georgios Kouroupetroglou, Greece
- Patrick M. Langdon, UK
- Barbara Leporini, Italy
- Tania Lima, Brazil
- Alessandro Marcengo, Italy
- Troy McDaniel, USA
- Ana Isabel Paraguay, Brazil
- Enrico Pontelli, USA
- Jon A. Sanford, USA
- Vagner Santana, Brazil
- Jaime Sánchez, Chile
- Anthony Savidis, Greece
- Kevin Tseng, Taiwan
- Gerhard Weber, Germany
- Fong-Gong Wu, Taiwan

The full list with the Program Board Chairs and the members of the Program Boards of all thematic areas and affiliated conferences is available online at:

http://www.hci.international/board-members-2017.php

HCI International 2018

The 20th International Conference on Human–Computer Interaction, HCI International 2018, will be held jointly with the affiliated conferences in Las Vegas, NV, USA, at Caesars Palace, July 15–20, 2018. It will cover a broad spectrum of themes related to human–computer interaction, including theoretical issues, methods, tools, processes, and case studies in HCI design, as well as novel interaction techniques, interfaces, and applications. The proceedings will be published by Springer. More information is available on the conference website: http://2018.hci.international/.

General Chair
Prof. Constantine Stephanidis
University of Crete and ICS-FORTH
Heraklion, Crete, Greece
E-mail: general_chair@hcii2018.org

http://2018.hci.international/

Contents – Part II

Non Visual and Tactile Interaction

Gesture and Gaze-Based Interaction

Contents – Part III

Universal Access to Education and Learning

Universal Access to Mobility

Universal Access to Information and Media

Design for Quality of Life Technologies

Contents – Part I

Accessibility and Usability Guidelines and Evaluation

User and Context Modelling and Monitoring and Interaction Adaptation

Sign Language Processing

Evaluation of Animated Swiss German Sign Language Fingerspelling Sequences and Signs

Sarah Ebling[1]([✉]), Sarah Johnson[2], Rosalee Wolfe[2], Robyn Moncrief[2],
John McDonald[2], Souad Baowidan[2], Tobias Haug[3], Sandra Sidler-Miserez[3],
and Katja Tissi[3]

[1] University of Zurich, Zurich, Switzerland
ebling@cl.uzh.ch
[2] DePaul University, Chicago, IL, USA
sarahej101@gmail.com, {wolfe,jmcdonald}@cs.depaul.edu,
{rkelley5,sbaowida}@mail.depaul.edu
[3] University of Applied Sciences of Special Needs Education (HfH),
Zurich, Switzerland
{tobias.haug,katja.tissi}@hfh.ch, sandysidler@gmail.com

Abstract. This paper reports on work in animating Swiss German Sign Language (DSGS) fingerspelling sequences and signs as well as on the results of a study evaluating the acceptance of the animations. The animated fingerspelling sequences form part of a fingerspelling learning tool for DSGS, while the animated signs are to be used in a study exploring the potential of sign language avatars in sign language assessment. To evaluate the DSGS fingerspelling sequences and signs, we conducted a focus group study with seven early learners of DSGS. We identified the following aspects of the animations as requiring improvement: nonmanual features (in particular, facial expressions and head and shoulder movements), (fluidity of) manual movements, and hand positions of fingerspelling signs.

Keywords: Sign language animation · Animation evaluation · Focus group

1 Introduction

Sign language animation, the process of creating a signing avatar, is a young field of research, looking back on about 20 years of existence. In contrast to videos of human signers, sign language animations are capable of providing an anonymous representation of a signer. This minimizes the likelihood of legal implications arising from, e.g., display on the web. Moreover, the content of a sign language animation can typically be modified more easily than that of a self-contained video. Using sign language animation also bears the possibility of tailoring the avatar's appearance (gender, level of formality, etc.) and speed of signing to a user's needs [7].

© Springer International Publishing AG 2017
M. Antona and C. Stephanidis (Eds.): UAHCI 2017, Part II, LNCS 10278, pp. 3–13, 2017.
DOI: 10.1007/978-3-319-58703-5_1

Sign language animation can be used as a part of tools for learning *finger alphabets*, i.e., communication systems associated with sign languages in which dedicated signs are used for each letter of a spoken language[1] word. Figure 1 shows the finger alphabet of Swiss German Sign Language (*Deutschschweizerische Gebärdensprache*, DSGS). Note that it features separate signs for -Ä-, -Ö-, and -Ü- as well as for -CH- and -SCH-. Traditional fingerspelling learning tools display one still image corresponding to the prototypical hand configuration for each letter of a sequence, thereby merely visualizing the holds (static postures) of that sequence. In contrast, sign language animation is capable of accounting for all of the salient information inherent in fingerspelling, namely both holds and transitions (movements).

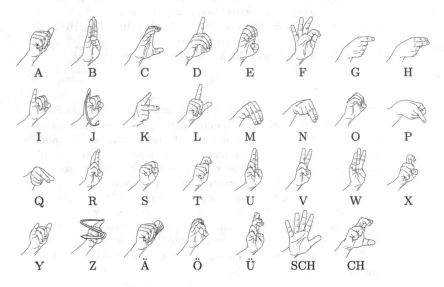

Fig. 1. Finger alphabet of DSGS [3]

We hypothesize that sign language avatars additionally have the potential to increase motivation and interest in young learners of sign language, thus evoking the *Persona effect* [15] that has been observed in pedagogical agents for children in spoken languages. Our aim is to conduct a study in which the items of a Receptive Skills Test (RST) for DSGS [10] are signed by an avatar instead of a human. The DSGS RST is completed by Deaf children between ages four and eleven. The test assesses morphological constructions of DSGS such as spatial verb morphology, negation, number, distribution, and verb agreement through 46 items. In its current form, an item consists of a video of a human signer performing a DSGS sequence, such as BÄR KLEIN ('BEAR SMALL'), APFEL VIELE ('APPLE MANY'), or BUB SCHAUEN-oben ('BOY LOOK-upward').

---

[1] *Spoken language* refers to a language that is not signed, represented as speech or text.

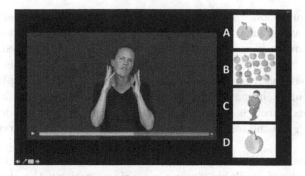

Fig. 2. Item APFEL VIELE ('APPLE MANY') in the DSGS Receptive Skills Test [10]

Test takers are then asked to pick the correct one among three or four images, i.e., the image that best matches the content previously signed. Figure 2 shows the options given for the sequence APFEL VIELE, where B is the targeted response.

The first step in our study designed to gauge the potential of sign language avatars in sign language assessment consists of creating animations of the test items.[2] This paper reports on the results of a study evaluating the acceptance of (1) a subset of these animations and (2) DSGS fingerspelling sequences generated through the DSGS fingerspelling learning tool described above. The study was a focus group conducted with seven early learners[3] of DSGS and a Deaf[4] moderator.

The remainder of this paper is structured as follows: Sect. 2 discusses previous work on sign language animation (Sect. 2.1) and evaluation of sign language animation (Sect. 2.2). Section 3 presents work on animation of DSGS fingerspelling sequences (Sect. 3.1) and signs (Sect. 3.2). Section 4 presents the setup and the results of the focus group study conducted to evaluate the DSGS sign and finger-spelling animations. Finally, Sect. 5 offers a conclusion and an outlook on future work.

2   Previous Work

2.1   Sign Language Animation

Sign language animations are typically created through one of three approaches: animation by hand (traditional animation), motion capturing, or fully synthesized

---

[2] The 46 test items contain 91 unique signs, both lexicalized and productive.

[3] This term refers to Deaf persons who learned DSGS in a family situation from birth or as pre-schoolers/in their very first primary school years. Limiting the subject pool to native signers is generally not an option for DSGS due to the small population upon which one could draw.

[4] It is a widely recognized convention to use the upper-cased word *Deaf* for describing members of the linguistic community of sign language users and the lower-cased word *deaf* for describing the audiological state of a hearing loss [17].

(procedural) animation. Animation by hand consists of manually modelling and posing an avatar character in a purpose-built tool or commercially/freely available software such as Maya, 3ds Max, or Blender. This procedure is highly labor-intensive but generally yields very good results. A signing avatar may also be animated based on information obtained from motion capturing, which involves recording a human's signing. While the quality of sign language animations obtained through motion capturing tends to be high, major drawbacks of this approach are the long calibration time and the extensive postprocessing required.

Both with hand-crafted animation and with animation from motion capturing, the inventory of available signing comprises precisely the sign forms previously created and their combinations. The sublexical structure of the signs is usually not accessible at runtime. This is different for the fully synthesized animation approach: Here, animations are created from a gesture/form notation, which means at execution time there is access to the sublexical structure of signs at whatever level of detail the underlying notation system offers. In case of, e.g., the Hamburg Notation System for Sign Languages (HamNoSys) [9,19], the place of articulation of a sign and other parameters can be adjusted on the fly to take account of coarticulation effects. The fact that fully synthesized animation allows for signs to be modified in context *ad hoc* renders it the most flexible of the three approaches to sign language animation. At the same time, this approach typically results in the lowest quality, as controlling the appearance of all possible sign forms that may be produced from a given notation inventory is virtually impossible [5].

The avatar that is at the core of the work described in this paper, Paula, relies on both hand animation and procedural animation. Paula has been used to develop a fingerspelling learning tool for American Sign Language (ASL) [22,24,28], which served as the basis for the DSGS fingerspelling learning tool described in Sect. 3.1. While individual signs in ASL can be used to represent whole words, fingerspelling allows signers to spell out names, proper nouns, acronyms, and other words for which there are no explicit signs [18]. In a survey of hearing students learning ASL, participants cited the understanding of fingerspelling as the most challenging aspect of learning the language [23]. While a student may learn the alphabet early in their coursework, spelling a word in practice involves not just each individual letter, but also the movement of the transitions between them [1], giving the entire word a unique shape [8]. This was the main motivation in designing the ASL fingerspelling software mentioned above, which includes not just still frames of each letter, but also animated transitions to more accurately replicate native fingerspelling. However, there is no way for an animator to individually recreate every possible word, and real-time procedural generation of the transitions carries a high computational cost. In response to these problems, unique transitions between every possible two-letter combination in the alphabet were hand-animated. This makes it possible to create any arbitrary word with greatly reduced computational requirements, natural movement, and no awkward penetrations between the fingers during the transitions from one shape to the next [26].

Similar to the fingerspelling software, an ASL sentence generator [25] takes individual, hand-animated signs as a motion base, and procedurally transitions between them to form unique sentences using any combination of pre-animated signs. The sentence generator has the additional feature of allowing procedural incorporation of modifiers in order to scale the range of the movement, change its speed, and, in the future, convey a wide variety of emotions. The use of human-generated animation reduces the robotic movements that seem mechanical and awkward to Deaf people, similar to how computer-generated voices sound stilted and unnatural to hearing people. The procedural automation allows for cheap and quick generation of arbitrary sentences and phrases without the exorbitant time and labor costs of hand animation.

2.2 Sign Language Animation Evaluation

No automatic procedure exists for assessing the quality of signing avatars. Sign language animation evaluation studies so far have been carried out in the form of user studies. Here, a distinction is typically made between two concepts: the degree to which a user understands the content of an animation (*comprehension*) and the degree to which he or she accepts it (*acceptance*) [11]. While these two concepts cannot be taken to be independent (most importantly, comprehension is likely to affect acceptance), distinguishing between them makes sense in light of the method used to assess each concept: Comprehension is typically assessed through objective comprehension tasks, while acceptance is commonly assessed via subjective participant judgments. Several studies assessing the comprehension of signing avatars have been carried out [11,12,14,16,20,21]. [13] conducted what is to date the most comprehensive acceptance study; other acceptance studies include those of [4,16,20]. The study introduced in this paper (cf. Sect. 4) represents an acceptance study as well.

3 DSGS Animation

3.1 Animation of DSGS Fingerspelling Sequences

Departing from work on an ASL fingerspelling learning tool (cf. Sect. 2.1), development of a DSGS fingerspelling learning tool has recently begun [6]. Just like with ASL, synthesizing the DSGS finger alphabet consisted of producing hand postures (handshapes with orientations) for each letter of the alphabet (as shown in Fig. 1) and transitions for each pair of letters. Recall that the DSGS finger alphabet contains signs for -Ä-, -Ö-, -Ü-, -CH-, and -SCH-, which are not present in the ASL finger alphabet. In addition, four handshapes, -F-, -G-, -P-, and -T-, are distinctly different from ASL. Further, the five letters -C-, -M-, -N-, -O-, and -Q- have a similar handshape in DSGS, but required smaller modifications, such as a different orientation or small adjustments in the fingers. Hence, the DSGS finger alphabet features 14 out of 30 hand postures that needed modification from the ASL finger alphabet.

We conducted an online study to assess the comprehensibility of the resulting animated DSGS fingerspelling sequences among Deaf and hearing participants; details of this study are given in [6]. Participants saw 22 names of places in Switzerland fingerspelled by either a human or the Paula signing avatar and were asked to type the letters of the word in a text box. The resulting comprehension rate of the signing avatar was highly satisfactory at 90.06%. In the general comments section, one participant encouraged the introduction of speed controls for the signing avatar.

While the participants of the study reported on in [6] were shown isolated videos of animated DSGS fingerspelling sequences, in the meantime, a Desktop interface for Windows similar to the one available for ASL[5] has been developed (cf. Fig. 3). This interface was demonstrated to the participants of the focus group study described in Sect. 4. Among other functionality, the interface offers the possibility of adjusting the speed of fingerspelling, a feature implemented in response to the previous user study.

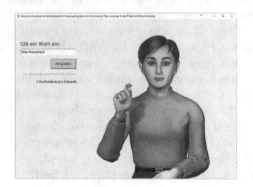

Fig. 3. Fingerspeller interface and presentation in the focus group

3.2   Animation of DSGS Signs

While the ASL and DSGS finger alphabets are similar, there are some key differences between these two languages. For one, DSGS heavily relies on mouthing,[6] i.e., making a mouth movement as if to pronounce a spoken language word but with no vocalization, along with the manual sign for full comprehension. This process seems to be less dominant in ASL. For an initial expansion into DSGS, we animated ten signs using a transcriber software [27] that allows for animating lexical signs by hand in a linguistically informed way: APFEL ('APPLE'), AUTO ('CAR'), BALL ('BALL'), BÄR ('BEAR'), BETT ('BED'), BLEISTIFT ('PENCIL'), BUB ('BOY'), DA ('THERE'), ESSEN ('EAT'), and FRAU ('WOMAN').

---

[5] http://fingerspellingtutor.com/.

[6] According to [2], 80–90% of signs in DSGS are accompanied by a mouthing.

Fig. 4. Animation of DSGS sign BETT ('BED')

The ten signs were from the DSGS RST described in Sect. 1. Figure 4 shows a screenshot of the animation of BETT.

For this preliminary study, we did not include the mouthing motions, as we were more focused on portraying the mechanics of the hands and body as accurately as possible for review by our focus group. We understand the importance of this part of the language, and fully intend to include it in future animations. Other non-manual features such as head and upper-body movements (cf. Fig. 4) were included.

Additionally, the transcriber software described above was expanded to include a wider variety of handshapes based on HamNoSys. This allows users more flexibility in animating a variety of different sign languages, making the overall animation workflow faster and more efficient.

4 Focus Group Study

We conducted a focus group study to evaluate the acceptance of the animated DSGS fingerspelling sequences and signs described in Sects. 3.1 and 3.2. Seven early learners of DSGS between ages 32 and 55 participated in the study, all but one of whom were certified DSGS instructors working for the Swiss Deaf Association. The study took place on the premises of the Swiss Deaf Association in Zurich and was moderated by a Deaf DSGS user not affiliated with our research. The study took 1.5 h.

The focus group consisted of three activities: Firstly, participants were shown three examples of avatars producing continuous signing and asked to evaluate them (cf. Fig. 5). The avatars presented were Paula signing content in ASL, Mira by Braam Jordaan with many features of sign language poetry,[7] and an avatar produced by MocapLab in collaboration with Gallaudet University signing the ASL nursery rhyme "My Three Animals".[8] The avatars had been selected to

---

[7] http://braamjordaan.com/.

[8] http://www.mocaplab.com/projects/gallaudet-university/.

Fig. 5. Three avatars shown: Paula, Mira, and MocapLab/Gallaudet

represent different possible use cases of avatars; this was to stimulate a discussion among the participants as to what additional fields of application of sign language avatars could be. Participants were then presented with ten animated DSGS signs from the DSGS RST (cf. Sect. 3.2) and asked for their feedback. Following this, the moderator demonstrated the DSGS fingerspelling learning tool (cf. Sect. 3.1) and again solicited feedback.

When evaluating the three different avatars (Activity 1), participants stressed the importance of facial expressions, of which they stated Mira had a lot (one participant even deemed it too much), the MocapLab/Gallaudet avatar a bit less, and Paula too little. Mira's expressiveness was the reason why this avatar was not envisioned in a public information setting (e.g., for conveying train or air travel announcements). The participants agreed that Paula would be most suitable for such purposes.

With regard to the ten DSGS signs (Activity 2), participants pointed out the lack of mouthings. Another aspect that came up for the majority of signs shown was facial expression, of which the participants requested there should be more. Additionally, they wished to see more movement of the head, shoulders, and upper body for two of the signs (APFEL, AUTO). Regarding manual activity, mention was made of some movements being executed too abruptly: For example, with BLEISTIFT, the movement back to neutral position at the end of the sign was taken to be too instantaneous, and the initial movement of the hand to the ear in FRAU was judged as being too fast. The handshapes and/or hand positions of some signs were also deemed as needing improvement.

For the fingerspelling learning tool (Activity 3), the participants remarked that many of the handshapes were correct but that some hand positions (e.g., of -P- and -D-) were not. They also commented on the absence of *glides*, i.e., single executions of a letter combined with a horizontal movement to represent double letters (as opposed to two successive executions of the letter). Similarly, they noted that while a single sign for -SCH- existed, the sign was not used in the fingerspelling sequences but instead replaced with S-C-H. Further feedback targeted the height at which some fingerspelling signs were executed. For example, the participants remarked that the signing location of -M-, -N-, and -Q- was too low.

5   Conclusion and Outlook

This paper has reported on work in animating DSGS fingerspelling sequences and signs as well as on the results of a study evaluating the acceptance of the animations. We have described ongoing work in developing a DSGS fingerspelling learning tool and including sign language animations in sign language assessment. As a result of the focus group study we conducted, we identified the following aspects of the animations as being in need of improvement: non-manual features (in particular, facial expressions as well as head and shoulder movements), (fluidity of) manual movements, and hand positions of fingerspelling signs.

Our future work will focus on improving these aspects. In addition, we will implement routines that replace S-C-H and C-H with -SCH- and -CH-, respectively, where appropriate and incorporate glides for double letters in the fingerspeller interface.

Acknowledgments. We are grateful to the Swiss Deaf Association for hosting the focus group.

References

1. Akamatsu, C.: Fingerspelling formulae: a word is more or less than the sum of its letters. In: Proceedings of Sign Language Research 1983, pp. 126–132. Linstok Press, Silver Spring (1985)
2. Boyes Braem, P.: Functions of the mouthing component in the signing of deaf early and late learners of Swiss German Sign Language. In: Brentari, D. (ed.) Foreign Vocabulary in Sign Languages: A Cross-Linguistic Investigation of Word Formation, pp. 1–47. Erlbaum, Mahwah, NJ (2001)
3. Boyes Braem, P.: A multimedia bilingual database for the lexicon of Swiss German Sign Language. Sign Lang. Linguist. 4(1/2), 133–143 (2001)
4. Ebling, S.: Evaluating a Swiss German Sign Language avatar among the deaf community. In: Proceedings of the 3rd International Symposium on Sign Language Translation and Avatar Technology (SLTAT), Chicago, IL (2013). http://www.zora.uzh.ch/85717/1/CAMERA_READY_sltat2013_submission_14.pdf. Accessed 20 Nov 2015
5. Ebling, S.: Automatic translation from German to synthesized Swiss German Sign Language. Ph.D. thesis, University of Zurich (2016)
6. Ebling, S., Wolfe, R., Schnepp, J., Baowidan, S., McDonald, J., Moncrief, R., Sidler-Miserez, S., Tissi, K.: Synthesizing the finger alphabet of Swiss German Sign Language and evaluating the comprehensibility of the resulting animations. In: Proceedings of the 6th Workshop on Speech and Language Processing for Assistive Technologies (SLPAT), Dresden, Germany (2015)
7. Glauert, J.: Animating sign language for deaf people. Lecture held at the University of Zurich, October 9, 2013. Unpublished
8. Groode, J.: Fingerspelling: Expressive and Receptive Fluency (videotape). Dawn Sign Press, San Diego (1992)
9. Hanke, T.: HamNoSys-representing sign language data in language resources and language processing contexts. In: Proceedings of the 1st LREC Workshop on Representation and Processing of Sign Languages, Lisbon, Portugal, pp. 1–6 (2004)

10. Haug, T., Perollaz, R.: Verständnistest Deutschschweizer Gebärdensprache (2015)
11. Huenerfauth, M., Zhao, L., Gu, E., Allbeck, J.: Evaluating American Sign Language generation through the participation of native ASL signers. In: Proceedings of the 9th International ACM SIGACCESS Conference on Computers and Accessibility (ASSETS), Tempe, AZ, pp. 211–218 (2007)
12. Kipp, M., Heloir, A., Nguyen, Q.: Sign language avatars: animation and comprehensibility. In: Vilhjálmsson, H.H., Kopp, S., Marsella, S., Thórisson, K.R. (eds.) IVA 2011. LNCS (LNAI), vol. 6895, pp. 113–126. Springer, Heidelberg (2011). doi:10.1007/978-3-642-23974-8_13
13. Kipp, M., Nguyen, Q., Heloir, A., Matthes, S.: Assessing the deaf user perspective on sign language avatars. In: Proceedings of the 13th International ACM SIGACCESS Conference on Computers and Accessibility (ASSETS), pp. 107–114. Dundee, Scotland (2011)
14. Lefebvre-Albaret, F.: DictaSign deliverable D7.4: prototype evaluation synthesis. Technical report, DictaSign project (2011)
15. Lester, J.C., Converse, S.A., Kahler, S.E., Barlow, S.T., Stone, B.A., Bhogal, R.S.: The persona effect: affective impact of animated pedagogical agents. In: Proceedings of the ACM SIGCHI Conference on Human Factors in Computing Systems (CHI), Atlanta, GA, pp. 359–366 (1997)
16. McDonald, J., Wolfe, R., Moncrief, R., Baowidan, S.: A computational model of role shift to support the synthesis of signed language. In: Presented at the 12th Theoretical Issues in Sign Language Research (TISLR), January 4–7, Melbourne, Australia (2016)
17. Morgan, G., Woll, B.: The development of complex sentences in British Sign Language. In: Morgan, G., Woll, B. (eds.) Directions in Sign Language Acquisition: Trends in Language Acquisition Research, pp. 255–276. John Benjamins, Amsterdam (2002)
18. Padden, C.: The acquisition of fingerspelling by deaf children. In: Fischer, S.D., Siple, P. (eds.) Theoretical Issues in Sign Language Research, pp. 191–210. University of Chicago, Chicago (1991)
19. Prillwitz, S., Leven, R., Zienert, H., Henning, J.: HamNoSys: Version 2.0: An Introductory Guide. Signum, Hamburg (1989)
20. Schnepp, J., Wolfe, R., McDonald, J., Toro, J.: Generating co-occurring facial nonmanual signals in synthesized American sign language. In: Proceedings of the Eighth International Conference on Computer Graphics Theory and Applications (GRAPP), Barcelona, Spain, February 21–24, pp. 407–416 (2013)
21. Smith, R., Nolan, B.: Emotional facial expressions in synthesised sign language avatars: a manual evaluation. Univ. Access Inf. Soc. 15, 567–576 (2016)
22. Toro, J.A., McDonald, J., Wolfe, R.: Fostering better deaf/hearing communication through a novel mobile app for fingerspelling. In: Proceedings of the 14th International Conference on Computers Helping People with Special Needs (ICCHP), Paris, France, pp. 559–564 (2014)
23. Wilcox, S.: The Phonetics of Fingerspelling. John Benjamins, Amsterdam (1992)
24. Wolfe, R., Alba, N., Billups, S., Davidson, M.J., Dwyer, C., Gorman Jamrozik, D., Smallwood, L., Alkoby, K., Carhart, L., Hinkle, D., Hitt, A., Kirchman, B., Lancaster, G., McDonald, J., Semler, L., Schnepp, J., Shiver, B., Suh, A., Young, J.: An improved tool for practicing fingerspelling recognition. In: Proceedings of the International Conference on Technology and Persons with Disabilities, Los Angeles, CA, pp. 17–22 (2006)

25. Wolfe, R., Cook, P., McDonald, J.C., Schnepp, J.: Linguistics as structure in computer animation: toward a more effective synthesis of brow motion in American Sign Language. Sign Lang. Linguist. **14**(1), 179–199 (2013)
26. Wolfe, R., McDonald, J., Davidson, M., Frank, C.: Using an animation-based technology to support reading curricula for deaf elementary schoolchildren. In: Proceedings of the 22nd Annual International Technology and Persons with Disabilities Conference, Los Angeles, CA (2007)
27. Wolfe, R., McDonald, J., Schnepp, J.: An avatar to depict sign language: building from reusable hand animation. In: Presented at the International Workshop on Sign Language Translation and Avatar Technology (SLTAT), January 10–11. Federal Ministry of Labour and Social Affairs, Berlin (2011)
28. Wolfe, R., McDonald, J., Toro, J., Baowidan, S., Moncrief, R., Schnepp, J.: Promoting better deaf/hearing communication through an improved interaction design for fingerspelling practice. In: Antona, M., Stephanidis, C. (eds.) UAHCI 2015. LNCS, vol. 9175, pp. 495–505. Springer, Cham (2015). doi:10.1007/978-3-319-20678-3_48

Sign Search and Sign Synthesis Made Easy to End User: The Paradigm of Building a SL Oriented Interface for Accessing and Managing Educational Content

Eleni Efthimiou$^{(\boxtimes)}$, Stavroula-Evita Fotinea, Panos Kakoulidis, Theodore Goulas,
Athansia-Lida Dimou, and Anna Vacalopoulou

Institute for Language and Speech Processing/ATHENA RC, Athens, Greece
{eleni_e,evita,panosk,tgoulas,ndimou,avacalop}@ilsp.gr

Abstract. Accessibility of electronic content by deaf and hard-of-hearing WWW users is crucially depending on the possibility to acquire information that can be presented in their native sign language (SL), from the vast amounts of text sources being constantly uploaded. Similarly crucial is the ability to easily create new electronic content that can enable dynamic message exchange, covering various communication needs.

Given that during the last decade, there have been created considerable language resources for a number of SLs worldwide, integration of a set of deaf accessibility aids in combination with standard Language Technology (LT) tools for text handling in the various platforms serving tasks of current everyday life, may drastically improve access to Web services by deaf and hard-of-hearing (HoH) populations.

In this paper, we present the example of integration of a set of tools which enable written content accessibility and dynamic student-student/student-teacher interaction via SL, as applied on the official educational content platform of the Greek Ministry of Education for the primary and secondary education levels, exploiting Greek Sign Language (GSL) resources.

Keywords: Web accessibility via SL · SL oriented HCI · Dynamic sign language synthesis · Fingerspelling for search input · Deaf communication · Deaf education · Deaf accessibility tools evaluation

1 Introduction

The development of Web 2.0 technologies has made the WWW a rich source of information to be exploited at business, at all levels of education, and in various communication situations as in the cases of e-Health and e-Government. In parallel, the WWW has become a place where people constantly interact with each other, by posting information (e.g. on blogs or discussion forums), by modifying and enhancing other people's contributions (e.g. in Wikipedia), and by sharing information (e.g. on Facebook and other social networking websites).

However, as effective as these technologies might be to non-native signers, they seem to create considerable difficulties to native signers, since they require a good

© Springer International Publishing AG 2017
M. Antona and C. Stephanidis (Eds.): UAHCI 2017, Part II, LNCS 10278, pp. 14–26, 2017.
DOI: 10.1007/978-3-319-58703-5_2

command and extensive use of the written language. On the other hand, although the cloud receives vast amounts of video uploads daily, SL videos have two major problems: first, they are not anonymous, and second, they cannot be easily edited and reused in the way written texts can.

To address this problem, a number of research efforts [1, 2] have been reported towards making Web 2.0 accessible for SL users by allowing interactions in SL via the incorporation of real time SL technologies. These technologies are based on available monolingual and bilingual resources with emphasis on dynamic production of SL. The signed utterance is presented via a signing avatar (Fig. 1).

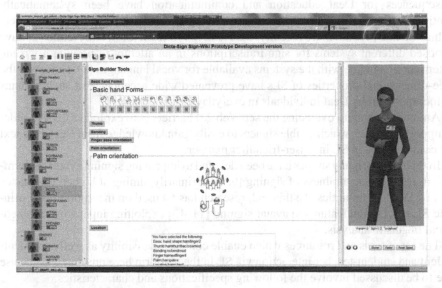

Fig. 1. Sign building and representation environment in the sign-Wiki of the Dicta-Sign demonstrator

In this paper, we attempt to demonstrate that Web content may become more accessible to deaf and hard-of-hearing users by combining a set of language technology tools that have been developed for handling SL and vocal/written language. Such tools may incorporate bilingual and monolingual dictionary look-up and fingerspelling facilities as well as a dynamic SL synthesis environment. The proposed architecture exploits bilingual vocal-SL lexicon resources, monolingual SL resources, and language technology (LT) tools including a tagger and a lemmatizer to handle the written form of the vocal language. In the rest of the paper, we present the different components of a workbench with integrated LT tools and technologies. The result was enabling the use by deaf and HoH users of (a) the official educational content platform of the Greek Ministry of Education for the primary and secondary education levels, and (b) the platform's Graphical User Interface (GUI) characteristics and evaluation procedures. The ultimate aim of this venture was to showcase the accessibility potential of the proposed approach.

2 Integrated Language Technology Tools and Resources

In [3] we extensively discussed the limitations posed by the use of SL videos, while there was also reference to the issues relating to creation of SL resources that are needed to drive SL synthesis engines, along with issues of signing avatar technology and its acceptance by end users. Emphasis was also put on the discussion of various currently implemented interfaces to serve deaf users and suggestions were made as to the tools that would enable better reach to Web content by native signers [3].

The limitations in composing, editing and reusing SL utterances as well as their consequences for Deaf education and communication have been systematically mentioned in the SL literature since the second half of the 20th century. Researchers such as Stokoe [4] and, more recently, the HamNoSyS team [5, 6] and Neidle [7] have proposed different systems for sign transcriptions in an attempt to provide a writing system for SLs in line with the systems available for vocal languages [8]. However, the three-dimensional properties of SLs have prevented wide acceptance of such systems for incorporation by Deaf individuals in everyday practice.

An intuitive way to overcome the set Web 2.0 barriers is to exploit (S)LTs in order to support interfaces which enable signers to easily gain knowledge from electronic text and communicate in SL in a user-friendlier manner.

In this context, many studies have been devoted to improving signing avatar performance in respect to naturalness of signing [9, 10] primarily aiming at higher acceptance rates by Deaf communities. To this end, research has focused on incorporation of principle SL articulation features in avatar signing [11–13] exploiting input from SL theoretical linguistic analysis.

The set of tools and resources which enable content accessibility as well as student-student and student-teacher interaction via SL in the platform here presented as the use case to be discussed involve the following specifications and characteristics:

From the part of SL technologies, the tools integrated to the platform entail:

1 A bilingual dictionary for the language pair Modern Greek (MG) – Greek Sign Language (GSL), linked with the textbooks uploaded in the platform. Word search is possible by:
   1.1 double clicking on the encountered words while reading (Fig. 2);
   1.2 typing the search item in a search box;
   1.3 providing search input by means of a virtual fingerspelling keyboard;
   1.4 copying words and pasting them in the search box. The system then retrieves the correct dictionary entry, irrespective of the inflectional form in the Greek text where originally encountered.
2 A dynamic sign phrase synthesis tool [3], which allows composition of signed content on the fly, according to users' communication needs and makes use of a signing avatar to represent the instantly created content.
3 A virtual fingerspelling keyboard of the Greek alphabet characters and the digits 0–9 that enables search and representation of proper names and various number formations via the set of handshapes corresponding to alphabet characters and digits, thus,

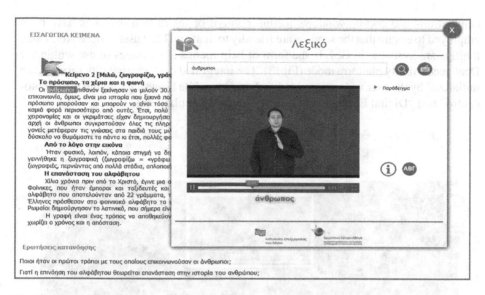

Fig. 2. Association of "unknown" words in a Web text with their equivalent signs by exploitation of the proposed LT toolkit

facilitating accessibility and learning of primarily named entities in all subject areas in the curriculum – from History and Geography to Biology and Mathematics.

4 To further facilitate the presentation and reuse of SL content, a link to the multilingual SL resources of the Dicta-Sign FP7 (http://www.sign-lang.uni-hamburg.de/dicta-sign/portal/) project is also available.

From the part of vocal/written LTs, the platform currently makes use of:

1. A segmentation tool that simply segments strings of characters in a text,
2. A tagger, which runs on segmented items and provides labels with grammar information such as morphological tags and tags for syntactic category, and
3. A lemmatizer that associates each string in text with a lemma, which can be checked for match in the bilingual lexicon database.

The abovementioned tools for handling the lexical items found in Greek written texts are all part of the ILSP language tool suite [14], which has been developed by the Institute and is subject to constant improvements. These tools are necessary for the implementation of the integrated accessibility tools, since MG is a highly inflected language and there are many instances of complete change of the form of a lemma in its different syntactic use environments. This, in general, poses a significant extra load to text comprehension by deaf users, who need to become bilingual in the written form of a highly inflected vocal language. Morphological complexity also makes checking different morphological forms against a lexicon a difficult issue demanding numerous filters and raises the retrieval error risk, unless handled in a systematic way by means of LT tools. In the user interface, the initialization of the integrated services is done through the use of help buttons of appropriate shape and size, while color code conventions and pop-up windows for informative or interaction purposes have been employed to ensure that the services are friendly to deaf and HoH users. Moreover, video tooltips are available in GSL in the form of help menus at all stages of use within the Deaf accessibility platform mode (Fig. 3). The integrated deaf accessibility services are initialized by the user and are provided as Add-Ons while browsing through the "Photo-dentro" and "Digital Educational Content" educational platforms.

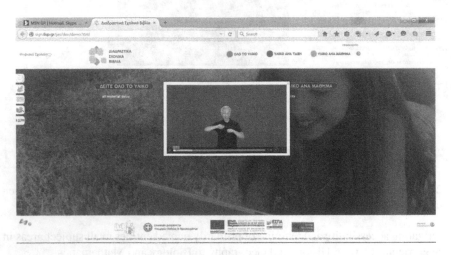

Fig. 3. Platform main page with activated deaf accessibility facilities and instructions in GSL

The integrated tools are run through a web browser with the help of java applets, currently supporting Mozilla Firefox, Chrome and Internet Explorer. The supported operating systems are Microsoft Windows (XP or above) as well as Mac OS X with Safari browser.

3 Workbench with Integrated LT Tools and Technologies

Within the framework of the implementation presented here, the functionalities facili-tating sign search are connected to a look-up environment that can be utilized either in direct link with the viewed text or as an independent dictionary look-up tool activated by demand. The bilingual dictionary, the virtual fingerspelling keyboard and the dynamic sign phrase synthesis tool, described next in more detail, are incorporated in the use case workbench in an interoperable manner in order to support accessibility to text content and communication between platform users [15].

3.1 Bilingual Dictionary: MG-GSL

While browsing through any digital educational text uploaded on the supported educa-tional websites, deaf or HoH users may seek explanation in GSL for any word present in the text. The selected word is then checked against the system's lexicon of signs using any of the methods described in Sect. 2 above to enter a specific query. The unknown word is looked up in the database of correspondences between written lemmas of MG and the respective GSL sign and, if found, users are presented with information regarding the video lemma representation in GSL, examples of use, synonyms (Fig. 4) linked to senses, or expressions linked to lemmas.

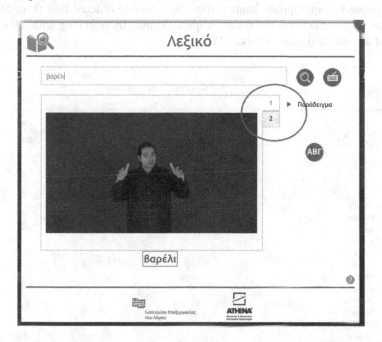

Fig. 4. Presentation of the lemma "barrel", associated with two forms (synonyms) in GSL

The task to be executed, however, is by no means trivial, since in many cases the morphological form of a word in a text differs considerably from the form associated with a headword in a common dictionary, especially in languages with very rich morphology such as MG. Thus, the successful execution of a given query demands an initial processing step of morphological decomposition of the selected word prior to its accurate association with the corresponding entry in the bilingual dictionary, as mentioned in Sect. 2. The search procedure, therefore, entails morphological queries for any given word inserted while it also takes into account any grammatical/semantic differentiation among lemmas in order to filter the search results as, for instance, in the case of the stress position in word sets «θόλος» [th'olos] - «θολός» [thol'os] or semantic differences between two morphologically different types of the same word (e.g. «αφαιρώ» [afer'o]- «αφηρημένος» [afirim'enos]).

The dictionary that supports the accessibility of the textual material currently comprises approximately 10,000 bilingual entries (MG-GSL). A detailed report on its compilation and selection of example sentences along with the methodology followed for the lexicon database creation is provided in [16].

When the use of the dictionary is selected as a standalone platform tool, users may also employ the alphabetically ordered search option. This search option is, in general, considered appropriate for video databases of signs and it has been already applied in some educational and/or e-government internet-based applications [3]. This approach provides the alphabetical ordering of the entailed concepts' written form, allowing the user to choose the appropriate lemma from the available ordered lists (Fig. 5). This method prevents the delay in the system response caused by searching within the entire content of an extended video database [17].

Fig. 5. Alphabetically ordered lemma look-up

In all cases, the information provided incorporates different senses and/or GSL synonym signs with which a MG lexical equivalent may be associated, GSL examples of use for each sense and/or sign available as well as expressions linked to different lemmas.

3.2 Virtual Fingerspelling Keyboard

The fingerspelling keyboard facility comprises a set of virtual keys that correspond to the GSL fingerspelling alphabet. Each key depicts the handshape that represents each letter of the alphabet, while the digits 0–9 are also included. Thus, users can select a sequence of preferred handshapes corresponding to the desired alphanumeric string, while on the screen they can visually inspect the selected sequence being fingerspelled in GSL.

The tool can either run as an external service (Fig. 6) or be interconnected with the lexicon and the dynamic sign synthesis tool as a string input mode of search data (i.e. lemmas). Such tools allow the fingerspelling of proper names [18] and can generally support deaf users while inserting data of the type names, numbers etc. in web forms and also in various other communication situations [19]. Furthermore, when incorporated in the synthetic signing environment, this tool enables the visualization of proper names in the context of a signed utterance and also fingerspelling of "unknown words", so preventing performance failure. The user interface provides help in GSL in the form of a video tooltip.

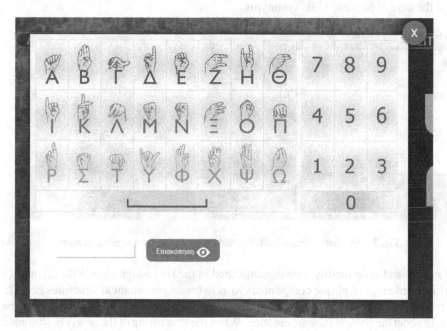

Fig. 6. Characters and digits fingerspelling keyboard activated as a search facility both in the dictionary and the synthetic signing environment

3.3 Dynamic Sign Synthesis Tool

Sign phrase representation is being performed via a virtual signer through the use of a java applet, which runs in the web browser. The user selects the components of the phrase to be synthesized among the available lexical items that are appropriately coded for synthesis (namely, those containing information not visible to users yet important for synthetic representation). The user interface is designed to allow for different word orderings of the phrase to be synthesized, while the signing phrase may, at this point, consist of up to four components. The composition of new synthetic sign phrases is achieved by selecting the desired phrase components from a list of available, appropriately annotated lexical items [6, 7]. The HamNoSys notation system has been used for the phonological annotation of sign lemmas, along with features for the non-manual activity present in sign formation, while the UEA avatar engine [20] has been used to perform signing. End users interact with the system via a simple search-and-match interface to compose their desired phrases. Phrase components are marked by different color frames indicating which items in the phrase are signed and which are fingerspelled. Users select the desired element by clicking on it and the respective GSL gloss is then included in the sign stream/phrase to be performed by the avatar (Fig. 7). In case a word is not present in the synthesis lexicon, users are provided with the option to fingerspell it. This option proves especially helpful in the case of incorporating proper names in the signed phrase. Furthermore, search results may provide options among which to choose as in the case of possible GSL synonyms.

Fig. 7. Synthetic phrase building and presentation by a signing avatar

A drag-and-drop facility, first demonstrated in the Dicta-Sign sign-Wiki [2], allows multiple orderings of phrase components so as to create grammatical structures in GSL. Verifying user choices is important at any stage of this process, so that users can be certain about the content they are creating. When the structuring of the newly built signed phrase is completed (Fig. 7), this phrase is performed by a signing avatar for final verification. Users may select to save, modify, or delete each phrase they have built. They may keep the saved phrases or parts of them for further use depending on their communication needs (e.g. a non-native signer could make use of this utility for language learning purposes).

Since the mainstream school environment is not usually familiar with SL, the sign synthesis tool may also be used by SL illiterate individuals. Thus, in the current implementation, a template-based GSL grammar guide is incorporated in the sign synthesis environment to help non-signers compose grammatically correct GSL utterances. This guide contains a list of core GSL grammatical structures relating to sentence formation, negation, question, and noun-phrase formation, as well as the use of GSL-specific particles (such as the "pa" particle, used to indicate completed actions).

4   Case Study Evaluation

The platform described in this paper underwent different types of evaluation in three stages:

The first stage included a thorough internal technical evaluation process relating to the success of the integration of tools and their effective use in the platform itself. This was carried out by experts on each of the areas involved, who had to evaluate not only each tool individually but also the platform as an integrated whole. Technical evaluation run in parallel to integration work and, in its final stage, focused on issues of robustness and performance stability of the virtual machine (VM) accommodating the platform in the cloud, while receiving huge numbers of parallel requests.

The second evaluation stage involved a small team of five GSL experts, including three native GSL signers, who tried out the platform as end users, acting as informants to provide valuable feedback on the usability and content of the platform. All team members kept a logbook of the part of the content they checked with notes on vocabulary content, GSL example phrases and avatar performance of the signs. The team of experts met regularly to discuss their findings and propose corrections and improvements which were then incorporated in the platform's database. The same team was consulted regarding the design of the platform GUI.

Finally, the last stage of the evaluation involved real end users themselves. This was carried out during a series of visits at the Deaf School of Argiroupoli, one of the largest Deaf schools established in the area of Athens, including both primary and secondary educational settings. The evaluation was carried out in the form of pilot uses by both teachers and pupils. After becoming familiar with the platform and having used it for an amount of time which allowed them to navigate it with ease, users were asked to provide comments based on their experience with the platform. The comments were collected in the form of subjective evaluation questionnaires with questions on the GUI structure, the provided content and users' opinions on synthetic signing. The comments that were collected were then studied, grouped (e.g. comments about content or usability, comments with teaching and/or learning implications) and analyzed by the developing team as a means to make possible improvements or additions/extensions.

In general, the platform was positively scored by both user groups. Young pupils tended to find it especially amusing to be able to synthesize signed phrases, while they were pleased with the avatar performance. This result indicates a radical change in signers' attitude, since previous experience had shown that users are rather concerned as regards SL performance by avatars. The subjective evaluation results presented high scores for the option to compose one's own wished utterances, which may be one of the reasons that can explain the positive attitude towards avatar performance.

More particularly, search of unknown written content with direct linking to GSL lexicon presentation was among the features which received particularly high scores in respect to their usability as an educational support mechanism.

The most striking result from the part of the teachers was that they considered the platform as a very helpful mechanism to be exploited in bilingual deaf education. To this end, they pointed out that they would like to also see information on grammatical gender of the Greek lemmas in parallel of viewing the Greek equivalent to the presented

GSL sign in the vocabulary display window. Finally, the fingerspelling facility was accepted by all users as something natural in the school environment, while several users noted that there are too many proper names to be memorized.

5   Conclusion

Based on the pilot use of the platform and the analysis of user evaluation results, several additions or improvements can be foreseen. For instance, one of the options considered for inclusion in future extensions of the platform is that of search by handshape, so that users will not have to be restricted by using words while searching. This will be utilized following the appropriate grouping of these handshapes within the alphabetical index of the lexical content, so as to limit the number of the search items that are returned by the system.

The composition of synthetic signing phrases may facilitate communication over the Internet and it can also be crucial for class and group work, since it allows for the direct participation and dynamic linguistic message exchange, in a manner similar to what hearing individuals do when writing.

The emerging technology of sign synthesis opens new perspectives with respect to the participation of deaf and HoH individuals in Internet-based everyday activities, including access and retrieval of information and anonymous communication.

Moreover, if advanced SL technology tools and SL resources are combined with standard LT tools and resources for vocal/written language, they may provide workbench environments to radically change the deaf accessibility landscape in the next period. For example, one may envisage the incorporation of sign synthesis environments in machine translation (MT) applications targeting SLs and, thus, opening yet new perspectives as regards their potential and usability [21].

Acknowledgements.   The research leading to these results has received funding from POLYTROPON project (KRIPIS-GSRT, MIS: 448306) and is based on insights, technologies, and language resources initially developed within the Dicta-Sign project (FP7-ICT, grant agreement n°: 231135).

References

1. Dicta-Sign project, Deliverable D8.1: Project demonstrator: Sign-Wiki, February 2012. http://www.dictasign.eu/attach/Main/PubliclyAvailableProjectDeliverables/DICTA-SIGN_Deliverable_D8.1.pdf
2. Efthimiou, E., Fotinea, S.-E., Hanke, T., Glauert, J., Bowden, R., Braffort, A., Collet, C., Maragos, P., Lefebvre-Albaret, F.: The dicta-sign wiki: enabling web communication for the deaf. In: Miesenberger, K., Karshmer, A., Penaz, P., Zagler, W. (eds.) ICCHP 2012, Part II. LNCS, vol. 7383, pp. 205–212. Springer, Heidelberg (2012)
3. Efthimiou, E., Fotinea, S.-E., Goulas, T., Kakoulidis, P.: User friendly interfaces for sign retrieval and sign synthesis. In: Antona, M., Stephanidis, C. (eds.) UAHCI 2015. LNCS, vol. 9176, pp. 351–361. Springer, Cham (2015). doi:10.1007/978-3-319-20681-3_33
4. Stokoe, W.C.: Sign Language Structure, 2nd edn. Linstock Press, Silver Spring MD (1978)

5. Prillwitz, S., Leven, R., Zienert, H., Hanke, T., Henning, J.: HamNoSys. Version 2.0. Hamburg Notation System for Sign Language: An Introductory Guide, Signum, Hamburg (1989)
6. Hanke, T.: HamNoSys - representing sign language data in language resources and language processing contexts. In: Proceedings of 1st Workshop on Representing and Processing of Sign Languages (LREC-2004), Paris, France, pp. 1–6 (2004)
7. Neidle, C.: SignStream™: a database tool for research on visual-gestural language. In: Bergman, B., Boyes-Braem, P., Hanke, T., Pizzuto, E. (eds.) Sign Transcription and Database Storage of Sign Information, special issue of Sign Language and Linguistics, vol. 4(1), pp. 203–214 (2002)
8. Pizzuto, E., Pietrandrea, P.: The notation of signed texts: Open questions and indications for further research. Sign Lang. Linguist. 4(1/2), 29–45 (2001)
9. McDonald, J., Wolfe, R., Wilbur, R.B., Moncrief, R., Malaia, E., Fujimoto, S., Baowidan, S., Stec, J.: A New tool to facilitate prosodic analysis of motion capture data and a datadriven technique for the improvement of avatar motion. In: Proceedings of 7th Workshop on the Representation and Processing of Sign Languages: Corpus Mining (LREC-2016), Portorož, Slovenia, pp. 153–158, 28 May 2016
10. Huenerfauth, M.: Evaluation of a psycholinguistically motivated timing model for animations of american sign language. In: 10th International ACM SIGACCESS Conference on Computers and Accessibility (ASSETS 2008), pp. 129–136 (2008)
11. Adamo-Villani, N., Wilbur, Ronnie B.: ASL-Pro: American sign language animation with prosodic elements. In: Antona, M., Stephanidis, C. (eds.) UAHCI 2015. LNCS, vol. 9176, pp. 307–318. Springer, Cham (2015). doi:10.1007/978-3-319-20681-3_29
12. Huenerfauth, M.: A linguistically motivated model for speed and pausing in animations of american sign language. ACM Trans. Access. Comput. 2(2), 9 (2009)
13. Wolfe, R., Cook, P., McDonald, J.C., Schnepp, J.: Linguistics as structure in computer animation: toward a more effective synthesis of brow motion in American sign language. Sign Lang. Linguist. 14(1), 179–199 (2011)
14. Prokopidis, P., Georgandopoulos, B., Papageorgiou, C.: A suite of NLP tools for Greek. In: The 10th International Conference of Greek Linguistics. Komotini, Greece (2011)
15. Efthimiou, E., Fotinea, S.-E., Goulas, T., Kakoulidis, P., Dimou, A.-L., Vacalopoulou, A.: A complete environment for deaf learner support in the context of mainstream education. In: Proceedings of the Conference Universal Learning Design, vol. 5, Linz, 13–15 July, pp. 35–44 (2016). ISSN 1805-3947
16. Efthimiou, E., Fotinea, S.-E., Dimou, A.-L., Goulas, T., Karioris, P., Vasilaki, K., Vacalopoulou, A., Pissaris, M., Korakakis, D.: From a sign lexical database to an SL golden corpus – the POLYTROPON SL resource. In: Proceedings of 7th Workshop on the Representation and Processing of Sign Languages: Corpus Mining (LREC-2016), Portorož, Slovenia, pp. 63–68, 28 May 2016
17. Fotinea, S.-E., Efthimiou, E.: Tools for Deaf accessibility to an eGOV environment. In: Miesenberger, K., Klaus, J., Zagler, W., Karshmer, A. (eds.) ICCHP 2008. LNCS, vol. 5105, pp. 446–453. Springer, Heidelberg (2008)
18. Ebling, S., Wolfe, R., Schnepp, J., Baowidan, S., McDonald, J., Moncrief, R., Sidler-Miserez, S., Tissi, T. Synthesizing the finger alphabet of Swiss German Sign Language and evaluating the comprehensibility of the resulting animations. In: 6th Workshop on Speech and Language Processing for Assistive Technologies (SLPAT), pp. 10–13 (2015)

19. Wolfe, R., McDonald, J., Toro, J., Baowidan, S., Moncrief, R., Schnepp, J.: Promoting better deaf/hearing communication through an improved interaction design for fingerspelling practice. In: Antona, M., Stephanidis, C. (eds.) UAHCI 2015. LNCS, vol. 9175, pp. 495–505. Springer, Cham (2015). doi:10.1007/978-3-319-20678-3_48
20. Glauert, J., Elliott, R.: Extending the SiGML notation - a progress report. In: Second International Workshop on Sign Language Translation and Avatar Technology (SLTAT-2011), Dundee, UK (2011)
21. Efthimiou, E., Fotinea, S.-E., Goulas, T., Dimou, A.-L., Kouremenos, D.: From grammar based MT to post-processed SL representations. In: Wolfe, R., Efthimiou, E., Glauert, J., Hanke, T., McDonald, J., Schnepp, J. (eds.) Special issue: recent advances in sign language translation and avatar technology, Universal Access in the Information Society (UAIS) Journal, vol 15, pp. 499–511. Springer, Heidelberg (2016)

Synthesizing Sign Language by Connecting Linguistically Structured Descriptions to a Multi-track Animation System

Michael Filhol[✉], John McDonald, and Rosalee Wolfe

DePaul University, Chicago, IL, USA
michael.filhol@limsi.fr, {jmcdonald,wolfe}@cs.depaul.edu

Abstract. Animating sign language requires both a model of the structure of the target language and a computer animation system capable of producing the resulting avatar motion. On the language modelling side, AZee proposes a methodology and formal description mechanism to build grammars of Sign languages. It has mostly assumed the existence of an avatar capable of rendering its low-level articulation specifications. On the computer animation side, the Paula animator system proposes a multi-track SL generation platform designed for realism of movements, programmed from its birth to be driven by linguistic input.

This paper presents a system architecture making use of the advantages of the two research efforts that have matured in recent years to the point where a connection is now possible. This paper describes the essence of both systems and describes the foundations of a connected system, resulting in a full process from abstract linguistic input straight to animated video. The main contribution is in addressing the trade-off between coarser natural-looking segments and composition of linguistically relevant atoms.

Keywords: Sign language · Computational linguistics · Computer animation · Avatar

1 Introduction

Being a comparatively young field of research, Sign Language (SL) linguistics is still one of lively debate more than a set of tested and established scientific theories. Linguistic features and properties, for which a wide theoretical consensus exists, are not numerous. Most propositions to formalize SLs remain in question, including the most basic premises of language studies such as the nature or even existence of lexical units and a phonological level [1–3].

Computer generation is therefore a goal located between two potentially unfortunate choices. One would be to choose a set of description formalisms arbitrarily. The other would be to keep playing back recorded (e.g. with motion capture) or hand-crafted (drawn) data with no model of it at all, which would never allow or foster content editing tasks. This paper presents our first exploration of a way forward between those two problematic paths. It combines a language description model set on making as few assumptions as possible about language structure, and an animation system built on the

© Springer International Publishing AG 2017
M. Antona and C. Stephanidis (Eds.): UAHCI 2017, Part II, LNCS 10278, pp. 27–40, 2017.
DOI: 10.1007/978-3-319-58703-5_3

principle that the language description should drive the animation while making as few assumptions and limitations on how language processes can combine to affect avatar motion.

2   The AZee Language Description

The initial goal of the AZee framework was to enable formal description, without assuming any of the still debated hypotheses, especially when they would lay the foundations of the entire system.

For example, all formal approaches to NLP assume not only a syntactic level of description but also a clear-cut and finite list of categories (e.g. N, V, Adj…), and a fixed mapping from a set of known lexical units to those categories. Whereas, the nature, relevance or even existence of such categories and a syntactic level are not agreed on when considering Sign Languages.

To enable SL description and synthesis without unwisely categorizing language objects, the AZee model proposed to fall back on three very weak linguistic assumptions before formalizing its visible features [4], which are explained in turn below.

Language productions create observable forms carrying intended meaning. Observable *forms* are visible states and movements of any of the language's articulators, and synchronisation features between them. For example, A, B and C below are all visible form descriptors.

> A: "eyelids closed"
> B: "left fingertip in contact with left-hand corner of mouth"
> C: "orient palm downwards"

When two or more articulations are involved on a shared time line, synchronisation constraints between them such as "B starts before A ends" or "C is fully contained in A" are also form descriptors.

AZee calls a *function* any meaning that could be associated with such forms, whether intended (when the forms are produced) or interpreted (when the forms are perceived). For example, D, E and F are functions in this sense.

> D: "house" (as a concept carried by this word in English)
> E: "pejorative judgement on [person/object]"
> F: "[date & time] form the context of [event]"

Systematic links between the two are what specifies the language. The idea behind this assumption is that language is a system, i.e. is governed by rules, shared between the users of the language, and that an experimental approach can identify. So we define the modelling problem as one of finding systematic associations between forms and functions. In other words, AZee proposes to capture every:

- invariant combination of forms observed for the occurrences of an identified function, which yields a *production rule* that can be animated by SL synthesis software;

- function consistently interpreted from the occurrences of a given form, which yields an *interpretation rule* that can support recognition software.

  With our objective of synthesis, the former rule type is the one we will be referring to in this paper.

Languages allow for compositional structures. Compositionality in language is an essential premise of all language studies, admittedly already assumed in both sections above since they refer to "combinations" of forms and "pieces" of the meaning. This is why AZee allows for rule parametrisation, whereby a structure is defined as a process applied to its arguments. Comparably to common formal grammars, it also allows recursion.

These assumptions have two noteworthy corollaries:

- **Multi-linearity**: allowing to describe any sort of form combination, enrolling multiple articulators and defining potentially complex synchronisation patterns calls for the ability to partition and layer articulation tracks on top of one another, like a music score arranges multiple instrument productions on a single time line.
- **No functional partitioning of the articulator set**: any form feature, articulation or synchronisation constraint can be associated with a function if systematically observed, and a single articulator can take part in many different functions.

These are novel properties for a formal model describing SL, which we have argued were an advantage over those generally used to this day [5]. For example, the wide-spread standard HamNoSys [6] relies primarily on manual activity as the vector for the lexical function, and builds SL utterances as a strings of juxtaposed lexical units, which makes it mostly linear.

The AZee framework proposes a methodology to identify, and a language to formalise, production rules turning interpretable functions into the forms to articulate, and parametrise them to account for rule composition. Every rule is a <H, P, f(P)> triplet:

- H is the rule **header**, usually named after the function it carries, e.g. "house";
- P is a list of **parameters** on which both the interpretation and the form might depend, e.g. the location of the house;
- f(P) is a description of the **form** to produce if the rule is applied and given its necessary parameters, including all necessary and sufficient articulations and synchronisations, e.g. finger extension, duration of contact, etc. (by analogy with production rules in formal grammars, we call this part the *right-hand side* of the rule, RHS henceforth).

For example in LSF, expression of non-subjectivity in a measure, estimate or judgement X (in the sense that the speaker reckons X is generally not disputed), requires that lips be moved forward over the time used to sign X, see [1]. This yields a rule:

- header: "non-subjectivity";
- parameters: X = the estimated value or judgement;
- RHS: see box diagram in Fig. 1, and the lip form to produce in Fig. 2.

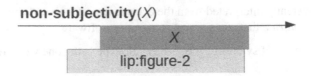

non-subjectivity(*X*)

Fig. 1. RHS box diagram for "non-subjectivity"

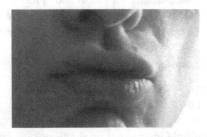

Fig. 2. Lip form used in RHS of "non-subjectivity"

Rules being combinable, any rule's production can be used in place of a parameter for another rule. For example, consider the LSF rule "good", named after the English word for its meaning, with no parameters and whose RHS results in the fixed manual form in Fig. 3. One can use the product of this rule as parameter *X* for "non-subjectivity", nesting the former function inside the latter in an AZee expression:

(E1) non-subjectivity(good())

This *composes* the meaning of "generally deemed good", and directly *produces* the resulting form (Fig. 4) by combining the RHS of the invoked rules, which results in a multi-track time-line specification of the full arrangement. In the case of (E1), this means

Fig. 3. Manual form for "good"

layering the lip pout of Fig. 2 over the manual form of Fig. 3. We call the resulting arrangement a sign score.

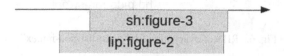

Fig. 4. Resulting score for (E1)

An AZee expression is generally represented by a tree structure, called a functional tree, whose nodes are the contained rules' headers used in the expression, and in which node A has child nodes B_i, if B_i are the arguments of A in the expression. The tree for our simple expression (E1) is:

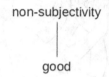

We give another example, of a more complex tree below, for expression (E2):

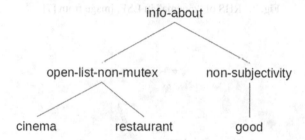

(E2) info-about(open-list-non-mutex(cinema(), restaurant()), non-subjectivity(good()))

where:

- "info-about" has parameters A and B, carries function "B is the information given about A" [4] and has the RHS of Fig. 5;

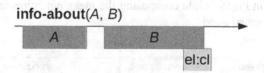

Fig. 5. RHS of "info-about"

- "open-list-non-mutex" has any number of parameters Ei, carries the function of itemising every Ei to form a non-exhaustive list of non-mutually exclusive items, and whose RHS is the succession in time of a Fig. 6 for each Ei;

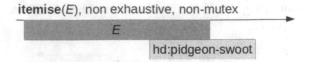

Fig. 6. RHS of every item for "open-list-non-mutex"

- "cinema" and "restaurant" have an optional point parameter each for location, carry the respective concepts they are named after in English, and have the manual RHSs illustrated in pictures Figs. 7 and 8.

Fig. 7. RHS of "cinema" in LSF, image from [7]

Fig. 8. RHS of "restaurant" in LSF, image from [7]

Layering all the RHS forms contained in the rules invoked in the expression, (E2) results in the score in Fig. 9, while composing the meaning: "cinema[s], restaurant[s], etc. are generally deemed good".

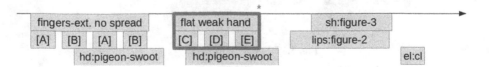

Fig. 9. Resulting score for (E2)

The hope from there is that there exists a set of rules able to cover all language productions by combination, and that it remains small enough to be acceptable as a grammar model.

3 The Paula Animation System

Animating signed languages with an avatar is an ongoing challenge with difficulties arising both from the nature of human motion and the requirements of the input linguistic model. The flexibility and multi-track nature of the AZee description requires a commensurate level of flexibility in an animation system. An animation system such as [8], which is based on the HamNoSys and SiGML representations, scripts animation in a sequential manner and would present many challenges in connecting to AZee. The Paula sign synthesis system [9] provides a multi-track animation system that resembles AZee's representation. This section explores the nature of computer animation as it relates to sign synthesis, and provides an overview of the Paula system.

Synthesizing sign directly from linguistic descriptions that specify key poses is well known to create robotic motion, but does have the advantage of being able to convey any utterance that can be encoded. Several other options for human character animation are also available, including traditional keyframe, procedural and motion-capture based animation. Each of these has distinct advantages and challenges when applied to the animation of signed languages.

Traditional hand-crafted key frame techniques rely on an animator for the composition of the movements of the avatar. The movements are controlled by setting key postures and interpolation data [9]. Depending on the skill of the artist, the resulting animations can be extremely natural and appealing, with the advantage that the sparse nature of the keyframe data can be relatively easy to edit, modify and connect together to build animations from individual segments [10]. The main disadvantage of hand-crafted keyframe animation is the high cost of animator time and the fact that new animations cannot be produced at will based on linguistic descriptions such as AZee.

Motion capture can produce some of the most realistic animation on an avatar since it is recording all of the subtleties of human motion. It can also be an invaluable tool for studying the motion of signers. Mocap recordings have provided insight into many aspects of sign including prosody and ambient non-linguistic motion [11, 12].

Mocap does come with challenges that make it difficult to use in a flexible sign synthesis system. First, motion capture can be nearly as costly to record and clean as hand-crafted animation is to produce [13]. It relies heavily on clean-up artists to both remove ambient noise in the system [12] and also to fill in segments that are missing due to occluded sensors [14]. Second, the simple fact that mocap records all of the small details of human motion makes it challenging to stitch mocap recordings together in a natural way.

Another challenge with motion capture from a synthesis perspective is that the sheer detail and data density can often record more than we actually want when trying to layer linguistic forms. A motion capture clip will have all of the linguistic relevant forms (the ones meant to be described by the AZee framework) the signer is expressing baked in with all other observable forms, and swapping out only part of the effects on a set of joints for a different form will be akin to attempting to remove the sugar from a baked cake to try to replace it with honey. In contrast, a skilled animator with knowledge of sign language structure can produce animations which are very clean in their expression of the linguistic parameters of the utterance. This facilitates layering linguistic processes in synthesized utterances.

Finally, procedural techniques in animation model the movements of the body mathematically and are useful for synthesis in several situations including:

- Providing time saving utilities for keyframe animation [15]. Such tools can shorten the time that animators need to spend in fine tuning details of the animation and reduce the cost of this form of animation.
- Modelling the motion for linguistic forms that affect specific parts of the body [16]. Such processes can be provided with a set of parameters to tune the motion to the linguistic form.

In addition, procedural techniques can be used to produce non-linguistic forms that nevertheless increase legibility of sign synthesis by adding carefully tuned procedural noise to an avatar's joints to simulate the ambient motion that all human signers exhibit even when still or holding a pose [12].

In short, different animation techniques are useful or appropriate for different situations, and the Paula animation system is designed to leverage multiple animation techniques and capitalize on each technique's strengths. It strives to use coarser hand-animated blocks to increase the naturalness of the motion while leveraging procedural blocks to both increase the naturalness of the motion and layer additional linguistic functions over the base movement. The Paula animation system is thus a multi-level

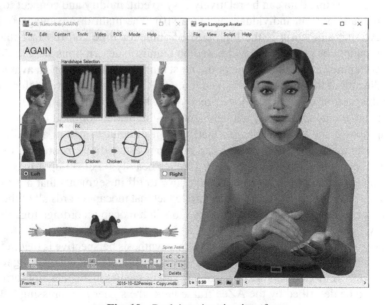

Fig. 10. Paula's animation interface

hybrid system that strives to strike a balance between flexibility and naturalness in the avatar's motion through two components.

The first component is a set of hand-crafted animations built in a sign transcriber that resembles a traditional animation package, but with controls tied to the linguistic components of sign language, see Fig. 10. This component allows the animation of basic lexical signs and other animation components that rely on artist-driven key-frame techniques [9].

The artist's work is augmented by procedural techniques such as a spine assist computation that augments the forward and inverse kinematics controls on the model's arms to move the torso in a natural way, thus reducing work for the artist [10]. Another important aspect of these controls and procedural techniques is that they help assure that animations encode as many linguistic parameters as possible and are as sparse, i.e. contain as few "key postures", as possible to enable easier editing and combining of animations.

The second component of the Paula system composes complete signed utterances. The system structures signed language animation as a collection of parallel tracks. Each track contains a sequence of animation blocks which can be timed and synchronized arbitrarily, much like a sound recording.

Unlike traditional animation systems, each track can affect entire sections of the avatar's anatomy, and multiple tracks can affect the same anatomy without disruption or conflict. For example, in the example in Fig. 11, the system animates several overlapping processes present in (E2). The base lexical items previously animated are combined with a collection effects that influence the face, torso and head. For more details on the techniques used by this system see [9].

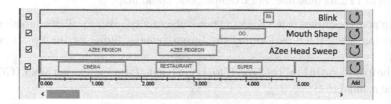

Fig. 11. Paula's sentence generation component

In summary, the Paula animation system provides a flexible framework in which

1. Animations can be built from a sequence of tracks, each of which contains a sequence of animation blocks.
2. Tracks can manipulate any part of the avatar's anatomy, and multiple tracks can manipulate the same anatomy.
3. Track blocks can use a variety of animation techniques including key-frame and procedural techniques. In the future we plan to support other techniques such as motion capture and synthesis directly from linguistic input parameters.

4 Appropriateness of the Two Systems for Connection

As we have explained, Paula implements a time line of parallel tracks, on which timed animation blocks are placed so that performing the tracks simultaneously produces a full Sign Language utterance. The animation blocks on the time line have so far mainly been filled with:

- hand-crafted animations, more or less computer-assisted at the time of creation but ultimately fixed to be played back;
- procedural specifications, i.e. parametrised descriptions directly producing articulations, e.g. extent and duration of mouth aperture or position of a hand in space.

In the Paula system, virtually any contents can fill an animation block, as long as it specifies an articulation.

On the AZee side, by construction, a node in a functional tree can only exist if a production rule was identified, i.e. together with a parametrised description of a form to produce (the rule's RHS). This RHS mixes *invariant descriptors* (fixed articulations like the lip pout in "non-subjectivity") with *parameter dependencies* like X in the same rule, usually containing more *function calls*. In any case, it always results in a score of synchronised parallel blocks, containing the layered fixed articulations contained in the RHS terms of the input expression.

In short, AZee provides with a mechanism that turns any functional tree into a resulting score that is similar to the internal animation format of the Paula animation system. We propose to take advantage of this by mapping every fixed form descriptor to a Paula animation block. This way, any resulting score from AZee would be trivially translated to a Paula time line. For example, one could map:

- the lip pout descriptor in the RHS of "non-subjectivity" over to a Paula mouth shape animation block [OO] performing the lip movement, fitting on the lip articulator track;
- and the fixed form in Fig. 3 of "good" to, say, a hand-crafted animation block [GOOD] on the manual track.

Expression (E1) generates a Paula timeline with [OO] and [GOOD] directly in place. And similarly for (E2) if all blocks of the resulting score in Fig. 9 is mapped to a Paula block.

This proposition allows to consider full synthesis of Sign Language animations straight from semantically-loaded linguistic expressions. We emphasise that it is possible mostly thanks to the fact that the two corollaries of AZee's axioms were assumed in the design of Paula from the start. That is, both systems use parallel tracks and free block synchronisation, with no need to project unit composition a 1D time axis or split the tracks early in the process.

However, linguistically meaningful (i.e. systematically interpretable) compositions in SL are meant to be accounted for in AZee, even within an RHS. For example, the form for "restaurant" in LSF involves an iconic weak hand shape reference to a flat surface, in this case of a waiter's notepad (see Fig. 8). This flat palm and finger arrangement being interpretable in other contexts the same way, good AZee practice would be to incorporate a function call "flat surface" in the RHS of "restaurant".

This basically captures the morphemic function of the hand shape, and is a token of AZee's flexibility as it can capture any sort of linguistic function in any sort of context. This has the power of accounting for as much compositionality of the language as possible. But in our circumstance of generating realistic animations, we understand that this proposition leads us to generate and combine many low-level animation blocks, which we know leads to robotic gestures, and is generally unacceptable for final rendering [17]. Thus, the connection between the two systems is guided by the following principle:

Guiding principle: The coarser the basic animation blocks, the more natural the final animation.

To generate coarser elements and honour this principle, we have to avoid processing the deeply nested AZee parts, and recognise subtrees for which we could have Paula blocks available, whether as pre-recorded natural-looking animations or as procedures defined on the Paula side.

For example, function "resto" applied with no arguments, represented by the simple one-node subtree, always generates the same form, namely that in the picture in Fig. 8 and enclosed in the thick box (*) in Fig. 9. If we have that sign recorded, we can shortcut the AZee production rule and avoid reading and developing its RHS (incl. its flat weak hand description). We may play back the recorded form directly from the recognised subtree, which allows for a natural looking play back of the whole rule's RHS. Generalising this, an alternative solution is to match Paula animation blocks from full AZee expressions instead of just the basic AZee form descriptors. Applied to our first example (E1), this causes the system to search for a Paula block ready for play-back and meaning "generally deemed good".

Clearly, pushing the principle to the extreme rapidly goes out of scale. There is no formal limit against wishing for direct Paula matches for higher-level subtrees, or indeed for entire inputs like the full expression (E2), which would require an infinite number of recorded forms. So, we need some counter-balance.

We thus propose to prefer coarse building blocks when they are available, but allow the system to fall-back on finer pieces otherwise. Therefore, we propose to create mappings to Paula animation blocks from both of the following sets:

- a subset of all possible AZee expressions;
- the complete set of basic AZee form descriptors.

From any AZee input, we only then need to read the functional tree from the root down, try matching the full subtree against the inventory of available Paula blocks at every step (giving preference to the taller tree matches when they exist), and developing the RHS if no match is found (which takes the process one level down inside the score building expression).

5 Validation and Moving Forward

The expression (E2) is a first example that validates the direction of this mapping and makes a first test of the two systems as potential components of a complete synthesis solution. Initially, the two systems were each built as separate research efforts, yet:

1. The design of the Paula animation system has always had as a goal the eventual connection to a structured linguistic system such as AZee. To this point, however, the linguistic features expressed by the avatar have been incorporated in an ad-hoc manner, driven partially by the physical capabilities of the avatar. The result has been a system that displays increasingly fluid, legible sign, but which needs a more complete linguistic structure to drive its animation.
2. AZee also has been designed with the intention of connecting to an animation system, but to this point has had to itself perform all the work of translating its forms into articulatory specifications for connection to an avatar that would simply interpolate those articulator specifications.

So, while both recognized the need and intention to connect to a system much like the other, they have each pursued their own goal and separate evaluations. However, each have now reached a level of maturity that the bridge between them described in the last section is feasible.

Expression (E2) applied the AZee to Paula mapping for a set of test utterances in French Sign language (LSF). In each case, AZee built the required LSF structure and produced a high level score that coordinated linguistic forms as shown in Fig. 9. This score was translated in to a preliminary version of the XML encoding of the utterance. An excerpt of this XML encoding is displayed in Fig. 12. Notice that in the XML output, AZee explicitly produces a series of hooks for the Paula system to use to shortcut if it has the capability.

```
<block_score>
        <block id="gl1">
                <paulablock name="CINEMA"/>
                <sync/>
        </block>
        <block id="pn1">
                <paulablock name="AZEE-PIDGEON"/>
                <sync>
                        <param name="dur" value=".8"/>
                        <param name="end" value="gl1:-1:.25"/>
                </sync>
        </block>
```

Fig. 12. AZee XML output of the utterance

The XML encoding was then used to populate the tracks of the Paula sentence generator, as seen in Fig. 11. It is up to Paula to translate and interpret the timing hints in such a way as to ensure smooth transitions between animation blocks on a given track and to preserve an overall flow in the animation. The head sweeps, mouth shapes and blinks are layered as procedures on top of the hand-crafted animations that provide a shortcut for the three hand-animated blocks CINEMA, RESTAURANT and GOOD. The resulting animation can be seen at the following URL: http://asl.cs.depaul.edu/ Paula-Azee/Paula-Azee-Example.mp4

The mapping between the two systems provides a first validation of each system's approach from a technical standpoint, gives evidence of feasibility, and lays the groundwork for further development of both systems.

6 Conclusion

The results presented in this paper demonstrate the feasibility of the mapping between AZee and Paula and also an initial validation of the proposition in Sect. 4. The power of this mapping, and thus the method for animating structured Sign Language linguistics lies in the fact that higher levels of animation can be used to animate entire sections of the AZee tree thus leveraging hand-animated or captured motion. In addition, the structured nature of the linguistic model allows us to exploit the layered nature of the AZee score to structure the corresponding animation. These lessons are important for any system that wishes to synthesize Sign Language animation based on a structured linguistic description.

It is, however, important to note that the details of some of the elements presented here, such as the XML format in Fig. 12 are preliminary and will need further study to expand into a full system. Moving forward, we plan to expand the mapping between these two systems to more fully encompass the structures encoded by AZee and the range of expression available in Paula.

References

1. Cuxac, C.: La langue des signes française, les voies de l'iconicité, Editions Ophrys (2000)
2. Van der Kooij, E.: Phonological categories in Sign Language of the Neth-erlands: the role of phonetic implementation of and iconicity, Utrecht: Ph.D. Thesis (2002)
3. Stokoe, W.C.: Semantic phonology. Sign Lang. Stud. **71**(1), 107–114 (1991)
4. Filhol, M., Hadjadj, M.N.: Juxtaposition as a form feature; syntax captured and explained rather than assumed and modelled. In: Language Resources and Evaluation Conference (LREC), Representation and Processing of Sign Languages, Portorož, Slovenia (2016)
5. Filhol, M., Hadjadj, M.N., Choisier, A.: Non-manual features: the right to indifference. In: Language Resource and Evaluation Conference (LREC), 6th Workshop on the Representation and Processing of Sign Language: Beyond the Manual Channel, Reykjavik, Islande (2014)
6. Prillwitz, S., Leven, R., Zienert, H., Hanke, T., Henning, J.: HamNoSys version 2.0, Hamburg Notation System for Sign Languages: An Introductory Guide. Signum Press, Hamburg (1989)
7. Moody, B.: Dictionnaire bilingue LSF/français, IVT edn. (1998)

8. Elliott, R., Glauert, J., Kennaway, J., Marshall, I., Safar, E.: Linguistic modelling and language-processing technologies for Avatar-based sign language presentation. Univ. Access Inf. Soc. **6**(4), 375–391 (2007)
9. Parent, R.: Computer animation: algorithms and techniques. Newnes, Boston (2012)
10. McDonald, J., Wolfe, R., Schnepp, J., Hochgesang, J., Jamrozik, D., Stumbo, M., Berke, L., Bialek, M., Thomas, F.: An automated technique for real-time production of lifelike animations of American Sign Language, pp. 1–16 (2015)
11. Wilbur, R.B., Malaia, E.: A new technique for analyzing narrative prosodic effects in sign languages using motion capture technology. In: A. H. &. M. S. (eds.) Linguistic foundations of narration in spoken and sign languages, Amsterdam, John Benjamins (in Press)
12. McDonald, J., Wolfe, R., Wilbur, R., Moncrief, R., Malaia, E., Fujimoto, S., Baowidan, S., Stec, J.: A new tool to facilitate prosodic analysis of motion capture data and a data-driven technique for the improvement of avatar motion, Portoroz (2016)
13. Dent, S.: What you need to know about 3D motion capture, Engadget, 14 August 2014. https://www.engadget.com/2014/07/14/motion-capture-explainer/. Accessed 21 Jan 2017
14. Gleicher, M.: Animation from observation: Motion capture and motion editing. ACM SIGGRAPH Comput. Graph. **33**(4), 51–54 (1999)
15. Wolfe, R., McDonald, J., Moncrief, R., Baowidan, S., Stumbo, M.: Inferring biomechanical kinematics from linguistic data: a case study for role shift. In: Symposium on Sign Language Translation and Avatar Technology (SLTAT), Paris, France (2015)
16. McDonald, J., Wolfe, R., Moncrief, R., Baowidan, S.: Analysis for synthesis: Investigating corpora for supporting the automatic generation of role shift. In: Proceedings of the 6th Workshop on the Representation and Processing of Sign Languages: Beyond the Manual Channel. Language Resources and Evaluation Conference (LREC), Reykjavik, Iceland (2014)
17. Kipp, M., Nguyen, Q., Heloir, A., Matthes, S.: Assessing the deaf user perspective on sign language avatars. In: The Proceedings of the 13th International ACM SIGACCESS Conference on Computers and Accessibility. ACM (2011)

An Improved Framework for Layering Linguistic Processes in Sign Language Generation: Why There Should Never Be a "Brows" Tier

John McDonald[✉], Rosalee Wolfe, Sarah Johnson, Souad Baowidan,
Robyn Moncrief, and Ningshan Guo

DePaul University, Chicago, IL, USA
{jmcdonald,wolfe}@cs.depaul.edu, sarahej101@gmail.com,
{sbaowida,rkelley5,nguo4}@mail.depaul.edu

Abstract. Creating legible animations of sign language that satisfy the needs of native users requires drawing from the fields of computational linguistics, computer animation and user experience research. This paper explores the problem of layering the many linguistic processes that contribute to a sign language utterance in avatar animation. A new framework is presented that satisfies requirements from each of these fields, and yields a flexible architecture for sign language avatars capable of leveraging a wide range of animation techniques to generate rich multi-layered animations of sign.

Keywords: Sign language avatars · Computational linguistics · Computer animation · Hierarchical models · User interface

1 Introduction

In many countries access to spoken and written language remains an extreme challenge for those who use sign languages as their preferred means of communication. Automatic translation technologies have the potential to help bridge this gap. Because sign languages are expressed on the human body and face rather than in a written form, avatars capable of displaying the full naturalistic motion of sign language are essential for such translation systems.

In this paper, the term *sign language* will be understood to refer to all fully-qualified linguistic systems (independent languages) that are visual/gestural in their modality. This distinguishes these languages from other signed communication systems such as Signed English [1]. Unlike spoken or written languages, sign languages communicate in multiple channels concurrently. The hands and arms often form the primary manual channel that conveys lexical information, but additional signals co-occur on the torso, neck and face that can add linguistic and paralinguistic information to intensify, invert or otherwise modify the meaning of this information [2].

Current sign language avatars are capable of displaying a stream of lexical units [3, 4], but how best to represent and coordinate information beyond the manual channel has proved to be a challenge, and is still an open question. This paper presents a novel

M. Antona and C. Stephanidis (Eds.): UAHCI 2017, Part II, LNCS 10278, pp. 41–54, 2017.
DOI: 10.1007/978-3-319-58703-5_4

framework for layering linguistic processes for avatar technology that facilitates greater expressivity, naturalness and legibility beyond the manual channel. This new framework allows for both synchronous and asynchronous coordination of processes among channels while avoiding the robotic motion often associated with avatars. In addition, the framework provides an elegant and parsimonious method to facilitate a high degree of flexibility in the way each channel can influence the avatar's motion.

Developing this framework required a multidisciplinary approach. Automated sign language generation draws on a number of disciplines, including computational linguistics, computer animation and user experience which all inform the software engineering design. To motivate the new framework, this paper analyzes sign language avatar technology from each of these perspectives. In the following three sections, we discuss relevant features of each discipline that will impose constraints on the system, which will be addressed in the final section of the paper that lays out the architecture of the system.

These disciplines require a high level of flexibility and naturalness in an avatar framework. In particular, the framework cannot limit a physical feature such as brows to a single linguistic or animation process, yet each process will affect a wide range of physical features on the avatar. Additionally, the avatar framework cannot be limited to a single method of animation. The implementation presented is an elegant solution to enable this flexibility, and it requires little additional code beyond the traditional services provided by animation systems to support key frame, procedural and motion capture animation.

2   Computational Linguistics

Avatars have several promising uses in computational linguistics, and the requirements of these applications yield important priorities for the structure and quality of avatar animation technology. Since an avatar is the most appropriate target for any spoken-to-sign translation system, it must be capable of expressing all aspects of sign language. To date, avatars have struggled to provide the flexibility, fluidity and legibility desired by native signers.

Second, avatars can serve as a helpful component for improving the annotation of video. Applications such as Elan, iLex, and Anvil allow researchers to annotate videos of sign language in multi-tier organizations [5–7], and validation is a continual concern. If annotations are used to drive an avatar automatically, the resulting output can be compared with the initial video for discrepancies. This provides an independent method of verification [8].

Finally, avatar technology shows potential as a hypothesis-testing tool. One possible method is to apply the hypothesis to an avatar, generate animations and then review the animations with the Deaf community. In this capacity, avatars have a distinct advantage over video technologies, since they can allow for a single process to be included or excluded in isolation. It is much more difficult to ask a signer, "please do the exact same thing, but without the Y/N question indication" [9]. However, for avatars to be used in this way, they must produce a more realistic depiction of sign than currently possible.

To create an avatar capable of serving these applications, one must consider the linguistic structures that the avatar must express. As independent, natural languages, sign languages have grammars that do not correspond directly to the linguistics of spoken languages. Animating sign languages flexibly and efficiently requires drawing on a deep understanding of sign language structure. The discipline of sign language linguistics yields a wealth of information that can be used for this purpose. Linguistics also poses several challenges in the coordination of channels, which heretofore has not been satisfactorily addressed in avatar technology.

Initial findings in the field [10] have been extraordinarily helpful for structuring avatar motion by categorizing the manual parameters of an utterance into handshapes, positions, palm orientation and motions. However, such elemental parameters are only the beginning of the structure that a sign language avatar will need to express. More recent research has revealed rich nonmanual signals on the face and torso [11], a system of interacting referential frames for communicating reported speech [12], and many other structures such as classifier predicates [13]. All of these processes can co-occur, and can even individually involve multiple co-occurring movements.

Further research has also indicated that language processes do not lay claim over a particular subset of human anatomy to the exclusion of co-occurring processes. Instead, a complex structure of linguistic forms will layer onto multiple parts of the body to express the intended utterance [14]. This extends and reinforces initial studies on features of the body which indicate that multiple linguistic processes can combine to influence a single part of the body. Consider the following examples of co-occurring processes.

- Sign languages often communicate syntactic information, such as whether an utterance is a statement or a question, by raising and lowing the brows. In addition, brows can be used to communicate emotional content in utterances such as joy and anger.
- The neck can be used to communicate syntactic information in some sign languages such as the use of a head-nod to enumerate a list in Langue des Signes Française. In addition, the neck can be turned when reporting the discourse of third parties.

Such processes will not occur in a synchronous manner. The onset of information in a nonmanual channel may or may not coincide with the onset of lexical items, and the duration of the nonmanual signal may differ from the duration of the lexical item [15]. Thus, multiple linguistic processes can simultaneously influence the position and/or orientation of an individual anatomic feature.

For example, consider a fan of the Cleveland baseball team who asks sadly, "CUBS WIN?" This phrase consists of two lexical signs, along with two co-occurring nonmanual signals. The final blink is a prosodic indicator for the end of the phrase, as presented in (1).

$$
\begin{array}{cc}
& \underline{\text{bl}} \\
& \underline{\text{sadness}} \\
& \underline{\text{q}} \\
\text{CUBS} & \text{WIN}
\end{array} \tag{1}
$$

To analyze the layering of linguistic processes in this phrase, we visualize them as a block diagram in Fig. 1.

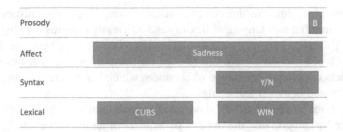

Fig. 1. Layered structure of the utterance "CUBS WIN?"

The processes are manifested as movements or positions on the signer's body. Multiple processes can affect a single joint or position. Though, the movements or positions are sometimes in conflict, the utterances are legible to a fluent signer. For example, research has shown that multiple processes influence the timing and movement of the brows [16, 17]. Both the question marker and the sadness expressed in (1) are communicated by the brows. In the former, the brows are raised to indicate a y/n question, and in the latter the brows are lowered, communicating sadness. However, the timing and intensity of the two brow transitions allow a signer who views the utterance to identify both processes easily.

For all of these reasons it is clear that a complete framework for communicating sign language should not have a single "brows" tier, as a single tier would have difficulty encoding the multiple influences affecting the brows. This asynchronicity presents several challenges for a framework in the coordination of channels. From a linguistics perspective, the framework should focus on language processes, not anatomy. It must allow any combination of linguistic processes in an utterance, and the sign language avatar technology should provide clear labelling of the linguistic processes. In particular, the framework should satisfy the following requirements based on the analysis in this section:

(**L1**) Multiple processes can and will affect the same geometry.
(**L2**) Processes may start and end asynchronously.
(**L3**) Processes may be enabled and disabled at the user's discretion.

3   Computer Animation

The quality of an avatar's signing hinges on the quality of the underlying computer animation. Its usefulness in the previously discussed applications is dictated by the flexibility of the graphical architecture and the types of animation techniques that it supports. Interestingly, the requirements for animating a sign language avatar differ from and are, in some ways, more demanding than those for animating film characters and game avatars.

Avatars for sign languages do share some similarities with animated characters from film and computer games, but they also have additional requirements that set them apart. This can be quite surprising at first blush since realistic animated characters are so ubiquitous in today's film industry. Viewers expect that realism to carry over to signing avatars. Unfortunately, the two are very different since film is not an interactive nor a generative medium. The motion of the characters in Pixar's *Toy Story* is the same today as it was when the film was released in 1995 [18]. The film, once rendered, is set for all time, and editing can only be done at the greatest of expense.

Compare this to sign languages which, being productive, can express a functionally infinite range of utterances. If an avatar is to be used for sign language generation rather than simple playback of prerecorded sequences, then the system must support the generation of novel utterances at the whim of the user. Such flexibility is closer to what a user expects from a computer game avatar, but such avatars usually only have a limited number of movements such as swinging a baseball bat and sliding into a base. Further these predefined movements can only be combined in predefined ways [19].

Another difference between signing avatars and animated film/game characters is that cartoon animators utilize labor-saving shortcuts such as using simplified hands consisting of only three fingers and a thumb. Such simplifications would be inappropriate for sign languages, since there would be no way to distinguish between the 7 and 8 handshapes of ASL. Even when animated characters are rigged with realistic hands, there is further complexity in generational avatar systems such as automatic collision avoidance which is necessary for such actions as entering and leaving the letter "T" in ASL fingerspelling, see Fig. 2.

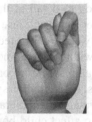

Fig. 2. ASL Handshape 'T'

Several distinct approaches exist for animating avatars all of which have been exploited over the years in various sign synthesis systems including:

1. artist-driven keyframe animation [20],
2. motion capture [21],
3. key-frame synthesis from linguistic descriptions [22],
4. procedural techniques [23].

Each of these methods has its own advantages. Artist driven keyframe animation can be highly realistic, and provides a sparsity of data that can facilitate editing and combining animation clips, but its realism depends largely on the skill of the artist.

Motion capture, can produce extremely realistic motion, as long as the body type of the avatar matches the body type of the recorded person. Unfortunately, motion capture also produces a density of data that causes extreme challenges for editing and combining recorded motions. Doing so relies on large libraries of recorded clips that enable searching not only for the nature of the desired motion but also for the motion at the boundary of the clip in order to smoothly combine them in sequence [24]. Research into this is ongoing.

Reconciling the need to drive an avatar from linguistic data with the demands of producing natural human motion is an ongoing challenge. This is especially true given the requirements of the target audience who expect legible flowing sign, and can find it difficult to read stiff robotic motion. Synthesizing sign exclusively using linguistic descriptions results in such robotic motion. However, such an avatar has the flexibility to combine any lexical items that the linguistics encodes. Conversely, natural and realistic avatar motion relies on extensive animator time or motion capture data at the expense of flexibility. Such systems can only express what has been either animated or pre-recorded.

Procedural animation techniques may also be useful for driving a sign language avatar. For example, consider the fact that the joints in the human body do not start and end their movements simultaneously. In a role shift, the head rotates first, followed by the hips and then the upper spine and shoulders [25]. Such subtleties are already baked into motion capture recordings, but they must be handled manually or modeled procedurally in a key-frame animation system. Experienced animators are skilled in incorporating asynchronicity of this kind, but it is time consuming. Procedural techniques can add such effects and shorten the animator's time and expense [15].

Ideally, an avatar framework would have the capacity to incorporate any and all of the four animation techniques, employing the one best suited for any given language process. Regardless of the underlying animation technique, creating natural, convincing animation requires an acute attention to detail at the biomechanical level, including subtle changes to the avatar's movement that cause no distinguishable change at the linguistic level but affect the legibility of the generated utterance. The framework should support the tuning of such motions within the confines of the linguistic constraints.

Understanding how these four animation approaches can cooperate in an avatar framework requires a deeper analysis. All animation systems will model the human body as a skeleton of articulated bones arranged in a hierarchy so that rotating bones closer to the root of the hierarchy will also affect child bones, see Fig. 3. In this articulated figure, the upper spine, neck, head, shoulders and arms are all children (descendants) of the waist bone. When the waist moves, they also move.

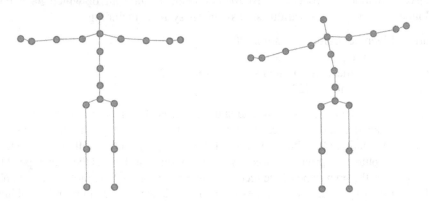

Fig. 3. Hierarchical Skeleton: the waist influences the orientation of all bones descending from the waist.

In the case of a key-frame animation system, a set of controllers for each bone will interpolate a set of key positions or rotations using a variety of methods [26]. The result is then multiplied by the parent's transformation to get the overall transformation of the bone.

The challenges of using computer animation to produce sign language thus lead us to the following requirements:

(A1) Multiple processes will affect each bone and combine to produce the final orientation of each bone.

(A2) Any process that affects multiple bones may have differing start and end times on each bone but will need to controlled in concert.

(A3) These processes may require different animation techniques, interpolation schemes or procedural computations.

To better understand how these requirements present challenges for an animation system, consider the sentence in (1). The linguistic processes become layers of animation that must be combined. See Fig. 4. Several of these animation blocks may affect any given part of the body, such as the brows. These include the syntactic marker for a Y/N question and the extralinguistic expression of sadness. Suppose also that in the animation of WIN the artist added a subtle movement of the brows to enhance the legibility and naturalness of the sign, and perhaps also added a colorful nonmanual embellishment associated with the lexical item CUBS.

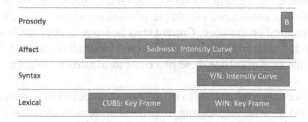

Fig. 4. Animation techniques for different processes in an utterance

On the lexical track we have the two signs CUBS and WIN. These are built as keyframe animations and each consists of a sequence of orientations specified at a subset of the joints. Layered on these lexical items is the Y/N question nonmanual marker which raises the eyebrows. This action begins slightly before the WIN sign and ends slightly after it. The extralinguistic emotion of sadness lowers the eyebrows, combining with the raising from the question. This action encompasses the whole utterance. Finally the eyes blink at the end of the phrase, which may also lower the eyebrows very slightly. Each of these processes is specified as a strength of expression defined by an intensity curve.

Mixing different types of computations on a given bone can be a challenge, as the avatar framework will need to compute the value of each process at each frame and multiply them to obtain the final orientation of the bone. Figure 5 motivates how each of these processes are manifested mathematically. Consider the time t indicated at the end of the production of the sign WIN in the figure. Four processes affect the eyebrows at time t. Each of these processes will create a transformation, M_{proc}, affecting the brow as indicated in the figure. The final transformation of the brow is the combination of all of these effects, some raising and some lowering the brows. Since each is a rotation on a bone that moves the eyebrow, the total transform can be built as a product of these transformations:

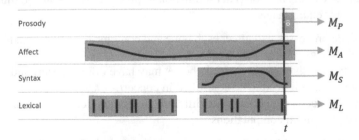

Fig. 5. Transformations that affect the eyebrows

Using the linear algebra convention of pre-multiplication, the final transformation on the brows will be:

$$M_P * M_A * M_S * M_L$$

A system that can manage such processes and combine them properly for a bone will also be able to handle requirement **A3** above since it does not matter whether the underlying representation is procedural, key-frame or motion capture. Each are individually evaluated and combined on the bone. Current sign language avatars are limited by either lacking the capability of layering these processes on some or all of the joints in the avatar's body, or lacking the facility to tune these processes as dictated by linguistic and physical constraints.

The next two sections explore how to manage these processes from the perspectives of user experience and software engineering. In particular, the next section explores how the linguistic and animation requirements will inform the requirements of the user experience.

4 User Experience

The user interface will tie the linguistic descriptions to the animation techniques while also giving necessary control to adjust avatar movement within the linguistic constraints. The interface must accommodate three different types of users:

1. Linguists who will be primarily concerned with the structure of the utterance.
2. Animators who will be primarily concerned with the realism and flow of the avatar's motion.
3. Machine translation researchers, who will want the software to output natural correct sign with as little user intervention as possible.

Animators are concerned with the appearance of an anatomic feature, as contrasted with linguists, who identify the language processes that influence that feature. Returning to the example in (1), consider the difference between raising an eyebrow in an animation and determining what combination of processes in the language caused the motion. A linguist will want to designate the time of onset and offset of each process. An animator will want to adjust the finer details of timing, including transition shapes (attack and decay) of the envelope as well as adjusting the envelope's steady state. The interface must support the goals of each type of user, while quietly taking care of other details.

The linguistic (**L1–L3**) and animation (**A1–A3**) requirements share commonalities in terms of flexibility for both timing and affected components of the avatar. To satisfy these, the framework's interface must visualize the temporal component as signed utterances unfold over time. Further, this temporal component must be subdivided into the various process tracks or tiers that control the avatar's motion. As in many annotation systems, the new framework displays the time axis horizontally and the tracks organized vertically, see Fig. 6. This organizational scheme is familiar to sign language researchers, and is similar to sign language annotation systems. It allows easy temporal comparison and coordination of elements.

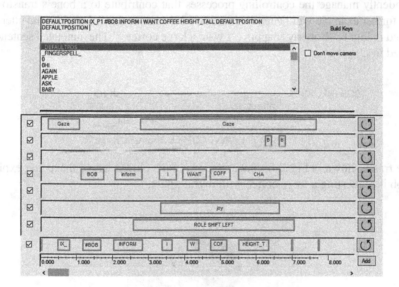

Fig. 6. Paula sentence generator interface

This interface has several features that satisfy requirements **L1-3** and **A1-3** above:

1. A given bone in the hierarchy may be influenced by multiple tracks (**L1, A1**).
2. Timing of animation segments can be controlled independently in each track, and thus tracks may independently control the configuration and timing of multiple sections of the avatar (**L2, A2**).
3. As disparate parts of the human anatomy may be involved in a specific process, bones may not necessarily be contiguous in the hierarchy (**L2, A2**).
4. The check-boxes at the left of each track allow the track to be enabled and disabled at the user's discretion. In addition, tracks may be individually edited without affecting the processes in other tracks (**L3**).

The only requirement not specifically addressed in the user experience here is **A3**, but this requirement is a lower level issue that will be addressed in the next section dealing with the software engineering and implementation of the framework.

5   Software Engineering and Implementation

To support both the linguistic (**L1–L3**) and animation (**A1–A3**) requirements, the underlying architecture must be structured to manage controllers at each articulatory site on the avatar. Commercial animation packages support this through layered animation controllers [27]. Avatar system developers don't often have the luxury of time and resources to implement such systems, however, with an elegant change to the avatar's skeleton, we can satisfy both the linguistic and animation requirements with no added code in the underlying display technology.

To support the combining of effects scripted by the user in Fig. 6 the system must independently manage the controlling processes that contribute to a bone's transformation. A further example will better illustrate how this can be done. Consider the utterance displayed in Fig. 6, "Bob says happily, 'I want a large coffee'." The annotated sentence is displayed in (2)

$$
\begin{array}{ll}
_a\text{BOB INFORM} < \qquad\qquad\qquad\qquad\qquad\qquad _a\text{shift}> \\
\qquad\qquad \text{affect:joy}\underline{\qquad\qquad\qquad\qquad\qquad\qquad} \\
\qquad\qquad\qquad\qquad\qquad\qquad\qquad \text{nms:CHA}\underline{\qquad} \\
\qquad\quad (_a\text{SHIFT) I WANT COFFEE Bbent-CL"large"}
\end{array}
\qquad (2)
$$

The frame shown in Fig. 7 occurs at the end of the phrase where the avatar explains that Bob is requesting a large coffee with joyful affect.

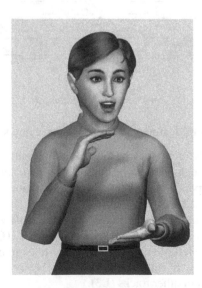

Fig. 7.   Avatar indicating that a large cup of coffee is desired

Several manual and nonmanual processes affect the spine of the avatar during the production of LARGE including:

1. The manual channel will raise the shoulders and give a small lean of the spine away from the raised hand. This process uses artist driven key-frame animation.
2. The role-shift used to mark reported dialog will turn the spine along the axis of the body. This process uses a procedure that rotates the body to take the role of a previously indexed discourse participant. This procedure manages the asynchronicity of the spine bones in the shift [15].
3. The emotion of joy will tend to raise the shoulders and arch the spine slightly. This process uses a pre-generated pose controlled by an intensity curve.
4. To increase realism throughout the utterance, a small amount of noise is applied to the joints in the spine to "liven" the avatar. This is a procedural application of Perlin noise [23].

The avatar framework should manage all four of these processes without letting them interfere with each other. Each has its own method of computation at a specific time in the animation. Consider the single bone "Waist" in the hierarchy displayed in Fig. 8. To allow the avatar to combine these four effects, we split this bone into four *sub-bones* as displayed.

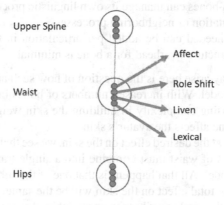

Fig. 8. Bone structure in the torso

Each sub-bone is a fully-qualified bone in the animation engine with its own transformation controller. We call them sub-bones because each has identical positions to the main waist articulator. They are hierarchically organized from parent to child in the order dictated by the tracks in the sentence generator interface seen in Fig. 6. In this case, the hierarchy is:

Waist_Lexical

Waist_Liven

Waist_RoleShift

Waist_Affect

This framework satisfies the linguistic **L1–L3** and animation **A1–A3** requirements in the following ways:

1. **L1** and **A1**: Since each sub-bone has its own animation controller, each will be set and controlled independently. The hierarchical nature of the skeleton automatically combines the effects to produce a final transform on the overall bone.
2. **L2** and **A2**: The timing of effects or processes in each sub-bone's controller is completely independent of the other sub-bones.
3. **A3**: Each sub-bone's controller may use any animation technique to compute its transform including key-frame interpolation, procedure or motion capture.
4. **L3**: Each controller acts independently and can therefore be altered or even enabled and disabled independently of all the other processes.

The new framework also has several additional advantages:

1. It uses the existing structure of the avatar's animation hierarchy, requiring no extra coding of layered controllers, or of process management systems in the sentence generator.
2. The computational burden is no greater than it would be with other options. No matter the system, the four contributing processes must be evaluated and their transformation matrices multiplied.
3. Each of the four sub-bones can manage its own linguistic process and will not interfere with the computation of neighboring processes.
4. As many bones as needed can be added per articulation in the avatar. The extra memory and data structure overhead for a bone is minimal.

One concern that may arise here is the question of how such an organization would affect the skin of the model. With increased numbers of bones in an avatar that affect the skin, there is increasing complexity in building the skin weighting factors, which determine how each bone affects the avatar's skin.

However, if we look at the desired effect on the skin, we see that each of the processes that affect the sub-bones of waist must combine into a single transformation that will affect the skin of the model. All that happens is that one of the sub-bones can rotate the waist a little farther. The total effect on the skin will be the same. The proposed framework here assumes that these all contribute to one combined effect on both the torso and the model's skin. As long as the most distal sub-bone in the waist controls the skin, the avatar will deform as expected. Thus no additional complexity in computing the deformation is introduced.

6 Conclusion and Future Work

The new framework presented in this paper allows for a flexible specification of many processes in sign simultaneously that all can influence any part of the anatomy. This is accomplished by replicating bones on a per-process basis so that each process can control its own bone independent of the others, thus allowing not only independent timing, but possibly completely different animation procedures or data controlling each. As long as the interactions between the bones is minimal, the animation hierarchy will properly combine the process effects by multiplying their resulting transformation matrices.

Moving forward, there are a limited number of cases where interactions among tracks would be desirable. Consider situations where the transformation in one process will be influenced by the transformation in another. For example, the IK system on an arm may need to take into consideration some processes on the arm and torso and ignore others. Another example is the eyebrow motion described in [16]. In her study she found that in some cases the presence of one process can alter the range of motion in co-occurring processes. Such interactions will be addressed in a follow-up study.

References

1. Signed Language vs. Sign Language, Canadian Cultural Society of the Deaf. http://www.deafculturecentre.ca/Public/Default.aspx?I=569&n. Accessed 17 Jan 2017
2. Valli, C., Lucas, C.: Linguistics of American Sign Language: An Introduction. Gaulladet University Press, Washington D.C. (2000)
3. Elliott, R., Glauert, J.R., Kennaway, R., Marshall, I., Safar, E.: Linguistic modelling and language-processing technologies for Avatar-based sign language presentation. Univ. Access Inf. Soc. 6(4), 375–391 (2008)
4. Kipp, M., Heloir, A., Nguyen, Q.: Sign language avatars: animation and comprehensibility. In: International Workshop on Intelligent Virtual Agents (2011)
5. Crasborn, O., Sloetjes, H.: Enhanced ELAN functionality for sign language corpora. In: Proceedings of the 3rd Workshop on the Representation and Processing of Sign Languages: Construction and Exploitation of Sign Language Corpora (2008)
6. Hanke, T., Storz, J.: iLex – a database tool for integrating sign language corpus linguistics and sign language lexicography. In: Workshop on the Representation and Processing of Sign Language, at the Sixth International Conference on Language Resources and Evaluation (LREC 2008), Marrakech, Morocco (2008)
7. Kipp, M.: Multimedia annotation, querying and analysis in ANVIL. In: Multimedia Information Extraction, vol. 19 (2010)
8. Hanke, T.: Lexical sign language resources: synergies between empirical work and automatic language generation. In: Language Resources and Evaluation Conference (LREC), Libson (2004)
9. Thorpe, D.: Certified ASL Interpreter. Personal Communication, Chicago (2016)
10. Lidell, S., Johnson, R.: American sign language: the phonological base. Sign Lang. Stud. 64(1), 195–277 (1989)
11. Wilbur, R.: Phonological and prosodic layering of nonmanuals in American sign language. In: Emmorey, K., Lane, H.L., Bellugi, U., Klima, E. (eds.) The Signs of Language Revisited: Festscrift for Ursula Bellugi and Edward Klima, pp. 213–241 (2000)
12. Morgan, G.: Event packaging in British Sign Language discourse. In: Wiinston, E. (ed.) Storytelling & Conversation: Discourse in Deaf Communities, pp. 27–58. Gallaudet University Press, Washington, DC (1999)
13. Schick, B.: Classifier predicates in American Sign Language. Int. J. Sign Linguist. 1(1), 15–40 (1990)
14. Filhol, M.: «Grammaire récursive non linéaire pour les langues des signes,» chez Conférence sur le Traitement Automatique des Langues Naturelles, Marseille (2014)

15. Wolfe, R., McDonald, J., Moncrief, R., Baowidan, S., Stumbo, M.: Inferring biomechanical kinematics from linguistic data: a case study for role shift. In: Symposium on Sign Language Translation and Avatar Technology (SLTAT), Paris, France (2015)
16. Weast, T.P.: Questions in American Sign Language: A quantitative analysis of raised and lowered eyebrows, ProQuest (2008)
17. Wolfe, R., Cook, P., McDonald, J., Schnepp, J.: Linguistics as structure in computer animation: Toward a more effective synthesis of brow motion in American Sign Language. Nonmanuals Sign Lang. Spec. Issue Sign Lang. Linguist. **14**(1), 179–199 (2011)
18. Lasseter, J.: Director, Toy Story. [Film]. Walt Disney Pictures/Pixar Studios, USA (1995)
19. Lee, J., Lee, K.H.: Precomputing avatar behavior from human motion data. Graph. Models **68**(2), 158–174 (2006)
20. Wolfe, R., McDonald, J., Schnepp, J.: An Avatar to Depict Sign Language: Building from Reusable Hand Animation, Berlin, Germany, 10–11 January 2011
21. Gibet, S., Courty, N., Duarte, K., Le Naour, T.: The SignCom system for data-driven animation of interactive virtual signers: methodology and evaluation. ACM Trans. Interact. Intell. Syst. (TiiS) **1**(1), 1–26 (2011)
22. Jennings, V., Elliott, R., Kennaway, R.: Requirements for a signing avatar. In: Workshop on Copora and Sign Language Technologies (CSLT), LREC, Malta (2010)
23. McDonald, J., Wolfe, R., Wilbur, R., Moncrief, R., Malaia, E., Fujimoto, S., Baowidan, S., Stec, J.: A new tool to facilitate prosodic analysis of motion capture data and a data-driven technique for the improvement of avatar motion. In: Lanugage Resources Evaluation Conference (LREC), Portoroz (2016)
24. Lefebvre-Albaret, F., Gibet, S., Turki, A., Hamon, L., Brun, R.: Overview of the Sign3D Project High-fidelity 3D recording, indexing and editing of French Sign Language content. In: Third International Symposium on Sign Language Translation and Avatar Technology (SLTAT), Chicago (2013)
25. McDonald, J., Wolfe, R., Schnepp, J., Hochgesang, J., Jamrozik, D., Stumbo, M., Berke, L., Bialek, M., Thomas, F.: An automated technique for real-time production of lifelike animations of American Sign Language, pp. 1–16 (2015)
26. Parent, R.: Computer Animation: Algorithms and Techniques. Newnes, Boston (2012)
27. Autodesk, Animation Layers (Layer Controller) Documentation. 15 November 2016. https://knowledge.autodesk.com/support/3ds-max/learn-explore/caas/CloudHelp/cloudhelp/2017/ENU/3DSMax/files/GUID-ACAD407C-B079-4DAB-9DD0-6C8DC22389EF-htm.html. Accessed 19 Jan 2017

Coarticulation Analysis
for Sign Language Synthesis

Lucie Naert[✉], Caroline Larboulette, and Sylvie Gibet

IRISA, Université Bretagne Sud, Vannes, France
{lucie.naert,caroline.larboulette,sylvie.gibet}@univ-ubs.fr
http://lsf.irisa.fr

Abstract. A sign language utterance can be seen as a continuous stream
of motion, involving the signs themselves and inter-sign movements or
transitions. Like in speech, coarticulation constitutes an important part
of the language. Indeed, the signs are contextualized: their form and,
most of all, the transitions will greatly depend on the surrounding signs.
For that reason, the manual segmentation of sign language utterances
is a difficult and imprecise task. Besides, annotators often assume that
both hands are synchronous, which is not always true in practice. In this
paper, we first propose a technique to automatically refine the segmentation by adjusting the manual tags isolating signs from transitions. We
then study motion transitions between consecutive signs and, in particular, the duration of those transitions. We propose several computation
techniques for the transition duration based on the analysis we have conducted. Finally, we use our findings in our motion synthesis platform to
create new utterances in French Sign Language.

Keywords: Coarticulation · Sign language segmentation · Transition
duration · Kinematic features analysis · Synthesis · French Sign Language (LSF)

1 Introduction

French Sign Language (LSF) is the natural language of deaf people in France
and is therefore used as their first means of communication. As the linguistic
mechanisms used in LSF are very different from those used in French, deaf
people may face difficulties using written French. In LSF, the grammatical rules,
as well as the nature and the spatial organization of the linguistic concepts
are completely different from those used in French. However, most sources of
information available on the Web and on other media are in French (written or
oral), thus restraining Deaf access to information in their everyday life.

Virtual humans or *avatars* are a new and promising way to improve Deaf
access to information. With avatar technologies, the anonymity of the signer is
preserved. Furthermore, the content of sign language can be edited, manipulated, and produced more easily than with a video medium. Indeed, videos lack

© Springer International Publishing AG 2017
M. Antona and C. Stephanidis (Eds.): UAHCI 2017, Part II, LNCS 10278, pp. 55–75, 2017.
DOI: 10.1007/978-3-319-58703-5_5

flexibility and operations such as copy/paste fail to deal with transitions in the context of editing new utterances.

Several approaches for synthesizing signed language utterances have been exploited over the years including keyframe techniques, procedural synthesis and data-driven synthesis. **Keyframe techniques** and **procedural synthesis** have been extensively developed in the international community. It allows a fine control at the language specification level which results in a precise behavior of the avatar. In return, the specification step is fastidious and time-consuming. Moreover, the avatar may be poorly accepted by the deaf community due to the lack of realism of the resulting animations. To compensate for this realism issue, McDonald et al. [23] analyzed noise in motion capture data in order to extract linguistic and kinematic information. They injected this information into their keyframe-based synthesis tool to give their avatar a more life-like appearance. **Data-driven synthesis** often involves motion capture which is a very powerful tool to analyze movement features. Furthermore, as the synthesis is based on the movements of a real signer, the produced animations are more human-like. However, the capture of motion, the post-processing of data, the skeleton reconstruction and the annotation are costly both in time and resources. Besides, the corpus has to be large enough to account for the variability of sign languages.

Over the last ten years, we have worked on a data-driven approach for sign language synthesis. In our two last projects, *SignCom* [8] and *Sign3D* [9], we have developed a system in which we edit and compose new sentences that keep some linguistic coherence and are visually acceptable when played by an avatar. Some editing and animation issues have already been studied, implemented and discussed in [9]. Currently, our synthesis system relies on manually annotated data by expert annotators (deaf signers). However, manually segmenting sign language movements is a laborious and time-consuming process. Furthermore, this process depends on linguistic studies. In particular, the phonetic work proposed by Liddell and Johnson [15], as well as the annotation template proposed by Johnston and De Beuzeville [16] have largely inspired our annotation scheme in the *SignCom* project [8]. This template has been slightly refined in the *Sign3D* project to ease the annotation by avoiding the labeling of transition segments [9].

One of the main difficulties in the annotation process is that it is subject to variability due to the fact that all annotators do not agree with the starting and ending frames of the semantic segments [12]. Furthermore, as the signs in sequences appear in a continuous stream, one signer may start the subsequent movement before fully completing the previous one. This contextual dependency between signs, called *coarticulation*, makes the labeling more complex. Besides, the level of details of the annotation scheme greatly influences the way the avatar will be controlled.

This paper focuses on the analysis of inter-sign transitions to make the segmentation process as automatic and precise as possible, and to find motion invariants, in order to interactively improve the animation of the novel utterances signed by an avatar. Our final objective is to be able to incorporate coarticulation mechanisms into our concatenative synthesis system in order to generate a natural articulation between signs, while preserving the linguistic intelligibility. Two sub-challenges are considered in this paper: first, the segmentation of the transitions between signs is analyzed, leading to a refinement of the manual annotations; second, the duration of the transitions is deeply studied. The results are illustrated through interactive tools that are directly incorporated into our synthesis system.

2 Related Work

Segmentation of human motion is the process of breaking a continuous sequence of movement data into smaller and meaningful components, that range from actions to movement primitives. It is important here to emphasize that the segmentation may depend on its further use; in particular, this process is more constraining when the motion primitives relate to movement generation. The segmentation process consists in identifying the starting and ending frames for each segment corresponding to a movement primitive. The definition of the segments themselves is challenging due to the high-dimensional nature of human movement data and the variability of movement. For sign language movements, this is even more challenging since the segments depend on how the linguistic element boundaries are defined, according to phonetic, phonological and semantic rules, as well as coarticulation between signs. We review hereafter some segmentation work applied on general motion capture data and on sign language motion.

For general motion capture data segmentation, a frequently used approach is to identify segment boundaries by detecting sudden changes or threshold crossings in kinematic features, such as position and orientation and their derivatives (velocity, acceleration, curvature). For example, an indexing system has been developed by using joint positions relatively to other points or 2D planes [25] or by detecting the zero crossings in the angular velocity of the arm joints [6]. If these methods are easy to implement and can be efficiently applied on various data sets, they may give over or under segmentation boundaries and do not take into account semantic content.

Boundaries can be determined by other metric thresholds, using for example data analysis principles such as Principal Component Analysis (PCA), Probabilistic PCA, or Gaussian Mixture Models (GMM) [14], deriving Bayesian methods [5], or temporal application of Hilbert space embedding of distributions [10]. These methods, by projecting the motion capture data into low-dimensional representation spaces, give effective results, but fail to represent semantic data.

Other segmentation approaches use supervised learning techniques to take into account the semantic content of motion data. Among the proposed approaches, Müller et al. [24] used a genetic algorithm to identify characteristic keyframes while Brand et al. [2] used Hidden Markov Models.

Segmentation of sign language data has first been studied using video sequences. The complexity of the signs, characterized by many features (including hand movement, hand configuration and facial expression), requires the development of specific approaches. Lefebvre-Albaret et al. [21] developed a method to semi-automatically segment sequences of signs in French Sign Language (LSF) using region aspects: temporal boundaries are identified from a set of features including symmetry, repetition of movements, hand velocity and stability of the configuration. It introduces an interactive segmentation tool: first, a one-frame segment called *seed* is picked out by the user for each sign; this *seed* is then used by the region-detection algorithm to determine intervals containing all features of a sign. The resulting segmentation can be checked by a sign language annotator. Gonzalez et al. [11] have proposed to define an automatic two-level segmentation process: the first one, based on a robust tracking algorithm, uses hand movement features; the second one uses hand configuration to correct the first level. A segmentation approach, based on a Hidden Markov Model and a state automata, has also been developed for Korean Sign Language segmentation [17]. Yang et al. [27] use Conditional Random Fields to distinguish transitions and signs in American Sign Language.

Coarticulation has given rise to a few works. Linguistically motivated models have been defined and validated through various approaches. Huenerfauth [13] has found that adding pauses and variations in sign durations improved the performance of virtual avatars by making the synthesized sentences more comprehensible by ASL signers. Pauses and temporal variations within signs were also introduced in LSF utterances by Segouat [26] to highlight the coarticulation effects in animations. A coarticulation model, incorporated into an inverse kinematic model has been developed for synthesis purpose [19]. Transitions have also been studied. A transition-inclusive system, separating the Strokes (S) conveying the meaning of the signs from the Preparation (P) and Retraction (R) phases characterizing inter-sign movements, has been initially proposed by [18] and used for LSF [1]. The transition shape has then been studied for recognition [20] or synthesis purposes [4].

Segmenting signs into significant components is still an open issue. Since the building of new sentences relies on the quality of the segmentation, we focus on this problem and we analyze inter-sign timing for synthesis purposes.

3   Our Synthesis System

Our synthesis system aims to build new utterances in LSF. To this end, it creates sentences concatenatively by:

(i) retrieving motion chunks corresponding to isolated signs, glosses (groups of signs with a specific meaning), or semantic components from our motion database, and

(ii) adding transitions between those chunks to create a continuous motion.

3.1   Data-Based Concatenative Synthesis

The system is based on a dual heterogeneous database containing both a database indexed by linguistic annotations and a second one indexed by the motion signal that has been recorded using motion capture. Furthermore, movements are annotated on different linguistic levels corresponding to grammatical indications, two-hand glosses, and finer phonological or phonetic levels (including right and left handshapes, hand placement and mouthing [4,9]). These different levels are annotated on different channels.

To create a new LSF utterance, the user first edits the sentence by selecting a sequence of glosses organized in an order that is grammatically correct in LSF. The motion chunks corresponding to the glosses are then extracted from the motion database using the annotations. The concatenative synthesis then consists in concatenating those motion chunks by adding transitions between each glosse (see for example Fig. 1). This process is based on the assumption that the semantic annotation is accurate.

Note that in our system, we could query the database to retrieve motion primitives by channel, and we will show in Sect. 4 that this would be more accurate, although the proposed synthesis presented at the end of the paper does not yet take advantage of this possibility.

Segmentation. The aim of the segmentation is to explicitly identify at which frame a sign or a component of sign starts and at which frame it ends. One of the main difficulties of this process relies on the identification of the starting and ending of the meaningful part of the sign (called *meaning*).

Unlike speech in which transitions between words is silence, movement never stops and there is no reference starting point in space or rest hand configuration. However, there is a phase when the hand (or arm) prepares to move towards the starting position/configuration of the hand for the sign about to be executed. This phase is called *preparation* of the sign. For the same reason, before preparing to make the next sign, the hand/arm system first needs to retract to be ready to prepare for the next sign. This phase is named *retraction*. As we capture full sentences of LSF, each sign recorded in our database will be of the following form: *Preparation-Meaning-Retraction*. The annotation identifies the *meaning* part of each sign, the *preparation* and *retraction* being respectively the frames before and after the *meaning*.

Transition Synthesis. We implemented two algorithms to synthesize transitions between two signs: the *Interpolation* and the *Blending* techniques.

The Motion Interpolation Method: it consists in doing a linear **interpolation** of both joint orientations and joint positions between the last posture of the first sign and the first posture of the second sign (see Figs. 1 and 13). In that case, we do not use the *retraction* motion of the first sign nor the *preparation* motion of the second sign. The duration of the interpolation (i.e. the number of frames n being added between both motion chunks) is based on the distance between M_{1_N} and M_{2_0} and the mean velocities of M_1 and M_2 (see Sect. 5.2, SIMPLE_DURATION, for details on the computation). This method is simple to compute but does not take into account the transition data recorded in the

Fig. 1. Transition using the motion *Interpolation* method based on the last posture of the first sign and the first posture of the second sign.

database. As a result, it gives visually poor results when the duration exceeds a certain threshold.

The Motion Blending Method: it is computed as a linear **blending** of two motions: the movement following the first sign (*retraction* of M_1) and the movement preceding the second sign (*preparation* of M_2) in the *Sign3D* database (see Fig. 2). The transition length, i.e. the number of frames n used for the blending, is computed as previously (see Sect. 5.2, SIMPLE_DURATION, for details on the computation). This method gives better results in terms of realism (partial conservation of the context) and robustness with respect to a longer duration. However, the quality of the resulting movement greatly depends on the content of the database. For instance, if there is no captured motion before the second sign or after the first sign in the database, the transition will be less realistic (use of an idle skeleton with a default posture instead).

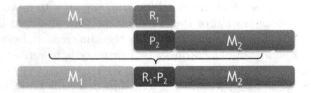

Fig. 2. Transition using the motion *Blending* method with the n first frames of the *retraction* phase R_1 of the first sign and the n last frames of the *preparation* phase P_2 of the second sign.

For both methods, the quality of the original annotation that will identify the *meaning* phase of a sign is of prime importance. However, when the annotation is manually done, usually by watching the corresponding video, it is not always easy to find the actual starting and ending frames of the *meaning* phase, let apart that both hands are not always synchronous as we will show in Sect. 4.1.

The second important parameter of the concatenative synthesis is the choice of the length of the transition to be constructed. Considering the organization of the database, if the computed duration is too long, part of another sign could be extracted in addition to the *preparation* or *retraction* part. For example, in our database, a transition lasts on average about 0.30 s (i.e. 30 frames) and never exceeds 50 frames while a sign may last about 20 frames. It is straightforward that if the computed transition time exceeds by 20 frames or more the transition time recorded in the database (>50 frames), the transition will be computed using the previous sign and the *preparation* of the next sign when it should only use the *preparation* phase of the next sign. This results in a quite unrealistic motion that will appear as an hesitation from the avatar in the final synthesis. For the same reason, if the annotation is shifted by 10 frames from the actual point in time from where it should be, it will impact the final synthesis in the same way or by creating truncated motions.

This illustrates the need of a good computation of the transition duration as well as an accurate annotation of the database.

3.2   Overview of the Paper

In this paper, we first study the segmentation of the motion, by looking at the manual annotation provided by deaf experts in annotating LSF data as well as at an automatically refined annotation that we compute. Both annotations are then used to study the transitions in captured data to derive rules and metrics to use in our concatenative synthesis system to create new utterances in LSF (see Fig. 3).

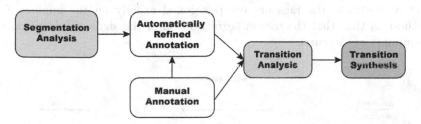

Fig. 3. Overview of the paper: we first study the segmentation of the captured data and improve the manual annotation; we then use both annotations to study the nature and length of transitions; we finally show some results using our findings in our synthesis system.

4   Segmentation

In sign languages, the signer alternates between signs and transitions. When processing recordings of sign language utterances, the first step consists in manually isolating signs from inter-sign movements using an annotation software such as ELAN [3,22]. This step consumes both time and resources as at least one person has to review each video in order to produce a correct annotation. Another drawback of this manual annotation step is that it is a subjective task that greatly depends on the annotator's criteria and on the quality of the data to be processed. Indeed, it is often difficult to point out with certainty the beginning and end of a sign due to the inter-sign coarticulation and the continuous aspect of movement.

4.1 Kinematic Features of LSF Motion

In order to study a possible correlation between the kinematic properties of the hand motions and the sign/transition segmentation, sequences of LSF composed of two or three signs separated by transitions were examined. Those sequences, considered as the ground truth, are raw motions directly extracted from the *Sign3D* database which contains different utterances in French Sign Language. We have computed several kinematic features on those motions for various joints and observed that the speed (i.e. the norm of the velocity) of both wrists had interesting properties.

The Figs. 4 and 5 show the speed of both hands (left wrist and right wrist) for two different sign sequences. A green plain vertical line marks the beginning of a sign while a green dotted vertical line shows the end of the sign and the beginning of the transition, according to the manual segmentation. The dotted blue and red lines show the local minima of the two curves, respectively depicting the speed of the right hand and the left hand. The values were processed using a lowpass filter to prevent the algorithm from detecting all the incidental minima due to noise in the data.

According to the manual segmentation, the transitions seem to be delimited by two local minima in the norm of the velocity even though, due to the manual aspect of the task, the tags are not positioned exactly on the minima. Our hypothesis is thus that the correct segmentation of the signs should be on the local minima of the curves.

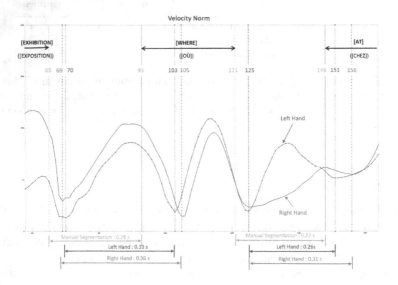

Fig. 4. Norm of the velocity of the left (red line with markers) and right (blue line) hands with respect to the frame number. The vertical lines show the edge of the transition defined by the annotator (green lines), the local minima of the right hand (blue lines) and the local minima of the left hand (red lines). (Color figure online)

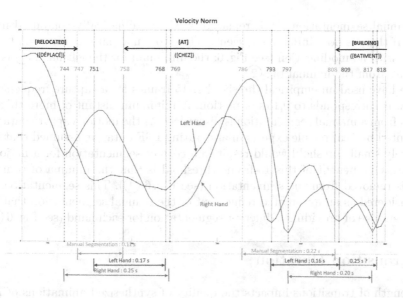

Fig. 5. Norm of the velocity of the left (red line with markers) and right (blue line) hands with respect to the frame number. The vertical lines show the edge of the transition defined by the annotator (green lines), the local minima of the right hand (blue lines), and the local minima of the left hand (red lines). An offset between the minima for each hand is visible. (Color figure online)

Furthermore, when doing manual segmentation, the whole body is considered. So, the starting and ending time of a sign is considered to be the same for all the skeleton joints. However, that is not always true in practice. On Fig. 5, we can note that, assuming that minima delimit a transition, the transition of the left hand does not occur at the same time than the transition of the right hand. Indeed, there is an offset between the minima for each hand.

Therefore, we decided to refine the manual segmentation of motion capture data of French Sign Language by:

(i) detecting the speed minima of hand motions, and
(ii) assuming that the joints of the two hands are partially autonomous.

This refinement aims to improve the quality of the segmentation in order to perform a more accurate analysis and synthesis of LSF utterances.

4.2   Semi-automatic Segmentation

The detection of the speed minima of the hand motions is a fully automated process. However, it presents mixed results when used for LSF segmentation because of false positives when a sign is too noisy or complex (like the sign [AFTERNOON] which is a contraction of [AFTER] and [NOON] in LSF).

We have thus used a combination of the manual annotation and the local minima computation. When a minimum is close to a manual segmentation tag, the manual segmentation tag is replaced by the automatically computed minimum. If there is no minimum sufficiently close to a manual segmentation tag, it is kept with no modification (see Fig. 6: the minimum for the left hand ③ is too far away from the manual tag ②).

We have used an empirical threshold of 15 frames for a capture frequency of 100 Hz: it corresponds to 0.15 s of motion. A minimum distant of more than 15 frames from a manual segmentation is discarded. As the motion capture data was segmented by deaf people experts in annotating LSF data, we assumed that this relatively small threshold would result in a correct segmentation for a majority of cases. One benefit of this 15-frame threshold is that the minima of complex signs is removed from the segmentation (see Fig. 6 ④). This segmentation can be considered as an automated refinement of the manual segmentation that has the advantage of providing a different segmentation for each hand (see Fig. 6 ①).

5 Transition Duration

The length of transitions impacts the quality of synthesized animations of LSF utterances. A too short or too long transition will be perceived as strange and will often have repercussions on the general comprehension of the sentence [13]. The computation of a correct duration for transitions is therefore necessary.

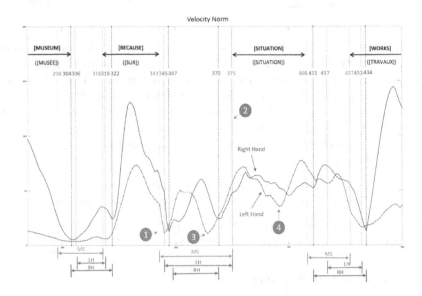

Fig. 6. Norm of the velocity of the left (red line with markers) and right (blue line) hands with respect to the frame number. The vertical lines show the edge of the transition defined by the annotator (Manual Segmentation (MS) with green lines) and refined by the segmentation procedure (blue lines for the right hand (RH) and red lines for the left hand (LH)). (Color figure online)

5.1   Analysis

In order to define some empirical laws and invariants for the transition duration, we considered 89 transitions extracted from two sequences of motion capture data in the *Sign3D* database [9]. The first sequence (SIG_S1_X04) is a presentation of the opening and closing times of various town places (swimming pool, museum, etc.). The second sequence (SIG_S3_X02) explains the change of location of various exhibitions due to some incidents. Table 1 shows an example extracted from each sequence. The 89 transitions are the motions between two consecutive signs. They are extracted from the sequences using the annotations, either manual or the automatically refined annotation presented in Sect. 4.2.

Table 1. Example of utterances contained in the database

Sequence	Extracted utterances (*English translation*)
SIG_S1_X04	The swimming pool in front of the theater is open from 12:00 a.m to 11:00 p.m
SIG_S3_X02	The museum exhibition was moved to the theater due to construction works

Duration with Respect to the Distances Between Postures. The **duration** of each transition was computed from the annotation times of the beginning tag and end tag of the transition.

The average distances between the last posture of the previous sign and the first posture of the next sign were computed. Two types of distances were used: the **Geodesic Distance** between the joint orientations and the **Euclidean Distance** between the joint positions of the two skeletons. Each distance was averaged on the number of joints.

Considering two skeletons S1 and S2 composed of oriented joints, the Geodesic distance between the orientations (quaternions) of S1 and S2 is defined as the mean of the Geodesic distances between the orientations of each joint of S1 and the corresponding joint of S2:

$$\text{GeodesicDistance}(quaternion\ a, quaternion\ b) = ||log(a^{-1} * b)|| \qquad (1)$$

The Euclidean distance between S1 and S2 is defined as the mean of the Euclidean distances between the positions of each joint of S1 and the corresponding joint of S2:

$$\text{EuclideanDistance}(vector3d\ a, vector3d\ b) = ||a - b|| \qquad (2)$$

To take into account the two types of distances, we normalized them (by subtracting the mean value and dividing by the range of values) and computed the average distance.

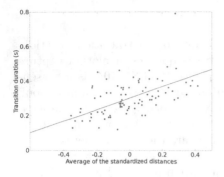
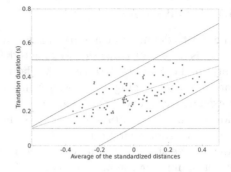

Fig. 7. Duration of the transitions in function of the average of the two normalized distances.

Fig. 8. More than 90% of the values is contained in the area bounded by the lines.

Observations using Manual Annotations: Figures 7 and 8 show the duration of the transitions with respect to the distances between the postures at the beginning and end of the transitions.

Considering our examples, we can note that:

1. The general tendency of the duration is to increase with the distance.
2. Apart from a single outlier, the duration never exceeds 0.5 s.
3. The duration never goes under 0.1 s.
4. More than 90% of the values is contained in a diamond shaped bounding box (see Fig. 8).
5. The mean duration of a transition is 0.303 s with a standard deviation of 0.098 s.

Comparison with the Refined Segmentation (Sect. 4): Figure 9 shows the transition duration as a function of the mean Euclidean distance for the left joints (on the left) and for the right joints (on the right). The transition lengths of the left and right hand are considered independently and are, therefore, different for each hand. As each hand uses a different segmentation, only the arm joints (from the shoulder to the tip of the fingers) were studied and the mean Euclidean distance is, once again, computed between the last skeleton of the first sign and the first skeleton of the second sign. The blue diamond shaped markers represent the values for the manual segmentation whereas the red circle markers show the results considering the segmentation described in Sect. 4.2. The lines between the pairs of markers depict the differences between the results of the two methods of segmentation.

Figure 9 confirms that there is an important difference, visible in the length of the lines connecting each two markers, between the segments defined by annotators and by the refinement using the velocity minima. However, the benefits of this new segmentation have to be ascertained using a quantitative and/or a perceptual evaluation.

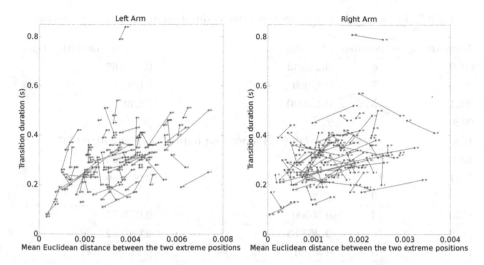

Fig. 9. On the left (right resp.): transition duration with respect to the mean of Euclidean distances of the left joints (right resp.) for the manual segmentation (blue diamond markers) and for the refined segmentation (red disk markers). The line between each pair of markers represents the difference in duration and distance between both segmentations. (Color figure online)

Duration with Respect to the Type of the Surrounding Signs. To determine if the length of the transitions is related to the nature of the surrounding signs, two different features of signs in LSF were examined in order to quantify their impact on the transition duration:

1. The number of hands used in the execution of the sign:
   - 0 = one hand ([MUSEUM] sign, for example),
   - 1 = two hands as in the [SWIMMING POOL] sign, and
   - 2 = one hand is doing a one-hand sign and the other is preserving the context: for example a [POINTING] gesture (one-hand sign) toward the other hand showing the remnant of the previous [EXHIBITION] sign (context). This is a case of contextualized signs.
2. The symmetry of the sign (only in the case of a two-hand sign). A sign is considered as symmetric if the two hands perform a symmetric motion:
   - 0 = the movement is not symmetric (e.g., [HOUR] sign), and
   - 1 = the movement is symmetric as in the [SWIMMING POOL] sign.

A transition was thus defined with four digits, the first two digits designating the features of the previous sign and the last two the features of the following sign. For example, a transition associated with the number 1011 is a transition between a two-hand asymmetric sign (10) and a two-hand symmetric sign (11). The transition 0010 is a transition between a one-hand and thus asymmetric sign (00) and a two-hand asymmetric sign (10). Table 2 lists all of the possible types of transition, their distribution in our data set and the mean duration and standard deviation according to the type of transition and the manual segmentation.

Table 2. List of all the transition types, mean duration and standard deviation

Transition type	Number	Meanduration (s)	Standard deviation (s)
0000	6	**0.26833**	0.095167
0010	7	0.31000	0.090000
0011	5	**0.32000**	0.069642
0020	0	/	/
1000	9 (8)	0.36778 (0.3150 without outlier)	0.16292 (0.041057)
1010	9	**0.33444**	0.098629
1011	11	0.29273	0.054789
1020	0	/	/
1100	4	0.30500	0.077675
1110	16	**0.25813**	0.081912
1111	6	0.31667	0.14528
1120	6	0.29500	0.089610
2000	0	/	/
2010	1	0.30000	0
2011	5	0.30400	0.10761
2020	4	0.30250	0.078049

The shortest transitions are obtained for the transitions from two-hand symmetric signs to two-hand asymmetric signs (1110) and for the passage from one-hand signs to other one-hand signs (0000). Apart from the 1000 transitions whose result is impacted by the outlier (average without outlier: 0.3150 s), the longest transitions are between two-hand asymmetric signs (1010). Figure 10 shows the mean duration of the transitions depending on the number of hands (type 2 considered as two-hand signs). The transition between two one-hand signs (1H → 1H) and two two-hand signs (2H → 2H) is shorter (and might be interpreted as easier) than adding or removing a hand between signs (1H → 2H and 2H → 1H). However, as the standard deviation is quite high compared to the mean values, the conclusion that can be made is that the number of hands and the symmetry of the signs surrounding a transition do not significantly impact the duration of the transition. An analysis of a higher number of transitions could lead to more conclusive results.

5.2   Synthesis

Computation of Transition Duration. By using the results of our analysis, we aim to find a transition duration that best emulates the behavior of a real LSF signer in order to synthesize more natural and intelligible utterances.

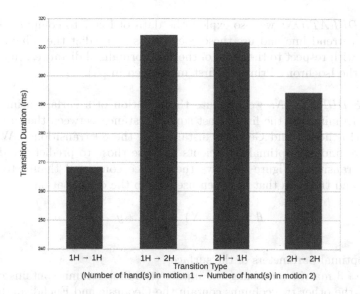

Fig. 10. Mean duration considering the number of hands involved in the first and second signs.

SIMPLE_DURATION: previously to this analysis, the computation of the duration was based on the distance between the extreme positions $S1$ (end of the first movement M_1) and $S2$ (beginning of the second movement M_2) and the mean velocity of the two surrounding signs:

$$simpleDuration = (\alpha * \frac{2 * \text{EuclideanDistance}(S1, S2)}{MeanVel_{M_1} + MeanVel_{M_2}}$$

$$+ (1 - \alpha) * \frac{2 * \text{GeodesicDistance}(S1, S2)}{MeanAngVel_{M_1} + MeanAngVel_{M_2}} \quad (3)$$

This method produces visually acceptable results for small distances and high velocities (short duration) but the computed transition duration is often longer than the ground truth equivalent. It reaches sometimes unacceptable values (sometimes as high as 1.5 s) that give unrealistic results with a slow down or an "hesitation" depending on the type of synthesized transition (*Interpolation* or *Blending* respectively).

Using the results of our analysis we propose three new computation methods of the transition duration.

SIMPLE_BOUNDED_DURATION: a first, simple measure is to put an empirical lower limit at 0.1 s and a higher limit at 0.5 s using the items #2 and #3 of the observations (Sect. 5.1). The transitions with inconsistent duration are thus automatically changed to more correct values. We visually note an improvement in the rendering of the animation for the transitions involved.

LINEAR_DURATION: we also exploit the data of Fig. 7 to compute the coefficients of a trend line and use those coefficients to predict the value of a new transition with respect to the mean of the two normalized distances. In this way, we follow the Isochrony Principle (first mentioned in [7]).

SURFACE_DURATION: we compute the equation of a surface using normal equations to minimize the linear least square distance between the surface and the data (Euclidean and Geodesic distances of the 89 transitions). With this method, we find the optimal coefficients and use those to predict the duration of a new transition. Figure 11 shows the surface computed thanks to normal equations and the data that has been used to do the computation.

$$\theta = (X^T * X)^{-1} * X^T * y \tag{4}$$

- θ: the optimal parameters of the surface,
- X: a $89 * 3$ matrix containing the inputs (the first column contains only the value 1, the other two columns contain the Geodesic and Euclidean distances of each transition respectively), and
- y: a vector containing the durations of the transitions.

Using the Eq. (4) and our data, we found:

$$\theta = \begin{pmatrix} 0.148777 \\ 0.663958 \\ 0.275229 \end{pmatrix}$$

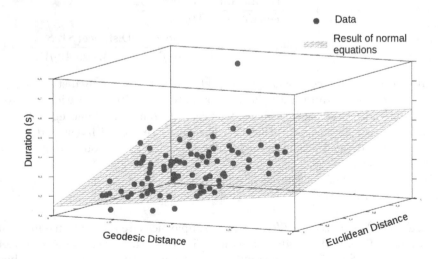

Fig. 11. Surface computed using normal Eq. (4) with the manual annotation data.

The mean error between the real and computed duration for our 89 transitions can be calculated as:

$$MeanError = \frac{1}{89} \sum_{i=1}^{89} \sqrt{(y_i - (X_i * \theta))^2} = 0.06075 \, s \qquad (5)$$

As the analysis of Sect. 5.1 concluded that the number of hands and symmetry of the surrounding signs did not have a great impact on the transition duration, these two parameters were not taken into account in the duration computation.

Results. In this section, we compare and visualize the results of the various computations methods of the transition duration.

We first compare **synthesized transitions with their ground truth equivalent** on a limited number of examples. The ground truth is the original motion capture signal segmented according to the manual annotation. The transition synthesis methods (*Interpolation* or *Blending*) and the duration computation methods (XXX_DURATION) are tested by comparing the resulting animation with the ground truth equivalent. Figure 12 illustrates the transition between the signs [BUILDING] and [THEATER]: an offset between the two skeletons is visible when playing the animation. This offset changes with the parameters of the transition. While the duration of the ground truth is of 0.27 s, the LINEAR_DURATION method gives the closest result with a duration of 0.30 s whereas the SIMPLE_DURATION method is the farthest with 0.37 s.

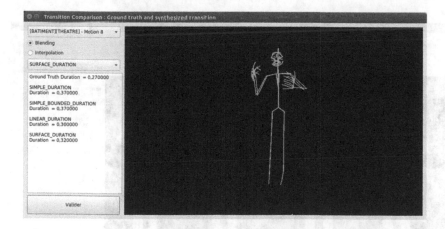

Fig. 12. Comparison of the ground truth with the synthesized transitions. The two skeletons representing the ground truth (in white) and the synthesized motion (in cyan) are superimposed. (Color figure online)

Then, we compared the **synthesized transitions with each other** by choosing to pair any, not necessarily consecutive, signs in the database. It is thus impossible to compare the performances of the generated transition with the ground truth which does not exist but, instead, we can compare the synthesized transitions with one another.

On Fig. 13, the user has chosen to analyze the transition between the sign [TO PAY] and the sign [MUSEUM]. The duration of the corresponding transition has been computed for each of the methods. We can see that the SIMPLE_DURATION method gives an abnormally high value of 1.47 s. Indeed, the Euclidean distance between the two extreme skeletons of the transition is equal to 1.08172 and the Geodesic distance is 0.103753. The high value of the Euclidean distance can be explained by the fact that [TO PAY] is a two-hand sign and [MUSEUM] is a one-hand sign (see Fig. 13).

The resulting transition is not convincing using either the *Interpolation* (slow-down) or *Blending* (artifacts due to unwanted sign chunks added to the animation) generation techniques.

The SURFACE_DURATION gives a much more acceptable result with a transition of 0.51539 s:

$$duration = \theta_0 + \theta_1 * GeoDist + \theta_2 * EucDist$$
$$= 0.148777 + 0.663958 * 0.103753 + 0.275229 * 1.08172$$
$$= 0.51539s$$

The other methods do not allow the duration to exceed the 0.5 s boundary and their results are also more convincing than the SIMPLE_DURATION method.

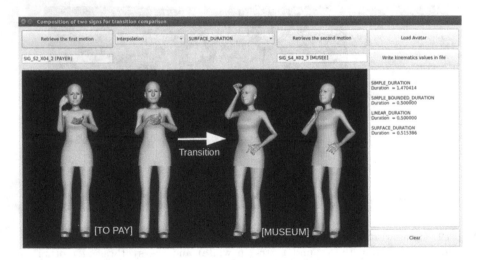

Fig. 13. Composition of two signs for transition comparison. The last posture of the first movement is quite far from the first posture of the second movement.

Improvement of Motion Retrieval. The previous analysis shows that the distance between two consecutive motions has an impact on the transition duration. We also know that a long duration will often be less realistic than a shorter duration. We thus implemented a new motion retrieval method based on those observations. This method retrieves a motion from a range of possible motions in order to minimize the average distance of this motion with the previous and/or following motion. By minimizing the distance, the duration of the transition is naturally shorter than if we had taken a random motion among all of the possible motions.

6 Conclusion

In this paper, we studied the coarticulation aspect of sign languages by focusing on the transition segmentation and duration.

We first proposed a new way of segmenting LSF utterances by analyzing some kinematic properties of sign language motions and, more specifically, by detecting local minima in the norm of the velocity for each hand. The manual annotations done by deaf experts were then refined by selecting the nearest corresponding minima for each manual segment.

In a second phase, the transition duration was analyzed with respect to the distance covered during a transition and to the type of the surrounding signs. Based on our observations, we defined new methods to compute transition durations based on our observations. An extremely simple and effective method resulting in a visual improvement of the animation is to introduce a lower and upper limit in the duration. Other approaches using basic statistics on the data were implemented. For our dataset, the nature of the surrounding signs did not impact significantly the duration of the transition. An analysis of a higher number of transitions could lead to more conclusive results. This approach raises questions concerning the synchronization of the sign language channels. Indeed, our segmentation is based on the observation that each hand has a partially autonomous behavior. The offset between both hands will be the focus of future studies.

Using these observations, we aim to improve our synthesis engine by handling the two hands separately. This process will be evaluated thanks to perceptual studies with native LSF signers testing, on the one hand, the intelligibility and comprehensibility of the produced sentences and, on the other hand, the acceptability and realism (3D rendering, smoothness, etc.) of the animation. Other issues may be addressed such as the advantages of segmenting each channel (hand configuration, placement, orientation, non-manual features, etc.) separately both for retrieving signs in our database and for synthesizing sentences. In the future, we would like to use our semi-automatic segmentation on a larger corpus composed of carefully chosen utterances to perform further analyses.

Acknowledgements. The observations of this paper were based on the motion capture data and annotations of the *Sign3D* project [9].

References

1. Awad, C., Courty, N., Duarte, K., Naour, T., Gibet, S.: A combined semantic and motion capture database for real-time sign language synthesis. In: Ruttkay, Z., Kipp, M., Nijholt, A., Vilhjálmsson, H.H. (eds.) IVA 2009. LNCS (LNAI), vol. 5773, pp. 432–438. Springer, Heidelberg (2009). doi:10.1007/978-3-642-04380-2_47
2. Brand, M., Kettnaker, V.: Discovery and segmentation of activities in video. IEEE Trans. Pattern Anal. Mach. Intell. **22**(8), 844–851 (2000)
3. Crasborn, O., Sloetjes, H.: Enhanced ELAN functionality for sign language corpora. In: Proceedings of LREC, Sixth International Conference on Language Resources and Evaluation (2008)
4. Duarte, K.: Motion capture and avatars as portals for analyzing the linguistic structure of sign languages. Ph.D. thesis, Université Bretagne Sud (2012)
5. Endres, D., Christensen, A., Omlor, L., Giese, M.A.: Segmentation of action streams human observers vs. Bayesian binning. In: Proceedings of KI 2011: Advances in Artificial Intelligence, 34th Annual German Conference on AI, pp. 75–86 (2011)
6. Fod, A., Matarić, M.J., Jenkins, O.C.: Automated derivation of primitives for movement classification. Auton. Robots **12**(1), 39–54 (2002)
7. Freeman, F.N.: Experimental analysis of the writing movement. Psychol. Monogr. **17**, 1–57 (1914)
8. Gibet, S., Courty, N., Duarte, K., Le Naour, T.: The *SignCom* system for data-driven animation of interactive virtual signers: methodology and evaluation. Trans. Interact. Intell. Syst. (Tiis) **1**, 6:1–6:23 (2011)
9. Gibet, S., Lefebvre-Albaret, F., Hamon, L., Brun, R., Turki, A.: Interactive editing in french sign language dedicated to virtual signers: requirements and challenges. Univ. Access Inf. Soc. **15**(4), 525–539 (2016)
10. Gong, D., Medioni, G., Zhu, S., Zhao, X.: Kernelized temporal cut for online temporal segmentation and recognition. In: Fitzgibbon, A., Lazebnik, S., Perona, P., Sato, Y., Schmid, C. (eds.) ECCV 2012. LNCS, vol. 7574, pp. 229–243. Springer, Heidelberg (2012). doi:10.1007/978-3-642-33712-3_17
11. Gonzalez, M.: Un système de segmentation automatique de gestes appliqué à la langue des signes (French) [An automated gesture segmentation system applied to sign language]. In: JEP-TALN-RECITAL, p. 9398 (2012)
12. Hanke, T., Matthes, S., Regen, A., Worseck, S.: Where does a sign start and end? Segmentation of continuous signing. In: Language Resources and Evaluation Conference (2012)
13. Huenerfauth, M.: A linguistically motivated model for speed and pausing in animations of American sign language. ACM Trans. Access. Comput. **2**(2), 9:1–9:31 (2009). doi:10.1145/1530064.1530067. Article no. 9. ACM, New York, USA
14. Barbic, J., Safonova, A., Pan, J.-Y., Faloutsos, C., Hodgins, J.K., Pollard, N.S.: Segmenting motion capture data into distinct behaviors. In: Graphics Interface, May 2004
15. Johnson, R.E., Liddell, S.K.: A segmental framework for representing signs phonetically. Sign Lang. Stud. **11**(3), 408–463 (2011)
16. Johnston, T., De Beuzeville, L.: Researching the linguistic use of space in Auslan: guidelines for annotators using the Auslan corpus. In Technical report, Department of Linguistics, Macquarie University (2009)
17. Kim, J.-B., Park, K.-H., Bang, W.-C., Bien, Z.Z.: Continuous Korean sign language recognition using gesture segmentation and Hidden Markov Model. In: Proceedings of the 2002 IEEE International Conference on Fuzzy Systems (2001)

18. Kita, S., van Gijn, I., van der Hulst, H.: Movement phases in signs and co-speech gestures, and their transcription by human coders. In: Wachsmuth, I., Fröhlich, M. (eds.) GW 1997. LNCS, vol. 1371, pp. 23–35. Springer, Heidelberg (1998). doi:10. 1007/BFb0052986

19. Lebourque, T., Gibet, S.: High level specification and control of communication gestures: the GeSsyCa system. In: Proceeding of Computer Animation, Genova, Switzerland (1999)

20. Lefebvre-Albaret, F.: Traitement automatique de vidéos en LSF. Modélisation et exploitation des contraintes phonologiques du mouvement (French) [Automatic processing of LSF videos. Modelling and exploitation of the phonological constraints of motion]. Ph.D. thesis, Université Paul Sabatier - Toulouse III (2010)

21. Lefebvre-Albaret, F., Dalle, P., Gianni, F.: Toward a computer-aided sign segmentation. In: Language Resources and Evaluation Conference (LREC). European Language Resources Association (2008)

22. Max Planck Institute for Psycholinguistics, The Language Archive, Nijmegen, The Netherlands. http://tla.mpi.nl/tools/tla-tools/elan/

23. Mcdonald, J., Wolfe, R., Wilbur, R.B., Moncrief, R., Malaia, E., Fujimoto, S., Baowidan, S., Stec, J.: A new tool to facilitate prosodic analysis of motion capture data and a data- driven technique for the improvement of avatar motion. In: Proceedings of the 7th Workshop on the Representation and Processing of Sign Languages: Corpus Mining Language Resources and Evaluation Conference (LREC), vol. 7 (2016)

24. Müller, M., Baak, A., Seidel, H.-P.: Efficient and robust annotation of motion capture data. In: Symposium on Computer Animation (2009)

25. Müller, M., Röder, T., Clausen, M.: Efficient content-based retrieval of motion capture data. ACM Trans. Graph. **24**(3), 677–685 (2005)

26. Ségouat, J.: Modélisation de la coarticulation en Langue des Signes Française pour la diffusion automatique d'informations en gare ferroviaire à l'aide d'un signeur virtuel (French) [Modelling coarticulation in LSF for automatic broadcast of information in train stations using an avatar]. Ph.D. thesis, Université Paris Sud - Paris XI (2010)

27. Yang, R., Sarkar, S.: Detecting coarticulation in sign language using conditional random fields. In: Proceedings of the 18th International Conference on Pattern Recognition, vol. 2, pp. 108–112. IEEE Computer Society, Washington, DC, USA (2006)

Investigation of Feature Elements and Performance Improvement for Sign Language Recognition by Hidden Markov Model

Tatsunori Ozawa, Hirotoshi Shibata, Hiromitsu Nishimura,
and Hiroshi Tanaka$^{(\boxtimes)}$

Kanagawa Institute of Technology, 1030 Shimo-ogino,
Atsugi-Shi, Kanagawa, Japan
{s1321059, s1585009}@cce.kanagawa-it.ac.jp,
{nisimura, h_tanaka}@ic.kanagawa-it.ac.jp

Abstract. Sign language is commonly used as one means of communication for hearing-impaired or speech-impaired people. However, there are many difficulties in learning sign language. If automatic translation for sign language can be realized, it would be extremely valuable and helpful not just to those who are physically impaired but to unimpaired people as well. The cause of the difficulty in automatic translation is that there are many kinds of specific hand motions and shapes, which make it difficult to discriminate each motion. Consequently, this has a negative impact on accurate recognition. This paper presents a recognition method that is able to maintain accurate recognition of different signs that encompass a multitude hand motions and shapes. The main feature of our approach is the use of colored gloves to detect hand motions and shapes. For our investigation, a recognition scheme using HMM (Hidden Markov Model) has been introduced to enhance recognition performance. In this scheme, performance depends on the feature elements extracted from each sign language motion. Feature elements of sign language motions and their unification are investigated, and the recognition performance is clarified using these feature elements and compared with each result. Although the percentage of recognition successes for each feature element is low, from 21.7% to 42.7%, it was shown that recognition success for the combined element results increased from 55.2% to 61.9% for 25 different sign language motions. In addition, the removal of candidates was also examined to enhance performance as a form of preprocessing using a threshold obtained from DP matching. It is also confirmed through experiments that the recognition success rate increased by a few percentage.

Keywords: Sign language · Color gloves · Optical camera · Hidden Markov Model · Feature elements · DP matching

1 Introduction

Sign language is a widely used communication method for hearing or speech impaired people. It is quite difficult to learn sign language. If automatic translation for sign language could be realized, it would become very meaningful and valuable to both

© Springer International Publishing AG 2017
M. Antona and C. Stephanidis (Eds.): UAHCI 2017, Part II, LNCS 10278, pp. 76–88, 2017.
DOI: 10.1007/978-3-319-58703-5_6

impaired people and physically unimpaired people. Although interpretation from sign language to speech has also been studied for many years, the technologies have not yet matured to the level at which they can be put into practical use. Specifically, some methods that use a special sensor or device [1, 2] are associated with high introduction costs or sensors must be attached to the body. The detection target is mainly limited to hand motions and hand shape, and finger motions are not included. For this reason, achieving highly accurate recognition is difficult and the number of words that can be recognized using these methods is limited [3, 4]. Thus, the results that can be obtained with existing technologies are insufficient in terms of developing a system that can be put into practical use. In addition, because the scenario for usage has necessarily been limited in experiments, in previous studies, researchers have not even attempted to put them to practical use.

The authors have been investigating a method of sign language recognition using the optical camera and colored gloves shown in Fig. 1 [5, 6]. Since an optical camera is implemented in smartphones, this configuration can be used anywhere, although the colored gloves are also necessary. By using an optical camera and colored gloves, each finger can be discriminated by color and therefore hand shape can be correctly detected.

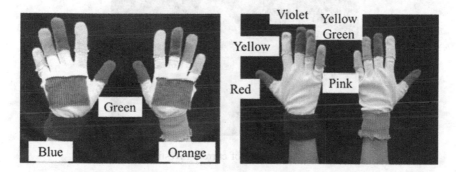

Fig. 1. Proposed colored gloves (Color figure online)

Automatic translation is our final goal, but remains too difficult to realize with current technology. Therefore, the authors are now trying to produce a kind of learning tool for sign language. Video data relevant to sign language can be obtained from the web site. Figure 2 shows an image from an instruction video demonstrating sign language motion. A learner memorizes the motions of each sign from this video. However, it is quite difficult not only to memorize the motion but also to confirm the validity of the motion memorized from the video. A tool for checking the learned motion is essential. An example of the use of our current research technology is shown in Fig. 3. After memorizing the sign language motion, the learner displays the same motion in front of a web camera connected to a PC. If the PC recognizes his/her motion, the positive result shows on the display. The learner uses this system as a review tool for sign language.

Fig. 2. Instructional video for sign language motions

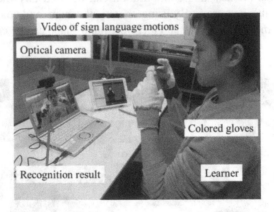

Fig. 3. Application of current investigation

In this paper, we describe recognition schemes for sign language motions, and experimental results. The hidden Markov model (HMM), which is used for recognition in several fields such as voice recognition, was used in this investigation. Since this method can easily be adapted to the recognition of a wide variety of feature elements of motions, excellent recognition performance can be expected.

2 Preparation of Learning Models for Recognition

The authors used DP matching [7] for sign language recognition in an earlier investigation [5, 6]. Hand motions were detected as the motion of the center of gravity of the colored region on the wrists. We decided to use the HMM recognition method, as this model can include many kinds of feature elements from video image data representing sign language motion, which can be useful in the instructional process. Improved recognition can be expected when the appropriate feature elements of sign language motions are used.

The instructional video data for sign language words included in Smart Deaf [8] is divided into 35 categories based on the usage areas of each sign. Each category includes roughly 50 to 100 words. In this study, recognition targets in sign language motions are selected according to the words included in each category. Demand for words relevant to medical and health issues is high, so we selected 25 words from this category (Table 1).

Table 1. Target sign language words

1.アトピー	2.おしっこ	3.ガン	4.コンタクト	5.喘息
1. Atopic	2. Urinary	3. Cancer	4. Contact lens	5. Asthma
6.体調	7.ハゲ	8.発熱	9.病気	10.盲腸
6. Physical condition	7. Bald	8. Fever	9. Sickness	10. Cecum
11.顔が赤い	12.カテーテル	13.禁煙	14.喫煙	15.薬を飲む
11. Blushing	12. Catheter	13. No smoking	14. Smoking	15. Take medicine
16.呼吸	17.耳鼻科	18.頭痛	19.摘出	20.糖尿病
16. Breath	17. Otorhinology	18. Headache	19. Remove	20. Diabetes
21.脳卒中	22.吐き気	23.鼻水	24.昼寝	25.虫歯
21. Stroke	22. Nausea	23. Runny nose	24. Nap	25. Tooth decay

One of the most important tasks in a recognition investigation is to compose the dataset for a recognition experiment and its evaluation. It is especially important to have sufficient motion data for each sign language word in order to create the learning model for HMM. Multiple motion data sets from multiple operators are required for the learning process. The recognition process uses HMM and calculates the likelihood values that the input motion data represents each possible sign language motion. The word with the highest likelihood value is selected as the recognition result.

Clearly, it is quite important to gather correct motion data. Therefore, the authors asked for the cooperation of the person in charge of making the motion video of Smart Deaf to compose the set of motion data used in this investigation. Figure 4 shows the signer directing and checking the sign language motions of the experimenter. The motion data for 25 words were recorded for learning and evaluation. The number of persons used for collecting motion data, and the number of samples for each motion are indicated in Table 2. The total number of collected motion data samples was 2250 $(60 \times 25 + 30 \times 25)$. The number of experimenters and the number of samples for each word were based on the pre-study as the optimum for applying the learning HMM and recognition performance. The conditions under which the motion data were captured are as follows.

(i) Camera image resolution of 800×600 pixels is selected.
(ii) Illumination is set at about 200 lx for both the camera side and singer side.
(iii) Frame rate is 30 fps (frames per second). This is the maximum rate for a standard Web camera and smartphone.
(iv) The distance between the camera and signer is one mater, as this distance is considered to coincide with a real situation.

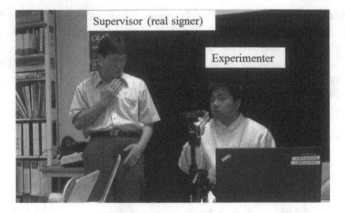

Fig. 4. Scene of sign language instruction

Table 2. Collected motion data for learning and evaluation

	Singers	Sample/Signer	Total
Data for learning	A, B, C	20	60
Data for evaluation	D, E, F	10	30

(v) The color of the signer's clothes and the background wall is black to facilitate easy detection of the colored region of colored gloves.

(vi) The height in the field of view of the camera is set at a position that prevents the wrists of the signer being detected when he/she lowers his/her arm in order to make clear the beginning and the end of a sign language motion.

We are now trying to compose sign language motion data as a corpus for analysis. Therefore, these conditions will be included the next time we collect motion data.

3 Feature Elements

DP matching was used for the recognition of hand motions in the previous investigation. However, hand speed and hand position are also important features of sign language motions. The following features were extracted from the motion data for each sign.

(i) Shape of hand motion

The sequence of positions recorded as x and y coordinates indicates the shape of the hand motion. Since the size of the motion differs for each user, a normalization scheme for these data was applied, based on the normalization process represented by expression (1). Figure 5 shows the shape of a hand motion, i.e. the progressive positions of the center of the gravity of the wrist. The figure on the left is from the raw data before normalization, and the one on the right is the result of normalization. In addition, linear interpolation was applied when there was no color region detection due to occlusion or no color detection.

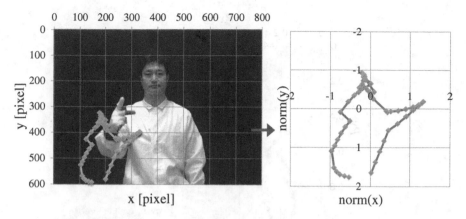

Fig. 5. Shape of hand motion before and after normalization

$$norm(x_i) = \frac{(x_i - \bar{x})}{\sqrt{\frac{1}{n}\sum_{i=1}^{n}\left((x_i - \bar{x})^2 + (y_i - \bar{y})^2\right)}}$$
$$norm(y_i) = \frac{(y_i - \bar{y})}{\sqrt{\frac{1}{n}\sum_{i=1}^{n}\left((x_i - \bar{x})^2 + (y_i - \bar{y})^2\right)}} \Bigg\} \quad (1)$$

Here,

i: i^{th} frame of motion data

n: the total number of frames of sign language motion data

(ii) Speed of hand motion

The speed of motion sometimes indicates meaning. The hand-position difference in each successive video frame can be regarded as a measure of the speed of motion, and

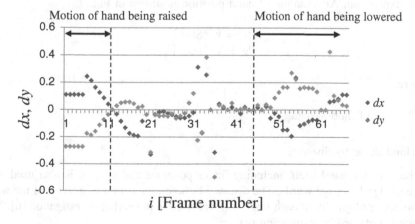

Fig. 6. Hand motion speed

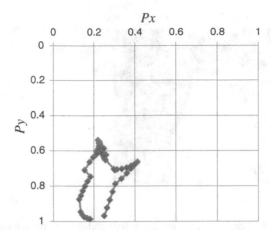

Fig. 7. Hand position

is used as such for this feature element. Hand speed is defined by the following expression. An example of hand motion speed is shown in Fig. 6.

$$
\left. \begin{array}{l} dx_i = x_i - x_{i-1} \\ dy_i = y_i - y_{i-1} \end{array} \right\}
\tag{2}
$$

Here,
i: i^{th} frame of motion data

(iii) Position of hand

The position of the hand includes meaning, so it should be included as a feature element, identified by its position in the image frame. Of course, the division by frame size (x:800, y:600) was used in the normalization process as represented by the following expression. An example of hand position is shown in Fig. 7.

$$
\left. \begin{array}{l} Px_i = x_i \,/\, 800 \\ Py_i = y_i \,/\, 600 \end{array} \right\}
\tag{3}
$$

Here,

i: i^{th} frame of motion data

(iv) Hand shape by distance

The shape of the hand itself, including finger positions and shapes, is also used as a feature of sign language words. The distance between the center of gravity of the wrist and the center of gravity of each finger-tip was used in the earlier investigation [6]. The distance is obtained by expression (4).

$$d_i = \sqrt{(fx_i - w_x)^2 + (fy_i - w_y)^2} \tag{4}$$

Here,

d: distance of center of gravity of wrist and each finger tip
i: Each finger
   (1: Thumb, 2: Forefinger, 3: Middle finger, 4: Ring finger, 5: Little finger)
(f_x, f_y): Center of gravity of colored region of each finger tip
(w_x, w_y): Center of gravity of colored region of wrist (Fig. 8)

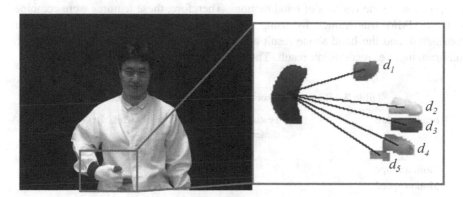

Fig. 8. Hand shape by distance

(v) Hand shape by number of pixels

When a finger is hidden, the distance represented by expression (4) is undefined. Nevertheless, the value 0 is set in method (iv). In this investigation, the number of visible pixels of each finger is also used as feature element for comparison. Of course, each value is divided by each maximum value as normalization. Either of (iv) or (v) is used in the recognition experiment.

4 Recognition Experiment Results

4.1 Recognition Experiment Result for Each Feature

All feature elements were used for the HMM learning process. The HMM learning and likelihood calculations were carried out with HTK. The dimensions of the state and initial values for the HMM, and the number of experimenters and samples used for HMM learning were determined in the pre-investigation. The data set shown in Table 2 was used for HMM learning and the recognition performance evaluation experiment.

The recognition success percentage for each feature element is shown in Table 3. The dimensions of each feature element and the number of HMM states are also shown in this table. The success ratios of the first through third ranks are shown in this table. The hand shape, i.e. the feature based on the number of pixels in each finger-tip image brought the best result.

4.2   Recognition Experiment Using Combined Feature

This experiment was carried out using HTK (Hidden Markov model toolkit) [9]. Table 3 shows the recognition success percentage as well as the learning value of each feature. It is expected that recognition performance can be raised by combining features. Two methods were used to examine the potential for improving the recognition performance. One involved combining three features (shape, speed and position) for HMM learning, and the other was to sum the rankings of the recognition results obtained with each feature. The ranking was in the order of likelihood, that is, 1, 2, 3 ⋯, 25, where 25 was the total number of words that might be recognized. Shape, speed and position are the features of hand motions. Therefore, these features were combined and the HMM was trained by using these features. Of course, both methods are considered, and the hand shape result and their ranking were added to determine the total ranking, i.e. recognition result. The results are shown in Tables 4 and 5.

Table 3. Recognition success ratio by each feature element

Feature value	Feature element dimension	Number of states	Recognition success ratio	
			1st	1st-3rd
Motion shape	2	4	21.7%	41.2%
Motion speed	2	4	28.5%	51.9%
Motion position	2	4	34.0%	69.6%
Hand shape (Distance)	5	3	39.7%	70.4%
Hand shape (Number of pixels)	5	3	42.7%	68.1%

Table 4. Recognition results by combining feature elements

Feature element		Success ratio	
		1st	1st-3rd
A	{Shape, Speed, Position}	Hand shape (Distance)	61.2%	84.1%
B	{Shape, Speed, Position}	Hand shape (Number of pixels)	55.2%	80.3%

Table 5. Recognition results by sum of ranking of each result

Feature element				Success ratio	
				1st	1st-3rd
A	Shape	Speed	Position	I land shape (distance)	61.9%	82.1%
B	Shape	Speed	Position	Hand shape (Number of pixels)	58.8%	81.1%

Similar results were obtained by both methods. The success percentage rose to around 60%, and increased to over 80% when 3rd rankings were included. It seems possible to use this method as a review tool for confirming the correctness of a learner's sign language motions.

5   Enhancement of Recognition Performance

The recognition results shown in Tables 4 and 5 are not sufficient for practical use. This section shows the methods we used to enhance recognition performance.

5.1   Selection of Candidates

As the number of words to be recognized increases, the more difficult it becomes to maintain recognition performance. The basic idea is that some of the recognition candidates should be eliminated before the HMM recognition process by using a number of relevant criteria. DP matching is used as the criterion in this investigation. This method has been widely used in voice and motion recognition [10]. There were experiences in the past investigation [5] where recognition using DP matching includes correct result when we selected the half of the recognition target words. This means that although the performance of DP matching cannot necessarily achieve the high recognition results obtainable using the HMM schemes, the possibility that correct results will be achieved is high if we take multiple candidates. Therefore, the authors used the results of DP matching to select the candidates of the recognition results before applying the HMM recognition scheme. DP matching calculates the distance of two vector elements, which is the motion data shown in Fig. 9. This is obtained from the movement of the center of gravity of the colored region of the wrist. This is an example of the motion of representing the word of "Diabetes". These motion data in a time sequence are used for DP matching. The more similar two motions are the smaller the distance for two motions by DP matching.

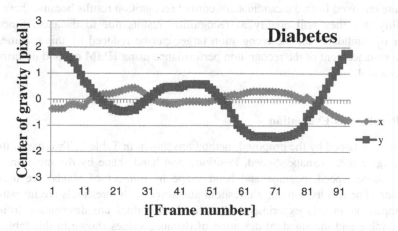

Fig. 9. Example of motion data for DP matching

The proposed recognition process sequence is shown in Fig. 10. Before the initiating the recognition process using HMM, the threshold values are decided for each word to be recognized as a pre-process, and these values are used for selection of

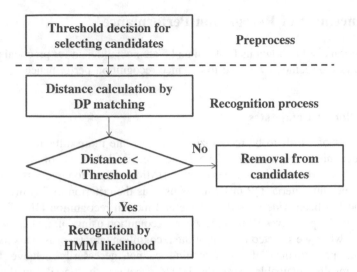

Fig. 10. Performance enhancement by introduction of threshold

correct candidates by sigh language recognition using HMM. The authors add a data set for this purpose (Table 6) as data for the threshold. Since the similarity of two motions is obtained as the distance of two motions, the distance of each word was used as the criterion for motion data to be recognized. We obtained 1800 (60 × 30) pieces of distance data from 60 samples for learning and 30 samples for deciding the threshold. The threshold values were determined from these distance values. If the distance of data for learning and the data for evaluation exceeds this threshold, these words are removed from the candidate of correct recognition results because there is no possibility that they will qualify as recognition results due to distance. Since the number of candidates for the recognition target can be reduced by this scheme, this leads to enhancement of the recognition performance using HMM method described in Sects. 3 and 4.

5.2 Results and Evaluation

The results obtained by the proposed method are shown in Table 7. Two cases, that is, combining feature ({Shape, Speed, Position} and hand shape by distance) and each feature (shape, speed, position and hand shape by number of pixels) are used for evaluation. The results without a threshold and some with thresholds are investigated for comparison in this experiment. The threshold values are determined from the average value and the standard deviation of distance values shown in this table. It is verified that the recognition performance can be enhanced, from 61.2% to 63.7% (from 81.6% to 85.6%) and 55.8% to 61.3% (from 81.1% to 84.5%), by setting appropriate threshold values in the experiment.

We confirmed the validity of this removal method. While the correct candidates must be retained, any word that has no possibility of a correct answer should be

Table 6. Dataset for experiments for proposed method

	Signers	Sample/Signer	Total
Data for learning	A, B, C	20	60
Data for evaluation	D, E, F	10	30
Data for threshold	G, H, I	10	30

Table 7. Recognition results by threshold

Threshold	Recognition success rate			
	Combining feature		Each feature	
	1st	1st-3rd	1st	1st-3rd
None	61.2%	81.6%	58.8%	81.1%
$\mu - \sigma$	55.9%	68.7%	53.2%	68.4%
μ	63.7%	85.6%	61.3%	84.5%
$\mu + \sigma$	63.5%	85.1%	60.8%	83.6%

Table 8. Evaluation of eliminated candidates

Number of samples (incorrect)			Number of samples (correct)		
Total	Removed	Percent	Total	Removed	Percent
18,000	8,733	48.5%	750	17	2.3%

removed by the proposed method. Among 25 words to be recognized, the number of correct samples is 750(= 1 × 25 × 30), and the number to be eliminated is 18,000 (= 24 × 25 × 30). We checked the eliminated samples using the proposed methods in each feature case. The results are shown in Table 8. The table on the left shows the removed candidates from incorrect candidates and the table on the right shows the results from correct samples. Almost half of the incorrect candidates and about 2% of the correct candidates can be eliminated. This shows the validity of the proposed method.

6 Conclusion

HMM learning and likelihood techniques were used to recognize sign language motions. The authors composed a sign language motion data set for model learning and performance evaluation together with supervision from a human signer. Each feature element that could be used for recognition was investigated and extracted from the motion data generated from video recordings of sign language. The percentage success of the two proposed methods was around 60% based on the 1st rank rating, and over 80% based on the 1st through 3rd ranks for 25 words. In addition, the selection of candidates of correct answer was introduced to enhance the recognition percentage by using the DP matching results. The success percentage was increased from 61.2% to 63.7% (from 81.6% to 85.6%) and 55.8% to 61.3% (from 81.1% to 84.5%) by setting an appropriate threshold value.

It seems quite possible to use the proposed method as a learners' reviewing tool. However, it is necessary to enhance the performance by adding features, for example, hand direction, the visibility of the palm and other features. It is considered that the final ranking should be arrived at by considering the sum of the reliabilities, i.e. a weighted summation of the recognition success percentage for each word. Rejection criteria for a recognition result should be introduced to enhance the reliability of recognition methods. These investigations will be undertaken in future studies.

References

1. Baatar, B., Tanaka, J.: Comparing sensor based and vision based techniques for dynamic gesture recognition. In: The 10th Asia Pacific Conference on Computer Human Interaction (APCHI), Poster 2P-21 (2012)
2. Matsuda, Y., Sakuma, I., Jimbo, Y., Kobayashi, E., Arafune, T., Isomura, T.: Development of finger braille recognition system. J. Biometrical Sci. Eng. 5(1), 54–65 (2010)
3. Humphries, T., Padden, C., O'Rourke, T.: Basic Course in American Sign Language. T. J. Pub., Inc., Silver Spring (1994)
4. Murakami, K., Taguchi, H.: Gesture recognition using recurrent natural networks. In: CHI 1991 Conference Proceedings, pp. 237–242 (1991)
5. Sugaya, T., Tsuchiya, H., Iwasawa, H., Nishimura, H., Tanaka, H.: Fundamental study on sign language recognition using color detection with an optical camera. In: International Conference on Imaging and Printing Technologies(ICIPT), Bangkok, Thailand, pp. 8–13 (2014)
6. Shibata, H., Nishimura, H., Tanaka, H.: Basic investigation for improvement of sign language recognition using classification scheme. In: Yamamoto, S. (ed.) HIMI 2016. LNCS, vol. 9734, pp. 563–574. Springer, Cham (2016). doi:10.1007/978-3-319-40349-6_55
7. KCC Corporation, Smart Deaf. http://www.smartdeaf.com/
8. HTK version 3.4.1. http://htk.eng.cam.ac.uk/
9. Sakoe, H.: Two-level DP-matching algorithm – a dynamic programming based pattern matching algorithm for continuous speech recognition. IEEE Trans. Acoust. Speech Sig. Process. 27(6), 588–595 (1979)
10. Tanaka, H., Kimura, R., Ioroi, S.: Equipment operation by motion recognition with wearable wireless acceleration sensor. In: Next Generation Mobile and Services and Technologies, Cardiff, Wales, United Kingdom, pp. 114–118 (2008)

Towards Automatic Recognition
of Sign Language Gestures Using Kinect 2.0

Dmitry Ryumin[1,2] and Alexey A. Karpov[1,2(✉)]

[1] St. Petersburg Institute for Informatics and
Automation of the Russian Academy of Sciences, SPIIRAS,
St. Petersburg, Russian Federation
dl_03.03.1991@mail.ru, karpov@iias.spb.su
[2] ITMO University, St. Petersburg, Russian Federation
http://hci.nw.ru

Abstract. We present a prototype of a new computer system aimed at recognition of manual gestures using Kinect 2.0 for Windows. This sensor allows getting a stream of optical images having FullHD resolution with 30 frames per second (fps) and a depth map of the scene. At present, our system is able to recognize continuous fingerspelling gestures and sequences of digits in Russian and Kazakh sign languages (SL). Our gesture vocabulary contains 52 fingerspelling gestures. We have collected a visual database of SL gestures, which consists of Kinect-based recordings of 2 persons (a man and a woman) demonstrating manual gestures. 5 samples of each gesture were applied for training models and the rest data were used for tuning and testing the developed recognition system. Model of each gesture is presented as a vector of informative visual features, calculated for the hand palm and all fingers. Feature vectors are extracted from both training and test samples of gestures, then comparison of reference patterns (models) and sequences of test vectors is made using the Euclidian distance. Sequences of vectors are compared using the dynamic time warping method (dynamic programming) and a reference pattern with a minimal distance is selected as a recognition result. According to our experiments in the signer-dependent mode with 2 demonstrators from the visual database, the average accuracy of gesture recognition is 87% for 52 manual signs.

Keywords: Sign language · Assistive technology · Automatic gesture recognition · Image processing · Kinect sensor

1 Introduction

Sign languages (SLs) are known as a natural means for verbal communication of the deaf and hard-of-hearing people. All the SLs use visual-kinetic clues for human-to-human communication combining manual gestures with articulation of lips, facial expressions and mimics. At present there is no universal SL all over the world, and almost each country has its own national SL. Any SL has a specific and simplified grammar, which is quite different from that of spoken languages. In addition to conversational SLs, there are also fingerspelling alphabets, which are used to spell whole

© Springer International Publishing AG 2017
M. Antona and C. Stephanidis (Eds.): UAHCI 2017, Part II, LNCS 10278, pp. 89–101, 2017.
DOI: 10.1007/978-3-319-58703-5_7

words (such as names, rare words, unknown signs, etc.) letter-by-letter. All the fingerspelling systems depend on national alphabets and there are both one-handed fingerspelling alphabets (in France, USA, Russia, Kazakhstan, etc.) and two-handed ones (in Czechia, UK, Turkey, etc.). Russian SL (RSL) is a native communicative language of the deaf people in the Russian Federation, Belarus, Kazakhstan, Ukraine, Moldova, also partly in Bulgaria, Latvia, Estonia, Lithuania, etc.; almost 200 thousand people use it daily. Many of these countries also have own national SLs like Kazakh SL (KSL), which is very similar to RSL. In RSL, there are 33 letters, which are demonstrated as static or dynamic finger signs, and in KSL, there are 9 additional letters (42 letters in total); so the whole gesture vocabulary contains 52 different items.

Thus, the creation of computer systems for automatic processing of SLs such as gesture recognition, text-to-SL synthesis, machine translation, learning systems and so on is a current and useful topic for research. There are quite many recent articles both on recognition [1–3] and synthesis [4, 5] of hand gestures of a sign language and fingerspelling (finger signs) [6, 7]. SL recognition is also one of key topics at the recent HCI conferences [8–11].

At present, Microsoft Kinect sensors are very popular in edutainment domain and they are quite efficient for the task of SL recognition too [3, 12, 13]. MS Kinect 2.0, which is the last version of the video sensor released by Microsoft in 2014, provides simultaneous detection and automatic tracking of up to 6 people at the distance of 1.2–3.5 m from the sensor. In the software, a virtual model of human's body is presented as a 3D skeleton of 25 points.

2 Architecture of the Recognition System

The recognition system must identify a shown gesture as precisely as possible and minimize the recognition error. Figure 1 shows a functional scheme of the system for sign language automatic recognition using MS Kinect 2.0. MS Kinect 2.0 is connected to the workstation via USB 3.0. The viewing angles are 43.5° vertically and 57° horizontally. Resolution of the video stream is 1920 × 1080 pixels with a frequency of 30 Hz (15 Hz in low light conditions) [14]. The inclination angle adjuster is pointed at changing vertical viewing angle within the range of ± 27°. Workstation (a high-performance personal computer) has software GestureRecognition of the sign language recognition system and a database, part of which is used for training, and the rest for experimental studies.

Practical studies revealed that the most optimal model of the database design, capable of storing the multidimensional signals (received from the sensor Kinect 2.0), is a hierarchical model [15]. The root directory of the database consists of 52 subdirectories, 10 of which contain information about gestures showing the numbers 1–10. The rest of the directories store static and dynamic gestures of finger alphabets (Russian and Kazakh dactylology), consisting of 42 letters. The RSL has 33 letters that are shown in the form of static gestures. In the KSL the Russian finger alphabet is supplemented by 9 letters that are reproduced dynamically.

A single subdirectory includes 30–60 video files with one and the same recorded gesture shown by demonstrators many times in a monochrome light or dark-green

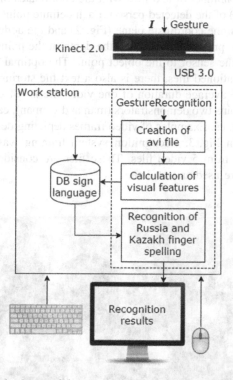

Fig. 1. Functional scheme of the automatic recognition system for sign language

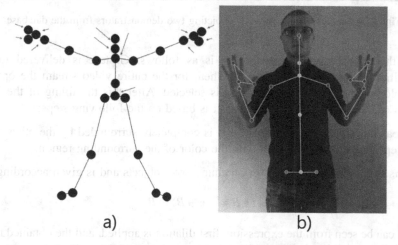

Fig. 2. Human's body model: (a) 25-point model of the human skeleton; (b) detection of a user in the frame

background; the same number of text files with the coordinates of the skeleton pattern (divided into 25 joints) of the detected person. Each definite point is the intersection of the two axes (X, Y) on the coordinate plane (Fig. 2) and the additional value of the Z coordinate with double precision, indicating the depth of the point, which is measured by the distance from the sensor to the object point. The optimal distance is 1.5–2 m. Besides the above-mentioned files, there is also a text file storing service information about the gesture. The average duration of one video file is ≈4–5 s.

The database contains two demonstrators (man and woman), each of whom showed the same gesture 30 times. Examples of video frames depicting demonstrators from the database are shown in Fig. 3. Recognition system training was carried out on the extracted visual signs from 5 video files. These files are considered benchmark gestures, while the rest are used as test data.

Fig. 3. Examples of video frames depicting two demonstrators from the database

Method for extracting visual cues is as follows. Gesture is delivered to the recognition system as a video signal. Then, for the entire video stream the optimal threshold value of reducing brightness is selected. After this the filling of the inner regions of the objects (closing) occurs. It is based on the following steps:

(1) Searching for one color square that is completely surrounded by the other one;
(2) Replacing the found region with the color of the surrounding region.

This operation is necessary for obtaining solid objects and is given according:

$$A \bullet B = (A \oplus B) \ominus B$$

As can be seen from the expression, first dilation is applied, and the obtained result is subjected to erosion [16].

Removal of minor noise and uneven borders around objects is carried out with the help of masking in the form of a structural element consisting of a matrix of zeros and ones, forming an oval square. The diameter is selected based on the best results. With increasing the diameter, small objects disappear. Objects, which have color characteristics matching hands color, but much smaller in diameter, are excluded likewise.

Finally, an square, which contains the coordinates from a set of text data obtained from MS Kinect 2.0, will be a hand.

When testing on prerecorded gesture database, it was revealed that the deviations from the normal functioning occur when the hand tilt angle exceeds 45°. This is due to the fact that the sensor MS Kinect 2.0 is unable to identify the key point around the hand center. This problem is solved by the method of averaging the last 7 previous horizontal and vertical peaks of the hand contour, which allows us to predict in what place the peaks will be in the subsequent time moment.

Next, using the skeleton data, obtained from the sensor MS Kinect 2.0, a demonstrator's hand is represented as an ellipse (Fig. 4), on condition that it constitutes one object. The semi-major axis runs through the points that are in wrist, the center of the hand and vertices of middle and ring fingers. The semi-minor axis runs perpendicular to the major axis through the point with the coordinates of the hand center.

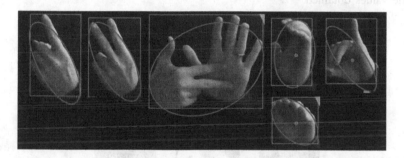

Fig. 4. Representation of hands in the form of an ellipse

After finding the ellipse, the first geometrical informative feature in the form of the orientation of hands is defined. The value is the angle between the x-axis of the coordinate plane and the major axis of the object (hand), as illustrated in Fig. 5.

Other interrelated necessary features are the lengths of the ellipse's axes. It should be noted that MS Kinect 2.0 does not allow for high-precision determination of the coordinates of the vertices, which can be reflected in false values. Therefore, a pre-colored image of hands is transferred into binary. This allows us to separate background from the hand and get the optimum values of lengths of both minor and major axes of the ellipse.

Then eccentricity is determined by dividing the major axis length by the minor axis length. The resulting value is added to the found features.

Other features are the topological properties of the binary object, such as the number of holes inside the object and the Euler number, calculated based on the difference in the number of objects and their inner holes in the image [17].

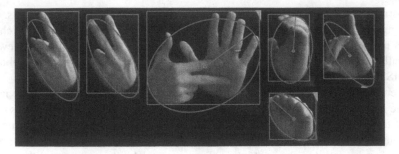

Fig. 5. Orientation of hands (the angle between the x-axis and the major axis of the object)

In continuation of analysis of the binary object, the square and convexity coefficient are determined. The convexity coefficient is defined as the ratio of the square of the object to the square of the quadrilateral that completely encompasses the object.

Using the Sobel operator [18] we obtain hand border (examples are shown in Fig. 6) and find its length and diameter. Finally, we complement an array of features with the values obtained.

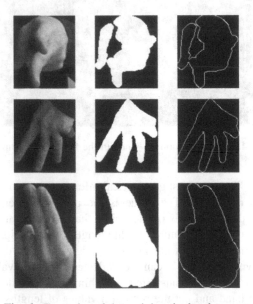

Fig. 6. Examples of determining the hand contour

In total, the defined informative features characterize the hand in the general view, without determination of a shown gesture with a high probability. Therefore, the hand opening process is performed using the structural element in the form of a circle with a diameter of 1/5 of the length of the ellipse's minor axis. Such a diameter allows clipping the fingers from the central region of the hand, as shown in Fig. 7 in the

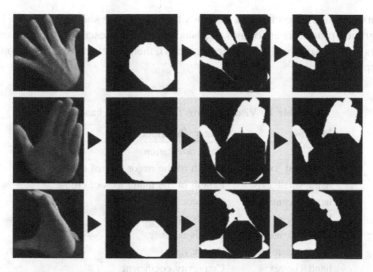

Fig. 7. Examples of clipping fingers from the central region of the hand in the image

second vertical row on the left. Then, a matrix, subjected to opening, should be excluded from the binary matrix with an object in the form of a hand. This procedure leads to separation of the central region of the hand from the fingers, as illustrated in Fig. 7 (the second column to the right).

As a result, we receive fingers in the form of objects with a preliminary removal of minor noises (as shown in Fig. 7 in the right column), for which the same features as for the hand are determined. This procedure allows us to have an idea about the hand as a whole and of its components in the form of fingers. The values of features are stored in the identifiers, the names of which do not coincide with each other. This allows using features in any order during recognition. Figure 8 shows a diagram of the method of calculating the visual features of hands.

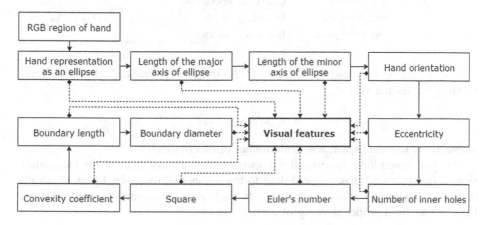

Fig. 8. Diagram of the method of calculating the visual features of one hand

Vectors of visual video features of hands and fingers are shown in Tables 1 and 2. The recognition process is as follows. If visual images are described using quantitative descriptors (length, square, diameter, texture, etc.), then the elements of decision theory can be applied.

Table 1. Visual features for describing a hand

Identifier	Feature description
hand_or	Hand orientation
hand_maj_axis_len	Length of the major axis of ellipse
hand_small_axis_len	Length of the minor axis of ellipse
hand_eccentr	Eccentricity
hand_open	Number of inner holes
hand_eul_num	Euler's number
hand_square	Square (area)
hand_convex	Convexity coefficient
hand_bord_len	Boundary length
hand_bord_diam	Boundary diameter

Table 2. Visual features for describing each finger

Identifier	Feature description
fing_or	Finger orientation
fing_maj_axis_len	Length of the major axis of ellipse
fing_small_axis_len	Length of the minor axis of ellipse
fing_eccentr	Eccentricity
fing_open	Number of inner holes
fing_eul_num	Euler's number
fing_square	Square (area)
fing_convex	Convexity coefficient
fing_bord_len	Boundary length
fing_bord_diam	Boundary diameter

Every gesture is represented as an image. An image is an arranged set of descriptors forming the feature vectors:

$$X = (x_1, x_2, \ldots, x_n)$$

where $x_i - i$ is a descriptor; n – total number of descriptors.

Images, which have some similar properties, form a class. In total, the recognition system comprises 52 classes (according to the number of recognized gestures in the database) referred to as $w_1, w_2, \ldots, w_{52}$. In each class, there are 5 records that are benchmarks for a proper showing of a certain gesture.

Fig. 9. Examples of gesture recognition

The process of matching the reference vectors with test ones is based on the calculation of the Euclidean distance between them. Belonging of an object to any class is based on the minimum distance between the reference (prototype) and unknown objects as shown in Fig. 9.

A static classifier by the minimum Euclidean distance is as follows. A reference class is the expectation of images vectors of the selected class:

$$m_j = \frac{1}{N} \sum_{x \in w_j} x_j$$

where $j = 1, 2, \ldots, W$ is the number of classes, N_j is the number of vectors of objects descriptors of the class w_j.

Summing is carried out over all vectors. A proximity measure based on the Euclidean distance is calculated according to the formula:

$$D_j(x) = \|x - m_j\|$$

where $j = 1, 2, \ldots, W$ is the number of classes, x is an unknown object, m_j is mathematical expectation calculated according to the previous formula.

Thus, the unknown object x will be correlated with a certain probability to such a class w_j, or which the proximity measure $D_j(x)$ will be the least.

Reaching the least (on average) error probability for the classification is carried out as follows. The probability that a certain object x belongs to the class w_j is $p(w_j|x)$. If the classifier refers an image (object) to the class w_j, which actually belongs to w_i, this indicates that there is a loss in the form of the classification error. These errors are referred to as L_{ij}. Since any image x в may be attributed to any of the existing classes W, the average loss value (error), associated with the attribution to the class w_j of the object x is equal to the average risk. The calculation is made according to the formula:

$$r_j(x) = \sum_{k=1}^{W} L_{kj} p(w_k|x)$$

Thus, an unknown image may be attributed to any class W. The sum of the average loss values over all admissible solutions will be minimal, because for the input image x the functions $r_1(x), r_2(x), \ldots, r_w(x)$ are calculated. This classifier is based on the Bayes classifier, i.e. it attributes the image x to the class w_i if $r_i(x) < r_j(x)$ on condition that $j = 1, 2, \ldots, W$ is the number of classes and the class j is not equal to the class i.

In our computer system, we employ some freely available software such as Open Source Computer Vision Library (OpenCV v3) [19], Open Graphics Library (OpenGL) [20] and Microsoft Kinect Software Development Kit (Kinect SDK 2.0) [21].

3   Experimental Research

The automated system was tested on different computers with various performance characteristics, parameters of which are presented in Table 3.

Table 3. The speed of frame processing with different computers

Processor	RAM, GB	Storage type	Video adapter	Processing speed, ms
Intel Core i7 3.4 GHz	8	HDD	Nvidia GeForce GTX 650 Ti	≈180
Intel Core i7 3.4 GHz	4	SSD	Nvidia GeForce GTX 650 Ti	≈140
Intel Atom Z250 1.33 GHz	2	HDD	GMA500	≈415
Intel Xeon E5-2690	128	SSD	NVIDIA Tesla K20X, NVIDIA Quadro K5000 (SLI)	≈70
Intel Core i5-3470	8	HDD	NVIDIA GeForce GT 640	≈270

The average processing time of one frame of the video sequence is 215 ms (Table 3), which allows processing up to 5 frames per 1 s. Current results do not allow processing video stream by an automation system in real time. However, there is a possibility of processing the recorded video fragments with the camera Kinect 2.0 together with the values obtained from the depth sensor in the synchronous mode.

The average recognition accuracy was 87%. Calculation is done according to the formula:

$$x_c = \frac{x_1 + x_2 + \ldots + x_n}{n},$$

where n is the number of gestures, x_n is the gesture recognition accuracy.

These results were obtained for the recorded database.

Gestures, for which it is necessary to put the fingers quite close to one another at different angles, showed the least recognition accuracy. In this case, the increasing of accuracy is possible by increasing the number of benchmarks and developing an algorithm capable of performing the processes of opening and closing not only a binary image, but also color one. This will allow controlling color parameters flexibly and more accurately determine not only the coordinates of objects, but also their descriptors.

4 Conclusions and Future Work

In this paper, we presented the computer system aimed at recognition of manual gestures using Kinect 2.0. At present, our system is able to recognize continuous fingerspelling gestures and sequences of digits in Russian and Kazakh SLs. Our gesture vocabulary contains 52 isolated fingerspelling gestures. We have collected a visual database of SL gestures, which is available on request. This corpus is stored as a hierarchical database and consists of recordings of 2 persons. 5 samples of each gesture were applied for training models and the rest data were used for tuning and testing the developed recognition system. Feature vectors are extracted from both training and test samples of gestures, then comparison of reference patterns and sequences of test vectors is made using the Euclidian distance. Sequences of vectors are compared using the dynamic programming method and a reference pattern with a minimal distance is selected as a recognition result. According to our preliminary experiments in the signer-dependent mode with 2 demonstrators from the visual database, the average accuracy of gesture recognition is 87% for 52 manual signs.

In further research, we plan to apply statistical recognition techniques, e.g. based on some types of Hidden Markov Models (HMM) such as multi-stream or coupled HMMs, as well as deep learning approaches with deep neural networks [22]. We have plans to apply a high-speed video camera with >100 fps in order to keep dynamic gesture dynamics and to improve gesture recognition accuracy [23]. Also we plan to create an automatic lip-reading system for the full SL recognition system and to make a gesture-speech analysis [24] for SL. Our visual database should be extended with more gestures and signers to create a signer-independent system for RSL recognition. In future, this automatic SL recognition system will become a part of our universal assistive technology [25], including ambient assisted living environment [26, 27].

Acknowledgements. This research is partially supported by the Russian Foundation for Basic Research (project No. 16-37-60100), by the Council for Grants of the President of the Russian Federation (project No. MD-254.2017.8), by the state research (№ 0073-2014-0005), as well as by the Government of the Russian Federation (grant No. 074-U01).

References

1. Koller, O., Forster, J., Ney, H.: Continuous sign language recognition: Towards large vocabulary statistical recognition systems handling multiple signers. Comput. Vis. Image Underst. **141**, 108–125 (2015)
2. Cooper, H., Ong, E.J., Pugeault, N., Bowden, R.: Sign language recognition using sub-units. J. Mach. Learn. Res. **13**, 2205–2231 (2012)

3. Guo, X., Yang, T.: Gesture recognition based on HMM-FNN model using a Kinect. J. Multimodal User Interfaces **11**, 1–7 (2016). doi:10.1007/s12193-016-0215-x. Springer

4. Karpov, A., Kipyatkova, I., Zelezny, M.: Automatic technologies for processing spoken sign languages. Procedia Comput. Sci. **81**, 201–207 (2016)

5. Karpov, A., Krnoul, Z., Zelezny, M., Ronzhin, A.: Multimodal synthesizer for Russian and Czech Sign Languages and Audio-Visual Speech. In: Stephanidis, C., Antona, M. (eds.) UAHCI/HCII 2013. LNCS, vol. 8009, pp. 520–529. Springer, Heidelberg (2013). doi:10.1007/978-3-642-39188-0_56

6. Kindiroglu, A., Yalcin, H., Aran, O., Hruz, M., Campr, P., Akarun, L., Karpov, A.: Automatic recognition of fingerspelling gestures in multiple languages for a communication interface for the disabled. Pattern Recogn. Image Anal. **22**(4), 527–536 (2012)

7. Hruz, M., Campr, P., Dikici, E., Kindiroglu, A., Krnoul, Z., Ronzhin, A.L., Sak, H., Schorno, D., Akarun, L., Aran, O., Karpov, A., Saraclar, M., Zelezny, M.: Automatic fingersign to speech translation system. J. Multimodal User Interfaces **4**(2), 61–79 (2011)

8. Sousa, L., Rodrigues, J.M.F., Monteiro, J., Cardoso, P.J.S., Lam, R.: GyGSLA: a portable glove system for learning sign language alphabet. In: Antona, M., Stephanidis, C. (eds.) UAHCI 2016. LNCS, vol. 9739, pp. 159–170. Springer, Cham (2016). doi:10.1007/978-3-319-40238-3_16

9. Shibata, H., Nishimura, H., Tanaka, H.: Basic investigation for improvement of sign language recognition using classification scheme. In: Yamamoto, S. (ed.) HIMI 2016. LNCS, vol. 9734, pp. 563–574. Springer, Cham (2016). doi:10.1007/978-3-319-40349-6_55

10. Nagashima, Y., et al.: A support tool for analyzing the 3D motions of sign language and the construction of a morpheme dictionary. In: Stephanidis, C. (ed.) HCI 2016. CCIS, vol. 618, pp. 124–129. Springer, Cham (2016). doi:10.1007/978-3-319-40542-1_20

11. Sako, S., Hatano, M., Kitamura, T.: Real-time Japanese sign language recognition based on three phonological elements of sign. In: Stephanidis, C. (ed.) HCI 2016. CCIS, vol. 618, pp. 130–136. Springer, Cham (2016). doi:10.1007/978-3-319-40542-1_21

12. Halim, Z., Abbas, G.: A Kinect-based sign language hand gesture recognition system for hearing- and speech-impaired: a pilot study of Pakistani sign language. Assistive Technol. **27**(1), 34–43 (2015)

13. Chong, W., Zhong, L., Shing-Chow, C.: Superpixel-based hand gesture recognition with Kinect depth camera. IEEE Trans. Multimed. **1**(17), 29–39 (2015)

14. Microsoft Developer Network. Skeletal Tracking. https://msdn.microsoft.com/en-us/library/hh973074.aspx

15. Sharma, D., Vatta, S.: Optimizing the search in hierarchical database using Quad Tree. Int. J. Sci. Res. Sci. Eng. Technol. **1**(4), 221–226 (2015). Springer

16. Sreedhar, K., Panlal, B.: Enhancement of images using morphological transformations. Int. J. Comput. Sci. Inf. Technol. **4**(1), 33–50 (2012)

17. Sossa-Azuela, J.H., Santiago-Montero, R., Pérez-Cisneros, M., Rubio-Espino, E.: Computing the Euler number of a binary image based on a vertex codification. J. Appl. Res. Technology. **11**, 360–370 (2013)

18. Chaple G., Daruwala R., Gofane, M.: Comparisons of Robert, Prewitt, Sobel operator based edge detection methods for real time uses on FPGA. In: Proceeding International Conference on Technologies for Sustainable Development ICTSD-2015. IEEEXplore (2015)

19. Kaehler, A., Bradsky, G.: Learning OpenCV 3. O'Reilly Media, California (2017)

20. OpenGL library. https://www.opengl.org

21. Kinect for Windows SDK 2.0. https://www.microsoft.com/en-us/download/details.aspx?id=44561

22. Kipyatkova, I.S., Karpov, A.A.: Variants of deep artificial neural networks for speech recognition systems. SPIIRAS Proc. **49**(6), 80–103 (2016). doi:10.15622/sp.49.5

23. Ivanko, D.V., Karpov, A.A.: An analysis of perspectives for using high-speed cameras in processing dynamic video information. SPIIRAS Proc. **44**(1), 98–113 (2016). doi:10.15622/sp.44.7

24. Sargin, M., Aran, O., Karpov, A., Ofli, F., Yasinnik, Y., Wilson, S., Erzin, E., Yemez, Y., Tekalp, M.: Combined gesture-speech analysis and speech driven gesture synthesis. In: Proceeding IEEE International Conference on Multimedia and Expo ICME-2006, Toronto, Canada. IEEEXplore (2006)

25. Karpov, A., Ronzhin, A.: A universal assistive technology with multimodal input and multimedia output interfaces. In: Stephanidis, C., Antona, M. (eds.) UAHCI/HCII 2014. LNCS, vol. 8513, pp. 369–378. Springer, Cham (2014). doi:10.1007/978-3-319-07437-5_35

26. Karpov, A., Akarun, L., Yalçın, H., Ronzhin, A.L., Demiröz B., Çoban A., Zelezny M.: Audio-visual signal processing in a multimodal assisted living environment. In: Proceeding of 15th International Conference INTERSPEECH-2014, Singapore, pp. 1023–1027 (2014)

27. Karpov, A., Ronzhin, A., Kipyatkova, I.: Automatic analysis of speech and acoustic events for ambient assisted living. In: Antona, M., Stephanidis, C. (eds.) UAHCI/HCII 2015. LNCS, vol. 9176, pp. 455–463. Springer, Cham (2015). doi:10.1007/978-3-319-20681-3_43

Universal Access to Virtual and Augmented Reality

On Capitalizing on Augmented Reality to Impart Solid Geometry Concepts: An Experimental Study

Bruno Alves[1], Diego R. Colombo Dias[2], Simone de S. Borges[3],
Vinicius H.S. Durelli[3], Paulo Alexandre Bressan[4], Valéria Farinazzo Martins[5],
and Marcelo de Paiva Guimarães[1,6(✉)]

[1] Faculdade Campo Limpo Paulista, São Paulo, Brazil
bruno_finus@hotmail.com
[2] Universidade Federal de São João Del Rei, São João del Rei, Brazil
diegocolombo.dias@gmail.com
[3] Universidade de São Paulo, São Paulo, Brazil
{s.borges,durelli}@icmc.usp.br
[4] Laboratory of Educational Technology,
Federal University of Alfenas, Alfenas, Brazil
paulo.bressan@gmail.com
[5] Universidade Presbiteriana Mackenzie, São Paulo, Brazil
valeria.farinazzo@mackenzie.br
[6] Universidade Aberta do Brasil (UAB/UNIFESP),
São Paulo, Brazil
marcelodepaiva@gmail.com

Abstract. Spatial reasoning is key to success in several fields, including learning solid geometry concepts. Due to their lack of spatial skills, some students struggle with solid geometry concepts. Part of this difficulty stems from the fact that textbooks illustrate inherently three dimensional content using two dimensional images, which causes some students to score lower than others on these tests that require spatial reasoning. We believe that students with poor spatial skills can benefit from our augmented reality environment. This study investigated the benefits of using augmented reality to teach solid geometry concepts and boost spatial reasoning. During our investigation, 24 students were randomly assigned to two groups. The 12 students in the experimental group engaged in an introductory geometry lesson using augmented reality, while the students in the control group received instruction in a traditional fashion. Before being exposed to the contents of both introductory lessons, a pre-test was carried out. Following the completion of the introductory geometry lesson, a post-test was conducted. Afterwards, a statistical test was performed on the scores of both groups. Our results seem to indicate that using augmented reality can be a slightly more effective approach to teach solid geometry concepts. More specifically, after being exposed to solid geometry concepts through augmented reality, all but three of the participants improved their previous test scores while eight of the 12 participants obtained perfect scores. Thus, we conjecture that augmented reality can be used to better impart solid geometry knowledge to

© Springer International Publishing AG 2017
M. Antona and C. Stephanidis (Eds.): UAHCI 2017, Part II, LNCS 10278, pp. 105–117, 2017.
DOI: 10.1007/978-3-319-58703-5_8

students while at the same time engaging students and increasing their rapport throughout the learning process.

Keywords: Poor spatial skills · Augmented reality · Geometry

1   Introduction and Motivation

Many efforts have been carried out to come up with new learning methodologies as well as improve upon existing ones. Moreover, researchers have been investigating what other factors play an important role in supporting the learning process. Towards this direction, the development of teaching material that better reflects the characteristics of the subject matter and thus makes the learning process more approachable has been gaining a lot of attention.

Geometry is an important branch of mathematics [3]. Throughout elementary school, students are exposed to several geometry concepts: shapes and their attributes and shape classification using lines and angles. In hopes of supporting the learning process of geometry-related concepts, researchers have developed educational applications with the goal of helping students to better explore geometry concepts through dynamic manipulation of geometric objects as lines, circles, and dots [5,7,18]. These applications are often termed interactive geometry software (IGS; interactive geometry, IG; dynamic geometry environments, DGEs; dynamic geometry systems, DGSs; or dynamic geometry, DG). The fundamental premise of these applications is the learning-by-doing method where, through the manipulation of a geometric space, students can construct their knowledge [7].

There is evidence of the benefits of using IG systems in classroom [4,6,7]. For example, several studies have shown that using IG software to teach geometry, tends to result in more committed students in comparison with students learning with traditional tools, such as rulers and compasses [4]. Moreover, current research indicates that IG software encourages students to develop their own hypotheses and find new ways to solve proposed problems [1, 6, 9]. When using IG software, students interact with the subject being presented through the graphical user interface, being able to alter the contents on the fly. This rapid feedback can play an important role in the learning process of elaborate concepts [20]. However, the majority of the IG software developed to date are desktop-based. That is, the interactions between user and the system take place through conventional input and output devices such as keyboard, mouse, and monitor. It turns out that there is a shortage of material tailored towards teaching abstract math concepts that takes advantage of more recent technological advances: for example, when teachers have to impart knowledge about three dimensional concepts, they have to resort to two dimensional illustrations. We argue that in such scenarios not all students are able to fully grasp the implications of these concepts because they are ill-represented. Hence, these students might end up with a subpar knowledge of the subject at hand.

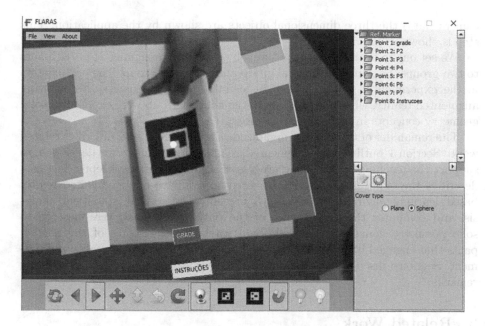

Fig. 1. User investigating an augmented reality object mapped to the marker.

Many of the learning initiatives have been trying to tap into technological advances such as augmented reality to support the learning process [11, 12, 22]. One of the advantages of using augmented reality is that this technology can be applied to teach students of any age. Another advantage of this technology is that it provides students with an improved depth perception, which is not possible via orthodox learning materials such as textbooks. Consequently, we conjecture that augmented reality can be used to teach concepts whose comprehension is rather difficult without visual aids. We hypothesize that solid geometry concepts fall into this category of concepts that can be better assimilated by students when the learning process is supported by technology. According to Kaleff [8], visualizing abstract concepts is key. Kaleff states that it is important for students to differentiate between the flat representation of an object and its corresponding three dimensional form.

Given that spatial skills can be learned, we believe that students with poor spatial skills can benefit from our augmented reality environment. To evaluate the effectiveness of augmented reality in supporting the learning process of solid geometry concepts, we created a set of learning material that capitalizes on this technology. This material is based on the requirements elicited during an interview with an elementary school teacher. Essentially, this material is presented using web-based technologies, and augmented reality is introduced to allow students to better visualize the concepts. More specifically, our application uses marker-based augmented reality, hence students have to point the camera at the underlying marker; and only after recognizing the marker (i.e., while acquiring camera data) the three dimensional objects are shown by the application. This step is shown in Fig. 1.

We set out to evaluate our hypothesis by randomly assigning 24 participants to two groups: i.e., an experimental group and a control group. The participants in the experimental group engaged in an introductory geometry lesson using augmented reality, while the students in the control group were exposed to solid geometry concepts in a traditional fashion.

The remainder of this paper is organized as follows. Section 2 describes related work. Section 3 outlines the augmented reality environment we developed to support the teaching and learning process of solid geometry concepts. Section 4 describes the experimental design we used to evaluate our augmented reality based learning environment. Section 5 presents the results, statistical analysis, and compares the performance of the participants that were exposed to solid geometry concepts in a traditional way with the scores of the participants that engaged in a geometry lesson through our augmented reality environment. Section 6 discusses the threats to validity and Sect. 7 presents concluding remarks.

2   Related Work

Computer systems and human beings interact through a graphical user interface (GUI). Ill-designed GUIs (i.e., interfaces that do not meet usability criteria) often hamper how users interact and access the underlying functionality. Thus, users may end up performing wrong operations, thus reducing their productivity. In the context of educational software for teaching geometry, the development of interfaces can play a key role in how learners explore and understand the concepts shown on the computer screen. Nevertheless, despite the importance of a judiciously designed GUI, there are not many studies exploring novel ways of interaction with the user. That is, there are many under explored technologies that can be used to improved the interaction user-computer and the learning process as a whole. In [17] Reis et al. describe the state of the art in terms of the technology used to implemented GUI for IG systems. According to Reis et al., most forms of interaction with IG systems are either keyboard or mouse based (or both), while most of the information is shown in regular monitor screens. Few efforts have been trying to take advantage of more advanced technology as augmented reality.

Meiguins et al. [14] employed augmented reality to allow students to manipulate solids and Oliveira and Kirner [15] developed an augmented reality environment within which students can create solids by specifying several properties and then these solids can be visualized after pointing the underlying cameras to the pre-configured markers. The assumptions of these studies is that augmented reality is an effective way of imparting knowledge related to shapes that are inherently three dimensional. Nevertheless, both studies fail to provide evidence of the benefits of employing augmented reality to boost the learning experience.

Silva and Ribeiro [21] implemented a tool to support the teaching of spatial geometry: this tool represents three dimensional shapes along with their definitions. Silva and Ribeiro evaluated this augmented reality environment in terms of its usability (according to the participants) and whether or not the participants were able to learn from it. Similarly to the aforementioned studies, several other studies have also investigated the application of augmented reality to support and boost the learning process [2,9,16].

Kirner et al. [10] proposed an interactive book where the markers in each page allow users to visualize three dimensional objects as well as information about these objects. This book, named GeoAR, was tailored to elementary school students, hence covering only the main geometric shapes and related information. According to Kirner et al., retrofitting augmented reality to textbooks promotes students' interest and engagement. However, the authors fail to report the results of the pilot study they conducted to evaluate their interactive book. They claim that the prototype yielded "very positive results concerning the educational potential of GeoAR", but evidence of such benefits are omitted from the study. Martins et al. [13] devised an educational application geared towards supporting the teaching and learning process of geometry. Martins et al. also carried out an usability evaluation.

Although the aforementioned studies deal with improving the learning experience by exploiting augmented reality to engage and motivate students, none of these studies carried out a randomized controlled experiment to assess whether augmented reality contributes to the learning process. To some extent, most of the previous studies evaluate their approaches based only on the feedback of the students. One of the prime contributions of our study is that, apart from developing an augmented reality environment, we also evaluated the benefits of augmented reality in educational settings.

3   An Augmented Reality Based Environment for Teaching and Learning Solid Geometry Concepts

Our learning environment was devised based on an interview with an elementary school teacher at the target school. This interview shed light on the needs of whose ranges from eight to nine years. Moreover, according to the results of the interview, there is a shortage of learning material covering solid geometry concepts for elementary school students. In addition, the available material is not interactive, i.e., in the sense that it does not give the student the ability to manipulate the content. According to the interviewed teacher, when teaching solid geometry, teachers have to resort to elementary resources such as textbooks [19] in which the shapes are represented (i.e., discretized) as flat, two dimensional images.

It was this lack of innovative learning material that motivated us to try and bridge this gap by tapping into augmented reality to foster learning. After deciding on the basic functionality, we investigated what sort of technology could be used to implement the planned application. We developed a web-based environment in HTML (HyperText Markup Language) that enables students to visualize three dimensional shapes using augmented reality. Our augmented reality application was developed using the authoring tool Flaras (Flash Augmented Reality Authoring System). The objects rendered by this tool were selected from a open repository [1]. After putting together all these technologies we were able to create an interactive, augmented reality-based learning environment for teaching solid geometry.

Figure 2 shows the web-based module of our learning environment. By clicking on the several options at the top left side of the GUI the user can browse by content or the learning experience can be guided by the teacher. The user can, for instance, access the option that renders a tetrahedron or assess their knowledge in the environment's test mode. The center of the web page shows the object that is currently being rendered. Overall, the environment was designed to increase student engagement during the learning process by promoting active, student-centered learning. The environment features four learning modules: one covering solid geometry concepts and three involving interactive games tailored towards enforcing retention of the underlying concepts.

Fig. 2. Web-based module of our learning environment.

4   Experiment Setup

This section describes the randomized experiment we carried out to evaluate the benefits of using augmented reality to teach solid geometry. More formally, we set out to answer the following research question (RQ):

RQ: Is augmented reality a more effective approach to teach solid geometry than the traditional approach?

The aforementioned RQ outlines the issue that this study is intended to investigate. As detailed in the following subsections, the RQ was used as the basis to formulate the hypotheses we used in this study.

4.1 Scoping

Experiment Goals. Basically, defining the scope of an experiment boils down to setting its goals. Towards this end, we used the Goal/Question/Metric (GQM) template [23]. Following this template, our experiment can be summarized as follows:

Analyze an augmented reality tool for teaching solid geometry
for the purpose of evaluation
with respect to the scores of 8/9-year-old children in a solid geometry test
from the point of view of a researcher
in the context of rural primary school children from 8 to 9 years.

As mentioned, we are particularly interested in examining whether augmented reality is beneficial in introducing solid geometry concepts to children. More to the point, we set out to find if incorporating augmented reality can yield better results than the traditional method (i.e., expositive lecture) when used to impart solid geometry concepts to students.

Variable Selection and Metrics. Here we clarify the dependent variable we set out to measure. Since it is complex to gauge the effectiveness of the teaching and the amount/quality of learning taking place, we settled on evaluating the students' knowledge by giving them a test on solid geometry concepts. So the operational definition of our variable is the score of the subject students on a solid geometry test: we will answer our RQ by comparing the score of students that were introduced to solid geometry concepts through an augmented reality tool with the scores of students that learned the same concept via the traditional method (i.e., expositive lecture).

Hypothesis Formulation. We formalized our RQ into hypotheses so that statistical tests can be carried out. Throughout this section we refer to the approach based on augmented reality as ARBA and the traditional approach as TA.

- **Null hypothesis, H_0:** there is no difference in terms of effectiveness (wherein the quality of teaching and learning are evaluated in terms of how students fare in a test) between the two approaches (i.e., expositive lecture and using an augmented reality tool to introduce concepts to students) to impart solid geometry knowledge. H_0 can be formalized as follows:

$$H_0 = \mu_{ARBA} = \mu_{TA}$$

- **Alternative hypothesis, H_1:** there is a significant difference in efficiency between the two approaches (measured in terms of the students' scores), which can be formalized as follows:

$$H_1 = \mu_{ARBA} \neq \mu_{TA}$$

Setup. 24 subjects participated in our experiment. The ages of these subjects range from 8 to 9 years old. To evaluate our conjecture, the subjects were assigned to the two different treatments at random: 12 subjects were assigned to ARBA and 12 subjects were assigned to TA. As mentioned, in this experiment, the main dependent variable is the scores of the subjects in a solid geometry test. More specifically, this dependent variable is defined in terms of the number of questions that they correctly answered.

Our experiment was broken down into four steps. These steps are listed in chronological order:

- **Pre-test:** all students answered questions on solid geometry. This step lasted 8 min.
- **Random assignment:** as mentioned, subjects were assigned to treatments at random.
- **Learning step:** during this step each of the groups was introduced to solid geometry concepts. Subjects in the ARBA group were introduced to these concepts through a 10-minute interaction with an augmented reality tool. Subjects in the TA group attended a 30-minute lecture on solid geometry.
- **Post-test** over the course of this step, subjects had to answer questions related to the concepts they were previously introduced to. We allocated 8 min for the subjects to go over all the questions.

5   Analysis of the Results

Figure 3 shows the scores of the students in the TA group in the pre- and post-tests. As indicated in Fig. 3, the traditional method seems to be an affective approach to introduce students to solid geometry concepts given that most subjects retained the information imparted to them and performed well on the post

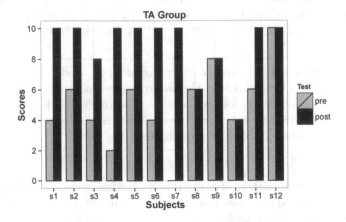

Fig. 3. Pre- and post-test scores obtained by the subjects in the TA group.

Table 1. Summary of the scores obtained by the subjects in the TA group.

	TA group	
	Pretest	Post-test
Median	5.0	10
Mean	5.0	8.83
Std	2.63	1.99
Max	10	10
Min	0	4

test. As shown in Table 1, during the pre-test, subjects answered on average 5 questions correctly. Five subjects (i.e., s1, s3, s4, s6, and s7) did not perform well on the pre-test. In particular, s7 answered all questions incorrectly. Almost all subjects performed better during the post-test. During the post-test, on average, subjects answered approximately 9 questions correctly (Table 1).

During the pre-test (Table 2), the subjects in the ARBA did not performed as well as the subjects in the TA group did . On average, subjects answered 4.83 questions correctly (Fig. 4). However, the high standard deviation (3.46) indicates that the scores varied widely. Our results seem to indicate that using augmented reality to introduce students to solid geometry concepts can be an effective approach. During the post-test, that is, after being exposed to solid geometry through an augmented reality tool, all but three subjects improved their scores. As shown in Fig. 4, eight of the 12 obtained perfect scores on the post-test. Similarly to the TA group, on average, subjects in the ARBA answered 8.83 questions correctly during the post-test.

Owing to the small size of the groups and given that the results do not follow a normal distribution, in order to compare each treatment (i.e., TA and

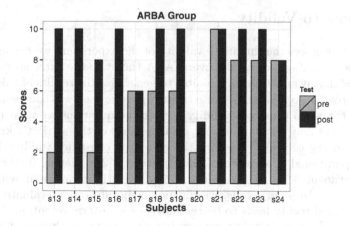

Fig. 4. Pre- and post-test scores obtained by the subjects in the ARBA group.

ARBA) we carried out a non-parametric test: Wilcoxon signed rank test. More specifically, we compared whether there was a significant improvement between the scores obtained during the pre- and post-test in each treatment. It turns out that both treatments showed significant improvements on the post-test. The p-value for the TA was 0.013, while the p-value for ARBA was 0.009. Since that the p-value for ARBA was even smaller we conjecture that ARBA is an approach slightly more suited for presenting solid geometry concepts than TA, which is a static, chalkboard-based approach. However, the difference between these two treatments is not statistically significant. Thus, further comparisons are necessary to increase our confidence in the results.

Table 2. Summary of the scores obtained by the subjects in the ARBA group.

	ARBA group	
	Pretest	Post-test
Median	6	10
Mean	4.83	8.83
Std	3.46	1.99
Max	10	10
Min	0	4

Despite the results of our statistical analysis, we argue that augmented reality can be a positive addition to the classroom. According to the teacher, some of the participants in the ARBA group outdid expectations. It seems that the main reason is that students in the ARBA group developed more positive attitudes towards the material being exposed.

6   Threats to Validity

This section discusses the threats to validity of the experiment we carried out to evaluate the advantages of ARBA over TA. A threat to the external validity of this study is that it might not be possible to generalize the results of this experiment to a broader population because the sample size used was somewhat small. A possible threat to construct validity is that the questions we used to evaluate the subjects may result in a poor measurement of the subject's knowledge of solid geometry concepts. Another threat to the construct validity is inadequate preoperational explication of the constructs [23]: that is, in the context of our experiment it is not possible to be sufficiently clear about what being "better" means. In other words, we did not elaborate on or evaluate whether using augmented reality leads to better short- or long-term retention. Basically, the benefits of both approaches were evaluated in terms of the scores obtained by the participants: that is, the scores obtained by participants were the only concept operationalized as experimental measure. However, test scores are an incomplete gauge of how much students have learned, they can be seem as a starting point, a basic means of comparison. Therefore, to better examine the advantages of augmented reality in this context, the scores of the participants should not be the sole factor involved in the investigation.

7   Concluding Remarks

Many students struggle with solid geometry concepts due to the limitations in the way these concepts are presented to them (i.e., three dimensional content is usually presented using two dimensional images). In this direction, and based on our believe that augmented reality has the potential to provide a myriad of benefits to the learning environment, we took an initial step towards probing into these benefits. An experiment using a control and a experimental group should be conducted throughout a period of one to three months. In this experiment, the control group should be exposed to the underlying concepts only through traditional instruction while the experiment group should also receive traditional instruction along with being exposed to augmented reality based material, which should be employed in expository and hands-on learning activities. This way it would be possible to focus on how much each approach helps the students to improve, taking into account the fact that students start with different sets of knowledge. Such an experiment will yield more conclusive results concerning the pros and cons of adopting either approach in the long run: that is, how much augmented reality contributes to student growth during the time students are in the classroom. Moreover, it is worth mentioning that using multiple measures further helps ascertain the effectiveness of each approach. Hence, as mentioned in Sect. 6, follow-up experiments should also gather other information besides student achievement gains: for instance, surveys could be carried out throughout the conduction of such experiments along with systematic observations of the students' behavior in classroom. Such information can help to shed light on the advantages of augmented reality in comparison to the traditional approach to teaching inherently three dimensional concepts.

It is also worth mentioning that all efforts in this context must emphasize and employ user-friendly technologies, which are easier to adopt. Otherwise, adopting these educational applications may be difficult even for teachers willing to adopt innovative approaches as augmented reality.

References

1. 3D Warehouse: Model repository. https://3dwarehouse.sketchup.com/index.html. Accessed Aug 2015
2. Banu, S.: Augmented reality system based on sketches for geometry education. In: International Conference on E-learning and E-technologies in Education (ICEEE), pp. 166–170 (2012)

3. Clements, D.H., Battista, M.T.: Geometry and spatial reasoning. In: Handbook of Research on Mathematics Teaching, Learning: A Project of the National Council of Teachers of Mathematics, pp. 420–464 (1992)

4. Erbas, A.K., Yenmez, A.A.: The effect of inquiry-based explorations in a dynamic geometry environment on sixth grade students' achievements in polygons. Comput. Educ. **57**(4), 2462–2475 (2011)

5. Erez, M.M., Yerushalmy, M.: "If You Can Turn a Rectangle into a Square, You Can Turn a Square into a Rectangle ..." young students experience the dragging tool. Int. J. Comput. Math. Learn. **11**(3), 271–299 (2007)

6. Hollebrands, K.F.: The role of a dynamic software program for geometry in the strategies high school mathematics students employ. J. Res. Math. Educ. **38**(2), 164–192 (2007)

7. Isotani, S., de Oliveira Brandão, L.: An algorithm for automatic checking of exercises in a dynamic geometry system: iGeom. Comput. Educ. **51**(3), 1283–1303 (2008)

8. Kaleff, A.M.M.R.: Looking at and Grasping Geometrical Objects: From Drawing Them to Working Out Their Volumes Through Puzzles and Other Solid Materials. Universidade Federal Fluminense, Niteroi (2003). (In Portuguese)

9. Kaufmann, H., Schmalstieg, D., Wagner, M.: Construct3D: a virtual reality application for mathematics and geometry education. Educ. Inf. Technol. **5**(4), 263–276 (2000)

10. Kirner, T., Reis, F., Kirner, C.: Development of an interactive book with augmented reality for teaching and learning geometric shapes. In: Iberian Conference on Information Systems and Technologies (CISTI), pp. 1–6 (2012)

11. Kolstee, Y., van Eck, W., Gogh's, The augmented van : augmented reality experiences for museum visitors. In: IEEE International Symposium on Mixed and Augmented Reality - Arts, Media, and Humanities (ISMAR-AMH), pp. 49–52 (2011)

12. Lu, W., Nguyen, L.-C., Chuah, T.L., Do, E.-L.: Effects of mobile AR-enabled interactions on retention and transfer for learning in art museum contexts. In: IEEE International Symposium on Mixed and Augmented Reality - Media, Art, Social Science, Humanities and Design (ISMAR-MASH'D), pp. 3–11 (2014)

13. Martins, F.V., Delgado, M., Guimaraes, M.P.: An application to support the teaching and learning process of geometry. In: Congresso Brasileiro de Recursos Digitais na Educação (2012). (In Portuguse)

14. Meiguins, B.S., Almeida, I.A., Oikawa, M.A.: On using markers in augmented virtual reality environments. In: VIII Symposium on Virtual Reality, pp. 1–4 (2006). (In Portuguese)

15. Oliveira, F.C., Kirner, C.: Exploring spatial geometry in virtual reality and augmented reality environments using the tool RA-educacional. Technical report, Universty of Sao Paulo (2006). (In Portuguese)

16. Purnama, J., Andrew, D., Galinium, M.: Geometry learning tool for elementary school using augmented reality. In: International Conference on Industrial Automation, Information and Communications Technology (IAICT), pp. 145–148 (2014)

17. Reis, H.M., Borges, S.S., Griffiths, P.A., Moro, L.F.S., Isotani, S.: Interaction in graphical user interfaces of interactive geometry software (From the paper in Portuguese: Interação em Interfaces de Softwares de Geometria Interativa: Um Mapeamento Sistemático). Simpósio Brasileiro de Informática na Educação, pp. 255–264 (2013)

18. Roanes-Lozano, E., Roanes-Macías, E., Villar-Mena, M.: A bridge between dynamic geometry and computer algebra. Math. Comput. Model. **37**(9–10), 1005–1028 (2003)
19. Sanchez, L.B., Liberman, M.P.: Understanding mathematics (from the Portuguese title: "Fazendo e Compreendendo Matemática"). Saraiva (2011)
20. Shimomura, Y., Hvannberg, E.T., Hafsteinsson, H.: Haptic cues as a utility to perceive and recognise geometry. Univ. Access Inf. Soc. **12**(2), 125–142 (2013)
21. Silva, W.A., Silva, M.W.S.: An augmented reality based tool to support the teaching of spatial geometry. In: Workshop de Aplicações de Realidade Virtual Aumentada (2008). (In Portuguese)
22. Sin, A.K., Badioze Zaman, H.: Tangible interaction in learning astronomy through augmented reality book-based educational tool. In: Badioze Zaman, H., Robinson, P., Petrou, M., Olivier, P., Schröder, H., Shih, T.K. (eds.) IVIC 2009. LNCS, vol. 5857, pp. 302–313. Springer, Heidelberg (2009). doi:10.1007/978-3-642-05036-7_29
23. Wohlin, C., Runeson, P., Höst, M., Ohlsson, M.C., Regnell, B., Wesslén, A.: Experimentation in Software Engineering. Springer, Heidelberg (2012)

WebAR: A Web-Augmented Reality-Based Authoring Tool with Experience API Support for Educational Applications

André Barone Rodrigues[1], Diego R. Colombo Dias[2], Valéria Farinazzo Martins[3],
Paulo Alexandre Bressan[4], and Marcelo de Paiva Guimarães[5(✉)]

[1] Faculty of Campo Limpo Paulista, Campo Limpo Paulista, SP, Brazil
andre.barone@gmail.com
[2] Federal University of São João Del Rey, São João Del Rey, MG, Brazil
diegocolombo.dias@gmail.com
[3] Computing and Informatics Program, Mackenzie Prebisterian University, São Paulo, SP, Brazil
valeria.farinazzo@mackenzie.br
[4] Laboratory of Educational Technology, Federal University of Alfenas, Alfenas, MG, Brazil
paulo.bressan@gmail.com
[5] Brazilian Open University (UAB/UNIFESP)/Master Program of Faculty Campo Limpo
Paulista, São Paulo, Brazil
marcelodepaiva@gmail.com

Abstract. Learning objects are reusable teaching units that are supported by various learning management systems, such as Moodle and Blackboard. Once learning object standards are followed, several types of media can be used as learning objects, such as augmented reality applications. We propose the use of augmented reality content as media for e-learning systems. Therefore, this paper presents an Web Augmented Reality-based Authoring called WebAR. It is compatible with Experience API (xAPI) which is a standard learning object that is based on the Shareable Content Object Reference Model (SCORM). Learning objects based on augmented reality can also be used to assist students with difficulties related to spatial skills.

Keywords: Augmented reality · Learning objects · E-learning

1 Introduction

The use of technological resources in the teaching and learning process has grown in recent years. One of these resources is learning objects, which can be defined in general terms as a way to organize and structure digital educational materials. According to Wiley [18], learning objects include any digital resource that can be reused to support teaching and learning. Thus, learning objects can be characterized as different types of media, such as images, videos, graphics, and sounds.

The use of learning objects to promote sharing content has been discussed in the context of e-learning [17], which can be defined as a way to deliver information and instruction to someone through the Internet. The possibility of delivering and sharing

© Springer International Publishing AG 2017
M. Antona and C. Stephanidis (Eds.): UAHCI 2017, Part II, LNCS 10278, pp. 118–128, 2017.
DOI: 10.1007/978-3-319-58703-5_9

content across multiple locations is appealing. However, it requires the adoption of standards in order to be successful. The Sharable Content Object Reference Model (SCORM) was proposed to handle this challenge. According to Bailey [3], SCORM aims to incorporate various specifications of teaching objects, thus enabling compatibility with various types of learning management software (LMS). In other words, the SCORM defines the interface between web-based content and learning technology using existing specifications. The advanced distributed learning (ADL) model developed the SCORM in agreement with the US Department of Defense in order to formulate a strategy for education and training.

Several types of media can be used as learning objects. However, new needs arise regularly as new media possibilities, such as using virtual reality (VR) and augmented reality (AR), are developed. AR is defined as a variation of VR [4], but while VR completely immerses the user in a computer-generated environment, AR adds virtual artifacts to real viewing, giving the impression that these artifacts are part of the physical environment.

The early development of AR and VR can be traced back to Ivan Sutherland who created the Ultimate Display in 1965 where matter could be controlled by a computer [14]. Three years earlier, Sutherland constructed the first VR system, complete with a head-mounted display and seeing throw optics. This research was conducted during the 1970s and 1980s by members of the United States Air Force Armstrong Laboratory, NASA Ames Research Laboratory, Massachusetts Institute of Technology and North Carolina University at Chapel Hill [15].

This paper presents a new tool called Web Augmented Reality-based Authoring (WebAR), which can be used with Experience API (xAPI). This tool allows teaches to create educational applications of AR that can benefit the learning process. For example, the applications can assist students with difficulties related to spatial skills. This paper's major contributions are:

- A discussion about AR applications as valuable didactic material;
- A tool that can generate AR applications easily;
- A tool that packages AR applications compatible with xAPI;
- A discussion about the sharing of AR applications through repositories.

This study is structured as follows: Sect. 2 discusses previous work related to this research; Sect. 3 describes AR and provides details about the tracking system used in our solutions; Sect. 4 discusses e-learning systems and the xAPI; and Sect. 5 presents the WebAR tool, as well as conclusions and suggestions for future work.

2   Related Works

Jee, Lim, Youn, and Lee [11] have created an authoring tool called An Immersive Authoring Tool for Augmented Reality-based E-learning Applications. In their paper, they show that online teaching has evolved from models without interaction to those that use a list of activities and questions and answers as a form of interaction and capturing the attention of students. However, they find these activities to be dull and unintuitive, and believe that AR can be more efficient in these respects. The paper also identifies the existence of libraries that allow applications with AR authorship to be constructed, such as ARToolKit, which uses computational vision resources to identify markers for 3D model overlays. The efficiency of this system was evaluated by a comparative experiment with primary school students in English and science classes, in which half of them took a class with traditional audiovisual material and the other half were exposed to the immersive e-learning system. Teachers and students reported that they saw more benefits from the immersive system because the students concentrated and participated more actively in class.

Farias, Dantas, and Burlamaqui [9] published a study presenting the creation of the Educ-AR Application Programming Interface based on ARToolKit. The main contribution pointed out by the authors is that it does not require the instructor to have programming knowledge, AR applications, or 3D modeling. Instead, they created a web tool where educators could register themselves, create classes, and submit markers and 3D objects. AR artifacts are generated within a class by associating 3D objects with markers. The application also allows for the management and creation of custom bookmarks. Through experiments, the researchers concluded that the use of AR technology could not be considered an efficient solution by itself.

This paper by Farias, Dantas, and Burlamaqui [12] presented AR as an assistance technology for students with special needs, particularly with communication difficulties. The current paper identifies the possibility of using a hybrid method, that is, not only recognition made through computer vision, but also through the use of a global positioning system (GPS) to add the virtual objects to the display of the real content.

Cubillo et al. [5] mentioned that new technologies such as Web 2.0, mobile devices, virtual environments, and AR environments have the potential to transmit information and acquire knowledge. According to the authors, the AR environment proves to be timely for teaching subjects that involve practical training and outside the classroom, where students need interaction with the real world. However, many educational applications of RA are subject-specific, fixed content that was made available by developers.

This analysis of the literature shows that AR has been the object of study of some researchers who aim to ally it with the learning process through electronic tools, such as E-learning systems. The objectives of the papers analyzed here were to create tools that would make the process of authoring AR comfortable for anyone, without the need for the involvement of AR specialists.

An important point raised in our paper is the flexibility of the tools. Some applications aim to use AR in education. However, these programs are restricted to a discipline and, with the flexibility of the tools, it becomes possible to create content that is applicable to several areas of education and, especially, disciplines that require interaction with the real-world medium. It is also noted that the use of AR can help people with special needs learning, thus leading to greater social inclusion.

3   Augmented Reality

AR is most commonly presented to the user through a video display in real time, although the system needs to track the environment to decide how to display the virtual objects. Figure 1 depicts a sequence of tasks performed when an AR scenario is assembled on a handheld device, such as a smartphone [16].

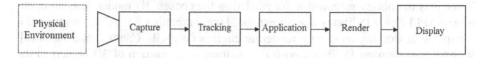

Fig. 1. Sequence of events to assemble an AR scenario on a handheld device.

Each phase can be described as follow:

- Physical environment: the real environment is seen by the user without any interference of the computer system;
- Capture: the video camera of the device captures the physical environment scene;
- Tracking: the system tracks the markers;
- Application: the system interprets the markers to decide how and what virtual objects will be added to the scene;
- Render: the system draws the virtual objects; and
- Display: the system combines the real image from the environment and the virtual objects to display to the user or users.

The tracking technique employed in our solution is based on fiducial markers, which are based on and performed by the JavaScript (JS) library JS-Aruco, which is a JS port of ArUco, a library based on OpenCV for AR [2]. JS-Aruco is capable of detecting markers with a 7×7 pattern in the external border, as depicted in Fig. 2(a). Figure 2(b) provides an example of a complete marker.

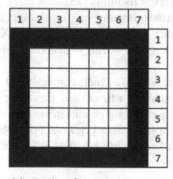

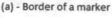
(a) - Border of a marker   (b) - Complete Marker

Fig. 2. (a) A pattern of a JS-Aruco expected marker; (b) a complete marker, using the inside patterns for rows (1, 2, 3, 4, 1).

A combinatorial analysis shows the number of possible markers that can be distinctly used by JS-Aruco:

- Possible rows (P): 4;
- Number of rows at one Marker (N): 5; and
- Distinct possibilities: $Ar(P, N) \rightarrow PN = 4^5 \rightarrow 1024$.

This combination shows that JS-Aruco can detect up to 1024 different markers. Three.js is the library responsible for rendering the chosen 3D model. It is an open-source API/Library JS library that allows for 3D programming for web browsers and it is capable of working on several rendering engines (WebGL, Canvas, and SVG) [8]. WebAR also supports JS library posit that estimates the position of 3D objects in the rotation and position axes, x, y, and z [1].

4　E-learning Systems and Experience API

The first generation of e-learning systems released in the early 1990s was similar to a black box. These were proprietary systems with no user tracking [6] that were commonly designed for a specific course. On the other hand, e-learning standards were coming on the scene, such as Dublin Core, IMS Learning Resource Metadata, and IEEE Learning Object Metadata. In 1997, two important learning management systems (LMSs) had come to light—Web Course Tools (WebCT) and Blackboard—and the following year saw the birth of the Modular Object-Oriented Dynamic Learning Environment (Moodle).

In 2000, ADL released the first version of a reference model called SCORM. It was designed as a set of unified specifications for content packaging and description that also determined how the content would communicate with an LMS. SCORM was designed to support interoperability and portability for web and has been widely adopted. However, the appearance of new platforms and the requirements for learning records with analytic purposes have contributed to the development of proprietary or middleware technologies, indicating that SCORM has achieved its limits [13].

With the intention to standardize new elements in the e-learning platforms, especially learning records, ADL issued a call to the community that led to the creation of Xapi, which is focused on defining an interoperable data model for storing data about students and sharing this data among systems [7].

xAPI is focused on tracking learning experiences (LE), which can reside in any activity executed in the learning environment. To achieve a functional way store and share LE, xAPI specified a data model that cognitively called statements in the following format: <actor> <verb> <object>, with <result>, in <context> [7]. JavaScript Object Notation (JSON) is the chosen format to present this data. Figure 3 depicts a JSON xAPI statement.

```
{
    "id": "6690e6c9-3ef0-4ed3-8b37-7f3964730bee",
    "actor": {
                "name": "Andrew Downes",
                "mbox":mailto:xapi@adlnet.gov
    },
    "verb": {
        "id": "http://adlnet.gov/expapi/verbs/attended",
        "display": {
            "en-US": "attended"
        }
    },
    "result": {
        "success": true,
        "completion": true,
        "duration": "PT1H0M0S"
    },
    "context": {
        "registration": "ec531277-b57b-4c15-8d91-d292c5b2b8f7",
        "contextActivities": {
            "category": [
                {
                    "id": "http://www.example.com/meetings/categories/teammeeting",
                    "objectType": "Activity"
                }
            ],
            "instructor" :
            {
                "name": "Andrew Downes",
                "account": {
                    "homePage": "http://www.example.com",
                    "name": "13936749"
                },
                "objectType": "Agent"
            }
        }
    }
}
```

Fig. 3. Adapted example of a JSON xAPI statement

This statement is compounded by the properties exposed in Table 1.

Table 1. Properties of an xAPI statement.

Property	Type	Description	Required
Id	Universally unique identifier (UUID)	Assigned by LRS or LRP. Can be any format of variant in RFC4122 and must be String formatted	Recommended
actor	Object	Who performed the action	Required
verb	Object	Action between the actor and the activity	Required
object	Object	Activity or agent/group that the object was acted upon	Required
result	Object	Represents a measure outcome	Optional
context	Object	Gives the statement a meaning	Optional
timestamp	Timestamp - ISO 8601 format	Timestamp of event occurrence Sets LRS if not provided	Optional
stored	Timestamp	Timestamp of when the statement was record in LRS. Set by LRS	Set by LRS
authority	Object	Agent or group asserting the statement	Optional
version	Version	Associated xAPI version	Not recommended
attachment	Ordered array of attached objects	Headers for statements to attach to	Optional

A generic architecture for xAPI may consist of the following three components [10]:

- Learning record provider (LRP), previously called the activity provider (AP);
- Learning record store (LRS); and
- Learning record consumer (LRC).

The LRS is a server that receives, stores, and gives access to the records generated during an LE. The experiences are tracked by an LRP, the entity in charge of sending the records to the LRS. An LRC is a client to the LRS that can access the records after authentication. Figure 4 overviews this architecture, showing that an LRS can have several clients in an 1..n relationship, as the LRP and LRS have 1..1 relationships.

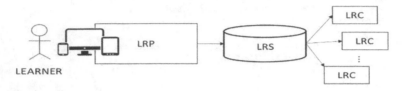

Fig. 4. xAPI Architecture overview.

5 WebAR: Web-Based Tool for AR with Support for xAPI

Figure 5 presents an overview of the WebAR architecture, according to the teacher's view. The teacher uses this architecture to create the learning objects based on AR and stores them in a learning object repository. To develop the application, it is fundamental to consider the content of a given class and the teaching strategy used.

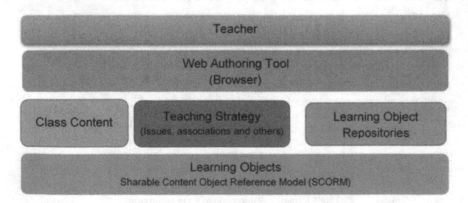

Fig. 5. Teacher's view of the WebAR.

Figure 6 presents an overview of the WebAR architecture from the student´s point of view. Students have two options for using objects: (1) via an LMS, such as Moodle, teachers can import objects into the virtual learning environment; or (2) via a mobile viewer running on Android or iOS. In this case, the student needs to install the application on their smartphone in order to be able to import the previously available objects into a repository.

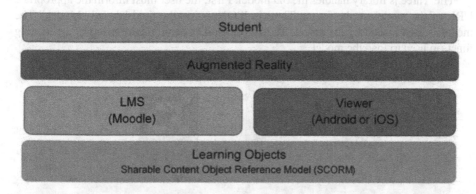

Fig. 6. Student's view of the WebAR.

WebAR uses navigator.getUserMedia API to acquire access to the device camera where the user is authoring the AR scene, at which point the video is called back to an HTML5 <video> as a stream. This stream also feeds the object AR.Detector through its method detect(), helped by a HTML5 <canvas> where the ImageData object is

```
<video id="video" width=320 height=240 autoplay="true" style="display:none;"></video>

<canvas id="canvas" style="width: 320px; height: 240px; float: left; border: solid 1px black;
display:none"></canvas>

                              (a) HTML5 part
```

```
navigator.getUserMedia({video: true},
                  function (stream) {
                        if (window.URL) {
                              video.src =
                  window.URL.createObjectURL(stream);
                        } else if (video.mozSrcObject !== undefined) {
                              video.mozSrcObject = stream;
                        } else {
                              video.src = stream;
                        }
                  },
                  function (error) {
                        alert("Erro ao acessar dipositivo de vídeo");
                  }
            );
canvas = document.getElementById("canvas");
context = canvas.getContext("2d");
context.drawImage(video, 0, 0, canvas.width, canvas.height);
imageData = context.getImageData(0, 0, canvas.width, canvas.height);

detector = new AR.Detector();
var markers = detector.detect(imageData);

                              (b) JavaScript Part
```

Fig. 7. (a) The HTML5 elements for video handling; (b) JavaScript implementation for the Marker detection.

captured. Figure 7 contains the HTML code (a) and the JavaScript part of the implementation described above (b).

The Three.js library handles the 3D model. First, the user must inform the appropriate URL of the model on the format Three.js JSON, using the field labeled "Model." The model is then loaded by the object, THREE.ObjectLoader(). Figure 8 shows the loading function used to load the model.

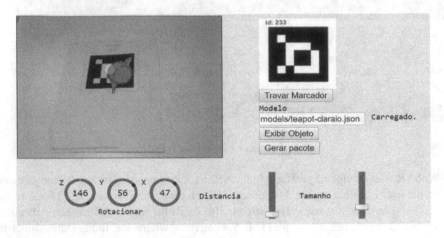

Fig. 8. Screenshot of WebAR with a model of a teapot on a detected ID-233 marker.

The function implemented on WebAR also captures the three axes (x, y, and z) of the model to provide its manipulation. Figure 6 shows the implementation of this function. Figure 9 also shows the controllers that allow the user to adjust the model on the referenced marker, including the rotation, distance marker, and the size of the model.

```
function createModel3d(url) {
        if(!modelLoaded){
            var objectLoader = new THREE.ObjectLoader();
            var ambient = new THREE.AmbientLight(0x444444);
            var directionalLight = new THREE.DirectionalLight(0xffeedd);
            scene4.add(ambient);
            scene4.add(directionalLight);
            directionalLight.position.set(0, 0, 1).normalize();
            objectLoader.load(url, function (obj) {
                model = obj;
                modelLoaded = true;
                rot_x = model.rotation.x;  rot_y = model.rotation.y;  rot_z = model.rotation.z;
                enableControls(true);
                scene4.add(model);

                document.getElementById("objectLoaded").innerHTML = 'Carregado.';

        }}
```

Fig. 9. Function CreateModel3d (url) responsible for inputting the 3DModel in the AR scene.

As soon as the user detects the desired marker, he can push it and work freely to load and manipulate the model. This feature facilitates the authoring process. The *Gerar pacote* button packages the AR application into an xAPI-compliant package. When the user presses this button, WebAR collects the relevant information about the scene, including the marker ID, the model position, rotation and size, and copies the model files to a temporary directory. Next, the tool uses a template to create an HTML file that implements the scene adjusted by the user.

The last part of this task consists of creating a zip file containing the HTML file, model files, and the manifest file in the XML format used by LRS.

6 Conclusions

The use of AR as a learning tool can support educators in several disciplines. In order to do this, educators must have authoring tools that are capable of facilitating the entire development process of AR applications and simplifying everything from creating content (3D objects, images, and sounds) to using them in educational institutions. Another important issue addressed in this paper is that while these tools are capable of generating educational AR applications for any context, different teachers do not reuse them. None of these tools deals with, for example, packaging applications in the format of learning objects. Therefore, an opportunity and challenge exists to create authoring tools that are easy to use and are reusable by educators. In line with the related literature, this research shows that there is a need to create user-friendly authoring tools, but that there are still challenges that need to be overcome. Moreover, none of these articles addressed the reuse of such applications by other teachers.

Thus, our paper present an authoring tool that is capable of generating easy-to-use AR content that can also be reused. The main idea is to package these applications in the format of learning objects in order to satisfy the reuse of the xAPI standard. In the future, we intend to improve the WebAR interface, and we also aim to create AR applications that can assist students with specific learning disorders.

References

1. Aforge.net::3D pose estimation. http://www.aforgenet.com/articles/posit/. Accessed 30 Jan 2017
2. Javascript library for augmented reality applications. https://github.com/jcmellado/js-aruco. Accessed 30 Jan 2017
3. What is ADL SCORM? http://zone.cetis.ac.uk/lib/media/WhatIsScorm2_web.pdf. Accessed 30 Jan 2017
4. Billinghurst, M., Clark, A., Lee, G.: A survey of augmented reality. Found. Trends Hum. Comput. Interact. **8**(2–3), 73–272 (2015)
5. Cubillo, J., Martn, S., Castro, M., Diaz, G., Colmenar, A., Botiki, I.: A learning environment for augmented reality mobile learning. In: Proceedings of the IEEE Frontiers in Education Conference (FIE), pp. 1–8, October 2014

6. Dagger, D., O'Connor, A., Lawless, S., Walsh, E., Wade, V.P.: Service-oriented-learning platforms: from monolithic systems to flexible services. IEEE Internet Comput. **11**(3), 28–35 (2007)
7. del Blanco, A., Serrano, A., Freire, M., Martnez-Ortiz, I., Fernández-Manjón, B.: E-learning standards and learning analytics. Can data collection be improved by using standard data models? In: 2013 IEEE Global Engineering Education Conference (EDUCON), pp. 1255–1261, March 2013
8. Evans, A., Romeo, M., Bahrehmand, A., Agenjo, J., Blat, J.: 3D graphics on the web: a survey. Comput. Graph. **41**, 43–61 (2014)
9. Farias, L., Dantas, R., Burlamaqui, A.: Educ-AR: a tool for assist the creation of augmented reality content for education. In: Proceedings of the 2011 IEEE International Conference on Virtual Environments, Human-Computer Interfaces and Measurement Systems, pp. 1–5, September 2011
10. Glahn, C.: Using the ADL experience API for mobile learning, sensing, informing, encouraging, orchestrating. In: Proceedings of the 2013 Seventh International Conference on Next Generation Mobile Apps, Services and Technologies, NGMAST 2013, pp. 268–273, Washington, DC. IEEE Computer Society (2013)
11. Jee, H.-K., Lim, S., Youn, J., Lee, J.: An immersive authoring tool for augmented reality-based E-learning applications. In: 2011 International Conference on Information Science and Applications (ICISA), Jeju Island, pp. 1–5 (2011)
12. Lucrecia, M., Cecilia, S., Patricia, P., Sandra, B.: AuthorAR: authoring tool for building educational activities based on augmented reality. In: 2013 International Conference on Collaboration Technologies and Systems (CTS), pp. 503–507, May 2013
13. Poltrack, J., Hruska, N., Johson, A., Haag, J.: The next generation of SCORM: innovation for the global force. In: Proceedings of the 2012 Interservice/Industry Training, Simulation, and Education Conference (I/ITSEC), pp. 1–9 (2012)
14. Schmalstieg, D., Hollerer, T.: Augmented Reality: Principles and Practice. Game Design/ Usability. Addison Wesley Professional, Boston (2015)
15. van Krevelen, D.W.F., Poelman, R.: A survey of augmented reality technologies, applications and limitations. Int. J. Virtual Real. **9**(2), 1–20 (2010)
16. Wagner, D., Schmalstieg, D.: First steps towards handheld augmented reality. In: Proceedings of the 7th IEEE International Symposium on Wearable Computers, ISWC 2003, Washington, DC, p. 127. IEEE Computer Society (2003)
17. Welsh, E.T., Wanberg, C.R., Brown, K.G., Simmering, M.J.: E-learning: emerging uses, empirical results and future directions. Int. J. Train. Dev. **7**(4), 245–258 (2003)
18. Wiley, D.A.: Connecting learning objects to instructional design theory: A definition, a metaphor, and a taxonomy. The Instructional Use of Learning Objects (2002)

How Augmented Reality Technology Consolidates the SMB Ecosystem of the Tourism Industry in Taiwan

Ya-Hui Chan[1], Jung-Yu Lin[2(✉)], Yu-Hsiu Wang[2], I-Ying Lu[2], and Yueh-Hsin Hsu[2]

[1] Department of Business Administration, Big Data Research Center, Asia University,
Taichung, Taiwan (R.O.C.)
yahui0219@gmail.com
[2] Data Analytics Technology & Applications Research Institute,
Institute for Information Industry, Taipei, Taiwan (R.O.C.)
{jylin,angiewang,iyinglu,emmahsu}@iii.org.tw

Abstract. Taiwanese tourism industry has been consisting largely of small and micro businesses (SMBs). Compared to medium and large corporations who achieve quality service by standardizing operations, these SMBs usually provide quality service by emphasizing local cultures, and relying heavily on storytelling and face-to-face interactions with their customers. However, these interactions are neither systematic nor efficient, resulting in random and scattered contact points; and the lack of marketing resource left these SMBs with weak distribution channels. In the meantime, the tourism landscape is experiencing a shift - a shift in travelers' preference from escorted tours toward independent tours with profound local experiences. Even if the shift lessens the profits of individual shops around top tourism destinations, it still sheds light on formations of mutually beneficial local offline business networks for small and micro businesses.

This shift also increases the importance of applying of Augmented Reality (AR) technology in tourism because of its high efficiency and interactiveness. In this research, we set up a project that adapts multiple location-based techniques to provide on-site information and interactions, and display travel information on user's camera screen by calculate camera position and angle and layering corresponding images. The project also introduces virtual currency into our AR service models, aiming to motivate more travel behaviors.

The purpose of this research is to discuss the effects of applying AR technology on forming an offline business network of SMBs, and consequently building a business model with the use of virtual currency in the offline business network. In other words, this research investigates how the AR applications motivate travelers in engaging in more extensive and deeper travel experiences, and consequently transform travel-related non-consumer behaviors into travel-related consumer behaviors. Besides motivating travelers, the circulation of the virtual currency further facilitates mutually beneficial operation of the offline business network.

This research also illustrates how the technology development of the service system and the operational process of augmented reality can be further applied to future researches. After two months of Proof of Services, the project in this research brought nearly 11,000 visits and circulation of 1.9 million of virtual currency, demonstrating that the integration of augmented reality technology and

© Springer International Publishing AG 2017
M. Antona and C. Stephanidis (Eds.): UAHCI 2017, Part II, LNCS 10278, pp. 129–143, 2017.
DOI: 10.1007/978-3-319-58703-5_10

business model can effectively build an offline business network and a new form of tourism service value system.

Keywords: Augmented reality · Offline business network · Virtual currency · Human-computer interaction · Tourism

1 Background and Motivation

According to the World Travel and Tourism Council (WTTC), as of 2015, the size of the global tourism industry, was about US$7.17 trillion, nearly 9.8% of the global GDP, making the tourism industry the second largest industry in the world. WTTC also estimates output value will be about US$10.98 in 2026, nearly 20.8% GDP. In contrast, Taiwan's tourism industry made up only 2.48% of the GDP in 2015, with its nearly 10 million travelers. This comparison seems to indicate there is still significant potential growth for Taiwan.

Taiwanese tourism industry has been consisting of more than 95% small and micro businesses (SMBs), including dining, accommodation, transportation, entertaining, and shopping industry. Compared to medium and large corporations who achieve quality service by standardizing operations, these SMBs usually provide quality service by emphasizing local cultures, and relying heavily on storytelling and face-to-face interactions with their customers. However, these interactions are neither systematic nor efficient, resulting in random and scattered contact points, and creating gaps in the service chain. Gaps in the service chain have led to the lack of seamless consumer accessibility, leaving travelers poorly guided, and not able to fully experience the beauty of Taiwan. SMBs usually find marketing costly, without seeing the benefits of increased consumption. Fragmented services do not help to create a clear image of tourism in Taiwan, and make it harder to compete with other countries.

In the meantime, the tourism landscape is experiencing a shift - a shift in travelers' preference from escorted tours toward independent tours with profound local experiences. The tourism industry is currently in need of technology-based integrated value-added services, which are highly dynamic and offer interactivity and entertainment (García-Crespo et al. 2009). Latest mobile technologies have revolutionized the way people experience their environment. This development has led to increased popularity of augmented reality (AR) applications to project augmented information on objects or users' immediate surroundings. Recent research explored the opportunities of using marker-based or GPS-based AR in order to enhance the overall tourism experience (Han et al. 2014; Yovcheva et al. 2012; Claudia tom Dieck and Jung 2015). As such, one could say that mobile AR applications allow users to explore the world by adding new layers to their reality, thus resulting in an interactive and highly dynamic experience (Kounavis et al. 2012; Yovcheva et al. 2014). The change in travelers' behavior results in a shift of tourism landscape - a shift that leaves SMEs who have yet to adapt online advertisements and mobile technologies behind. One of the biggest issue that Taiwanese tourism industry needs to resolve now is how the SMEs can quickly adapt to the travelers' behavior and create new business models to overcome current bottleneck with limited resource.

2   Research Purpose

Recent advances in mobile computing, computer graphics, wireless and sensor technologies allow for the fast development of AR applications on smartphones (Azuma et al. 2001; Yovcheva et al. 2012). AR technologies could project virtual messages in a 3D space, thus creating an interface that agrees to human cognitive experience through smartphones. These AR applications are considered more intuitive than conventional presentations of information, and are widely used to elevate user experience. They enhance B2C business relations, achieving the goal of creating value. However, the act of travelling is not restricted to a single B2C relation, but it is instead multiple BN2C (business network to customer) business relations (ref. Fig. 1). The challenge for the travel industry is to build a shared value ecosystem for business networks. This illustrates the needs of a more open ecosystem business concept through partnerships in the vertical supply chain or even horizontal cross-industries cooperation.

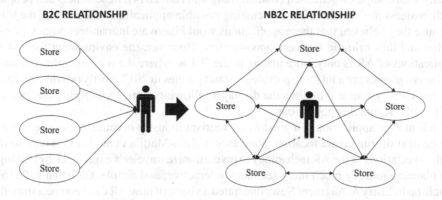

Fig. 1. B2C and BN2C conceptual model

Thus, this research will propose an API-Centric Architecture integrating AR-Based Virtual Currency Solution in tourism, especially applying AR technology on forming a more extensive and deeper travel experiences, and consequently building a business model with the use of AR and virtual currency mechanisms. The purpose of this research is to investigate how the AR applications motivate travelers to transform travel-related non-consumer behaviors into travel-related consumer behaviors and support cross-industry integration and operation, enabling new service models to integrate the tourism-based value chain effectively and create a shared, common platform with dining, transportation, shopping, and other entertaining business.

3   Literature Review

3.1   Online to Offline (O2O)

Travelling is an extensive offline activity. It cannot be replaced by online experiences, but it can be greatly assisted and reinforced by online information and services. With the continued growth of population who regularly surf the Internet, the World Wide Web (WWW) has become the indispensable channel for people seeking to use tourism information (Buhalis and Law 2008). Online-to-Offline Commerce is a business strategy to link online information to offline stores and services. Our research is applying the concept of O2O onto mobile services. Smart phones are prevalent and universal tools for bridging online information to offline context, thus providing an environment for O2O interactions and business opportunities. The most primitive form of O2O business model consist of "search than purchase" (Wang and Lai 2014), meaning that the information flow is consistent through online channel to offline shops. The application of AR technology allows us to provide a more context-specific environment for O2O business.

3.2 Augmented Reality in Tourism

Augmented Reality (AR) technology refers to any enhancement or augmentation on our reality with computer-generated content. (Jung and Han 2014). Researchers and people with business acumen have been discussing possible applications of AR since the 90s because they believed that these applications would innovate human-technology interaction and thus bring in business opportunities. However, the environment for wider applications of AR is only more mature in the 2010s, where the wireless infrastructure and smart phones are a lot more prevalent. Smart phones in 2017 mostly provide internet access, GPS system and multimedia displayer, allowing more applicability and possibilities of AR mobile applications.

AR mobile application is a great fit for tourism industry because AR is relevant to the context of immediate location (Väänänen-Vainio-Mattila et al. 2015). Many have high expectations of the AR technology to revolutionize traveler's experience by making the planning journey much more seamless, interactive, and simple. Christina's (2016) article on Industry & Augment News illustrated a vision of how AR can become a smooth user interface in tourism technology. Using AR, services such as booking hotels, accessing information locally, navigating around destinations, translating written or spoken signs or conversations, and locating dining and entertainment options can all be done simply through an app on your mobile devices.

In the 2010s, many travel mobile applications have started to adapt AR technology. There is ample literature on analyzing functions and technologies of these mobile applications. The table below draws upon the studies from Kounavis et al. (2012), Yovcheva et al. (2012), Buhalis and Yovcheva (2016) and our own research. Exemplary applications that provide AR view on smartphones were summarized in Table 1.

Several scholars pointed out the directions of future development of AR applications in tourism. Han et al. (2014) stated that the application of AR technology is "becoming a necessity of many destinations to stay competitive and attractive to the modern tourist [sic.]". However, they argue that the early employment of AR on mobile applications mainly focused on pushing information onto users, lacking the interactive aspect. Their research proposed to draw more attention to the end-user's point of view and consider engaging them more in the development of AR in tourism. And in order to attract travelers and encourage regular use, their research provides the design guidelines to tend to multi-language functionality, ease of use and personalization.

Table 1. AR on mobile applications

Functionality	Application name	Description
Context-aware push	Field Trip, Travel Guide	Using ibeacons, GPS location or even Google Awareness API to push context-specific messages
m-Commerce	Concerto Timer, IKEA catalog	Exhibit items in 3D mode thus attracting users to purchase the item
Feedback & social network	Aure, WhosHere, Circle	Location Based information sharing
Routing and navigation	iOnRoad	Planning and directing the users to a destination
Interactive AR view	Yelp Monocle, Wikitude, Panoramascope, Spyglass, Peaks, Nearest Tube	Serving as an alternative user interface, providing information that is augmented on the reality
Visual augmentation	Timetraveler Die Berliner Mauer, Theodolite, Layar	Augmenting image layers on camera view to provide more information, such as overlapping an old picture on the current street view or showing POI (Points of Interest) names and information on the camera view
Image recognition	Google Goggles, Google Translate, Word Lens	Recognizing images and able to decipher writings on the images
Marker detection	In2AR, Digital Binocular Station	Detecting markers to trigger 3D contents
Responsive gaming	Pokemon go, Ingress, TimeWarp	Incorporating gamified interactions designed

Yovcheva et al. (2012) also offer valuable reference for future design decisions. They pointed out the major drawbacks of these applications are (1) the structure of information is not clear on AR interface, often resulted in "overloaded and cluttered display". And (2) besides map-based services and communication, further tourism-related function-alities such as m-Commerce, feedback, routing and tour generation are rarely supported in these AR applications.

3.3 Economic Effects and Network

AR technology is expected to have high potential in economic impacts. However, none of the above studied applications incorporate substantial business model. Jung and Han (2014) pointed out several ways that AR can create commercial benefits: because it provides a new channel and more contact points for a travel product, and the publication of information and marketing is relatively low-cost and flexible. Therefore, they indicate that business has started to implement the technology to encourage customers to make purchase decisions.

The concept of network in economics combined with location-specific context would be appropriate for applying on tourism economy. In economics, the definition of net paradigm refers to the linkages, relevant to market competitiveness, that exist among firms and an array of complementary industries. Becattini et al. (2003) provide a definition that gave more emphasis on the economic benefits: "network refers to the relationships among firms, stakeholders, and other institutions of a region, which generate socioeconomic benefits, as in models of local development."

Asero et al. linked the concept of networks to geographical proximity. Dollinger (1990) regards points of interests (POIs) as nodes, and found that through spatial mobility, the travelers define their reference networks that they build around nodal destinations. The tourism industry is essentially the economic sector with the most inter-organizational networks (Bickerdyke 1996).

In a highly competitive environment, many argue that it's better for small and micro businesses in tourism to form networks and develop strategic cooperation (Asero et al. 2016; Dollinger 1990). The networks cannot be simply based on geographical vicinity; they have to have an electronic infrastructure as well (Ndou and Passiante 2005).

4   AR-Based Virtual Currency Solution

4.1   Service Model and Human-Computer Interaction Design

The applications of AR within the tourism industry are extremely varied and each is designed to satisfy different needs. Yet, in essence, a mobile AR application needs to take into account the particular needs of travelers and the businesses' potential to maintain and manage it. In this research, we proposed an AR-Based Virtual Currency Solution to achieve innovative travel experiences; and we implemented the solution to two models: Non-regional AR Model and Regional AR Model. We hope to encourage cross-store business cooperation by motivating travelers to explore more POIs and purchase more; and this solution would eventually facilitate the growth and sustainability of Business Networks (ref. Fig. 2). The solution includes two core modules as follows:

AR Exploration and Navigation
This research applied the AR technology of camera view on smart phones, which allows the users to explore and browse nearby POIs in 360-degree view thus providing intuitive spatial coordination. We also applied AR navigation technology, which leads the users to their chosen POI with map view and an AR icon layered on the camera view.

In terms of user interface design, for AR Exploration, we created a 360-degree exploring window. Using their smart phones, travelers will be able to browse nearby POIs and their information in all direction on the camera view. The information includes POI names, distance and the number of reviews. The number of review is presented in the number of "sprouts" on a green field (ref. Fig. 3). These reviews can be in forms of

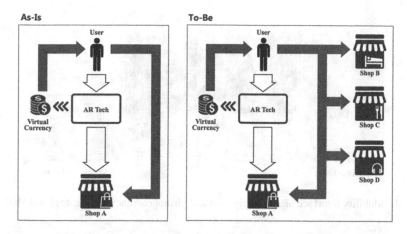

Fig. 2. Service model of AR-Based Virtual Currency Solution

texts, pictures and videos; we believed the number and the quality of these multimedia-based reviews would influence the visit rate of a POI.

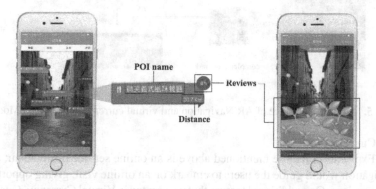

Fig. 3. Mobility interface of AR Exploration

As for AR Navigation, the user interface on mobile devices is consisted of two parts (ref. Fig. 4): the upper screen shows camera view with an icon layered on the intended direction; and the lower screen shows the planned route on the map view. After a traveler chooses a POI that he/she would like to visit, the map view provides the shorted route for the traveler to follow. The traveler can also turn their screens toward different directions to find the AR icon, which marks the direction of the chosen POI. The AR icon is customized according to POI features to accentuate local characteristics. For example, Nanzhuang is a township famous for its spectacular scene of white Tung flower blossoms. Therefore, we designed a Tung flower image as the AR icon, hoping that the connection between user interface and the local POIs can further intrigue travelers, and motivate them to explore the local POIs (Fig. 5).

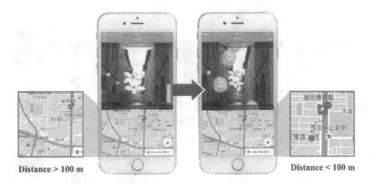

Fig. 4. Mobility interface of AR Navigation and virtual currency in Non-regional Model

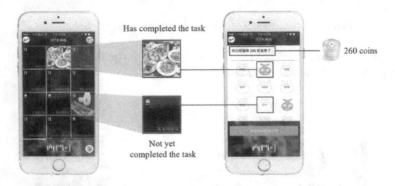

Fig. 5. Mobility interface of AR Navigation and virtual currency in Regional Model

Virtual Currency

The AR Exploration feature mentioned above is an online service mechanism; and the AR Navigation would guide the users to embark on an offline visit, giving opportunities to offline services. One additional feature that we created is Virtual Currency. Our system would award travelers with virtual coins when they perform certain tasks, such as writing a review (ref. Figs. 4 and 6). The virtual coins can be collected and further circulated in different shops by forms of discount coupons.

This research chooses virtual coins to be the operational drive for the AR-Based Virtual Currency Solution, not only because it enhances the novelty in AR technology, but also because it is expected to lead continual travel and consumer behaviors (Bogliolo et al. 2012). The left part of Fig. 2 illustrated that if virtual coins are provides by a shop's own system, they can only be circulated in the particular shop, and the travelers' further purchase would be limited to a single shop. The right part of Fig. 2 shows that our system allows travelers to redeem their virtual coins in different shops, thus encourage travelers to explore more shops.

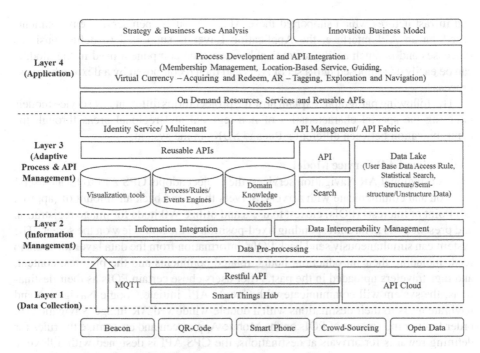

Fig. 6. API-Centric Architecture of AR-Based Virtual Currency Solution

4.2 Architecture and Mechanism Design

In order to realize the AR-Based Virtual Currency Solution in Fig. 2 and to be able to adjust flexibly with different regional features, the project of this research adopts API (Application Programming Interface) for platform development. Through connecting frontend and backend application programs in displaying, transmitting, and through the exchanges and storage of data between servers, users can use web-based applications on iOS and Android Mobile App to communicate fully with the platform.

The platform (ref. Fig. 6) is consisted of four layers of subsystems: Data Collection Layer, Information Management Layer, Adaptive Process & API Management Layer and Application Layer. The Data Collection Layer is at the very bottom layer and is designed to collect various real-time and batch data from IoT devices, open data, crowd-sourcing, and external data sources into the platform to achieve syntactic interoperability. The next layer is the Information Management subsystem. The purpose of this system is to achieve semantic and concept interoperability and provide a common data service framework for the platform. The Adaptive Process & API Management Layer is mainly formed by an API management subsystem designed to export all the services with API and provides its monitoring and manage. Since the operation of a business case is governed by various business processes, the design starts from making rules, data and analytics easily reusable, customizable, and can be connected into a business process which itself also needs to be flexibly modifiable. Each step of the business process systematically binds to other services via APIs. In this way, it makes it possible that the business process steps can be mapped to a set of isolated underlying computing services and infrastructures which supported these APIs. Through open service environments based on an API interface, the Application Layer is supported to define business processes and is much easily customizable since each component used in the module can be easily decomposed into a set of APIs and then recomposed by a flexible business process.

The following paragraphs explain how the project forms different AR service models targeting the special characteristics of non-regional and regional areas through the communication between different APIs and SDKs in the system.

Non-regional AR Service Model

For Non-regional AR Navigation services, the project adopts GPS API to locate users' location and communicate with servers. Servers then send back an amount of (approx. 20) Point of Interests (POIs) closest to users and utilize Wikitude for image registration and present POIs in its corresponding fixed-position in the 360° view on the screen. The system can simultaneously send back POIs' information from the data layer for users to read, including their introduction, hours, related comments and the pictures, content, and tags travelers uploaded in the past. After users chose certain POIs as their destinations, the system will communicate with Google API, initiate Google Navigation and navigate users to their destinations with a double-windowed AR Image Navigation. In order to filter the amount of POIs on the Mobile App screen and customize the rules for defining rewards for arrivals at destinations, the GPS API is designed with a flexible definition of arrival distance. For example, GPS API will locate users when they are approximately one hundred meters away from chosen POIs and communicate with servers to define it as meeting the standard for virtual coins rewards. Servers then trigger corresponding dialogues on APP screen to notify users to confirm the completion of their navigation mission and reward users with virtual coins. Next, the system will document the amounts of coins users receive in each mission into the Coins table and the accumulated amount of coins acquired by individual users into the Users table in database. These records then enable users to use virtual coins to redeem rewards in local shops in their upcoming trips.

Regional AR Service Model

Compared to non-regional AR service model, the application of this study's AR service model in regional area is specialized in its business model of directing travelers to specifically defined travel regions. For instance, the system will send users notification when it locates users within 2–5 km around specifically defined regions through GPS API. After users click to start the regional exploration services, the mobile app will send request to server API and further make a table query to get all regions information in database. API then gets the corresponding ID and related information of that specific region from the data layer. In addition to operating the virtual coins rewarding system with defined location, the system also verifies each regional store's coins-rewarding requirement settings for travelers' behaviors such as check-ins and story writing to enhance the gamification elements in regional exploration. Since all the information are in dynamic control by APIs, changes can be displayed on users' mobile app in real-time

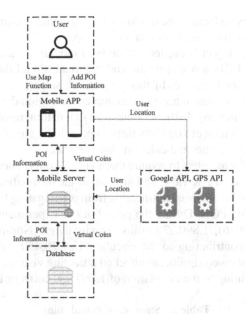

Fig. 7. Interaction of user, app, servers, and APIs database

if any store is added onto or removed from the store list, or changes its setting for rewards requirements.

In conclusion, this project's flexible API structure, connection to external Google API and GPS API and the mechanism of virtual coins are key elements to successfully support cross-industry services and business model. First of all, the system guided travelers to specifically defined regions with Google API and GPS API, and acquire the POI-specific rewards requirements information of travelers' behavior such as social media sharing or story-writing (Fig. 7). This enhancement of gamification elements is also strengthened by the usage of IoT technologies such as Beacon and QR Code. This gamification mechanism not only encourage users to interact with regional stores and experience local travels in a profound way, its AR technologies can further inspire users to share service information with more travelers and increase the numbers of our potential service users.

While travelers enjoy the AR services, the system will document the virtual coins travelers obtain in each mission and its overall record of the virtual coins users obtained into different tables of database, which further enhance users' motivation in engaging in travel-related consumer behaviors. This study also aims to form a tourism ecosystem consisted of travelers and stores through the circulation of virtual coins between POI stores and further realize the goal of building an offline business network.

5 Empirical Result

We incorporated virtual currency system to motivate travelers to explore more, and visit more shops in order to stimulate economic prowess in Taiwanese tourism. The design of the virtual currency redeem system allows users to redeem coins collected in their travels for discounts of merchandises in another shop.

Our experimental project is carried out on both models: Non-regional Model that encompasses normal POIs across Taiwan, and Regional Model that includes selected POIs and designed user interface. In this project, we selected 5 districts, each with different characteristics to charm travelers, to implement regional AR project on. Some districts are bustling shopping districts, some have rich natural resources, and some are quaint, artsy districts. A total of 103 POIs signed up, including local shops, chain stores, popular attractions, restaurants and cafes and bike rentals.

There are 3 ways for travelers to acquire these virtual coins in both models: (1) using the navigation function on AR view, and arriving at the destination POI, (2) scanning QR code or getting the broadcasted notification from participating POIs, and (3) leaving reviews or feedback on POIs. During the period of our experimental project (Oct. 1st 2016 to Dec. 31st 2016), 1,890,330 coins are circulated: Non-regional AR Model attracted 236 visits, contributing to the circulation of 20,450 coins. In comparison, Regional AR Model showed significant effect on attracting visitors, because it attracted 10,645 visits, contributing to the circulation of 1,869,880 coins (ref. Table 2).

Table 2. Statistics of virtual coins

AR Model	Visits generated	Coins redeemed	Max. of visits by traveler
Non-regional	236 visits	20,450 coins	17
Regional	10,645 visits	1,869,880 coins	28

Users will be able to use these coins to redeem rewards such as items in other shops, or 35 NTD discount in local convenient stores. Other redeemable items are periodic, for example, in October, users can choose to donate these virtual coins, and we donate corresponding values to Chinese Children home & Shelter Association, a local orphanage institute. The value of virtual coins circulated equals to 140,000 New Taiwan Dollars (NTD).

We also looked into the behavioral pattern of the travelers' visit to POIs (ref. Fig. 8) and found that the variance of the number of visited POI is higher in Non-regional AR Model (given that the interval of 1 to 33) - most travelers only visit 1 to 2 POIs. Whereas in Regional AR Model, the variance is smaller, and the average of number of visited POI is 20 for a three day trip. This shows that the Regional AR Model is 1.5 times more effective than the Non-regional AR Model. Our assumption is that when travelers are exploring in an undefined environment, they have higher uncertainties for time and space, thus limiting their motivation to explore the next POI. In contrast, Regional AR Model more effectively engages travelers in more extensive travel experiences.

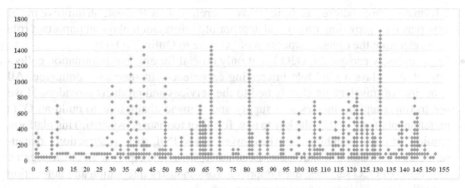

(a) Non-regional AR Model

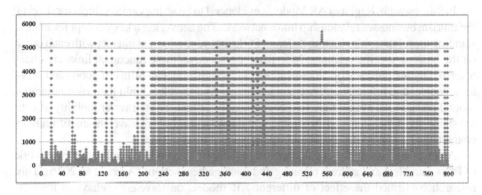

(b) Regional AR Model

Fig. 8. Circulation of virtual coins

6 Conclusion

New technology has been seen as a way for many businesses in the tourism industry to stay competitive and enhance their marketing campaign in various ways. AR has evolved as the buzzword of modern information technology and is gaining increasing attention in the media as well as through a variety of use cases (Jung and Han 2014). However, although research on AR has been conducted in various fields, the majority of studies focus on technical aspects of AR, while others are tailored to specific applications. Therefore, this research aims to examine the current implementation of AR in the SMB Tourism context that is required to guide the early stages of AR implementation in a purposeful way to enhance both the travelers' experiences and businesses' relationship which are as bellows:

- Intuitive Travel Experience: End-to-end travel includes the course of before, during and after trips. As travelers start a tour, they have to obtain large volume of information from different channels, providers and even industries. It takes efforts and time for travelers to collect and sort out useful information from the large and diverse information, both before and during trips. Therefore, how to create an intuitive travel experience by providing timely and appropriate information plays an important role in accelerating the organic expansion of "Online to Offline" (O2O).

- Cross-industry ecosystem: O2O is not only crucial for efficient information collection; it also plays a vital role in creating experiences in seamless commerce. All behaviors of travelers are closely tied to the services and products providers. If we see travelers and businesses as a supply and demand chain, how to build an O2O matching platform will be the key to new forms of tourism ecosystem. This platform would customize matchings between travelers and POI, such as attractions, restaurants, accommodations, stores, etc. Eventually, it would help to achieve the organic expansion of O2O services, even improve cross-industry integration and innovation as well as the efficiency of commerce process.

In this research, Regional AR Model is evidenced to be an important vehicle for driving the tourism businesses relationship into a network. The network is a key concept for understanding the relationships linking different POIs that cooperate and interact with each other on the basis of specific relations. In a spatial perspective, these functional links are characterized by the presence of "dominant nodes," which attract an influx of goods and services, people, and information (Asero et al. 2016). And travelers build their own networks around nodal POIs, even if they are geographically distant. Thus, traveler mobility affects the shape, the dimension, and the structure of the networks, where travelers are different in characteristics, trip-related behaviors, and type of holiday chosen.

As POIs are complex dynamic systems, a "smart" system to consolidate the network of POIs can affect and address planning and management actions (Asero et al. 2016). This research confirmed the effect of different AR models on travelers' behaviors through primary research. However, we did not personalize POI suggestions based on individual traveler's behavior. We also did not go as far as customizing distribution rules of the virtual currency based on individual preferences - we standardized the distribution rules for each action. Therefore, future research can further investigate how to optimize POI suggestions and virtual currency distribution based on analyses of traveler's behaviors.

Acknowledgement. Thanks to the Department of Industrial Technology in the Ministry of Economy Affairs, R.O.C. for their support and resource in the 4G Advanced Commerce and Multimedia Service Promotion Program (4G 先進商務與影音服務平台推動計畫).

References

Azuma, R., Baillot, Y., Behringer, R., Feiner, S., Julier, S., MacIntyre, B.: Recent advances in augmented reality. IEEE Comput. Graph. Appl. **21**(6), 34–47 (2001)

Becattini, G.: From the industrial district to the districtualisation of production activity: some considerations. In: Belussi, F., Gottardi, G., Rullani, E. (eds.) The technological evolution of industrial districts, pp. 3–17. Springer, US (2003)

Bickerdyke, I.: Australia: the evolving structure and strategies of business networks. In: OECD (ed.) Networks of Enterprises and Local Development: Competing and Co-operating in Local Productive Systems, pp. 203–216. Organisation for Economic Cooperation and Development, Paris (1996)

Bogliolo, A., Polidori, P., Aldini, A., Moreira, W., Mendes, P., Yildiz, M., Ballester, C., Seigneur, J.M.: Virtual currency and reputation-based cooperation incentives in user-centric networks. In: 2012 8th International Wireless Communications and Mobile Computing Conference (IWCMC), pp. 895–900. IEEE, August 2012

Buhalis, D., Law, R.: Progress in information technology and tourism management: 20 years on and 10 years after the Internet–The state of eTourism research. Tourism Manage. **29**(4), 609–623 (2008)

Kounavis, C.D., Kasimati, A.E., Zamani, E.D.: Enhancing the tourism experience through mobile augmented reality: challenges and prospects. Int. J. Eng. Bus. Manag. **4**, 1–6 (2012)

Christina: Augmented Reality Applications in the Tourism Industry. Industry & Augment News, 6 January 2016. http://www.augment.com/blog/augmented-reality-in-tourism/

Dollinger, M.J.: The evolution of collective strategies in fragmented industries. Acad. Manag. Rev. **15**(2), 266–285 (1990)

Han, D.-I., Jung, T., Gibson, A.: Dublin AR: implementing augmented reality in tourism. In: Xiang, Z., Tussyadiah, I. (eds.) Information and Communication Technologies in Tourism 2014, pp. 511–523. Springer, Cham (2014). doi:10.1007/978-3-319-03973-2_37

Buhalis, D., Yovcheva, Z.: The digital tourism think tank: reports and best practice. Produced in partnership with YAHOO! and Bournemouth University (2016). https://thinkdigital.travel/wp-content/uploads/2013/04/10-AR-Best-Practices-in-Tourism.pdf

García-Crespo, A., Chamizo, J., Rivera, I., Mencke, M., Colomo-Palacios, R., Gómez-Berbís, J.M.: SPETA: social pervasive e-Tourism advisor. Telemat. Inform. **26**, 306–315 (2009)

Jung, T., Han, D.: Augmented Reality (AR) in Urban Heritage Tourism. e-Review of Tourism Research (2014). ISSN: 1941-5842

Claudia tom Dieck, M., Jung, T.: A theoretical model of mobile augmented reality acceptance in urban heritage tourism. Curr. Issues Tour. (2015). http://www.du.se/PageFiles/139207/A%20theoretical%20model%20of%20mobile%20augmented%20reality%20acceptance%20in%20urban%20heritage%20tourism.pdf

Ndou, V., Passiante, G.: Value creation in tourism network systems. In: Frew, A.J. (ed.) Information and Communication Technologies in Tourism 2005, pp. 440–451. Springer, Vienna (2005)

Väänänen-Vainio-Mattila, K., Olsson, T., Häkkilä, J.: Towards deeper understanding of user experience with ubiquitous computing systems: systematic literature review and design framework. In: Abascal, J., Barbosa, S., Fetter, M., Gross, T., Palanque, P., Winckler, M. (eds.) INTERACT 2015. LNCS, vol. 9298, pp. 384–401. Springer, Cham (2015). doi:10.1007/978-3-319-22698-9_26

Asero, V., Gozzo, S., Tomaselli, V.: Building tourism networks through tourist mobility. J. Travel Res. **55**(6), 751–763 (2016)

Wang, F.S., Lai, G.H.: Empirical study to design field applications for O2O (Online to Offline) business model in tourism with mobile computing and cloud service supports. 産研論集 **46**(47), 193 (2014)

Yovcheva, Z., Buhalis, D., Gatzidis, C.: Empirical evaluation of smartphone augmented reality browsers in an urban tourism destination context. Int. J. Mob. Hum. Comput. Interact. **6**(2), 10–31 (2014)

Yovcheva, Z., Buhalis, D., Gatzidis, C.: Overview of smartphone augmented reality applications for tourism (2012). http://citeseerx.ist.psu.edu/viewdoc/download?doi=10.1.1.910.2465&rep=rep1&type=pdf

AR Based User Interface for Driving Electric Wheelchairs

Shigeyuki Ishida[1][✉], Munehiro Takimoto[1], and Yasushi Kambayashi[2]

[1] Department of Information Sciences, Tokyo University of Science,
2641 Yamazaki, Noda-shi, Chiba-ken, Japan
6316604@ed.tus.ac.jp
[2] Department of Computer and Information Engineering,
Nippon Institute of Technology, 4-1 Gakuendai, Miyashiro-machi,
Minamisaitama-gun, Saitama 345-8501, Japan
yasushi@nit.ac.jp

Abstract. Todays, the electric wheelchair has been an essential tool for handicapped people. It may be difficult, however for hand-impaired people to operate the electric wheelchair with the conventional joystick. For hand-impaired people, we have to provide other operations such as eye-tracking. Traditional eye-tracking method, however, is tiresome, because the user has to fix his or her eyes to the direction of the destination. In this paper, we propose an user interface with eye tracking extended by the augmented reality (AR) technology. In our user interface, the sight in front of the electric wheelchair is displayed on the PC screen. Furthermore, an oval is overlaid at user's view point in the sight on the screen as if a search light spots focus at the specified location. The user can decide the location at the oval as a temporary destination, to which the electric wheelchair moves. Repeating the process, the user can intuitively drive his or her electric wheelchair to the final destination without the burden of operations.

Keywords: Electric wheelchair · Eye tracking · Augmented reality

1 Introduction

The electric wheelchair is an indispensable tool for handicapped people. It especially has a great value for ones with impaired legs. It is not, however, always easy to use for those who have invalidity with hands. Most electric wheelchairs are designed to be operated through a joystick, which requires operations with hand; therefore, other operation manners have to be given for hand-impaired people. One of such improvements of an electric wheelchair is intelligence. The purpose of intelligence is to realize safer and friendlier driving assistance by giving intuitive operations for driving electric wheelchairs.

Eye tracking is one of the most leading candidates of hands-free operations [1,2]. In traditional eye tracking operations, users have to focus their attentions to the direction by their eyes. When driving a electric wheelchair, the user has

© Springer International Publishing AG 2017
M. Antona and C. Stephanidis (Eds.): UAHCI 2017, Part II, LNCS 10278, pp. 144–154, 2017.
DOI: 10.1007/978-3-319-58703-5_11

to fix his or her eyes to the destination or goal of the electric wheelchair. It is not only unintuitive, but also tiresome. In this paper we propose a user interface that allows users to intuitively control their electric wheelchairs through eye tracking. Our electric wheelchair has a laptop PC, which displays the sight in front of the electric wheelchair with a web camera. The user can observe the sight as if he or she looks through the window.

The user interface for driving uses AR technique. AR is a technique and a method for expanding reality by adding "something different information" to human-perceivable information in the real world. In order to provide feedback to the user so that he or she can confirm the destination of the electric wheelchair, the front sight displayed on the PC includes an oval shape as a destination sign. The highlighted oval shape indicates the spot on the floor the user looks at, as if he or she plays search light on the floor. This feature let the user confirm he or she is driving the wheelchair in the right direction. Thus, iteration of AR based specification of the destination and move to it contributes to intuitively driving electric wheelchair without using hands or legs.

2 Related Work

There are roughly two approaches proposed for making of electric wheelchairs intelligent. The first approach is autonomous movement such as giving map information or recognizing surrounding environments through several sensors, so that the electric wheelchair can autonomously avoid obstacles and traveling along the wall without troublesome operations. This approach is effective for prevention of accidents due to user's mistakes in judgment or operation errors. The second one is improvement of the user interface, which introduces an alternative method to replace the joystick which is a conventional operation for input interface. This approach is effective for users such as a hand-impaired people.

2.1 Autonomous Traveling

Many intelligent electric wheelchairs have been developed to realize autonomous traveling by recognizing the surrounding environment using multiple sensors [3–5]. They have infrared sensors and ultrasonic sensors as distance sensors, and touch sensors as contact sensors. Once these sensors recognize some obstacles, the electric wheelchairs calculate suitable roundabout routes. Furthermore, some systems that drive a wheelchair through visualizing a destination based on electroencephalogram [6]. In these driving systems, users specify the destination instead of the traveling direction; the specification manner reduces the burden on the user. Our user interface also aims at reduction of users' burden in the same direction.

2.2 User Interface Improvements

Some control utilize facial expression methods through recognizing gestures of user's face with the web camera [7], and the inclination of the user's face [8].

Also, some electric wheelchairs are equipped with an interface that selects and manipulates buttons on a GUI (Graphical User Interface) built on the laptop PC screen with gaze [9,10]. In addition, electric wheelchairs with a voice input interface have been developed [11]. In our proposal, we mainly improve the user interface, but we have also included autonomous driving features in two aspects.

3   Device Overview

3.1   Concept of Our Electric Wheelchair

Figure 1 shows the concept of our electric wheelchair. Users drive the wheelchair with a laptop PC on his knee. As shown in the figure, the laptop PC has an eye tracker sensor and a web camera. The web camera takes the sight in front of the electric wheelchair, and displays it on the screen of the PC. Also, an eye tracking sensor is equipped at the joint of the laptop so as it faces with the user to give the coordinates of the viewpoint on the PC screen. In order to track the user's eye correctly, the display of the PC is inclined with right angle as the display and the user's line of sight crosses perpendicularly.

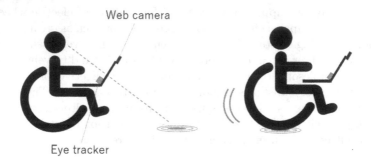

Fig. 1. Overview of our electric wheelchair

3.2   AR Based User Interface

The sight in front of the user, which is a floor in most cases, is displayed on the screen of PC. The user can see the sight on the screen as if he or she is looking at the front sight through a physical window. On the screen, the user can see the spot corresponding to the destination of a line of sight on the floor, as shown in Fig. 2. It looks as if a small oval area of the floor is lighted up by a search light. Since the spot is on the line of sight, the user feels as if light would be emitted from his or her eyes to the floor as shown by the dotted line in Fig. 1.

Even though the destination spot moves along the line of sight, once the user determine the destination, it is not necessary to make the destination spot move. We provide a means to fix the destination. For example, the user can fix the spot through a trigger like blinking his or her eyes. In our current prototype,

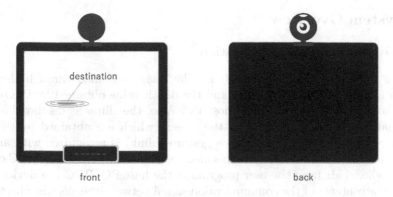

Fig. 2. Image on the display

we tentatively use a specific key on the PC to fix the destination spot. When the destination spot is fixed, the wheelchair moves forward until the destination spot comes under its wheels, as shown in the right side of Fig. 1.

3.3   Operations of the Electric Wheelchair

We can summarize the manner for driving our electric wheelchair using our user interface as follows:

1. Move the oval on the screen with the line of sight to the coordinates of the user's destination.
2. When the user matches the oval to the destination, he or she blinks one eye for 0.5 s or more.
3. A signal is sent from the PC to the electric wheelchair, and the electric wheelchair move to the destination.
4. Once the electric wheelchair reaches to the destination, return to Operation 1. The user can reach the final destination through repeating this set of operations. If the user wants to stop halfway, he or she blink one eye.

Basically, the operations that the user is responsible are only to determine the destination with gaze, and to blink one eye for start and stop.

Notice that eye tracking is not performed during movement of the wheelchair. In general, continuous eye tracking imposes a burden on users. In our user interface, on the other hand, the user does not need to fix his or her stare at a point for operations. Our user interface liberates the users from concentration of eye-tracking. The user can see anything during the movement of wheelchair once he or she decides the destination.

It is rare for users to directly specify the final destination, because the display of laptop PC is not big enough. Also, there may be some obstacles on the path to the destination. Thus, we have designed our user interface to let the user reset partial destinations repeatedly while approaching to the final destination.

4   System Overview

4.1   Overall System Configuration

Figure 3 is an overview of our system. The image obtained through the web camera is displayed on the screen, and the depth value obtained by the sensor is sent to the user program of the host PC. Also, the ellipse is displayed at the coordinates of the line of sight on the screen, which are obtained by the eye tracker connected to the PC. Once a gesture (blink) is recognized with an eye tracker, a signal for moving to the specified coordinates is sent to the RRC of the electric wheelchair from the user program of the host PC. RRC is a device that adjusts the contents of the communication signal between the electric wheelchair and the host PC.

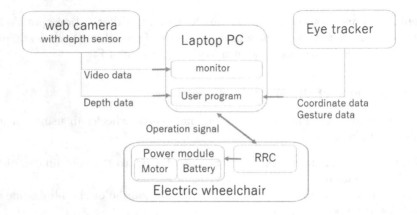

Fig. 3. System configuration diagram

4.2   State Transition of Electric Wheelchair

Figure 4 is a state transition diagram of the electric wheelchair with our user interface. Basically, when we use interface, state of our system is Run mode, and then, the state transits to output mode of (vi) in Fig. 4. In this state, the host PC sends a signal with output command to the RRC. Table 1 describes the output mode and output command.

4.3   Driving Controls

Figure 5 shows flows of data or commands in our system. In order to make an electric wheelchair move to the destination on the floor, the degree θ of the destination for the front of the wheelchair, and the distance d from the wheelchair to the destination on the floor (DoF). Therefore, our system calculates them based on the coordinates of the destination on the screen (DoS), which is given

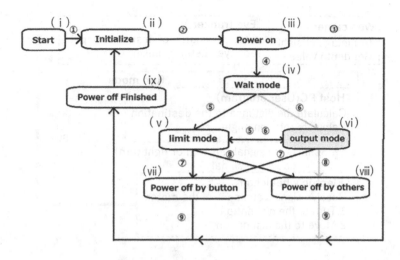

Fig. 4. State transition diagram of electric wheelchair

Table 1. Output mode and output command description

Output mode	A state in which the joystick operation by the user is prohibited and the wheelchair is operated by the program with set value
Output command input method of command	An output signal from the host PC
	"output" + 2hex#1 + 2hex#2 ※ #1 = [−100, 100] = Translational output value ※ #2 = [−100,100] = Rotational output value

※ example command
output1e00: Drive at a speed of 30% in the straight direction

by an eye tracker as a view point on the screen, and depth information, which is given by a depth sensor.

Once user's Gesture is recognized, the turning direction, i.e. the left turn or the right turn, is first determined. The direction can easily be determined based on DoS. The turn off degree θ can be calculated as follows: $\theta = \arctan(Gx/depth)$ as shown in Fig. 6(b). Gx is the x-coordinate in global coordinates obtained from the depth sensor with depth value. As well, the distance from the Web camera ($WtoD$) to DoF can also be calculated using Gx and depth as follows: $WtoD = \sqrt{Gx^2 + depth^2}$.

Once $WtoD$ is obtained, assuming that the height from the floor to the web camera is fixed at $height = 0.85$ [m], as shown in Fig. 6(a), the distance to the destination can be calculated as follows: $d = \sqrt{WtoD^2 - 0.7225}$

Finally, PC sends a command for turning in degree θ and then a command for going straight distance d to the electric wheelchair.

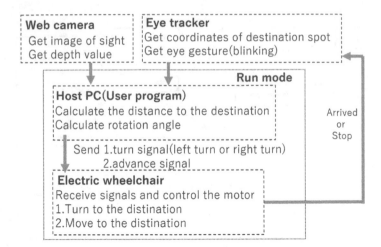

Fig. 5. Overview of control system

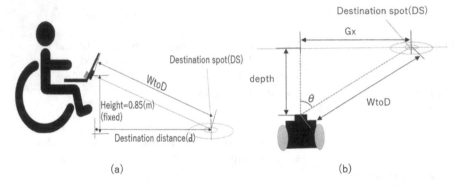

Fig. 6. (a) Destination distance from the web camera; (b) Angle to the destination

5   System Implementation

As shown in Fig. 7, we have implemented our user interface on a real electric wheelchair. Main components are as follows:

- A laptop PC with the proposed user interface
  This is the core of the entire intelligent wheelchair control system. All the data are processed on this laptop PC, which send all the control signals to the electric wheelchair driving system (RRC).
- Web camera with depth sensor
  This is mounted on a rack at the front of electric wheelchair. The depth sensor is used to measure the distance to the destination.
- Eye tracker
  This is equipped on the joint of the laptop PC. It recognizes the user's line of sight coordinates and gesture.

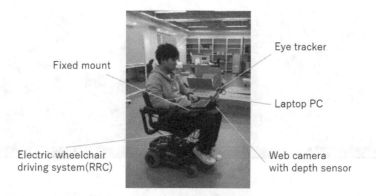

Fig. 7. Implementation of our user interface

- RRC (driving system)
  This is used to supply energy to the motors of wheelchair based on control signals sent by PC.

Figure 8(a) shows a screen shot of the destination on the floor and the screen of overlaid oval. Figure 8(b) is a screen shot of the destination specified by an oval. Notice that the size of oval varies in proportion to the distance. This feature gives users intuitiveness similar to physical perspective.

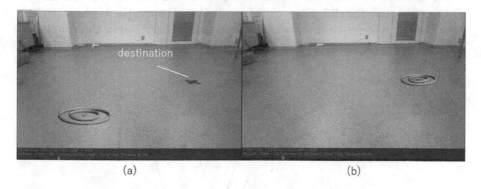

Fig. 8. (a) Destination set on the floor and oval; (b) Match the destination and the coordinates of line of sight

Figure 9(a) shows a screen when one eye is closed and a command for fixing the destination, and the signal is transmitted to the electric wheelchair. At this time, the color of the oval turns to red, and the color is kept until the electric wheelchair reaches the destination or stops. The color representation of the oval contributes to intuitive operations. Also, Fig. 9(b) shows the screen after arriving at the destination. As mentioned above, when one of the eyes is closed while traveling, it stops and returns to the state of Fig. 8.

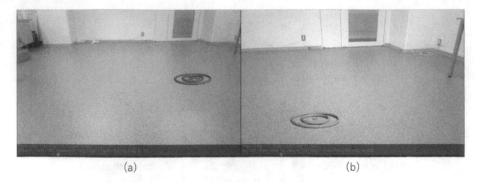

(a)   (b)

Fig. 9. (a) Immediately after gesture (command transmission); (b) After arrival at the destination (Color figure onine)

6   Experimental Results

In order to demonstrate the effectiveness of our AR based user interface, we have conducted experiments, and measured accuracy for arriving at the destination and tracing cranked route, and the number of executed operations.

1. **error for reaching point**
   As shown in Fig. 10, for some cases, where the direction is set to the right turn and the left turn, the distances are set to 1.2 [m], 2.4 [m], 3.6 [m], we have measured the difference of the positions between the destination and the electric wheelchair after arrival five times. Table 2 shows the results. As shown in the table, the farther the destination is, the more errors occur.

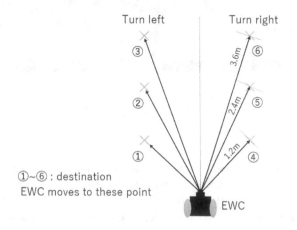

Fig. 10. Measuring the accuracy of arrival at the destination

Table 2. Differences between the positions of the destination and the wheelchair actually reached.

	Left			Right		
Destination num	①	②	③	④	⑤	⑥
Destination distance [m]	1.2	2.4	3.6	1.2	2.4	3.6
Position error [m]	0.07	0.12	0.16	0.06	0.14	0.20

2. **tracing cranked route and the number of operations**
   Figure 11 shows the cranked route we employed for the electric wheelchair passes through, and how many times the user had to perform the operations. The dotted line is the path through which the electric wheelchair passed. Although we conducted the experiment several times, the number of operations until reaching the final destination was roughly four times.

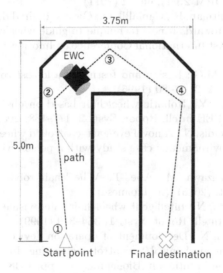

Fig. 11. Cranked road and traveling route of WC

7   Conclusion and Future Work

There are some electric wheelchairs (EWC) controlled with gaze have already been developed, but most of them lack intuitiveness or impose a burden through gazing at the direction during operation. Therefore, we have proposed and developed an ergonomic user interface for controlling an electric wheelchair. As the interface, we have adopted the operation manner to designate the destination instead of the direction to control the electric wheelchair. This reduces user's fatigue during operation. In addition, the gaze based approach enables handicapped people to operate the electric wheelchair easily and intuitively through AR technology. However, the results of the experiments showed that Table 2 shows that specifying far positions tend to cause certain errors. Also, we have observed that complex routes such as a crank intend to require too many operations. In future works, we plan to combine our approach with the traditional obstacle avoidance algorithm in order to enhance autonomous driving. This should allow the user to reach the destination while avoiding obstacles in an unexpected environment and reduce the number of operations. Also, since the operating range of the oval is restricted on the screen of the PC, the use of wearable device would make operation for turning around easy, and enable to decrease the number of operations.

References

1. Arai, K., Mardiyanto, R.: A prototype of electric wheelchair controlled by eye-only for paralyzed user. JRM **23**(1), 66–74 (2011)
2. Al-Haddad, A., Sudirman, R., Camallil, O.: Gaze at desired destination, and wheelchair will navigate towards it.new technique to guide wheelchair motion based on EOG signals. In: First International Conference on Informatics and Computational Intelligence (2011)
3. Miller, D.P., Slack, M.G.: Design and testing of a lo-cost robotic wheelchair prototype. Auton. Robot. **2**, 77–80 (1995)
4. Nakanishi, S., Kuno, Y.: Robotic wheelchair based on observations of both user and environment. IEEE Intell. Robot. Syst. **2**, 177–188 (2002)
5. Eid, A.M., Giakoumidis, N.: A novel eye-gaze-controlled wheelchair system for navigating unknown environments: case study with a person with ALS. IEEE Access **4**, 558–573 (2016)
6. Takahashi, K., Nakazawa, M., Abe, T.: Wheelchair robot control system using EEG. IPSJ Interact. (2015). (in Japanese)
7. Adachi, Y., Shimada, N.: Intelligent wheelchair using visual information from the human face. IEEE Intell. Robot. Syst. **1**, 354–359 (1999)
8. Terashima, S., Aida, N.: Development of operation device for electric wheelchair by ocular movement mechanical & control engineering. In: Proceedings of the ... JSME Conference on Frontiers in Bioengineering, pp. 1348–2939 (2006)
9. Ino, T., Matsumoto, Y.: Development of intelligent wheelchair system with face and gaze based interface. In: Robot and Human Interactive Communication, pp. 262–267 (2001)
10. Katevas, N.I., Sgouros, N.M.: The autonomous mobile robot scenario: a sensor aided intelligent navigation system for powered wheelchairs. IEEE Robot. **4**, 60–70 (2002)
11. Simpson, R.C., Levine, S.P., Bell, D.A., Jaros, L.A., Koren, Y., Borenstein, J.: NavChair: an assistive wheelchair navigation system with automatic adaptation. In: Mittal, V.O., Yanco, H.A., Aronis, J., Simpson, R. (eds.) Assistive Technology and Artificial Intelligence. LNCS, vol. 1458, pp. 235–255. Springer, Heidelberg (1998). doi:10.1007/BFb0055982

Geomorphology Classroom Practices
Using Augmented Reality

André Luiz Satoshi Kawamoto[1]([✉]) and Maristela Denise Moresco Mezzomo[2]

[1] Computing Department, Federal University of Technology – Paraná,
Campo Mourão, PR, Brazil
kawamoto@utfpr.edu.br
[2] Environmental Department, Federal University of Technology – Paraná,
Campo Mourão, PR, Brazil
mezzomo@utfpr.edu.br

Abstract. This article presents a set of classroom practices created for the discipline of Geomorphology that use an Augmented Reality installation known as SARndbox. This set was developed respecting the characteristics and according to a set of usability guidelines for applications that make use of Natural User Interfaces (NUI). The characteristics of Natural Interfaces, as well as the usability guidelines used in the development of these practices are presented.

Keywords: Augmented reality · Classroom practices · Natural user interfaces · Usability guidelines

1 Introduction

Augmented Reality (AR) applications aim to enhance the perception and effectiveness of the user by providing additional visual information. The user stays aware about the real world, but, ideally, is not able to distinguish between information coming from the real or the virtual world [1].

The use of RA systems has been investigated since the early 1990s, and includes medicine, production processes, aeronautics, robotics, entertainment, tourism, marketing, social networking and education [2].

The Augmented Reality has also benefited from several technological advances that have occurred in recent years, which have given rise to more natural and low-cost interfaces and human-computer interaction devices. Among these devices, depth sensors attract attention by implementing advanced interfaces in various Augmented Reality applications, from advertising to serious games for physical rehabilitation [3–8].

The present work presents a set of classroom practices for Geomorphology based on an Augmented Reality installation, known as SARndbox [9]. This set was developed based on guidelines developed for systems that use Natural Interfaces, as well as the pedagogical needs intrinsic to the teaching practices of the topics covered.

This paper is organized as follows: Sect. 2 presents some applications that use Augmented Reality in Education; In Sect. 3 the concept and characteristics of Natural User Interfaces; Sect. 4 presents the SARndbox, an installation used to support

© Springer International Publishing AG 2017
M. Antona and C. Stephanidis (Eds.): UAHCI 2017, Part II, LNCS 10278, pp. 155–166, 2017.
DOI: 10.1007/978-3-319-58703-5_12

classroom practice; Sect. 5 describes the guidelines that have guided the development of practices and a brief description of practices created and finally, in Sect. 6, the final considerations and future work.

2   Applications of Augmented Reality in Education

Specifically, in Education, there are applications that aim to promote teaching from elementary to higher education, in several areas of knowledge. An extensive listing of examples of the application of RA in teaching, varying from Biology, Physics, Mathematics, to Religious Education is presented in [2, 10]. Some RA systems applied to Teaching are presented in the following sections.

2.1   3D Pop-up Book

The 3D Pop-up Book is an Augmented Reality book used for teaching English with students in Thailand, which uses markers to combine characters and objects in a book (Fig. 1) [11].

Fig. 1. 3D Pop-up Book [11]

The results presented in [11] corroborate with other usability assessments, which always demonstrate the great interest of users in this technology, highlighting its playful and innovative aspects, as well as its possibilities in other studies.

2.2   Augmented Chemistry Reactions

To facilitate the understanding of Chemistry, especially the spatial structure of molecules and their behavior in some reactions, Maier Klinker proposed a visualization tool to display and control molecules as well as the dynamics between them [12].

This tool uses a cube with a handle that contains imprinted patterns (markers) on its faces (Fig. 2). Students should manipulate the cube to visualize the molecules and thus rotate and be aware of their atomic structure (Fig. 3).

Fig. 2. Marker cube for molecular manipulation and visualization [12]

This system, implemented with ARToolkit [13], is representative of the first implementations of RA, which makes use of markers to introduce virtual objects into the scene.

2.3   Augmented Reality Magic Mirror

In teaching Anatomy, Meng et al. propose a system that uses an "AR mirror" [14]. In this system, the depth camera is used to track the posture of the user standing in front of a screen. A computed tomography (CT) scan of the user is generated, creating the illusion that it is possible to observe the inside of your body, as shown in Fig. 4.

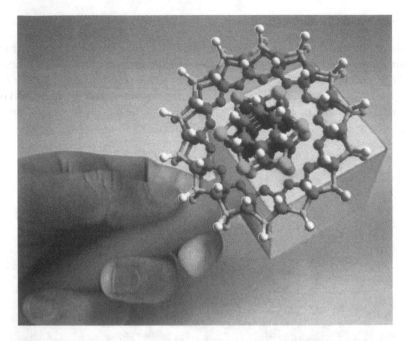

Fig. 3. Visualização de Moléculas usando augmented chemistry reactions [12]

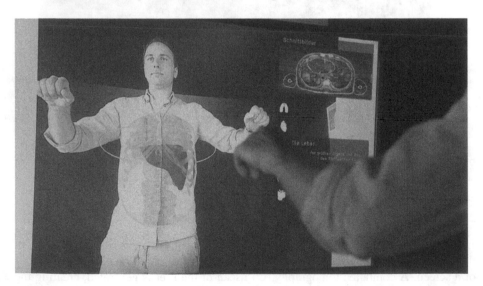

Fig. 4. Augmented reality magic mirror [14]

Gestures are used to select different layers of the tomography and a set of photographic data can be chosen for viewing. This system is also capable of displaying 3D models of internal organs, textual information, and anatomy images. The interaction with this system dispenses markers and uses depth data, increasing, or decreasing the visibility of the hands based on their distance from a virtual interaction plan. According to the authors, this helps the user to perceive the spatial relationships between his body and the virtual interaction plane.

Most of the examples found in the literature have been used by educators to provide preconceived teaching experiences. This can lead to situations where AR only develops lower order reasoning skills, rather than encouraging integrative skills such as analysis, evaluation, and creation.

Thus, using AR applications to stimulate critical thinking should be a main goal, allowing students to interact and act actively in these systems, instead of being mere spectators.

3 Natural User Interfaces

In recent years, the technological evolution allowed the creation of a range of devices that allowed the emergence of a new mode of interface. This new paradigm is known as Natural User Interfaces (NUI). These can be defined as "interfaces designed to reuse existing skills for direct interaction with content" [15].

Historically, NUIs can be inserted into an evolving line of Human-Computer interfaces, in which three paradigms can be highlighted (Fig. 5): **Command Line Interfaces** (CLI), **Graphical User Interfaces** (GUI), and, more recently, **Natural User Interfaces**.

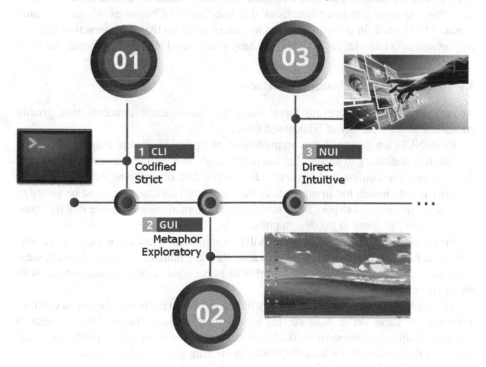

Fig. 5. Evolution of interface paradigms

In command-line interfaces, successive lines of text (command lines) are sent by the user to the system. This interface is found on older operating systems, such as MS-DOS, early versions of Unix, and more. Generally, its implementation consists of a prompt that is able to accept the text commands and convert them into calls to system functions. This is the type often preferred by advanced users interface, it provides a concise and powerful way to control a system.

Graphical interfaces are currently the most common, especially those based on the WIMP (Windows, Icons, Menus, Pointer) paradigm. In this paradigm, the mouse, or some similar device, is used to manipulate elements on the screen (windows, buttons and menus) and thus perform tasks. From a usability perspective, graphical interfaces introduce benefits such as the ease of remembering actions and constructing models that remain coherent for several similar tasks. Visual feedback is immediate when indicating the effects of a given action. For example, when you delete a file, its icon is removed from the screen. The great advantage of this type of interface is that they make the operation of the computer more intuitive and easy to learn.

Finally, the Natural User Interfaces can be found in various systems and applications of our everyday life: touch screens on computers and smartphones; applications using voice commands; gesture commands to control televisions and games; BCI (Brain-Computer Interface) systems, where brain commands trigger the execution of tasks.

NUIs refer to interfaces between humans and computers that use unconventional devices and are based on natural elements. The word "natural" in this case is used in opposition to most computer interfaces that use "artificial" devices whose operation needs to be learned. In this type of interface, one can affirm that the interaction is based on previous user knowledge and, thus, it is easy to learn and to become experienced [15].

3.1   Characteristics of Natural Interfaces

According to Blake, there are three important fundamental concepts that greatly contribute to the usability of NUI-based systems [15].

First, NUIs are designed, are premeditated and prior efforts are employed in their design. It is necessary to ensure that the interactions in a NUI are appropriate for both the user and the content and context. The simple fact of grouping several concepts together is not enough for an interface to be considered natural. One must be aware of the role designers need to play in creating natural interactions and ensure that the same design priority is given to the design phase.

Furthermore, NUIS reuse existing skills. Application users are experts in various skills that have been acquired simply because they are human. For several years, these users have practiced communication, verbal or non-verbal, as well as interactions with the environment.

The computing power and technology have evolved to the point where you can take advantage of these skills. Nuis do this by allowing users to interact with computers through intuitive actions such as touch, gesture and speech, and have interfaces which users can first understand with metaphors drawn from real-world experiences.

Finally, NUIs have direct interaction with content, that is, the focus of interaction is on the content itself and on direct interaction with it. That does not mean controls such as buttons and check boxes are totally absent in the interface. It simply means that such controls should be considered secondary when compared to content, and that direct manipulation should be the primary interaction method

4   Augmented Reality SandBox - SARNdBox

The Augmented Reality Sandbox (SARndbox) is an installation that aims to integrate an Augmented Reality system with graphical effects and simulations to physically created topographic models that have their surface scanned by a computer in real time [9].

A SARndbox aims to integrate an augmented reality system into physically created topographic models that have their surface scanned by a computer in real time. These models are used as background for a variety of graphic effects and simulations.

The installation consists of a computer, a projector, a 3D surface reading device (in this case, the Microsoft Kinect) and a box containing material that can be manipulated, such as sand, to create topographies interactively and with low need for supervision by a specialist (Fig. 6). All software required to configure SARndbox is available for free under the GNU General Public License. For its implementation is recommended a computer with Intel Core i7 processor, clocked at at least 3 GHz, a video card with graphics processor (recommended NVidia GeForce GTX 970), and Linux Mint 64-bit operating system.

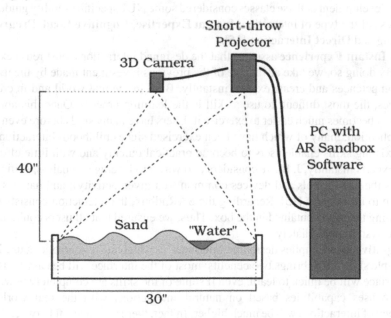

Fig. 6.   SARndbox installation [9]

Initially, the potential use of SARndbox in the educational environment was investigated through questions inserted into a usability assessment applied to 100 participants, including students and teachers of elementary, middle, and high school.

The evaluation consisted of two sets of questions: one to obtain the user profile (age and school education) and other to evaluate efficiency issues, prior knowledge of the topic addressed in the application (contour lines), prior knowledge of AR, ergonomics (comfort feeling when using the application, ease of use, satisfaction when using) and whether they consider that the use of the tool would facilitate learning.

The answers obtained in the usability assessment indicate that there is a great public interest in using innovative teaching technologies. The adoption of these technologies can introduce many benefits. The entire evaluation is presented in [16].

5   Geomorphology Classroom Practices

Despite AR technology is widespread in the Computer Science academic environment and used in entertainment and advertising, there is still a niche to be explored in Education. Although about half of the answers affirm already knowing this technology, it can be observed, from the answers provided, that AR applications, with great visual impact, still arise a lot of fascination and interest in people.

To enhance the teaching of Geomorphology concepts, we propose some classroom practices using the SARndbox, with the indication of auxiliary tools.

The development of these classes considered some NUI-specific usability guidelines, regardless of the type of interaction: **Instant Expertise, Cognitive Load, Progressive Learning** and **Direct Interaction** [15].

The **Instant Experience** assumes that the designed interactions must reuse existing skills. By doing so, we take advantage of the previous investment made by the users in their competences and create experts instantly. Both in the real world and in creating interfaces, the most difficult to use a skill is the learning process. Once this ability is learned, it becomes much easier to exercise it. Users have many skills before even using any application, many of which have been exercised since childhood. Interactions that reuse existing skills enable users to become practical quickly and with little effort. To create experts instantly, J. Blake considers two ways: to leverage domain-specific skills (such as the use of tools and devices common to a given activity); and harness skills common to all humans [15]. Regarding the SARndbox, the interaction consists solely of handling the sand contained in the box. Thus, we ensured that all users could interact with the system immediately.

Cognitive Load implies designing interfaces in which most interactions use innate and simple skills. This brings two benefits: most of the interface will be easy to use and the interface will be quick to learn, even if some of the skills are completely new. If the interface uses capabilities based on natural interactions with the real world, the frequency of interactions will be much higher. In fact, there is a trade-off between Instant Experience and Cognitive Load. These guidelines may conflict when users are already endowed with a useful skill, such as using the mouse. The focus, in these cases, should keep on minimizing a cognitive load for a majority of interactions, reusing it as existing simple skills. There was no concern about this guideline for the development of class-room practices, since the interaction was quite simple and straightforward.

Progressive Learning provides a smooth learning curve from basic tasks to advanced tasks. Natural Interfaces should allow your users to learn and evolve progres-sively, from beginners to expert level. At the same time, the interfaces cannot make it difficult for experienced users to perform advanced tasks in the best way. This guideline implies allowing the application to be used at the same time as more complex tasks are learned. In the case of class practices created, there was a concern to establish a growing and constant learning curve of the concepts addressed, from basic concepts to the subjects that need more critical thinking and analysis.

The **Direct Interaction**, in its turn, states that interactions should relate directly to the content; occur at high frequency and be appropriate to the context. Since our inter-actions with the real world show this effect, the adoption of direct interactions results in more fluid and natural interfaces, and allow access to many features without over-whelming the user presenting them all at once. In the case of SARndbox, the means of interaction is not only direct, but also tangible, allowing free manipulation (within the limits of the box), and giving this system a highly playful appeal to users.

Moreover, in [17] is highlighted the need to provide constant feedback to the user, so that it is aware of what is happening and what to expect as a result of their interactions. In the case of SARndbox, the results of interactions (sand movement) occur immediately with each action taken by the user (Fig. 7).

Fig. 7. User interacting with the SARndbox

The broad sense of these practices involves activities related to both basic and higher education, as well as consulting projects, public and/or private companies, among other projects that have the landform as the focus of analysis. The classroom practices proposed include:

- **types of terrain**, which consists of building different landforms, working concepts related to each shape, its genesis and evolution. The landforms to be built can be hills, plateaus, flatlands, among others;
- **hydrographic basins**, that is, to build in the sand a basin with its characteristics: main river, watershed, tributary and sub-tributaries rivers;
- **slope**, that is, building landforms for calculus of declivity and, later, classification of the landform as flat, slightly hilly, hilly, strongly hilly, hilly terrain and steep terrain;
- **relief and the Brazilian Forest Code**, that is, to reproduce relief forms with declivities within the limits of use established by the New Brazilian Forest Code (Brazil's Law number 12.651/2012) [18];
- **rivers and the Brazilian Forest Code,** which consists of constructing different types of riverbeds and applying the provisions of both the former Brazilian Forest Code and the new Brazilian Forest Code [18], showing the differences between them in terms of delimiting the Permanent Preservation Areas along the riverbanks.

The Fig. 8 illustrates some contours created for each of the classroom practices.

Relief   Hydrographic basin   Slope

Relief and the   Rivers and the
Brazilian Forest Code   Brazilian Forest Code

Fig. 8. Sample contours for each classroom practice

The application of this set of practices should be associated with a set of pedagogical guidelines, which aims to evaluate the efficiency of this approach.

Basically, the instructional aspect of SARndbox should be well understood before using it, and after the activity, the topic addressed should be discussed.

The instructor should be able to assess whether the use of the tool was more efficient than the use of conventional teaching techniques, such as lectures, animations, videos, and illustrations.

6 Conclusions and Future Work

In this paper, we present a set of classroom practices based on an Augmented Reality tool that uses as a interaction device a depth sensor created to provide Natural User Interfaces, called the SARndbox. This set of practices was created considering both characteristics required for Natural User Interfaces and specific usability guidelines for this interaction paradigm.

The great visual appeal of this tool, associated with its inherent playful aspect, mainly due to the interaction mechanism, were the main factors that motivated the investigation of the viability of its use in the classroom environment.

The practices created take into account issues addressed in both higher education in the areas of Environmental Engineering, Civil Engineering, Geography, as well as in High School courses, and can be used, with different degrees of depth, at all levels of education.

Future Works include measuring the impact of technology adoption on teaching. To do so, it is necessary to investigate ways to obtain an accurate, results-based, replicable and applicable evaluation not only for the area of Geomorphology, but also to contribute to the evaluation of other Augmented Reality devices applied to the teaching of several other areas of knowledge.

References

1. Milgram, P., Kishino, F.: A taxonomy of mixed reality visual displays. IEICE Trans. Inf. Syst. **77**(12), 1321–1329 (1994)
2. Bower, M., et al.: Augmented Reality in education–cases, places and potentials. Educ. Media Int. **51**(1), 1–15 (2014)
3. Biswas, K.K., Basu, S.K.: Gesture recognition using Microsoft Kinect. In: 2011 5th International Conference on Automation, Robotics and Applications (ICARA), pp. 100–103. doi:10.1109/ICARA.2011.6144864
4. Da Gama, A.E.F., Chaves, T., Figueiredo, L., Teichrieb, V.: Poster: improving motor rehabilitation process through a natural interaction based system using kinect sensor. In: 2012 IEEE Symposium on 3D User Interfaces (3DUI), pp. 145–146. doi:10.1109/3DUI.2012.6184203
5. Gerling, K., Livingston, I., Nacke, L., Mandryk, R.: Fullbody motion-based game interaction for older adults. In: Proceedings of the 30th International Conference on Human Factors in Computing Systems, CHI 2012, Austin, Texas, USA, pp. 1873–1882
6. Martin, C.C., Burkert, D.C., Choi, K.R., Wieczorek, N.B., McGregor, P.M., Herrmann, R.A., Beling, P.A.: A real-time ergonomic monitoring system using the Microsoft Kinect. In: 2012 IEEE Systems and Information Design Symposium (SIEDS), pp. 50–55. doi:10.1109/SIEDS.2012.6215130

7. Parajuli, M., Tran, D., Ma, W., Sharma, D.: Senior health monitoring using kinect. In: 2012 Fourth International Conference on Communications and Electronics (ICCE), pp. 309–12. doi:10.1109/CCE.2012.6315918
8. Yeh, S.-C., Hwang, W.-Y., Huang, T.-C., Liu, W.-K., Chen, Y.-T., Hung, Y.-P.: A study for the application of body sensing in assisted rehabilitation training. In: 2012 International Symposium on Computer, Consumer and Control (IS3C), pp. 922–925. doi:10.1109/IS3C. 2012.240
9. Reed, S.E., et al.: Shaping watersheds exhibit: an interactive, augmented reality sandbox for advancing earth science education. AGU Fall Meeting Abstracts, vol. 1 (2014)
10. Zagoranski, S., Divjak, S.: Use of augmented reality in education, vol. 2. IEEE (2003)
11. Vate-U-Lan, P.: An augmented reality 3D Pop-up Book: the development of a multimedia project for English language teaching. In: 2012 IEEE International Conference on Multimedia and Expo, Melbourne, VIC, pp. 890–895. doi:10.1109/ICME.2012.79
12. Maier, P., Klinker, G.: Augmented chemical reactions: 3D interaction methods for chemistry. Int. J. Online Eng. 9, 80–82 (2013)
13. Kato, H., Billinghurst, M.: Marker tracking and HMD calibration for a video-based augmented reality conferencing system. In: Proceedings of the 2nd IEEE and ACM International Workshop on augmented reality (IWAR 1999), San Francisco, CA, pp. 85–94 (1999). doi: 10.1109/IWAR.1999.803809
14. Meng, M., et al.: Kinect for interactive AR anatomy learning. In: 2013 IEEE International Symposium on Mixed and Augmented Reality (ISMAR), Adelaide, SA, pp. 277–278 (2013). doi:10.1109/ISMAR.2013.6671803
15. Blake, J.: Natural User Interfaces in. Net Manning Pubs Co Series. Manning Publications Company, Greenwich. ISBN 9781935182818. http://books.google.com.br/books? id=mmMCkgEACAAJ
16. Mezzomo, M.D., Kawamoto, A.: Dispositivo de Baixo Custo para Interfaces Naturais como Ferramenta de Apoio Didático no Ensino de Geomorfologia. In: XI Simpósio Nacional de Geomorfologia (SINAGEO), Maringá (2016). http://www.sinageo.org.br/2016/trabalhos/ 5/5-198-1664.html
17. Microsoft Corporation: Kinect for windows human interface guidelines v1.8.0 (2013). https:// msdn.microsoft.com/en-us/library/jj663791.aspx
18. Brasil: Código Florestal Brasileiro. Lei n° 12.651, de 25 de maio de 2012. Presidência da República do Brasil (2012)

Head-Mounted Augmented Reality Displays on the Cheap: A DIY Approach to Sketching and Prototyping Low-Vision Assistive Technologies

Frode Eika Sandnes[1,2(✉)] and Evelyn Eika[1]

[1] Oslo and Akershus University College of Applied Sciences, Oslo, Norway
{frodes,Evelyn.Eika}@hioa.no
[2] Westerdals Oslo School of Art, Communication and Technology, Oslo, Norway

Abstract. Several wearable augmented reality devices have emerged in recent years. Although these devices target users with 20/20 vision, they have also been explored as low vision aids. However, such devices are still relatively inaccessible and expensive. This study explores one of the inexpensive commercial head-mounted see-through display, google cardboard, and a simple homemade wearable augmented reality display. The experimentation reveals that, although not perfect, the homemade device built using a smartphone and common household scrap items is the most promising platform for experimenting with visual aids.

Keywords: Low vision · Augmented reality · Prototyping · Pepper ghost · Equirectangular panoramas · Wearable computing

1 Introduction

Several wearable augmented reality (AR) displays have emerged in recent years such as Google glass and Microsoft HoloLens. These devices allow users to see the real world with additional visual information superimposed on top. Although such technologies are intended for the general user, they also pose exciting opportunities for individuals with low vision. Visually impaired individuals may not be able to identify essential details in a scene and a digital visual aid based on augmented reality may help provide essential information such as navigation, people identification, reading signs, etc. The cool-factor of general devices is more likely to reduce the stigma associated with specialized assistive technologies. For instance, Google glass has been used to compensate for colour blindness [1] and edge enhancement for low vision wearers [2].

Still, several of these technologies are costly and not widely available. It may take several years before such devices are commonplace. The limited availability means that large user groups around the world are unable to experiment, develop ideas, and design new applications to suit their needs. This study focused on low cost devices. Experimentation was conducted with one of the less expensive see-through displays on the market, namely EPSON BT200, the inexpensive Google Cardboard [3] and cheap homemade head-mounted augmented reality display built from a smartphone and widely available scrap materials that can be found around the home.

© Springer International Publishing AG 2017
M. Antona and C. Stephanidis (Eds.): UAHCI 2017, Part II, LNCS 10278, pp. 167–186, 2017.
DOI: 10.1007/978-3-319-58703-5_13

2   Background

Visual impairment takes many forms. Examples include no visual perception, various levels of visual acuity [4], tunnel vision, colour blindness [5–7], nystagmus, etc. Research into digital visual aids goes back several decades to the early work by Peli et al. [8, 9]. Peli et al.'s early work mostly focused on various filters to enhance face recognition among visually impaired individuals. Over the decades various aspects of reduced vision have been addressed. Everingham et al. [10] experimented with a head-mounted device that helped with the classification of scenes. Harper et al. [11] developed a digital visual aid that performed magnification of the scene. Colour blindness is a topic that has drawn the attention of several researchers. Approaches for enhancing colour images such that they are more easily perceivable by individuals with reduced colour perception have been proposed and also implemented in a wearable device [1]. Various approaches addressing tunnel vision have focused on condensing wide fields of view and displaying these in the narrow field of view where the user can perceive visual stimuli [12].

Edge enhancement is also a recurring topic in the research literature [2, 13, 14] where several attempts at enchanting the views using wearable displays have been explored. In particular, edge detection can be used to highlight important features such as the edges of the steps of stairs to prevent a visually impaired person falling, or it can be used to highlight pedestrian crossing zones for safer navigation in busy traffic with moving vehicles. Others have proposed to provide depth cues [15] where objects closer to the viewer are given a brighter colour than objects further away. A more direct approach is obstacle detection and identification, for instance, using stereoscopic vision [16] and laser range scanners [17].

Although quite a few exciting solutions to various aspects of low-vision have been proposed, there are comparatively fewer studies on what visually impaired individuals want and what they actually need. One exception is the qualitative study by Cimarolly et al. [18] that emphasized visually impaired individuals' need for social interaction and getting around. Similar findings were identified in [19], which more specifically identified the needs as being able to recognize faces and texts in various physical contexts. Text is especially important when travelling and utilizing public transport, finding locations such as shops and offices, and identifying specific products within shops. The detection of text and digits is well researched [20, 21]. Several studies have specifically focused on wearable devices capable of recognizing text in the wild intended for visually impaired users [22, 23]. The recognition of people is important in order for visually impaired people to be able to participate and to function in social settings and be involved in society in general. Faces are the most widely used cue for recognizing individuals. However, faces can be hard to identify from a distance for individuals with low visual acuity, and impossible for individuals without vision. Surprisingly, there are very few studies on face recognition applied to low-vision aids despite the fact that the research field of face recognition is vast and the algorithms are well-developed [24].

Another issue is the desire to be "normal" and not to stand out [19, 25]. It has been found that older individuals with reduced function tend to abandon their assistive aids [25]. Generally, people have a desire to look cool and blend in [25] while assistive technologies can be stigmatizing. The long-term goal of this research endeavour is to achieve invisible assistive technology that does not draw attention. The alternative view to assistive technology is universal design where there is one, non-stigmatizing, solution to be used by all, for instance, readable language [26–28], dyslexia [29–33], motor disabilities [34–37], low-vision [38, 39], etc.

3   Wearable AR-Display Evaluations

Three augmented reality displays were evaluated to assess their suitability for prototyping and evaluating AR-based assistive technologies for users with low vision, namely, the commercial EPSON BT200 see-through display, Google Cardboard, and a homemade DIY (do it yourself) AR device.

3.1   Commercial See-Through Display

First, the suitability of a set of commercial display glasses was evaluated, i.e., the EPSON BT300 see-through mobile viewer. This display kit is relatively inexpensive (approximately 800 Euro) and therefore used by researchers [40–42]. The glasses have a display area in the middle of each lens that reflects the displays to the viewer with the light source embedded in the frames. A standalone handheld android unit with buttons and a touch pad controls the device. The device is intended for individuals with uncorrected vision or with low corrections as the device can be worn with eyeglasses. A tinted sunscreen in front of the glasses filters bright external light. The device is intended for entertainment purposes.

Figure 1 shows visual results of simple tests performed with the kit. The immediate impression is that the display area is too small to be perceivable for anyone with low visual acuity (see Fig. 1a and b). The documentation states that the display has a viewing angle of 23°. Some low vision users may be able to perceive icons and simple symbols if the entire display is used for displaying such symbols.

Figure 1c shows how the semi-transparent display areas cause large shadows in the center of the visual fields. These shadows are especially noticeable when the device is switched-off. It is likely that this shadow can be visually disturbing to users when focusing on the real-world scene. However, Fig. 1d shows that the display is visible even when viewed in very bright lighting conditions such as looking towards the sky. Overall, the small display with its shadow obstructing the important part of the view makes this device not suitable as a platform for developing and experimenting with low-vision aids.

3.2   Google Cardboard

Google cardboard [43, 44] has received much attention as it can provide relatively powerful virtual reality experiences at moderate costs. While other virtual reality headsets are based on specialized hardware, google cardboard simply relies on using ordinary smartphones for computation, networking, sensing, sounding, and displaying [43]. The cardboard framework thus consists of a simple headset and software. The name

a) Display area in the field of view.   b) Display area enlarged.

c) Display off – shadow in view.   d) Visibility in bright conditions.

Fig. 1. ESPON BT200 See through mobile viewer.

cardboard stems from the simple proof-of-concept headset built from cardboard and a set of lenses allowing focusing on the close display. Moreover, cardboard comes with an open API and new cardboard applications are added regularly.

Cardboard can also be used for AR applications. To test this, a simple 20 Euro plastic cardboard headset was used (see Fig. 2). It has adjustable lenses, straps to hold it to the head, and an opening allowing the camera to be used to capture the scene. Figure 2 bottom right shows how the camera view on the display appears with the headset.

A simple experiment was conducted with the mobile phone in camera monitor mode. The test was performed walking around with the headset only and relying on the live video captured by the camera. The results were less than optimal. The camera update is quite slow to be practical as there is a noticeable lag of a fraction of a second. Moreover, the dynamic range is low and camera response slow as the camera takes a long time to adjust when walking from a dark area to a light area and vice versa, turning the head rapidly, etc. In conclusion, the limitations with current smartphone cameras do not make Cardboard suitable for real-time real-world AR-aids for the visually impaired.

3.3   Homemade AR-Device

The proposed approach applies a similar technique to that of many existing augmented reality systems [45] where visual elements are superimposed on the worldview via a heads-up display [46, 47]. Heads-up displays often exploit the pepper ghost effect [48] traditionally used to create the illusion of ghosts via transparent glass reflections.

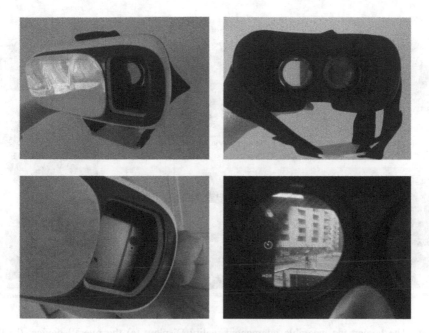

Fig. 2. Variation on Google cardboard for AR using the mobile camera.

A simple system can be built using a smartphone as smartphones are commonplace, affordable, and easy to program. The display of the smartphone is placed perpendicular to the viewing direction of the user (see Fig. 3). A flat transparent plastic plate is positioned at an angle of 45° relative to the smartphone display and viewer such that the image displayed on the smartphone display is reflected into the eyes of the user. The user sees a combination of the real-world view behind the transparent glass and the smartphone displays image reflected via the glass.

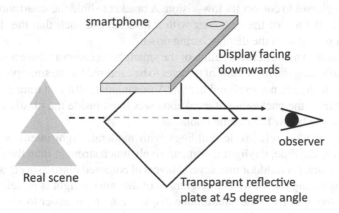

Fig. 3. The augmented reality device utilizing the Pepper ghost effect. The real scene is viewed through the plastic film and virtual scene shown on the smartphone display is reflected into the same view via the transparent and reflective film positioned at a 45° angle.

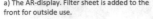

e) Slot for Smartphone.

a) The AR-display. Filter sheet is added to the front for outside use.

b) The AR-display in use. Content only visible to wearer.

f) Inside opening for Smartphone display.

c) Example application: navigation.

d) Example application: people recognition.

g) Opening for camera mirror fixture.

Fig. 4. The homemade wearable augmented reality Display. (a) the overall device, (b) the augmented information is not visible to onlookers, (c) and (d) augmented information as seen by the user, (d) and (e) the augmented image from the smartphone and (f) camera-mirror fixture. (Color figure online)

Various approaches were explored using various household items. One solution involved a plastic detergent container with the open end to view the world and the back end cut out for the eyes (see Fig. 4). This plastic container had sufficient stiffness to carry the mobile phone. An Apple iPhone 6 was used in this prototype. Enough space was made such that the device could be worn with eyeglasses as individuals with low vision may wear eyeglasses to correct for low-vision. A bracket to hold the smartphone in place was created at the top of the container with a hole cut out such that the display was visible when placed with the display facing down.

A hole was also made at the location of the smartphone camera where a small mirror can be fixed allowing the front view of the user to be captured by the smartphone camera. Note that this feature is not explored herein. A rectangular, stiff and transparent plastic sheet cut out from the packaging of a cakebox was fixed inside the plastic container at a 45-degree angle below the mobile phone.

This setup works well inside buildings with moderate light-intensity. However, outdoors during daytime, daylight is comparatively much stronger than the smartphone display. Therefore, for outdoor use, several layers of coloured plastic sheets were placed at the opening facing the view. The brightness of the outside light is therefore reduced compared to the light from the smartphone display, making it easier to view the information. Many individuals with low vision use sunglasses outside and often sunglasses which blocks disturbing light coming in from the sides. The configuration is thus consistent with the viewing environment preferred by many low-vision individuals.

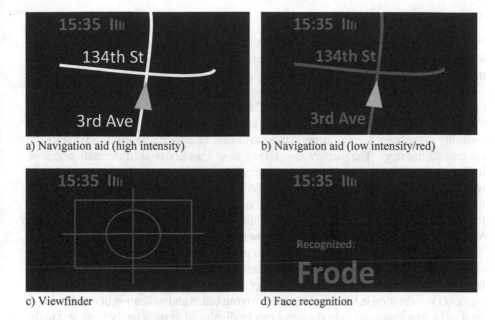

a) Navigation aid (high intensity)   b) Navigation aid (low intensity/red)

c) Viewfinder   d) Face recognition

Fig. 5. Augmented information as displayed on the smartphone. Only the non-black visual elements are reflected and perceivable by the user when superimposed on the view. (Color figure online)

The amount of information displayed should be minimized so as not to disturb the real-world view. Black is used as the background on the display as it is not reflected into the viewers' eyes. Information is highlighted in bright colours to make the information clearly visible. Figure 5 shows the augmented views used in the examples in Fig. 4. The remainder of this paper will focus on applications of this homemade AR-device.

In conclusion, the homemade AR device is able to augment information across most of the field of view, and there is no lag in the background information. It thus appears more suitable than the two other technologies for visually impaired users.

4   Example Applications and Techniques

Several issues have been explored with wearable visual aids, such as text recognition [19] and edge enhancement [15]. Edge enhancement requires calibration to ensure that the image overlaps with the view. Other applications do not require calibration. Transportation, recognizing text, and recognizing faces are key challenges for low-vision individuals [9].

4.1 Navigation Aid

Projecting key map information may help a low-vision individual navigate a city without losing track of traffic. Figure 4c shows a sketch of how the device could be used to track the progress of reaching a target on the map, while seeing the scene.

Figure 5a shows the information displayed on the smartphone. As mentioned, the black background is not reflected and visible to the user. The important information, that is, the roads and name of the roads, is displayed in white that gives maximum visibility to the user. A green arrow is used to indicate the user's position and orientation relative to the map. The display also shows how less important information can be included, such as the current time and battery level of the device. In this example, red was used as well as a smaller text size in order not to draw attention away from the main information displayed. Figure 4b shows the same view with the key information in red. Practical tests suggest that red may be difficult to see under varying lighting conditions. Note that the user will not be able to perceive the information if the scene is very bright.

The user does not have to look down to inspect the content of a navigation device or smartphone and thereby creating dangerous situations by shifting the visual attention from the traffic. The augmented reality display may also be used to show local public transport information in real-time, such as arriving buses and indication of nearby shops. Text or faces recognized from the scene can be displayed in sufficiently large text to the viewer.

4.2 Face Recognition

Figure 4d shows a sketch of how the device could be used to recognize people. The device is pointed towards the person the user is looking at through the viewfinder. The camera captures the image of the person, face recognition software identifies the person, and the name is displayed as a textual cue. Alternatively, a familiar photograph of the person can be displayed. Other modalities can also be used such as audio.

Figure 5d illustrates the view as it is displayed by the smartphone using red-coloured large text on a black background. Note that the text is positioned towards the bottom right of the display in order not to completely overshadow the face. Moreover, it is likely that the scene maybe less dark towards the bottom than in the middle, especially if the person stands by a window or with the sky as background.

5   Augmenting 3D Sketches

Sketching is a useful tool for exploring and communicating ideas [49]. Also, hand-drawn sketches signal unfinished work [50]. Sketches are usually associated with 2D drawings or flat drawings of 3D objects and scenes [51]. However, they have also been extended to the panoramic domain [52–54] where the observer gets a three-dimensional experience of being immersed inside the sketch. For instance, panoramic views are used in Google street view [55] and for creating richer museum experiences [56], often with additional technology such as RFID [57]. A method for sketching augmented reality visual aids is demonstrated next.

5.1 Sketching Panoramas

The approach involves superimposing a 3D sketch on top of the view that changes according to the movement of the head. This is achieved by treating the 3D sketch as a panoramic image. The panoramic image is sketched using the PanoramaGrid grid paper proposed in [53]. This grid paper allows the designer to draw sketches directly onto the equirectangular space. The equirectangular space represents the viewing sphere around the viewer. The original panoramic sketch is then twice as wide as it is tall as the horizontal axis represents "longitude" from 0° to 360° around the viewer, and the vertical axis represents the tilt or latitude from −90° to 90° below and above the viewer [58, 59]. By tracing the lines of different colours on the grid paper, the designer "moves" in x, y, and z dimensions in 3D space.

The sketches were made in a simple sketching software package (Microsoft Paint). Figure 6 (top) illustrates how the sketch is drawn on the grid paper. The grid paper has a cube configuration with four horizontal planes organized in 90° in relation to each other (the center line has a horizontal distance of 90°). These four planes are represented by the cyan, magenta, yellow, and green grids where the green grid wraps around the edges to achieve a full 360° panorama. In addition, two horizontal planes representing the floor and the ceiling are represented by the two black grids. The simple sketch contains the handwritten word "LOOK" aligned with the magenta gridlines and three filled hand-drawn squares aligned with the yellow gridlines. Since the magenta and yellow gridlines represent two planes perpendicular to each other, the word "LOOK" and the three squares also appear perpendicular to each other when viewed as a panorama.

5.2 Post-processing Sketches

Next, the sketches were inverted such that the background became black and the sketch white in order for the sketch and not the background to be visible to the viewer. Figure 6 (middle) shows the example sketch inverted with the gridlines included for illustrative purposes, and Fig. 6 (bottom) shows a binarized [60] inverted image where the gridlines were removed with a morphological closing operator. The open source image-processing framework ImageJ [61] was used to perform these post-processing operations.

The inverted sketches were mirrored across the horizontal axis to counterbalance the mirroring that occurs when the displayed image is mirrored to the user via the reflective transparent plate. Figure 7 illustrates the effect of mirroring the panoramic sketch across the horizontal axis.

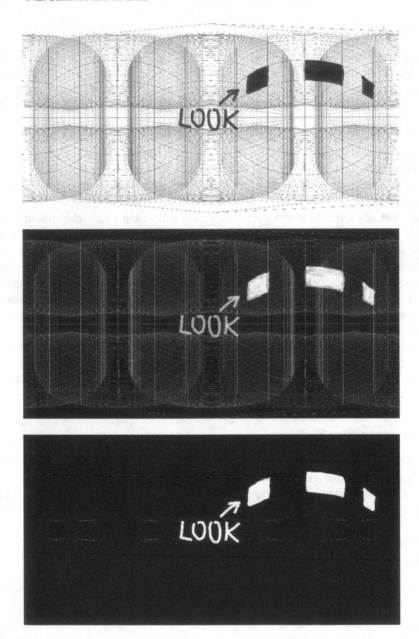

Fig. 6. Making a panoramic sketch: (a) sketching by tracing panoramic gridlines by hand, (b) panoramic sketch inverted, (c) inverted panoramic sketch binarized and subjected to a morphological closing operator for gridline removal. (Color figure online)

Fig. 7. Panoramic renderings of a panoramic sketch (left), mirrored around the horizontal axis to ensure correct viewing (right)

5.3 Rendering Panoramic Sketches

The panoramic images were rendered using the freely available FSPviewer panoramic viewer [62]. Alternatively, the sketches could be viewed in a smartphone panoramic viewer where the viewing tilt and direction is controlled by the orientation and tilt of the mobile handset. This allows the sketch to be updated in conjunction with the head movements of the user. Note that this strategy will not allow the user to move around the scene (translation). However, the purpose is to give a convincing experience, not actual functionality.

A suitable horizontal viewing range had to be set in the panoramic rendering software. The horizontal viewing angle parameter controls the size of the viewport onto the panorama specified as a horizontal angle. The front opening of the viewing box was 7.5 cm high and 16.8 cm wide, and the depth of the box was 14 cm. The viewing angle can be found simply as $2atan(W/2D)$ where W is the width of the opening and D is the depth of the viewing chamber (the distance from front opening to the back opening).

The vertical viewing range of the opening was therefore approximately 30° while the horizontal viewing range of the opening was 60°. The vertical and horizontal displayable viewing range by the reflected image of the smartphone was 34° and 58°, respectively. This is because the dimensions of the iphone 6 display are 10.4 × 5.6 cm and the distance from the smartphone to the viewer was 9.5 cm. The distance between the smartphone to the viewer is calculated as the sum of the distance from the smartphone to the mirror and the distance from the mirror to the viewer (see Fig. 8). The images were thus rendered with a viewing angle of 60°.

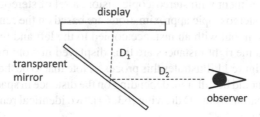

Fig. 8. Measuring the distance to the display as a sum of the distance between the display and the mirror (D_1) and the distance between the mirror and the observer (D_1).

Figure 9 illustrates how the sketch in Fig. 6 is rendered with the view pointing in different directions with different tilts. Gridlines were included for reference. Figure 10 shows renderings of several panoramic sketches without gridlines. Note that these renderings were not mirrored across the horizontal axis for presentation purposes.

Fig. 9. Panoramic renderings of the panoramic sketch in Fig. 6 for various directions and tilts using FSPviewer. Gridlines are included and rendered with a horizontal viewing range of 70° for illustrative purposes.

5.4   Stereoscopic Views

A trait of full vision is the ability to perceive depth through stereoscopic views where each eye views a scene from a slightly offset vantage point relative to each other. A common trait of reduced vision is the lack of depth vision. One reason for this is probably that the human visual system is complex and a fully working stereoscopic vision requires a fine-tuned visual system. Because of this, the focus herein is on monoscopic views as it is assumed that the target user group may have varying degrees of depth vision.

However, to experiment with stereoscopic vision, a set of stereographic renderings were created. These stereoscopic approximations are based on the renderings explained in the previous section, but with an instance copied to the left and the right side of the display. The left and the right instances are thus displayed in front of the left and right eyes, respectively. Figure 11 illustrates this process. Note that to be theoretically correct, the two renderings should be different depending on the distance in space. As it is difficult to infer depth information from 2D drawing [63, 64], two identical renderings were used as a simple substitute.

Fig. 10. Panoramic renderings of three panoramic sketches without gridlines for various directions and tilts using FSPviewer. Rendered with a horizontal viewing range of 70°.

Fig. 11. Stereoscopic panoramic renderings of panoramic sketches (not mirrored around the horizontal axis and with a horizontal viewing range of 70° for more simple presentation).

5.5 Augmenting Panoramic Sketches

Figure 12 shows example sketches viewed using the homemade AR headset. The scenes were aligned manually and photographed indoors. An underground garage was chosen as it is not too bright yet large. Note that views were rendered with an angular horizontal range of 48° since it is assumed that the camera was located approximately 10 cm from the opening of the displays.

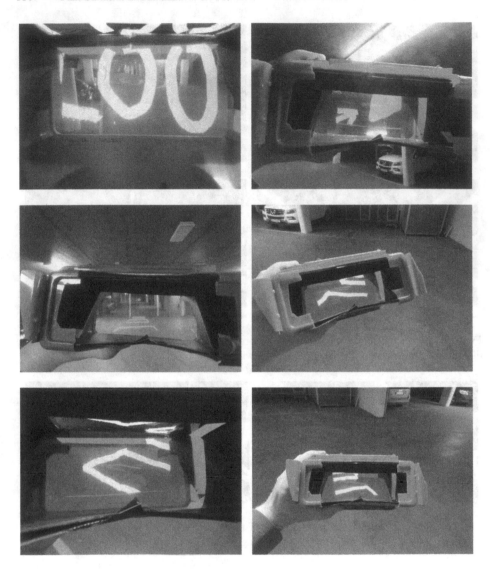

Fig. 12. Panoramic sketches superimposed on the real-world views. The four examples in the middle row and bottom row show the outline of a zebra crossing and a virtual gate.

The photographs reveal that the information is easily perceivable. Moreover, the perspective projections of the sketches align quite well with the lines in the scene. Figure 12 (top left) shows the handwritten word "LOOK" occupying the entire view-finder. The white text nearly occludes the background that can just nearly be seen through the limited transparency. The top right image shows an arrow pointing towards the square perpendicular in an angle positioned high up in the scene.

The following four images show a zebra crossing and a virtual gate. The first image (middle left) is obtained with medium mobile phone display intensity and a horizontal angular range of 70° with the camera further away, while the three other images are obtained with maximum intensity and a horizontal angular range of 48°. The first image depicts the scene looking ahead revealing both the virtual gate and the zebra crossing. The three other images depict looking down showing the zebra crossing from various orientations.

5.6 Lighting Conditions

Finally, some simple tests were conducted to assess the property of the headset under various lighting conditions (see Fig. 13). Obviously, it was no problem perceiving the reflected information indoors. However, it was not possible to perceive the information outside on a bright day except from when looking towards darker regions (see Fig. 13c). A simple test with coloured filters was thus performed.

The filters were made from a green transparent plastic sheet. Four identical sheets were cut out in the size of the headset opening allowing various levels of filtering to be explored. Figure 13a shows the four layers of film placed on the front of the headset. Figure 13b shows that the two filters had no effect when looking at the sky, while four filters did help make the information visible when looking at the sky (see Fig. 13d) or looking at the ground (see Fig. 13e). Figure 13f shows that the indoor views were perceivable even when using the filter.

Although the filter helped block out bright light making it possible to perceive the displayed information, the filter made the scene unclear. The main reason for this was the low quality filter effect with the plastic sheets used that were not intended for optical purposes. The results would be better if one had used a more suitable material, such as the material used in sunglasses lenses. However, there is still the problem of moving from bright to dark or dark to light locations as it is not practical to add or remove the filter on the fly as one walks around. One possible remedy is to use a controllable screen that could be used to block out light according to the level of background light. Moreover, the intensity of the light emitted from the display should obviously be adjusted automatically to match the given lighting conditions.

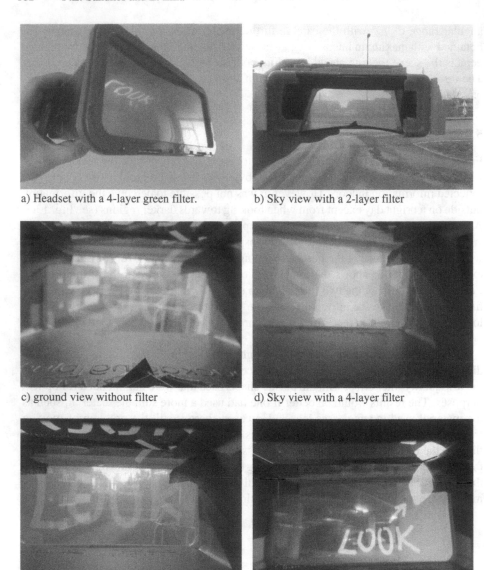

a) Headset with a 4-layer green filter.   b) Sky view with a 2-layer filter

c) ground view without filter   d) Sky view with a 4-layer filter

e) ground view with a 4-layer filter   d) inside view with a 2-layer filter

Fig. 13. Perceiving AR-display information. The balance between intensity of the display and scene lighting. (Color figure online)

6   Conclusions

Prototyping of AR applications with the visually impaired as target group was explored. The experimentation revealed that the display of the commercial see-through display was too small and obstructive, and that a smartphone camera based Cardboard system was responding too slowly to be practical. Instead, a method for prototyping simple wearable augmented reality displays was shown. Examples of how sketches can be combined with the real world were illustrated. The proposed approach allows experimentation with augmented reality visual aids. Augmented reality may not be useful for individuals with very low vision as they often find visual stimuli stressful and thus may prefer to receive information via other modalities, especially audio. Future work will focus on improving the DIY display by making it smaller and moving the weight of the mobile handset closer to the body to make it more practical in use.

References

1. Tanuwidjaja, E., Huynh, D., Koa, K., Nguyen, C., Shao, C., Torbett, P., Weibel, N.: Chroma: a wearable augmented-reality solution for color blindness. In: Proceedings of the 2014 ACM International Joint Conference on Pervasive and Ubiquitous Computing, pp. 799–810. ACM (2014)
2. Hwang, A.D., Peli, E.: An augmented-reality edge enhancement application for Google glass. Optom. Vis. Sci. **91**, 1021–1030 (2014)
3. Boffoli, N., Foley, J.T., Gasperetti, B., Yang, S.P., Lieberman, L.: Enjoyment levels of youth with visual impairments playing different exergames. Insight Res. Pract. Vis. Impairment Blindness **4**, 171–176 (2011)
4. Sandnes, F.E.: Designing GUIs for low vision by simulating reduced visual acuity: reduced resolution versus shrinking. Stud. Health Technol. Inform. **217**, 274–281 (2015)
5. Sandnes, F.E.: Understanding WCAG2.0 color contrast requirements through 3D color space visualization. Stud. Health Technol. Inform. **229**, 366–375 (2016)
6. Sandnes, F.E., Zhao, A.: A contrast colour selection scheme for WCAG2. 0-compliant web designs based on HSV-half-planes. In: Proceedings of SMC2015, pp. 1233–1237. IEEE (2015)
7. Sandnes, F.E., Zhao, A.: An interactive color picker that ensures WCAG2.0 compliant color contrast levels. Procedia-Comput. Sci. **67**, 87–94 (2015)
8. Peli, E.: Image enhancement for the visually impaired - simulations and experimental results. Invest. Ophthalmol. Vis. Sci. **32**, 2337–2350 (1991)
9. Peli, E., Lee, E., Trempe, C., Buzney, S.: Image enhancement for the visually impaired: the effects of enhancement of face recognition. J. Opt. Soc. Am. **11**, 1929–1939 (1994)
10. Everingham, M.R., Thomas, B.T., Troscianko, T.: Head-mounted mobility aid for low vision using scene classification techniques. Int. J. Virtual Reality **3**, 3 (1999)
11. Harper, R., Culham, L., Dickinson, C.: Head mounted video magnification devices for low vision rehabilitation: a comparison with existing technology. Brit. J. Ophthalmol. **83**, 495–500 (1999)
12. Luo, G., Peli, E.: Use of an augmented-vision device for visual search by patients with tunnel vision. Invest. Ophthalmol. Vis. Sci. **47**, 4152–4159 (2006)
13. Kálmán, V., et al.: Wearable technology to help with visual challenges-two case studies. Stud. Health Technol. Inform. **217**, 526–532 (2015)
14. Satgunam, P., Woods, R.L., Luo, G., Bronstad, P.M., Reynolds, Z., Ramachandra, C., Peli, E.: Effects of contour enhancement on low-vision preference and visual search. Optom. Vis. Sci. **89**, E1364 (2012)
15. Hicks, S.L., Wilson, I., Muhammed, L., Worsfold, J., Downes, S.M., Kennard, C.: A depth-based head-mounted visual display to aid navigation in partially sighted individuals. PLoS ONE **8**, e67695 (2013)

16. Costa, P., et al.: Obstacle detection using stereo imaging to assist the navigation of visually impaired people. Procedia Comput. Sci. **14**, 83–93 (2012)
17. Gomez, J.V., Sandnes, F.E.: RoboGuideDog: guiding blind users through physical environments with laser range scanners. Procedia Comput. Sci. **14**, 218–225 (2012)
18. Cimarolli, V.R., Boerner, K., Brennan-Ing, M., Reinhardt, J.P., Horowitz, A.: Challenges faced by older adults with vision loss: a qualitative study with implications for rehabilitation. Clin. Rehabil. **26**, 748–757 (2012)
19. Sandnes, F.E.: What do low-vision users really want from smart glasses? Faces, text and perhaps no glasses at all. In: Miesenberger, K., Bühler, C., Penaz, P. (eds.) ICCHP 2016. LNCS, vol. 9758, pp. 187–194. Springer, Cham (2016). doi:10.1007/978-3-319-41264-1_25
20. Huang, Y.-P., Chang, T.-W., Chen, J.-R., Sandnes, F.E.: A back propagation based real-time license plate recognition system. Int. J. Pattern Recogn. Artif. Intell. **22**, 233–251 (2008)
21. Huang, Y.-P., Chen, C.-H., Chang, Y.-T., Sandnes, F.E.: An intelligent strategy for checking the annual inspection status of motorcycles based on license plate recognition. Expert Syst. Appl. **36**, 9260–9267 (2009)
22. Merino-Gracia, C., Lenc, K., Mirmehdi, M.: A head-mounted device for recognizing text in natural scenes. In: Iwamura, M., Shafait, F. (eds.) CBDAR 2011. LNCS, vol. 7139, pp. 29–41. Springer, Heidelberg (2012). doi:10.1007/978-3-642-29364-1_3
23. Zhao, Y., Szpiro, S. Azenkot, S.: ForeSee: a customizable head-mounted vision enhancement system for people with low vision. In: Proceedings of the 17th International ACM SIGACCESS Conference on Computers and Accessibility, pp. 239–249. ACM (2015)
24. Zhao, W., et al.: Face recognition: a literature survey. ACM Comput. Surv. **35**, 399–458 (2003)
25. Dougherty, B.E., Kehler, K.B., Jamara, R., Patterson, N., Valenti, D., Vera-Diaz, F.A.: Abandonment of low vision devices in an outpatient population. Optom. Vis. Sci. **88**, 1283 (2011)
26. Eika, E.: Universally designed text on the web: towards readability criteria based on anti-patterns. Stud. Health Technol. Inform. **229**, 461–470 (2016)
27. Eika, E., Sandnes, F.E.: Authoring WCAG2.0-compliant texts for the web through text readability visualization. In: Antona, M., Stephanidis, C. (eds.) UAHCI 2016. LNCS, vol. 9737, pp. 49–58. Springer, Cham (2016). doi:10.1007/978-3-319-40250-5_5
28. Eika, E., Sandnes, F.E.: Assessing the reading level of web texts for WCAG2.0 compliance—can it be done automatically? In: Di Bucchianico, G., Kercher, P. (eds.) Advances in Design for Inclusion. Advances in Intelligent Systems and Computing, vol. 500, pp. 361–371. Springer, Cham (2016)
29. Berget, G., Mulvey, F., Sandnes, F.E.: Is visual content in textual search interfaces beneficial to dyslexic users? Int. J. Hum.-Comput. Stud. **92–93**, 17–29 (2016)
30. Berget, G., Sandnes, F.E.: Do autocomplete functions reduce the impact of dyslexia on information searching behaviour? A case of Google. J. Am. Soc. Inf. Sci. Technol. **67**, 2320–2328 (2016)
31. Berget, G., Sandnes, F.E.: Searching databases without query-building aids: implications for dyslexic users. Inf. Res. **20** (2015)
32. Habib, L., Berget, G., Sandnes, F.E., Kahn, P., Sanderson, N.C., Fagernes, S., Olcay, A.: Dyslexic students in higher education and virtual learning environments: an exploratory study. Comput. Assist. Learn. **28**, 574–584 (2012)
33. Berget, G., Herstad, J., Sandnes, F.E.: Search, read and write: an inquiry into web accessibility for dyslexics. Stud. Health Technol. Inform. **229**, 450–460 (2016)
34. Sandnes, F.E., Thorkildssen, H.W., Arvei, A., Buverad, J.O.: Techniques for fast and easy mobile text-entry with three-keys. In: Proceedings of the 37th Annual Hawaii International Conference on System Sciences. IEEE (2004)

35. Sandnes, F.E., Aubert, A.: Bimanual text entry using game controllers: relying on users' spatial familiarity with QWERTY. Interact. Comput. **19**, 140–150 (2007)
36. Sandnes, F.E.: Can spatial mnemonics accelerate the learning of text input chords? In: Proceedings of the Working Conference on Advanced Visual Interfaces, pp. 245–249. ACM (2006)
37. Sandnes, F.E.: Directional bias in scrolling tasks: a study of users' scrolling behaviour using a mobile text-entry strategy. Behav. Inf. Technol. **27**, 387–393 (2008)
38. Hagen, S., Sandnes, F.E.: Toward accessible self-service kiosks through intelligent user interfaces. Pers. Ubiquit. Comput. **14**, 715–721 (2010)
39. Sandnes, F.E., Jian, H.L., Huang, Y.P., Huang, Y.M.: User interface design for public kiosks: an evaluation of the Taiwan high speed rail ticket vending machine. J. Inf. Sci. Eng. **26**, 307–321 (2010)
40. Wright, R., Keith, L.: Wearable technology: If the tech fits, wear it. J. Electron. Resour. Med. Librar. **11**, 204–216 (2014)
41. Bai, H., Lee, G., Billinghurst, M.: Free-hand gesture interfaces for an augmented exhibition podium. In: Proceedings of the Annual Meeting of the Australian Special Interest Group for Computer Human Interaction, pp. 182–186. ACM (2015)
42. Avila, L., Bailey, M.: Advanced display technologies. IEEE Comput. Graph. Appl. **35**, 96–96 (2015)
43. Yoo, S., Parker, C.: Controller-less interaction methods for Google cardboard. In: Proceedings of the 3rd ACM Symposium on Spatial User Interaction, pp. 127–127. ACM (2015)
44. Yan, X., Fu, C.W., Mohan, P., Goh, W.B.: CardboardSense: interacting with DIY cardboard VR headset by tapping. In: Proceedings of the 2016 ACM Conference on Designing Interactive Systems, pp. 229–233. ACM (2016)
45. Van Krevelen, D.W.F., Poelman, R.: A survey of augmented reality technologies, applications and limitations. Int. J. Virtual Reality **9**, 1 (2010)
46. Park, H.S., Park, M.W., Won, K.H., Kim, K.H., Jung, S.K.: In-vehicle AR-HUD system to provide driving-safety information. ETRI J. **35**, 1038–1047 (2013)
47. Tufano, D.R.: Automotive HUDs: the overlooked safety issues. Hum. Factors J. Hum. Factors Ergon. Soc. **39**, 303–311 (1997)
48. Ailsa, B., Trout, J., Debenham, P., Thomas, G.: Augmented reality in a public space: the natural history museum, London. Computer **7**, 42–47 (2012)
49. Buxton, B.: Sketching User Experiences: Getting the Design Right and the Right Design: Getting the Design Right and the Right Design. Morgan Kaufmann, Amsterdam (2010)
50. Sandnes, F.E., Jian, H.L.: Sketching with Chinese calligraphy. Interactions **19**, 62–66 (2012)
51. Israel, J.H., et al.: Investigating three-dimensional sketching for early conceptual design-Results from expert discussions and user studies. Comput. Graph. **33**, 462–473 (2009)
52. Sandnes, F.E.: Communicating panoramic 360 degree immersed experiences: a simple technique for sketching in 3D. In: Antona, M., Stephanidis, C. (eds.) UAHCI 2016. LNCS, vol. 9738, pp. 338–346. Springer, Cham (2016). doi:10.1007/978-3-319-40244-4_33
53. Sandnes, F.E.: PanoramaGrid: a graph paper tracing framework for sketching 360-degree immersed experiences. In: Proceedings of the International Working Conference on Advanced Visual Interfaces, pp. 342–343. ACM (2016)
54. Sandnes, F.E., Huang, Y.P.: Translating the viewing position in single equirectangular panoramic images. In: Proceedings of IEEE SMC 2016. IEEE (2016)
55. Anguelov, D., et al.: Google street view: capturing the world at street level. Computer **6**, 32–38 (2010)

56. Kwiatek, K., Woolner, M.: Transporting the viewer into a 360 heritage story: panoramic interactive narrative presented on a wrap-around screen. In: 16th International Conference on Virtual Systems and Multimedia. IEEE (2010)
57. Huang, Y.P., Wang, S.S., Sandnes, F.E.: RFID-based guide gives museum visitors more freedom. IT Prof. Mag. **13**, 25 (2011)
58. Sandnes, F.E.: Where was that photo taken? Deriving geographical information from image collections based on temporal exposure attributes. Multimedia Syst. **16**, 309–318 (2010)
59. Sandnes, F.E.: Determining the geographical location of image scenes based on object shadow lengths. J. Sig. Process. Syst. **65**, 35–47 (2011)
60. Huang, Y.P., Hsu, L.W., Sandnes, F.E.: An intelligent subtitle detection model for locating television commercials. IEEE Trans. Man Cybern. B **37**, 485–492 (2007)
61. Abràmoff, M.D., Magalhães, P.J., Ram, S.J.: Image processing with ImageJ. Biophotonics Int. **11**, 36–42 (2004)
62. Senore, F.: FSPViewer. http://www.fsoft.it/FSPViewer/. Accessed 20 Nov 2015
63. Ku, D.C., Qin, S.F., Wright, D.K.: What is on the backside of the paper? From 2D sketch to 3D model. In: The 20th BCS HCI Group Conference. British Computer Society (2006)
64. Naya, F., Jorge, J., Conesa, J., Contero, M., Gomis, J.M.: Direct modeling: from sketches to 3D models. In: Proceedings of the 1st Ibero-American Symposium in Computer Graphics SIACG, pp. 109–117 (2002)

Effect of Difference in Information Between Vision and Vestibular Labyrinth on a Human Body

Akihiro Sugiura[1,2(✉)], Kunihiko Tanaka[1], Hiroki Takada[3], and Masaru Miyao[2]

[1] Department of Radiology, Gifu University of Medical Science, Seki, Japan
{asugiura,ktanaka}@u-gifu-ms.ac.jp
[2] Graduate School of Information Science, Nagoya University, Nagoya, Japan
mmiyao@is.nagoya-u.ac.jp
[3] Graduate School of Engineering, University of Fukui, Fukui, Japan
takada@u-fukui.ac.jp

Abstract. For development of motion sickness or visually induced motion sickness (VIMS) caused by sensory conflict, we can set the hypothesis that positive correcting differences in information among afferent input from each sensoria lead to the suppression of symptoms attributed to sensory conflict. In this study, as fundamental verification of above hypothesis, we verified the effect on the human body in case of stimulating only vision, only vestibular-labyrinth system, and vision and vestibular-labyrinth system (in phase and opposite phase), simultaneously. For the stimulating to the vestibular-labyrinth system, the method of delivering electrical stimulus called galvanic vestibular stimulation (GVS) from body surface is utilized. As a result, 2 conclusions were obtained. First was the disruption between subjective and objective evaluation was recognized. It was assumed that the task included vision and GVS with opposite phase had other factor of sensory conflict, which was not considered in this study. Second was significant changes between each task were not confirmed from HRV and RRIV analysis. In addition, there was disruption between the results of subjective and objective evaluation. Therefore, further verification is required with changing study conditions and settings such as posture.

Keywords: Galvanic vestibular stimulation (GVS) · Visually induced motion sickness (VIMS) · Visual stimulation · Body sway · Vestibular labyrinth

1 Introduction

Recently, with advances in display technologies (e.g., larger size, high definition, 4 K resolution, and stereoscopy), users can enjoy virtual experiences that provide the "sense of being there," [1] whether at home or at an amusement parks. On the other hand, there has been an increase in opportunities to cause the symptoms that are similar to motion sickness, referred often to as visually induced motion sickness (VIMS) or cyber sickness [2, 3], which is experienced by as user during or after enjoying these virtual experiences. Stanney has shown that 88% of virtual environment participants developed VIMS when viewing virtual reality movies for an hour [4]. Thus, the current state of the virtual

© Springer International Publishing AG 2017
M. Antona and C. Stephanidis (Eds.): UAHCI 2017, Part II, LNCS 10278, pp. 187–198, 2017.
DOI: 10.1007/978-3-319-58703-5_14

experience with the objective of amusement eventually becomes stressor in some instances.

The pathogenic mechanism and reason for onset of the complex symptoms are not sufficiently understood. However, one of the leading hypotheses for the pathogenic mechanism includes sensory conflict theory, which suggests that the presence of conflicts among afferent input from each sensoria (vision, equilibrium sense, somato-sensory) and the subject's experience causes the complex symptoms because of the irrelevant correction of differences in information [5, 6]. In particular, VIMS is evoked by differences in information between vision and other senses.

Allowing for the development of the complex symptoms caused by sensory conflict, we can set the hypothesis that positive correcting differences in information among afferent input from each sensoria lead to the suppression of these symptoms induced by sensory conflict. This hypothesis is easy to understand viscerally, and humans may be able to display behavior like positive correcting sensory conflict subconsciously. However, there is almost no scientific verification to demonstrate this human behavior.

Our study group has a system that gives artificially created independent information, which assumes the feeling of acceleration or obliquity to the vision and vestibular-labyrinth system. Thus, this system has the capability to provide the condition of sensor conflict or that of accordance artificially. The input to vision, such as visual information like motion in a movie (amount of movement, motion in the direction) is controlled by computer graphics software. For the input to the vestibular-labyrinth system, the method of delivering electrical stimulus to the vestibular-labyrinth system from body surface is utilized. This method is called galvanic vestibular stimulation (GVS), and provides a sense of obliquity or that of constant period fluctuation in the side direction. Our system creates quantitative condition of sensor conflict/accordance because it simultaneously provides input to both the vision and vestibular-labyrinth system. In this study, as fundamental verification of above hypothesis, we verified the effect on the human body by using our artificially providing the condition of sensor conflict/accordance system in case of stimulating only vision, only GVS, and vision and GVS, simultaneously.

2   Materials and Methods

2.1   Galvanic Vestibular Stimulation (GVS)

GVS (See the review of GVS [7]) is stimulation technique allows humans to perceive the sensation of acceleration or gradient by applying small electrical current behind the ear. The GVS technique is older, and has been used for over a century as a means to discover and understand the function of the vestibular-labyrinth system. Bohemian physiologist Johann Purkyne [8] reported that a galvanic current flowing through the head upset balance and equilibrium in his dissertation. GVS generally places electrodes on both mastoid processes, as shown in Fig. 1. Then, direct current or alternating current (AC) (<2 mA) is passed between the electrodes. Sinusoidal motion in the side (anode) direction is felt when AC is applied because GVS induces a sensation of acceleration or gradient according to the magnitude of the electrical current. This study archived GVS follows:

1. Self-built stimulus waveform software based on LabVIEW 2016 (National Instruments, Austin, TX, USA) was used to generate the pre-input-waveform.
2. The pre-input waveform was inputted into an Isolator (SS-203J, NIHON KOUDEN, Tokyo, Japan) through the external power unit.
3. The Isolator adjusted the current value and then outputted GVS.

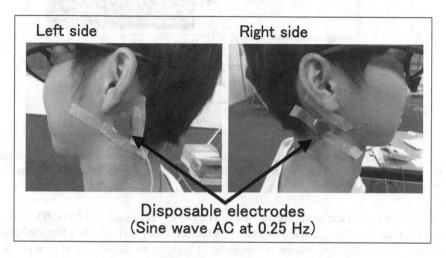

Fig. 1. Galvanic vestibular stimulation (GVS). In GVS, electrodes are placed on both mastoid processes, and a direct current or alternating current (AC) (<2 mA) is passed between electrodes. This study used GVS with an 0.25-Hz AC sine wave.

We perform GVS (maximum current value: 2 mA and period: 0.25 Hz) using this system. If the participant did not remain in the standing position during the GVS task, the maximum current of GVS was set at 1 mA (1 male and 1 female).

2.2 Visual Stimulation

The visual stimulation used was a movie created using 3ds Max 2015 computer graphics software (Autodesk, San Rafael, CA, USA). A screenshot of the movie that was used in this study is shown in Fig. 2. The basic construction of the movie consisted of several color balls, which were displayed at random positions, and a green cross that was shown at the center position as the point of reference.

The direction of motion in the movie was along the side direction (X-direction) because the conformation of both motions directions induced visual stimulation and GVS. The motion in the movie also was sinusoidal at 0.25 Hz and was generated by moving camera-simulated ocular globes (the balls themselves did not move). The amplitude of the sinusoidal motion was set to 150 software setting.

As regards the presentation of the movie, the movie was projected onto a rear projection screen that was 150 cm in front of the participant with a domestic three-dimensional (3D) projector (EH-TW5100, Seiko Epson Corporation, Suwa, Japan). The projected movie size was 157.5 cm × 280 cm and the matrix size was 1,920 × 1,080. The

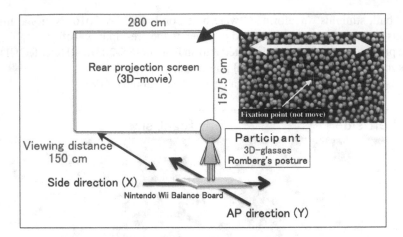

Fig. 2. Screenshot of the movie and the experimental setup. In order to measure the position of the COP, participants were asked to stand on a Wii Balance Board with Romberg's posture. (Color figure online)

participants watched the experimental 3D movies using 3D glasses (ELPGS03, Seiko Epson Corporation, Suwa, Japan) as a parallax barrier. Our previous study reported that continuously viewing this motion movie induced body sway that was in sync with the motion in the movie [9].

2.3 Procedure and Design

Ten university students (4 males and 6 females; 20–24 years, motion sickness susceptibility questionnaires-short (MSSQ-short [10]) adult score: 10.58 (average) ± 5.9 (S.D.), total score: 23.04 (average) ± 14.0 (S.D.)) who did not have vision or equilibrium problems participated in this study. Through the MSSQ-short that the participant performed before examination, we confirmed that the distribution of participants did not have sensitivity bias attributable to sensory conflict. The study was approved by the Research Ethics Committee at Gifu University of Medical Science. Written consent was obtained from the participants after the purpose and significance of the study and the nature and risk of the measurements were explained, both orally and in writing. In addition, the study was conducted in line with the 1964 Declaration of Helsinki and its later amendments or comparable ethical standards.

The experimental setup utilized in this study is shown in Fig. 2. We performed the experiments in a controlled environment (illuminance: 10 lx) in order to avoid any variations that were caused by visual stimuli. In order to measure the position of the center of pressure (COP) as body sway, participants stood on a Wii Balance Board (Nintendo Co., Ltd., Kyoto, Japan) with Romberg's posture. As regards the study protocol, first, a participant stood on the Wii Balance Board with eye-opening, and watched a static (nonmoving) movie for 60 s as the pretest (control). Further, participants performed four tasks in a random sequence to avoid the order effect. Task-interval was set at more than 5 min. (Table 1).

Table 1. Types of experimental tasks.

Task	Time (min)	Detail of the task
GVS	2	GVS with eye-closing
Movie	2	Watching movie without GVS
Reversed phase	2	Watching movie with GVS (opposite phase)
In phase	2	Watching movie with GVS (same phase)

2.4   Analysis

During the duration of the tasks, position of the COP was continuously recorded using the Wii Balance Board and custom-built stabilometry software WiimoteLib [11]. The COP measurements were recorded at 20 Hz, which is a basic sampling setting in clinical gravimetric tests. The continuous COP data were separated at intervals of 60 s of task time in order to only use stable second-half 60 s-data for various types of analysis. Our previous study reported that the position of the COP moved in synchronization with the phase in the motion movie, when the participants watched movie with low-frequency global motion [9]. Moreover, we assumed that the effect of the GVS on the change in the position of the COP indicated the same tendency. Thus, in order to evaluate the synchronization accuracy of the phase of movie and the GVS, the COP data unit underwent a frequency analysis with a fast Fourier transform with a Hamming window along both the X- and anteroposterior direction (Y-direction). Moreover, the total locus length, area, and standard deviation (S.D.) of the COP data for the two directions, which are generally indexes of body sway, were calculated. Then, a Tukey–Kramer method was performed using ORIGIN Pro 8.5 (OriginLab, Corporation, Northampton, MA, USA).

In order to evaluate heart rate variability (HRV) and RR interval variability (RRIV), a lead II ECG and thoracic movement, which is an index of respiration, were monitored and recorded (DL-320, S&ME, Tokyo, Japan). These data were separated at 60-s intervals in order to only use stable second-half 60 s-data for various types of analysis, as was the case with the COP data. Then, we calculated heart rate (HR), normalized low-frequency component (LF, 0.04–0.15 Hz)/high-frequency component (HF, 0.15–0.40 Hz), Normalized HF and Total power by using Memcalc/win (Ver.1.2, GMS, Tokyo, Japan), which is a time series analysis software that uses the maximum entropy method. Then, the Tukey–Kramer method was performed out using ORIGIN Pro 8.5.

As for the subjective measurements, motion sickness or VIMS symptoms were measured. The participants completed a simulator sickness questionnaire (SSQ) [12], which has been used in a number of previous studies, after each task. The total score and three subscores (nausea, oculomotor discomfort, disorientation,) were calculated for each task (See for the SSQ calculation methods [12]). Then, the Scheffe's multiple comparison was performed using ORIGIN Pro 8.5.

3   Results

3.1   Stabilometry

A typical stabilogram result calculated from the second-half 60 s-COP data (22 years old, male) is shown in Fig. 3a–d. The stabilogram indicated a continuous change along the side direction. Comparison of the Movie task (Fig. 3b) and other tasks (Fig. 3a, c, and d) show that the COP size in the side direction in the tasks with GVS was wider than that without GVS. Moreover, the change in the COP in the side direction of the GVS task with movie (Fig. 3c and d) increased than that without movie (Fig. 3a). A significant difference between the In phase task and the Reversed phase task was not identified in the stabilogram.

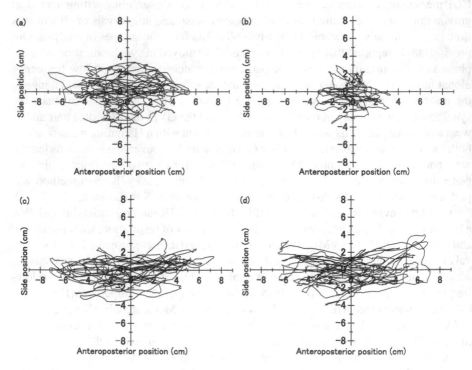

Fig. 3. Stabilogram result of the second-half 60 s-COP. (22 years old, male). (a) GVS task, (b) Movie task, (c) Reversed task, (d) In phase task.

The index of the COP (body sway) in each task was calculated, as shown in Fig. 4a–e. Figure 4a–d show the results for body sway indexes calculated from the second-half 60 s-COP; Fig. 4e shows the body sway indexes for power spectral density (PSD) at 0.25 Hz, which were obtained from the frequency analysis using the second-half 60 s-COP. The all body sway indexes and the PSD at 0.25 Hz show similar results. First, the In phase task indicated the highest index value among all tasks, and the value of the Reversed phase task was the second highest. Second, compared the result for In phase task with that for the Movie task, the index values of the In phase showed significantly higher than that of the Movie task. Third, comparison of result for S.D. in the X-direction and in the Y-direction showed that body sway spread not only in the X-direction but also in the Y-direction owing to the effect of tasks; however, each task had an effect on the body sway only along the X-direction.

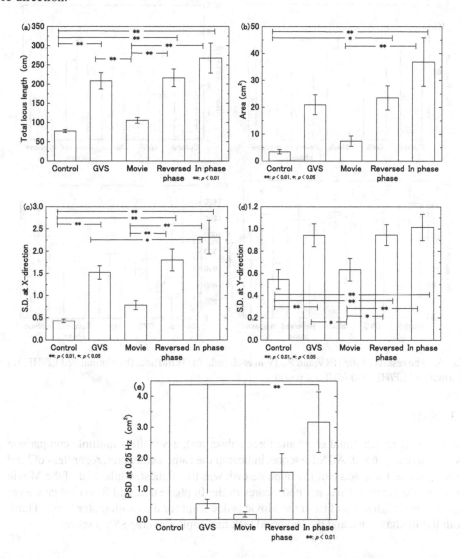

Fig. 4. Body-sway index of the each task and the PSD at 0.25 Hz. (a) Total locus length, (b) Area, (c) S. D. at X-direction, (d) S.D. at Y-direction, and (e) PSD at 0.25 Hz.

3.2 HRV and RRIV

Figure 5a–d show the results for the HRV and the RRIV using of the second half. No significant changes were observed. Moreover, a consistent tendency that could be attributed to the difference in the type of task was not also observed.

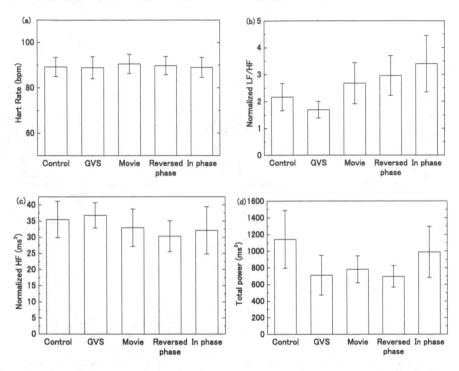

Fig. 5. The results of the HRV and RRIV in each task. (a) Hart Rate, (b) Normalized LF/HF, (c) Normalized LF/HF, and (d) Total power.

3.3 SSQ

For the SSQ results (total score and three subscores), a Scheffe's multiple comparison as shown in Fig. 6a–d. All SSQ scores indicated the same tendencies, regardless of kind of SSQ score. First, score of the In phase task was the highest, while, that of the Movie task was the smallest. Second, both scores of the In phase task and Reversed task were significantly higher than that of the Movie task except for the Oculomotor score. Third, both the In phase task and the Reversed task had similar average SSQ score.

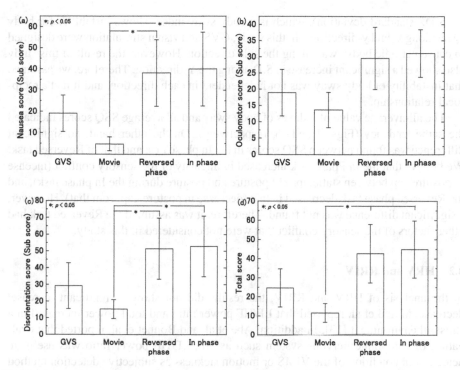

Fig. 6. The results of Simulator sickness questionnaire (SSQ). (a) Nausea (Subscore), (b) Oculomotor (Subscore), (c) Disorientation (Subscore), and (d) Total score.

4   Discussion

4.1   Body Sway

We compared the GVS task with the Movie task for the body sway test (Fig. 4) and found that instability and synchronization accuracy of the GVS task was higher than that of the Movie task. The reason was attributed to between relationship the current setting of GVS and motion settings in the experimental motion movie as follows. The effect of the GVS task (2 mA current setting) was higher than that of the Movie task (150 software setting). Thus, the body sway in both the In phase task and Reversed phase task was mainly due to the GVS. We compared the In phase task and the Reversed phase task and found that the indexes of the body sway in the In phase task was higher than that in the Reversed task, although no significant difference was found. We considered that the vision stimulation was treated as accessory component on body sway in this study. In the In phase task, vision stimulation worked as adding component toward GVS. By contrast, that in the Reversed task worked as subtraction component toward that because both stimulations impinged on body sway, mutually. All experimental settings, such as the current of GVS, movie contents, viewing condition, and difference in phases, were factors of change in body sway. Therefore, we assumed that adjustment of these settings enabled the control of changes in the body sway freely.

S.D. (standard deviation), which is a body sway index, shows instability for body sway along x- and y-directions. In this study, GVS and visual stimulation were designed to cause periodic body sway along the side direction. However, the result of this study also showed a significant increase in S.D. along the Y-direction. Therefore, we assumed that instability of body sway was not independent in each direction, and it had a reciprocal relationship.

The all-average value of indexes of body sway and all average SSQ scores indicated the same tendency (Figs. 4 and 6, respectively). On the other hand, no significant difference was found between SSQ scores in the In phase task and that of Reversed task. We believe that the In Phase task increased in intensity of the sensory conflict (incense in posture gap between static upright posture and posture during the In phase task), and the Reversed phase task decreased in that (decrease in posture gap from that). However, a significant difference was not found. Therefore, it was assumed the Reversed task had other factors of the sensory conflict that were not considered in this study.

4.2 HRV and RRIV

In the analysis of HRV and RRIV, the results did not show a significant increase/decrease. Marco et al. reported that LF/HF power ratio and total power increased in a stressful environment [13]. In addition, Abe et al. and Bonnet et al. reported that evaluation of autonomic nervous system such as HF, LF/HF power ratio was useful in detection of condition of the VIMS or motion sickness as subjective detection method [14, 15]. However, significant changes in conditions from the control condition (upright posture with opening eye) in each task were not found from the HRV and RRIV analysis. Considering previous studies, the results of HRV and RRIV indicated that the task did not cause a change in the condition regardless of the kind of task. However, the SSQ scores in both the In phase task and Reversed task increased significantly, as compared to the Movie task. Thus, the disruption between subjective and objective evaluations was recognized. Previous studies have shown that the HR and LF component in the upright posture is relatively higher than that in sitting posture. Considering previous studies, it was assumed that effect of the task was overshadowed by the effect of difference in the posture. Therefore, usefulness of the detection of symptoms induced by the sensory conflict using HRV and RRIV requires further verification with changing study conditions such as posture.

5   Conclusion

In this study, we verified the hypothesis that positive correcting differences in information among afferent input from each sensoria lead to the suppression of various symptoms induced by the sensory conflict. In addition, we verified effect on the human body in case where only vision, only GVS, and vision and GVS were stimulated simultaneously. The following conclusions can be drawn:

1. The instability of body sway and the synchronization accuracy increased in the following order: Movie < GVS < Reversed phase < In phase. Moreover, the result

of SSQ score changed in the following order: Movie < GVS < Reversed phase = In phase. Therefore, the disruption between subjective and objective evaluation was recognized. It was assumed that the Reversed task had other factor of the sensory conflict, which was not considered in this study.

2. From HRV and RRIV analysis, significant changes between each task were not confirmed. In addition, there was disruption between the results of subjective and objective evaluation. Therefore, further verification is required with changing study conditions and settings such as posture.

Acknowledgments. I would also like to thank the ten participants who participated in this experimental study. This work was supported by a JSPS KAKENHI Grant-in-Aid for Scientific Research (C), 15K00702.

References

1. Held, R.M., Durlach, N.I.: Telepresence. Presence Teleop. Virtual Environ. **1**, 109–112 (1992). doi:10.1162/pres.1992.1.1.109
2. Kennedy, R.C.S., Drexler, J., Kennedy, R.C.S.: Research in visually induced motion sickness. Appl. Ergon. **41**, 494–503 (2010). doi:10.1016/j.apergo.2009.11.006
3. Stanney, K.M., Kennedy, R.S., Drexler, J.M., Harm, D.L.: Motion sickness and proprioceptive aftereffects following virtual environment exposure. Appl. Ergon. **30**, 27–38 (1999). doi:10.1016/S0003-6870(98)00039-8
4. Stanney, K.M., Kingdon, K.S., Kennedy, R.S.: Dropouts and aftereffects: examining general accessibility to virtual environment technology. In: Proceedings of Human Factors Ergonomics Society Annual Meet, pp. 2114–2118. SAGE Publications, California (2002). doi:10.1177/154193120204602603
5. Oman, C.M.: Motion sickness: a synthesis and evaluation of the sensory conflict theory. Can. J. Physiol. Pharmacol. **68**, 294–303 (1990). doi:10.1139/y90-044
6. Reason, J.T.: Motion sickness adaptation: a neural mismatch model. J. R. Soc. Med. **71**, 819–829 (1978)
7. Fitzpatrick, R.C., Day, B.L.: Probing the human vestibular system with galvanic stimulation. J. Appl. Physiol. **96**, 2301–2316 (2004). doi:10.1152/japplphysiol.00008.2004
8. Purkyne, J.: Commentatio de examine physiologico organi visus et systematis cutanei. In: Opera Selecta Joannis Evangelistae Purkyne. Pragagae: Spolek ceskych lékaru (1819)
9. Sugiura, A., Tanaka, K., Takada, H., Kojima, T., Yamakawa, T., Miyao, M.: A temporal analysis of body sway caused by self-motion during stereoscopic viewing. In: Antona, M., Stephanidis, C. (eds.) UAHCI 2015. LNCS, vol. 9176, pp. 246–254. Springer, Cham (2015). doi:10.1007/978-3-319-20681-3_23
10. Golding, J.F.: Predicting individual differences in motion sickness susceptibility by questionnaire. Pers. Individ. Dif. **41**, 237–248 (2006). doi:10.1016/j.paid.2006.01.012
11. Managed Library for Nintendo's Wiimote. http://wiimotelib.codeplex.com
12. Kennedy, R.S., Lane, N.E., Berbaum, K.S., Lilienthal, M.G.: Simulator sickness questionnaire: an enhanced method for quantifying simulator sickness. Int. J. Aviat. Psychol. **3**, 203–220 (1993). doi:10.1207/s15327108ijap0303_3

13. Pagani, M., Montano, N., Porta, A., Malliani, A., Abboud, F.M., Birkett, C., Somers, V.K.: Relationship between spectral components of cardiovascular variabilities and direct measures of muscle sympathetic nerve activity in humans. Circulation **95**, 1441–1448 (1997). doi: 10.1161/01.CIR.95.6.1441

14. Chu, H., Li, M.-H., Huang, Y.-C., Lee, S.-Y.: Simultaneous transcutaneous electrical nerve stimulation mitigates simulator sickness symptoms in healthy adults: a crossover study. BMC Complement. Altern. Med. **13**, 84 (2013). doi:10.1186/1472-6882-13-84

15. Yokota, Y., Aoki, M., Mizuta, K., Ito, Y., Isu, N.: Motion sickness susceptibility associated with visually induced postural instability and cardiac autonomic responses in healthy subjects. Acta Otolaryngol. **125**, 280–285 (2005). doi:10.1080/00016480510003192

Exploring Location-Based Augmented Reality Experience in Museums

Tsai-Hsuan Tsai[1(✉)], Ching-Yen Shen[1], Zhi-Sheng Lin[2], Huei-Ru Liu[2], and Wen-Ko Chiou[1]

[1] Department of Industrial Design, Chang Gung University, Taoyuan, Taiwan
ttsai.cgu@gmail.com
[2] Formosa Plastics Group Museum, Taoyuan, Taiwan

Abstract. Augmented reality and beacon technology have gradually attracted considerable attention as the technology has matured, and is now applied in many areas, including museums. This study uses AR and beacons to develop a new museum tour guide app and then design the content and functions of the app based on media richness theory. The tour guide app is expected to provide immediate information guiding service and various education and entertainment functions that are more interactive. Finally, the present study measured the usability of the system by a mobile-specific heuristic evaluation checklist.

Keywords: Augmented reality · Beacon · Media richness theory · Mobile-specific heuristic guideline · Tour guide app · Museums

1 Introduction

Since smartphones have become popular, humans' lives have been closely related to apps (applications). Everything becomes more convenient via apps. Mobile devices are not only generally used in formal educations [1] but also in informal situations such as touring a museum [2]. Mobile guiding decreases the limits of visiting. Users can learn anytime they want by using their mobile devices because mobile learning is free from time and space, is low cost and is easy to access [3]. Also, mobile guiding can provide personal information according to different users' needs. Therefore, mobile applications have become a mainstream guiding technique today. For example, the "My visit to the Louvre" app developed by the Museum Du Louvre [4] contains 3D museum models, suggested itinerary, cultural events, 600 comprehensive descriptions of artworks and 600 audio commentaries on the artworks. The "British Museum Guide" app was developed by the British Museum [5], which contains HD images, the history of exhibits and an interactive map. The "Explorer: The American Museum of Natural History" app was developed by the American Museum of Natural History [6], which contains the function of sharing on social network, testing your knowledge and purchasing tickets. "The Metropolitan Museum of Art, NYC" app developed by The Metropolitan Museum of Art [7] contains the function of saving favorite art. The "Discover NPM" app developed by the National Palace Museum (Taiwan) [8] contains traffic Information, location services and funny games.

© Springer International Publishing AG 2017
M. Antona and C. Stephanidis (Eds.): UAHCI 2017, Part II, LNCS 10278, pp. 199–209, 2017.
DOI: 10.1007/978-3-319-58703-5_15

1.1   Taking Advantages of Augmented Reality Technology in Museum Visiting Experience

Digital media definitely provides a lot of convenience, but sometimes people focus too much on the interaction between the human and the device and ignore the interaction between the human and the context. This has occurred in many museums with mobile guiding [2, 9]. For these situations, it is important to lead users' attention during the guiding process. Augmented reality technology that bridges the gap between the digital and physical connects the virtual objects created by computers and the real scenes [10] and improves the interaction between audiences and exhibits, and the knowledge becomes more expressive and interesting. The AR technology has been widely used in education, for example, to show the collision effects in a physics class [11] and the chemical reactions in a chemistry class [12]. Research found that the attractive method, such as an AR learning game for children, seemed to have a positive effect on children's long-term knowledge, as demonstrated by Zarzuela et al. [13]. Sommerauer and Müller [14] found that using AR technology in a museum can efficiently improve the audience's knowledge and considered that AR is a valuable technology in museum exhibitions. AR technology connects the real exhibits and the information from the past to the future, allows the museum visitors to be immersed in the exhibition via virtual objectives and environments, turns education into entertainment and creates different visiting experiences. Also, the AR apps can let museum visitors check the visual tour guides and information they need by using their everyday mobile devices.

1.2   Using Beacons to Enhance Location-Based Interactivity in Museums

In addition to the AR technology, museums have begun to use micro-location technology beacons to provide visitors new experiences. Instead of searching through an audio tour for the right section, with beacons providing accurate locations, an app can detect users' exact location and then offer them static or dynamic information about the exhibits. So beacons are very appropriate for museum guiding and can be used to create experiences that are more convenient [15]. Besides, compared with other indoor location technologies, beacons have the advantage of low energy and low cost [16]. Beacon technology has been used to set up an interaction system between users and exhibits in a recently study [17] in order to develop different interaction systems [18] and to promote learning or consumption by providing personal guiding information based on users' locations. The National Slate Museum in England developed the Slate Museuml Amgueddfa Lechi app in 2014 [19] and applied beacon technology to the museum so that visitors can use the guiding app to sense 25 beacons located in different places and then experience the information guiding service immediately via their mobile devices, and it is the first organization to use beacons in a museum.

1.3   Media Richness, Interactivity and Retargeting to Mobile Devices

Since museums improve the visiting experience through various digital technology nowadays and provide rich interactive education and entertainment functions, it is important to clarify whether the rich information is correctly and effectively transferred to users and achieves the expected result. Media richness theory (MRT) is widely used to investigate the communicating ability of information. Media richness theory emphasizes that information and knowledge transferred by media can help the receiver understand information and new knowledge. It was used to investigate the communication between the members of a business organization and to evaluate the communicating effect of media with varying degrees of media richness. Recently, digital media and mobile devices have become common. MRT has been used to investigate the actual benefit of the Internet applied in organization communication [20], evaluate the learning effect of digital media and improve the satisfaction [21], use MRT and TAM to evaluate the usability of multimedia messaging service [22] and integrate MRT, TAM and flow theory to investigate the acceptance of students' digital learning by using streaming media [23]. In addition, the Formosa Plastics Group Museum (FPGM) applied MRT to build a digital museum (www.fpgmuseum.com.tw) in 2014, which prompted the museum to become a resource website that efficiently transfers education information and achieves the effect of distance learning [24]. Therefore, the present study will use augmented reality and beacon technology to develop a new museum tour guide app and then design the content and functions of the app based on media richness theory. The tour guide app is expected to provide immediate information guiding service and various education and entertainment functions that are more interactive. Finally, the present study measured the usability of the system by a mobile-specific heuristic evaluation checklist.

2 FPGM Pocket Navigator App Design and Development

The Formosa Plastic Group Museum chose 24 special exhibits from numerous exhibits on different floors in 2015 and developed 24 independent guiding apps that can be downloaded by a QR code to help visitors learn and better know the Formosa Plastic Group. But scanning the QR code to get the app is not intuitive enough today. Since new technology appears, such as AR and beacons, we would like to create a more instinctive guiding process via these new technologies. The Chang Gung University Digital Media Lab combines the AR and beacon technology, builds a new guiding system (FPGM Pocket Navigator) based on the digital context used in apps that the Formosa Plastic Group Museum created in 2015 and designs the guiding functions according to the media richness theory. The initial guidance will be triggered through image recognition or sensor beacons. The FPGM Pocket Navigator supports the official version of Android 4.4 or higher for all Android operating systems. It was published in May 2016 on Google Play for consumers to download (https://play.google.com/store/apps/details?id=com.fpgm.ibeaconguide&hl=zh_TW), and it is updated and modified constantly (Fig. 1). The system architecture of the FPGM Pocket Navigator is shown in Fig. 2.

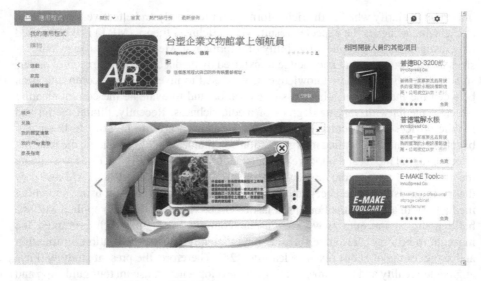

Fig. 1. FPGM Pocket Navigator on Google Play

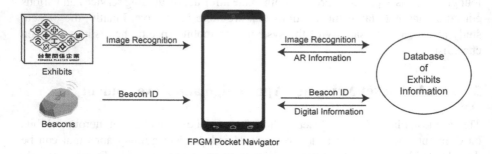

Fig. 2. System architecture.

The FPGM Pocket Navigator designs the functions of the guiding app based on four items of the media richness theory: Immediate Feedback, Multiple Cues, Language Variety and Personal Focus. It allows visitors to use the app in an intuitive way during their personal visiting, and the information will be conveyed more correctly and rapidly in order to approach the goal of education learning in museum.

2.1 Immediate Feedback

In order to strengthen the initiative hint and the interaction during the guidance, we integrate the AR and the micro-location beacon technology. We use different forms according to the exhibitions with different features. Users can use the AR camera aim for specific exhibits, and then the system will start the image recognition and show available information (Fig. 3). The beacons are used in those regional exhibits. When users are in range of the beacons' signal with the FPGM Pocket Navigator, the systems will know which region the users are located and then immediately provide the exhibits' digital information to users (Fig. 4).

Fig. 3. Image recognition.

Fig. 4. Beacon locations.

2.2 Multiple Cues

The FPGM Pocket Navigator takes advantage of the initiative notification of beacons to provide the most intuitive guiding service. We set up beacons at the location of 24 special exhibits, the elevators on every floor and the main entrance (Fig. 5). The system will provide the available digital information right there and show where the user is on the map in a different color when he/she is in range of the beacons' signal. Besides, the system will automatically offer a map of the current floor each time a user reaches a different floor. Every time a beacon is triggered, the FPGM Pocket Navigator not only provides a clear hint on the user interface but also makes a sound to instruct users that something is available now. For every exhibit, the system provides text commentary, audio commentary, Facebook links, interactive questions and the unique buttons of each exhibit (Fig. 6). It allows users to contact the exhibits in many different ways.

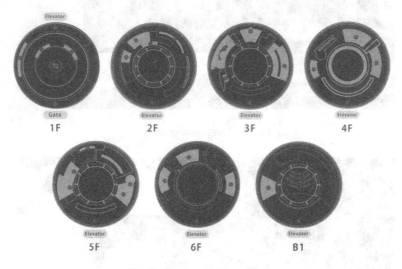

Fig. 5. Beacons in every floor.

2.3 The Audio Function Based on Language Variety

Language variety can be conveyed via signs. For instance, numbers can provide clearer meaning than natural language, and natural language can help the understanding of concepts and ideas. Therefore, the FPGM Pocket Navigator not only provides texts, images and realism, but audio commentary functions are also used in the system (Fig. 7). Through the guide's real speaking tone, the listener will be immersed in the situation and have a feeling of listening to a story, and learning will be more interesting in this way. In addition, the system has the function of interactive questions. It will ask users some questions and let them seek the answers on their own during the visit.

Fig. 6. Text commentary, Facebook link and independent button.

Fig. 7. Audio commentary and interaction question.

2.4 Leading Users by Personal Focus

Personal focus means that the message will be conveyed more completely when a person includes his/her own feeling or emotion. Some messages can be conveyed according to different users' needs or current situations. The FPGM Pocket Navigator can offer exhibit introductions according to users' current location. Besides, the system provides introductions of each floor (Fig. 8). The user can rapidly understand the theme of each floor and quickly approach the region he/she would like to visit.

Fig. 8. Floor guides.

3 Validation

In the present study, we use 10 Usability Heuristics [25] for the User Interface Design, as proposed by Nielsen as the heuristic evaluation (HE) method because it is low cost, accurate and fast. HE is generally used to measure the usability of system user interfaces. However, with the continuously updating technology and devices, the traditional HE method is necessary to adapt to today's generation. Yáñez Gómez et al. [26] proposed a mobile-specific heuristic guideline according to today's generation, and they developed a modified version of heuristic evaluation checklists for mobile devices. We use the heuristic evaluation checklists for mobile devices to validate our tour guide system, but functions of the FPGM Pocket Navigator do not contain some of the items. So some subheuristics were removed from the original 13 heuristics in this study. We invited four experts: two of them are interactive interface designers and the other two are very senior museum staffs who work in the group of education promotion. The two interactive interface designers have the background of digital media design and the experience of interface design of mobile apps. One of the museum staff members has worked in FPGM more than 10 years, and the others have the experience of being guided for 8 years. The experts used the heuristic evaluation checklists for mobile devices to test the usability of the FPGM Pocket Navigator, exchange opinions and identify/discuss the weakness of the system. The results of the evaluation, based on 12 usability heuristics, were as follows:

(1) Visibility of the system's status: The FPGM Pocket Navigator can allow the user to understand the system's current status and which step is easier for the user.

(2) Match between the system and the real world: The visual element used on the buttons conforms to people's cognition. The users can understand it well without additional explanation, and it conforms to their logical thinking.

(3) User control and freedom: Users can use the functions for free, which are instinct and unlimited. They can check information they need whenever they want.

(4) Consistency and standards: The color, font and icons displayed in the system are consistent. The buttons with the same function will be located in the same position on the screen. Also, the texts, images and buttons perform in a fixed way.

(5) Error prevention: The size and the space between the buttons are appropriate. Users can easily tap the buttons, and the user interface design allows them to correctly understand the meaning without making mistakes.

(6) Recognition rather than recall: It is very intuitive to use the FPGM Pocket Navigator. Users don't need to perform special operations.

(7) Flexibility and efficiency of use: The functions in the systems are easy to operate and can be recognized easily.

(8) Aesthetic and minimalist design: The graphical interface design is clear and beautiful. Also, the system will not provide unnecessary information.

(9) Helps users recognize, diagnose and recover from errors: The system has some weaknesses in this part when the sensor is not working very well. Experts suggest that the system should inform the user about the interface when this occurs.

(10) Skills: Everybody has the operational abilities for this system.

(11) The help and documentation: The system offers the tutorial only once at the beginning. Experts noticed this situation. A good system should allow the user to receive tutorial information whenever he/she does not clearly understand all the functions.

(12) Pleasurable and respectful interaction: The interaction is interesting during the guidance so that the user can enjoy it.

4 Conclusion

Since new technologies also appear, the guiding method is also under constant innovation. New technologies provide various guiding methods but prevent the users from becoming confused after receiving too much information. It is important to lead users during the guidance. In this study, we currently use two popular technologies in museum guiding: AR and beacons are used to make guidance more intuitive and then investigative and measurable items are used from the media richness theory to design guiding functions. The usability of the system was tested by experts in the HE method. Experts affirmed the design of the FPGM Pocket Navigator and provided some valuable advice. The result demonstrated that the FPGM Pocket Navigator conforms to the usability standards and can provide a positive experience during people's visit with the FPGM Pocket Navigator. In the future, we will conduct further usability evaluations with audiences after fixing some issues according to experts' advice.

Acknowledgments. The authors owe much gratitude to Ming-Jun Yu, Yu-Wen Lin, Jia-Yu Chang, and Xiao-Xuan Chen for all the work they contributed during the production of this system.

References

1. Virvou, M., Alepis, E.: Mobile educational features in authoring tools for personalised tutoring. Comput. Educ. **44**, 53–68 (2005)
2. Hsi, S.: A study of user experiences mediated by nomadic web content in a museum. J. Comput. Assist. Learn. **19**, 308–319 (2003)
3. Chabra, T., Figueiredo, J.: How to design and deploy and held learning. Retrieved June 22, 2006 (2002)
4. Museum Du Louvre. https://itunes.apple.com/tw/app/my-visit-to-the-louvre/id1100629786?mt=8
5. Vusiem Ltd. https://itunes.apple.com/tw/app/british-museum-guide/id551275212?mt=8
6. American Museum of Natural History. https://itunes.apple.com/tw/app/explorer-american-museum-natural/id381227123?mt=8
7. The Metropolitan Museum of Art. https://itunes.apple.com/tw/app/metropolitan-museum-art-nyc/id910622872?mt=8
8. National Palace Museum. https://itunes.apple.com/tw/app/discover-npm/id588676047?mt=8
9. Exploratorium: Electronic Guidebook Forum Report. The Exploratorium, San Francisco (October 11 and 12, 2001) (2001)
10. Milgram, P., Kishino, F.: A taxonomy of mixed reality visual displays. IEICE Trans. Inf. Syst. **E77-D**, 1321–1329 (1994)
11. Irawati, S., Hong, S., Kim, J., Ko, H.: 3D edutainment environment: learning physics through VR/AR experiences. In: Proceedings of the 2008 International Conference on Advances in Computer Entertainment Technology, pp. 21–24. ACM (2008)
12. Tan, K.T., Lewis, E.M., Avis, N.J., Withers, P.J.: Using augmented reality to promote an understanding of materials science to school children. In: ACM SIGGRAPH ASIA 2008 Educators Programme, p. 2. ACM (2008)
13. Zarzuela, M.M., Pernas, F.J.D., Martínez, L.B., Ortega, D.G., Rodríguez, M.A.: Mobile serious game using augmented reality for supporting children's learning about animals. Procedia Comput. Sci. **25**, 375–381 (2013)
14. Sommerauer, P., Müller, O.: Augmented reality in informal learning environments: a field experiment in a mathematics exhibition. Comput. Educ. **79**, 59–68 (2014)
15. Koühne, M., Sieck, J.: Location-based services with iBeacon technology. In: 2014 2nd International Conference on Artificial Intelligence, Modelling and Simulation (AIMS), pp. 315–321. IEEE (2014)
16. Newman, N.: Apple iBeacon technology briefing. J. Direct Data Digital Market. Pract. **15**, 222–225 (2014)
17. He, Z., Cui, B., Zhou, W., Yokoi, S.: A proposal of interaction system between visitor and collection in museum hall by iBeacon. In: 2015 10th International Conference on Computer Science & Education (ICCSE), pp. 427–430 (2015)
18. Sykes, E.R., Pentland, S., Nardi, S.: Context-aware mobile apps using iBeacons: towards smarter interactions. In: Proceedings of the 25th Annual International Conference on Computer Science and Software Engineering, pp. 120–129. IBM Corp., Markham (2015)
19. National Museum of Wales. https://itunes.apple.com/tw/app/national-slate-museum-amgueddfa/id1122132874?mt=8

20. Otondo, R.F., Van Scotter, J.R., Allen, D.G., Palvia, P.: The complexity of richness: media, message, and communication outcomes. Inf. Manag. **45**, 21–30 (2008)
21. Sun, P.-C., Cheng, H.K.: The design of instructional multimedia in e-learning: a media richness theory-based approach. Comput. Educ. **49**, 662–676 (2007)
22. Lee, M.K.O., Cheung, C.M.K., Chen, Z.: Understanding user acceptance of multimedia messaging services: an empirical study. J. Am. Soc. Inform. Sci. Technol. **58**, 2066–2077 (2007)
23. Liu, S.-H., Liao, H.-L., Pratt, J.A.: Impact of media richness and flow on e-learning technology acceptance. Comput. Educ. **52**, 599–607 (2009)
24. Tsai, T., Lin, Z., Lu, L., Chiou, W.: Research on media richness theory's application in the digital museum. In: 2014 Asia Design Engineering Workshop (A-DEWS 2014), Taipei, Taiwan (2014)
25. Nielsen, J.: 10 usability heuristics for user interface design. Nielsen Norman Group 1 (1995)
26. Yáñez Gómez, R., Cascado Caballero, D., Sevillano, J.-L.: Heuristic evaluation on mobile interfaces: a new checklist. Sci. World J. (2014)

Non Visual and Tactile Interaction

BrailleTap: Developing a Calculator Based on Braille Using Tap Gestures

Mrim Alnfiai[✉] and Srinivas Sampalli

Faculty of Computer Science, Halifax, Canada
mrim@dal.ca, srini@cs.dal.ca

Abstract. Touchscreen calculators require a user to visually locate a button on the screen. This poses a challenge for individuals with limited or no vision. To overcome this challenge, prior to use these individuals must invest additional time and energy into memorizing the calculator layout. There is currently no application that simplifies the calculator user-interface for individuals with limited or no vision. To fill this void, this paper proposes BrailleTap. BrailleTap is a button-free calculator application for touchscreen devices that utilizes tap gestures to operate. Using finger tap, the user can input a number in braille and the application will compute the braille code to its corresponding numerical value. Alternatively, using a swipe gesture, the user will be orally prompted to select the desired arithmetic operations. This paper presents our pilot study of BrailleTap that was conducted with two blind users. Results indicate that BrailleTap is faster and more accessible to blind users than the traditional touchscreen calculator. However, in order to increase the efficiency of BrailleTap further development of the underlying algorithm is required.

Keywords: Visually impaired · Braille · Touchscreen calculator · Mobile apps

1 Introduction

There have been significant improvements in the accessibility of touchscreen devices in recent years. One of the most significant improvements is the screen reader. The visually impaired user can touch the screen to identify the screen layout, and the screen reader reads out the item under the user's finger. This includes text, object names, and application labels. In order to activate an object, a user performs a double tap when he/she finds the location of the intended object.

Despite these improvements, locating an object on a touchscreen is a challenging task for people with limited or no vision [1]. For example, it is difficult for blind people to insert text on a touchscreen, even with audio feedback. The user has to find a particular character on the QWERTY keyboard and double tap to insert it. This is time consuming as users have to listen to every character when they explore the screen. The possibility of inserting the wrong character is high because the keys are small. Performing basic arithmetic operations on touchscreen calculator applications present a similar challenge: blind users have to search for their desired character through a time-consuming process that is prone to errors [1]. The calculator is considered to be the most commonly used

© Springer International Publishing AG 2017
M. Antona and C. Stephanidis (Eds.): UAHCI 2017, Part II, LNCS 10278, pp. 213–223, 2017.
DOI: 10.1007/978-3-319-58703-5_16

application at home, school, and while shopping [5]. As such, there is a need for accessible touchscreen calculator applications for the visually impaired.

To address this issue, we propose the BrailleTap calculator, a novel calculator specifically designed for blind users. The core idea is to permit users to insert numbers using braille, which is the fundamental writing system used by visually impaired people. The BrailleTap calculator relies on tap patterns, as opposed to tap locations, allowing visually impaired users to perform both simple and complex calculations in less time and with fewer errors. Previously, we presented the design of SingleTapBraille, a nonvisual text entry keyboard for smartphone devices [2, 3]. In contrast, the BrailleTap application enables for numerical computation thus allowing users to perform simple calculations using their language. BrailleTap was developed based on a similar technique to that used for SingleTapBraille. We integrated the single tap concept in the BrailleTap calculator application to make it accessible to individuals who are visually impaired. We also improved the algorithm accuracy to insert numbers on touchscreen devices.

The BrailleTap calculator is also a nonvisual number entry method which can be used for basic mathematic calculations and can potentially be used for different tasks, for example, entering phone numbers in a contact list, entering addresses in a map application and entering information in calendar applications. However, our initial design has implemented BrailleTap on a calculator. The BrailleTap calculator allows users to tap braille patterns on the screen to enter a number and uses defined gestures to allow users to select the operations and edit their entries. We provide an initial study to examine the performance of BrailleTap calculator with a blind user. The initial evaluation shows that BrailleTap is faster and more accessible than the TalkBack calculator.

2   Braille Code

Braille is a special code that uses a combination of up to six dots. Each character has a specific combination of these dots that distinguish it from others. The dots are organized in two columns, each column with three spaces [4]. Visually impaired users can read these characters using their fingertips. The codes of numbers in Braille are similar to the first ten characters, as shown in Fig. 1.

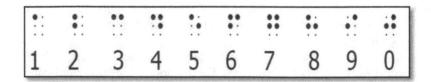

Fig. 1. Braille numbers

3   Related Work

Apple and Android have applied screen readers to smartphone devices to improve accessibility for blind people. Users can move their finger over the screen and the

TalkBack service speaks the object name under the user's finger. Despite this improvement, inserting numbers or arithmetic operations using the standard calculator with the TalkBack service is challenging [2, 3, 5]. The basic TalkBack calculator has one layer, with four operations on the right of side and the numbers 0–9 on the left side. The result of each calculation is displayed on the top of the screen. The user has to move his finger over the calculator screen and TalkBack reads out numbers or operations that are located under the user's finger. Thus, the user has to move his finger over the screen until he finds the desired number. If the user enters a wrong number, the user is required to find a clear button to delete the error. Thus, the main drawback of this method is that it is time consuming as it requires users to listen to all the keys until the desired key is heard [3, 14]. This technique also consumes time when the user makes mistakes since she has to reenter the numbers and operations from the beginning. However, the main strength of the TalkBack calculator is that it provides audio feedback that helps users ensure they enter the correct number.

In addition to the standard keyboard with TalkBack, researchers have proposed several other text entry techniques [6–12], which also predominantly require users to find a specific object location. Several developers have also introduced accessible text entry methods to overcome navigation problems, but they require users to remember particular gestures to enter text or numbers [5, 13].

Limited research has been done in the field of accessible number entry for blind users, and only one method has been integrated with an application for a particular aim, in this case an accessible calculator mainly for this population [5]. Previous work by Hesselman et al. [6] developed a number entry method on a large screen, where a blind user taps on the screen with the number of fingers of the entry number. Thus, in this application, users need to use two hands to interact with a touchscreen. It also allows audio feedback to help users confirm they have entered the intended number. Drawbacks of this technique are that it is limited to entering numbers only from 1 to 10 and requires users to use two hands to interact with a screen, which may be difficult as blind users tend to use one hand to hold a cane or a guide dog [2]. Another input method was proposed by Azenkot [14], which is called DigiTaps. This method was designed mainly for small screens where a user only needs three fingers to interact with the screen, but this application requires several steps to just input one digit. After inserting a digit, the app provides haptic and optional audio feedback.

The H4-writer is a text and number entry method introduced by MacKenzie et al. [6], which uses optimal prefix-free codes based on Huffman codes [15] to insert numbers as well as text. The H4-writer user interface has four buttons and the user need only use one thumb. Thus, it creates navigation issues and requires users to memorize the defined prefix codes. This is similar to Tapulator, a non-visual calculator, which was designed mainly for blind people. It uses prefix-free codes to enter numbers on a touchscreen; users tap on touchscreens using one to three fingers and swipe the screen to insert a number. It requires users to perform specific gestures to perform operations, such as a two consecutive swipes up to down to represent addition. The clearest advantages of this calculator are that it overcomes navigation problems by allowing users to tap anywhere on the screen and it provides audio feedback. Like BrailleTap, there are no numbers represented on the user interface; users can enter numbers on a screen based on braille patterns. However, the major limitation of this method is that it is not easy to learn because users are required to memorize the defined prefix codes to enter a number or operation. It is also time consuming because users are required to complete more than three steps to enter a number.

4   The Design of the BrailleTap Calculator

Our main goal is to design an accessible calculator on a touchscreen device that allows blind users to tap braille numbers anywhere on a touchscreen using their thumb or finger without the need to find a particular number or operation on a calculator layout. In our proposed calculator, users are not required to navigate the calculator keys.

The calculator is designed based on braille codes. As mentioned above, the code has two columns and three rows. Blind users generally enter braille dots from left to right and from one to six. Our calculator follows the same principle, allowing users to insert braille dots from left to right and from one to six. Users can activate braille dots individually using their thumb or a finger to tap on the screen. In order to activate the first braille dot, users can tap once anywhere on the screen and this will represent the number "1". In case the user wants to activate more than one dot, he/she can tap the screen quickly to create braille shapes. Once the user stops tapping on the screen for a short time, our algorithm will interpret the braille pattern and the corresponding letter. At the same time, a text-to-speech function will read out the resulting number. Our approach allows users to hold the smartphone device using one hand while they interact with the touchscreen using their thumb to tap braille dots anywhere on the screen. This follows Paisios [16], who found that the most accessible way for blind users to interact with a touchscreen is by using one finger.

In order to determine the corresponding number when users tap braille dots on a screen, our algorithm analyzes the relationship between all activated dots in each braille pattern based on the active dots' coordinates. For instance, the number two will be represented when a user taps the first dot followed by the second dot on the touchscreen. Our algorithm is mainly based on the clustering of active dots for each number and identifying the relationship between those active dots. The algorithm clusters all the inserted taps on a touchscreen and analyzes all these taps based on the number of taps, the shape of these taps, as well as each tap's coordinates. When the user stops tapping on the screen for a short interval, the taps are analyzed and the algorithm will compute the corresponding number. Table 1 and Fig. 2 represent the algorithms that have been used to examine the relationship between dots.

Table 1. Categorization of braille numbers based on number of dots

a. Character that has one dot	e. Characters that have four dots
Number 1 0 1 2 3 4 5 6 7 X One tap anywhere in a mobile screen	Number 7 0 1 2 3 4 5 X |X1-X2|<e; |X3-X4|<e; X2<X3; |Y1-Y3|<e; |Y2-Y4|<e; Y3<Y2
b. Characters that have two dots	
Number 2 0 1 2 3 4 5 6 X |X1-X2|<e	Number 3 0 1 2 3 4 5 X |Y1-Y2|<e
Number 5 0 1 2 3 4 56X X1-X2<0; Y1-Y2<0	Number 9 0 1 2 3 4 5X X1-X2>0; Y1-Y2<0
c. Characters that have three dots	
Number 4 0 1 2 3 4 5 6 X Y1-Y2= 0; X2-X3=0	Number 0 1 2 3 4 5 X X1-X2=0; Y1-Y3=0
d. Characters that have three dots	
Number 8 0 1 2 3 4 5 6 X X1-X2=0; Y2-Y3=0	Number 0 0 1 2 3 4 5 6 X X1-X2<0; X2-X3=0; Y1-Y3=0

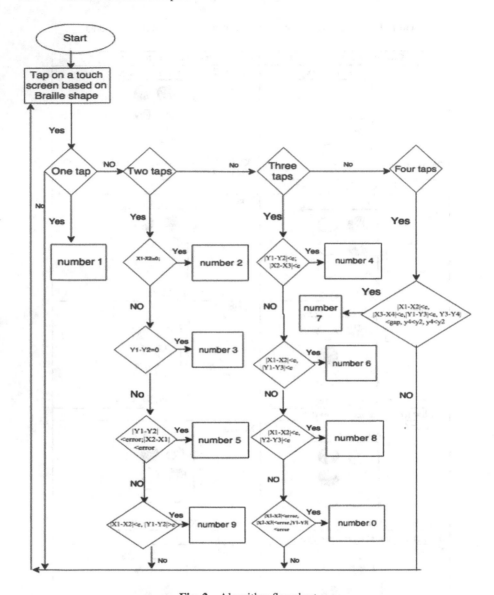

Fig. 2. Algorithm flowchart

The factors that indicate the relationship between braille dots are:

1. The value of coordinates (X, Y) for each tap on the screen
2. The number of dots in each number in braille

As seen in table above, each braille dot's position is reflected by both an x and y coordinate. These coordinates are used by the algorithm to create an equation that reflects the relationship between the position of the dots in each braille code. These equations are represented below each braille code in the table above. Once the pattern of braille code is recognized the algorithm will present the corresponding number.

The error variable "e" is a defined value that is used as a threshold for whether two floating numbers are in a vertical or horizontal line. If the difference between the x or y values of two taps is smaller than the error value, the algorithm will accept it because it is difficult for a user to insert two taps in an exact vertical or horizontal line.

5 Representing Braille Numbers Using BrailleTap

BrailleTap allows operations to be entered in a way that is accessible and effective using swiping gestures with a single thumb. This is in accordance with Paisios and Richard et al. [16, 17], who found that using swiping and tapping to interact with a touchscreen is the easiest gesture and most accessible methods for blind users. In order to insert an operation, users can swipe vertically in a loop to activate a particular operation. The first swipe will activate the first operation and TalkBack service will speak the operation name. Then, if the users swipe vertically twice, they will obtain the second operation. For example, when the user performs the first vertically swipe from bottom to top, the app will say "addition". In case the user does not want the addition operation, he/she can swipe again from bottom to top to select subtraction instead of addition. Performing a vertical swipe from top to bottom will insert division operation. A second swipe from top to bottom will insert multiplication instead of division. They can also swipe horizontally to edit their typing (see Table 2). After the users enter the mathematics equation, they can perform a long press gesture to obtain the result.

Table 2. Braille keyboard interaction techniques and their purposes.

Interaction techniques	Purposes
Swipe from bottom to top	Addition, subtraction
Swipe from top to bottom	Division, multiplication operations operations operations
Swipe from left to right	Clear operation
Swipe from right to left	Backspace
Long press	equal

The BrailleTap interface is based mainly on audio feedback and does not use any buttons on the screen. Users can tap and perform gestures anywhere on the screen (as shown in Fig. 3). The TalkBack accessibility service in Android platforms reads out the written text on the screen.

Fig. 3. BrailleTap user interface

6   Pilot Study

We evaluated the BrailleTap calculator to examine the performance of the calculator as well as to compare it with the TalkBack calculator. Other touch-based methods that aim to increase the accessibility of calculators to visually impaired individuals include Tapulator and DigiTaps. However, in contrast to TalkBalk these methods are not available on smartphone devices. In addition, DigiTaps does not enable numerical computation. As a result, the researchers only compared BrialleTap to the TalkBalk calculator. This evaluation was conducted with two participants who are completely blind and who are fluent in braille. The participants were involved from the initial phase of the calculator's design and provided some suggestions about choosing the appropriate touchscreen gestures for operations. After we designed the application, they were asked to perform eight mathematics equations using both the BrailleTap calculator and the TalkBack calculator.

During a brief training period of approximately five minutes, participants learned how to use the BrailleTap calculator. This pilot study utilized the counterbalance methodology meaning that participant 1 used the BrailleTap application prior to the button calculator and vise versa. Participants stated that they liked the application because they can use braille code, the language they are most familiar with, to input their commands.

We asked the participants to perform several mathematical equations using both the TalkBack calculator as well as the BrailleTap calculator. Table 2 indicates the amount of time that each participant spent to compute each mathematical equation on both calculators.

Table 3 shows that BrailleTap was faster than the button keyboard because it overcomes the navigation problem and the user can tap anywhere on the screen. BrailleTap is also faster because it eliminates noisy audio feedback that is used to help the user identify where he is on the calculator interface or identify the button name. In the interview, she stated that the BrailleTap calculator is a promising tool that allows users to enter numbers based on braille and perform operations using accessible gestures. She also likes being able to perform several tasks on the touchscreen without having to identify an object location. She also found it helpful to delete everything at once using a simple gesture.

Table 3. The time spent to use both the button calculator and the BrailleTap calculator

Mathematical equation	Average time spent using button calculator	Average time spent using BrailleTap
51 + 36	28 s	23 s
54 + 34−15	71 s	27 s
50*200	96 s	48 s
450/5	108 s	15 s
50 + 25/4	87 s	35 s
600/5−50	119 s	39 s
200 + 40*2	109 s	64 s

Overall, the initial result indicates that the proposed calculator is easy to learn, more accessible than the TalkBack calculator, and it overcomes most of the limitations that are associated with the previously discussed calculators. In the BrailleTap calculator, users are not required to learn specific techniques to enter a number. Unlike Tapulator, where users have to memorize the prefix codes to be able to interact with the screen, BrailleTap allows them to simply use their experience with braille. Based on our observation of the participants' interaction with both calculators, we noticed that there are noticeable improvements in both accessibility and speed of the BrailleTap calculator over the button calculator. However, the most noticeable error that occurred during the study is that the users forgot where they had first tapped the screen when the braille code had more than three dots, like in the number 7. This type of error leads to typing the wrong number. When their attention was focused on where they tapped the screen, they correctly typed the number 7. Although it is common for these types of studies to use one or a few participants, the main limitation of the current study was being unable to recruit a large number of blind participants.

7   Conclusion

We have presented BrailleTap, a non-visual number entry application with audio feedback based on braille coding. The proposed calculator allows visually impaired people to perform basic operations on touchscreen devices more easily than presently available calculators. It does so by overcoming their main limitation, which is requiring visually impaired individuals to locate an object on a touchscreen.

Based on the initial study, there are certainly opportunities for improvement to the BrailleTap calculator. Firstly, we need to test the calculator with larger groups of people via both qualitative and quantities methods in order to better understand its strengths and weaknesses. We will also measure total typing time, digits per minute, as well as identifying types of errors. We will improve the calculator based on the participant's suggestions, for example, by adding other mathematics operations using accessible touchscreen gestures for blind users.

Acknowledgements. We thank the Canadian National Institute for Blind, and especially the study volunteers. We also gratefully acknowledge support from Taif University and the Saudi Arabian Cultural Bureau in Canada.

References

1. Nicolau, H., Guerreiro, T., Jorge, J., Gonçalves, D.: Proficient blind users and mobile text-entry. In: Proceedings of the 28th Annual European Conference on Cognitive Ergonomics (ECCE 2010), pp. 19–22, New York, NY, USA. ACM (2010)
2. Alnfiai, M., Sampalli, S.: SingleTapBraille: developing a text entry method based on braille patterns using a single tap. In: The 11th International Conference on Future Networks and Communications (FNC 2016) (2016)
3. Alnfiai, M., Sampalli, S.: An evaluation of SingleTapBraille keyboard: a text entry method that utilizes braille patterns on touchscreen devices. In: Proceedings of ASSETS 2016, 24-26 October 2016, Atlantis Casino Resort Spa - Reno, Nevada, US. ACM (2016)
4. what is braille. The Tennessee Council of the Blind (TCB) (2008). http://www.acb.org/tennessee/braille.html
5. Ruamviboonsuk, V., Azenkot, S., Ladner, R.E.: Tapulator: a non-visual calculator using natural prefix-free codes. In: Proceedings of the 14th International ACM SIGACCESS Conference on Computers and Accessibility (ASSETS 2012), pp. 221–222. ACM, New York (2012). DOI=http://dx.doi.org/10.1145/2384916.2384963
6. Hesselmann, T., Heuten, W., Boll, S.: Tap2Count. In: Proceedings of ITS 2011, pp. 256–257. ACM Press, New York (2011)
7. Mattheiss, E., Georg, R., Johann, S., Markus, G., Schrammel, J., Garschall, M., Tscheligi, M.: EdgeBraille: braille-based text input for touch devicesnull. J. Assist. Technol. **9**(3), 147–158 (2015)
8. Mascetti, S., Bernareggi, C., Belotti, M.: TypeInBraille: a braille-based typing application for touchscreen devices. In: Proceedings of ASSETS 2011, pp. 295–296 (2011)
9. MacKenzie, S., Soukoreff, R.W., Helga, J.: 1 thumb, 4 buttons, 20 words per minute: design and evaluation of H4-writer. In: Proceedings of the 24th Annual ACM Symposium on User Interface Software and Technology (UIST 2011), pp. 471–480. ACM, New York (2011). doi:http://dx.doi.org/10.1145/2047196.2047258
10. Frey, B., Southern, C., Romero, M.: BrailleTouch: mobile texting for the visually impaired. In: Stephanidis, C. (ed.) UAHCI 2011. LNCS, vol. 6767, pp. 19–25. Springer, Heidelberg (2011). doi:10.1007/978-3-642-21666-4_3
11. Oliveira, J., Guerreiro, T., Nicolau, H., Jorge, J., Gonçalves, D.: BrailleType: unleashing braille over touch screen mobile phones. In: Campos, P., Graham, N., Jorge, J., Nunes, N., Palanque, P., Winckler, M. (eds.) INTERACT 2011. LNCS, vol. 6946, pp. 100–107. Springer, Heidelberg (2011). doi:10.1007/978-3-642-23774-4_10
12. Azenkot, S., Ladner, R., Wobbrock, J., Borning, A., Landay, J., Levow, G.-A.: Eyes-free input on mobile devices. ProQuest Dissertations and Theses (2014)
13. Shabnam, M., Govindarajan, S.: Braille-coded gesture patterns for touch-screens: a character input method for differently enabled persons using mobile devices. In: International Conference on Communication, Computing and Information Technology (ICCCMIT-2014) (2014)

14. Azenkot, S., Bennett, C.L., Ladner, R.E.: DigiTaps: eyes-free number entry on touchscreens with minimal audio feedback. In: Proceedings of the 26th Annual ACM Symposium on User Interface Software and Technology. ACM (2013)

15. Huffman, D.A.: A method for the construction of minimum-redundancy codes. Proc. IRE **40**(9), 1098–1102 (1952)

16. Paisios, N.: Mobile accessibility tools for the visually impaired. Ph.D. Thesis (2012). http://cs.nyu.edu/web/Research/Theses/nektariosp.pdf. Accessed 19 Sep 2012

17. Ladner, R.E., Kane, S.K., Wobbrock, J.O.: Usable gestures for blind people: understanding preference and performance. In: Proceedings of the 2011 Annual Conference on Human Factors in Computing Systems. ACM (2011)

Technology-Enhanced Accessible Interactions for Visually Impaired Thai People

Kewalin Angkananon[1(✉)] and Mike Wald[2]

[1] Suratthani Rajabhat University, Surat Thani, Thailand
k.angkananon@gmail.com
[2] University of Southampton, Southampton, UK

Abstract. This research addresses the lack of an existing, comprehensive method to help developers evaluate and gather requirements for the evaluation and/or design of technological solutions for the visually impaired. This paper, utilizing interviews with experts and the visually impaired, focuses on using the "Technology Enhanced Accessible Interaction Framework Method".

Keywords: Accessible interaction · Visual impairment · Thailand

1 Introduction

The Technology Enhanced Interaction Framework (TEIF) Method was developed to technologically enhance accessible interactions between people, technology, and objects, particularly in face-to-face situations involving people with disabilities. It was successfully validated by three developer experts, three accessibility experts, and an HCI professor for use with hearing impaired people [1]. The TEIF Method supports other design methods by providing multiple-choice questions to help identify requirements, the answers to which help provide technological suggestions that support the design stage. This paper described how the TEIF Method has been extended for use with visually impaired people. Ten experts, 20 visual impaired students and 10 visual impaired adults were interviewed in order to create scenarios, and investigate problems of visual impairment problems and their subsequent technological solutions.

2 Literature Review About Visual Impaired Requirements

The Individuals with Disabilities Education Act (IDEA) defines the term "visual impairment" as impairment in vision that, even with correction, adversely affects a child's educational performance. The term includes both partial sight and blindness [2]. Nearly 11% of Thailand's registered disabled population in 1996 had a visual Impairment, and the National Statistics Office 2007 data estimates that nearly two million women and men in Thailand, or approximately 3% of the population, or 2209,000 people had a registered visual impairment disability, [3].

To reduce discrimination in access requires accessible technology solutions, an accessible environment, accessible documents and accessibility awareness.

© Springer International Publishing AG 2017
M. Antona and C. Stephanidis (Eds.): UAHCI 2017, Part II, LNCS 10278, pp. 224–241, 2017.
DOI: 10.1007/978-3-319-58703-5_17

2.1   How Can Blind People Get Information?

Golledge [4] analyzed the four senses involved in a navigation task:

1. Touch is a tactile perception ability which acquires information from objects pressed against the skin, using Mechanoreceptors. These utilize neural receptors to detect a pressure on human skin when it is touched e.g. pressure on hands, feet, follicle, tongue and body skin.
2. Sight is vision perception, which includes focusing, interpreting, and detecting visible light that bounces off and reflects from objects into the eyes. It provides information such as images, colours, brightness, and contrast.
3. Audition is sound perception, namely the ability to detect and interpret the vibration into various frequencies of noise in the inner ears. Hearing capability using both ears also provides the ability to echolocate, that is, detect orientation of the sound source. (Milne et al. [5]; Wallmeier and Wiegrebe [6]).
4. Olfaction is Odour perception, ability to smell objects in the environment, utilizing the Olfactory neural receptor.

Visual impairment obstruction detection at different levels is shown in Table 1. For example, visually impaired people use a white can to detect obstructions at ground level. They use guide dogs to avoid the obstruction and/or sighted people to avoid the obstruction.

Table 1. Shows the relationship between activities and internal perceptions (Watthanasak [7] via Williams et al. [8])

Activities	Internal Perceptions			External Helpers		
	Touch	Audition	Olfaction	White Cane	Guide Dog	Sighted People
Obstacle detection (ground level)				✓		✓
Obstacle detection (body level)	✓		✓	✓	✓	✓
Obstacle detection (eye level)			✓			✓
Obstacle avoidance					✓	✓
Crossing the street with high traffic		✓		✓	✓	✓
Walking though a loud noise area (daytime) e.g., urban, shopping mall, construction area, etc	✓	✓	✓	✓	✓	✓
Walking through a silent area (night time) e.g., inactive construction area	✓		✓	✓	✓	✓

2.2   Problem and Solutions of Visual Impairment

Problems and solutions experienced by the visually impaired and blind. People are shown in Table 2.

Table 2. Problems and solutions experienced by visually impaired and blind.

Topics	Problem	Solutions	References
Unfamiliar places	Difficulties in navigating inside unfamiliar places which are usually large, complex, wide-open, full of crowds and noise, and have accessibility information. A guide dog sometimes is not allowed in some buildings, for example, hospital ICU	Sighted Guide Guide Dog Accessible Map (limited)	Williams et al. [8, 9] Guidedogs.org.au [10]; Guidedogs.org.uk [11]
Accessibility information	Difficulties in navigating inside the buildings due to lack of accessibility information such as tactile pavement, stair information, stairs, escalators, drop-offs, room number & name, etc. which are usually not provided	Sighted Guide Accessible Map (limited)	Williams et al. [9]; Zeng [12]
Map for blind	Information provided in maps, both commercial or Public service, is limited and not enough for people with visual impairment. To provide more confidence in Navigation, objects and accessibility information should be integrated into the maps	Proposed Framework	Miao et al. [15]; Google [14]; Apple [16]; OpenStreetMap [17]; Kolbe et al. [18]; Li and Lee [19]; Lee et al. [20]; Ryu et al. [21]
Indoor navigation system	No matter what indoor positioning techniques have been used in the indoor navigation system, maps are the primary navigational tool, and these are normally proprietary and lack information required by blind	Proposed Framework	Indoors [22]; Wifarer [23]
Obstacle detection and avoidance	Difficulties in detecting and dodging obstacles installed or placed in the environment during the navigation	Echolocation Sensor: Ultrasound	Finkel [13]; Williams et al. [9]
Unpredictable obstacles	Difficulties in detecting or receiving information regarding unpredictable objects such as crowds, noise, etc	Sensor: Camera	Williams et al. [9]
Studying in class	Difficulty hearing recordings properly with background noise, difficulty in seeing/understanding what is	OrCam MyEye software, Assisted Vision Smart Glasses,	Quek and Olivereira [24]

(continued)

Table 2. (*continued*)

Topics	Problem	Solutions	References
	being written/drawn on board, difficulty in seeing/understand what is being pointed at	FingerReader software	
Visit museums	Difficulty in seeing text which explain exhibits, and in understanding exhibits which can not be touched or which move	Audio description, 3D tactile diagram	
Crossing roads	Difficulty crossing roads independently, and, and traveling independently in new environments	vibrating system at the traffic lights	
Shopping in grocery	Difficulty in identifying things like cans of soup, cereal boxes, cartons of milk, and other things by touch, and inability to see product detail	OrCam MyEye, braille labels, audio description, FingerReader	

3   TEIF Interactions

Table 3 shows the five TEIF interactions while Fig. 1 shows the TEIF architecture. Someone pointing at something while referring to it as this, it is an example of Diexis.

Table 3. Interactions and Communication in the Technology Enhanced Interaction Framework

Interaction	Explanation and example
People-People (P-P)	People communicate verbally (speak, listen, ask, answer) and non-verbally (lip-read, smile, touch, sign, gesture, nod). When communicating, people may refer (speak or point) to particular objects or technology – this is known as 'deixis'
People-Objects (P-O)	People interact with objects for two main objectives: controlling (e.g. touch, hold or move), and retrieving information (e.g. look, listen, read, in order to get information or construct personal understanding, and knowledge)
People-Technology (P-T)	People control technology, (e.g. hold, move, use, type, scan, make image, press, swipe,) transmit and store information (e.g. send, save, store, search, retrieve)
People-Technology-People (P-T-P)	People use technology to communicate/transmit information (e.g. send sms, mms, email, chat, instant message) other people
People-Technology-Objects (P-T-O)	People use technology (e.g. point, move, hold, scan QR codes, scan AR tag, use camera, use compass) to transmit, store, and retrieve information (send, save, store, search, retrieve) to, in, and from objects

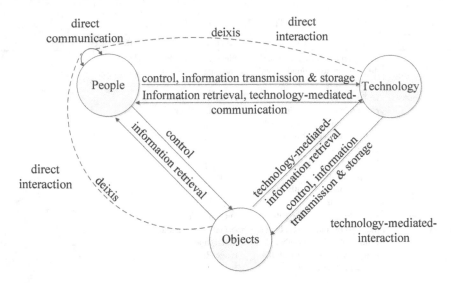

Fig. 1. The TEIF Architecture.

4 Developing TEIF for Blind

4.1 Interviews

The research analyses the information gathered from the experts and visually impaired people to develop requirement questions, five possible scenarios with actions, interaction issues, and possible technologies.

4.2 Transforming Requirements into Questions and Multiple Choices

The TEIF Method helps developers gather and evaluate requirements by using TEIF based multiple-choice questions. The questions help identify issues for which a technology solution is required.

In the following example, requirement questions □ means more than one answer can be chosen and ○ means only one answer can be chosen. The example requirement questions which are shown below only include questions for which correct answers in the given scenario are provided.

1) What is the main purpose of the technology solution?
   - ☐ a. improve communication and interaction
   - ☐ b. make the service more interesting and exciting
   - ☐ c. improve the service efficiency in terms of time and ease of use
   - ☐ d. improve the storage and retrieval of information
   - ☐ e. improve the service's more realiasm and authenticity,
   - ☐ f. improve interaction accessibility.

2) Where and when does the scenario take place?
   - O a. same time / same place
   - O b. same time / different place
   - O c. different time / same place
   - O d. different time / different place

3) What main role do people have in the scenario?
   - ☐ a. presenter – audience. Presenter gives information to the 'audience'- one or more persons- and controls the interaction. The audience can ask the presenter questions).
   - ☐ b. peer -> peer. Any person can give information or ask questions to any other person and therefore no one person controls the interaction)
   - ☐ c. no communication between people, only interaction with technology or objects
   - O Number of presenters and audience members
   - O a. one presenter – one audience member
   - O b. one presenter – many audience members
   - O c. many presenters – one audience member
   - O d. many presenters – many audience members

4) Does the presenter have a disability?
   - O a. Yes
   - O b. No

5) What language does the presenter use?
   - ☐ a. English
   - ☐ b. Thai
   - ☐ c. other language
   - ☐ d. I do not know

6) What language does the audience use?
   - ☐ a. English
   - ☐ b. Thai
   - ☐ c. other language
   - ☐ d. I do not know

7) Does the audience have a disability?
   - O a. Yes
   - O b. No

8) What kind of disability do the audience members have?
   - ☐ a. hearing impaired
   - ☐ b. visually impaired
   - ☐ c. physically impaired
   - ☐ d. none

9) What level of visual impairment does the presenter have?
   - ☐ a. blind
   - ☐ b. some useful sight

☐ c. Unknown

10) What interaction types occur in the scenario?
    ☐ a. people to people
    ☐ b. people to objects
    ☐ c. people to technology
    ☐ d. people to technology to people
    ☐ e. people to technology to objects

11) What type of technology would be appropriate for the solution to the scenario?
    ○ a. online technology (Internet)
    ○ b. off-line technology
    ○ c. either
    ○ d. Unknown

12) What type of technology devices would be appropriate for the solution to the scenario?
    ○ a. mobile devices
    ○ b. non-mobile devices
    ○ c. either
    ○ d. Unknown

13) What media is used to provide information?
    ☐ a. Non-text image
    ☐ b. Printed text
    ☐ c. Handwritten text
    ☐ d. non accessible electronic files
    ☐ e. accessible electronic files e.g. pdf

14) Is live support available?
    ○ a. Yes
    ○ b. No

15) Is there "Deixis"?
    ○ a. Yes
    ○ b. No

16) Where does the situation take place?
    ○ a. indoors
    ○ b. outdoors
    ○ c. both
    ○ d. Unknown

17) What are the two main environmental considerations identified that impact the scenario?
    ○ a. noise (Background noise affects everyone's ability to hear and understand what is said.)
    ○ b. room acoustics (surface (e.g. walls, windows, tile) and objects within every room interact to produce reverberation.)

○ c. distance (How far is the audience standing from the presenter? The further a student is from the presenter or sound source, the softer the sound they receive.)

○ d. visual access (How well can the audience see everything in different locations?)

○ e. lighting (Inadequate lighting or large banks of windows can be challenging for deaf or hard of hearing audience because they cannot see the speakers face well or an interpreter may be located in shadows)

18) Does the customer require a low cost solution?
   ○ a. Yes
   ○ b. No
   ○ c. Unstated

19) Should the technology solution work on a smart phone?
   ○ a. Yes
   ○ b. No
   ○ c. Unstated

4.3 Develop Scenario to Test Requirement Questions and Multiple Choices

In order to ensure that the TEIF has broad applicability,, five scenarios and technology solutions were considered during the development process: a blind person shops for groceries, crosses the road, finds rooms and buildings, studies at the University, and visits the Shadow Puppet Museum. The process illustrated TEIF suitability in these complex situations involving visual imparement, and addressed the specific aspects of these technologically- enhanced interactions.

Table 4 shows how the questions can be applied to the relationship between the multiple-choice requirement questions and answers for these five scenarios.

Table 4. How questions can be applied for five scenarios

Requirement questions	Scenarios for blind person				
	Grocery shopping	Crossing road	Finding rooms or buildings	Studying at University	Shadow Puppet Museum
(1) What is the main purpose of the technology solution?	a. Improve communication and interaction	f. Improve interaction accessible	f. Improve interaction	a. Improve communication and interaction	a. Improve communication and interaction
(2) Where and when does scenario take place?	a. Same time/same place	a. Same time/same place	a. Same time/same place	a. Same time/same place	a. Same time/same place
(3) Role of persons?	b. Peer - peer	c. No communication between people, only interaction with technology or objects	a. Presenter - audience	a. Presenter - audience	a. Presenter – audience

(continued)

Table 4. (*continued*)

Requirement questions	Scenarios for blind person				
	Grocery shopping	Crossing road	Finding rooms or buildings	Studying at University	Shadow Puppet Museum
					c. interaction with technology or objects
(4) Number of presenters audience members present	b. One presenter – one audience member	a. One presenter – one audience member	a. One presenter – one audience member	b. One presenter – many audience members	b. One presenter – many audience members
(5) Does the presenter have a disability?	b. No	b. No doesn't have disability	b. No doesn't have disability	b. No	b. Doesn't have disability
(6) Presenter's language	b. Thai	b. Thai	b. Thai	b. Thai	b. Thai
(7) Audience Language?	b. Thai	b. Thai	b. Thai	b. Thai	b. Thai
(8) Audience diability status	a. Yes	a. Yes, user has disability	a. Audience has disability	a. Yes	a. Audience has disability
(9) Type of audience disability?	b. Visually impaired	b. Visually impaired	b. Visually impaired	b. Visually impaired	b. Visually impaired
(10) Level of presenters visual imparement	a. Blind	a. Blind	a. Blind	a. Blind	a. Blind
(11) Scenario interaction types	c. People to objects	b. People to objects c. People to technology	a. People to people b. People to objects c. People to technology d. People to technology to people	c. People to technology d. People to technology to people	a. People to people b. People to objects c. People to technology d. People to technology to people
(12) Appropriate technological solution	d. I do not know	d. I don't know	c. Either online or offline technology	c. Either	c. Either
(13) Appropriate type of technology	a. Mobile devices	d. I don't know	a. Mobile devices	a. Mobile devices	a. Mobile devices

(*continued*)

Table 4. (*continued*)

Requirement questions	Scenarios for blind person				
	Grocery shopping	Crossing road	Finding rooms or buildings	Studying at University	Shadow Puppet Museum
(14) Media information source	a. Non-text image (touching can) b. Printed text	d. Non accessible technology	b. Printed text	a. Non-text image b. Printed text c. Handwritten text d. Non accessible electronic files	b. Printed text
(15) LIVE support available?	a. Yes	b. No	b. No	b. No	b. No
(16) "Deixis" Available?	a. Yes	b. No	a. Yes	a. Yes	a. Yes
(17) Situation location.	a. Indoors	c. Both	c. Both	a. Indoors	a. Indoors
(18) Two primary environmental influences	a. Noise b. Room acoustic c. Distance	a. Noise	a. Noise	a. Noise	a. Noise
(19) Customer requires low cost solution?	a. Yes	a. Yes	a. Yes, low cost solutions	c. Not mention	a. Yes, low cost solutions
(20) Solution smart phone compatibility	c. Not mention	c. Not mention	c. Yes, visitors' mobile devices	c. Not mention	c. Yes, visitors' mobile devices

Scenario 4: Problem of a blind students studying at the University

Space limitations allow only one of the scenarios to be described in detail. "Golf" is the only blind student in the law faculty class. Golf normally sits in a front of the class as he wants to record the lectures. However, (1) there is a lot of noise as teachers do not use microphones and other students are also talking during the class. Therefore, the sound quality of the media file that he records is not so good. Golf uses Braille to take notes from the lecture sometimes but not so often because he is not very familiar with braille. During the class, the teacher speaks Thai, as all class members are Thais. (2) When the teacher writes notes on the blackboard, Golf does not know what the teacher writes. Golf sometimes asks a friend to read it for him. Also, (3) when the teacher refers to material by pointing at the board, Golf does not know what the teacher is pointing towards. Sometimes, (4) the teacher asks questions related to information on the board, but Golf is not able to answer as he does not understand the question as he cannot see the board. Sometimes (5) the teacher gives students a hard copy case study to read and analyse in class individually. Golf cannot read it so the teacher allows Golf to work in a pair. Golf mentions to the teacher that if she provides him a word file or information on the web then he will be able to read it, but the teacher tells him that she only has a .pdf file.

At the end of the class, (6) the teacher shows an important book that every student needs to read. Golf is not sure what is the book looks like, so he asks the teacher if he can touch the book and feel it's size and thickness. Despite not receiving any financial support from friends or the university, he normally incurs considerable personal expense by having friends or professionals type the books and convert them into text files. While expensive, this is required, as otherwise the lack of accessible materials would result in him failing the course. (7) Golf find it particularly difficult when pictures, graphs or multimedia are required.

In this scenario Golf requires on or offline problem-solving mobile devices that he can use in the class and at home. Following are potentially appropriate technologically-based adaptions, an analysis of which assists in the developer choosing practical solutions.

Action 1: Golf records teacher voice in the noisy environment
Interaction issues: (P-T-P) Golf unable to hear the recording properly with background noise
Possible solutions:

i. (P-T-P) Teacher uses microphone when talk to students that can reduce the noise.

Action 2: Teacher writes/draw on board
Interaction issues: (P-T-P) Golf unable to see/understand what is being written/drawn on board
Possible solutions:

  i. (P-T-P) Teacher only uses pre-prepared accessible slides which Golf has access to before the lecture
 ii. (P-P) Teacher or another student or helper read information aloud/explain it for Golf
iii. (P-T-P) Helper annotates drawing on screen with text information
 iv. (P-T-P) Golf uses camera focused on board with Optical Character Recognition (OCR) and Screen Reading Technology (SRT) used to read text
  v. (P-T-P) Teacher & Golf uses electronic whiteboard with OCR & SRT to read text
 vi. (P-T-P) Golf uses pre-prepared tactile diagram
vii. (P-T-P) Golf uses electronic tactile display
viii. (P-T-P) Golf uses OrCam MyEye, an intuitive wearable device with a smart camera to read from any surface
 ix. (P-T-P) Golf uses Assisted Vision Smart Glasses, a wearable device by the University of Oxford, could be used in this case
  x. Digital Trends http://www.digitaltrends.com/mobile/blind-technologies)
 xi. Hand Writing Recognition (HWR) & SRT

Changes required:

i. Teacher behavior
ii. Teacher or other students' behaviour or additional helper
iii. Technology with in class helper
iv. Technology
v. Technology
vi. Technology pre-prepared by helper
vii. Technology
viii. Technology
ix. Technology
x. Technology

Action 3: Teacher points to writing/drawing on board
Interaction issues: (P-T-P with diexis) Golf unable to see/understand what is being pointed at
Possible solutions:

i. (P-P) A teacher or another student or helper explains what the teacher is pointing at
ii. (P-T-P) A teacher provides pre-prepared tactile diagram with camera tracking of teacher's pointing and haptic glove (further development is required before this can be a feasible and affordable solution) **REF** Quek and Oliveira
iii. (P-T-P) A teacher uses Camera focused on board with OCR used to read text
iv. (P-T-P) A teacher uses an electronic tactile display with camera tracking of teacher's pointing and haptic glove (further development is required before this can be a feasible and affordable solution)
v. (P-T-P) A teacher uses an OrCam MyEye software which is an intuitive wearable device with a smart camera to read from any surface
vi. (P-T-P) Golf uses an Assisted Vision Smart Glasses, a wearable device by the University of Oxford, which could be used in this case

Changes required:

i. Teacher/other students: behaviour or additional helper
ii. Technology pre-prepared by helper
iii. Technology
iv. Technology
v. Technology
vi. Technology

Action 4: Teacher asks a question that related to the information on a board
Interaction issues: (P-T-P with diexis) Golf unable to see/understand what is referring to
Possible solutions:

i. (P-P) Teacher or another student or helper explains to what the teacher is referring.

ii. (P-T-P) Teacher provides pre-prepared tactile diagram with camera tracking of teacher's referring and haptic glove (further development is required before this can be a feasible and affordable solution)

iii. (P-T-P) Teacher uses camera focused on board with OCR used to read text.

iv. (P-T-P) Teacher uses an electronic tactile display with camera tracking of teacher's pointing and haptic glove (further development is required before this can be a feasible and affordable solution)

v. (P-T-P) Golf uses an OrCam MyEye software which is an intuitive wearable device with a smart camera to read from any surface

vi. (P-T-P) Golf uses an Assisted Vision Smart Glasses, a wearable device by the University of Oxford, could be used in this case.

Changes required:

i. Teacher/other students: behaviour or additional helper

ii. Technology pre-prepared by helper

iii. Technology

iv. Technology

v. Technology

vi. Technology

Action 5: Teacher gives a case study hard copy paper to Golf to read
Interaction issues: (P-T-P) Golf unable to see/understand what is being written
Possible solutions:

i. (P-P) Teacher or another student or helper reads it for Golf

ii. (P-T-P) Teacher uses a camera focused on board utilizing OCR for text recognition

iii. (P-T-P) Teacher uses an electronic tactile display with camera tracking of teacher's pointing and haptic glove (further development is required before this can be a feasible and affordable solution)

iv. (P-T-P) Golf uses an OrCam MyEye software which is an intuitive wearable device with a smart camera to read from any surface

v. (P-T-P) Golf uses the Assisted Vision Smart Glasses, a wearable device by the University of Oxford, could be used in this case

vi. vi. (P-T-P) Golf uses the MIT 'FingerReader' device software to read the book scanning text with a finger. **REF** Follmer et al. [25]

Changes required:

i. Teacher/other students: behaviour or additional helper

ii. Technology pre-prepared by helper

iii. Technology

iv. Technology

v. Technology

vi. Technology

Action 6: Teacher shows a book to students
Interaction issues: (P-T-P) Golf unable to see/understand what is being written
Possible solutions:

   i. (P-P) Teacher or another student or helper reads it for Golf
  ii. (P-T-P) Camera focused on board with OCR used to read text
 iii. (P-T-P) Electronic tactile display with camera tracking of teacher's pointing and haptic glove (further development is required before this can be a feasible and affordable solution)
  iv. (P-T-P) Use OrCam MyEye, an intuitive wearable device with a smart camera to read from any surface
   v. (P-T-P) Assisted Vision Smart Glasses, a wearable device by the University of Oxford, could be used in this case
  vi. (P-T-P) FingerReader is providing an ability to read the book by scanning text with a finger.

Changes required:

   i. Teacher/other students: behaviour or additional helper
  ii. Technology pre-prepared by helper
 iii. Technology
  iv. Technology
   v. Technology
  vi. Technology

Action 7: Teacher shows a graph/diagram to students
Interaction issues: (P-T-P) Golf unable to see/understand what is being written
Possible solutions:

   i. (P-P) Teacher or another student or helper reads it for Golf
  ii. (P-T-P) Electronic tactile display with camera tracks teacher's pointing and haptic glove (further development is required before this can be a feasible and affordable solution)
 iii. (P-T-P) Electronic file that has alt tag with detailed explanation using an audible screen reader

Changes required:

   i. Teacher/other students: behaviour or additional helper
  ii. Technology pre-prepared by helper
 iii. Technology

Table 5 shows a few of the suggested technologies which could be used to address these issues, and the tick or cross indicates whether it could address the requirements identified. Only the first 11 columns are shown due to space restrictions. Some of the technology suggestions are still at prototype stage and so further development would be required before considered practical and feasible.

Table 5. Technology suggestion table

Technology description	1a improve communication &interaction	2a same time/same place	3a presenter – audience	4b one presenter – many audience members	5b Presenter has no disability	6b Thai	7b Thai	8a Audience have disability	9b visually impaired	10a blind	11c P-T
1. Microphone	✓	✓	✓	✓	✓	✓	✓	✓	✓	✓	✓
2. Pre – prepared accessible slides	✓	✓	✓	✓	✓	✓	✓	✓	✓	✓	✓
3. Camera focused on board with OCR/HWR to read text & SRT Enables text on a non-electronic board in class to be read by a screen reader	✓	✓	✓	✓	✓	✓	✓	✓	✓	✓	✓
4. Electronic whiteboard with OCR/HWR to read text & SRT Enables text on an electronic board in class to be read by a screen reader	✓	✓	✓	✓	✓	✓		✓	✓	✓	✓
5. Pre-prepared paper tactile diagram Static 3D representation of a diagram that can be explored by touch by a blind person	✓	✓	✓	✓	✓	✓		✓	✓	✓	✓
6. Electronic tactile display	✓	✓	✓	✓	✓	✓	✓	✓	✓	✓	✓
7. OrCam MyEye An intuitive wearable device with smart camera empowering the blind, visually impaired, or those with a reading disability or other conditions to read from any surface	✓	✓	✓	✓	✓	✓	✓	✓	✓	✓	✓
8. Assisted Vision Smart Glasses A wearable device by the University of Oxford	✓	✓	✓	✓	✓	✓		✓	✓	✓	✓
9. "FingerReader", a device designed by MIT, providing an ability to read the book by scanning text with a finger	✓	✓	✓	✓	✓	✓		✓	✓	✓	✓
10. Diagram mediated text annotation Adds text to a diagram	✓	✓	✓	✓	✓	✓		✓	✓	✓	✓

(continued)

Table 5. (continued)

Technology description	1a improve communication & interaction	2a same time/same place	3a presenter – audience	4b one presenter – many audience members	5b Presenter has no disability	6b Thai	7b Thai	8a Audience have disability	9b visually impaired	10a blind	11c P-T
11. Optical Character Recognition (OCR) Converts a text image into text that can be read by a screen reader	✓	✓	✓	✓	✓	✓	✓	✓	✓	✓	✓
12. Handwriting recognition (HWR) Converts a handwritten image into text that can be read by a screen reader	✓	✓	✓	✓	✓	✓	✓	✓	✓	✓	✓
13. Screen Reading Technology (SRT) Automatically reads displayed text aloud and allows blind user to navigate screen	✓	✓	✓	✓	✓	✓	✓	✓	✓	✓	✓
14. Camera and haptic glove tracking of teacher's pointing using tactile diagram/display Information regarding teacher's's focus via electronic glove vibration	✓	✓	✓	✓	✓	✓	✓	✓	✓	✓	X
15. Live electronic tactile display Dynamic 3D representation of a diagram that can be explored by touch by a blind person	✓	✓	✓	✓	✓	✓	✓	✓	✓	✓	✓

5   Conclusion and Future Work

Interviews with experts and Thai visually impaired individuals permits extension of the TEIF Method, allowing developers to create technological solutions, thereby facilitating visually impaired individuals' interactions with people, technologies and objects. Planned future research will evaluate its use with developers and visually impaired students at Suratthani Rajabhat University, Surat Thani, Thailand.

Acknowledgement. This research was funded by The Thailand Research Fund.

References

1. Angkananon, K., Wald, M., Gilbert, L.: Developing and evaluating a technology enhanced interaction framework and method that can enhance the accessibility of mobile learning. Themes Sci. Technol. Educ. **7**(2), 99–118 (2014)
2. http://www.specialeducationguide.com/disability-profiles/visual-impairment
3. http://www.ilo.org/wcmsp5/groups/public/—ed_emp/—ifp_skills/documents/publication/wcms_112307.pdf
4. Golledge, R.G.: Wayfinding behavior: Cognitive mapping and other spatial processes. JHU Press (1999)
5. Milne, J.L., Goodale, M.A., Thaler, L.: The role of head movements in the discrimination of 2-d shape by blind echolocation experts. Atten. Percept. Psychophys. **76**(6), 1828–1837 (2014). Masateru Minami, Yasuhiro Fukuju, Kazuki Hirasawa
6. Wallmeier, L., Wiegrebe, L.: Self-motion facilitates echo-acoustic orientation in humans. R. Soc. Open Sci. **1**(3), 140185 (2014)
7. Watthanasak, J.: Unpublished interim PhD Report University of Southampton, UK (2016)
8. Williams, M.A., Hurst, A., Kane, S.K.: Pray before you step out: describing personal and situational blind navigation behaviors. In: Proceedings of the 15th International ACM SIGACCESS Conference on Computers and Accessibility, p. 28. ACM (2013)
9. Williams, M.A., Galbraith, C., Kane, S.K., Hurst, A.: Just let the cane hit it: how the blind and sighted see navigation differently. In: Proceedings of the 16th International ACM SIGACCESS Conference on Computers & Accessibility, pp. 217–224. ACM (2014)
10. Guidedogs.org.au. Frequently asked questions - guidedogs SA/NT (2016). https://www.guidedogs.org.au/frequently-asked-questions. Accessed 5 Nov 2016
11. Guidedogs.org.uk. Are dogs allowed everywhere? - All access areas|guide dogs (2016). https://www.guidedogs.org.uk/supportus/campaigns/access-all-areas/are-dogs-allowed-everywhere. Accessed 5 Nov 2016
12. Zeng, L.: A survey: outdoor mobility experiences by the visually impaired. In: Mensch und Computer 2015–Workshopband (2015)
13. Finkel, M.: The blind man who taught himself to see (2012). http://www.mensjournal.com/magazine/the-blind-man-who-taught-himself-to-see-20120504. Accessed 13 Nov 2016
14. Google. Google - indoor maps (2016). https://www.google.co.uk/maps/about/partners/indoormaps/. Accessed 17 Dec 2016
15. Miao, M., Spindler, M., Weber, G.: Requirements of indoor navigation system from blind users. In: Holzinger, A., Simonic, K.-M. (eds.) USAB 2011. LNCS, vol. 7058, pp. 673–679. Springer, Heidelberg (2011). doi:10.1007/978-3-642-25364-5_48
16. Apple. Apple maps (2016). http://www.apple.com/ios/maps/. Accessed 17 Nov 2016

17. OpenStreetMap. Openstreetmap - indoor mapping (2016). http://wiki.openstreetmap.org/wiki/Indoor_Mapping. Accessed 17 Apr 2016
18. Kolbe, T.H., Groger, G., Plumer, L.: Citygml: interoperable access to 3D city models. In: van Oosterom, P., Zlatanova, S., Fendel, E.M. (eds.) Geo-information for Disaster Management, pp. 883–899. Springer, Heidelberg (2015)
19. Li, K.J., Lee, J.Y.: Basic concepts of indoor spatial information candidate standard indoorgml and its applications. J. Korea Sp. Inf. Soc. 21(3), 1 (2013)
20. Lee, J., Li, K.J., Zlatanova, S., Kolbe, T.H., Nagel, C., Becker, T.: Ogc R indoorgml (2014)
21. Ryu, H.-G., Kim, T., Li, K.-J.: Indoor navigation map for visually impaired people. In: Proceedings of the Sixth ACM SIGSPATIAL International Workshop on Indoor Spatial Awareness, pp. 32–35. ACM (2014)
22. Indoo.rs. indoo.rs guides blind travellers at san francisco international airport (2015). http://indoo.rs/sfo/. Accessed 13 Nov 2016
23. Wifarer. Wifarer - indoor positioning | indoor gps | location analytics (2016). http://wifarer.com. Accessed 13 March 2016
24. Quek, F., Oliveira, F.: Enabling the blind to see gestures. ACM Trans. Comput. Hum. Interact. 20(1), 4 (2013)
25. Follmer, S., Leithinger, D., Olwal, A., Hogge, A., Ishii, H.: inFORM: dynamic physical affordances and constraints through shape and object actuation. In: Proceedings of the 26th Annual ACM Symposium on User Interface Software and Technology (UIST 2013), pp. 417–426. ACM, New York (2013)

Mobile Audio Games Accessibility Evaluation for Users Who Are Blind

Maria C.C. Araújo[1]([📧]), Agebson R. Façanha[1], Ticianne G.R. Darin[1],
Jaime Sánchez[2], Rossana M.C. Andrade[1], and Windson Viana[1]

[1] Graduate Program in Computer Science,
Federal University of Ceara, Fortaleza, Brazil
mariaaraujo@great.ufc.br, agebson@ifce.edu.br,
{ticianne,windson}@virtual.ufc.br, rossana@ufc.br
[2] Department of Computer Science, University of Chile, Santiago, Chile
jsanchez@dcc.uchile.cl

Abstract. Digital games have become increasingly popular for both entertainment and education purposes. However, making these games universal and accessible poses a challenge for interface designers and game developers, since they are usually unfamiliar with the peculiarities of gamers who are blind. More effort is necessary for contributing to a universal game design and, ultimately, helping to promote the inclusion of people with disabilities to take full advantages of digital games. In this research, we present a study concerning existent guidelines and recommendations for accessibility in digital games. As a result, we propose ten recommendations for the design of mobile audio games, targeting gamers who are blind. We also present an evaluation instrument assembled from the recommendations we propose. We used this instrument to assess ten audio games labeled as inclusive. Results indicate that only three from a total of ten games were considered "good", which means they met the fundamental aspects of the guidelines.

1 Introduction

During the past decades, the way of enjoying the playful universe of digital games evolved regarding style, meaning, and available platforms (e.g., arcades, consoles, PCs, mobile devices). In turn, the purpose of games has been widened beyond sheer entertainment. For instance, we can find games as learning support software (edugames), marketing tools (advergames), or even games for improving physical conditioning (fitness games) [19,22]. Digital games are now more socially relevant than when they were conceived. Despite performing a significant social role in many sectors and communities, most games do not contribute to the inclusion of people with disabilities. In fact, the majority part of digital games has not design, user interface, or mechanics adapted to gamers who have some disability [12,32].

R.M.C. Andrade—Researcher scholarship - DT Level 2, sponsored by CNPq.

M. Antona and C. Stephanidis (Eds.): UAHCI 2017, Part II, LNCS 10278, pp. 242–259, 2017.
DOI: 10.1007/978-3-319-58703-5_18

According to the United Nations (UN), there are more than 600 million people with some physical, cognitive, hearing, or visual disability in the world. The World Health Organisation estimates 285 million inhabitants with visual impairments. 40 million of them are totally blind. The majority (90%) live in developing countries such as Brazil and India [1]. Game designers and developers devote feeble efforts for implementing accessibility in their games despite this significant number of people with disabilities [12,25].

Groups of researchers, game communities, and specialized game companies have mobilized themselves to develop games targeting users with disabilities in various platforms [3,32]. Some communities compile and make available such games, such as the Game Accessibility Web sites[1] and Audiogames.net[2]. Another notorious initiative is the proposal of accessibility guidelines and recommendations for designers and game developers. However, the most important guidelines available nowadays are scattered in many works and demand compilation.

In this research, we present a study concerning these guidelines and recommendations for accessibility in mobile games. The research focused on accessibility recommendations for gamers who are blind. As a result, we propose ten recommendations for the design of mobile audio games, which are a set of games in which the primary interaction occurs through audio.

In the first phase of this research, we gathered and studied six collections of guidelines. Then, we resumed these guidelines focused on the most relevant accessibility characteristics provided in mobile audio games for users who are blind. Based on this study, we identified ten recommendations that can be considered recurrent or minimal requirements to meet in the design and development of a mobile audio game. These recommendations contain simple considerations and design decisions that apply to most game mechanics. However, these are the recommendations that benefit the biggest number of players and are easy to implement.

Moreover, we developed an evaluation instrument based on the Web Content Accessibility Guidelines (WCAG) 2.0 classification and organization [24]. The assessment instrument offers a simplified way to evaluate the minimal accessibility requirements that a mobile audio game should meet. To validate the instrument, we applied it to the evaluation of ten mobile audio games (e.g., Nebula, Inquisitor, GBraille Hangman). Finally, we implemented an evaluation process with the assistance of two individuals who were blind. Results indicate that only three from a total of ten games were considered "good", i.e., met the fundamental aspects of the guidelines. Two games were found unsatisfactory, and three games were insufficient mainly due to the absence of an audio tutorial and no level configuration available to the gamers.

The remainder of the paper is organized as follows: Sect. 2, after the introduction, gives an explanation about accessibility in games in a broader context and also discusses the audio games available for mobile devices. Next, Sect. 3 presents the study of the Recommendations for Accessibility in Digital Games. Section 4

---

[1] http://game-accessibility.com/game/.
[2] http://audiogames.net/.

details the assessment of ten audio games implemented using our instrument. It also presents the results obtained by this evaluation. Section 5 takes up on related works and, finally, Sect. 6 closes the paper showing final considerations and future work.

2   Game Accessibility

"Accessibility for games can be defined as the ability to play a game despite limiting conditions. Limiting conditions can be temporary functional limitations or permanent disabilities - such as blindness, deafness or reduced mobility" [14].

Accessibility features in digital games are often limited to change of resolution, volume adjusts, subtitles activation, and remapping of game controllers [25]. These mechanisms promotes on some level the universal design of the games, but several limitations are still unaddressed. Game audio is an important immersion aspect. However, rarely, it receives the same attention received by the game visual project. Frequently, sound feedback provided by games is not enough to indicate all the essential information for understanding the scene or the possible navigation paths. Players who are blind also experiment a generalized incompatibility of screen readers and games since these systems require access to hidden text descriptions in each element of interaction. Also, even players with low vision need options for increasing the size or contrast of game elements [31,32].

2.1   Audio Games Accessibility

Audio games are focused on an audio-based gameplay. These techniques allow a user to play a game without the need for a graphical user interface to understand the game context or to interact with the application [7]. It is also important to emphasize that these audio-based games are not always accessible due to its target audience. For example, the game Zombie, Run! [29] is an immersive running audio game in which users are put into zombie's universe focused on a street running.

Accessible audio games have as target audience people with visual impairments. These games reinforce audio solutions to guarantee the interaction. Originally, amateurs have developed the majority part of the accessible audio games. They started with adaptations from existing games, trying to make them partially or entirely accessible. Nevertheless, they also aroused the interest of sound artists, researchers, developers, and gamers [16]. Most of the audio games don't have a graphical interface. In some cases, a primary visual interface is available since games can also aim at universal design. Then, people who are blind can also play with or against people who are sighted.

The main characteristic of accessible audio games is the treatment of routines and narrative in games through sound resources. Games use both recorded sounds or TTS (Text-To-Speech) techniques to generate audio from text information. In these games, the player can differentiate several sound patterns quickly.

Additionally, audio games could include tactile and haptic feedback (e.g., feed-backs with vibration or sound). With this approach, a complete game atmosphere can be built, offering to individuals who are blind a good level of interaction [12,26,32].

Audio Quake, *Serialization*, and *Audio Icons* are the most commonly used techniques to provide accessibility in audio games [3,26,33].

- **Audio Quake** - It simulates a radar and uses sound metaphors to indicate the position of mobile and fixed objects. For example, sounds are emitted from the enemy's position. They gain intensity (or alarms) according to the approximation of the opponent [4]. Some authors indicates Audio Quake as the first adaptation technique produced [33].
- **Serialisation** - This technique treats game priorities in the sound playing. Distinct levels of information (e.g., enemies, obstacles, etc.) have different levels of priority concerning sonorization time. Therefore, the correspondent sounds should be serialized according to this priority, which indicates its importance for the game comprehension. In that sense, several paradigms of priority might be used in this technique [5,33].
- **Audio Icons and Audio Cues** - This technique proposes adding sound effects to the game (audio icons) or sound clues for promoting the object identification or for describing actions in the game [26,33]. For example, the game plays a collision sound, and, just a few seconds later, it executes other audio indicating that there is a wall in front of the gamer's avatar [12].
- **3D Audio Cues** - 3D audio cues use sound levels and sound source position (e.g., sound from the north, from behind the user) for directional guidance. Nowadays, smartphones and PCs have binaural audio, which reproduces 3D effect to systems that have 5.1 sound (5 channels for simple sounds - medium and acute sounds - and a channel for deep sounds) in stereo headphones or speakers. Frequently, this technique is combined with the other ones to provide a fully immersive 3D game. Nevertheless, games incorporating 3D audio and directional simulation may not always provide high-quality experience, since it also depends on the user's device audio system (speakers position, headphone quality) [12].

There are several academic work related to developing of audio games that incorporate these techniques [7,8,18,27,28]. For example, Audiopolis [28], a game focused on stimulating navigation and orientation abilities in a virtual city by interaction with audio and tactile interfaces.

Web repositories maintained by users communities contains a list of accessible audio games. Take as an example the website Augiogames.net, an international repository with more than 100 games (http://www.audiogames.net/). The available games range from adaptations of board games (e.g., chess) to RPG (Role Playing Games) and action games. For example, "Nicolas Eymerich, Inquisitor" is a PC adventure game, in which Eymerich is called to investigate a complex case that reveals a new face of Evil. The player finds and collects objects through sound feedback of scenery elements.

2.2 Mobile Audio Games

Audio Games may also be developed for mobile platforms. It is similar to any other digital game with audio and video output. In other words, it has a narrative, and the player interaction uses audio and other native resources of the mobile device. For instance, sensors and gestures may also be used to guarantee and improve player's immersion. Audio games that are in a mobile context present the same gender variety that console-based or PC games, such as adventure games, action, terror, running, RPG, among others [6,23].

Mobile game developers also work with binaural audio. Sound effects provide an identification of where the player is, and device gestures can be translated into game commands. These sound effects allow them to build an immersive world around the player, making him able to identify direction and distance from game objects. Besides, the mobile game could take advantages of the resources available in Smartphones and tablets as the a compass, GPS, accelerometer, and other sensors [12,20,26].

Accessibility implementation in mobile games involves several specific issues. Mobile devices provide freedom to the user, which can play games everywhere using a multitude of input methods (text, gestures on the screen, gesture with the mobile phone, etc.). However, these characteristics imply more interaction limitations for players with disabilities.

While designing games for mobile devices, game designers and developer must consider items related to alternative inputs (e.g., "buttons" configuration, controlling customization). Some games include a capacity of spinning the device in space by using a gyroscope to control the game avatars. Other games require interaction with the device's touchscreen. In both situations, developers must provide alternative controllers. For instance, the game should have alternative buttons in the interface, allowing those that cannot properly hold the device to be able to play the game by using the screen buttons [12,17]. High contrast and design options for color-blind people are important for players with low vision or color blindness so they can distinguish critical areas related to the game menu and navigation.

Web repositories also contain a list of mobile audio games that are accessible for people who are blind. Papa Sangre, Blind Legend, VBHangman, and GBraille Asteroids are examples of these audio games. Their download is available at the virtual stores of Android and iOs. For instance, Papa Sangre is an audio-based navigation game with a terror thematic. Gamers walk or run by tapping left and right on the bottom of the screen. Sliding gestures on the screen will turn the user's virtual "avatar". The game plays 3D audio cues for directional guidance. It is available for both Android and iOS. Another example is VBHangman, in which the user plays the game and tries to determine what word is dictated, given its length and a limited number of guesses [18].

3   Methodology

The methodology followed in this research followed four phases: Analysis of Accessibility Guidelines, Proposal of Guidelines for Audiogames, Development of Evaluation Instrument, and Evaluation of Audiogames. The starting point of the work was the search and studying of papers concerning accessibility in both digital and audio games. This study also includes the investigation of the main accessibility guidelines for digital games. In the beginning, the goal was to find a guide or group of patterns, such as WCAG 2.0, that could help in the design of mobile games for people with visual impairment. However, the first searches and readings indicated an inconsistency in the guidelines and recommendations, which led to the decision of carrying this research out.

The research second stage consisted of the study, classification, and compilation of the guidelines and recommendations. We focus on the accessibility features for people who are blind. We adapted these guidelines for an evaluation performed, focused on the most relevant accessibility characteristics provided in mobile audiogames for people with visual impairment and blindness. Based on this study, we identified ten recommendations that can be considered recurrent or minimal requirements to meet in the design and development of a mobile audiogame. We then create an evaluation instrument that allows the assessment of these recommendations in mobile audio games. This guide was used throughout the whole process of design and development of an accessible audio game. In the fourth part of the study, we applied the instrument in the evaluation of ten mobile audiogames (e.g., Nebula, Inquisitor, GBraille Hangman). This evaluation was held with the assistance of two individuals who were blind. The results and their analysis are shown in Sect. 4.

3.1   Accessibility Guidelines Investigation

In the first phase of this research, we gathered and studied six collections of guidelines:

- Accessibility in Games: Motivations and Approaches - IGDA (International Game Developers Association) [14];
- Game Accessibility Guidelines *Top Ten* - IGDA GASIG - Game Accessibility Special Interest Group [14];
- Guidelines for the development of entertaining software for people with multiple learning disabilities - UPS Project [23];
- Guidelines for the Development of Accessible Computer Games - Roland Ossmann [20];
- Blind Computer Games: guidelines for building blind-accessible computer games - J. Bannick [15];
- A Pratical Guide to Game Acessibility (Includification) - The AbleGames Foundation [17].

These guides present - through similar structure and points of view - recommendations and accessibility guidelines focused specifically on the assessment and support for the development of accessible digital games. These six guidelines are the most cited by the game development community.

The guidelines deal with the relevance of game items that maximize the accessibility, considering aspects concerning the user, the game theme, and the characteristics of the interactions. For example, the IGDA Game Access SIG (Game Accessibility Special Interest Group) proposed, in 2004, nineteen accessibility guidelines. The group derived the guidelines from a research of 20 accessible games. Most games included applications for blind users, individual with a motor disability, and games for users who are hearing impaired.

Norwegian organization Medialt has sponsored the UPS project aim at creating guidelines to adjust existing games to become more accessible to a larger audience. They propose a set of 34 accessibility recommendations.

A group of developers, specialists, and scholars published two guidelines: the *Guidelines for the Development of Accessible Computer Games* and *Blind Computer Games: guidelines for building blind-accessible computer games*. In both cases, the authors gathered efforts to increase the number of recommendations available. The last guide studied, called Includification, brings definitions and approaches that developers must implement to promote accessibility in digital games. They propose guidelines for the general themes of visual impairment, cognitive disability, motor disability, and hearing impairment. English organizations created a Web portal[3] with an illustrated version of the Includification guidelines.

3.2   Top 10 Recommendations

There is a variety of possible approaches that game designers and developers can follow considering the main items in accessibility that are applicable for mobile platforms. The set of recommendations in the guidelines studied deals with all types of disabilities. However, our focus is game accessibility for gamers who are blind. To do so, we made a simplification of the recommendations having in mind the assessment of mobile audio games. Hence, after the study of the six guidelines, we identified the ten most relevant game accessibility characteristics that must be provided for gamers who are blind.

These ten recommendations can be considered recurrent or minimal requirements to meet in the design and development of a mobile audio game. These recommendations contains simple considerations and design decisions that apply to most game mechanics. However, these are the recommendations that benefit the biggest number of players and are easy to implement if they are taken into account since the Game Design Document (GDD) creation. The following list detail each of the ten recommendations and tests to identify their correct application:

– **R1 - Game level and speed adjustments.** The game should allow players to choose between a wide range of challenges and speeds.

---

[3] http://gameaccessibilityguidelines.com.

Goal: People might benefit from slower and easier versions to adjust the game, adapting to their needs.

Test: Does the game allow these settings to be changed? If yes, can the title be adjusted to a mode in which is much harder to fail or to be hit?

- **R2 - Free exploration and tutorial modes.** The game should offer a way in which the player can explore the game without failures. Another possibility includes a tutorial mode that explains how to play the title.

Goal: This game feature helps in the understanding, control adjustment, skill development and to offer a fun way for those who interact with the standard game while playing alone.

Test: Is the game free exploration mode easy to enable? Does it have attractive commands to catch the players attention? Is the player free to try and learn on his/hers own pace?

- **R3 - High contrast interfaces.** The game should offer high contrast color schemes. Essential items and the menu selection must follow the same approach. Also, the game should allow background deactivation in 2D/3D games.

Goal: It increases the visibility of text items that are important for players who are visual impaired.

Test: First, the tester should run the game on a low-resolution computer screen. Is it possible to read and navigate by its menu or is it too difficult? If it is hard to navigate, the game is not following this recommendation correctly.

- **R4 - Friendly design for people with color blindness.** Game developers should avoid color combinations that are hard or impossible for a person with color blindness to distinguish.

Goal: The goal is to allow access to information in all color shapes and also offer alternative configurations to transmit the meaning of the color combination.

Test: How is the color information in the display? Are only two colors being used to give options? Is there a color palette showing all colors in a way that allows color-blind people to change it?

- **R5 - Accessible menu.** Game interface customization should be ease to access by people who are blind. For this, the menu should have fast starting modes, alternative texts, and navigation for the menu entry (e.g., text-to-speech and a description of symbols).

Goal: For a game with a complex interface, the goal is to provide a simplified interface that shows only the most common used controls. All the resources will continue available. However, they are hidden from the users in a first place.

Test: Do the players face difficulties when navigation through the menu? Is there a way to access most of the game functions in 3 menu options or less?

– **R6 - Standard presentation of texts.** Game messages and labels should be compatible with screen readers. Gamers should be able to use simple gestures to access the majority of the text messages, which should be read by the screen readers. When the game shows a visual message, it should be recommended to present an equivalent audio message to indicate what has been done.
Goal: Users with visual impairment will be able to identify and understand texts presented in the game.

Test: Use a screen reader provided by the mobile operational system or one that is compatible with it. Are the items and descriptions read correctly by the tool?

– **R7 - Speech-generating features.** This recommendation is a derivation of R6. The main idea is to use text-to-speech technologies to improve the user immersion. Texts can be presented in different languages and be correctly read by game-integrated voice synthesizers, even there is no screen reader installed.

Goal: R7 allows users with visual impairment situate themselves in the game dialogues and the sequence of narrative texts.

Test: Navigate through the game with a personal with no visual impairment and an another one with visual impairment. Do the navigation of all control combinations properly return visual and hearing feedback for both users?

– **R8 - Accessibility resources easily found.** Developers should implement features that assure easy access to accessibility configurations. Gamers should access and understand in the first contact with the game where are the accessibility features (e.g., color customization, audio cues enabling, additional audio feedback).

Goal: The goal is to permit players to know that they will be capable of enjoying the game before purchasing the title or start playing. This information must be mainly in the dissemination platforms of these games on the web, for example.

Test: Is there a way to quickly check the accessibility features, options and requirements of the game right in the first contact with the title?

– **R9 - Game tutorials and help.** Developers should hierarchize game tutorial and helps to guide the gamer through the help items, providing feedback. This resource would be useful for almost all players, especially, for people with learning disabilities that have low attention span or lack lasting attention to focus on a long instruction guide.

Goal: Following R9, the game provides the players with objective indicators assisting the players in situations of bewilderment.

Test: Is the player forced to read long information passages? Can he properly continue with his game through fast orientation?

– **R10 - Orientation.** Players should be able to use the physical keyboard or the touchscreen to guide the avatar in many directions and receive feedback about its direction. For example, using the sliding gesture to the right the avatar will turn its face to the right in a standard angle (e.g., turn 45 degrees). An audio feedback will be played describing the users orientation (e.g., North).

Goal: To guide specific avatar movements and receive orientation feedback.

Test: Is there a way to offer the player to be guided based on the cardinal points, for example?

4 Accessibility Assessment Instrument for Mobile Audio Games

From the top ten recommendations, we created an assessment instrument to help game developers in the testing of the mobile audio games. The questionnaire comprises a total of 32 questions distributed in six categories. These categories are inspired by WCAG 2.0, which is a W3C stable and referenceable technical standard for accessibility assessment. The six categories are:

[C1]-**Alternative texts:** The game mobile interface should provide textual alternatives for non-textual content. The idea is to map visual elements to speech and textual messages. This additional information should be available as text, aiming the proper use of screen reader programs that provide a sound return of textual information.

– [C2]-**Adaptability:** Game interfaces and contents should be adaptable according to the mobile device characteristics. So, they could be presented in many forms on the mobile devices (for example, in minor resolution or only audio), without losing essential information.

– [C3]-**Atmosphere:** Navigating in the mobile interface, players should be able to comfortably situate themselves in the scenery from the content, including through separate sound return.

– [C4]-**Operability:** Interface, Interaction, and navigation components should be operable, easy to understand, and intervene by players. Fast start options should be included for avoiding multiple levels of information overloading the players. Players should have appropriate times of interaction with game features.

– [C5]-**Configuration Facility:** the game should allow the player to adjust, simplify, and change controls and game settings. Language issues, screen resolution, speech resource, screen readers, volume, among others features should be properly addressed in this category.

- **[C6]-Assistance and Tutoring:** Provide documentation, tutorial mode, and help features to assist the player in the understanding of the gameplay.

All 32 questions are classified as **A**, **AA** and **AAA**. Level attendance suggests effort in support of game accessibility features for people who are blind.

- **Level A**- 17 questions: The conformity level A (minimal level) comprises satisfactory criteria that could be implemented with low or moderate technical effort. This level includes most of the part of game mechanics and interface.
- **Level AA**- 12 questions: The conformity level AA guarantees that the game attends a more accurate list of successful criteriums. However, the technical effort to implement these features may be high. Some mobile devices and platforms may not support these features, which implies in an extra implementation effort.
- **Level AAA**- 3 questions: AAA ensures that the game contemplates satisfactory criteria that widen game experience. However, meeting the criteria is so specific that recommendations apply to a limited game list. This level will not be easily accomplished by games targeting a large audience, being suitable for games developed focusing on a particular player profile (e.g., totally blind users).

We attribute one point for all 32 questions. But, each level (A, AA or AAA) has a distinct weight, being 3 to level A, and 2 to level AA, and 1 to AAA. In this sense, the assessment can attribute to level A (the most critical one) a maximum of 51 points, level AA 24 points, and level AAA 3 points. Therefore, a game can reach the maximum of 80 points. Then, a game is going to be evaluated as *insufficient* when the score is from 0 to 39 points; *unsatisfactory*, when is from 40 to 60 points; and *good* when the score is from 61 to 78 points.

The assessment instrument is available on https://goo.gl/np7PrR.

5   Mobile Audio Game Evaluations

The final step of our study consisted of accessibility tests by using the proposed assessment instrument. Tests have evaluated ten audio games aiming at better refine the investigation of accessibility features found in mobile audio games recurrently. The assessment also tried to measure the conformity level of these applications according to the top ten game accessibility recommendations. Tables 1 and 2 show a summary of the evaluation results.

5.1   Users

We carried out the evaluation process with the assistance of two individuals who were visually impaired and collaborated with the research group. One user was 26 years old, and the other was 32 years old. Both users receive scholarships and work in the IFCE research center. They assist accessibility tests of the prototypes and software developed by the research group. They have great knowledge and experience using touchscreen mobile devices.

5.2   Audio Games

We evaluated eight distinct games and two versions of a ninth game:

- **Mine Sweeper Accessible - BFG.** The aim of this freeware game[4] is to find and mark all the hidden bombs on the game board map. The game includes many accessibility resources and uses tactile feedback for interaction (screen vibration). Blind Faith Games has developed this arcade game for Android Platform 2.2 or superior versions.
- **Golf Accessible - BFG.** This arcade and freeware game[5] works on Android 2.2 or superior versions. It provides a Golf game experience in an accessible format. The Blind Faith Games has created a Golf game with many game modes and levels.
- **Zarodnik - BFG.** The aim of this strategy game[6] is to collect rewards while defending and avoiding an attack from an ocean monster. Also developed by Blind Faith Games, this freeware Android game uses audio effects by implementing 3D binaural sound, and it also provides tactile feedback during the game interaction.
- **GBraille HangMan v3.0 and 3.1 - GREat Lab.** Its an educational quiz game based on the hangman game[7]. It runs on Android 4.0 and uses GBraille Keyboard data entry. The game requires a previous installation of a voice synthesizer for its full functioning (e.g., eSpeak or Acapela). GBraille Hangman Version 3.1 has added new game features, corrected some accessibility problems, and included more language options.
- **Nebula.** Gray Company developed this action and strategy game[8] for iOS. Nebula has an arcade style of spatial battles. It targets as players both people with or without visual impairment. Players need to trust their hearing to move forward and win. The game also offers a multiplayer mode.
- **Inquisitor Audio Game Adventure.** An inquisitor, Eymerich, is called to investigate an unclear case of heresy, which can reveal a new face of Evil. The game is available for both Android and iOS platforms[9]. It can be played by blind, myopic, visually impaired, and sighted people.
- **Flarestar.** The mission is to discover Icarus spaceships, fly to explore deep space, avoiding collisions, fighting training drones, and trained strikers. Audiogame.it developed this arcade game[10] for iOS 8.1.
- **GBraille Asteroids v.6.0 - GREat Lab.** The goal of the game[11] is to practices Braille characters by using a Braille-based virtual keyboard. In this battle arcade game, players are in a spacecraft and have to avoid hits from

---

[4] https://play.google.com/store/Apps/details?id=es.eucm.blindfaithgames.
minesweeepe.
[5] https://play.google.com/store/apps/details?id=es.eucm.blindfaithgames.golfgame.
[6] https://play.google.com/store/apps/details?id=es.eucm.blindfaithgames.zarodnik.
[7] https://play.google.com/store/apps/details?id=com.gbraille.forca.
[8] http://www.applevis.com/forum/ios-gaming/nebula.
[9] http://www.eymerich.it/index.php?center=audiogame.
[10] http://www.applevis.com/apps/ios/games/flarestar.
[11] https://play.google.com/store/apps/details?id=com.gbraille.asteroids.

asteroids. To do so, users must destroy the asteroids by firing missiles. To trigger them, the user uses gestures on the screen that correspond to the writing of Braille characters.

- **Papa Sangre II - the museum of memories.** This paid iOS app is a first person adventure game[12]. The player is in a posthumous world and the game atmosphere makes him access memories to evolve. He has to find a way back to the living world. For this, the player explores a museum of memories, the Papa Sangre's Museum, a place where his existence depends on the knowledge of the living world. In the museum, there is a danger of being lost forever as a spirit without purpose or memories of his origin.

5.3   Materials

Users have played the games in two mobile devices: (i) Apple iPhone 5 S with iOS 8.13 system, and (ii) Motorola MOTO G 2nd generation with Android 4.4.4 operational system (KitKat).

5.4   Procedures

Section 5.2 describes in detail all the games evaluated. They are available in Web repositories, such as Audiogames.net, Grey Company, Google Play Store, Universal Access, and Audiogame.it. We selected these games based on their popularity. We also evaluated three games developed by our research group.

The evaluation lasted four days. Each user has tested two games per day, and in the fourth day, they evaluate the last one. Each game evaluation section lasted for 50 min. One assistant filled the assessment instrument according to the answers given by each user.

5.5   Results

Tables 1 and 2 present an evaluation summary, as well as the scores obtained for each game. Results indicate that only two from a total of ten games have a right level of accessibility meeting the top ten recommendations. Two games were considered unsatisfactory and three presented insufficient results mainly concerning questions of level A, which are those indispensable in the implementation of game accessibility features.

Test results also indicate the categories of recommendations identified as critical for each game. The most common errors are related to operability category [C4]. Minor errors are related to Alternative Texts [C1]. It means that these ten games have basic accessibility levels, but features that are more complex are not receiving the same attention.

---

[12] https://itunes.apple.com/br/app/papa-sangre/id407536885.

Table 1. Accessibility evaluation results - Part 1

Game	Critical Categories	Score	Evaluation
BFG- Mine Sweeper	[C4] Configuration presents problems related to memorization and lack of agility when accessing rules, commands, and game objectives; [C5] Some Incompatibilities with screen readers;	Level A: 12 pts (x3) Level AA: 7 pts (x2) Level AAA: 2 pts (x1) Final Score: 52 pts	Unsatisfactory
Accessible Golf	[C2]- The game has simple versions of menu options and interfaces, but it not has options for enabled/disabled them; [C3]- The audio descriptions of some commands are not executing correctly;	Level A: 8 pts (x3) Level AA: 6 pts (x2) Level AAA: 1 pt (x1) Final Score: 37 pts	Insufficient
Zarodinik BFG	[C4] Time to read, understand, and use content is insufficient [C4] In order to start a new game, user must navigate through multiple levels of screens and menus	Level A: 8 pts (x3) Level AA 6 pts (x2) Level AAA: 2 pts (x1) Final score: 38 pts	Insufficient
GBraille HangMan v.3.0	[C3] Sound feedback is not enough to indicate all essential information for the understanding of the game scenes. Audio descriptions are not sufficient to orient the navigation in menus and input/output screens; [C6] The game does not have a tutorial mode.	Level A: 8 pts (x3) Level AA: 6 pts (x2) Level AAA: 1 pts (x1) Final Score: 37pts	Insufficient
GBraille HangMan v.3.1	Gbraille Hangman 3.1 improved some interaction problems (e.g., navigation, menu, audio feedback, speed) of the 3.0 version, but the game is still not meeting [C4] and [C6] adequately.	Level A: 11 pts (x3) Level AA: 6 pts (x2) Level AAA: 1 pts (x1) Final Score: 46 pts.	Unsatisfactory

Table 2. Accessibility evaluation results - Part 2

Game	Critical Categories	Score	Evaluation
Nebula	[C2] Low vision players need options that widen the size or the contrast of elements; [C4] The game has some problems with screen readers settings. It does not warn users whether the screen reader is disabled or enabled;	Level A: 15 pts (x3) Level AA: 10 pts (x2) Level AAA: 2 pts (x1) Final Score: 67 pts.	Good
GBraille Asteroids	[C3] Sound feedback is not enough to indicate all essential information during game sessions; [C6] The game does not have a tutorial mode.	Level A: 14 pts (x3) Level AA: 6 pts (x2) Level AAA: 1 pts (x1) Final score: 56 pts	Unsatisfactory
Inquisitor	[C2] Low vision players need options that widen the size or the contrast of elements;	Level A: 14 pts (x3) Level AA: 9 pts (x2) Level AAA: 2 pts (x1) Final Score: 62 pts	Good
Flarestar	[C5] Incompatibilities and configuration problems with screen readers; [C1] Many alternative texts are absent;	Level A: 13 pts (x3) Level AA: 8 pts (x2) Level AAA: 2 pts (x1) Final Score: 57 pts	Unsatisfactory
Papa Sangre II	[C5] Incompatibilities and configuration problems with screen readers; [C1] Some alternative texts are absent;	Level A: 16 pts (x3) Level AA: 12 pts (x2) Level AAA: 2 pts (x1) Final Score: 74 pts	Good

6   Final Considerations

The focus of this paper was a preliminary proposal of structuration and organization of the main guidelines of accessibility for audio games in mobile platforms. As the first contribution, the research produced a simplified list of ten accessibility recommendations focused on gamers who are blind. Second, we offer a WCGA-style manual test instrument to assess these recommendations in mobile audio games.

We implemented an initial evaluation with ten mobile audio games. The results suggest a low level of accessibility in a part of the mobile audio games investigated. From this research, we noted how complex is to trace profiles or evaluation patterns for accessible games in the mobile context because of the mobile device heterogeneity. For this study, we did not take into account the many device screen sizes, the standard gestures on the touchscreen, and also the use of device sensors in the games. Recommendations to deal with these issues should be further investigated.

The tested samples of this work are not sufficient to obtain more precise information about the mobile gaming scenery. Due to this factor, we consider this as an initial study on the identification of necessary refinements for the group of proposed guidelines and recommendations. However, the study provides evidence that the instruments and compiled recommendations are a good starting point for game designers and developers seeking a way to make their games more accessible in mobile platforms.

Acknowledgments. This paper is a partial result of the project GBraille supported by CNPq (MCT/CNPq 14/2013 - Universal) under grant number 484255/2013-4. It was also partially funded by the Program of Scientific Cooperation called STIC-AmSud-CAPES program/CONICYT/MAE. The sponsored project is entitled Knowing and Interacting while Gaming for the Blind (KIGB), 2014.

The research was also funded by the Fondo Nacional de Desarrollo Científico y Tecnológico (FONDECYT), Fondecyt 1150898; and the Basal Funds for Centers of Excellence, FB0003 project, from the Associative Research Program of CONICYT. Mobile applications have been developed with the support of MCTI-SECIS/CNPq No. 84/2013 - Assistive Technology project, registered under grant number 458825/2013-1.

References

1. Visual impairment and blindness fact sheets. World Health Organization (2014). http://www.who.int/mediacentre/factsheets/fs282/en/. Accessed Sep 2015
2. Antona, M., Stephanidis, C. (eds.): UAHCI 2015. LNCS, vol. 9177. Springer, Cham (2015). doi:10.1007/978-3-319-20684-4
3. Archambault, D., Ossmann, R., Gaudy, T., Miesenberger, K.: Computer games and visually impaired people. Upgrade **8**(2), 43–53 (2007)
4. Atkinson, M.T., Gucukoglu, S., Machin, C.H., Lawrence, A.E.: Making the mainstream accessible: redefining the game. In: Proceedings of the 2006 ACM SIGGRAPH Symposium on Videogames, pp. 21–28. ACM (2006)
5. Atkinson, M.T., Gucukoglu, S., Machin, C.H.C., Lawrence, A.E.: Making the mainstream accessible: what's in a game? In: Miesenberger, K., Klaus, J., Zagler, W.L., Karshmer, A.I. (eds.) ICCHP 2006. LNCS, vol. 4061, pp. 380–387. Springer, Heidelberg (2006). doi:10.1007/11788713_57
6. Attewell, J.: Mobile technologies and learning. London: Learning and Skills Development Agency 2(4) (2005)
7. Beksa, J., Fizek, S., Carter, P.: Audio Games: Investigation of the Potential Through Prototype Development. In: Biswas, P., Duarte, C., Langdon, P., Almeida, L. (eds.) A Multimodal End-2-End Approach to Accessible Computing. HIS, pp. 211–224. Springer, London (2015). doi:10.1007/978-1-4471-6708-2_11
8. da Araújo, M.C.C., Silva, A.R.S., Darin, T.G.R., de Castro, E.L., Andrade, R.M.C., de Lima, E.T., Sánchez, J., de Castro Filho, J.A., Viana, W.: Design and usability of a braille-based mobile audiogame environment. In: Ossowski [21], pp. 232–238. http://doi.acm.org/10.1145/2851613.2851701
9. Cheiran, J.F.P.: Jogos inclusivos: diretrizes de acessibilidade para jogos digitais (2007). http://www.lume.ufrgs.br/handle/10183/77230

10. Cheiran, J.F.P., Nedel, L., Pimenta, M.S.: Inclusive games: a multimodal experience for blind players. In: Proceedings of the 2011 Brazilian Symposium on Games and Digital Entertainment, SBGAMES 2011, pp. 164–172. IEEE Computer Society, Washington, DC (2011). http://dx.doi.org/10.1109/SBGAMES.2011.24

11. Cheiran, J.F.P., Pimenta, M.S.: "eu tambem quero jogar!": Reavaliando as praticas e diretrizes de acessibilidade em jogos. In: Proceedings of the 10th Brazilian Symposium on on Human Factors in Computing Systems and the 5th Latin American Conference on Human-Computer Interaction, IHC+CLIHC 2011, pp. 289–297. Brazilian Computer Society, Porto Alegre, Brazil (2011). http://dl.acm.org/citation.cfm?id=2254436.2254485

12. Csapó, Á., Wersényi, G., Nagy, H., Stockman, T.: A survey of assistive technologies and applications for blind users on mobile platforms: a review and foundation for research. J. Multimodal User Interfaces **9**(4), 275–286 (2015). http://dx.doi.org/10.1007/s12193-015-0182-7

13. Grabski, A., Toni, T., Zigrand, T., Weller, R., Zachmann, G.: Kinaptic - techniques and insights for creating competitive accessible 3d games for sighted and visually impaired users. In: 2016 IEEE Haptics Symposium (HAPTICS), pp. 325–331, April 2016

14. IGDA, I.G.D.A.: Accessibility in Games: Motivations and Approaches (2004). http://archives.igda.org/accessibility/IGDA_Accessibility_WhitePaper.pdf

15. J. Blind, B.: Computer Games: guidelines for building blind-accessible computer games (2012). http://www.blindcomputergames.com/guidelines/guidelines.html

16. de Lima, L.S.: A produção de subjetividade nos jogos eletrônicos. Ph.D. thesis, Pontifícia Universidade Católica de São Paulo (2011)

17. Mark, C.B., Spohn, S.D.: A pratical guide to game acessibility (2012). http://www.includification.com/AbleGamers_Includification.pdf

18. Milne, L.R., Bennett, C.L., Ladner, R.E.: Vbghost: a braille-based educational smartphone game for children. In: Proceedings of the 15th International ACM SIGACCESS Conference on Computers and Accessibility, ASSETS 2013, pp. 75:1–75:2. ACM, New York (2013). http://doi.acm.org/10.1145/2513383.2513396

19. Morelli, T., Foley, J., Folmer, E.: Vi-bowling: a tactile spatial exergame for individuals with visual impairments. In: Proceedings of the 12th International ACM SIGACCESS Conference on Computers and Accessibility, ASSETS 2010, pp. 179–186. ACM, New York (2010). http://doi.acm.org/10.1145/1878803.1878836

20. Ossmann, R., Miesenberger, K.: Guidelines for the development of accessible computer games. In: Miesenberger, K., Klaus, J., Zagler, W.L., Karshmer, A.I. (eds.) ICCHP 2006. LNCS, vol. 4061, pp. 403–406. Springer, Heidelberg (2006). doi:10.1007/11788713_60

21. Ossowski, S. (ed.): Proceedings of the 31st Annual ACM Symposium on Applied Computing, Pisa, Italy, 4–8 April 2016. ACM (2016). http://doi.acm.org/10.1145/2851613

22. Pereira, J.C., Rodrigues, M.E., Campos, H.O., Amorim, P.R.d.S.: Exergames como alternativa para o aumento do dispêndio energético: uma revisão sistemática. Revista Brasileira de Atividade Física & Saúde **17**(5), 332–340 (2013)

23. Project, U.: Guidelines for the development of entertaining software for people with multiple learning disabilities (2012). http://www.medialt.no/rapport/entertainment_guidelines

24. Reid, L.G., Snow-Weaver, A.: Wcag 2.0: a web accessibility standard for the evolving web. In: Proceedings of the 2008 International Cross-disciplinary Conference on Web Accessibility (W4A), pp. 109–115. ACM (2008)

25. Rutter, R., Lauke, P.H., Waddell, C., Thatcher, J., Henry, S.L., Lawson, B., Kirk-patrick, A., Heilmann, C., Burks, M.R., Regan, B., et al.: Web Accessibility: Web Standards and Regulatory Compliance. Apress, Berkeley (2006)
26. Sánchez, J., Darin, T.G.R., Andrade, R.M.C.: Multimodal videogames for the cognition of people who are blind: trends and issues. In: Antona, M., Stephanidis [2], pp. 535–546. Springer (2015). http://dx.doi.org/10.1007/978-3-319-20684-4_52
27. Sánchez, J., Flores, H.: Audiomath: Blind children learning mathematics through audio. Int. J. Disabil. Human Dev. 4(4), 311–316 (2005)
28. Sánchez, J., Mascaró, J.: Audiopolis, navigation through a virtual city using audio and haptic interfaces for people who are blind. In: Stephanidis, C. (ed.) UAHCI 2011. LNCS, vol. 6766, pp. 362–371. Springer, Heidelberg (2011). doi:10.1007/978-3-642-21663-3_39
29. SixToStart: Zombies, Run! (2015). https://www.zombiesrungame.com/
30. Wake, J.D.: Mobile, location-based games for learning: Developing, deploying and evaluating mobile game technology in education. The University of Bergen (2013)
31. Yuan, B.: Towards Generalized Accessibility of Video Games for the Visually Impaired. Ph.D. thesis, University of Nevada, Reno, NV, USA (2009)
32. Yuan, B., Folmer, E., Harris, Jr., F.C.: Game accessibility: a survey. Univers. Access Inf. Soc. 10(1), 81–100 (2011). http://dx.doi.org/10.1007/s10209-010-0189-5
33. Yuan, B., Folmer, E., Harris Jr., F.C.: Game accessibility: a survey. Univ. Access Inf. Soc. 10(1), 81–100 (2011). http://dx.doi.org/10.1007/s10209-010-0189-5

Read It Aloud to Me

Sergio Celaschi[1(✉)], Mauricio Sol Castro[2], and Sidney Pinto da Cunha[1]

[1] Centro de Tecnologia da Informação Renato Archer, Campinas, Brazil
{sergio.celaschi,sidney.cunha}@cti.gov.br
[2] Fundação de Apoio à Capacitação em Tecnologia da Informação,
Rod. D.Pedro I, km 143,6, Campinas, SP 13069-901, Brazil
https://www.cti.gov.br

Abstract. The universal design applied to assistive technologies can help visually impaired person perform some day-to-day tasks as well as everybody. With this aim, the present work focuses on development of photo-to-speech instruments for the visually impaired person. It allows the user to hear text typed on a sheet of paper or written/posted on a wall. To achieve that aim a set of image capture and processing frameworks such as Optical Character Recognition (OCR) and Text to Speech Synthesis (TTS) were integrated. The first versions of the OCR based speech synthesis systems were developed for our native language, Portuguese. A preliminary desktop version was designed under Windows OS, and a version for mobile devices was developed as an application for Android devices. In this paper, we summarize efforts to develop and test a desktop and a mobile version of autonomous photo-to-speech instruments for the visually impaired. The project consisted of integration of selected components, and the CPU applications governing several functionalities: capture of images by the CCD camera; image preprocessing; OCR framework for text recognition; and finally the process of TTS, producing a synthesized voice.

Keywords: Assistive technology · Text reading · Speech synthesis · OCR · Photo-to-speech · Blind · Visually impaired · Universal design

1 Introduction

Many software and applications are especially dedicated to visually impaired person, some that improve accessibility like Talkback (Android) and Voice Over (IOS), and screen readers. Others example are: ZoomReader (iOS) [1], o CapturaTalk [2], Google Translator [3], LookTel Money Reader [4] (Money reader-iOS), TapTapSee (iOS) [5] that identify objects to blind person out loud, a Brazilian Portuguese TTS Alcance-CPqD [6], helping blind person to access a lot of smart phone services. See the appendix A, for a list of applications. The present paper describes the development of photo-to-speech instruments for visually impaired persons [7] with the following prerequisites: to be free of charge to users in general, easy to install and easy to use, available locally in the country, useful and very understandable in Brazilian Portuguese, locally processed

M. Antona and C. Stephanidis (Eds.): UAHCI 2017, Part II, LNCS 10278, pp. 260–268, 2017.
DOI: 10.1007/978-3-319-58703-5_19

without internet and cloud connections, low memory space requirements and compatible with most common used operational systems such as windows, IOS and Android. Specifically, this engine gives access to printed information, leading images of printed texts to audio voice. It allows the user to hear text typed on a sheet of paper or written/posted on a wall, in outdoors and billboards. The application has the following sequence: capture of images by the CCD camera of A4 printed text, preprocess the image, optical character recognition with an OCR - Optical Character Recognition software [8], extraction of the text [12], and synthesized voice generation with a TTS-text-to-speech application.

2   Used Technologies

2.1   Image Acquisition

The specifications of the digital camera are mandatory, which require mobile devices with 6–8 Megapixels resolution, main camera to capture images from an A4 size paper. The quality and resolution of the image are crucial for the pre-processing stage and character recognition. The OCR efficiency requires roughly up to 10×10 pixels per character. The preprocessing stage improves the overall performance of the text recognition providing feedback to the OCR framework. Finally the TTS framework provides the audio stream to the internal Digital Signal Processing-DSP unit to drive the speakers. The text classification is a binary output in which an input text image is considered readable or non-readable without any character recognition. The OCR will be described in the next subsection. Figure 1 shows a flowchart of steps in the process, as taking a picture of the document, preprocessing as binarization, some small corrections in the skews, submitting to the OCR, calling the voice synthesizer, and the output to user.

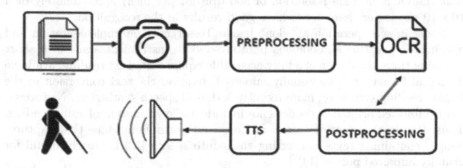

Fig. 1. Flowchart of software operation.

2.2   Optical Character Recognition Tesseract

The Tesseract technology of Optical Character Recognition (OCR) does part of the task. It enables the extraction of texts from image data. Tesseract began as a PhD research project in HP Labs, Bristol. Today, Tesseract is an open-source OCR engine distributed by Google Inc. This technology has been used in photographed documents which one can play and listen to the content in audio formats, using TTS - resembling the spoken form of the same text, as read by a native. Well established in the field of computer science, early approaches to language research focused on automating the analysis of the linguistic structure of language. This research also relied on developing basic technologies such as fast digital processors, multi megapixel CCD cameras, OCR, machine translation, speech synthesis, among others. Nowadays, such tools are employed in real-world applications, creating spoken dialogue systems and speech-to-speech translation engines. Google Translate - GT is one such a practical application. It is a multilingual machine for text translation, speech, or real-time text images, from one language into another. It offers a web interface, and cloud interfaces for Android and IOS mobiles. It has one requirement: the photo-to-speech GT functionality is not autonomous, but depends on cloud processing. To improve system quality performance [9], a preprocessing stage of the image was carried out before submitting it to character recognition. The preprocessing stage improves the overall performance of the text recognition providing feedback to the OCR framework. The preprocessing include the following sequence of operations: color to gray scale transformation - 8 bits/pixel, image "binarization" (1 bit/pixel), image rotation and median filtering. Those image operations used OpenCV functions library.

OpenCV [10] written in optimized C/C++, with multi-core processing and real-time applications is very useful for our software. EmguCV [11] was used as a cross platform to .NET framework to call functions of OpenCV, to capture image of the printed text to be recognized. The Ziggi HD camera employed with 3264×2448 pixels, has resolution enough to recognize the characters. The captured images needs to be rotated to be in portrait position. It was observed that the OCR needs a resolution of 300 dpi(dot per inch) approximately or a 10×10 pixels per character to have good results in the recognition.

Some image operation are done inside Tesseract. The implementation and optimization of this autonomous photo-to-speech instrument aims, in a short period of time, the design of a fully accessible equipment. Text reading, available in digital format, for the visually impaired, requires the text conversion to the Braille reading system or, more recently, a digital speech synthesizer. Nowadays, most published printed works does not include audio versions nor Braille reading. Thus, the development of an autonomous and portable machine that captures images containing texts, converting them into speech [13] is greatly useful for visually impaired person [14].

Figure 2 shows relations, for an A4 paper, of resolutions, width, height and size of images. In our case it is necessary resolutions about 300 dpi, for better recognitions

| Resolution - dpi | A4 paper | 29.7x21 cm | |
	width in pixels	height in pixels	size of image - Mpixels
50	413	584	0.24
75	620	876	0.54
96	793	1122	0.89
150	1240	1753	2.17
200	1654	2338	3.87
300	2481	3507	8.70
600	4962	7014	34.8

Fig. 2. Size of A4 and the image resolution, comparisons.

2.3 Voice Synthesizer

The software application can use the embedded voice synthesizer [15] of the operational system or could use such free screen reader such as NonVisual Desktop Access-NVDA, eSpeak, or Alcance Voice Synthesizer, a Brazilian initiative project including voice synthesizer.

3 Operation and Features

Aiming to be very easy and friendly to use, the app needs few commands to be operated, as seen by the list of commands below. The accessibility of the desktop application version relies fully on the keyboard as follows:

- (1) Return/Enter if the program is in idle mode, triggers a frame capture, and the whole cycle shown in Fig. 1.
- (2) Esc if the program is in idle mode, closes the application - if a speech is playing, it is canceled.
- (3) Left/Right keys decrease/increase speech rate.
- (4) Space pause/resume a speech.
- (5) Bar language choice.

4 Architecture

Figure 3 shows an operation with a stand to fix camera. So, better pictures of the texts can be obtained. In close up photos is necessary to avoid camera shakes. The Fig. 4 below shows the state machine model for a desktop software [17]. Using version for mobiles, to take close-up photos of text, is better to use a stand as shown in figure below. Figure 5 shows a special stand with four legs, designed for mobiles. It has the right distance for picture a A4 text, and the legs could guide the position of the paper.

For example, the accessibility of the mobile previous version operates under the native voice assistant Samsung. One touch on the screen triggers a frame

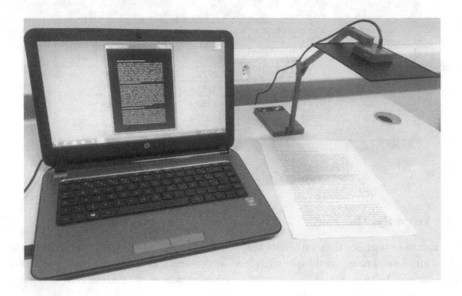

Fig. 3. Desktop configuration, with a camera and adjustable stand.

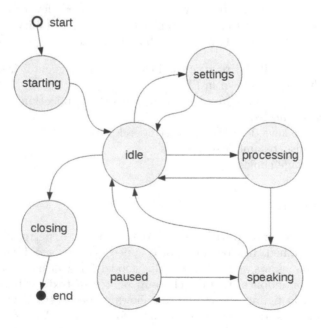

Fig. 4. Architecture - state machine model.

Fig. 5. FourPod - stand for mobile capture - patent pending.

capture, and the whole cycle. The "LETEX" app applies small corrections misalignment for angular position of text columns, up to 30°. The text could be positioned upside-down.

5   Blind Users Review and Performance

5.1   Review

According a reviewer a digital reader like this one has good impact over the users' lives, as in the case of independence and privacy when used with head phones, for example. Independence because the user can digitalize a text or a document alone without any help. The program is easy to open and run, and there are few buttons to push. Also the alignment of the paper is guided by a frame. The user can choose the speed and pitch of the voice synthesizer. Compared to equivalent commercial equipments this one is affordable, using a personal computer and/or mobile devices. In the case of mobile devices it is more useful in reading written characters in signs and outdoors. Although is not so easy to capture sharp photos through mobile caused by the vibrations. So, is better to use a stand as shown to have good text pictures.

5.2   Performance

Summarizing the pros and cons of performance pointed out by users and also observed in the preliminary tests are the following: Fig. 6 shows a two-columns text, that was inverted to negative image, and could be recognized by Tesseract OCR.

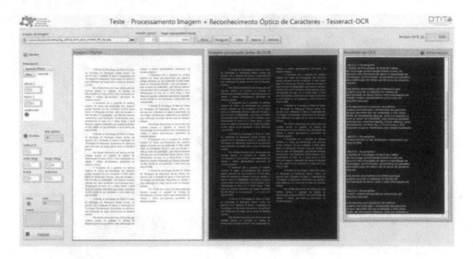

Fig. 6. Two-columns text, that also can be recognized by Tesseract-OCR.

Figure 7 shows results of tests, with a very few errors, and a short elapsed time in the processing, indicating that the project can succeed, and the software is useful for blind persons to use. Following the premises of simplicity, few commands, affordability, few equipment requirements.

Digital Reader	Words/ A4	ASCII/ A4	Preprocessing	OCR-Processing	OCR-speed	OCR-errors	TTS-errors
Model	#	#	elapsed time(s)	elapsed time(s)	words per s	%	%
Prototype	546±48	2741± 186	7±2	21±3	27±3	0,5%	0,5%

Fig. 7. Figure shows some data about performance of the reader.

5.3   Pros

- The software is a direct access to a document after the picture shot.
- With a guide platform it is very easy to align a document to be photographed.
- Its a very simple and intuitive to use and quite cheap to acquire.
- Desktop version is very useful for documents reading and the mobiles version is better to read outdoors, indoor building directions and street signs.
- User can choose the speed of speech and the voice pitch.

5.4 Cons

- It will be practical if users could save the file (not implemented yet).
- It will be useful if the program warns the users about impossibilities and causes of not reading certain documents or texts (not implemented yet).
- Blind users have difficulties in framing an A4 printed paper with a smart phone/mobile.
- Vibrations in the smartphone cause bad images and difficulties in the OCR.
- The mobile version is very useful for outdoors sign reading as compared to document reading.

6 Conclusion

The proof of concept has shown feasibility of the project [18]. It has practical importance mainly for visually impaired persons to access printed matter in general. The independence of connection with internet implies no money waste with data plans for smartphones. The software and application are friendly and very easy to use, with few commands. The version for desktop is better for reading printed texts in A4 format and the version for mobiles is useful for street signs and outdoors.

7 Future Work

The results of the preliminary work with this project has shown the possibility of adding other functionalities like saving the read text in any desired format, even in audio formats. Without enhancing complexity, integrating the Brazilian voice synthesizer, Alcance-CPqD, as the default choice, and voice warns, like "there is no text!", "please realign the paper!".

8 Final Comments

By the end of 2011, the Brazilian federal government created a plan for people with disability. The plan entitled "Living without Limits" [16] has four main branch areas: access to education, health care, social inclusion and accessibility. It involves cooperation of 15 federal agencies, states and municipalities. This project has been supported by one of these Brazilian federal agencies - FINEP, under contract number 01.13.0038.00 coordinated by Funda de Apoio Capacitao a Tecnologia da Informao - Facti. Shown in caption of Fig. 5, the FourPod - stand for mobile capture has a patent pending [19].

Acknowledgments. We have to thank FINEP for the financial support of the project and CTI Renato Archer for providing the supporting infrastructure.

A   Appendix

It is possible to check on the internet the available commercial products. Check the addresses below:

- Sara CE - http://www.freedomscientific.com/Products/LowVision/SARA
- Eye-pal   Solo   -   http://www.freedomscientific.com/Products/Blindness/EyePalSOLO
- Poet Reading Machine - http://www.baum.de/cms/en/poetcompact2/
- LavoiceSolo Reading - https://www.maxiaids.com/
- Zoo-Ex - http://www.abisee.com/Zoom-EX.html
- Magnilink   Voice   -   http://lviamerica.com/products/readingmachine/magnilink-voice

References

1. ZoomText, ZoomReader. http://www.zoomtext.com/products/zoomreader/
2. iansyst Ltd.: CapturaTalk. http://www.capturatalk.com/
3. Google Inc.: Google Tradutor. https://play.google.com/store/apps/details?id=comgoogle.android.apps.translatehl=ptBR
4. LookTel: LookTel Money Reader. http://www.looktel.com/moneyreader
5. Image Searcher Inc.: TapTapSee. http://www.taptapseeapp.com/
6. https://www.cpqd.com.br/solucoes/cpqd-alcance/
7. Netoa, R., Fonseca, N.: Camera reading for visually impaired people. Procedia Technol. **16**, 1200–1209 (2014). In: International Conference on Health and Social Care Information Systems and Technologies - HCIST 2014
8. Smith, R.W.: The extraction and recognition of text from multimedia document images. Ph.D. Thesis, University of Bristol, Bristol (1987)
9. Mithe, R., Indalkar, S., Divekar, N.: Optical character recognition. Int. J. Recent Technol. Eng. (IJRTE) **2**(1), 72–75 (2013). ISSN: 2277-3878
10. Itseez: OpenCV (Open Source Computer Vision). http://www.opencv.org
11. Emgu: Emgu CV. http://www.emgu.com/wiki/index.php/Main
12. GitHub: Tesseract Open source OCR Engine (main repository). https://github.com/tesseract-ocr/tesseract
13. Hirschberg, J., Christopher D.M.: Advances in natural language processing. Sci. Mag. **349**(6245), 261–266 (2015)
14. Rodrigues, A., Montague, K., Nicolau, H., Guerreiro, T.: Gettingsmartphones to talkback: understanding the smartphone adoption process of visually impaired users. In: Proceedings of the 17th International ACM SIGACCESS Conference, ASSETS 2015, Lisbon, pp. 23–32 (2015)
15. Dutoit, T.A.: Short Introduction to Text-to-Speech. Kluwer Academic Publishers, Dordrecht, Boston, London (1997)
16. http://zeroproject.org/policy/brazils-billion-dollar-national-plan-for-inclusive-education/
17. Singla, S.K., Yadav, R.K.: Optical character recognition based speech synthesis system using LabVIEW. J. Appl. Res. Technol. **12**(5), 919–926 (2014)
18. Leitor Digital. https://www.youtube.com/watch?v=SEM6slss2ls
19. Instituto Nacional da Propriedade Industrial, Depsito de pedido nacional de Patente, pedido BR 10 2013 0295515 A2. http://www.inpi.gov.br/

Providing Dynamic Access to Electronic Tactile Diagrams

Tyler Ferro and Dianne Pawluk[(✉)]

Virginia Commonwealth University, Richmond, USA
{ferrot,dtpawluk}@vcu.edu

Abstract. A significant problem for individuals who are blind or visually impaired is the lack of access to graphical information. In this paper, we describe our work on components of a system to make this access available in real-time, on demand, and through effective means. We start by discussing our current work on converting visual diagrams and images into a representation that can be more effectively interpreted by individuals who are blind or visually impaired. We then describe previous and ongoing work in our laboratory on computer I/O devices we are developing to provide the given representation to the user immediately and interactively. Finally, we describe dynamic methods that we have developed to help manage the information presented more effectively given the constraints of the tactile system.

Keywords: Blindness · Visually impaired · Tactile graphics · Assistive technology

1 Introduction

Visually, graphical information is increasingly being used as the sole method for conveying information whether due to the ease of capturing/creating, storing and transmitting digital pictures and other graphics, or the increasing acknowledgement that visual graphics are a more effective method of communicating information than words for the majority of the population (i.e., sighted individuals). In fact, it is estimated that even in current textbooks that over 70% of information is relayed solely in graphical form (Hasty 2007). This has created an enormous obstacle for the more than 25 million individuals who are blind and visually impaired (American Foundation for the Blind website 2011) as there is no effective independent access to graphical information (as with screen readers). This subsequently limits these individuals' advancement, or even placement, in their education and careers (of which only 38% of the more than 18.7 million adults of working age are employed, AFB website 2011), and their independence/quality of life in everyday living. Providing individuals who are blind and visually impaired access to the content of these visual graphics would increase their independence and empower them at work, in school, at home, or at play.

Tactile diagrams are the most common alternate representation of visual graphics. Currently, most of these diagrams are made manually, whether by hand or by using a drawing program, and involve a complex method of development in order to be effectively interpreted by touch. Access to electronic tactile diagrams typically uses

© Springer International Publishing AG 2017
M. Antona and C. Stephanidis (Eds.): UAHCI 2017, Part II, LNCS 10278, pp. 269–282, 2017.
DOI: 10.1007/978-3-319-58703-5_20

specialized microcapsule paper and a heater or a thermoforming machine to "print" the diagram. Some progress has been made in developing computer I/O devices as for vision and audition, but there are currently no affordable commercial devices. Advances in describing information that is normally presented graphically in written text or speech form can be very useful and are currently more accessible than the original graphics themselves. However, the ability to relay novel spatial forms, spatial patterns, and spatial relationships is typically lost when replacing the graphics with words.

Unfortunately, spatial information is usually very important when providing instructions for commercially available devices and machinery (whether for work, school, home, or play) or devices that the user may be developing themselves, whether alone or as part of a team. Photographs are commonly taken in a variety of scientific fields from which measurements, spatial relationships, and descriptions may need to be derived. However, the process of turning these photographs and diagrams into precise word descriptions is typically considered an important skill of the job as opposed to being incidental to it. In addition, diagrams are often used to describe biological organisms, processes, weather patterns, maps, and potentially unfamiliar content that is very difficult to put into words. Furthermore, basic graphs are used extensively in mathematics and science.

Pictures and diagrams are also important in the development of young children. For them, it is difficult to replace pictures with words as their vocabulary is not yet fully developed. In fact, young children acquire a basic vocabulary, as well as basic relational concepts, such as above and below, by looking at pictures. In contrast to the staggering resources for sighted children, there is a shortage of accessible material for children who are blind and visually impaired. This is critical, as serious limitations in the variety of information to which a child is exposed can negatively impact a child's "cognitive, emotional, neurological and physical development" (U.S. Dept. of Health and Human Services 2005).

2 Overview of Approach

An approach to the presentation of graphical information to individuals who are blind or visually impaired needs to be significantly different from that of multi-modal interfaces that include vision. This is not only due to the dominance of vision in multi-modal interfaces but also the extraordinary differences in the information processing capacities, strengths, and weaknesses between the senses. Our laboratory's approach for presenting graphical information primarily focuses on using haptics, taking into account its strengths and weaknesses, as well as the design recommendations and methods used by teachers of the visually impaired (TVIs) for creating tactile graphics for students. In addition, we use cognitive load theory to motivate the use of audio-haptic displays.

As compared to vision, touch has two primary weaknesses that we have taken into account in our approach. First, the spatial resolution of touch is significantly less than that of vision (Loomis et al. 2012). This suggests that spacing between elements should be larger than for vision and that details should be left out of any initial representation. It also suggests that software to provide zooming may help overcome this problem by increasing the size of local areas of the picture. Second, studies that have considered raised line drawings (2D geometric information) have found that the field of view for vision is considerably larger than that of touch. Most work examining this issue has found that the tactile field of view does not extend beyond a single finger (e.g., Loomis et al. 1991). This means that these diagrams are interpreted sequentially, one finger at a time, which is cognitively demanding and has limited access to top-down information processing.

However, the strength of the haptic system is its ability to simultaneously process material properties across multiple fingers (Lederman and Klatzky 1997). Work in our laboratory (Fig. 1 and Sect. 5) also found this to be true for interpreting tactile diagrams, where information needs to be *integrated* to understand what is in the diagram (Burch and Pawluk 2011). In this study, performance in an object identification task did not improve when multiple fingers were used (compared to a single finger) for raised line drawings (solely geometric information). However, performance did increase when texture was utilized for the representation, especially with multiple fingers (Fig. 1c).

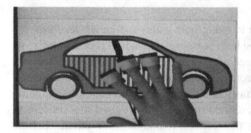

Fig. 1. Left, multi-finger tactile display in our lab with colors on the screen being scanned indicating different textures; Right, single tactile device showing a RGB senor in the middle, pinhole aperture for the sensor on the left, and piezoelectric actuator on the right. (Color figure online)

From the field of making tactile graphics, the most effective method of conveying information through tactile diagrams (Edman 1992), and the one mostly used by TVIs, is to create collages using different types of materials (string, fabric, etc.) to represent different items in the diagram. As with the psychological evidence, this suggests the importance of using texture (material properties) for interpreting tactile diagrams. The resulting tactile diagram also needs to be very different than the original visual diagram, or even an outline drawing, if it is to be used effectively. In addition to simplifying a diagram into objects and object parts, diagram makers are advised (Braille Authority of North America 2010) to: (a) eliminate unnecessary parts, (b) separate a graphic with too many components into sections or layers, (c) determine if objects or shapes need to be exactly reproduced or can be replaced by simpler symbols, (d) enlarge the diagram to fit the page, and (e) reduce clutter (where clutter is defined as when components of the graphics are too close together or not needed for the purpose of the task) (Fig. 2).

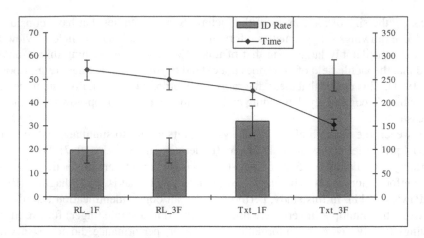

Fig. 2. Results from testing with individuals who are visually impaired; RL = raised line, Txt = textured, 1F = 1 finger, 3F = 3 fingers.

Perhaps the most significant advantage to using both audio and haptic feedback for presenting graphical information is that using both sensory systems is expected to improve performance by reducing cognitive load. Each sensory system is posited to have its own working memory, which can work simultaneously, mostly in parallel with others (Samman and Stanney 2006). Although working memory is not doubled, the amount does significantly increase. Work in our laboratory (described in Sect. 5) have used this concept to improve task performance involving maps that contain relational information, such as geography, weather, agricultural industry, etc. Another potential advantage is that using redundant dimensions in different modalities that are integral could improve retention. This could be beneficial in two cases: when cues are given near threshold and when there are noise sources. However, under typical conditions where neither of these are true, we have found that blind and visually impaired participants disliked this method because they found the feedback to be too much sensory stimulation (Adams et al. 2015).

To provide effective independent access to tactile graphics, one must consider the automation of the whole process and the provision of access tools (Fig. 3). If we imagine a diagram appearing on a page of a document or on a web page, it is desirable that the user who is blind or visually impaired can have access to this information instantaneously. This starts with the need to rapidly convert the visual diagram into an appropriate tactile form. Rather than physically print a tactile diagram, which is expensive and time consuming, computer I/O devices that can instantly and effectively provide access to a virtual tactile (or audio-tactile) diagram is desirable. One advantage of using a computer I/O device to display the information is that we can now provide tools for the user to dynamically interact with the diagram. This is necessary if we want to avoid overwhelming the user with information at a single point in time (which quickly becomes unmanageable through touch), while still providing them access to all the information (in contrast to current techniques, where, to reduce the number of diagrams to make, TVIs remove detail that a teacher, for instance, says is not needed). In the next few sections, we will talk about the work in our lab to address all these different aspects of the needed system.

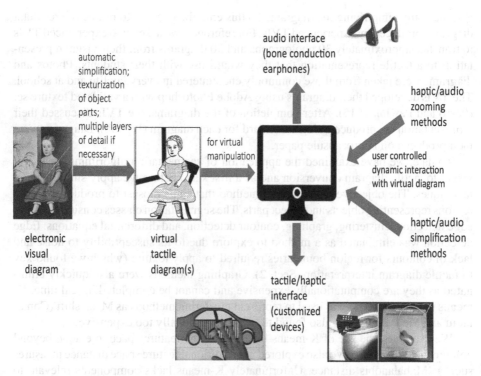

Fig. 3. Dynamic, immediate access to diagrams must start with the conversion of the electronic visual diagram into a form that can be effectively interpreted by individuals who are blind or visually impaired. This could either be a virtual tactile, audio or audio-tactile diagram. This process is much more than simply taking the outline of objects if it is to be effectively used. If one is to provide immediate, refreshable access, effective interfaces need to be developed for the computer. Audio interfaces are already very good, while tactile/haptic interfaces are still in need of improvement. Although not needed for immediate access to diagrams, software algorithms can be beneficial to manage the data being explored.

3 Visual to Tactile Diagram Conversion

Visual to tactile diagram translation is a key first step: If this cannot be done effectively and quickly, then it makes the development of tools for dynamic access a moot point. Several research groups (e.g., Ladner et al. 2005) have developed software algorithms to automatically convert visual graphs, such as line graphs and bar charts, into tactile form. There is both commercial and research software (e.g., Firebird Graphics Editor) to assist in developing graphics more quickly. Way and Banner (1997) have examined the use of basic segmentation techniques (blurring, edge detection, adaptive filtering using K-means segmentation, median filtering, and their combinations) to convert visual greyscale photographs automatically to tactile diagrams.

We are developing a rapid visual to tactile diagram conversion technique which includes more modern segmentation techniques and the additional key step of automatically simplifying the diagram. To this end, the intent is to mimic the resultant diagrams produced by experienced TVIs. For reference, we asked two experienced TVIs to translate approximately 30 photographs and 30 diagrams from their visual representation to a tactile representation that they would use with their students. Photos and diagrams were taken from those commonly encountered in everyday life and at school. The TVIs developed their diagrams using Adobe Photoshop with a validated texture set (Ferro and Pawluk 2015). After completion of the diagrams, the TVIs discussed their representations to produce a single standard for each diagram (Fig. 3b). Diagrams were then produced on microcapsule paper.

To date, we have examined the application of segmentation algorithms for use in visual to tactile diagram conversion and as a first stage before we apply simplification techniques. The objective was to find a method that came closest to producing closed regions representing objects and object parts. The segmentation classes considered were: edge detection, clustering, graphing, contour detection, and differential equations. Edge detection was eliminated as a method to explore due to its susceptibility to noise and lack of contours for region boundaries required to apply texture (which we found key to tactile diagram interpretation, Sect. 2). Graphing methods were also quickly eliminated as they are computationally expensive and cannot be completed in real time. K-means (Luo et al. 2003) was used to represent clustering methods as Mean shift (Comaniciu and Meer 2002) was also found to be computationally too expensive.

We examined the use of K-means by adapting the feature space to extend beyond color to include texture. We also explored nontraditional feature space distance measures such as Mahalanobis distance. Unfortunately K-means lacks components relevant to image space such as proximity. Level-set (e.g., Borx and Wieckert 2004) was used to represent differential equation methods as it builds on the other algorithms and has better speed and accuracy. Previous versions of this method considered pixel intensity, proximity to an intensity gradient, and contour stiffness as features in the algorithm. We added the use of texture gradients and examined different initialization structures, feature space and image space distance measures (Euclidean, dihedral, normalized Euclidean, Mahalanobis), feature weights, gradient extractors (central distance, monogenic signal, probability of boundary), a variety of filter sizes and configurations, and new models we developed for merging/splitting segments for better convergence. For both K-means and Level-set, we extensively explored the parameter settings, using the best-performing sets of parameters in our algorithm comparisons. For contour detection, we used the global probability of a boundary with an oriented watershed transform (gPb-owt) developed at Berkley (Arbelaez et al. 2011) with their optimized parameter set because of its recent success over many other segmentation algorithms in visual segmentation (Fig. 4).

The segmentation techniques described above produce images that display the outlines of the segmented parts. However, as described earlier (Sect. 2), texturing the regions significantly improves performance over the use of raised line drawings. Segments were textured according to the size of the area covered. The largest area, assumed to be background, received no texture and the following 6 largest areas received preselected textures. The algorithm used the same texture set as that used by the TVIs.

The algorithms were compared in performance by using both scoring metrics developed to assess segmentation performance and participant testing with individuals who

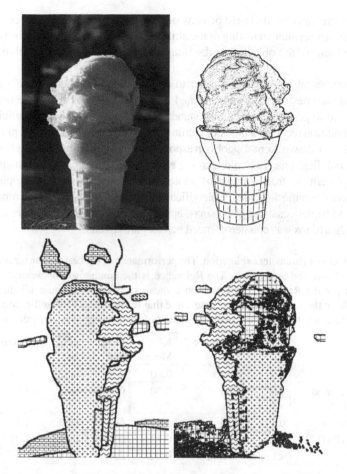

Fig. 4. Clockwise from top left: (a) original electronic photo, (b) tactile diagram produced by TVIs, (c) tactile diagram produced by using our Level-set algorithm and then texturizing segments, (d) tactile diagram produced by using gPb-owt and then texturizing segments.

are visually impaired. Some of the scoring metrics used were those commonly used for visual segmentation: the F-measure and the probabilistic rand index (PRI; Everingham and Winn 2012). Regression to PRI was also used to predict how individual parameters affected PRI while accounting for noise and outliers as opposed to using the absolute best that may be caused by chance. Time was also included because of the crucial need to approximate real time in converting diagrams.

One difficulty with these metrics is that they do not take into account the differences between the visual and tactile systems. Previously, Loomis (1990) developed a method that takes into account the differences in the spatial resolution between vision and touch. This method involves applying a low pass filter to the visual image that corresponds to the difference in resolution between vision and touch. Then a dissimilarity type distance is measured between the filtered versions of the results of the algorithm and the standard reference. We will refer to this as the Loomis Distance. However, this still does not take into account the more limited field of view of touch and the cognitive processing of the image. Hence, experimental testing of the ability of individuals who are blind or visually impaired to identify the object(s) in the image using the different algorithms was also examined.

For experimental assessment, in order to decrease testing time to three 3 h sessions, only the best parameter sets for gPb-owt and Level Set were selected to be tested. These were compared to performance with the standard reference set. For each participant, each algorithm condition received a block of tactile diagrams (based on 12 visual photos and 12 visual diagrams) drawn from a pool corresponding to 36 different visual photos and 36 different visual diagrams. To avoid learning effects, the diagrams, were drawn randomly (without replacement) from a triplet of photos or diagrams on the same topic and with approximately the same difficulty of identification in the standard reference representation (e.g., the food triplet consisted of bananas, apples and ice cream). The order of presentation of the algorithms was counterbalanced across participants.

Table 1. Results of parameter exploration. The performance of the best parameter set for a given algorithm is shown for each metric. The Reference is the comparison between the two TVIs. Calculations for the Reference are based on a mean consistency because all illustrators are expected to have the same level of expertise. Note that for time, the TVIs self-reported that they took greater than one hour for their planning phase before they began to construct the diagram.

Metric	Perfect	Reference	K-Means	Level Set	gPb-owt	Viability (1–5)
F-Score	1.0	0.85	0.80	0.81	0.82	2.14
Probabilistic Rand Index (PRI)	1.0	0.93	0.80	0.82	0.81	1.57
Loomis distance	0.0	45.4	68.3	66.7	62.3	2.14
Regression (PRI)	1.0	0.93	0.77	0.79	0.81	1.71
Ttime	<1 min.	30 min	0.2 s	20 s	40 s	

The task was to identify the shape of the object(s) in the diagram, their name and their category. The only hint participants were given was whether the diagram represented a single object, multiple objects or a scene. Although descriptive words are often provided with a diagram, none were included, by this means, we chose the most difficult condition to explore a diagram – namely, understanding an unknown object. Participants were all blind or visually impaired, and were blindfolded so that they relied solely on tactile information. Seven participants completed the experiment.

The comparison between the different segmentation methods using the scoring metrics mentioned above is given in Table 1. The results for the best performing parameter set for each metric is given. Based on these results all computational algorithms performed relatively similarly although notably different from the TVIs for the probabilistic rand index and Loomis distance. To determine which metric should be used for selecting the parameter set for further study, we had a laboratory intern determine the viability of each metric for tactile information processing based on their observation of similarity to the reference image, clarity, distinguishability, continuity and amount of noise. The intern rated each picture in a set corresponding to the given metric on these items on a scale of 1 (best) to 5 (worst). Both the metrics and human inspection suggest that further work is needed to produce tactile diagrams closer to that of the Reference.

However, we wanted to examine how well individuals who are blind or visually impaired can understand diagrams after only the segmentation techniques are applied. We were particularly interested in understanding what problems identified visually impeded tactile identification and which were unimportant due to the differences between the visual and tactile sensory systems. The parameter sets based on the regression analysis were chosen because of its more robust approach to calculating the PRI metric. Due to the time consuming nature of human testing, only two of the algorithms were used in our experiment: the Level Set algorithm and the gPb-owt-ucm algorithm. This was because, when examining the internal consistency of each algorithm the kMean algorithm was the most inconsistent. In contrast the Level Set algorithm was more consistent and the gPb-owt-ucm algorithm was the most consistent.

Perhaps the most surprising result from the human testing is that participants had less of a problem with the Level Set algorithm, which typically shows a fair amount of noise (Fig. 3c) as compared to the gPb-owt. In fact, users did not find the noise that distracting. In contrast, the gPb-owt algorithm had a tendency to underrepresent the needed lines, which made it more difficult for participants to interpret. For both algorithms, "stray regions", which were separated from the object to which they belonged, caused the most difficulty in interpretation and will be further considered in the simplification process. Another surprising result is that most participants found that there was too much use of texture and the textures presented should not be as strong as the edge lines. This suggests that, although textures improve performance (see Sect. 2), edge lines are still a critical component for diagram interpretation.

4   Tactile Hardware

Visual and auditory feedback displays have long benefited from commercial devices developed for other purposes (such as entertainment). Tactile and haptic displays have been much more limited in their development. To a large degree this has to do with the difficulty in developing feedback for a sense that requires physical interaction with the interface. A review of currently existing tactile and haptic displays that have been used to present graphical information is given in (Pawluk et al. 2015) and (Vidal-Verdu and Hafez 2007). Here we will describe three different displays that have been developed in our lab: fingertip vibratory displays, a moving pin display and a more complex display merging multiple approaches together.

The fingertip vibratory displays (Burch and Pawluk 2011) were designed to be low cost vibratory feedback displays that could each be attached to a pad of a finger, together providing separate feedback to different fingers, or even different segments of a finger. Each feedback device senses the color underneath it using a color sensor and renders it as a texture (vibration) on the tip of the finger (Fig. 1). The different colors on the diagram in the visual display were used to format the object so that different textures were used to distinguish different parts of an object as well as their orientation, the two primary difficulties with raised line drawings; this was similar to parallel work by Thompson and her colleagues (2006), who developed their representation for paper diagrams constructed by hand. As described in Sect. 2, the use of texture with multiple fingers greatly improved performance. In fact, it was actually surprising how well these simple, low-cost devices performed on, probably, the most difficult task that can be performed (i.e., an object identification task without cuing).

The moving pin display is a "mouse-like" display (Fig. 5) that can directly control vibratory feedback to individual pins in the display (e.g., Headley et al. 2011). It is similar to other displays in presenting a moving display of a matrix of pins. However, the frequency response range for our device is quite large in order to ensure that textures can be displayed. We also examined the use of four level of amplitudes, however, these were not easily distinguished and so only binary amplitude is used. The device consists of a single electronic Braille cell that is mounted on a hollow case. The cost of the device is less than $400 to prototype, which is a much more viable option compared to $50,000 commercial multi-pin graphics displays. These latter displays also cannot provide vibratory feedback as they work through the use of shift registers to turn pins on and off, to conserve costs, rather than direct drive.

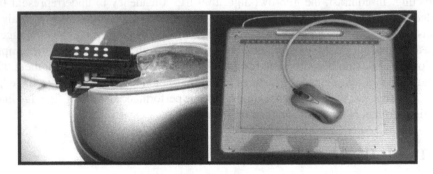

Fig. 5. One of the refreshable tactile displays in the PI's lab consisting of a Braille cell mounted on a hollow mouse case and using a graphics tablet to track its position.

The most important difference between this moving pin display and the previously mentioned fingertip display is that this display can provide distributed spatial information across the fingertip, which is expected to improve performance over a single contact point. Most of that improvement is expected to occur from changes the feedback from one point of contact to four (Weisenberger 2007). Besides the use of vibration to provide texture-like feedback to represent textured diagrams, the most important concept introduced by this display, compared to those previously, is the use of absolute positioning at the location of the pins rather than relative positioning at the location at the palm. We found these improvements significantly improved performance in understanding diagrams by improving the accuracy of the spatial representation (Rastogi et al. 2009).

The current incarnation of our display design is to obtain the benefits of using texture feedback over multiple fingers, like our fingertip displays, with multi-pin feedback at each finger, like our moving pin display. Based on our work with multi-finger feedback, we believe feedback to two fingers of each hand (one "mouse" per hand) will produce the largest performance benefit while limiting the increase in complexity. However, one difficulty with both of these feedback displays is that edges are not easily tracked. Although we found that using textured areas in addition to indicating the edges significantly improved task performance, edge information is still important. With the above mentioned devices, users found the need to move the devices side to side across edges to obtain spatial information about them. This greatly increased the exploration time compared to that when performing tasks with real physical diagrams. One possibility to improve smooth tracking and still allow exploration of textured areas is to use soft haptic fixtures. Currently we are developing a mobile, force feedback mouse using an omnidrive system (Lazea and Pawluk 2016) to provide these soft fixtures. Two Braille cells will be mounted within the mouse casing to provide textured tactile feedback to two fingers.

5 Dynamic Interaction

Direct interaction with virtual tactile diagrams on a computer is advantageous when considering access speed and long-term costs. However, another advantage of this interaction is that a user can manage the limited information processing capacity of touch while still having access to all the information in a diagram. This can be achieved by providing tools for the user to manipulate the diagram and decrease the amount of information observed at a time. Currently, TVIs who develop diagrams for students remove material from the diagram not related to the lesson plan for simplification and provide magnified versions of some components, again based on the lesson plan. However, this is problematic if the teacher changes their plan during class and also limits incidental learning. For dynamic interaction on a computer, there is no reason not to store all the information of a diagram in memory but allow the user to limit how much they explore at a time. We have been developing tools allowing users to zoom more effectively on a diagram and also simplify it in different manners through a point and a click.

Most previous researchers on zooming have considered the application of visual methods (both smooth and step zooming) to tactile diagrams (Magnuson and Rassmus-Grohn 2003; Walker and Salisbury 2003; Ziat et al. 2007). However, unlike vision, it is not possible to take a quick glance at a tactile diagram and decide whether the level of zoom is appropriate: instead, it is a time consuming process. Our objective was to develop a zooming method that would only produce zooming levels significantly different in content from the previous level. Schmitz and Ertl (2010) focused on using the density of streets in a city map to select zoom levels. Density works well for street maps.

However, we have focused more on pictures and images for which we wish to avoid clipping of objects or object parts because otherwise the displayed area becomes exceedingly difficult to tactually interpret. For these cases, we considered a diagram hierarchy based initially on objects and object groups (e.g., house with flowers beside it), and being broken down into object components (e.g., first house and each flower, then the door, windows, etc. of the house and the petals, stem, etc. of the flowers). We then allowed users to zoom between different levels of the picture/image hierarchy. Experimental testing with users who are visually impaired found that our image hierarchy method significantly increased performance and usability compared to step and smooth zooming methods (Rastogi and Pawluk 2013a).

We have developed and examined the use of two types of tools for simplification: boundary simplification and content simplification. Boundary simplification was motivated by the fact that TVIs do simplify shape boundaries, if possible, to help with exploration. We found this to be particularly relevant for our developed tactile I/O devices as users had previously commented that it was much easier to track straight lines than more squiggly ones with these devices (Fig. 6). We considered context simplification in terms of a geographical map that may have cities, roads, weather patterns, crops and industries. Such a map, as is, has too much clutter to be easily interpreted. However, a user often does not need to look at more than a couple aspects of the map at a time (e.g., weather patterns and crops). Allowing the user to remove the other information to answer the question, but still have that information available for other questions seems desirable.

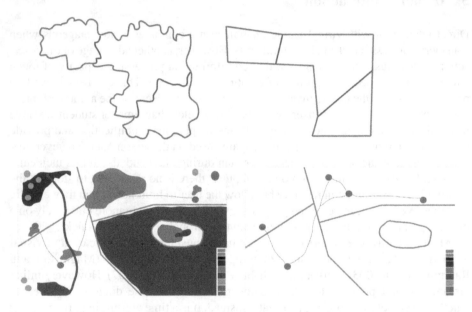

Fig. 6. Top left, original geographical drawing of a country with 3 states; Top right, boundary simplification to produce straight lines; Bottom left, original geographical diagram to indicate cites, roads, resources and topology; Bottom, right, simplified diagram showing only road and topological boundaries.

We found both simplification methods helpful: boundary simplification for answering general questions about borders on a geographical map, and contextual simplification in answering relational questions (Rastogi and Pawluk 2013b). The latter was also found to improve when feature sets (e.g., weather patterns and crops) were divided between the auditory and sensory modalities: presumably due to the improved ability to handle the cognitive load by using two senses.

6 Conclusions

Being able to have immediate access to any and all diagrams is expected to improve the accessibility of information for individuals who are blind or visually impaired. This is expected to allow these individuals more independence whether at work, school or home. Although the algorithms being developed for the automatic conversion from visual to tactile diagrams described here used microcapsule paper, the produced virtual diagrams can be used for computer I/O devices as well. For the devices that we have described, one would simply use vibratory feedback to produce pseudo-textures rather than the physical textures for the paper. However, more work is needed on the automatic conversion methods before the components are integrated into a complete system.

Acknowledgements. The work presented here was funded by NSF IIS Grants ##1218310 and ## 0712936, as well as NSF CBET Grant #0754629. We would also like to thank Megan Lavery, Janice Johnson and Kit Burnett for their assistance with the work on automatic visual to tactile diagram conversion.

References

Adams, R.J., Pawluk, D.T.V., Fields, M.A., Clingman, R.: Multimodal Application for the Perception of Spaces (MAPS). In: ACM ASSSETS 2015, Lisbon, Portugal, 26–28 October (2015)

Arbeláez, P., Maire, M., Fowlkes, C., Malik, J.: Contour detection and hierarchical image segmentation. IEEE Trans. Pattern Anal. Mach. Intell. 33(5), 898–916 (2011)

Brox, T., Weickert, J.: Level set based image segmentation with multiple regions. In: Rasmussen, C.E., Bülthoff, Heinrich H., Scholkopf, B., Giese, Martin A. (eds.) DAGM 2004. LNCS, vol. 3175, pp. 415–423. Springer, Heidelberg (2004). doi:10.1007/978-3-540-28649-3_51

Burch, D., Pawluk, D.: Using multiple contacts with texture-enhanced graphics. In: World Haptics 2011 Conference Proceedings, Istanbul Turkey, 21–24 June (2011)

Comaniciu, D., Meer, P.: Mean shift: a Robust approach toward feature space analysis. IEEE Trans. Pattern Anal. Mach. Intell. 24(5), 603–619 (2002)

Everingham, M., Winn, J.: The PASCAL Visual Object Classes Challenge 2012 (VOC2012) Development Kit, pp. 1–32 (2012)

Ferro, T., Pawluk, D.: Developing tactile diagrams with electronic drawing programs using a validated texture palette. In: AER Annual Conference on Becoming Agents of Change (2015)

Hasty, L.: Personal Communication (2007)

Headley, P.C., Hribar, V.E., Pawluk, D.T.V.: Displaying braille and graphics on a mouse-like tactile display. In: ACM ASSETS 2011, Dundee, Scotland, 24–26 October (2011)

Ladner, R.E., Slabosky, B., Martin, A., Lacenski, A., Olsen, S., Groce, D., Ivory, M.Y., Rao, R., Burgstahler, S., Comden, D., Hahn, S., Renzelmann, M., Krisnandi, S., Ramasamy, M.: Automating tactile graphics translation. In: Proceedings of the 7th International ACM SIGACCESS Conference on Computers and Accessibility - Assets 2005, vol. 150 (2005)

Lazea, A., Pawluk, D.: Design and testing of a haptic feedback active mouse for accessing virtual tactile diagrams. In: RESNA 2016, Arlington, VA, 12–14 July (2016)

Lederman, S.J., Klatzky, R.L.: Relative availability of surface and object properties during early haptic processing. J. Exp. Psychol. Hum. Percept. Perform. 23(6), 1680–1707 (1997)

Loomis, J.M.: A model of character recognition and legibility. J. Exp. Psychol. Hum. Percept. Perform. **16**(1), 106–120 (1990)

Loomis, J.M., Klatzky, R.L., Lederman, S.J.: Similarity of tactual and visual picture recognition with limited field of view. Perception **20**, 167–177 (1991)

Loomis, J.M., Klatzky, R.L., Giudice, N.A.: Sensory substiution of vision: importance of perceptual and cognitive processing. In: Assistive Technology for Blindness and Low Vision. CRC Press, Boca Raton (2012)

Luo, M., Ma, Y.-F., Zhang, H.-J.: A spatial constrained k-means approach to image segmentation. In: Proceedings of the 2003 Joint Conference of the Fourth International Conference on Information, Communications and Signal Processing, 2003 and Fourth Pacific Rim Conference on Multimedia, vol. 2, pp. 738–742 (2003)

Magnuson, C., Rassmus-Grohn, K.: Non-visual zoom and scrolling operations in a virtual haptic environment. In: Eurohaptics 2003, Dublin, Ireland, 6–9 July (2003)

Pawluk, D.T.V., Adams, R.J., Kitada, R.: Designing haptic assistive technology for individuals who are blind or vision impaired. IEEE Trans. Haptics **8**(3), 258–278 (2015)

Rastogi, R., Pawluk, D., Ketchum, J.M.: Issues of using tactile mice by individuals who are blind and visually impaired. IEEE Trans. Neural Syst. Rehabil. Eng. **18**(3), 311–318 (2009)

Rastogi, R., Pawluk, D.: Intuitive tactile zooming for graphics accessed by individuals who are blind and visually impaired. IEEE Trans. Neural Syst. Rehabil. Eng. **21**(4), 655–663 (2013a)

Rastogi, R., Pawluk, D.: Development of an intuitive haptic zooming algorithm for graphical information accessed by individuals who are blind and visually impaired. Assistive Technol. **25**(1), 9–15 (2013b)

Samman, S.N., Stanney, K.M.: Multimodal interaction. In: Karwowski, W. (ed.) International Encyclopedia of Ergonomics and Human Factors, 2nd edn., vol. 2. Taylor and Francis, Boca Raton (2006)

Thompson, L.J., Chronicle, E.P., Collins, A.F.: The role of pictorial convention in haptic picture perception. Perception **32**(7), 887–893 (2003)

Vidal-Verdu, F., Hafez, M.: Graphical tactile displays for visually-impaired people. IEEE Trans. Neural Syst. Rehabil. Eng. **15**(1), 119–130 (2007)

Walker, S., Salisbury, J.K.: Large haptic topographic maps: marsview and the proxy graph algorithm. In: ACM Siggraph 2003, pp. 83–92 (2003)

Way, P., Barner, K.E.: Automatic visual to tactile translation–Part I: human factors, access methods, and image manipulation. IEEE Trans. Rehabil. Eng. **5**(1), 81–94 (1997)

Weisenberger, J.M.: Changing the haptic field of view: tradeoffs of kinesthetic and mechanoreceptive spatial information. In: World Haptics Conference 2007, Japan (2007)

Ziat M., Gapenne, O., Stewart, J., Lenay, C., Bausse, J.: Design of a haptic zoom: levels and steps. In: World Haptics Conference 2007, pp. 102–108 (2007)

Towards Tangible and Distributed UI for Cognitively Impaired People

Ruzalin Galiev, Dominik Rupprecht[✉], and Birgit Bomsdorf

University of Applied Sciences, Fulda, Germany
ruzalin.galiev@gmail.com,
{dominik.rupprecht,birgit.bomsdorf}@informatik.hs-fulda.de

Abstract. Tangible systems are used for cognitively impaired persons to support activation of users' cognitive processes and to facilitate the understanding of according tasks. Motivated by the research results, a combined tangible and distributed user interface was realized by means of which users can navigate through and interact with a web form. The work is based on an existing accessible web form (AWF) that is to be filled out cooperatively by cognitively impaired and by cognitively non-impaired people assisting them. As proof-of-concept, Sifteo cubes were used that enable the user to interact with a system by pressing a cube's display, by tilting, shaking or flipping a cube, or by placing cubes side by side. In terms of an inclusive design the resulting AWF-Cube prototype was developed and evaluated by a user test with cognitively impaired people. They judged the use of the cubes to be simple although some problems were encountered. The results indicate that the participants understood the navigation and interaction concepts and do not have problems in switching their attention between the AWF main interface and the cubes at the right time.

Keywords: Tangible UI · Distributed UI · Inclusive design · Accessibility · Evaluation

1 Introduction

A tangible user interface (TUI), according to Fishkin [5], is broadly characterized by some input event caused by a user's manipulation of a physical object, and a computer system processing the event and providing feedback via a change of the object. The mapping between the physical object and the digital information or function enables new ways to human-computer interaction to overcome some of its current limitation. Different approaches have been concentrating on tangible interfaces especially for cognitively impaired people. The research mostly aimed at the application of a tangible interface for a cognitive training. The ASPAD ("Augmentation of the Support of Patients suffering from Alzheimer's Disease and their caregivers") project started explore the impact of employing tangible interfaces and robot programming tasks as a method for cognitive training (Demetriadis et al. [1, 2]). Furthermore, already in 2004 Sharling et al. [13] reported on a research of employing the "Cognitive Cubes" system. The authors summarized that tangible systems may offer a reliable and valid diagnose and cognitive

© Springer International Publishing AG 2017
M. Antona and C. Stephanidis (Eds.): UAHCI 2017, Part II, LNCS 10278, pp. 283–300, 2017.
DOI: 10.1007/978-3-319-58703-5_21

training technological tool. This motivated the work presented in this paper, i.e. to investigate a tangible UI for cognitively impaired people. The resulting UI, moreover, is also a distributed UI (DUI) since several interactive cubes extends an existing web form. A DUI is a UI whose "components are distributed across one or more of the dimensions input, output, platform, space, and time" (Elmqvist [4]).

The combined TUI/DUI presented in the following is built upon a former project (Rupprecht et al. [11, 12]) on the development of accessible web forms for people with dyslexia caused by cognitive impairments. The main objective had been to support understanding and interacting with a form in spite of cognitive impairments. The resulting accessible web forms (AWF) are used cooperatively in counseling interviews for planning their real life inclusion. The impaired people, also called clients, should work with the AWF as autonomously as possible. The other interview participants, referred to as assistants, provide help such as entering resulting data or pointing to navigation possibilities.

The general goal of our follow-up work is to enhance accessibility and to avoid situations in which assistants needlessly dominate the cooperation because they are operating the keyboard and mouse. A first step was done within the AWF-Cube project. Its basic idea was to enable navigation by interactive, tangible cubes on the one hand aiming at a more clear separation between form and navigation concepts. On the other hand, the clients should be supported to interact with the form in a more self-determined way by means of the cubes. In terms of an inclusive design (cf. Rupprecht et al. [11], Dubuc & Edge [3] or Newell [10]) clients should be involved as early as possible. Hence, a first prototype was realized even though with limited functionality. It uses Sifteo cubes (Merrill et al. [9]) that are 1.5-inch cubes with full-color, touch-sensitive screens functioning like a single button. A user can also interact with a system by tilting, shaking and flipping a cube, or by placing cubes side by side. We decided on the cubes because of their interaction possibilities in spite of their limitations, particularly caused by the small screen size reducing accessibility. A further advantage was that we got cost-efficiently early feedback from the clients.

In the remaining of this paper the work related to our approach is presented (Sect. 2). Afterwards (Sect. 3) the specific accessible web form the AWF-Cube prototype is based on is introduced, but only the features as relevant to the AWF-Cube are explained. In Sect. 4 the AWF-Cube prototype is introduced, namely the re-design as relevant for the subsequent presentation of the conducted user study in Sect. 5. The paper ends with a conclusion containing a discussion of the results and future work (Sect. 6).

2   Related Work

TUI and DUI are, besides the implementation of assistive technologies (Dubuc et al. [3]), generally researched for people with impairments in different directions. In Sitdhisanguan et al. [14], e.g., a tangible application for training shape matching skills for autistic children is proposed. The TUI is based on wooden, shaped blocks and a semi-transparent glass table top detecting the block laid on it. After a geometric shape is displayed on the table the child has to place the right tangible shaped block on it. Results of user studies show that the TUI is easier to use than a WIMP interface for the same application. Furthermore, the children learned more shapes with the TUI training system than with a conventional one using non-digital training artifacts. The TraInAb system (Guía et al. [6]) is a set of interactive games to train cognitive skills of people with intellectual disabilities. The UI is made up of a mobile device and smart objects, i.e. everyday physical objects using IR technology, and a main interface displaying the graphical game content. Interaction with the game takes place by moving an object closer to the mobile. Clients participating in the evaluation were highly motivated and interested in the system. The TUI of Virtual Kitchen (Hilton et al. [7]) is similar but this time physical objects became smart objects. The purpose is to train in stroke rehabilitation everyday tasks safely.

The Tangible Virtual Kitchen (Hoang et al. [8]) was created to support the rehabilitation of Alzheimer's patients. The task setting is very similar to that of the former Virtual Kitchen but the smart objects are replaced by Sifteo cubes. Each cube displays an object associated with the tasks, e.g. a coffee machine or a cup, while an action cube, showing a hand, serves users to transfer objects from cube to cube. The system's evaluation is postponed to follow-up work. PhysiCube (Vandermaesen et al. [15]) is a game-based system using Sifteo cubes to provide motivating physical training for the upper limbs rehabilitation for patients with physical disabilities. Therapists involved in the study showed appreciation for PhysiCube and would use it once the effectiveness for physical therapy has been shown. The purpose of Cognitive Cubes (Sharlin et al. [13]) is cognitive assessment and training. Plastic cubes (all 2 inch/edge) can be interconnected, forming both a physical shape and a network topology. The user has to build 3D shapes shown on a screen by means of the cubes. Results of user studies prove the benefit of the spatial TUI over conventional assessment and training systems.

The above mentioned approaches show directions of TUI and DUI applications to realize assistive technology or to support clinical diagnosis and therapies. The AWF-Cube, however, extends a UI by tangibles for the purpose of enhancing the inclusive design of a web form used by cognitively impaired people. The UI, besides the tangibles, is based on a main interface displaying the AWF, comparable to TraInAb and Virtual Kitchen. In spite of the two but as in the Tangible Virtual Kitchen and PhysiCube systems, the AWF-Cube prototype uses Sifteo cubes. Similarly to most of the mentioned related work, a user test was conducted with people of the target group. A common result is that the TUI system is enjoyable and attractive.

3   The Accessible Web Form

The tangible and distributed UI presented in this paper is a follow-up work of a former project on developing accessible web forms (AWF) [12]. Each of the resulting AWF implements an ICF based instrument. The International Classification of Functioning, Disability and Health (ICF) [16] is used as a classification of the health components of functioning and disability. Its purpose is to measure skills and limitations at both individual and population levels. An example of such an assessment is the question whether a person can carry out the coordinated tasks and actions of eating food that has been served (ICF Item d550: Eating). The ICF is applied to health-related domains such as rehabilitation, clinic care or planning central aspects of the participation in daily life.

The focus in our former AWF project as well as in the current AWF-Cube project is on people with dyslexia attributable to cognitive impairments, in the following referred to as clients. The specific purpose of the form is to determine required help and integration services. It is filled out cooperatively by clients and personal supporters of the clients like caregivers and relatives, referred to as assistants.

3.1   AWF Structure

The underlying structure of the specific AWF also used in the cube project is depicted in Fig. 1. The web form is subdivided hierarchically into form units and categories. Level 1, for example, consists of exactly one form unit and five main categories. A form unit is a semantically correlated part of the form and is as small as possible, e.g. dedicated to a single question. A form category is a bigger information entity and consist of zero or more (0…*) form units and/or zero or more (0…*) categories. Furthermore, category's form units that are interdependent and thus are to be processed in a strict order define a "form unit sequence". It was decided for a depth of maximal four for the purpose of a less complex navigation structure. Thus, the last level (level 4) of the hierarchy consists only of form units.

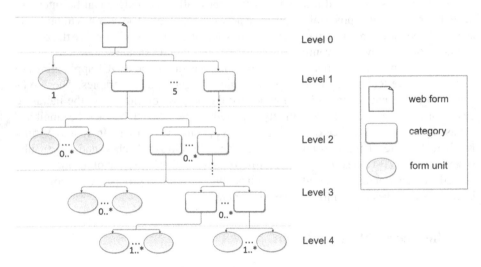

Fig. 1.   General AWF structure

3.2   Preliminary AWF Design

An already existing PDF based ICF instrument for determine required help and integration services was transformed into an AWF in the former project. The AWF was developed by an iterative, client-centered process in which also assistants and the company responsible for the original PDF were involved.

Basic Design and Navigation. The navigation structure is systematically derived from the form structure following a model-based approach (cf. Rupprecht et al. [12]). Each level of the form hierarchy results in a level in the navigation structure, whereby level 0 represents the form itself. The page resulting from the transformation of level 1 is shown in Fig. 2. The input field (single form unit of level 1) to enter a goal the client wants to reach within the next months is located at the top (see input field "Main goal"). It is visible all along as the form is filled in with respect to that goal. The five main categories, named "My situation", "My goals", "About me", "Working", and "Next steps", are represented by five, differently colored bars. If the user clicks on a category bar it opens and the next level becomes accessible.

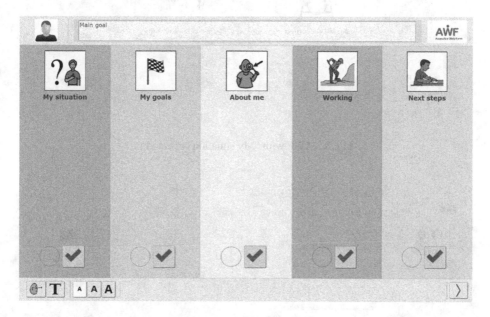

Fig. 2. AWF homepage

All next levels are structured as exemplified in Fig. 3, which shows the state of the application after selecting "My situation". Every form unit and category are represented by a so called tile. A unit tile has a white and a category tile a colored background to differentiate between the two types. If more than four tiles are to be presented navigation bars are inserted to navigate between the pages (labeled with "2" in Fig. 3).

The tiles enable the user to navigate through the form. Clicking on a unit tile the related form unit is shown on the screen. For example, after selecting the "Living situation" tile the associated form unit is presented to the user, as shown in Fig. 4. If a unit tile represents a form unit sequence, at each point in time only one of the units is accessible. Navigation bars enables the user to invoke the next unit once the prior units are filled out. Category tiles enable the user to navigate to the next level of the hierarchy. Clicking on a further category tile, e.g. on "Support or disability in relationship", the follow-up situation is similar to the one shown in Fig. 3.

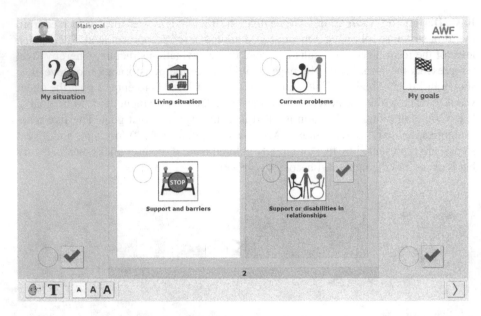

Fig. 3. AWF with "My situation" selected

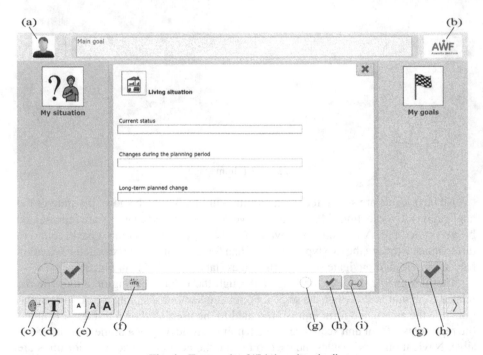

Fig. 4. Form unit of "Living situation"

Additional UI Elements. Additional UI elements are inserted to support working with the AWF (cf. Fig. 4). A picture of the current user (here an abstract image (a)) and a symbol representing the form (here the AWT logo by the authors, (b)) are placed at the top of an AWF page. Hereby it is indicated to which user the current AWF belongs and the type of the AWF since various ICF instruments may be generated by the tool described in [12]. Furthermore, by the two elements the user may enter an adaptation page, e.g. to set the simulation speed for opening a form unit or category.

The button (c) enables to invoke so-called clarifying elements for a category or a unit. Clarifying elements provide additional, simple explained information supporting the understanding of the AWF content. In addition, the AWF may be personalized (d), e.g. replacing a symbol or a label by the client's own content that is more understandable for this individual user. The elements (e) next to the T-Button enables as usual to change the size of the text.

The button (f) at the bottom, left side of a form unit enables to set that form unit to its initial state, i.e. clicking on a clear button removes all entries of the input fields and unset check- and radio-buttons. If clients fill out the form alone but still need assistant they may activate the button (i) right side to set a mark "assistant required" for the current unit. Furthermore, clients may set a "ready mark" (h) for a category or a unit that needs no or no more input (currently not set) while (g) is just a progress circle.

Current State. The AWF presented above is in use alternatively to the original PDF form. Reactions to the AWF were very positive by clients and assistants, particularly it supports more than the PDF version the understanding of the form and, most of all, the process of determine required help and integration services. However, we are aware that more work on accessibility for the AWF is needed.

The AWF, for example, should be enhanced by the possibility of more audio output and should enable audio input. The missing information about the current navigation path (e.g. visualized by a bread crump design pattern) seems also to be a drawback. Furthermore, a more clear separation between form and navigation concepts may easy the form filling process. The AWF project aimed at supporting the clients to interact with the form in a more self-determined way as the PDF form does. In cases, however, assistants fill in the data, they tend to perform all necessary navigation steps and interactions. Hereby, they are prone not only to prearrange the next actions within the form but also the next steps within the process of determine required help and integration services – both reducing inclusive design.

In addition, tangibles may support cognitively impaired people more than traditional UI using just mouse and keyboard, since current research shows positive effects on cognition by TUI. More research is needed on this.

As a first step within our follow-up work a prototype of an AWF using interactive cubes was implemented. The purpose was to get as early as possible feedback from clients, e.g. whether they will have problems with a combined TUI and DUI in general and if the AWF-Cube may contribute to accessibility and inclusive design.

4 The AWF-Cube Prototype

The AWF described above was taken as a proof of concept example. Sifteo cubes were used that enable the user to interact with a system by pressing a cube's display, by tilting, shaking or flipping a cube, or by placing cubes side by side (named neighbor action). As the created prototype uses cubes instead of a computer mouse for navigation, the UI of the former project was redesigned to be more compatible with the cubes navigation and interaction. The UI structure was modified but not the hierarchical structure of meaningful form units and categories. The labels and symbols[1], which were introduced for navigation and invocation of functionalities (cf. Rupprecht et al. [12]), were also kept.

4.1 Main Interface

The UI, besides the cubes, is based on a main interface displaying the AWF. Figure 5 shows an overview of the re-designed AWF. The input field to enter the goal remains located at the top (a). The picture of the user and the form symbol are grouped at the left side (d) since clicking on them has the same meaning, namely navigation to the adaptation page. Also on the left side the user may find the access to clarifying elements (e). The right side contains the UI elements to set the ready mark (f) (currently not set) and the mark assist (g), to clear a form unit (h), and to personalize the form (i).

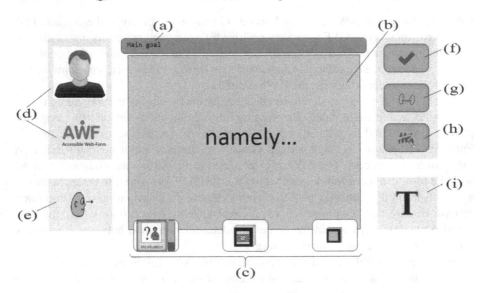

Fig. 5. Overview of the redesigned AWF

Access to a form unit is provided in the area (b). Thereby, a user does not see blocks or tiles of categories, sub-categories and form units not to overload the UI. The central area provides a hint to go forward with the cubes until a form unit is opened. Hence, in Fig. 5 the area is empty since currently no unit is activated. As soon as a form unit is selected it is displayed in the central area to be filled out. Cubes involved in navigation

---

[1] Most of them are Picture Communication Symbols ©1981–2011 by Mayer-Johnson LLC. All Rights Reserved Worldwide. Used with permission. www.mayer-johnson.com.

are replicated in the cube representation area (c) showing the tile images of the selected units or categories as on the Sifteo cubes. This approach follows the well-known bread-crumbs design pattern.

4.2   UI Cube Extension

Category Cubes. Three Sifteo cubes are used as category cubes to enable navigation between form categories and selection of form units. In Fig. 6 the three leftmost cubes are the category cubes, also referred to as cube-1, cube-2 and cube-3 in the following. Cube-1 holds the menu of the main categories; cube-2 and cube-3 contain menus of the sub-categories and form units of the subsequent hierarchical level 2 and level 3, respectively. The icons and labels of the preliminary AWF are adopted as menu items, whereby at each point in time exactly one of the icons is displayed. The user goes through a menu by tilting the cube to the right or to the left. The menu stops at an item once the cube is back in its horizontal position. The user selects an item by pressing on the display; thereupon the icon fills the entire screen to denote the current selection. Additionally, the next cube is activated providing access to the subsequent hierarchical level of the web form, i.e. the cube presents a menu of the sub-categories and/or units.

Fig. 6. Main category selected (on first cube), activating its sub-menu (on second cube)

Scenario. A short scenario exemplifies in the following the use of the AWF-Cube. In this scenario a client wants to give information about his personal living situation. As soon as the client presses on cube-1 while the option "My situation" is displayed this category is selected and the respective menu of the next level is activated on cube-2. This situation is shown in Fig. 6. The first category cube displays the enlarged icon of "My situation" while cube-2 enables the menu with one of its items visible and cube-3 remains inactive.

The representation area is changed at the same time to depict the current cube states (already shown in Fig. 5-c). Leftmost the first category cube is represented showing the same icon as cube-1. Cube-2 is represented by the next field, which currently contains a menu-is-active icon. The last field is empty since cube-3 is inactive.

The currently visible icon on cube-2, however, is not the wanted living situation options. Thus, tilting cube-2 the client searches for the "Living situation" item (see Fig. 7) and stops it once the required icon is displayed.

Fig. 7. User tilts second cube to go through menu items

Pressing then on cube-2, the AWF application loads the according form unit (cf. Fig. 4). Cube-1 and cube-2, as shown in Fig. 8, display a keyboard icon by which the client puts his attention to the main screen displayed on the laptop in front of him. Slightly before, he has looked shortly at cube-3. He has recognized the stop icon and has known that this cube cannot be used (since the current navigation sequence stops here).

The client recognizes the text fields in the AWF main area (Fig. 8) and asks someone to assist him. Immediately after the form unit was presented a prompt pops up on the main screen that explains how to go back into the menu on the cubes. The assistant first closes that window and starts to fill in the information provided by the client.

All in all, three Sifteo cubes are dedicated to navigation as the example AWF contains a maximum of three hierarchical navigation levels. In the case cube-2 contains only form units (leaf of the hierarchical AWF structure) the third cube is not used. If the menu item of a unit is pressed the central AWF area presents the respective form unit, which becomes an active unit waiting for input. A keyboard symbol appears on all active cubes to direct the user's attention to the web form on the main screen (where a clue popped up showing how the user can go back to cube interactions). However, pressing on the keyboard symbol restores the former state of all cubes und deactivates the form unit. Similarly, the user may switch to the menu of a higher level just by pressing the related cube.

Option Cube. The forth cube (named option cube or just cube-4) provides access to AWF functionalities frequently used by clients. Pressing the initial image (see e.g. Fig. 8) invokes a menu containing amongst others items representing ready, assist, clear and explain functionality. If one of these is selected semicircles appear on the top and

Fig. 8. Keyboard icon (on first and second cube), stop icon (on third cube)

bottom of the screen of the option cube and of all category cubes to which the selection is applicable. These semicircles indicate how the so-called neighbor action is to be utilized, i.e. how cubes are to be placed side by side.

Scenario. The client decides to finish his work with the "My situation" category and wants to note it with a *ready*-mark. Therefore, he presses on the option cube and tilts it until the ready icon is visible (Fig. 9). Cube-1 and cube-2 display again the beforehand selected items, so that the client can see to which categories and units he may apply the *ready*-mark.

Fig. 9. Activated option cube

Once the client selects ready by pressing on cube-4 a green and a red symbol is added to the icon on the first two category cubes (s. Fig. 10).

Fig. 10. Setting ready state for main category (Color figure online)

Generally, a category is marked to be finished when the option and the category cube are positioned in neighborhood so that the green semicircles are side by side. The red symbols enable to undo the mark. If clear is selected the two semicircles are green since in this case the user has two possibilities to arrange the cubes.

In the scenario the client connects the option cube with the first category cube so that two green semicircles starting to highlight. Meanwhile, the web application increases the ready-bar to the full height and on the right panel a *ready* icon is marked.

The cube actions *shake* and *flip* were implemented as well, but omitted in this paper since the cube navigation and interactions are introduced only to the extent as included in the evaluation.

Concluding the redesign, the structure of the AWF was hidden and due to additional areas (cf. Fig. 5-c) it imparted the consistency with the Sifteo cubes.

5   User Study

The purpose of the usability test was primarily to find out whether or not the AWF-Cube approach could contribute to inclusive design, and, furthermore, to determine usability strengths and weaknesses of the cube navigation and interaction implemented.

5.1   Study Design

Upon approval by the ethics commission of the authors' institution, the University of Applied Sciences in Fulda (Germany), an onsite usability test was conducted at assisted living residence of Caritas in Fulda where all participants live. The AWF was displayed on a laptop and the cubes in front of it. The test sessions were videotaped using a USB-Webcam that was positioned to focus on hand movements and cube interactions. The Morae Recorder software was used to record comments and to capture the on-screen activities and keyboard & mouse inputs. The test moderator, who was known to the participants from previous tests, and the observer, who took notes, was present in the test room. Each session duration including introduction and answering questions was between 19 and 25 min. Time of task execution, however, was not taken into account since it is influenced by the degree of cognitive impairment, particularly the current degree during the test.

The test moderator explained at the beginning of each session the test and the meaning of a consent form, which was provided in a simple language including explanatory illustrations. It was signed by the client to agree with being recorded. Afterwards, the cube interactions and their meanings were demonstrated. The moderator gave the client task scenarios and help in the case of problems. A printed version of the symbols or a simple text that was relevant for task execution was shown to the client. This was meaningless for the results since to remember symbols or to show writing skills was no subject of the test.

The sub-tasks, the actions required completing them, and special features of the tasks the clients should perform are presented in Table 1. The task find summarizes the tasks go through menu and stop with item; the cube action neighbor is used as an abbreviation for placing two cubes side by side regarding the red or green symbol.

The tasks were divided into two groups, navigation tasks (task N-1, …, N-6) and option tasks (task O-1, O-2, O-3). After each group, the moderator asked the client for improvements and for good and helpful features of the cube prototype. In a post-session the client were asked whether it was interesting to use it, whether it was easy to navigate with cubes and whether the single cube actions were comfortable to perform. There was no rating on a Likert Scale as former experiences shows that the clients feel more comfortable by getting just yes-no-questions. The moderator showed the keyboard & mouse and the disabled cube symbol to ask for the particular meaning. At the end of the

Table 1. Sub-tasks, involved cube actions and special features of test tasks

Task-ID	Sub-task	Cube action	Special features
N-1	find main category	tilt cube-1	just go through menu
N-2	find + open main category find given sub-category	tilt + press on cube-1 tilt cube-2	switch from cube-1 to cube-2
N-3	Invoke main menu find given + select category	press on cube-1 tilt + press on cube-1	switch from cube-2 to cube-1
N-4	find + open sub-category invoke form unit enter arbitrary data	tilt + press on cube-2 press on cube-3 (keyboard action)	switch to AWF & keyboard; ⌨ displayed
N-5	invoke main menu find + open category	press on cube-1 tilt + press on cube-1	switch back to cubes, directly to cube-1
N-6	find category + invoke unit enter arbitrary data	tilt + press on cube-2 (keyboard action)	switch to AWF & keyboard; ⌨ & ▣ displayed
O-1	open option menu find + invoke clear delete data from current unit	press on cube-4 tilt + press on cube-4 neighbor cube-4 and cube-2	switch to option-cube; neighbor correctly
O-2	invoke main menu find + open category open option menu find + invoke ready set main category ready	press on cube-1 tilt + press on cube-1 press on cube-4 tilt + press cube-4 neighbor cube-4 and cube-1	more complex task sequence; neighbor correctly regarding different colored semicircles
O-3	remove ready setting	neighbor cube-4 and cube-1	neighbor (cf. O-2)

interview the clients were asked what they liked most and least and to give further recommendations for improvement.

5.2 Participants

In the evaluation 6 adult clients (5 male, 1 female) participated, referenced to with P.A … P.F. The age was between 25 and 40 but not taken into account because in case of cognitive impairment skills often do not correspond to age. All clients live in the same assisted living residence and work in a sheltered workshop. They have no motor impairments except P.E who is unable to move the right arm and P.F who has slightly impaired function of the right hand and is sitting in a wheelchair. Both, P.E and P.F were slightly visual impaired. The combination of skills on reading & writing and using PC & web differs, cf. Table 2. Dyslexia caused by cognitive impairment is generally accompanied by reduced learning, perception, memory, attention, and thinking abilities in different degrees, affecting system usage as well as user tests. However, the clients have been participating four times in user studies of the former AWF. All of them did not have

Table 2. Skills of participants on reading and writing, and on uncomplicated PC and web usage

ID	Reading Skills	Writing Skills	Simple PC & web skills
P.A	can read hardly	can write hardly	low, no internet, listing to music
P.B	can read, with problems	low writing skills	high, daily use of internet
P.C	cannot read	cannot write	very low, no internet, watching pictures
P.D	can read hardly	can write hardly	medium, no internet, helping others
P.E	can read, with problems	can write hardly	high, daily use of internet
P.F	cannot read	cannot write	high, daily use of internet

problems with incomplete prototypes and were eager to participate in the tests. Furthermore, all clients were familiar with counseling interviews and the AWF.

5.3 Results

Task completion by all clients and the hints provided by the test moderator are presented in Fig. 11. All tasks of the navigation group were completed but in N-1 to N-4 sometimes help was needed. In a few of these cases a swipe instead of a tilt gesture was performed (P.B in N-1 and N-3, P.F in N-2 and N-3), but only P.B needed a hint at the first. In N-2 all clients except P.B and P.E did not notice the menu on cube-2. After a hint (see "Hints" in Fig. 11) navigation was no problem. In N-3 and N-4 some clients need only help with respect to the categories but switching between cubes and AWF & keyboard was without issues.

Starting with the tasks of the option group, all clients needed a hint to recognize that the options are on cube-4. This problem occurred solely at the beginning of O-1, probably since it was the first task including that cube. A further problem for P.B, P.D, P.E, and P.F in O-1 was to remember the neighbor action, but after a hint on "red and green marks" it immediately returned to mind and was correctly executed. In O-2 the clients recalled about marks but P.A, P.D, and P.E did not know on which cube the ready option was located. Furthermore, because of the exact arrangement (only one option to bring

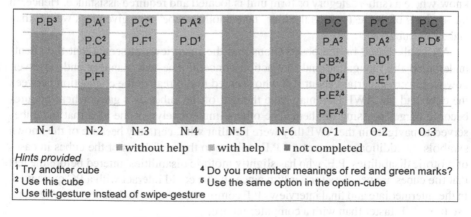

N-1	N-2	N-3	N-4	N-5	N-6	O-1	O-2	O-3
P.B[3]	P.A[1]	P.C[1]	P.A[2]			P.C	P.C	P.C
	P.C[2]	P.F[1]	P.D[1]			P.A[2]	P.A[2]	P.D[5]
	P.D[2]					P.B[2,4]	P.D[1]	
	P.F[1]					P.D[2,4]	P.E[1]	
						P.E[2,4]		
						P.F[2,4]		

■ without help   ■ with help   ■ not completed

Hints provided
[1] Try another cube
[2] Use this cube
[3] Use tilt-gesture instead of swipe-gesture
[4] Do you remember meanings of red and green marks?
[5] Use the same option in the option-cube

Fig. 11. Task completion by participants

the green semicircles together) they completed the sub-task set main category ready only with the second performance but without further help. O-3 was nearly identical to the last sub-task of O-2 and fulfilled by almost everybody without assistance. P.F completed O-3 with help only due to problems with the color red caused by visual impairment. P.C completed none of O-1 to O-3. Even after hints the client did not know how to perform, but was not bothered by this.

In former tests the authors experienced that the clients tend to respond quite positively within the interviews. This general behavior was carefully taken into account in analyzing the data. For example, the way of saying "yes", which was nearly a standard answer on all yes-no-questions, was interpreted and is summarized in this paper together with the verbal comments of the clients made within the interviews. Nevertheless, even taken this positive response behavior into consideration, the clients reacted at large positively to the cube actions and how they are utilized for task performance. They mentioned several times the simple use of the cubes. Particularly P.B, P.C, P.D, and P.F found it easy to open AWF categories and form units by tilt and press actions. A problem, however, was the speed of tilting. The menu moved too fast for the clients and from time to time they could not stop on the wanted item.

P.A rated the neighbor action more convenient than tilt and press. All other clients made no difference. Further comments related to the colored semicircles. They were regarded as helpful clues to arrange the cubes (emphasized by P.B) but were also considered too small. Particularly P.F could hardly recognize the red semicircles due to visual impairment.

All clients except P.E did not remember to have seen the disabled cube symbol during the test but could state its meaning. P.D could explain that by pressing on a keyboard & mouse symbol the menu is re-invoked on the cube. The other clients did not remember that but had applied it correctly during the test. However, cognitively impaired people generally have problems with short-term memory. The symbols, all in all, could be classified as correctly understood clues.

An astonishing result for us was that no problem occurred when attention was to be directed from cubes to the AWF and vice versa. The clients needed only few hints to switch between the cubes. However, even in the original AWF they sometimes did not know where a (sub-) category or form unit is located and required assistance. Hence, in the analysis of the test results the hint "take another cube" was given less weight than "take this cube".

All in all, based on the observations and the interviews, it seems that the clients understood the navigation and interaction concept. The test manager and observer, however, were uncertain about P.A who seemed not to realize the connection between the cube and the AWF, and may have thought of the cubes as a game where pictures become bigger pressing on them. The others immediately got the idea that the cubes served to navigate in the AWF they were familiar with, certainly because of the known symbols. In addition, comments of P.F indicate to the usefulness of the cubes in cases of motoric disabilities. P.F, who has slightly motoric disabilities, uttered before the test that the cubes are needless for her/him since she/he could interact with a PC quite well. In the intermediate and final interviews P.F commented that with the cubes she/he could use the AWF faster than with a computer mouse.

6   Conclusion

This paper presented a tangible application of web forms aiming at a more accessible navigation and interaction with an existing web form for people with dyslexia caused by cognitive impairments. The combined TUI and DUI is made up of a main UI displaying the web form and Sifteo cubes providing additional access to it. The current implementation, the AWF-Cube prototype, has some drawbacks. Actually, some of them were obvious from the beginning not only because of the cubes' technical limitations but also since not all ideas of the development team could be implemented. Primarily, the AWF-Cube prototype was created to get early feedback from the clients.

In the first user study we found no indication that the AWF accessibility could be reduced by AWF-Cube. On the contrary, the clients overall judged the use of the cubes to be simple. Two interaction problems occurred in using the cubes: The speed of tilting was too fast and should be adjustable in the next version. Secondly, the colored semi-circles were too small. Generally, the cubes themselves are too small and should be replaced. Bigger screens will not only provide better support for visually impaired clients but will also enable us to provide more clear clues on state information. This can be further enhanced by introducing sounds. Another subject of future work will be the implementation of a reading feature.

All in all, the navigation and interaction concepts were understandable for the clients. Furthermore, no problem occurred when attention was to be directed from cubes to the AWF and vice versa. The effectiveness for interacting with the form in a more self-determined way is to be verified. Although this was not covered by the conducted user study we assume that the cubes could have a possible impact on it. The TUI is used by the clients only and not shared with the assistants strengthening the client's position in the interviews.

References

1. Demetriadis, S., Giannouli, V., Sapounidis, T., Tsolaki, M.: Selection of Cognitive Training Programs and Design of Educational Robotics Applications. Project ASPAD Deliverable. ESPA, 2007–2013 (2013)
2. Demetriadis, S., Giannouli, V., Sapounidis, T.: Robot programming and tangible interfaces for cognitive training (2015)
3. Dubuc, L., Edge D.: TUIs to ease: tangible user interfaces in assistive technology. In: Clarkson, P.J., Langdon, P.M., Robinson, P., Goodman, J. (eds.) Proceedings of the 3rd Cambridge Workshop on Universal Access and Assistive Technology (CWUAAT 2006). Technical report. Cambridge University Engineering Department, pp. 1–10 (2006)
4. Elmqvist, N.: Distributed user interfaces: state of the art. In: Gallud, J.A., Tesoriero, R., Penichet, V.M.R (ed.) Distributed User Interfaces. Human-Computer Interaction Series, pp. 1–12. Springer, London (2011)
5. Fishkin, K.P.: A taxonomy for and analysis of tangible interfaces. Pers. Ubiquit. Comput. 8(5), 347–358 (2004)
6. Guía, E., Lozano, M., Penechet, V.: Tangible user interface applied to cognitive therapies. In: Schnelle-Welka, D., Radomski, S., Huber, J., Brdiczka, O., Luyten, K., Mühlhäuder, M. (ed.) Proceedings of the 3nd IUI Workshop on Interacting with Smart Objects, pp. 19–23 (2014)

7. Hilton, D., Cobb, S., Pridmore, T., Gladman, J.: Virtual reality and stroke rehabilitation: A tangible interface to an every day task. In: Sharkey, P., SikLányi, C., Standen, P.J. (ed.) Proceedings of the 4th International Conference on Disability, Virtual Reality and Associated Technologies (ICDVRAT 2002). The University of Reading, pp. 63–70 (2002)

8. Hoang, T., Foloppe, D., Richard, P.: Tangible virtual kitchen for the rehabilitation of Alzheimer's patients. In: 2015 IEEE Symposium on 3D User Interfaces (3DUI 2015), Arles, pp. 161–162 (2015)

9. Merrill, D., Sun, E., Kalanithi, J.: Sifteo cubes. In: Konstan, J.A., Chi, E.H., Höök, K. (eds.) CHI 2012 Extended Abstracts on Human Factors in Computing Systems, pp. 1015–1018. ACM, New York (2012)

10. Newell, A.F., Gregor, P., Morgan, M., Pullin, G., Macaulay, C.: User-sensitive inclusive design. Univ. Access Inf. Soc. **10**(3), 235–243 (2011)

11. Rupprecht, D., Blum, R., Bomsdorf, B.: User centered inclusive design for people with dyslexia: experiences from a project on accessibility. In: Sauer, S., Bogdan, C., Forbrig, P., Bernhaupt, R., Winckler, M. (eds.) HCSE 2014. LNCS, vol. 8742, pp. 307–314. Springer, Heidelberg (2014). doi:10.1007/978-3-662-44811-3_23

12. Rupprecht, D., Etzold, J., Bomsdorf, B.: Model-based development of accessible, personalized web forms for ICF-based assessment. In: Proceedings of the 7th ACM SIGCHI Symposium on Engineering Interactive Computing Systems, pp. 120–125. ACM, New York (2015). doi:10.1145/2774225.2775077

13. Sharlin, E., Itoh, Y., Watson, B., Kitamura, Y., Sutphen, S., Liu, L., Kishino, F.: Spatial tangible user interfaces for cognitive assessment and training. In: Ijspeert, A.J., Murata, M., Wakamiya, N. (eds.) Biologically Inspired Approaches to Advanced Information Technology. LNCS, vol. 3141, pp. 137–152. Springer, Heidelberg (2004)

14. Sitdhisanguan, K., Chotikakamthorn, N., Dechaboon, A., Out, P.: Evaluation the efficacy of computer – based training using tangible user interface for low-function children with Autism. In: Eisenberg, M., Kinshuk, C.M., McGreal, R. (eds.) 2008 Second IEEE International Conference on Digital Game and Intelligent Toy Enhanced Learning (DIGITEL 2008), pp. 70–74. IEEE (2008)

15. Vandermaesen, M., de Weyer, T., Luyten, K., Coninx, K.: PhysiCube: providing tangible interaction in a pervasive upper-limb rehabilitation system. Proceedings of the 8th International Conference on Tangible, Embedded and Embodied Interaction (TEI 2014), pp. 85–92. ACM, New York (2014)

16. World health organization. International Classification of Functioning, Disability and Health (ICF). http://www.who.int/classifications/icf/en/

Tactile Acoustic Devices: The Effect on Drowsiness During Prolonged Attentional Tasks

Patrick M. Langdon[1(✉)] and Maria Karam[2]

[1] Engineering Design Centre, Department of Engineering, University of Cambridge, Cambridge, UK
pml24@eng.cam.ac.uk
[2] Kings College London, London, UK
Maria.karam@kcl.ac.uk

Abstract. A study is presented, exploring the use of a tactile acoustic device (TAD); which presents full spectrum sound to participants through skin contact, to help increase alertness and reduce tiredness due to boredom during prolonged attentional tasks such as driving long distances. After a literature review on the background to sleepiness, an account is given of a pilot experiment looking at the effectiveness of the Tactile Audio Stimulation on wakefulness in a non-driving scenario. This was conducted, using a Stroop test to simulate the attention demands during long, boring task periods. The test results suggest that a TAD could potentially reduce fatigue during prolonged attentional tasks without compromising performance or increasing distraction. Results revealed that participants reported feeling significantly more alert and had higher KSS ratings after TAD condition then they did following the Music or Control conditions. The next stage experiments will proceed to a driving task with secondary distraction.

Keywords: Tactile acoustics · Somatosensory interfaces · Sleepiness · Driver fatigue · Automotive safety · Attention · Awareness

1 Introduction

Falling asleep at the wheel is one of the most common causes of accidents for drivers, despite their being fully awake and well rested at the outset of a journey. Sleepiness can occur due to fatigue, boredom, or tedium on the road, and is difficult to avoid when driving along long, monotonous, or dark stretches of roads. Drivers who become fatigued while on the road may experience attention drift, cognitive distractions, and tiredness despite having had significant rest, or having consumed caffeine. Some drivers either won't admit that they are tired, or continue to fight fatigue while continuing to drive. Long distance drivers may be unwittingly susceptible to drowsiness despite starting the drive awake and alert, and continue to drive despite feeling the onset of sleepiness. In this preliminary study we explore the use of tactile acoustic devices as a means of increasing cognitive stimulation, potentially reducing road weariness on monotonous sections of autonomous drives.

© Springer International Publishing AG 2017
M. Antona and C. Stephanidis (Eds.): UAHCI 2017, Part II, LNCS 10278, pp. 301–312, 2017.
DOI: 10.1007/978-3-319-58703-5_22

2 Background

Tactile acoustic devices (TADs) are systems that provide sound information to the body as an assistive technology to augment sound with sound vibration [1]. Tactile sounds have been shown to be effective at enabling deaf people to detect music and emotional aspects of sound on the body. However, if we consider using this assistive technology as a way to increase sensory stimulation, we could use this form of multimodal integration of sound and vibration to potentially increase cognitive stimulation through the combined and reinforced sense of sound on the skin. Tactile acoustic devices, or TADs are a technology explored in this work, to affect the somatosensory system and its tactile sensors to increase focus and awareness during monotonous tasks by adding ambient tactile stimulation to help increase focus and reduce tiredness.

2.1 Sleepiness, Fatigue and Tiredness

Early work on operator decision making under stress established that people's (and animal) responses to task demands may be affected by either low or high levels of demand. Hence, stress responses can be considered a useful enhancer of performance up till a particular level beyond which increasing the amount or intensity of stress leads to a deterioration of performance [16, 17] an effect originally suggested by Yerkes and Dodson in 1908. Following this widely accepted paradigm [17], we can see that the optimum level of "arousal" or stress is likely to be variable according to the individual and their adjustment to their circumstances as well as the nature of the source of stress in the task. In fact, it implies that the individual may respond with increased arousal (hence stress) in order to facilitate an optimal response. Low levels of stress in a driving task, for example, are related to poor performance. On the other hand, low levels (75 dB mixed intermittent noises consisting of traffic, music and general variable thumps) were found by Broadbent (1959) to improve visual vigilance tasks whereas louder continual sounds were deleterious [18], possibly because they raised arousal.

A key factor is the Physiology and psychology of sleepiness, fatigue and tiredness. This includes variability in arousal and boredom that may arise during driving. Definitions vary but broad agreement exist in the literature that this is a hazard for tasks during driving. For example, fatigue and falling asleep while driving as a primary activity account for around 15% of crashes in Australia [19–22]. In this study we initially address a tedious task without a primary driving task, as might be experienced during an autonomous driving episode.

2.2 Fatigue and Sleep-Deprivation

Although these may also be considered as processes linked to a general stress response, it is worth dealing with them as a special case of undesirable, unsafe and common problems that are experienced by drivers. In this case, we are interested in the identifiable cause, bodily responses, mitigations and interventions that may increase safety for drivers through good automotive HMI design [19]. A moment's introspection will reveal that hard tasks and difficult driving will produce Task related (TR) fatigue more quickly and that lack of sleep and diurnal rhythms are implicated in Sleep related (SR) fatigue. A number of causal factors in sleepiness have been examined as a means of classification of technologies for mitigation [20]:

- Sleep related fatigue is strongly related to performance lowering, as a result of disruption of patterns and sleep deprivation, and its effect on daily cycles of alertness;
- Task related fatigue is the most common form of fatigue [21];
    a. Active overload in high levels of traffic or adverse weather conditions and the requirements of secondary cognitive tasks;
    b. Passive monitoring of the driving environment in an undemanding and monotonous driving period as in autonomous driving.

2.3 Driver Sleepiness

Drowsiness is one of the leading causes of deaths and accidents on the roads [2]. One study suggests that 1 in 4 traffic accidents are due to momentary drowsiness [3].

Vigilance; the necessity to monitor and track some display and avoid distraction, requires mental effort and is fatiguing [18, 23]. Separating the physical workload from the driving task leaves us with the cognitive workload. Hence, it is likely that under demanding driving conditions the mental effort will be fatiguing and may lead to stress. This may occur in high traffic densities, during fast moving events, or in high risk environments with serious consequences of failure of a manoeuvre. It will also arise as a result of high levels of distraction within and without the vehicle, for example, from external driving events, or passenger communications.

Fatigue can also be caused by factors unrelated to the driver's initial state. One of the most prevalent approaches to reducing accidents due to sleepiness relies on the detection of tired behaviour, and subsequent warnings to the driver [4]. Different types of alarms can be used to notify the driver of the onset of sleep, however, this often leads to additional dangers in startling a driver out of sleep, potentially causing unpredictable or dangerous responses [2]. In addition, alarm sounds have shown to annoy some drivers, suggesting that more subtle sounds like music could be more effective as a warning [4].

Detecting sleepiness may not be the most effective way to avoid accidents due to drowsiness, with prevention being a desired approach. Detection methods may not always be accurate, or timely; once a driver exhibits head nodding, increased blink frequency, sharp steering wheel motions, or other sleepiness traits, a warning may likely be too late. Avoiding potential situations that can lead to fatigue during drives can potentially reduce the risk of becoming tired on the road on a drive: Peak times for drowsiness typically occurs between 2am-6am and 2 pm-4 pm, which could be avoided to help drivers avoid fatigue whenever possible [3].

Helping drivers stay awake may also be possible using haptics, which can alert the drivers of lane departures, or other dangers by vibrating steering wheels [5] or seats [6]. Haptic signals combined with audio signals are commonly used in combination to alert drivers, leading to more effective alertness alarms that can cause less distraction, fewer false positives, and have been shown to be more trusted by drivers than single alerts [7].

However, haptic notifications and alerts may require learning and identification, which can be difficult to interpret on the fly [8].

In this work, we are exploring techniques for increasing cognitive stimulus or activity without causing distraction. The aim being towards allowing the driver to ward off fatigue, while maintaining focus on a primary task; through the effects of stimulation of the somatosensory system.

Haptics target a specific kind of physical sensation that is highly effective at representing notification directional, or spatial information to the body that are effective as alarms or alerts. However, expanding the tactile signals to additional receptors in the somatosensory system using sound vibrations (tactile acoustics) has been shown to be effective at alerting drivers, for example, to sirens using sound vibrations as an alternative to haptic signals [9]. Tactile sound systems stimulate multiple receptors in the skin to provide a high-resolution tactile-acoustic signal to the body, as a means of communicating elements of sound as touch that are subtler than haptics, but that have a much broader range of potential messages and functions [10, 11].

2.4 Music and Driving Alert

Music is often used as an approach to warding off fatigue while driving, but studies have shown that music may not have an effect in keeping the driver alert [11]. Interactive cognitive stimulation however has shown to reduce the onset of fatigue while driving [12]. This is a novel approach to tactile interfaces, leveraging the benefits of an assistive technology to help increase sensory awareness for people without sensory impairments.

Tedium (TR) is a major problem for drivers, [13] noting that a tired brain tries to seek stimulation to help it stay alive, which makes it easily distracted. In order to provide an extra form of stimuli to the driver, tactile-acoustic displays may be an effective way of increasing stimulation, without leading to distraction or startling responses [11]. To explore the use of tactile sound as a source of physical stimulation to help drivers avoid fatigue, we consider the combination of music, and tactile acoustics, as a way to provide additional cognitive stimulation, without distracting or discomforting the driver.

3   Tedious Environment Study

We explore the hypothesis that adding tactile audio stimulation to music can increase alertness while performing a monotonous task. This study aims to recreate a scenario where the participant is performing a primary task that is monotonous (e.g. driving along a boring stretch of highway in autonomous mode) using the Stroop test to allow us to determine if using the TAD can reduce the sense of tedium. To test this hypothesis, we conducted an experiment to determine if the user's perception of being tired could be affected by the TAD condition. We also hypothesize that the addition of the TAD will not negatively affect the performance of the trials, or increase the number of errors on the task.

3.1 Study Design

The study aimed to create a boring yet critical set of tasks that the participant could perform while experiencing the different conditions. A Stroop test was used as the single primary task, asking participants to complete ten correct responses to a Stroop test indicating the colour of the text shown on the screen [14]. If an error occured, the test started again until all ten were answered correctly consecutively.

Variables included total time, number of errors for each trial, KSS reports before the trials start, and after each trial ends. In addition, we calculated an alertness variable, which represents the change in the original KSS ratings after completing each trial. Participants rated their alertness level at the start of the experiment using the Karolinska Sleepiness Scale (KSS) [15], which uses a scale of 1 (alert) – 9 (falling asleep) and were asked to provide alertness responses after each trial. A sheet of paper with the scale printed in large text was located in front of the participants during the experiment, and they were asked to pay attention to their ratings while they performed the tasks.

The conditions explored in this study are as follows:

1. TAD + Music
2. Music only
3. Ambient noise as the Control.

The TAD system displayed the audio from the music condition to the user as vibrations, using the standard classical music frequency split originally designed for the system [1]. A 2-track looping playlist was presented throughout the music and TAD conditions, selected for similarity in mood and style: Beethoven's Serenade in G, Eine kleine Nachtmusik – Allegro and Mozart's Symphony #40 in G Minor, K 550 - 3. Menuetto – Trio. The experiment was conducted in a semi-public usability lab in Toronto, where a TAD embedded theatre seat is located [9].

Participants were recruited from an experiment café and agreed to take part in accessible, non-invasive, short studies with minimal disruption to their daily routines. The study lasted around 30 min. Participants took part in four trials: one set as practice, and three sets of nine trials for each of the conditions: TAD, Music, and a Control. The goal was to replicate the cognitive state of a driver who is on a long, boring ride, using a Stroop test to simulate the dull, yet critical task of correctly answering questions that were demanding to one's attention. Participants were asked to complete Stroop tests as quickly as possible without making any mistakes. For each condition, (TAD, Music, Control), participants responded to ten questions for three sets of six trials for a total of 540 responses per participant, with an additional practice trial to ensure they were comfortable with the task.

The three conditions were TAD (tad + music), Music (music alone), and a Control (no music or tad). Quantitative data was recorded on the Stroop App, and included number of responses, and response times for each test and trial. The user was asked to pay attention to their state in response to the Karolinska Sleepiness Scale (KSS) [15] after each of the trial conditions.

3.2   Experimental Setup

A 16-channel tactile acoustic device was embedded into a set of theatre seats. The IPad running the Stroop test was used to run and collect responses for the trials. This represents the primary task, which we compare to driving on a boring road, as one must stay alert, despite the repetitive, seemingly mindless task. The setup is shown in Fig. 1 representing a reasonable substitution for an automotive seat. Participants were seated on the TAD theatre system, running a default classical music frequency split from earlier research [1]. The TAD is an 8 × 2 channel array (8 transducers array pairs) running 4 signals in parallel along the back and seat of the chair. Each was individually addressable, but for this work the audio signals were split into the 4 channels for the study. Levels for the music and the TAD were set at a starting level of 75db as the baseline for the participant, who was given the chance to indicate if either were uncomfortable.

Fig. 1. Tactile theatre seats used in the experiment

3.3   Tactile Acoustic Signals and Sound

Intensity levels for the music and the TAD were set at the default volume (75 db, with a JND level for the TAD), with the music played on stereo speakers. Participants were given the opportunity to become familiar with the vibrations before the trials to ensure they were detected, given the ambient nature of the tactile acoustic signals. Audio was played using a computer, with signal distributed through an audio mixer and studio sound system designed to distribute signals simultaneously to the sound system and to the TAD.

3.4   Method

Using the Stroop test application on an IPad air [14], participants responded to the colour of text by pressing the correct button on the screen. The pre-study questionnaire was short, focusing on their driving status, age group, and an open ended question about long distance drives and sleepiness. One of the randomly generated trial sets were initiated first, counterbalancing the three conditions. Each trial consisted of 6-stroop tests, with ten individual tests in each, for a total of 60 responses for each trial, and 90 responses in total of nine trials in total. All Stroop test experimental results were recorded on the Stroop app, and included number of runs, total time of the experiment, time for each trial, and results of each of the ten tests in the six trials.

3.5   Results

Using the KSS response at the beginning, the alertness variable was calculated by subtracting the KSS for each trial from the original KSS, and recording a positive (higher) or negative (lower) value as Alertness. The results showed a significant effect present for the three conditions with respect to the user reports of their KSS after each trial, using a variable measuring the alertness of the participants (Fig. 2).

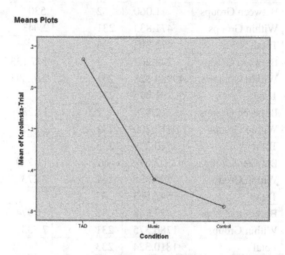

Fig. 2. Results show more alertness in the TAD condition than in the Music or Control.

Alertness was shown to be significant in the experiment at $p < 0.05$ for the three conditions, showing a positive mean for the TAD condition of .14 (sd 1.9), but negative means for each of the Music (mean $-.45$, sd 1.7), and the Control condition (mean $-.$ 58, sd 1.6), with details of the ANOVA reported in Table 1.

Individual KSS reports after each trial were also significant for the conditions, revealing a lower report (indicating greater alertness) in the TAD condition (mean 4.17, sd 1.47), compared to the increased tiredness after the Music (mean 4.75, sd 1.45) and the Control conditions (mean 4.88, sd 1.6). In response to our second hypothesis, the results suggest that there was no effect of condition on the error rate of the trials, or on the completion time of the tasks, based on the non-significant results of the Anova (n.s), The TAD did not negatively affect the users' performance on the task (Table 1). Results from Table 1 shows an average quicker response time in the TAD condition over Music and Control, but these were not significant. Further tests will aim to reveal more information about user differences and sensitivity levels to vibrations, noting that in some cases; especially with the female participants who had less experience with this kind of sensation, may have neglected to lower the intensity despite feeling distracted and overpowered by the vibrations. As tactile acoustics provide ambient information to maintain a user's awareness without dominating their attention, the user sensitivity level will be varied in future studies to ensure that the levels are appropriate for the individual.

Table 1. One-way ANOVA for the three conditions

ANOVA - Condition

		Sum of Squares	df	Mean Square	F	Sig.
Down time	Between Groups	.037	2	.019	.039	.962
	Within Groups	111.902	231	.484		
	Total	111.939	233			
Errors Per Trial	Between Groups	1.060	2	.530	.259	.772
	Within Groups	471.833	231	2.043		
	Total	472.893	233			
Total Time	Between Groups	294.267	2	147.133	.680	.508
	Within Groups	49986.828	231	216.393		
	Total	50281.095	233			
Alertness	Between Groups	22.579	2	11.289	3.634	.028
	Within Groups	717.700	231	3.107		
	Total	740.279	233			
Karolinska-Trial	Between Groups	22.579	2	11.289	4.966	.008
	Within Groups	525.085	231	2.273		
	Total	547.663	233			
Avg time per trial	Between Groups	23.948	2	11.974	1.548	.215
	Within Groups	1786.375	231	7.733		
	Total	1810.324	233			

Continued exploration of the data shows a large standard deviation for the total time variable (Table 1), suggesting that there may be other factors interacting with the results. Error rates were also shown to be higher in the TAD, but this was also not significant. A further test was performed to determine if there was a significance between conditions in the time between the tests (Down Time), which was also not shown to be significant in the analysis. We next consider other factors that may be influencing the time variable, and discuss the qualitative responses and observations made during this study.

3.6 Post Hoc Analyses

Post hoc analysis were carried out using the LSD (least significant difference) test, and the effects between the conditions on alertness and KSS suggest the TAD condition had a larger effect as compared to the Control condition, then between TAD and Music, or Music and Control. Significance on alertness is .016 for TAD-Music, which is not as significant as the higher at $p < .003$ responses between the TAD-Control conditions, which was, in turn, not significantly different than the Music condition (.587). This was an interesting result that is in line with existing research that suggests music may not be as effective at averting sleepiness as one might expect [12]. We also considered observed responses from the participants as potential results, noting that age appears to have an effect, although our groups were not evenly sampled and cannot effectively be analyzed based on our sample sizes. Other possible factors that appeared to have an effect include years of driving experience, long distance driving experience, and current driving status. A further note based on user responses suggests that, in line with existing research, participants did not openly or always admit to feeling tired, which may have been happening in this experiment. For examples, some participants who are drivers or who have had experience over long distance drives hesitated to lower their KSS, even though they felt that they may have been feeling tired, yet insisted that it was only a half step down, despite noticing feeling tired. Other participants did not like to say they were tired during the trials, and preferred to say they were distracted, or their thoughts were wandering. In a future study, we will be able to employ a simple driving simulator to provide a primary task along with eye trackers and other sensors to better gauge the physiological effects of TADs on driver sleepiness.

4 Discussion and Conclusions

The results of the experiment suggest that adding TAD to music as stimuli over boring repetitive task interactions can improve alertness from the perspective of the user. Results also suggest that there are no obviously negative effects due to TADs based on the number of errors made. Although the mean error rate for the TAD condition was slightly higher than the Music or Control conditions (Fig. 2), in general error rates were not significant across conditions or gender, supporting our claim that the TAD does not influence performance based on error rates.

The gender effects suggest that females were faster and made fewer errors on the tasks than males. There were, however, more female participants in the study than males, although the significance was strong (p < .01). Further gender effects may have been based on overall higher sensitivity levels in some of the female participants, who reported feeling distracted from the strong vibrations only after they had completed the tasks, despite being given an opportunity to lower the intensity at the start of the trials. This is likely due to the novelty of the system, and the sensations, which contribute to the discussion on some of the qualitative results. The intensity levels of the TAD system proved to be very important in terms of the individual sensitivity levels of different people. For example, most of the males taking part in the study asked to turn up the volume, so they could feel the vibrations more intensely, while several females requested that we turn down the vibrations, as they were distracted. The female participants who found the TAD to be distracting did show faster times and fewer errors in the Music and Control conditions, likely due to the distracting and intense sensations one can experience with haptics, or tactile acoustic signals that are either distorted or too intense. Further consideration of this could suggest that because the users stated that they liked the vibrations, they may have initially felt that the feelings were pleasant, but didn't anticipate that prolonged intense vibrations could be distracting, rather than focusing; a trait often associated with haptic notifications [14]. Although participants were given the opportunity to turn down the intensity, lack of experience with this kind of system may have prevented them from expressing discomfort until after the trials were completed.

In the next iteration or our research, we will be replicating this study in a driving simulator, to support testing to explore effects of using different music as stimuli to reduce tiredness or tedium on long drives, and to investigate other applications of somatosensory interactions in automotive settings.

Tactile acoustic devices use audio signals to communicate the physical elements of sound to the body, and have been used as a sensory augmentation system to reinforce what we hear using somatosensory system interactions. In the present study, a trial was conducted, using a Stroop test to simulate the attention demands placed during long, boring stretches of highway. The test results support our hypotheses, suggesting that TADs could potentially reduce fatigue for drivers over long boring rides, without compromising performance or increasing distraction. Results revealed that participants reported feeling significantly more alert and had higher KSS ratings after TAD condition then they did following the Music or Control conditions. There were no significant effects shown for error rate, indicating that TADs could effectively be considered as a tool to help driver's combat the problem of fatigue during long periods of one task; one of the most challenging problems drivers face daily.

The results revealed that there may be gender effects on task performance times, but the alertness levels were shown to be unaffected by gender, with higher ratings reported by users for the TAD condition. Tactile acoustic signals have been shown [1] to be effective at augmenting sound with related vibrations, supporting the attentional effects of multi-modal integration of sound and touch. This has the potential to help drivers maintain attention on the critical task of driving, while still having the ability to receive ambient information on the body's subtle cutaneous receptors. These ambient signals may also be used to augment other haptic signals with information and can help users become more sensitive to vibrations, allowing them to better understand and integrate tactile communications using TAD devices for sensory augmentation and substitution of sound and other stimuli to the body.

References

1. Karam, M., Russo, F., Branje, C., Price, E., Fels, D.I.: Towards a model human cochlea: sensory substitution for crossmodal audio-tactile displays. In: Proceedings of Graphics Interface 2008 (GI 2008). Canadian Information Processing Society, Toronto, Ont., Canada, pp. 267–274 (2008)
2. Sahayadhas, A., Sundaraj, K., Murugappan, M.: Detecting driver drowsiness based on sensors: a review. Sensors **12**, 16937–16953 (2012)
3. Thiffault, P., Bergeron, J.: Monotony of road environment and driver fatigue: a simulator study. Accid. Anal. Prev. **35**(3), 381–391 (2003). ISSN 0001-4575, http://dx.doi.org/10.1016/S0001-4575(02)00014-3

4. Fagerlönn, J., Lindberg, S., Sirkka, A.: Graded auditory warnings during in-vehicle use: using sound to guide drivers without additional noise. In: Proceedings of the 4th International Conference on Automotive User Interfaces and Interactive Vehicular Applications (AutomotiveUI 2012), pp. 85–91 ACM, New York, (2012). http://dx.doi.org/10.1145/2390256.2390269

5. Enriquez, M., Afonin, O., Yager, B., Maclean, K.: A pneumatic tactile alerting system for the driving environment. In: Proceedings of the 2001 Workshop on Perceptive User Interfaces (PUI 2001), pp. 1–7. ACM, New York (2001). http://dx.doi.org/10.1145/971478.971506

6. Telpaz, A., Rhindress, B., Zelman, I., Tsimhoni, O.: Haptic seat for automated driving: preparing the driver to take control effectively. In: Proceedings of the 7th International Conference on Automotive User Interfaces and Interactive Vehicular Applications (AutomotiveUI 2015), pp. 23–30. ACM, New York. http://dx.doi.org/10.1145/2799250.2799267

7. Lee, J.D., Hoffman, J.D., Hayes, E.: Collision warning design to mitigate driver distraction. In: Proceedings of the SIGCHI Conference on Human Factors in Computing Systems (CHI 2004), pp. 65–72. ACM, New York (2004). http://dx.doi.org/10.1145/985692.985701

8. Väänänen-Vainio-Mattila, K., Heikkinen, J., Farooq, A., Evreinov, G., Mäkinen, E., Raisamo, R.: User experience and expectations of haptic feedback in in-car interaction. In: Proceedings of the 13th International Conference on Mobile and Ubiquitous Multimedia (MUM 2014), pp. 248–251. ACM, New York (2014). http://dx.doi.org/10.1145/2677972.2677996

9. Karam, M.: Evaluating tactile-acoustic devices for enhanced driver awareness and safety: an exploration of tactile perception and response time to emergency vehicle sirens. In: Stephanidis, C., Antona, M. (eds.) UAHCI 2014. LNCS, vol. 8515, pp. 729–740. Springer, Cham (2014). doi:10.1007/978-3-319-07446-7_69

10. Karam, M., Langdon, P.M.: Designing human somatosensory system interactions: not just for haptics any more! In: Designing Around People: CWUAAT 2016. Langdon, Pat and Lazar, Jonathan and Heylighen, Ann and Dong, Hua, pp. 187–196 (2016). doi 10.1007/978-3-319-29498-8

11. Karam, M.: Multi-modal tactile displays for enhanced driver awareness and safety. In: Adjunct proceedings of the 5th International Conference on Automotive User Interfaces and Interactive Vehicular Applications (AutomotiveUI 2013), Eindhoven, The Netherlands, 28–30 October 2013, pp. 109–110 (2013)

12. Unal, A.B., de Waard, D., Epstude, K., Steg, L.: Driving with music: effects on arousal and performance. Transp. Res. Part F: Traffic Psychol. Behav. **21**, 52–65 (2013). doi:10.1016/j.trf.2013.09.004

13. Gershon, P., Ronen, A., Oron-Gilad, T., Shinar, D.: The effects of an interactive cognitive task (ICT) in suppressing fatigue symptoms in driving. Transp. Res. Part F: Traffic Psychol. Behav. **12**(1), 21–28 (2009)

14. Stroop, J.R.: Studies of interference in serial verbal reactions. J. Exp. Psychol. **18**(6), 643–662 (1935)

15. Carter, G.S.: Sleepfaring: a journey through the science of sleep. Arch. Neurol. **64**(8), 1205 (2007). doi:10.1001/archneur.64.8.1205

16. Shahid, A., Wilkinson, K., Marcu, S., Shapiro, C.M.: Karolinska Sleepiness scale (KSS). In: STOP, THAT and One Hundred Other Sleep Scales, pp. 209–210, 24 November 2011

17. Yerkes, R.M., Dodson, J.D.: The relation of strength of stimulus to rapidity of habit-formation. J. of Comp. Neurol. Psychol. **18**, 459–482 (1908)

18. Broadhurst, P.L.: The interaction of task difficulty and motivation: the Yerkes-Dodson Law revived. Acta Psychologica **16**, 321–338 (1959). doi:10.1016/0001-6918(59)90105-2

19. Broadbent, D.E.: Decision and Stress. Academic Press, NY (1971)

20. Dinges, D.F.: An overview of sleepiness and accidents. J. Sleep Res. **4**(Suppl. s2), pp. 4–14 (1995)
21. May, J.F., Baldwin, C.L.: Driver fatigue: The importance of identifying causal factors of fatigue when considering detection and countermeasure technologies. Transp. Res. Part F **12**(2009), 218–224 (2009)
22. Hancock, P.A., Verwey, W.B.: Fatigue, workload and adaptive driver systems. Accid. Anal. Prev. **29**(4), 495–506 (1997)
23. Armstrong, K., Obst, P., Banks, T., Smith, S.: Managing driver fatigue: education or motivation? vol. 19 No 3 September 2010 Road & Transport Research (2010)
24. Warm, J.S., Matthews, G., Finomore, V.S.: Workload, stress, and vigilance. In: Hancock, P.A., Szalma, J.L. (eds.) Performance under s tress, pp. 115–141. Ashgate, Brookfield (2008)
25. Bellisle, F., Blundella, J.E., Dyea, L., Fantinoa, M., Ferna, E., Fletchera, R.J., Lambeda, J., Roberfroida, M., Spectera, S., Westenhöfera, J., Westerterp-Plantenga, M.S.: Functional food science and behaviour and psychological functions. Br. J. Nutr. **80**(Suppl. S1), S173–S193 (1998)

Evaluating Vibrotactile Recognition Ability of Geometric Shapes by Using a Smartphone

Ray F. Lin[✉]

Department of Industrial Engineering and Management, Yuan Ze University,
135 Yuan-Tung Road, Chungli 32003, Taoyuan, Taiwan
juifeng@saturn.yzu.edu.tw

Abstract. Attempting to let visually impaired people perceive images instantly taken by a smartphone, Peng (2010) developed a mobile application that outlines images and vibrates the smartphone as user's finger was upon the outlined graphics. The intention is encouraging, but the extent to which people can recognize graphical information via the means is unclear. Hence, this study aimed at evaluating the vibrotactile recognition ability of geometric shapes. Six blindfolded college students participated in this study to discriminate geometric shapes displayed on a smartphone by touching its screen with their forefinger. The phone vibrated as long as the finger touched the graphics. Four shapes, three sizes, and three widths of shape edge were tested as independent variables. Correct rate of judgments and the response time were measured as dependent variables. The results showed that triangle shapes had the highest correct ratio (73.48%), whereas pentagon shapes had the lowest correct ratio (63.59%). Furthermore, the participants required the longest time to judge triangle shapes and the shortest time to judge shapes with width ratio set at 100%. The findings direct new coding methods for display geometric shapes and testing the vibrotactile recognition ability with visually impaired people.

Keywords: Vibrotactile · Recognition · Haptic interface · Graphical information · Smartphone

1 Introduction

To perceive graphical information, visually impaired people normally utilize tools such as thermoform paper, high-density Braille printing, or 3D printing. However, these tools have certain drawbacks of high costs and cumbersome for carrying around. With the rapidly developed technology of mobile devices, there has been researching that is working on mobile applications, attempting to help visually impaired people to perceive images using mobile devices. For instance, the 'Dark Angle' developed by Peng (2010) is a mobile application whose objective was to help visually impaired people to perceive simplified images instantly taken by a smartphone. The intention was encouraging, but the extent to which people can recognize graphical information via the means is unclear. To make practical contributions to similar designs so that to benefit visually impaired people, there is a necessity to study human capabilities and limitations corresponding to the means.

© Springer International Publishing AG 2017
M. Antona and C. Stephanidis (Eds.): UAHCI 2017, Part II, LNCS 10278, pp. 313–321, 2017.
DOI: 10.1007/978-3-319-58703-5_23

1.1 Perception of Visually Impaired People

According to United Nations (UN 2013) 285 million people among the world population are visually impaired, of which 39 million are blind and 246 have low vision. Because people who have total blindness have lost their visual ability entirely, they get information through remaining traditional senses: hearing, taste, smell, and touch. Mainly, hearing and touch are used by visually impaired people to perceive textual and graphical information. Hence, many techniques and methods are developed based on these two senses.

To obtain textual information, techniques of Braille and speech synthesizers are developed for visually impaired people. Braille is an embossed language that enables reading textual information through touch. Speech synthesizers are made to provide the spoken output of the information displayed on the computer screen. Recently, new techniques were further developed, such as mobile applications for navigating visually impaired people (Ciaffoni 2014) or even for telling them what are pictured by a smartphone (Image Searcher 2014). These techniques and methods mentioned above have greatly helped visually impaired people effectively perceive textual information. Compared with textual information, however, graphical information is relatively difficult to perceive by visually impaired people based on currently developed devices and techniques.

1.2 Traditional Ways Utilized by Visually Impaired People to Perceive Graphical Information

To perceive graphical information, techniques of collage (Edman 1992), embossed paper (Ina 1996), thermoform paper (Pike et al. 1992), microcapsule paper (McCallum and Ungar 2003), high-density Braille printing (Völkel et al. 2008), and 3D printing (Celani and Milan 2007) are developed for perceiving information such as geographic and orientation maps, mathematical graphs, and diagrams.

However, visually impaired people can only obtain limited graphical information based on the techniques and methods mentioned above. Moreover, they are expensive and cumbersome for personal use. Visually impaired people have difficulties in perceiving graphical information in their surroundings based on these techniques and methods. With the advantages of growing usage of mobile devices, there would be help for visually impaired people to perceive graphical information if relevant methods could be developed.

1.3 Utilization of Mobile Devices to Help Visually Impaired People

Utilizing the camera and vibration functions of new innovative mobile devices, researchers made efforts on developing mobile applications to help visually impaired people recognize environmental images taken by a mobile camera. The "Dark Angle" developed by Peng (2010) is a mobile phone application for helping visually impaired people. The application can simplify the image instantly taken by a smartphone and then process the image into an outlined graphic. It vibrates the smartphone as a moving finger is upon the graphic outlines. Via the vibrotactile feedbacks, the application with a smartphone was expected to help visually impaired people perceive graphical information in their surroundings. This intention of the application was ideal and encouraging. However, human capabilities of perceiving graphical information via the vibration function of the mobile device are unknown.

1.4 Vibrotactile Recognition Abilities of Two-Point Discrimination Threshold, Relative Judgment of Line Thickness, and Absolute Judgment of Line Thickness

To understand the vibrotactile recognition abilities via the vibration function of a smartphone, Lin et al. (2015) evaluated three vibrotactile recognition abilities. In their study, preliminary experiments were designed to assess (1) two-point discrimination threshold, (2) relative judgment of line thickness, and (3) absolute judgment of line thickness. Blindfold college students participated to measure their three vibrotactile recognition abilities. The results showed that (1) the two-point discrimination accuracy rate was great. When the distance between two points was set at 24 mm, the accuracy rate reached 99%; (2) the relative judgment accuracy rate reached the level of 88% when the two-line difference ratio was set at 1.3; (3) the absolute judgment accuracy rate reached the level of 72% when line thickness number was 3.

1.5 Research Objectives

Due to gaps in current findings and the knowledge of using applications such as the Dark Angle, the main objective of this study aimed at evaluating another vibrotactile recognition ability. In the previous study (Lin et al. 2015), the vibrotactile recognition abilities of two-point discrimination threshold, relative judgment of line thickness, and absolute judgment of line thickness were measured. Hence, this study aimed at measuring the vibrotactile recognition ability of geometric shapes. Similar to Lin et al. (2015), this study tested the ability based on the vibration function embedded in general mobile phones.

2 Method

2.1 Participants and Equipment

Three male and three female college students who were different from those participated in the study by Lin et al. (2015), participated in this study to test their vibrotactile recognition ability of geometric shapes. They were informed of the purpose of the study, which was carried out under the ethics of the Human Subject Protection Association in Taiwan.

An HTC Sensation of 4.7″ screen size with a resolution of 480 × 800 pixels was used in the experiment. The smartphone was fitted with an LCD (liquid-crystal display) capacitive touchscreen that allows the use of fingers to interact with.

A self-developed application, written in Java™ computer programming language using Eclipse Classic 4.2.2, was run on the smartphone. The application displayed geometric shapes on the screen and vibrated the phone as the outlines of graphic were touched.

2.2 Experimental Procedures

The experiment was conducted in a lighted room, in which the participants sat on a chair. After informed consent procedures, the participants were asked to wear a blindfold. As shown in Fig. 1 to perform experimental tasks, the participants held the smartphone with their left hand and sensed the geometric shapes by touching its screen with the forefinger of their right hand. The smartphone vibrated as long as their finger touched the graphics. The participant took their time to discriminate geometric shapes displayed on the screen. Their verbal responses of each experimental trial and the time took to make judgment were recorded.

Fig. 1. Executions of vibrotactile recognition of geometric shapes and the interface of the application.

2.3 Experimental Variables

The independent variables were Shape, Size, and Width Ratio and the dependent variables were the correct rate of judgments and the response time to make the shape judgment. The four Shapes were circle, regular triangle, square and regular pentagon. The three Size values corresponded to the following areas: 3600, 7200 and 14400 pixels

(58.98, 117.96 and 235.93 mm^2). The Width Ratio was defined as the edge width divided by the radius of a circle or the edge-to-center distance of the regular triangle, square and regular pentagon. Three Width Ratio values were 25%, 50%, and 100%. As shown in Fig. 2 a total of 36 graphics were measured (4 Shapes × 3 Sizes × 3 Width Ratios). When testing, the application rotated these graphics through a random angle from 0° to 359° with a scale of one degree. Each experimental combination was repeated four times, giving a total of 144 graphics for the experiment.

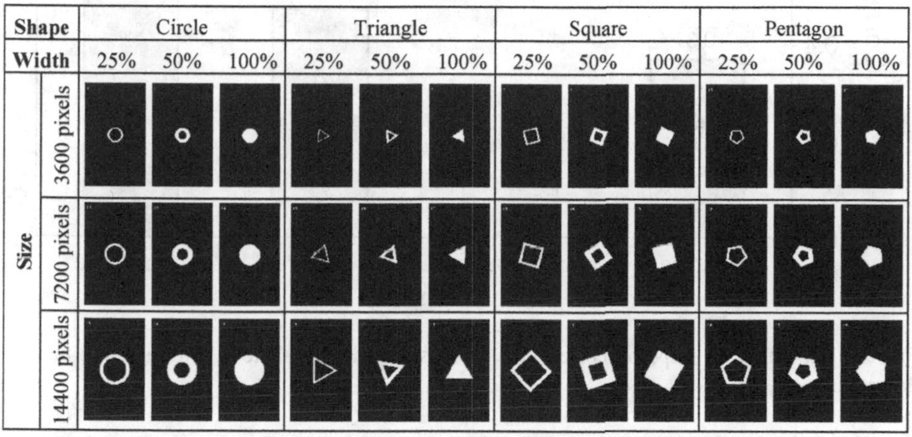

Shape	Circle			Triangle			Square			Pentagon		
Width	25%	50%	100%	25%	50%	100%	25%	50%	100%	25%	50%	100%
Size 3600 pixels												
7200 pixels												
14400 pixels												

Fig. 2. Geometric graphics tested in the experiment.

3 Results

3.1 Proportion of Correct Judgments

Analysis of variance was performed on the proportion of correct judgment using a mixed model with Shape, Size, and Width as fixed effects and Participant as random, in which the interaction effects among these three fixed effects were analyzed. The effect of Participant was considered as a blocking effect, which was not interested in. The results showed significant effects of Shape ($F_{3,823} = 15.02$, $p < 0.001$) on the proportion of correct judgments. As shown in Fig. 3 the proportion of correct judgments, from high to low, was triangle, square, circle, and pentagon. The triangle (54%) was significantly greater from circle and pentagon in performance and the pentagon (25%) was significantly lesser from triangle and square in performance. There was no significant main effect of Size on the proportion of correct judgment.

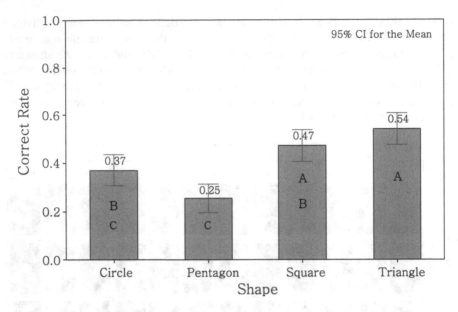

Fig. 3. The effect of shape on correct rate. Means that do not share a letter are significantly different.

3.2 Response Time

Analysis of variance was performed on the response time using a mixed model with Shape, Size, and Width as fixed effects and Participant as random, in which the interaction effects among these three fixed effects were analyzed. Again, the effect of Participant was considered as a blocking effect, which was not interested in. The results showed significant effects of Shape ($F_{3,823}$ = 2.77, p < 0.05) and Width ($F_{2,823}$ = 3.62, p < 0.05) on the proportion of correct judgments. As shown in Fig. 4 although a Tukey comparison showed no significant difference among shapes in response time, the participants spent relatively greater time (73.48 s) when judging shapes of triangle. As shown in Fig. 5 the participants spent significant lesser response time (63.59 s) while judging shapes with the width ratio at 100%. There was no significant main effect of Size on the response time, neither.

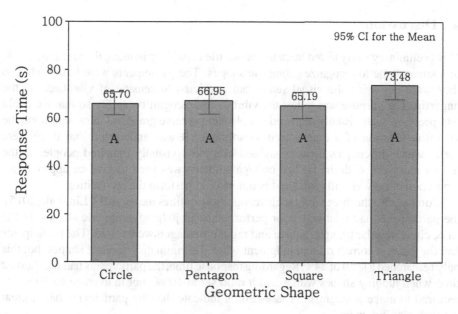

Fig. 4. The effect of shape on response time. Means that do not share a letter are significantly different.

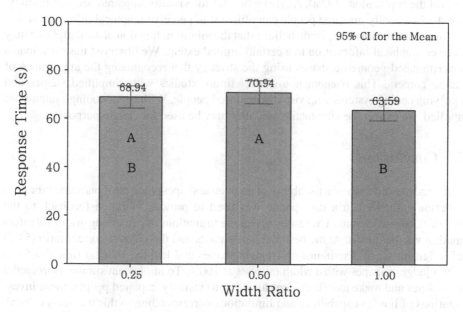

Fig. 5. The effect of width ratio on response time. Means that do not share a letter are significantly different.

4   Discussion

This preliminary study tested human vibrotactile capability in using the vibration mode of a smartphone to recognize geometric shapes. The participants were blindfolded so they were not using the visual sense, but restricted to sensing of vibration via the fingertip. The purpose was to test the vibrotactile recognition ability so that we could interpret how well visually impaired people can perceive graphical information via the vibration function of a touchscreen smartphone. It was anticipated that there were performance differences between sighted users and visually impaired people, so the results measured with the sighted college students was used to give an approximate prediction of how visually impaired people would perform the recognition.

Compared to the three vibrotactile recognition abilities measured by Lin et al. (2015), the participants had relatively poor performance in judging geometric shapes. In the case, circle, regular triangle, square and regular pentagon were tested. The participants had the greatest correct ratio of judgment when discriminating triangle shapes, but this only researched a level of 54%. Regarding response time, the participants had the shortest time when judging shapes with a width ratio set at 100%, but in average 63.59 s was required to make a judgment. These results indicate that the participants had a great confusion of judgment.

Based on the findings of this study and the previous study (Lin et al. 2015), how would the application of Dark Angle be helpful for visually impaired people? Frankly, we doubt visually impaired people can utilize it to perceive graphical information that is complicated. However, we do believe that the vibration function of a smartphone may deliver graphical information to a certain limited extent. We observed the participants discriminated geometric shapes using the strategy that recognizing the appearance of shape corners. This phenomenon directs future studies with simplified shapes and applying coding systems with visually impaired people. With better coding systems are applied, we expect the vibrotactile modality may be used for certain purposes.

5   Conclusions

This study tested a vibrotactile ability of geometric shapes when the monotonic vibration function embedded in a smartphone was used to provide vibration feedback to the blindfolded participants. The results reveal the limitations of perceiving graphical information via the means. At the best, the participants had the greatest correct ratio (54%) of judgment when discriminating triangle shapes and had the shortest time (63.59 s) when judging shapes with a width ratio set at 100%. To implement similar vibrotactile modalities and make mobile devices assistive to visually impaired people, more investigations of human capabilities and limitations corresponding to this means is critical. Future research should involve an adequate number of blind participants and test new coding systems.

Acknowledgements. I would like to acknowledge the grant support from Taiwan Ministry of Science and Technology (MOST103-2221-E-155-053-MY3) for funding the study and the paper presentation. Also, I would like to acknowledge Y.-Y. Wu, Z.-Y. Hong and J.-S. Zhan for helping with the data collection.

References

Celani, G.C., Milan, L.F.: Tactile scale models: three-dimensional info-graphics for space orientation of the blind and visually impaired. In: Virtual and Rapid Manufacturing: Advanced Research in Virtual and Rapid Prototyping, pp. 801–805. Taylor & Francis Group, London (2007)

Ciaffoni, G.: Ariadne GPS (Version 4.2.1) [Mobile application software] (2014). https://itunes.apple.com/us/app/ariadne-gps/id441063072?mt=8

Edman, P.: Tactile Graphics. American Foundation for the Blind, New York (1992)

Image Searcher: TapTapSee (Version 2.1.8) [Mobile application software] (2014). https://itunes.apple.com/us/app/taptapsee-blind-visually-impaired/id567635020?mt=8

Ina, S.: Computer graphics for the blind. ACM SIGCAPH Comput. Physically Handicapped **55**, 16–23 (1996)

Lin, R.F., Huang, C.-Y., Lee, Y.-W., Hsieh, Y.-H.: Evaluating vibrotactile recognition abilities of two-point threshold and line thickness by using a smart phone. In: Paper presented at the 19th Triennial Congress of the International Ergonomics Association, Melbourne, Australia (2015)

McCallum, D., Ungar, S.: An introduction to the use of inkjet for tactile diagram production. British J. Visual Impairment **21**(2), 73–77 (2003)

Peng, Y.-H.: The camera for the visually impaired people (2010). http://www.ccu.edu.tw/show_news.php?id=2336

Pike, E., Blades, M., Spencer, C.: A comparison of two types of tactile maps for blind children. Cartographica: Int. J. Geogr. Inf. Geovisualization **29**(3–4), 83–88 (1992)

UN: World Population Prospects: The 2012 Revision, Highlights and Advance Tables. Working Paper No. ESA/P/WP.228 (2013)

Völkel, T., Weber, G., Baumann, U.: Tactile graphics revised: the Novel BrailleDis 9000 pin-matrix device with multitouch input. In: Miesenberger, K., Klaus, J., Zagler, W., Karshmer, A. (eds.) ICCHP 2008. LNCS, vol. 5105, pp. 835–842. Springer, Heidelberg (2008). doi: 10.1007/978-3-540-70540-6_124

Non-visual Web Browsing: Beyond Web Accessibility

I.V. Ramakrishnan, Vikas Ashok, and Syed Masum Billah[✉]

Department of Computer Science, Stony Brook University, Stony Brook, NY, USA
{ram,vganjiguntea,sbillah}@cs.stonybrook.edu

Abstract. People with vision impairments typically use screen readers to browse the Web. To facilitate non-visual browsing, web sites must be made accessible to screen readers, i.e., all the visible elements in the web site must be readable by the screen reader. But even if web sites are accessible, screen-reader users may not find them easy to use and/or easy to navigate. For example, they may not be able to locate the desired information without having to listen to a lot of irrelevant contents. These issues go beyond web accessibility and directly impact web usability. Several techniques have been reported in the accessibility literature for making the Web usable for screen reading. This paper is a review of these techniques. Interestingly, the review reveals that understanding the semantics of the web content is the overarching theme that drives these techniques for improving web usability.

Keywords: Web accessibility · Web usability · Screen reader · Web content semantics

1 Introduction

The Web has permeated all aspects of our daily lives. We use the Web to obtain and exchange information, shop, pay bills, make travel arrangements, apply for college or employment, connect with others, participate in civic activities, etc. It has in effect become the indispensable ubiquitous "go-to utility" for participating in society. A 2016 report by Internet World Stats shows that Internet usage has skyrocketed by more than 1000% since 2000, to include almost half of the global population in 2016 (over 3.6 billion people) [38], making it one of the most widely used technologies.

About 15% of the world's population are living with some form of physical/sensory/ cognitive disability [57]. The Web has the potential to provide an even greater benefit to such individuals who once required human assistance with many of the activities mentioned earlier. The Web opens up opportunities to do them without assistance and thereby foster independent living.

People with disabilities rely on special purpose assistive software applications for interacting with the Web. It is left to web developers to ensure that their web sites are accessible, i.e., the web sites work with such assistive software. To aid web developers in this process, the W3C Web Accessibility initiative [55] has formulated the Web Content Accessibility Guidelines [56] on how to make web pages accessible. These guidelines are essentially recommendations to web developers. An example

© Springer International Publishing AG 2017
M. Antona and C. Stephanidis (Eds.): UAHCI 2017, Part II, LNCS 10278, pp. 322–334, 2017.
DOI: 10.1007/978-3-319-58703-5_24

recommendation states that web developers should provide text equivalents for images and semantically meaningful labels to links in web pages.

People with vision impairments browse the Web non-visually. They form a sizeable fraction of people with disabilities. Specifically, there are nearly 285 million people with vision impairments worldwide – 39 million blind and 246 million with low vision [58]. In the U.S. alone there are over 23 million Americans suffering from vision loss and over 1.5 million of them use the Internet [3]. This paper reviews the state of the art in non-visual browsing. Ever since the advent of the PC, visually impaired people have used Screen Readers (SRs), a special-purpose software application, to interact with digital content. SRs serially narrate the content of the screen using text-to-speech engines and let users navigate the content using touch or keyboard shortcuts.

Over the years there has been much progress on screen reading and more broadly on assistive technologies for a broad range of disabilities. It has been driven by several factors: (1) federal mandates such as the ADA [2] and the 21st Century Communications and Video Accessibility Act [1]; (2) companies specializing in the development of assistive technologies [18, 25, 33, 41]; large IT companies like Google, Apple and Microsoft incorporating support for accessibility in their products and services (e.g. Microsoft's MSAA and UI Automation [34, 35], Apple's NSAccessibility [9], and GNOME's ATK and AT-SPI [16]); (3) business and educational institutions adopting assistive technologies to enhance employment and educational opportunities for people with disabilities. Because of all this progress, these days visually impaired people have several high quality SRs to choose from, e.g., JAWS [25], Window-Eyes [33], Super-Nova [18], NVDA [41] and VoiceOver [53].

For visually impaired people, SRs remain the dominant technology for non-visual web browsing. Web sites that are designed based on WCAG guidelines are accessible to SRs. But making web pages accessible in and of itself does not make them usable – a problem that is primarily concerned with the "how to's" of providing a rich user experience in terms of ease of use, effectiveness in getting tasks done, etc. In this regard, SRs are not very usable or efficient for web browsing [14] and have several notable drawbacks [27]. Firstly, to be efficient, SR users have to remember an assortment of shortcuts and learn a number of browsing strategies; however, most users rely only on a small basic set of sequential navigation shortcuts, which leads to excessive interaction with computers even while performing simple browsing tasks [14]. Secondly, because one cannot judge the importance of content before listening to it; blind users typically go through reams of irrelevant content before they find what they need, thereby suffering from information overload. Thirdly, SRs are typically oblivious of the fact that web content is organized into semantic entities (e.g., menus, date pickers, search results, etc.), where each entity is composed of many basic HTML elements; the user may not know what entities are present on the page, whether s/he is navigating inside or outside an entity, where the entity's boundaries are, etc. These problems become particularly acute when performing tasks in content-rich web sites; for example, while sighted users can purchase something online or make a reservation in just a few minutes, screen-reader users often take 10 min or more [14, 45]. Yet another serious problem of not knowing the entity boundaries is that the SR's sequential readout intersperses content from different semantic entities, which can confuse and disorient the user. Lastly, in addition to not being able to get a quick overview of the entire web page and having to read through content one element at a time, blind users also have to endure the fact that SRs navigate web pages at the syntactic level instead of the semantic one. Consequently, while sighted people see the semantic structure of the web page, blind people have access only to its syntactic structure, and most often have to navigate and listen to individual HTML elements.

The root cause of the usability problems stems from the SR's limited knowledge of the semantics of web content. Research efforts in accessibility have sought to rectify this situation by incorporating *semantic awareness* in non-visual browsing. At their core, the techniques for semantic awareness infer the semantics by analysis of the content using syntactic and structural cues in web pages, optionally supplemented by explicit knowledgebase encoding the semantics of domain-specific web sites such as travel web sites, shopping web sites, etc. Semantic awareness goes beyond web accessibility. It embodies the state of the art in making web browsing usable for SR users. In the following sections this paper reviews how semantic awareness is incorporated in non-visual browsing with SRs.

2 Semantic Awareness in Non-visual Web Browsing

We begin with some terminology: A web page can be viewed as a collection of semantic entities. Informally, we define a semantic entity to be a meaningful grouping of related HTML elements. As an illustration, Fig. 1 is a web page fragment with six semantic entities, numbered 1 to 6. The number associated with an entity is shown in red at the corner of that entity. For example, entity numbered 4 corresponds to the search-result entity showing the results for an available flight. Notice that it is a grouping of related links, button, images and text. Similarly, an article entity in a news web page is a collection of paragraphs and possibly links; a list of items entity can be a simple HTML list or a tabulated list of products with their prices and short descriptions. Observe how the semantic entities in Fig. 1 have clear visual boundaries. Sighted people can easily identify and interact with these entities because of these boundaries and moreover are easy to distinguish from each other. In contrast, blind people have to use the screen reader to figure out and guess where the entity starts and ends and how it is organized. Early on there has been a lot of research effort on identifying the boundaries of semantic entities. The basis of these efforts is segmentation, described next.

2.1 Segmentation

A segment of a web page corresponds to a contiguous fragment of web elements in the page that are "semantically" related (e.g., the news headline and article summary, menu of categories, search results, etc.). As illustration: the fragments enclosed within the rectangles in Fig. 1 are examples of segments.

Organizing a web page into segments lets users navigate between "meaningful" pieces of information and results in much better comprehension of the content. This is

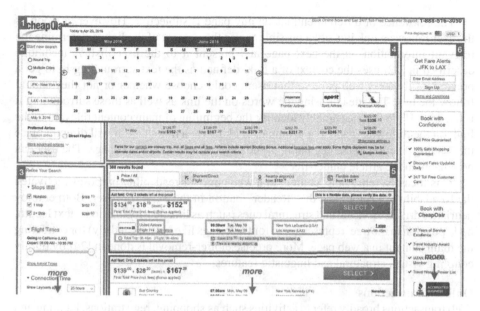

Fig. 1. Web page segmented into semantic entities (Color figure online)

especially useful for small screen devices where display area is at a premium, making it all the more important to focus on coherent and relevant chunks of content.

Several techniques for segmenting web pages have appeared in the research literature (e.g. see [5, 15, 20, 42, 49, 60–62]). They utilize a range of features in the pages from visual cues, to spatial locality information, to presentational similarity, to patterns in the content, etc.

Segmentation has been used in a variety of applications such as adapting content on small screen devices (e.g. [61]), data cleaning and search (e.g. [60, 62]) and web data extraction (e.g. [5, 49]). Recognizing the importance of segmentation, Apple's Voice-Over also segments web pages with its "auto web spot" feature. More importantly segmentation is an important component in many techniques that have been developed to enhance web usability for people with visual impairments. We review these techniques now.

2.2 Segmentation-Based Techniques for Enhancing Web Usability

Clutter-Free Browsing

As SR users browse the Web, they have to filter through a lot of irrelevant data, i.e., clutter. For example, most web pages contain banners, ads, navigation bars, and other kinds of distracting data irrelevant to the actual information desired by the users. Navigating to the relevant information quickly is critical for making non-visual web browsing usable. For finding information quickly, SRs allow keyword searching. This assumes that users already know what they are looking for, which is not necessarily true in all cases, especially in ad hoc browsing.

The relevance of different entities on any page is subjective. However, as soon as the user follows a link it is often possible to use the context of the link to determine the relevant information on the next page and present it to the user first. A technique described in [22] uses the context of a link, defined as the text surrounding it, to get a preview of the next web page so that users could choose whether or not they should follow the link. The idea of using the words on the link as well as those surrounding it is used in [31] to more accurately identify the beginning of main content relevant to the link, on the following page. For example, clicking on a news link, it will directly place the reading position to the beginning of the news article on the next page. The user can now listen to the article clutter-free.

This focus on removing "clutter" in a web page for readability purposes motivated the Readability [47] tool and the "Reader" button in the Safari browser. Both employ heuristics driven by visual and structural cues (such as link density in a node, text length, node position in the tree, representative font size, tags like headers and div) for extracting the main content in a web page. More precise clutter-removal is done in [24] by tightly coupling visual, structural and linguistic features.

Online Transactions

Web transactions broadly refer to activities such as shopping, registrations, banking and bill-payments online. Such transactions involve several steps that typically span several web pages. This can significantly exacerbate information overload on SR users and affect their productivity. In this regard, as was mentioned earlier, while sighted users can purchase something online or make a reservation in just a few minutes, SR users often take 10 min or more [14, 45].

Usually one needs to browse only a small fragment of a web page to perform a transaction. This observation is the basis of the method in [51] for doing web transactions

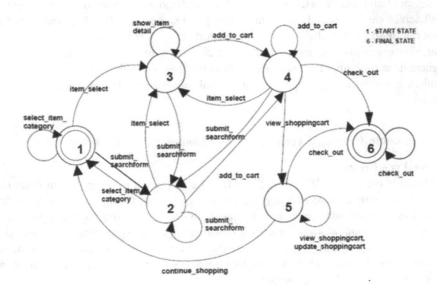

Fig. 2. Automaton fragment for online shopping

more efficiently and with less information overload. Specifically, a web transaction is modeled as a process automation (see Fig. 2). In that automaton, each node/state represents transaction-specific semantic entities (e.g., search results or product description) it expects to find in the web page that is given as the state's input and the edges/arrows are possible user actions corresponding to the entity represented by the state (e.g., clicking a button). Segmentation is used to identify transaction-specific semantic entities in that page.

Stepping through a transaction corresponds to making transitions in the automaton; at each step, only the entity relevant to that step in the transaction is presented thereby skipping all the other content in the page. The process automaton is learned from labeled training sequences gathered from click streams of user actions. In [30], the construction process of the automata was completely automated.

3 Skimming and Summarization

Skimming and summarization are complementary techniques that help the users obtain the gist of a text document. Summarization is a snippet of text, explicitly constructed from the document's text, which conveys the essence of the information contained in the document. Skimming, on the other hand, conveys it by identifying a few informative words in the document. These two topics have attracted the attention of the Information Retrieval and Natural Language Processing research community [32, 46]. Summarization and skimming are naturally applicable to web pages, especially for non-visual browsing as they give the users a "peek" into the content without having to make them listen to it in its entirety.

Using the notion of the context of a web page as a collection of words gathered around the links on other pages pointing to that web page, [17] uses this context to obtain a summary of the page. Summarization using context is also explored by the InCommonSense system [7], where search engine results are summarized to generate text snippets. In BrookesTalk [52] the web page is summarized as a collection of "significant" sentences drawn from the page. These are sentences containing key trigrams (phrases containing three words) that are identified using simple statistics. The AcceSS system [43] makes web pages accessible through a transcoding process comprised of summarization and simplification steps. The former uses the idea of context of a link from [22] to get a preview of the page and the latter identifies "important" sections to be retained. The Summate system picks a maximum of four sentences from a web page as its gist summary [23].

A method for non-visual skimming is described in [4]. It works as follows: Firstly, every sentence is parsed to extract grammatical relations amongst its words. Secondly, a lexical tree based on these relations is constructed, where each node of the tree represents a word in the sentence. Thirdly, for every word in this tree, it's grammatical (i.e., POS tags) as well as structural features (related to in-degree/out-degree, etc.) are extracted. These features are given to a trained classifier to determine whether or not to include the word in the skimming summary. Finally, a subtree consisting of the selected words is constructed. This subtree represents the skimming summary that users interact with via an interface.

4 Speech-Based Browsing

Speech input has long been recognized as a powerful interaction modality for non-visual browsing because of its potential to alleviate the shortcomings of a SR's keyboard-based press-and-listen mode of interaction. An exposition of these shortcomings and how speech modality can address them appears in [10]. Several systems support browsing with spoken commands.

Voice browsers like PublicVoiceXML [44] and JVoiceXML [48] have an interactive voice interface for browsing web content. Browsing the Web with these voice browsers requires the conversion of web pages to JVoiceXML [54], a document format that operates within a controlled domain. In some cases, voice navigation is used for improving one particular aspect of browsing, e.g., [21] focuses on making the menus and submenus appearing on a webpage voice-accessible; Windows Speech Recognition (WSR) [36] makes it possible to follow a link by speaking its ordinal number and enables a few other basic commands. Alas, neither is accessible to blind users. An Android accessibility service, JustSpeak [59], can be used with any Android app or accessibility service, and is able to process chains of commands in a single utterance. It is limited to a few basic browsing-related commands, specifically: activate, scroll, toggle switch, long press, toggle checkbox. Dragon NaturallySpeaking Rich Internet Application feature [40] enables the user to control certain websites by voice. It provides limited support to select parts of only four (4) websites in specific browsers, and lists many additional caveats and limitations, both general and browser specific. But usage of visual cues and a graphical user interface for listing possible utterances/commands significantly reduces Dragon's accessibility for blind people. Capti-Speak is speech-augmented Screen Reader developed recently [10]. Capti-Speak translates spoken utterances into browsing actions and generates appropriate TTS responses to these utterances. Each spoken utterance is part of an ongoing dialog. It employs a custom dialog-act model [11] that was developed exclusively for "speech-enabled non-visual web access" to interpret every spoken utterance in the context of the most recent state of the dialog, where the state, in some sense, encodes the history of previous user utterances and system responses.

5 Web Automation

Web automation broadly refers to methods that automate typical web browsing steps such as form filling clicking links and more generally any kind of repetitive steps, on behalf of the user. They therefore play an important role in making non-visual web browsing more usable.

There are several research prototypes that automate web browsing. The traditional approach to Web automation is via macros, which are pre-recorded sequences of instructions that automate browsing steps. The recorded macros are later replayed to automate the same sequence of recorded steps. Macros are usually created by the well-known process of programming by demonstration, where the developer demonstrates to the macro recorder what steps need to be done and in what sequence. With the exception of Trailblazer [13], which is built on top of the CoScripter system [28], most of the macro-based web automation systems are meant for sighted users.

The CoScripter system is a tool for recording macros to automate repetitive web tasks and replay them. CoCo [26] takes user commands in the form of (restricted) natural language strings in order to perform various tasks on the Web and maps these natural language commands to macros stored in the CoScripter Wiki [28] and CoScripter Reusable History (ActionShot [29]). While both CoScripter and CoCo are meant for sighted users, TrailBlazer [13] allows SR users to provide a brief description of their tasks for which it dynamically cerates new macros by stitching together existing macros in the CoScripter Wiki. It also attempts to adapt macros explicitly recorded for one website to similar tasks on other sites.

The main drawback with macros is that they lack the flexibility necessary to allow the user to deviate from the prerecorded sequence of steps, or to choose between several options in each step of the macro. Those difficulties make macro-based approaches too limiting to be useful for people with vision impairments. A flexible, macro-less model-based approach to web automation is described in [45]. The model is constructed based on the past browsing history of the user. Using this history and the current web page as the browsing context, the model can predict the most probable browsing actions that can be performed by the user. The model construction is fully automated. Additionally, the model is continuously and incrementally updated as history evolves, thereby, ensuring the predictions are not "outdated".

6   Web Screen Reading Assistants

Voice-activated Assistants are in vogue these days. The recent wave of such assistants include Apple's Siri [50], Samsung's S Voice [8], Google Now [19], Nuance's Nina [39], Microsoft's Cortana [37] and Amazon's Echo [6]. These assistants are typically used for factual question answering and doing common tasks such as finding restaurants and managing calendars. Users are finding them to be invaluable, so much so that it is fast becoming an integral part of their digital world. But Assistants fall short when it comes to general-purpose web browsing. Some, e.g., Siri, fall back to simple web search when they are unable to answer user's requests. Regardless, Assistants have the potential to become a transformative assistive technology and remains mostly unexplored in accessibility research. But a recent work that explores the applicability of Assistants in web screen reading suggests that it has the potential to significantly enhance web usability for SR users [12]. In this work, the web screen reading assistant, SRAA, is rooted in two complimentary ideas: First, it elevates the interaction to a higher level of abstraction - from operating over (syntactic) HTML elements to operating over semantic web entities. Doing so brings blind users closer to how sighted people perceive and operate over web entities. Second, the SRAA provides a dialog interface using which users can interact with the semantic entities with spoken commands. The SRAA interprets and executes these commands.

SRAA is driven by a Web Entity Model (WEM), which is a collection of the semantic entities in the underlying webpage. The WEM is dynamically constructed for any page using an extensive generic library of custom-designed descriptions of commonly occurring semantic entities across websites. The WEM imposes an abstract semantic layer over the web page. Users interact with the WEM via natural-language spoken commands (They can also use keyboard shortcuts). By elevating interaction with the web page to the more natural and intuitive level of web entities, SRAA relieves users from having to press numerous shortcuts to operate on low-level HTML elements - the principal source of tedium and frustration. Figure 3 below depicts a scenario snippet of how a user interacts with SRAA to review the search results for making a flight reservation in Expedia, depicted in Fig. 1.

USER ACTIONS	SPOKEN UTTERANCES	SRAA ACTIONS
Fill host and destination fields and navigate to departure date field		
Give speech command	"Select departure date 23"	
	"Departure date field value set to 10/23/2016"	Consult WEM for *Calendar* entity and call method to select 23 of current month
Use shortcuts to navigate to return date		
Give speech command	"Choose return date 28"	
	"Return date field value set to 10/23/2016"	Consult WEM for *Calendar* entity and call method to select 28 of current month
Press *Search* button		
Give speech command	"Go to search results"	
	"Search results first item [text content]"	Find *Search Results* entity in WEM and call method to move cursor to first result
Navigate results using screenreader shortcuts		
Give speech command	"Sort by price"	
	"Sort by price lowest or price highest?"	Find *Sort Options* entity in WEM and then ask user to resolve ambiguity for 2 *price*
Disambiguate	"Lowest"	
	"Search result sort by price lowest, first item"	Select price (lowest) option in *Sort Options* and move cursor to 1st item of *Search*
Navigate to next result item using shortcuts		
Give speech command	"What is the duration?"	
	"6 hours 21 minutes"	Find current result item in WEM and call method to obtain text value of *duration*

Fig. 3. Example user interaction scenario with SRAA

User actions (with keystrokes) and SRAA's internal operations corresponding to user commands appear in the left and right column respectively. Arrows pointing right and left in the middle column correspond to user's spoken commands and SRAA's synthesized-speech responses. The scenario sequence flows from left-to-right and top-to-bottom. As seen in Fig. 3, users no longer need to spend time and effort locating and getting the information they need; instead, they simply use speech commands to delegate this task to the SRAA, which also resolves any ambiguity in the process (e.g., "sort by price"). Observe the simplicity and ease of interaction with SRAA compared to using only a vanilla screen reader. While sighted users' interaction with the Web is implicitly driven by the semantics of web entities, SRAA makes it explicit to the blind users. It brings blind users closer to how sighted people perceive and interact with the Web – which is the highest degree of web usability any technology can expect to achieve.

7 Conclusion

This paper reviewed some of the important techniques reported in the accessibility research literature, for making web sites usable for screen reading. The review included clutter-removal techniques, support for online transactions, skimming and summarization, interacting using speech, web automations and Assistants. The overall aim of these techniques is to make the Web easy to use and navigate, and reduce information overload. The common thread underlying these techniques was their use of the semantic knowledge of the web content to improve the usability of the Web.

The reviewed techniques mostly focused on desktop computing as this is still the primary way visually-impaired people use computers at home, at school, and at work. Nowadays, smart phone devices are becoming an indispensable device in people's lives, including people with disabilities. These devices have numerous apps that assist users in performing various day-to-day activities. This raises several interesting research questions regarding the usability of these apps for people with vision impairments and how it can be further improved.

Acknowledgement. This research was supported in part by NSF awards: IIS-1447549, CNS-1405641; National Eye Institute of NIH award: R01EY026621; NIDILRR: 90IF0117-01-00. NIDILRR is a Center within the Administration for Community Living (ACL), Department of Health and Human Services (HHS). The content is solely the responsibility of the authors and does not necessarily represent the official views of NIH nor represent the policy of NIDILRR, ACL, HHS.

References

1. 21st Century Communications and Video Accessibility Act (CVAA). https://www.fcc.gov/consumers/guides/21st-century-communications-and-video-accessibility-act-cvaa
2. Introduction to the ADA. https://www.ada.gov/ada_intro.htm
3. AFB. Facts and Figures on American Adults with Vision Loss (2017). http://www.afb.org/Section.asp?SectionID=15&TopicID=413&DocumentID=4900
4. Ahmed, F., Borodin, Y., Soviak, A., Islam, M., Ramakrishnan, I.-V., Hedgpeth, T.: Accessible skimming: faster screen reading of web pages. In: Proceedings of the 25th Annual ACM Symposium on User Interface Software and Technology, pp. 367–378. ACM: Cambridge, Massachusetts, USA (2012)
5. Álvarez, M., Pan, A., Raposo, J., Bellas, F., Cacheda, F.: Finding and extracting data records from web pages. J. Sig. Process. Syst. **59**(1), 123–137 (2010)

6. Amazon. Echo (2015). www.amazon.com/echo
7. Amitay, E., Paris., C.: Automatically summarizing web sites: is there a way around it? In: CIKM 2000: Proceedings of the Ninth International Conference on Information and Knowledge Management, pp. 173–179. ACM Press (2000)
8. Android, S Voice (2012). http://www.androidcentral.com/tag/s-voice
9. Apple, NSAccessibility. https://developer.apple.com/reference/appkit/nsaccessibility
10. Ashok, V., Borodin, Y., Puzis, Y., Ramakrishnan, I.-V.: Capti-Speak: a speech-enabled web screen reader. In: Proceedings of the 12th Web for All Conference. ACM, Florence, Italy (2015)
11. Ashok, V., Borodin, Y., Stoyanchev, S., Ramakrishnan, I.-V.: Dialogue act modeling for non-visual web access. In: The 15th Annual SIGdial Meeting on Discourse and Dialogue, SIGDIAL, Philadelphia, PA, USA (2014). http://www.aclweb.org/anthology/W/W14/W14-43.pdf#page=143
12. Ashok, V., Puzis, Y., Yevgen, B., Ramakrishnan, I.-V.: Web screen reading automation assistance using semantic abstraction. In: 22nd ACM International Conference on Intelligent User Interfaces (2017)
13. Bigham, J.-P., Lau, T., Nichols, J.: Trailblazer: enabling blind users to blaze trails through the web. In: Proceedings of the 13th International Conference on Intelligent User Interfaces. ACM, Sanibel Island, Florida, USA (2009)
14. Borodin, Y., Bigham, J., Dausch, G., Ramakrishnan, I.-V.: More than meets the eye: a survey of screen-reader browsing strategies. In: Proceedings of the 2010 International Cross Disciplinary Conference on Web Accessibility (W4A), pp. 1–10. ACM, Raleigh, North Carolina (2010)
15. Cai, D., Yu, S., Wen, J.-R., Ma, W.-Y.: VIPS: a vision based page segmentation algorithm. Microsoft Technical report (2004)
16. GNOME Accessibility Architecture (ATK and AT-SPI). https://accessibility.kde.org/developer/atk.php
17. Delort, J.Y., Bouchon-Meunier, B., Rifqi, M.: Enhanced web document summarization using hyperlinks. In: Proceedings of the 14th ACM Conference on Hypertext and Hypermedia, pp. 208–215. ACM, Nottingham, UK (2003)
18. Dolphin, SuperNova Screen Reader. http://www.yourdolphin.com/productdetail.asp?id=1
19. Google. Google Now. http://www.google.com/landing/now/#utm_source=google&utm_medium=sem&utm_campaign=GoogleNow
20. Guo, H., Mahmud, J., Borodin, Y., Stent, A., Ramakrishnan, I.-V..: A general approach for partitioning web page content based on geometric and style information. In: Proceedings of the International Conference on Document Analysis and Recognition (2007)
21. Han, S., Jung, G., Ryu, M., Choi, B.-U., Cha. J.: A voice-controlled web browser to navigate hierarchical hidden menus of web pages in a smart-tv environment. In: Proceedings of the Companion Publication of the 23rd International Conference on World Wide Web Companion. International World Wide Web Conferences Steering Committee (2014)
22. Harper, S., Goble, C., Stevens, R., Yesilada, Y.: Middleware to expand context and preview in hypertext. In: Proceedings of the 6th International ACM SIGACCESS Conference on Computers and Accessibility (2004)
23. Harper, S., Patel, N.: Gist summaries for visually impaired surfers. In: Proceedings of the 7th International ACM SIGACCESS Conference on Computers and Accessibility (2005)
24. Islam, M.-A., Ahmed, F., Borodin, Y., Ramakrishnan, I.-V.: Tightly coupling visual and linguistic features for enriching audio-based web browsing experience. In: Proceedings of the 20th ACM International Conference on Information and Knowledge Management, pp. 2085–2088. ACM, Glasgow, Scotland, UK (2011)

25. JAWS. Screen reader from Freedom Scientific (2013). http://www.freedomscientific.com/products/fs/jaws-product-page.asp
26. Lau, T., Cerruti, J., Manzato, G., Bengualid, M., Bigham, J., Nichols, J.: A conversational interface to web automation. In: Proceedings of the 23nd Annual ACM Symposium on User Interface Software and Technology. ACM, New York, USA
27. Lazar, J., Allen, A., Kleinman, J., Malarkey, C.: What frustrates screen reader users on the web: a study of 100 blind users. Int. J. Hum.-Comput. Interact. **22**(3), 247–269 (2007)
28. Leshed, G., Haber, E.-M., Matthews, T., Lau, T.: CoScripter: automating & sharing how-to knowledge in the enterprise. In: Proceeding of the 26th Annual SIGCHI Conference on Human Factors in Computing Systems. ACM, Florence, Italy (2008)
29. Li, I., Nichols, J., Lau, T., Drews, C., Cypher, A.: Here's what I did: sharing and reusing web activity with ActionShot. In: Proceedings of the SIGCHI Conference on Human Factors in Computing Systems. ACM (2010)
30. Mahmud, J., Borodin, Y., Ramakrishnan, I.-V., Ramakrishnan, C.-R.: Automated construction of web accessibility models from transaction click-streams. In: Proceedings of the 18th International Conference on World Wide Web. ACM, Madrid, Spain (2009)
31. Mahmud, J.-U., Borodin, Y., Ramakrishnan, I.-V.: CSurf: a context-driven non-visual web-browser, In: Proceedings of the 16th International Conference on World Wide Web. ACM, Banff, Alberta, Canada (2007)
32. Manning, C.-D., Raghavan, P., Schütze, H.: Introduction to information retrieval. Cambridge University Press (2008)
33. GW Micro - Window-Eyes. http://www.gwmicro.com/Window-Eyes/
34. Microsoft, Microsoft Active Accessibility: Architecture. https://msdn.microsoft.com/en-us/library/windows/desktop/dd373592(v=vs.85).aspx
35. Microsoft, UI Automation Overview. http://msdn.microsoft.com/en-us/library/ms747327.aspx
36. Microsoft. Common commands in Speech Recognition (2014). http://windows.microsoft.com/en-us/windows/common-speech-recognition-commands#1TC=windows-7
37. Microsoft. Cortana contextual awareness (2014). http://www.bing.com/dev/en-us/contextual-awareness
38. Miniwatts Marketing Group. Internet Usage Statistics: The Internet Big Picture World Internet Users and Population Stats (2016). http://www.internetworldstats.com/stats.htm
39. Nuance. Nina (2012). http://www.nuance.com/landing-pages/products/nina/default.asp
40. Nuance. Dragon Naturally Speaking Rich Internet Application (2014). http://nuance.custhelp.com/app/answers/detail/a_id/6940/~/information-on-rich-internet-application-support
41. NVAccess, NV Access: Home of the free NVDA Screen Reader. http://www.nvaccess.org/
42. Zhai, Y., Liu., B.: Web data extraction based on partial tree alignment. In: Proceedings of the 14th international conference on World Wide Web. ACM (2005)
43. Parmanto, B., Ferrydiansyah, R., Saptono, A., Song, L., Sugiantara, I.-W., Hackett, S.: AcceSS: accessibility through simplification & summarization. In: Proceedings of the 2005 International Cross-Disciplinary Workshop on Web Accessibility (W4A). ACM, Chiba, Japan (2005)
44. Public Voice Lab, S., PublicVoiceXML. 2002
45. Puzis, Y., Borodin, Y., Puzis, R., Ramakrishnan, I.-V.: Predictive Web Automation Assistant for People with Vision Impairments. In: Proceedings of the 22th International Conference on World Wide Web. ACM, Rio de Janeiro, Brazil (2013)
46. Radev, D.-R., Hovy, E., McKeown, K.: Introduction to the special issue on summarization. Comput. Linguist. **28**(4), 399–408 (2002)
47. Readability. https://www.readability.com/

48. Schnelle,   JVoiceXML   (2013).   http://webdesign.about.com/gi/o.htm?zi=1/ XJ&zTi=1&sdn=webdesign&cdn=compute&tm=171&f=00&tt=14&bt=3&bts=31&zu=http %3A//jvoicexml.sourceforge.net/

49. Zhu, J., Nie, Z., Wen, J.-R., Zhang, B., Ma., W.-Y.: Simultaneous record detection and attribute labeling in web data extraction. In: Proceedings of the 12th ACM SIGKDD International Conference on Knowledge Discovery and Data Mining. ACM (2006)

50. Siri: The Personal Assistant on Your Phone (2013). http://siri.com/

51. Sun, Z., Mahmud, J., Ramakrishnan, I.-V., Mukherjee, S.: Model-directed Web transactions under constrained modalities. In: ACM Transactions on the Web (2007)

52. Zajicek, M., Powell, C., Reeves, C.: Web search and orientation with BrookesTalk. In: Technology and Persons with Disabilities Conference (CSUN) (1999)

53. VoiceOver, Screen reader from Apple (2015)

54. VoiceXML. W3C - Voice Extensible Markup Language (2009). http://www.w3.org/TR/ voicexml20

55. WAI. W3C Web Accessibility Initiative (1997). http://www.w3.org/WAI/

56. WCAG. W3C Web Content Accessibility Guidelines (2009). http://www.w3.org/TR/ WCAG10/

57. WHO-disability-data (2011). http://www.who.int/disabilities/world_report/2011/report/en/

58. WHO. Visual impairment and blindness (2014). http://www.who.int/mediacentre/factsheets/ fs282/en/

59. Zhong, Y., Raman, T.-V., Burkhardt, C., Biadsy, F., Bigham, J.-P.: JustSpeak: enabling universal voice control on Android. In: Proceedings of the 11th Web for All Conference. ACM, Seoul, Korea (2014)

60. Yi, L., Liu, B.: Eliminating noisy information in web pages for data mining. In: Proceedings of the ACM Conference on Knowledge Discovery and Data Mining (2003)

61. Yin, X., Lee, W.-S.: Using link analysis to improve layout on mobile devices. In: Proceedings of the International World Wide Web Conference (WWW). ACM (2004)

62. Yu, S., Cai, D., Wen, J.-R., Ma, W.-Y.: Improving pseudo-relevance feedback in web information retrieval using web page segmentation. In: Proceedings of the International World Wide Web Conference (WWW) (2003)

The 3D Printing of Tactile Maps for Persons with Visual Impairment

Roman Rener[✉]

Geodetic Institute of Slovenia, Ljubljana, Slovenia
Roman.rener@gis.si

Abstract. The safe and efficient mobility of persons with visual impairment may be secured with the development of new aids, based on new computer methods and technologies. The issue of mobility and accessibility is one of the central concerns in the development of »smart cities« and of accessible service for all inhabitants of urban areas. We will present an automated procedure for the production of tactile maps with the latest 3D printing technology for visually impaired persons. By employing a new method, which entailed the linking of geolocation data (digital maps, digital spatial images), new 3D tactile designing process and 3D print technology, we have reduced the costs and accelerated the production of tactile maps for visually impaired persons, and ensured the transportability of the products by converting them into a digital (STL) format. To exhibit the use of our new methodology, several production cases from Slovenia will be presented: the tactile map of the Slovene Ethnographic Museum, the tactile model of the Sečovlje Salina – the traditional production of salt, the tactile plate of the famous Schutze ceramic plate from 1886, the tactile map of the Library of the Union of the Blind and Partially Sighted of Slovenia, and the tactile map for orientation and mobility of the capital of Slovenia, Ljubljana.

Keywords: 3D tactile maps · Visually impaired persons · Indoor and outdoor accessibility

1 Introduction

When people lose their sight, they undergo significant changes. An important factor in the rehabilitation of people with disabilities is the degree to which they are able to move independently as that influences their employment prospects and inclusion in society, both directly and indirectly.

The safe and efficient mobility of persons with visual impairment may be secured with the development of new aids based on new computer methods and technologies. The article details various data sources, and the use of new computer technologies, such as 3D print, digital maps, digital spatial images, and open data. The issue of mobility and accessibility« is one of the central concerns in the development of »smart cities« and of accessible service for all inhabitants of urban areas. New technologies (smart phones, sensors, computers and the use of artificial intelligence) and the new paradigm

© Springer International Publishing AG 2017
M. Antona and C. Stephanidis (Eds.): UAHCI 2017, Part II, LNCS 10278, pp. 335–350, 2017.
DOI: 10.1007/978-3-319-58703-5_25

of data accessibility (open data, big data) offer the possibility to develop new utilities and services that would ensure the safe mobility of all sections of society.

The term 'people with disabilities' covers various groups of individuals: the blind and partially sighted, the physically disabled, the deaf and hard-of-hearing, and others. With the addition of senior citizens and families with children (getting around with prams), we come to the realization that ensuring mobility is not an established fact, but in fact the precondition for the active involvement of people with disabilities in micro- and macro- environments. Eventually, these products and services will benefit each and every one of us as we become the new generation of senior citizens, faced with a range of functional disabilities. The Geodetic Institute of Slovenia has been working towards new solutions for safe mobility in cities for many decades, focusing in particular on the needs of the visually impaired individuals.

In order to develop quality aids, it is essential to first recognize the needs of the users; each targeted group has its own needs and demands. From the point of view of the user (e.g. a blind individual), reaching a destination requires mapping out one's route in advance. This entails the following three processes: the individual's location in place, the process of navigation, and mobility. The major issue in navigation is having good information and being familiar with expert and optimal technological solutions. The main mobility enhancing sources of information are state and municipal »topographic« databases, upgraded occasionally with topical information for navigation (additionally acquired in the field and in the office), different orthoimages, Google Street View, etc.

The article will go on to describe the effects and requirements for the safe mobility of persons with visual impairment, our target group, and the state of the art automated production of tactile maps for the visually impaired with the help of new technologies.

2 The Safe Mobility of Persons with Visual Impairment – Definitions, Problems and Demands

From the point of view of the user – a blind individual – reaching a destination requires a detailed mapping out of one's route in advance. People with disabilities have none of the advantages that the sighted take for granted when navigating their hometown, travelling across countries or between continents. They have to meticulously plan their journey, as well as the activities required to reach their intended destination – we call these *pre-journey activities* – in advance. For better understanding, three key concepts which pertain to the mobility of visually impaired people must be formulated: orientation, navigation, and mobility.

- *Orientation*: the ability of a visually impaired person to orient themselves in space; i.e. to know where they are, to be aware of their location in space and of spatial relations.
- *Navigation*: a set of instructions that help a visually impaired person navigate from their current position to a different location in space. The instructions may be given in a number of ways, e.g. orally, or, as is more commonly the case, with the help of electronic navigation (e.g. with Trekker Breeze).

- *Mobility*: a complex notion that encompasses the orientation, navigation and movement of a blind individual in space to reach a new intended destination.

2.1 Objective

The objective of the project was to link a variety of input data and a number of different procedures and technologies into a single line. This entailed the acquisition and processing of data, the production of a 2D map with cartographic tools, designing a 3D model with computer software for solid modelling, and the production and re-production of the end products, e.g. by employing the thermo-vacuum method. The new procedure strived towards the automatization of production, the elimination of handwork, and the creation of tactile maps in a digital format that would enable easy access and the re-production (3D print) of the end product. The greatest flaw of standard tactile map production is that it is both a time-consuming and costly process and that the production of a larger number of copies is difficult (poor reproducibility).

2.2 The Difficulties and Challenges in the Navigation of Visually Impaired Persons

Navigating the city presents visually impaired people with a number of difficulties that arise from the lack of information in the environment [11]. To be able to move around independently, the visually impaired person has to be familiar with the city's urban areas and have the appropriate cognitive map formed. By using a white cane, the visually impaired individual can only sense their environment within a one metre radius of themselves. They obtain the rest of the information mostly through hearing.

I will address three of the most common problems the visually impaired person is confronted with when moving around the city.

Crossing the Road or Intersection. The level of difficulty for the visually impaired person rises with the number of lanes and the volume of traffic. They also have to be familiar with the geometry of the intersection. Accessible pedestrian signal (APS) devices offer substantial help to the visually impaired. Crossing the road without APS is impossible or extremely dangerous. Even so, the person has to locate their position in space, find an accessible pedestrian signal (a pedestrian pushbutton device), and direct themselves toward the identical device located on the other side of the road (Fig. 1).

Cycle Tracks and Cyclists. Being run over by a cyclist is the greatest fear and concern of every visually impaired person. Though the movement of cyclists is soundless, footways and cycle tracks tend to lie side by side. Cyclists often ride carelessly, speeding past the pedestrians. Because the visually impaired person cannot see them, bumping into them can be very dangerous. Luj Šprohar (the visually impaired person in the photograph, who usually moves around Ljubljana independently) has developed a special technique for crossing cycle tracks (Fig. 2).

Fig. 1. A visually impaired person crossing the road with no accessible pedestrian signals (Ljubljana Central Bus Station). He has to wait for a passer-by and ask for help.

Fig. 2. A visually impaired person crosses the road where the footway and the cycle track lie side by side.

Parking Violations. Vehicles parked illegally on pavements, in pedestrian zones, or stations prevent the visually impaired person from following a safe route. Often, the visually impaired person is forced to step on the road, placing themselves in danger and risking an accident. Scooters and motorcycles that a visually impaired person may bump into and knock over are equally dangerous. The risk of injury in these cases is high (Fig. 3).

Fig. 3. A blind person wants to reach his platform at the railway station. A motorcycle is parked on the footway, blocking his way.

3   Automated Production of Tactile Maps for Visually Impaired People – the Slovenian Experience

The idea of raised-relief maps, i.e. tactile maps, for the needs of the blind is more than a century old. Teaching the blind with the help of tactile maps has had a long tradition in Slovenia as well. The first institution for the visually impaired was founded in Ljubljana in 1919 [3].

The visually impaired are deprived of crucial information regarding space and the spatial relations of objects. The efficiency of their movement in space depends on their understanding of it, i.e. on the accuracy of their cognitive maps. The most frequent problem of the visually impaired is forming a comprehensive perception of space [5]. Often, the blind can locate objects in space correctly, but are unable to form a sense of the whole. This largely absent concept must therefore be introduced to the visually impaired person in an appropriate way. A lot of research has been done in this field since the 1950s, particularly in the last twenty years. Oral explanations, textual descriptions, and even training the blind by leading them in the field have proven to be less effective than orientation mobility maps. The combined use of tactile maps, computers and artificial sound has improved motivation, especially with young people, and produced better learning results as well [7]. Technologies well-established in the field of geomatics – e.g. GIS, GPS and, above all, smart phones and multimedia – have been applied to the field of accessibility for the visually impaired, opening new possibilities for their better and safer mobility.

3.1   The Selection of Optimal Content of Tactile Maps for the Mobility of Visually Impaired People

The most important idea behind tactile mobility maps is the selection of special content for the orientation and mobility of the visually impaired and multilevel representation. Tactile cartographic symbols, which serve the special needs of the visually impaired for their orientation in space, have been specifically arranged and selected as well. Slovenia has standardised more than 30 symbols for tactile orientation and mobility maps. These normally represent the following contents: roads and streets, urbane areas, buildings of particular significance to the visually impaired (schools, banks, post-offices, the opera, etc.), orientation data (barriers, staircases, subways, traffic lights, etc.), green plots, hydrography, and Braille letters.

Content differentiation is made possible by way of multilevel presentation (different height of layers content and symbols), the selection of appropriate tactile cartographic symbols, and their optimal distribution. Roads and streets play a major role on mobility maps. All roads and streets should be marked on tactile mobility maps [3]. As the content of tactile mobility maps is rather standardised, in addition to size, at least two other factors have to be considered:

- content density (the greatest density is to be found in old city centres),
- the size of the reproduced area.

Therefore, an appropriate scale must be determined so that, taking the rules of tactile cartography and the density of the represented area into consideration, it is still possible to show all the roads and streets with all the tactile cartographic symbols appropriately positioned. The Geodetic Institute of Slovenia has tested tactile orientation map scales ranging from 1:500 to 1:5000. The results have shown that there can be no straight limits between the scales. In the case of medium density population, experience has shown orientation maps scales in the range of 1:2000 to 1:3000 to be the most appropriate, and 1:500 to 1:1000 in the case of old city centres.

From the point of view of the visually impaired, the most important thing is that tactile mobility maps are simple and schematic, easy to decipher, and accurate in showing the locations within the scope of their type-reading abilities. This can be reached with the help of accurate cartographic generalisation, taking the special requirements of the users into account. The blind can only distinguish a limited number of tactile cartographic symbols in one representation. In practice, this is a range of approximately 10 symbols for an individual group of the point, linear or areal tactile symbols [9]. Research in this field up to the present day has identified a relatively small number of the type readable symbols that are effectively recognised by the blind.

3.2   3D Printing Technology for Tactile Maps

Blind and partially sighted people experience difficulties in communication, learning, and moving without aids. Tactile pictures and maps are specially designed aids that are read by touch. *The production of high quality tactile maps and pictures is a technologically demanding process that has caused numerous difficulties in the past.* The main difficulties are the high costs, a small number of printed copies, complex and time consuming elaboration, wide-spread locations in the centres for blind without the special expertise needed for the production. Visually impaired users feel the lack of good tactile graphics aids. The expenses may be simplified and reduced with the cooperation of different partners and their shared knowledge (tactile perception, cartography, geo-information, etc.), the latest technology solutions (ICT), knowledge about materials and the process of automated production including industrial tools. The article describes the automated process of the production of tactile maps and pictures with the latest *3D printing technology, which supports inclusion and gives opportunity for an individual approach to the blind person.* Each tactile map or picture is completed in a few hours or days, depending on the complexity of the image. New tactile maps or pictures are stored in a file, ready to be printed with 3D printers all over the word. Users can print as many copies as they want.

3.3   The Challenges of Providing a New Service for the Visually Impaired with 3D Print: On Demand Tactile Maps for Visually Impaired Users

It is crucial that with the help of 3D printing, tactile maps can be printed on demand of a user or a group of users (a visually impaired person, a school, society, municipality, museum, etc.). As shown in the image below, the user selects the desired area on a digital model (Fig. 4).

**On demand tactile maps for the visually impaired user:
the personal approach**

Fig. 4. The user selects the desired tactile map area on a topographic map

The data sources for tactile mobility maps are the existing cartographic and topographic digital data bases, orthoimages, aerial photographic images, thematic maps, terrain inspection records, Google Street View, open data and big data sources, etc. In order to produce a tactile orientation and mobility map, the source must be reproduced in a scale that is approximately two times smaller. Example: for a 1:2.500 scale orientation and mobility map a 1:5.000 scale topographic map, or an existing digital cartographic base, is used [8]. When the content is determined, the appropriate tactile cartographic symbols for the project are selected, and their digital library prepared. The fonts were prepared for the Slovenian set of the Braille letters.

With the appropriate data source selected, the digital orientation map is produced. Processing follows, i.e. the editing of the content. Here, the principles of tactile cartography apply, and an appropriate method of generalisation must be used. Visual data sources are used as the basis for the creation of a tactile map. As this is not a simple geometric/graphic transformation, but a sophisticated transformation of the content, direct transfer can be performed only by an experienced cartographer who is an expert in information technology. Some intermediate stages are otherwise necessary. The data that has been scanned or digitized is processed by way of the CAD software. On completion, all the special data for the orientation of the blind is added. This data is based on the terrain inspection performed by a specialist for the orientation of the blind.

Geographic Information Systems (GIS) are also used in the production process of tactile maps. They are used for capturing, storing and analysing spatial data, specifically, data required for the production of tactile mobility maps for the visually impaired. GIS issue a strict set of rules for capturing and storing data, i.e. topology of data.

In the production process, several inspections of the tactile maps are conducted in relation to their content and its logical sequence. A cartographer and a user representative inspect the content and review the control plot. A topologic inspection of the base follows so as to facilitate the processing of the data by the GIS tools. In our present projects, we have applied our own software, the AutoCad and Arc/Info.

The Steps of the Automated Production of Tactile Maps with the Help of 3D Print Technology

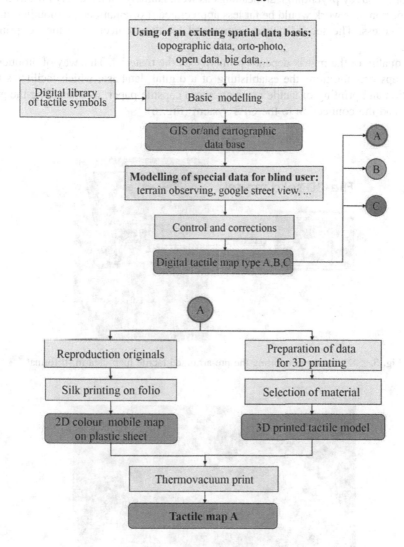

The tactile mobility map data processed in this way is prepared for three outputs:

- reproduction of the original plotting,
- data preparation for the 3D printer,
- the database for fast printing on micro capsule paper.

The reproduction originals are used for colour screen-printing. In our case, 4 films for black, red, blue and green colour were produced. The use of colours on orientation maps is essential for people with low-vision, the partially sighted and, ultimately, for the fully sighted, who cannot read the Braille letters.

Colours convey psychological meanings as well. Namely, in the eyes of the average sighted person, our work would be far less appreciated if orientation and mobility maps were colourless. The second output is prepared for the connection to the 3D printer (Fig. 5).

The quality of the matrix depends primarily on the material. This way of producing tactile maps preconditions the establishing of a digital database, which facilitates the preparation and printing of tactile maps on micro capsule paper, thus enabling the grid analysis and the connection to the GPS system (Fig. 6).

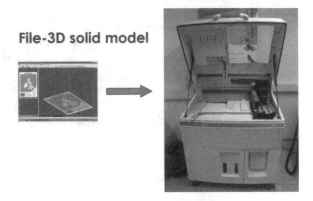

Fig. 5. 3D printer – importing the pre-arranged tactile map data in.stl format

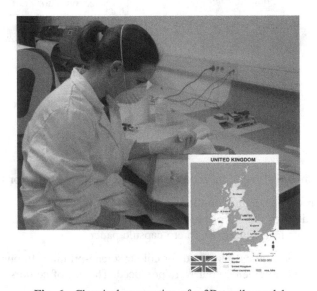

Fig. 6. Chemical preparation of a 3D tactile model

The procedure and step by step guide of the production of tactile maps with the help of 3D printing is outlined in the operation diagram. The production process consists of three key stages: the design and production of a 2D tactile map, matrix development, reproduction with the help of thermo-vacuum technology. The matrix was produced by means of 3D printing in a new, automated procedure. The entire model (matrix), with all its minor details – e.g. inscriptions in Braille, the cartographic signs – is produced in one go. Manual work and the subsequent sign sticking is no longer required.

Standardized production of tactile maps calls for a double perspective: the standardization of content and the standardization of the production process. The prime objective of the latter is the economy of the production.

A tactile cartographic sign key has been developed and approved for a tactile map orientation and mobility for the visually impaired group in Slovenia. Part of the cartographic sign was adapted from the Marburg standardization, the rest were developed in the joint effort of the Institute for Blind and Partially Sighted Children and the Geodetic Institute of Slovenia. The use of established and easily readable tactile cartographic signs is recommended.

3.4 The Results of the 3D Printing of Tactile Maps and Models and User Response

A number of 3D tactile maps, models and items have been produced in Slovenia with the help of 3D printing: for national parks, cities, and public institutions. We have also successfully manufactured a variety of items for different museums and their permanent collections.

The production of tactile maps with the help of 3D technology requires a high degree of technical expertise, data proficiency, and an excellent command of a variety of software tools. We have thus produced and printed over fifty tactile maps, models and items in the last years with the help of 3D printing. We have also printed several thousand tactile maps and images by means of reproducing the thermo-vacuum technique.

Some of our latest representative products are listed below:

- tactile map – Slovene Ethnographic Museum (Fig. 7)
- tactile model – Salt Works Museum – a tactile model of the Gulf of Piran, traditional salt production (Fig. 8)
- tactile plate – the famous Schutze ceramic plate from 1886 (Fig. 9)
- tactile map – the Union of the Blind and Partially Sighted of Slovenia Library (Fig. 10)
- tactile map for the capital of Slovenia, Ljubljana (Fig. 11)
- two awards: Excellence in Cartography for a tactile map (ICA – International Cartographic Association) and a Government of Slovenia award for innovation (Fig. 12)

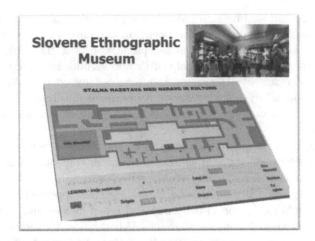

Fig. 7. Tactile map – Slovene Ethnographic Museum

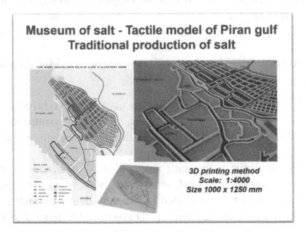

Fig. 8. Tactile model – Salt Works Museum

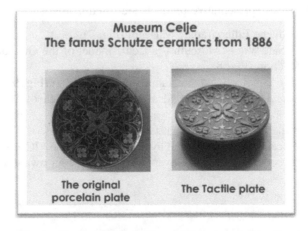

Fig. 9. Tactile plate – the famous Schutze ceramic plate

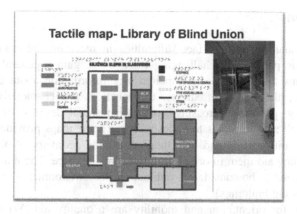

Fig. 10. Tactile map – the Union of the Blind and Partially Sighted of Slovenia Library

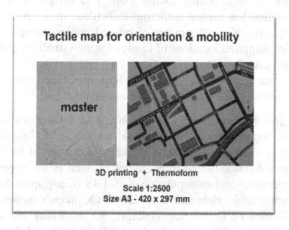

Fig. 11. tactile map for the capital of Slovenia, Ljubljana

Fig. 12. two awards: Excellence in Cartography for a tactile map (ICA – International Cartographic Association) and a Government of Slovenia award for innovation

4 Conclusion

Persons with visual impairment face difficulties in receiving information from the environment. It is particularly challenging for them to gain a general perception of space. This means that the visually impaired lack information about the position of objects in space, the layout of streets, the location and characteristics of traffic infrastructure (e.g. pedestrian crossings, pedestrian signal devices, the width of the road, etc.), as well as safe routes to choose from. Tactile maps provide blind persons with the missing information and help them assess the geometry of objects in urban environments. They aid them in orienting themselves in space. There are two types of navigation that need to be considered: outdoor (in the environment) and indoor navigation (inside public buildings).

Tactile maps for orientation and mobility are a quality aid. Without them, the mobility of visually impaired people would be difficult to imagine.

The production of high quality tactile maps and images is a technologically demanding process that has caused numerous difficulties in the past. The main difficulties were: high costs, a small number of printed copies, complex and time consuming elaboration, dispersed locations of centres for the visually impaired without the special knowledge needed for the production.

By completing our work of many years we have eliminated most of the problems listed above, and achieved the majority of our established goals:

- a variety of digital data sources, accessible on a local and national level – including other accessible (open data) and commercial sources (e.g. Google Maps, Google Street View, etc.) – have been integrated in the production of tactile maps,
- we have connected five different technologies, as well as the expertise from these fields: data processing and manipulation with GIS (Geographic Information System) tools, cartographic elaboration of 2D tactile maps (cartographic software, tactile generalisation of tactile map content), 3D modelling of tactile maps (3D model in STL format), 3D print technology (3D printer), and the thermo-vacuum technique of printing tactile maps (the industrial procedure of PVC foil stamping),
- we have accelerated the production of tactile maps and images, decreasing the production time from several weeks (3-5 weeks) to 2-5 days,
- the production costs have been reduced: the costs for the production of the first tactile map have been reduced by about 30%, the costs for the re-production have been reduced by about 50%.

The articles describes the results of a project which spanned over a number of years, and the efforts to bring together the technologies and expertise from a variety of fields. We experimented with several solutions in the process of achieving our established goals, but were often held back by difficulties that forced us back to the drawing board. For example: our 3D tactile models could not withstand the high temperature linked with printing a larger number of copies with the help of the thermo-vacuum technique. It took us more than a year to find the solution. We finally resolved the problem with the help of an expert from the automobile industry who had experience with a similar procedure.

New technologies, including 3D print technology, make the production of tactile maps simpler, faster, and cheaper. 3D printing also makes tactile maps more widely accessible; products thus developed can be printed with any 3D printer in the world, and any number of copies can be made,

Only the techniques and aids that have proven simple enough, efficient enough, and cost-effective are established and applied in the everyday life of the visually impaired user.

5 Ongoing Work

Setting up a (nation-wide, Europe-wide, and world-wide) digital library of tactile maps, stored in a variety of digital formats, is something to focus on in the future. Visually impaired users would be able to access this database free of charge, and print any number of copies (of tactile maps) they might need.

My next suggestion stems from our experience developing a new methodology for tactile map production. The side product of tactile map production is a variety of data that ought to be recorded in a multi-purpose digital database. This data might later on be used for the GPS navigation for visually impaired persons.

The third suggestion works toward standardizing the content of tactile maps for orientation and mobility. The new technique of tactile map production makes it possible for the content of tactile maps for orientation and mobility to be unified in an essentially better way, and to be permanently updated on the basis of new findings.

References

1. Bader, S.: The Designer Says. Princeton Architectural Press, New York (2012)
2. Berdman, D.: Do good Design - How Designers Can Change The World, Berkeley, USA (2009)
3. Brvar, R.: Geografija nekoliko drugače, Didaktika in metode pouka geografije za slepe in slabovidne učence, Zavod Republike Slovenije za šolstvo, Ljubljana, Slovenia (2000)
4. Dawidson, E.: Pedestrian navigation in Stocholm, how local data together with advanced positioning techniques can be used for detailed routing. In: Proceedings of the 16th ITS World Congress, Stocholm, Sweden (2009)
5. Eriksson, Y., Jansson, G., Strucel, M.: Tactile maps. The Swedish Braille Authority, Enskede (2003)
6. Hudson, B.: How to optimaze your design for FDM 3D printing (2016). https://www.3dhubs.com/knowledge-base/how-optimize-your-design-fdm-3d-printing
7. Kermauner, A.: Umetnost za vse. Revija za elementarno izobraževanje, znanstveni članek. Pedagoška fakulteta Maribor, Slovenia (2014)
8. Rener, R.: Tactile Maps and Diagrams, Master work, University of Ljubljana, Slovenia (1993)
9. Rener, R.: Tactile cartography: another view of tactile cartographic symbols. Cartographic J. **30**, 195–198 (1993)

10. Virtanen, A., Koschinen, S.: NOPPA-navigation and guidance system for the blind. In: Proceedings of the 11th ITS World Congress, Nagoya, Japan (2004)
11. Vovk, M.: Načrtovanje in prilagajanje grajenega okolja v korist funkcionalno oviranim ljudem, Urbanistični inštitut Slovenije, Ljubljana, Slovenia (2000)
12. The ASK-IT project (2009). http://www.ask-it.org

"I'm Blind, Can I Play?" Recommendations for the Development of Audiogames

Olimar Teixeira Borges[✉] and Marcia de Borba Campos[✉]

Faculty of Informatics (FACIN), Pontifical Catholic University
of Rio Grande do Sul (PUCRS), Porto Alegre, Brazil
olimar.borges@acad.pucrs.br, marcia.campos@pucrs.br

Abstract. While the areas of serious game and entertainment are growing, there is still a lack of games that are accessible, that people with disabilities can use. Audiogames are games based mainly on audio resources. In turn, accessible audiogames are games that should allow use without access barriers by people with visual disabilities. A literature review was performed using the Snowballing technique, resulting in the identification of 466 recommendations for the development of accessible games. These recommendations were organized, categorized and redesigned to 31 recommendations for the development of accessible audiogames to users with visual impairment. They were discussed with people with visual disabilities and developers of audiogames. This document presents the study performed as well as the analysis of 10 audiogames from the perspective of a blind user.

Keywords: Accessible games · Audiogames · Usability · Accessibility · Ergonomics · Visually impaired users

1 Introduction

In spite of the growth in the area of digital entertainment and of incentives to the area of Assistive Technology, there are still groups of users who face difficulties to use games. Among them are users with disabilities, as there are games that do not meet the accessibility criteria and, therefore, have access barriers.

The research presented in this article is related to accessible audiogames, which are accessible games bases mainly on a sound interface.

We studied the different ways that multimodal interfaces can be used for the creation of audiogames, allowing for a better user experience while using an audiogame, for people with visual disabilities.

Likewise, the usability, ergonomics, accessibility and gameplay criteria were considered.

Usability is one of the quality criteria in the use of interactive systems. In this article, the usability criteria proposed by Nielsen [23] were used, which are 10 usability heuristics.

According to Cybis, Betiol and Faust [11], ergonomics refers to a set of qualities an interface must have in order to improve user experience. The

© Springer International Publishing AG 2017
M. Antona and C. Stephanidis (Eds.): UAHCI 2017, Part II, LNCS 10278, pp. 351–365, 2017.
DOI: 10.1007/978-3-319-58703-5_26

authors proposed 10 ergonomics guidelines based on Nielsen's heuristics, on Shneiderman's Golden Rules, on the Dialog Principles of the ISO/ABNT 9241:110 norm, on the ergonomic criteria of Bastien and Scapin, and on the design principles of Android. They are: the power to mark the user's experience, conduction of user action, presentation quality, help and learning, work load, explicit control, adaptability, error management, homogeneity/coherence, and compatibility.

As written on the Accessibility Booklet from W3C Brazil [7], there are many definitions for accessibility. In this work, it is defined as: guarantee of the condition of use, with safety and autonomy, of systems and information technologies and communication, towards allowing people with disabilities and with changes due to aging equal use and access to information, communication and other services available in the area of information technology. And finally, the characteristic of a game's gameplay can be understood as the nature of interactivity. In other words, it is how and how much a player can interact with the game world, and how this world reacts to the player's choices (Schell, 2008 *apud* Ribeiro and Fernandes [26]).

Game mechanics were also considered in this study, as they are the actions the player lives and executes in a game. Lundgren and Bjordk [21] define game mechanics as any part of a game's rule system in which there is only one possible type of interaction that occurs during the game. The games' mechanics have many definitions, however some elements are commonly found, such as rules, objects and actions taken in a game.

Usability, ergonomics, accessibility, gameplay and game mechanics are part of the theoretical background needed to better understand this research's topic. With that knowledge, a few audiogames were selected, used alongside a user who is blind. The goal was to analyze the games in their context of use, identifying strengths and points for improvement.

In the games' analysis, we could not clearly understand the application of some of the guidelines for usability, ergonomics, accessibility and gameplay. Thus, a literature review based on the Snowballing technique [28] was performed to identify guidelines specific to the development of accessible games.

Initially, we identified 466 guidelines for the development of accessible games. The guidelines were then grouped and reorganized, eliminating the repetitions and focusing for the final user with visual disabilities. From that, a set of 31 guidelines was proposed. This set is presented and discussed in this work.

2   Audiogames

A practical study was performed with the purpose of investigating the use of audiogames by a real user, as well as identifying strengths and weaknesses regarding its use. We present 10 games which were used and analyzed by both a blind and a sighted user:

- Game 1: Tic Tac Toy[1], created in 2005, is a puzzle game developed by PB GAMES[2]. It is a traditional tic tac toe game, with online opponents. The game has its own voice. To move in the game board, the four directional arrow keys are used. The goal is to get five pieces in a line before your opponent. This line can be vertical, horizontal and even diagonal. Strengths: there is a very thorough game manual, with information on how to play; the game was easy to play; the game behaved in an accessible way; there is the option to play with an opponent in the same computer; the game's voice was clear and strong. Weaknesses: sometimes during the game, the speech became too fast, which could possibly disrupt beginner players; the game was too direct. There could have been a better goal development during the game; the game does not have the option to play against the computer or against another opponent online; The game could have more game board options, such as 3 × 3 instead of only 5 × 5.

- Game 2: Duck Blaster[3], created in 2004, is an action (subgenre shooting) game developed by PB GAMES. It is a fast and exciting game of manual and auditive coordination. The game's question is: "How many ducks can you shoot in five minutes?". The left and right arrow keys are used to move until the duck is centered in the speakers, and then a shot can be fired with the spacebar. Five minutes is the time for shooting as many ducks as possible. The game starts with one duck, then two, and so forth until the player reaches the maximum number of six ducks at once on screen. Strengths: it has a manual; the ducks' sound during the game was quite distinct; the game's sounds were very interesting; the game warns the player as to the remaining time in the play session. Weaknesses: In some moments, the game did not present feedback, such as when the game was over, there was no information as to how many ducks were hit in total; The game did not seem very accessible.

- Game 3: Audio Disc[4], created in 2008, is a puzzle game developed by Javier Mairena. It is an accessible game for people with visual disabilities. The goal is to launch a disk against the opponent, in an attempt to score a point. Each of the disk's movements has a distinct sound. In the game there is a tutorial where its functionalities are explained. There are 3 difficulty settings for playing against the computer. Strengths: There is a tutorial which explains clearly the game's goals; there is the option of playing against the computer; the game is great at stimulating attention; the game was divided in stages, which through wins increased in difficulty; the game's sounds are very creative; there is a good connection between player and narrator. Weaknesses: None identified.

- Game 4: The Secret of the Abbey[5], created in 2011, is an adventure game developed by Giovanni Simões Janjacomo, André Ricardo Azevedo and William. The game's story takes place circa 1400, where a young man named

---

[1] http://www.audiogames.com.br/jogos/tic-tac-toi/.
[2] http://www.pb-games.com/.
[3] http://www.audiogames.com.br/jogos/duck-blaster/.
[4] http://www.audiogames.com.br/jogos/125/.
[5] http://www.audiogames.com.br/jogos/o-segredo-do-mosteiro/.

John Stephens waits for the church's call to start his career in the catholic clergy. After many years of studying religion, he is chosen for a mission along with his church colleagues, in which he has to investigate reports of a mysterious creature that roams around an abbey in the Swiss Alps. The player starts in the first part of the story, described as number 1, and in the end of this part there are other numbers that represent the possible decisions the player must take in that moment in the game. The player must choose one of these numbers and this is the path he will follow in the adventure. Strengths: There is a very interesting manual with information and strategies on how to play; there are legends for the game's shortcuts, making it easy for the player to situate himself during play; the game stimulates reasoning very much; it has a good structure and is very creative; the game's audios are well elaborated; it offers sounds with music and quite interesting descriptions, with information on the character's commands and what is needed to proceed in the story; it offers restart options in different ways; it is interesting as it is based on a book narrative structure, with beginning, middle and end; it allows the player to elaborate his own solutions and problems; the questions and sounds are quite catching, as are the auto descriptions; the game explains well the principal characteristics of the place where the player is. Weaknesses: It could enable more interaction between player and computer; in some moments, the narration was very long; it could offer more options of life and experiences in the game; in some moments, the game ended and returned to the beginning, without informing the player about his defeat.

- Game 5: Operation BlackSquare[6] is an action (subgenre shooting) game developed by PB GAMES. It is a fast and action-packed shooting game, in which the player controls Max Fierros, guiding him through levels full of violence, trying to stay alive. The game's story begins when the player is woken up by one of his squad mates. Apparently, a secret terrorist group has taken control of one of the buildings used for investigation near New York city, and plans to blow it up. The player can move in four directions: up, down, left and right, using the arrow keys. Strengths: it has a manual with lots of information and description of the scenes; it has lots of action, in a way efficient to users with visual disabilities; the game proved to be very inclusive; the game demanded a lot of attention from the player; the game informed the commands of each shortcut key; a lot of attention on the game's sounds was needed in order to play. Weaknesses: There was no feedback when switching scenes. There could have been a description at the start of each scene with its name, or a level notification, for example, Level 1, Level 2, etc.
- Game 6: Last Crusade[7], created in 2006, is a Role-Playing Game (RPG) created by Patrick Dwyer and Peter S. VanLund. The player is a character with strength, defense, hit points, gold, potions, and a list of items. There are five types of items: Weapons, armor, gold, potions and special items. There are four types of characters: Enemies, allies, vendors and goblins. There are

---

[6] http://www.audiogames.com.br/jogos/blacksquare/.
[7] http://www.audiogames.com.br/jogos/last-crusade/.

interactions with enemies, allies, vendors, goblins and with the locals. The directional arrow keys are used for locomotion in the game world. Strengths: There are hit points; dynamics were very good, especially when interacting ,with certain characters; the characters offer advice during the game; the game allowed for fictitious shopping during play; the game demanded a great deal of concentration; the game has a map for localization. Weaknesses: There was difficulty in knowing which way to go during play; no information was found on the characters present in the beginning and end of the game, neither in the manual nor in the tutorial; the game did not inform the player when his destination was nearby.

- Game 7: Defender[8], created in 2006, is an action game developed by Luis Eduardo Oliveira. The game's main goal is to destroy enemy spaceships coming towards Earth, while avoiding the enemy's lasers. The player controls his ship with the directional arrow keys and fires his laser weapon, trying to identify the location of the enemies through hearing. Strengths: The possibility of guiding a spaceship. It is a curious feeling for a blind person, as it stimulates action techniques; the voice with the information draws the player's attention very much; direct and constant interaction with the computer; has a well-defined main menu, with information on the commands used; seemed very inclusive; it was easy to understand when an action was needed, such as attack for example; the voice during the menu was well chosen; it has difficulty levels; the game is quite long and this makes it interesting because the story also becomes long and good with time. Weaknesses: The attack sound could be better; there could be better feedback to indicate when the player dies; it would be interesting if there was a help guide, to indicate what actions are needed in order to play the game; the actions could be executed in a more practical manner; there could be more sound warnings when danger approaches; few ships and attack options; little interaction during combat; it could be more challenging; there could be the possibility of obtaining information on the whole battlefield, to check if there are still enemy ships nearby; there could be feedback on the attack, for example a defeated enemies counter; there is little distinction between the orientation voice and the game sounds; the orientation voice should be high pitched; it could offer more difficulty settings.

- Game 8: Super Mario Brothers[9], created in 2010, is an adventure game developed by Jaqocon Games. It is an adaptation of the original Nintendo classic game, in which the player is guided only through sound. The game uses the same idea from the original, as well as its way to play, soundtrack and sound effects. Strengths: Informed clearly the initial commands. Weaknesses: The game's music and sound effects continue to played even when presenting guidance sounds to the player. The music and sound effects could be toned down; music is too loud; it should warn when the player dies and the reason why; it should warn about obstacles during play.

---

[8] http://www.audiogames.com.br/jogos/defender/.

[9] http://www.audiogames.com.br/jogos/super-mario-brothers/.

- Game 9: Technoshock[10], created in 2007, is an action (subgenre shooting) game developed by Anatol Kamynin. It is a 3d individual shooter game in the style of the classic Doom. As other traditional shooter titles, Technoshock allows the player to navigate in a 3d environment. The story consists in escaping a prison filled with traps and controlled by well-armed robots. The player has to get to the sixth floor, free two scientists kept as hostages and call in the helicopter to pick them up. Strengths: None identified. Weaknesses: The possibility to return to the previous menu. This works by using the "ESC" key only, which is bad for less experienced users; it does not inform the player on the initial commands; it does not have an initial tutorial; it does not present the game's objective and what needs to be done.
- Game 10: Dark Destroyer[11], created in 2004, is an action game developed by PB GAMES. It is a very simple game. The player must press the left and right arrow keys to move his ship, and the spacebar to shoot his laser. When the player hears an enemy ship approaching, it must center it in a way that the enemy's sound is equal in both speakers. When in the correct shooting position, a sound will be played indicating the player's radar. The story consists in the Earth being invaded by an army of alien creatures, commanded by a cruel and evil overlord. The player is the hero Dark Destroyer, and the planet's defense is in his hands. Strengths: It informs the player when he dies during play; it informs the player on his score; it interacts with the player through dialog. Weaknesses: It does not have a tutorial; the sounds are not very clear, for example when the ship explodes, it could be more realistic.

3   Related Work

In this section we present the related work, identified after applying the snowballing technique [28].

As database, Google Scholar was used, which indexes most of the other query databases, such as IEEE, Springer, Elsevier, ACM and others.

After choosing the database, a search was performed using the following sentence: "accessible games development guidelines". The search was performed in September 2016, yielding 23,600 results. Though, for application of the technique, we chose the first 10 results found on the first page and, from them, start the Snowballing process.

During the initial set phase, after reading the titles and abstracts of each result, we kept only one article, as it was the only one containing a guideline proposal focused on the development of accessible games, named as P1 [8].

For the first iteration 1, from article P1, 89 references were evaluated through the backward snowballing method, and 6 articles were included, named as P2 [3], P3 [15], P4 [6], P5 [16], P6 [24] and P7 [25]. For the forward snowballing method, another article denominated as P8 [22] was included, from a total of 5 analyzed works. Thus, in the first iteration, we analyzed 94 works. The resulting

---

[10] http://www.audiogames.com.br/jogos/technoshock/.
[11] http://www.audiogames.com.br/jogos/dark-destroyer/.

articles from iteration 1 were evaluated in iteration 2, and the backward and forward snowballing methods were applied once again. In the second iteration, from the 7 articles added to the main set, 66 references were analyzed, 27 being from P4, 5 from P6 and 38 from P8, through backward snowballing. 3 works were then added, 2 being from P4 and 1 from P8. Using forward snowballing, we analyzed 39 works that cited the 7 articles, with 17 citing P4 and 22 citing P6. As result, 2 references were included from P6. The second iteration resulted in 5 articles, denominated as P9 [10], P10 [1], P11 [4], P12 [27] and P13 [13]. The new articles were evaluated in the third iteration, applying once again backward and forward snowballing.

Five articles were analyzed in iteration 3 by the methods and 4 new references were added to the study. With backward snowballing, we analyzed 82 references (45 from P11 and 37 from P12), resulting in 4 new articles, denominated P14 [30], P15 [5], P16 [12] and P17 [29]. In forward snowballing, 35 references were analyzed (3 from P10, 10 from P11, 19 from P12 and 3 from P13) and none brought forth new articles. The articles P9, P10 and P11 did not generate new articles to the study in either methods.

Finally, for the fourth iteration, 106 references (106 from P17) were analyzed through backward snowballing and 119 references (2 from P15 and 117 from P17) through forward snowballing, with 255 references in total only on this iteration. When added to the previous iterations, it totals to 541 works analyzed with the snowballing technique. None of the methods in this iteration brought new candidates for analysis. Thus, the application of the snowballing technique ended in the fourth iteration, giving us a total of 17 works.

From the resulting articles, we analyzed the proposed recommendations in each study as follows:

- **P1:** 16 guidelines proposed by Cheiran [8], based on visual, auditive, motor and mental disabilities, compiled from other sets of accessibility guidelines for games. Cheiran's study had the objective of proposing a restructuring of accessibility guidelines for digital games. To that end, different guideline proposals for digital games were analyzed, including the works of [3,6,15,16, 24,25]. Cheiran's guideline descriptions are organized according to the WCAG principles [9], which are perceptible, operable, comprehensible and robust.
- **P2:** 51 directives developed by Bannick [3] compose a guideline for the development of accessible games directed to blind users. It also proposes necessary care [2] when developing games in which the player uses screen readers such as JAWS, Window-Eyes, Supernova, NVDA, ZoomText or VoiceOver, for example.
- **P3:** 109 game accessibility guideline recommendations [15], in which 8 are applicable to more than one target audience. These directives were elaborated in collaboration with researchers of different institutions and companies. The recommendations are focused on games accessibility for users with motor, cognitive, visual, auditive and speech disabilities. General accessibility recommendations are also suggested.

- **P4:** 19 recommendations from the International Game Developers Association [6]. An online questionnaire was applied to game developers with the goal of identifying accessibility resources in games, indicated by each developer. This resulted in 20 answers, which allowed the authors to relate 20 accessible games by their target audience, identifying the game's genres and their assistive technology solutions, for example. The game's genres were: Action, Fighting, Racing, Shooting, Simulation, Strategy, RPG, Family Entertainment, Educational, Sports, Adventure, Gambling, Enigma, Exploration and Arcade. The study also discusses traditional games which meet the accessibility criteria for blind users.
- **P5:** 10 recommendations from the IGDA Game Accessibility SIG group [16], listed as the best practices for game developers. These recommendations can be found on other IGDA documents, listed by user groups [17–20].
- **P6:** 34 recommendations proposed by Ossmann and Miesenberger [24], considering the IGDA group [6] and Project UPS [25] recommendations. They are organized by Level/Progression, input, graphics, sound and installation/configuration. The process of elaborating the accessible game development guidelines is described in Ossmann and Miesenberger [24].
- **P7:** 25 recommendations proposed by Project UPS [25], elaborated for users with multiple learning disabilities, with recommendations for people with mental disabilities, and people with severe motor impairment that also have some sensorial disability.
- **P8:** 27 directives for accessibility in games for mobile devices, elaborated by Moura and Cheiran [22]. The recommendations consider users with visual, auditive, motor, cognitive and mental disabilities. According to the authors, different accessibility documents were analyzed and the content analysis technique was applied. The recommendations were also organized according to the WCAG 2.0 directives [9].
- **P9:** 12 recommendations proposed by Microsoft [10], similarly to Brannon Zahand's recommendations [30]. The proposals come from example scenarios, according to some types of groups of users with deficiencies. They describe some scenarios, related to a disability, and then list which recommendations are intended for that set of scenarios.
- **P10:** 20 suggestions described by CEAPAT [1], not enumerated explicitly. However, at first through a game called "Iredia", they observed and described 3 suggestions regarding the difficulty level and graphics. Secondly, they described 17 recommendations on how the subtitles of each game component should be treated.
- **P11:** 44 accessibility recommendations for digital games, proposed by Barlet and Spohn [4], where 16 can be found in more than one group of users. There are explanations on recommendations that need to be included to allow the access of users with motor, auditive, visual and cognitive deficiencies. The authors also discuss how each recommendation may benefit the final user.
- **P12:** 21 recommendations from Universally Accessible Games (UA-Games) [14], created together with "Game Over!", an accessible game in which, at each stage, one of the proposed accessibility directives is violated, showing

to the player in practice how bad it feels to not be able to perform basic functions during play.

- **P13:** 13 design directives for audiogames, created by Garcia and Almeida [13]. From a total of 50 mentioned to be in the group's website, none were found online. Thus, only the 13 described in the article were considered. The directives were created from a case study and user observations, where it was analyzed how audio is used in the creation of nine audiogames recommended by some users.
- **P14:** 11 directives written by Brannon Zahand [30], proposed from example scenarios which relate to the difficulties people with different types of disabilities may face in their daily lives when trying to play, such as: Auditive, Visual, Voice and Motor.
- **P15:** 14 orientations created by BBC [5], the television and journalism company, serving as norms to define the steps to be followed in order to guarantee that all games hosted on BBC sites are as accessible as possible to their target audience. They are intended specifically for web games created for use in BBC sites. They can be used as a starting point, for the development of any web-based browser game.
- **P16:** 20 recommendations proposed by Special Effect [12] as part of their project to create an objective classification system for games. Although the project seems to be in its beta version since 2011, the list is quite relevant and complete. These recommendations are especially proposed for the implementation of design characteristics in accessible games.
- **P17:** 20 strategies identified by Yuan et al. [29] in the analysis of accessible games. The study proposes an interaction model for games, defined in three stages: receiving stimuli, determining the answer and providing input. The authors analyze accessible games for user groups and, to each group, define accessibility strategies. They identify the following game genres: First-Person Shooter (FPS), Strategy, Sports, RPG, Puzzle, Racing, Dance/Rhythm and Adventure.

The 17 related articles present directive proposals for the development of accessible games, also considered for the proposal of directives for the development of audiogames for users with visual disabilities.

4 Proposal of Guidelines for the Development of Audiogames for Users with Visual Impairment

In this section, the 466 items were analyzed in their essence, with the goal of forming a general understanding in relation to the necessary directives for the development of audiogames destined to users with visual disabilities.

After a more thorough reading and analysis of the items, we filtered the ones who met important criteria for people with visual impairment, even if the item was not explicitly intended for that target audience. Without a consensus on the recommendation's presentation, we decided to gather them all, excluding the ones that could not be applied to audiogames. Naturally, many directives can be applied to other software categories, as stressed by Project UPS [25].

As a result, a new organization of the directives was generated, while keeping each author's references for, in a future analysis, verifying and identifying which directive contexts were the most proposed and suggested between all the guideline sets, strategies, recommendations and suggestions analyzed. In this stage, we opted to not include criteria related to the graphical interface. Initially, we rounded up 215 recommendations, and then eliminated repetitions and rewrote some of them, totaling 31 recommendations. The guidelines were reorganized in the following categories:

- Playing experience, level and progression: 59 guidelines, resulting in 12 recommendations:
  1. Use simpler and clearer dialogues so that the instructions in the game are easy to understand.
  2. Provide predictable and expected information, making game content, challenges and functionality consistent with the mechanics of the game, avoiding escaping your gameplay pattern.
  3. Offer varied levels of difficulty in the game activities, adaptively, during the game.
  4. Allow adjustment of difficulty levels of the game.
  5. Provide a training module.
  6. Include auxiliary modes, with shortcuts to game secrets ("auto-aim", "cheat"), such as direct access to secret areas and power steering.
  7. Enable the game to start quickly, without the need to navigate through several menus.
  8. Provide means to help players explore the environment through easy guidance such as making use of cardinal points and GPS to move the character in the environment.
  9. Provide menus that follow a logical sequence, and use the navigation patterns of the screen readers for easy navigation.
  10. Keep the player informed of what is happening in the game, avoiding loss of context.
  11. Allow the player to consult his progress summaries during the different phases of a game.
  12. Include haptic interface features such as vibration and touch features.
- Data entry for software and hardware: 79 guidelines, resulting in 9 recommendations:
  13. Provide a means of configuring time-dependent features such as speech speed control, events, movements, and game actions.
  14. Provide rescue mechanisms in the game, profile settings, automatically.
  15. In desktop games, allow the player perform all operations in the game through the keyboard.
  16. Avoid using simultaneous keys.
  17. Take care when using actions that require precision in character displacement in the game environment.

18. Predict the use of assistive technology features (voice control, extended keyboards, brain-computer interface, screen reader, etc.).
19. Avoid conflicts in the sound information that is emitted by the game and those that are transmitted by the screen reader.
20. Enable game controls and controls to be changed/reconfigured, as well as adjusted for their sensitivity and speed, ensuring they are as simple as possible.
21. When using voice commands, use individual words from a small vocabulary rather than more than one word or long words. For example, use "Yes", "No", "Exit", "Open", "Skip", "Save", etc.

- Installation, configuration and help: 44 guidelines, resulting in 7 recommendations:
22. Send immediate feedback according to the player's actions, so that he can know that his actions are being processed (for example, reporting to the player about the data entries, the need to close a dialog window, etc.).
23. Send tips and reminders to the player in order to help in cases of difficulty during the game.
24. Include mechanisms to reduce the occurrence of errors and favor their correction (for example, disable menu options that are not available for use, close a dialog after user action, allow the player to return to a secure point during play, provide messages clearly indicating the reason for the error, etc.)
25. Provide manuals, installation instructions and game setup mechanisms when needed, in an accessible manner.
26. Provide tutorial on how to play and interact in the game.
27. Allow the use of shortcut keys, for example, to interact in the game options (save, exit, pause, access help, etc.) and to access the game information (e.g. game score, lives, challenges, etc.).
28. Inform in the descriptions of the game, explicitly, if it is intended for use by people with visual impairment.

- Sound elements: 46 guidelines, resulting in 3 recommendations:
29. Offer as many interactive sound elements and sound effects such as 3D sound, binaural recording, surround sound, sonar style audio map, etc., providing fun sounds and audio tracks.
30. Use sound design and distinctive music for each event object, text area, lists, tables, controls, and other components of the game, emitting their sound when they gain prominence and preventing them from being difficult to understand by the player.
31. Offer mechanisms to configure the audios and sounds of the game.

5 Preliminary Analysis

This section presents analysis on the weak points and frailties of the audiogames, described in Sect. 2, by a blind user and a sighted user, according to the guidelines proposed by this study. Table 1 identifies the recommendations that were and/or could have been implemented in these audiogames.

Table 1. Relationship between the guidelines and the audiogames analyzed

GUIDELINES	AUDIOGAMES									
Playing experience, Level and Progression	Tic Tac Toy	Duck Blaster	Audio Disc	The Secret of the Abbey	Operation Black Square	Last Crusade	Defender	Super Mario Brothers	Technoshock	Dark Destroyer
1	P	OK	OK	NO	NA	NA	OK	OK	NA	OK
2	NA	NA	NA	OK	NA	NA	NA	NA	NA	NA
3	NO	NA	OK	NA	NA	NA	NO	NA	NA	NA
4	NO	NA	NA	NO	NA	NA	OK	NA	NA	NA
5	NA	NA	NA	NA	NA	NA	NO	NA	NA	NA
6	NA	NA	NA	NA	NA	NA	NA	NA	NA	NA
7	NA	NA	NA	NA	NA	NA	NA	NA	NA	NA
8	NA	NA	NA	NA	NA	NO	NA	NA	NA	NA
9	NA	NA	NA	NA	NA	NA	NA	NA	NA	NA
10	NA	NA	NA	OK	NA	NO	NO	NO	NA	OK
11	NA	OK	NA	NA	NA	OK	NO	NA	NA	OK
12	NO	NA	NA	NA	NA	NA	NA	NA	NA	NA
Data entry for Software and Hardware	Tic Tac Toy	Duck Blaster	Audio Disc	The Secret of the Abbey	Operation Black Square	Last Crusade	Defender	Super Mario Brothers	Technoshock	Dark Destroyer
13	NO	NA	NA	NA	NA	NA	NA	NA	NA	NA
14	NA	NA	NA	NA	NA	NA	NA	NA	NA	NA
15	NA	NA	NA	NA	NA	NA	NA	NA	NA	NA
16	NA	NA	NA	NA	NA	NA	NA	NA	NA	NA
17	NA	NA	NA	NA	NA	NA	NA	NA	NA	NA
18	NA	NA	NA	NA	NA	NA	NA	NA	NA	NA
19	NA	NA	NA	NA	NA	NA	NA	NA	NA	NA
20	NA	NA	NA	NA	NA	NA	NA	NA	NA	NA
21	NA	NA	NA	NA	NA	NA	NA	NA	NA	NA
Installation, Configuration and Help	Tic Tac Toy	Duck Blaster	Audio Disc	The Secret of the Abbey	Operation Black Square	Last Crusade	Defender	Super Mario Brothers	Technoshock	Dark Destroyer
22	NA	NO	NA	P	NA	NA	P	NO	NA	NA
23	NA	NA	NA	NA	NA	NA	NA	NA	NA	NA
24	NA	NA	NA	NA	NA	NA	NA	NA	NA	NA
25	OK	OK	NA	OK	OK	NO	NO	NA	NO	NO
26	NA	NA	OK	NA	NA	NA	NO	NA	NO	NA
27	NA	NA	NA	NA	OK	NA	NA	NA	NO	NA
28	NA	NA	NA	NA	NA	NA	NA	NA	NA	NA
Sound Elements	Tic Tac Toy	Duck Blaster	Audio Disc	The Secret of the Abbey	Operation Black Square	Last Crusade	Defender	Super Mario Brothers	Technoshock	Dark Destroyer
29	NO	NA	NA	NA	NA	NA	NO	NA	NA	NA
30	NA	NA	OK	OK	NA	OK	NO	NO	NA	NO
31	NA	NA	NA	NA	NA	NA	NA	NA	NA	NA
LEGEND:										
(NA - Not Applicable / Not Observed) - (P - Partially Implemented) - (NO - Not Answered) - (OK - Attends)										

Contextualizing, the cells that have "NA", "P", "NO" and "OK" mean, respectively, that the proposed directive to the column's audiogame: Does not apply or does not meet the directive, partly meets the directive, not answered and meets the directive. Thus, it was possible to verify which directives were the most observed, which were the least observed, which were partly observed and which do not apply to the audiogame tested.

In parallel, an online survey is being conducted with audiogame developers. In one of the questions, the 31 recommendations proposed by this study were listed and the question was which guidelines were implemented in the developers' audiogame projects. Likewise, another question brings forth the 31 recommendations and asks how relevant is their implementation during the development of an audiogame.

Due to the study still being in data analysis phase, until now only five developers have responded the survey, stressing the fact that this type of developer is

Table 2. Result of previous review of recommendations made by audiogame developers

GUIDELINES	Implementation of the Recommendation				Degree of Importance				
Playing experience, Level and Progression	Fully Implemented	Partly Implemented	Not Implemented	I do not know how to answer	High Priority	Average Priority	Low Priority	No Priority	I do not know how to answer
1	60%	40%			20%	80%			
2	80%	20%			40%	40%		20%	
3		40%	60%		40%	40%		20%	
4	20%		80%		20%	40%	20%	20%	
5	40%	20%	20%	20%	60%	20%	20%		
6		20%	80%		20%	20%	20%	40%	
7	20%	20%	60%			60%	20%	20%	
8	60%	40%			80%		20%		
9	40%	20%	40%		100%				
10	40%	40%	20%		100%				
11	40%	20%	40%		60%	40%			
12	40%		60%		20%	40%		20%	20%
Data entry for Software and Hardware	Fully Implemented	Partly Implemented	Not Implemented	I do not know how to answer	High Priority	Average Priority	Low Priority	No Priority	I do not know how to answer
13	20%	20%	60%		40%	20%	20%	20%	
14			80%	20%	20%	60%		20%	
15	80%		20%		40%	20%	20%	20%	
16	20%	40%	20%	20%		20%	20%	60%	
17	40%	40%		20%	60%	40%			
18	40%	40%	20%		40%	20%	20%	20%	
19	60%	40%			60%		40%		
20			100%		20%	80%			
21			80%	20%	20%	20%	40%		20%
Installation, Configuration and Help	Fully Implemented	Partly Implemented	Not Implemented	I do not know how to answer	High Priority	Average Priority	Low Priority	No Priority	I do not know how to answer
22	60%	20%	20%		80%		20%		
23	20%	20%	60%		20%	60%		20%	
24	40%	40%	20%		20%	80%			
25	20%		80%		40%	60%			
26	40%	20%	20%	20%	80%		20%		
27	40%	20%	40%		60%	40%			
28	40%	20%	20%	20%	60%	20%		20%	
Sound Elements	Fully Implemented	Partly Implemented	Not Implemented	I do not know how to answer	High Priority	Average Priority	Low Priority	No Priority	I do not know how to answer
29	40%	60%			80%		20%		
30	40%	40%	20%		60%	20%		20%	
31	20%	20%	60%		20%	60%	20%		

very rare and thus justifying the sample size of developers. The analysis' results so far can be seen in Table 2.

6 Final Considerations

After analysis of the 10 audiogames, performed by a blind user with the set of 31 guidelines proposed by this study, we conclude that, for the 10 audiogames analyzed in Sect. 2, 51% of the guideline set was identified in the *audiogames*, with the most implemented directives being numbers 1 and 25, both identified in four different games. We also observed that the directives most used to overcome the weaknesses of some games were numbers 1, 22 and 25, suggested in 4 distinct games.

The audiogames with the most guidelines implemented were "The Secret of the Abbey" and "Audio Disc", with a total of 5 and 4 different guidelines implemented, respectively. As for the audiogames with the most directive suggestions to overcome their weaknesses were "Defender" and "Tic Tac Toy", with a total of 8 and 6 different suggested directives, respectively, to overcome their weaknesses.

Some recommendations were not observed by the blind user, however, when analyzing the audiogames we identified recommendations 1, 2, 3, 4, 10, 11, 25, 26 and 30. Recommendations 1, 2, 8, 15, 19 and 22 were also identified in the online survey by audiogame developers, as the most implemented in their audiogames. As for recommendations 8, 9, 10, 11, 19, 22, 26, 29 and 30, they were marked as most important to be implemented. During analysis, in some games like "Tic Tac Toy" and "Audio Disc", we verified the player's desire to play online, or even to play on the same computer against another opponent. This need is not related to the initial directive set, being one of the points evaluated and analyzed with other audiogame players. It demonstrates that the proposed directives' scope must be revised, in order to verify which needs are really interesting for inclusion in this study's proposed directive set.

Many of the player's observations had emphasis when the games involved reasoning, attention, generating stimuli or that had a sharp and incentivizing sound interface. This question will also be taken into consideration, to verify if a specific directive, that makes this need very clear, should be included in the study.

With these analysis, the study was able to get a partial feedback on the recommendation set proposed, and with that it is possible to reassess which recommendations are really necessary and which are not so necessary as initially predicted. As the study is still ongoing, there will be new analysis and restructuration of the recommendation set, with the final goal of constructing a concrete and feasible guide, to be used by audiogame developers in the implementation of more stimulating, concise and accessible games for people with visual disabilities.

References

1. Abenójar, V., et al.: Buenas prácticas de accesibilidad en videojuegos. Colección Estudios (2012)
2. Bannick, J.: Blind computer games. http://www.blindcomputergames.com/howto/howto-screen-readers-games.html
3. Bannick, J.: Blind computer games: guidelines for building blind-accessible computer games. http://www.blindcomputergames.com/guidelines/guidelines.html
4. Barlet, M.C., Spohn, S.D.: Includification: A Practical Guide to Game Accessibility. The Ablegamers Foundation, Charles Town (2012)
5. BBC: Future media standards and guidelines. http://www.bbc.co.uk/guidelines/futuremedia/accessibility/games.shtml
6. Bierre, K., Hinn, M., Martin, T., McIntosh, M., Snider, T., Stone, K., Westin, T.: Accessibility in games: motivations and approaches. White paper, International Game Developers Association (IGDA) (2004)
7. W3C Brasil: Cartilha de acessibilidade na web. http://www.w3c.br/pub/Materiais/PublicacoesW3C/cartilha-w3cbr-acessibilidade-web-fasciculo-I.html
8. Cheiran, J.F.P.: Jogos inclusivos: diretrizes de acessibilidade para jogos digitais. Master's thesis, Instituto de Informática - UFRGS, Porto Alegre, RS, Brasil (2013). http://hdl.handle.net/10183/77230
9. Web content accessibility guidelines (WCAG) 2.0 WWW Consortium (2008)
10. Microsoft Corporation: The need for accessible games. https://msdn.microsoft.com/en-us/library/windows/desktop/ee415219(v=vs.85).aspx

11. Cybis, W.d.A., Betiol, A.H., Faust, R.: Ergonomia e usabilidade: conhecimentos, métodos e aplicações, vol. 3th. Novatec Editora (2015)
12. SpecialEffect: Accessible Gaming Wish List (2011). http://www.specialeffect.org. uk/accessible-gaming-wish-list
13. Garcia, F.E., Almeida Neris, V.P.: Design guidelines for audio games. In: Kurosu, M. (ed.) HCI 2013. LNCS, vol. 8005, pp. 229–238. Springer, Heidelberg (2013). doi:10.1007/978-3-642-39262-7_26
14. Grammenos, D.: Game over: learning by dying. In: Proceedings of the SIGCHI Conference on Human Factors in Computing Systems, pp. 1443–1452. ACM (2008)
15. Game Accessibility Guidelines: Game accessibility guidelines full list (2012). http://gameaccessibilityguidelines.com/full-list
16. IGDA Game Access SIG: Game accessibility topten. https://igda-gasig.org/ about-game-accessibility/game-accessibility-top-ten
17. IGDA Game Access SIG: IGDA game access SIG - on auditory disabilities (general) (2010). https://igda-gasig.org/about-game-accessibility/ development-frameworks/auditory/
18. IGDA Game Access SIG: IGDA game access SIG - on cognitive disabilities (general) (2010). https://igda-gasig.org/about-game-accessibility/ development-frameworks/cognitive/
19. IGDA Game Access SIG: IGDA game access SIG - on mobility disabilities (general) (2010). https://igda-gasig.org/about-game-accessibility/ development-frameworks/on-mobility-disabilities/
20. IGDA Game Access SIG: IGDA game access SIG - on visual disabilities (general) (2010). https://igda-gasig.org/about-game-accessibility/ development-frameworks/visual/
21. Lundgren, S., Bjork, S.: Game mechanics: describing computer-augmented games in terms of interaction. In: Proceedings of TIDSE, vol. 3 (2003)
22. Moura, E.J.R., Cheiran, J.F.P.: Diretrizes de acessibilidade para jogos em dispositivos móveis. ICCEEg-11 (2015). http://c3.furg.br/components/download_ categoria/baixar.php?arquivo=4122cb13c7a474c1976c9706ae36521d
23. Nielsen, J.: Usability Engineering. Morgan Kaufmann Publishers Inc., San Francisco (1993)
24. Ossmann, R., Miesenberger, K.: Guidelines for the development of accessible computer games. In: Miesenberger, K., Klaus, J., Zagler, W.L., Karshmer, A.I. (eds.) ICCHP 2006. LNCS, vol. 4061, pp. 403–406. Springer, Heidelberg (2006). doi:10. 1007/11788713_60
25. UPS project: Guidelines for the development of entertaining software for people with multiple learning disabilities (2012). http://www.medialt.no/rapport/ entertainmentguidelines
26. Ribeiro, G.L.H., Fernandes, N.M.P., Garone, P.M.C.: O design e a jogabilidade. In: Proceedings of the SBGames 2013. XII Brazilian Symposium on Games and Digital Entertainment, pp. 484–487. SBC (2013)
27. UA-Games: Game over! http://www.ics.forth.gr/hci/ua-games/index_main.php? l=e&c=563
28. Wohlin, C.: Guidelines for snowballing in systematic literature studies and a replication in software engineering. In: Proceedings of the 18th International Conference on Evaluation and Assessment in Software Engineering, p. 38. ACM (2014)
29. Yuan, B., Folmer, E., Harris Jr., F.C.: Game accessibility: a survey. Univ. Access Inf. Soc. 10(1), 81–100 (2011)
30. Zahand, B.: Developing for different types of disabilities. http://www.brannonz. com/accessibility/disabilities.html

Designing Interfaces to Make Information More Tangible for Visually Impaired People

Ikuko Eguchi Yairi[✉]

Graduate School of Science and Technology, Sophia University,
4-7, Yobancho, Chiyodaku, Tokyo, Japan
i.e.yairi@sophia.ac.jp

Abstract. This paper introduces our two research projects. One is to propose the graphic representation method with touch and sound as the universal designed touch screen interface for visually impaired people. Another is to investigate the good design of the collaborative work environment of the visually impaired. The proposed graphic representation method and interfaces are basic techniques for developing plug-ins which help blind people to use ordinary mass-produced computer devices with touch screens, such as smartphones and iPads. Our idea is so simple that musical scales enable users to trace graphics by their fingers and to memorize their position on the touch screen. Our recent progress including digital textbook application for visually impaired children is also reported. To investigate the design of the collaborative work environment, we have developed the collaborative music composition application with a tangible interface using daily goods that would attract the attention of both visually impaired and sighted people, and to induce collaborative communication among them. After evaluating this application, we focused our interest on the moment in which the visually impaired people are having fun, and on the factor of the excitement and concentration. This paper introduces our experimental system, which is a shooting game application without visual information, to investigate the factor of the excitement and concentration of the collaboration between visually impaired people. Recent analysis results of the collaboration are reported.

Keywords: Visually impaired people · Touch panel interface · Graphical representation · Collaborative work · Music composing application · Shooting game

1 Introduction

Protecting the lives and the rights of the visually impaired people and promoting their social participation is a paramount principle today. Especially for visually impaired people, information accessibility is the important issue under this digital society, so improvements of the interface to make information more and more accessible for visually impaired people are indispensable. This paper introduces our two research projects. One is to propose the graphic representation method with touch and sound as the universal designed touch screen interface for visually impaired people. Another is to

© Springer International Publishing AG 2017
M. Antona and C. Stephanidis (Eds.): UAHCI 2017, Part II, LNCS 10278, pp. 366–378, 2017.
DOI: 10.1007/978-3-319-58703-5_27

investigate the good design of the collaborative work environment of the visually impaired.

In this paper, Sect. 2 is the universal designed touch Interface and its' application. The digital divide problem of visually impaired people tends to be focused on the access difficulties of graphical information still today. We have been developing a new method which visually impaired people can intuitively recognize the graphical information using audio and touch panels. The method is universal-designed to enable not only the visually impaired people but also the sighted people to enjoy using interactive digital graphical contents together. The proposed method and interfaces are basic techniques for developing plug-ins which help blind people to use ordinary mass-produced computer devices with touch screens, such as smartphones and iPads. Our idea is so simple that musical scales enable users to trace graphics by their fingers and to memorize their position on the touch screen. Our recent progress including digital textbook application for visually impaired children is also reported.

Section 3 is the design of the collaborative work support environment. The collaborative work of visually impaired people and sighted people on equal ground plays a significant role for visually impaired people's social advance in society. Our developed collaborative application of music composition has a beautiful tangible interface that would attract the attention of both visually impaired and sighted people, and multiple functions that are likely to induce collaborative communication among users. After evaluating this application, we focused our interest on the moment in which the visually impaired were having fun, and on the factor of the excitement and concentration. This paper introduces our experimental system, which is a shooting game application without visual information, to investigate the factor of the excitement and concentration of the collaboration between visually impaired people. Recent analysis results of the collaboration are reported.

2   The Universal Designed Touch Interface and Its' Application

2.1   Basic Graphical Representation with ONE OCTAVE SCALE INTERFACE

This section introduces our research experiences on developing universal-designed interactive contents on touch panel for visually impaired people. We have been proposing "One Octave Scale Interface (abbr. OOSI) as a graphical representation interface on touch panels for visually impaired people. The OOSI is based on the view that all shapes of graphics are able to be divided into start/goal/relay points and line/curve segments. Each line/curve is divided into eight parts to be linked to a musical scale as showed in Fig. 1 [1]. When a user successfully traces a line/curve, continuous musical scale sound is played depending on the finger position. Proposed methods and interfaces are basic techniques for developing plug-ins which help blind people to use ordinary mass-produced computer devices with touch screens, such as smartphones and tablet computers.

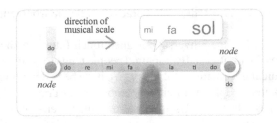

Fig. 1. The overview of the One Octave Scale Interface.

For improving the performance of the OOSI as the single-touch screen interface, several experiments with visually impaired people were done as showed in Fig. 2 (left) for investigating the node number effect, the stereo sound effect and the node regulation effect [2, 3]. Figure 2 (right) is the recognition results of the figures in three types of node regulation by eleven visually impaired people. In this figure, 'S' means the single-touch experiment, 'B' means the blind person, and 'L' means the masked low vision people. Despite these efforts of improving, the low recognition rate of curves still remained as unsolved problem. Looking at this problem from different angle, we decided to introduce the multi-touch screen in our development.

	M	⊃	⊐	□	⊃	N	⋛	∩
SBa	M	⌐	⊐	□	⊃	N	⋜	⊓
SBb	M	⊃	⊐	D	⊃	N	No answer	∩
SBc	M	⌐	⋜	⊍	⊃	N	⋜	∩
SBd	Λ	⊃	⊃	□	⊐	L	⌐	⌐
SBe	⊱	Z	⊐	R	⊃	N	Z	◻
SBf	⊓	⊃	⊐	D	⊃	Ν	⋝	⊓
SLg	M	⌐	V	⌐	⌐	N	⌐	∧
SLh	M	⌐	⊐	⌒	⊃	N	≈	∧
SBi	⊍	⊃	⋜	R	⊃	N	⋜	∩
SBj	I	⊐	⊐	▽	⊃	M	⋝	⌐
SLk	⊱	⋜	⋜	⊏	⋝	N	⋜	∧

Fig. 2. Left: Single touch display experiment (Symbols were not displayed on the screen.), and Right: Recognition results of the single-touch experiment drawn by participants

2.2 Improvements and Evaluation

To enrich the OOSI as a multi-touch screen interface, we thought that using multi timbre would provide useful clues to find the location of each finger on a displayed graphic for users [4]. We introduced the timbre of eight musical instruments into the OOSI's representation of lines and curves as shown in Fig. 3(a). To evaluate the OOSI's multi-touch function, an application was written by Cocoa for iPad, which allowed us to develop an eleven finger multi-touch application. The application consists of a training graphic in Fig. 3(b), and twelve graphics in three patterns as shown in Fig. 3(c). The size of each graphic is 10 cm × 10 cm as same as the previous experiments. Six blind people and five low vision people, who were staff members or former/recent students of braille training courses of Japan Braille Library, participated in our evaluation. People with low vision wore eye-masks, and all participants were given warm encouragement but no feedbacks about correct answers from examiners while evaluating. All figures were displayed in random order. Maximum time for examining one figure was strictly fixed

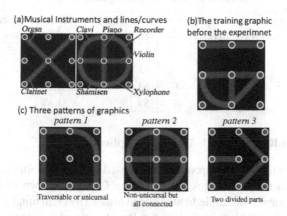

Fig. 3. (a) Sound mapping of figures, (b) A figure for training and (c) Figures for evaluation in three patterns

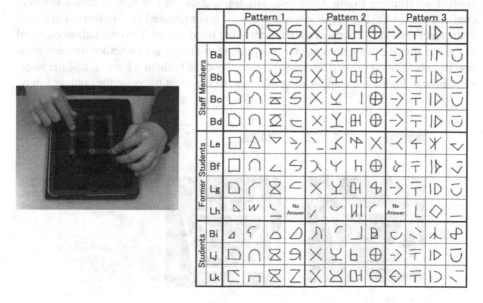

Fig. 4. Multi touch display experiment (Symbols were displayed on a iPad.), and Right: Recognition results of the multi-touch experiment drawn by participants

at four minutes. After examining, the recognition result was presented by the participants with fingertip drawing on a paper, and was traced by examiner with a pen. The recognition results by all participants are shown in Fig. 4 (right). An example of touchng display is shown in Fig. 4 (left). By comparing the recognition results of the same figure "∩" in two experiments shown in Figs. 2 and 4, the number of the perfect matching was zero in the single-touch evaluation and four in the multi-touch evaluation. The curve recognition ratio of single/multi-touch screens is compared in Table 1.

Table 1. The curve recognition ratio

	The number of lines + curves	The number of curves	Recognition ratio of curves	Misrecognition ratio of curves	Absence ratio
Single	43	7	31.2%	50.6%	18.2%
Multi-Pat1	25	7	45.5%	23.4%	31.2%
Multi-Pat2	26	6	63.6%	9.1%	27.2%
Multi-Pat3	18	2	59.1%	31.8%	9.1%

2.3   The Recent Research on E-learning Application

As a result of continuing to improve OOSI based on these evaluations, we are now developing an electronic textbook system using OOSI as shown in Fig. 5. An iPad application for students was implemented and evaluated by eight blind junior high school students to solve the problem of finding the length ratio of line segments and solving the problem of seeking congruent figures. As a result, it was verified that OOSI was useful as an interface of electronic textbooks and that it could be used as a learning content substituting Braille textbooks. An application for teachers to create learning contents using OOSI on the iPad was developed and evaluated by 7 university students in the teacher training course and 4 teachers of the blind school. The evaluation consisted of the quantitative evaluation on current application design as to whether contents creation of beforehand prepared ten questions can be done without a burden, and the interview how to improve the application in order for the users to create the content freely.

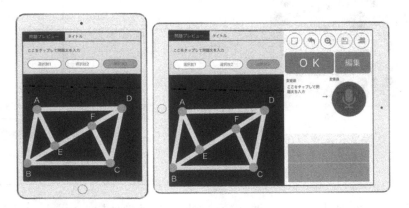

Fig. 5. The application for the students (left) and the application for the teacher (right)

As a result, it was shown that the proposed application can be used as the content creation system of electronic textbook for visually impaired students. We continue to refine and implement the electronic textbook system.

3   The Design of the Collaborative Work Support Environment

3.1   The Research on the Music Application

We started this research from interviews of blind people and a teacher who developed and researched assistive applications for visually impaired students. Agendas for designing the music application from the interviews were as follows; (1) composing music without memorizing or reading musical scores is a much-needed application for visually impaired people contrary to our expectation, (2) user friendly interface without making harsh sounds helps visually impaired people to enjoy the music application with others without embarrassment. For helping intuitive understanding of composing mechanism, we employed the method of laying out tangible objects on the table. A vision sensor (Kinect) detects the positions of the objects, and the detection results are directly changed into musical score as shown in Fig. 6. As the tangible objects, daily goods and stationeries were employed. After many trials, clip objects, such as paper clips, binder clips and clothespins with AR marker, and string objects, such as yarn, ropes and chains, to help users to trace and adjust the positions of clip objects were selected for the user evaluation. Single user evaluation and two user evaluation which two male and three female blinds, aged 18 to 33, and one sighted male aged 22 participated in, has been done. The result shows that all users preferred clothespins and chains to others, and that our proposed music composing interface by laying out tangible objects on the table was effective to help users' collaboration and communication [5].

As the 2nd phase system development, we made the workspace independent for each user so as to promote oral communication, as shown in Fig. 7. Two users sit on both sides of a table, create their own melody lines individually in the area A. In the area B, the dice-like shape box with six AR markers has a function to change sounds of musical instrument of the melody users composed. The six AR markers indicate high-pitched piano, low-pitched piano, guitar, drum kit, trumpet and violin respectively, and two users can select each instrument by rolling each box. In the area C, seven AR markers called "base marker" for base sounds are set on the center on the table. Seven sounds are the loop of percussion, drum, dance beat, pop beat, dance base, pop base and shaker. All base markers are laid upside down at the start. Users can add the base sounds to their music by turning over base markers. Six visually impaired and six sighted people participated in the evaluation. Figure 8 shows the appearance in the experiment. The results show that the proposed interface design helps visually impaired people sufficiently to have the initiatives of collaborative works, and that the developed collaborative application design enables the visually impaired people to enjoy composing music [6].

Fig. 6. A gesture and AR markers recognition result on the two users' collaboration.

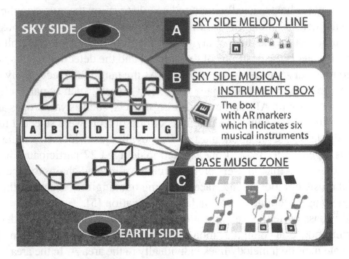

Fig. 7. Outline of the improved music application

Fig. 8. Appearance in the experiment

3.2   The Research on the Shooting Game

The purpose of this research is to elucidate the collaboration mechanism by manipulating information given to both visually impaired and sighted people and observing the state of changes in collaboration between users under multiple situations. The system configuration is shown in the Fig. 9. Three iPads are connected by Bluetooth, the two controllers iPad operate like a handle to manipulate the spaceship and send the tilt value measured by the gyro sensor to the server iPad. The server iPad moves the spaceship based on the tilt value and uses the vibration presentation device in Fig. 9 [7], which was developed with the vibration type loudspeaker, to feedback the distance between the spaceship and the enemy to the user in real time. Two users cooperate, navigate one spaceship, fire a beam and defeat more enemies. The spaceship will not move smoothly unless the directions of inclining the two iPads are not matched. In order to prevent random firing of the beam, it is set so that the next beam can not be struck for 1 s after the beam is emitted. Vibrations of a magnitude proportional to the square root of the distance between the spacecraft and the enemy are fed back to the speaker on the enemy side among the vibrating loudspeakers worn by the user on the two indexed fingers. When the spaceship is right under the enemy, the vibration will be zero.

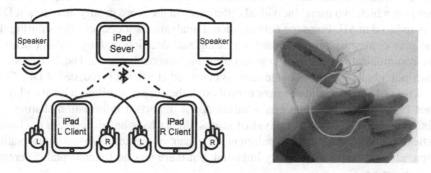

Fig. 9. Overview of the experimental system (Left) and the developed vibration presentation device (Right).

Four types of evaluation contents, (Single Enemy(SE), Double Enemy(DE)) × (Double Hands(DH), Single Hands(SH)), were prepared as shown in Fig. 10. In DE case, the spaceship may not move if there is a discrepancy in decision between users. In the case of SH, since the amount of information is insufficient to grasp the position of an enemy by each user, information sharing among users is indispensable to shoot the enemy. The collaboration changes in the order of SEDH, SESH, DEDH, DESH were examined for 7 pairs of severely visually impaired people near blindness and sighted people and 3 pairs of sighted people.

As a result, it turned out that 10 pairs can be classified into the following four groups from the transition of the score and the characteristics of the conversation. There is a group in which the score of SH is higher than that of DH and the score of DE is higher than that of SE, and conversely, there is another group which decreases in both. We define the former group as successful cases in collaboration, and the latter group as

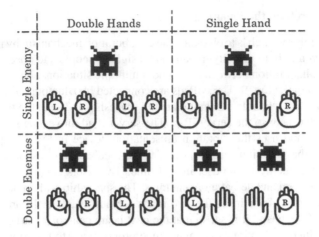

Fig. 10. Four evaluation contents for collaboration analysis.

unsuccessful cases in collaboration. There was a substantial difference between the number of conversations and the conversation contents of these two groups. The third group is in which two users' individual differences in the score greatly increases at DH, and is reduced at SH. From the conversational analysis, their conversations during the game play consist of only information sharing and decision making without heart to heart communications such as consideration and encouragement. The last group is whose individual differences in the score is observed at SE, but is reduced at DE. Their total scores of two users did not grow even though they enjoyed talking a lot and playing games because of insufficient conversation about important information sharing and decision making. In all cases, individual scores did not have any differences or characteristics related to the visual impairment. The pair of sighted had less conversation compared with the pair of visually impaired, but there was no fundamental difference in collaboration.

3.3   The Recent Research on Collaboration Analysis

In order to support the cooperative work of the visually impaired people, not only the universal design interface in which visual impairment does not affect tasks, but also the interface that encourages user's awareness and improves the quality of collaborative work are indispensable. Currently, we are exploring the design of the interface that encourages user's awareness. It was confirmed from additional experiments that the merely increasing amount of utterance could not improve the quality of cooperation. In the experiments, two smartphone applications that encourage users to speak to cooperators were implemented, and its effect was evaluated by six pair of users whose collaboration were thought to be going to fail by pre-surveys. The applications succeeded to increase the amount of conversation of all pairs, but the quality of the dialogue was never enhanced. In the case of four of six pairs, shooting score did not grow as the amount of conversation increases. It was confirmed that merely increased conversation was unrelated to improve the cooperative work. In order to encourage users' awareness, what kind of information should be designed to be more tangible is still pursued.

4 Related Work and Discussion

The authors started the research project of OOSI in 2008. After that, the spread of the iPhone and iPad and the realization of the morphing tactile display [8] have caused changes in the technical situation. The authors have confirmed that OOSI can more effectively support the visually impaired people's graphic recognition on the morphing tactile display than on the flat display like iPhone, iPad. As an academic research on the speech touch interaction, reading support system with interactive audio feedback more effective than VoiceOver has been developed in 2016 [9]. A recent research of the text input technology enables visually impaired users to tap the edges of the touch panel surface for high-speed text input without audio feedback by being assigned letters to the edge of the smartphone surface [10]. In recent years, problems concerning visually impaired people 's touch panel gesture learning have emerged, and researches on gesture sonification and corrective verbal feedback also have been done [11]. Research to provide image information to people with visual impairment had been done by conversion of graphics into tactile sensation of a tactile display or a force feedback device. Even in touch panel devices, research on image feature sonification to provide images with vibration or sound has been conducted [12]. However, due to advances in deep learning technology, conversion of images into natural language by automatic graphic annotion has reached a practical use level now [13]. Our proposed OOSI is the support technology of the graphical recognition and understanding of diagrams and charts, which are particularly important for students in science, technology, engineering, and mathematics (STEM) fields. That is a completely different approach from the image feature sonification and the automatic graphic annotion. Attempts have been made to support the use of large touch panels for the visually impaired by using tangible gadgets as a special option [15]. It is also expected as the future work to obtain synergistic effects by combining such a gadget with the proposed OOSI. As with our approach, there are a few latest researches aiming to develop graphic recognition/understanding support technology for visually impaired children, such as applying machine vision to the tactile graphics for realizing the tactile-audio graphics [16], and converting graphics previewed on a computer screen into tangible and scalable freely with the mini refreshable hyper-braille device on the base assembly and the gesture input ring device [17]. However, there is no research including development of e-learning contents and editor for visually impaired children that can be used in popular touch panel equipment like this research. The world wants to develop technology which is easier to obtain and less expensive [18].

   The mechanism of collaborative work between sighted and blind users across different modalities should be explicated [19]. But there are few researches even on collaborative work interface. One research example is that haptic virtual environments were evaluated to support the visually impaired children in an inclusive group work in school [20]. There are also researches on collaborative game applications including visually impaired people use case such as jigsaw puzzle playing [21]. There are few and few researches on collaboration analysis between sighted and visually impaired users such as a collaborative software engineering course between sighted college students and high school students with visual impairments [22]. We'll analyze the collaboration between sighted and blind users across different modalities and propose the ideal design of the collaborative work environment.

5   Conclusion

This paper described over several years' design and analysis research attempts to improve the touch panel usability of the visually impaired people and the collaborative work experience between the visually impaired people and the sighted. These trials can be summarized as follows: the information should be more and more tangible because the visually impaired people and the sighted people can make their daily life and social life better together. Future efforts will be expected for bringing the progress in this field.

Acknowledgments. We are deeply grateful to all participants of our experiments and development. Special Thanks to Mr. Naoki Kawasaki, Mr. Shotaro Ohmori, Mr. Takato Noguchi, Mr. Hiroki Ooe, Dr. Yusuke Fukushima, Mr. Masamitsu Takano, Dr. Yusuke Iwasawa, Prof. Makoto Kobayashi, Prof. Yasuhisa Tamura, Mr. Yoshiteru Azuma, Ms. Kumi Naoe, Mr. Ryo Eguchi, Mr. Tomoya Uchida and Mr. Takashi Yamaguchi. This work was supported by Grant-in-Aid for Young Scientists (B) No. 10358880 and Scientific Research (C) (General) No. 23500155 and No. 26350022 from the MEXT, Japan.

References

1. Yairi, I.E., Azuma, Y., Takano, M.: The one octave scale interface for graphical representation for visually impaired people. In: Proceedings of the 11th International ACM SIGACCESS Conference on Computers and Accessibility (ASSETS 2009), pp. 255–256. ACM, New York (2009) doi:http://dx.doi.org/10.1145/1639642.1639702
2. Naoe, K., Azuma, Y., Takano, M., Yairi, I.E.: Evaluation of sound effects and presentation position for universal designed interactive map with due consideration for visually impaired people. Int. J. Innov. Comput. Inf. Contr. **7**(5(B)), 2897–2906 (2011)
3. Naoe, K., Takano, M., Yairi, I.E.: Investigation of figure recognition with touch panel of visually impaired people from the perspective of braille proficiency. In: Proceedings of SICE Annual Conference 2010, SB06.04, Taipei, Taiwan, August 18-21 (2010)
4. Yairi, I.E., Naoe, K., Iwasawa, Y., Fukushima, Y.: Do multi-touch screens help visually impaired people to recognize graphics. In: The Proceedings of the 13th International ACM SIGACCESS Conference on Computers and Accessibility (ASSETS 2011), pp. 237–238. ACM, New York (2011). doi:http://dx.doi.org/10.1145/2049536.2049585
5. Yairi, I.E., Takeda, T.: A music application for visually impaired people using daily goods and stationeries on the table. In: Proceedings of the 14th International ACM SIGACCESS Conference on Computers and Accessibility (ASSETS 2012), pp. 271–272. ACM, New York (2012). doi:http://dx.doi.org/10.1145/2384916.2384988

6. Omori, S., Yairi, I.E.: Collaborative music application for visually impaired people with tangible objects on table. In Proceedings of the 15th International ACM SIGACCESS Conference on Computers and Accessibility (ASSETS 2013), Article 42, 2 p. ACM, New York (2013). doi:http://dx.doi.org/10.1145/2513383.2513403

7. Noguchi, T., Fukushima, Y., Yairi, I.E.: Evaluating information support system for visually impaired people with mobile touch screens and vibration. In: The Proceedings of the 13th International ACM SIGACCESS Conference on Computers and Accessibility (ASSETS 2011), pp. 243–244. ACM, New York (2011). doi:http://dx.doi.org/10.1145/2049536.2049588

8. http://tactustechnology.com/technology/optically-clear-film-for-tactile-interfaces/

9. El-Glaly, Y.N., Quek, F.: Read what you touch with intelligent audio system for non-visual interaction. ACM Trans. Interact. Intell. Syst. 6(3), 27 (2016). Article 24, doi:http://dx.doi.org/10.1145/2822908

10. Rajendran, C., Parab, C., Gupta, S.: EGDE, a soft keyboard for fast typing for the visually challenged. In: Proceedings of the 2016 CHI Conference Extended Abstracts on Human Factors in Computing Systems (CHI EA 2016), pp. 50–55. ACM, New York (2016). doi:https://doi.org/10.1145/2851581.2890635

11. Oh, U., Branham, S., Findlater, L., Kane, S.K.: Audio-based feedback techniques for teaching touchscreen gestures. ACM Trans. Access. Comput. 7(3), 29 (2015). Article 9, doi:http://dx.doi.org/10.1145/2764917

12. Yoshida, T., Kitani, K.M., Koike, H., Belongie, S., Schlei, K.: EdgeSonic: image feature sonification for the visually impaired. In: Proceedings of the 2nd Augmented Human International Conference (AH 2011), Article 11, 4 p. ACM, New York (2011). doi:http://dx.doi.org/10.1145/1959826.1959837

13. LeCun, Y., Bengio, Y., Hinton, G.E.: Deep learning. Nature **521**, 436–444 (2015)

14. Kane, S.K., Morris, M.R., Perkins, A.Z., Wigdor, D., Ladner, R.E., Wobbrock, J.O.: Access overlays: improving non-visual access to large touch screens for blind users. In: Proceedings of the 24th Annual ACM Symposium on User Interface Software and Technology (UIST 2011), pp. 273–282. ACM, New York (2011). doi:http://dx.doi.org/10.1145/2047196.2047232

15. Ducasse, J., Macé, M.J-M., Serrano, M., Jouffrais, C.: Tangible reels: construction and exploration of tangible maps by visually impaired users. In: Proceedings of the 2016 CHI Conference on Human Factors in Computing Systems (CHI 2016), pp. 2186–2197. ACM, New York (2016). doi:https://doi.org/10.1145/2858036.2858058

16. Fusco, G., Morash, V.S.: The tactile graphics helper: providing audio clarification for tactile graphics using machine vision. In: Proceedings of the 17th International ACM SIGACCESS Conference on Computers & Accessibility (ASSETS 2015), pp. 97–106. ACM, New York (2015). doi:http://dx.doi.org/10.1145/2700648.2809868

17. Namdev, R.K., Maes, P.: An interactive and intuitive stem accessibility system for the blind and visually impaired. In: Proceedings of the 8th ACM International Conference on PErvasive Technologies Related to Assistive Environments (PETRA 2015), Article 20, 7 p. ACM, New York (2015). doi:http://dx.doi.org/10.1145/2769493.2769502

18. Vashistha, A., Brady, E., Thies, W., Cutrell, E.: Educational content creation and sharing by low-income visually impaired people in India. In: Proceedings of the Fifth ACM Symposium on Computing for Development (ACM DEV-5 2014), pp. 63–72. ACM, New York (2014). doi:http://dx.doi.org/10.1145/2674377.2674385

19. Winberg, F., Bowers, J: Assembling the senses: towards the design of cooperative interfaces for visually impaired users. In: Proceedings of the 2004 ACM Conference on Computer Supported Cooperative Work (CSCW 2004), pp. 332–341. ACM, New York (2004). doi:http://dx.doi.org/10.1145/1031607.1031662
20. Moll, V., Pysander, E.-L.S.: A haptic tool for group work on geometrical concepts engaging blind and sighted pupils. ACM Trans. Access. Comput.4(4), 37 (2013). doi: 10.1145/2493171.2493172, http://doi.acm.org/10.1145/2493171.2493172
21. Grammenos, D., Chatziantoniou, A.: Jigsaw together: a distributed collaborative game for players with diverse skills and preferences. In: Proceedings of the 2014 Conference on Interaction Design and Children (IDC 2014), pp. 205–208. ACM, New York (2014). doi:http://dx.doi.org/10.1145/2593968.2610453
22. McMillan, C., Rodda-Tyler, A.: Collaborative software engineering education between college seniors and blind high school students. In: Proceedings of the 38th International Conference on Software Engineering Companion (ICSE 2016), pp. 360–363. ACM, New York (2016). doi:http://dx.doi.org/10.1145/2889160.2889188

A Generic Framework for Creating Customized Tactile User Interfaces

Francis Zinke, Elnaz Mazandarani, Marlene Karlapp[(⊠)], and Ulrike Lucke

Department of Computer Science, University of Potsdam, Potsdam, Germany
{francis.zinke,mazandar,mkarlapp,ulrike.lucke}@uni-potsdam.de

Abstract. The screen reader, the software which transforms the regular content of an application to audio and/or tactile output for visually disabled person have to be customized by a software developer for every single (version of an) application in order to have a sufficient result. Adapting screen reader to an application requires the capabilities of a software developer, is difficult and time-consuming. So far no solution is available to create an easy and customized screen reader for various applications. The necessity of a software developer to develop or adapt a screen reader especially for two-dimensional tactile braille displays is a barrier for blind users. For improving the inclusion of blind users a generic framework was developed to allow the customization of existing software for a tactile representation without any software engineering knowledge.

Keywords: Assistive environments · Design for all methods · Techniques and tools · Development methods · Interaction techniques · User interface adaptation for universal access

1 Introduction

Accessibility enable physical or mental disabled person to live their own lives independently in society [1]. Inclusion requires the equal participation of each person in the society, without a distinction between disabled and not disabled. Everyone could find themselves in the situation to be restricted in their quality of life due to barriers at any time. This viewpoint reinforces the relevance of user groups such as the elderly, temporarily sick people or people with low language skills [2] in today's society.

In the area of information and communication technology various assistive technologies exist which are intended to facilitate the use of computer technology e.g. screen readers. Visually disabled and blind person use this supporting software to transform an application to audio and/or tactile output displayed on a braille output device.

Two-dimensional tactile braille displays (TBD), like the BrailleDis [3], offer easy access to graphical applications for blind users. In contrast to common braille lines, they allow to visualize and interact with two-dimensional content like diagrams in real-time beside textual content. The usability of TBDs is only as good as the screen reader [4], the software which transforms the regular content of an application to audio and/or tactile output. There exist many screen readers for braille lines, like JAWS and NVDA, which support a lot of different applications. So far, screen readers for TBDs are limited to

M. Antona and C. Stephanidis (Eds.): UAHCI 2017, Part II, LNCS 10278, pp. 379–389, 2017.
DOI: 10.1007/978-3-319-58703-5_28

selected applications, like office software, travel routes or games [5, 6]. The relevant content information differs depending on the application. That's why screen readers for TBDs have to be customized by a software developer for every single (version of an) application in order to have a sufficient result [7].

Such adaptations and extensions are also necessary, because assistive devices are highly personalized and hardly shareable. Therefore screen reader have to be adapted individually for each application, every change in the application, and also every user.

Adapting screen readers to an application requires the capabilities of a software developer, is difficult and time-consuming. This is one reason why TBDs are not widely used. The hardware does already exist, but no adequate software for blind users. Furthermore, no framework is available to create an easy and customized screen reader for TBDs for various applications.

In this paper we present such a generic framework, its concept, toolkits and advantages [8]. It allows to customize existing software for a tactile representation without any software engineering knowledge. This paper is organized as follows: the following Sect. 2 will give an overview of the working methods of screen readers, Sect. 3 will introduce the proposed framework, the introduction of its architecture will follow in Sect. 4. The paper ends with a short conclusion and outlook section.

2   Related Work

A screen reader's work, converting content to tactile and/or audio output, is based on a non-graphical structure, e.g. a tree.

Such a tree structure is the result of filtering an application. Figure 1 shows the filtering of the Microsoft Word application in an abstract manner. Within a filtering process all control elements (with properties such as position and size) of the application are filtered and stored in a tree-like structure (e.g. off-screen model [9]). The filtered content stored in the tree can then be used to output it auditory or tactile.

Fig. 1. Workflow of a screen reader.

An application or its data can be filtered in various ways [10, 11]:

- via interfaces provided by the operating system in order to receive information from applications (e.g. Microsoft Active Accessibility[1], e.g. User Interface Automation[2] under Windows or the Assistive Technology Service Provider Interface[3] for Linux)
- through the Document Object Model (DOM) of the application, for example, to access HTML or XML documents
- the Java Access Bridge interface for reading Java applications
- the interfaces that an application provides itself
- working with screenshots of parts of an application and the use of optical character recognition (OCR)
- via the direct addressing of the Graphical Device Interface (GDI +) or the decoder

For a good filtering result all control elements and properties have to be detectable. For that purpose the application itself should be developed in consideration of accessibility. Guidelines therefor are available in ISO 9241-171. With regard to the blind, it is particularly important that[4]

- alternative texts are available for all graphic controls and images,
- content can be navigated and focused in an order that preserves meaning or operation and
- key board shortcuts are available for all/the most important actions, taking into account the platform specific guidelines.

For transferring the filtered elements to a TBD, the following three possibilities exist [12]:

- Direct control of the TBD
  Creation of bitonal pixel graphics (only black and white) of the application with dimensions of the TBD (e.g., 120×60) [13]. Each pixel corresponds to a pin. Texts must be translated beforehand in Braille. Registered events have to be transmitted into mouse actions.
- HyperReader
  HyperReader is a screen reader [10] for audio and tactile output which was developed within the HyperBraille project[5]. For adapting filters for different applications an add-in system was created in order to develop the corresponding filter mythology depending on the possibilities of the application.
- BrailleIO
  The BrailleIO framework [14] allows the control of various TBDs. The framework provides, among other things, the following functions: Converting texts into computer braille, rendering graphics, detecting basic gestures and detecting hardware buttons.

---

[1] https://msdn.microsoft.com/en-us/library/windows/desktop/dd373592(v=vs.85).aspx.

[2] https://msdn.microsoft.com/de-de/library/ms747327(v=vs.110).aspx.

[3] https://accessibility.kde.org/developer/atk.php.

[4] http://www-03.ibm.com/able/guidelines/ci162/accessibility_checklist.html.

[5] http://hyperbraille.com/.

3   Proposed Framework

The goal of the GRANT framework is to improve the inclusion of the blind and visually impaired by making screen readers easily and individually available for different braille devices. Along this process we find three different actors with specific roles and scopes: the blind user, the assistant and the software developer (see Fig. 2). The roles and scopes of the actors will be described next. Subsequently, the work steps for creating a screen reader and the framework with its functionalities are presented.

Fig. 2.   Roles for customizing tactile applications.

3.1   Roles and Scopes of the Actors of GRANT

The scope of the developer is the source code of the GRANT framework. If necessary, the proposed architecture allows exchanging basic functions in the framework (e.g. libraries for filtering or data handling). The framework will be available as open source software, and developers may add any desired library or screen reader which can be used for filtering. However, this is not mandatory for further use of the framework by the assistant.

The assistant is the core user of the proposed framework. It is used to create a customized screen reader without expenditure of time, efforts for developer or programming knowledge.

The blind user relies on the framework in order to interact with the application on a given TBD. Visualization and event handling are based on the customized screen reader provided by the assistant. Thus, the blind person is the end user of the product created in this process.

3.2   Work Stages of the Actor 'Assistant'

The process curried out by the assistant will now described in more detail with respect to the components of the GUI presented in Fig. 3. There are four main tasks to be fulfilled:

1. easy and customized content filtering of any application
   The assistant can adjust the filter for any application by choosing the application to be filtered, the filter library to be used, and the content to be filtered. Therefor the assistant starts with choosing the application to be filtered. The application which is focused by the mouse (1) will be filtered by the chosen filter library (2). Based on a strategy design pattern [15], which allows to select an algorithm of certain behavior, the libraries or a common screen reader can be selected.
2. customized content filtering for partial elements
   After filtering the application as a whole, a tree with all discovered elements (i.e. graphical components of the user interface) is displayed (3). This tree contains the captured elements of the application and their properties (4). If necessary, each node of the tree can be filtered repeatedly by another filter library. This might be useful since the quality of the filtering results (captured elements and properties) differs for particular elements.
3. designing output for the braille display
   For designing a specific visualization of the GUI on the chosen braille output device (e.g. TBD), the assistant has to define the display dimensions (5). Afterwards, he can decide for one of the following design methods:
   - Creating a customized design from scratch
     For that purpose, the assistant develops an output braille tree (6) by re-arranging the elements, their properties (7) and related events (8) for visualization on the TBD (9).
   - using an existing design concept
     Instead of developing a new output braille tree from scratch, an existing design template can be used (10) and mapped to the identified elements [16, 17]. The existing design templates will be introduced in detail in Sect. 4.2.
   - updating a customized design
     Blind people are accustomed to the GUI and memorize the positions and functions of the elements. If the GUI of the underlying application changes, blind (like elder or mentally disturbed) people face the challenge to re-discover the GUI. The framework allows to easily relate changes of the underlying application to a pre-defined output design. Furthermore, the same output design can be used for different applications of similar structure and behavior.
4. customized user events
   Both the original application and the adapted application must handle events (e.g. pressing the '7' button in the calculator (1)). The framework creates the possibility for the assistant to link the events of the output device (e.g. of a touch-sensitive braille display) with actions of the tactile representation, but also with those of the original application. Furthermore, the assistant can define additional events for the tactile display (e.g. clicking a hardware button on the TBD).

Based on the following example the workflow of the work stages of the assistant will be presented in detail:

The assistant wants to create a screen reader so a blind user is able to use the Windows Calculator on a TBD. For this purpose the assistant first set the desired filter library (2) with which the application should be filtered (in this example UIA was selected). To

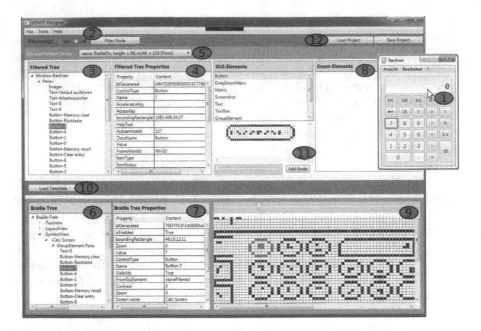

Fig. 3. The framework supports browsing the applications elements (top) and re-arranging them for tactile representation (bottom).

start the filter process, the assistant must focus the application (Windows Calculator) with the mouse (1) and press a shortcut key (e.g. F5). The result of the filtering is a tree with all filtered content (3).

In the tree view, all filtered elements are hierarchically arranged. The first node ('Window – Rechner') corresponds to the entire application. This has several child elements like 'Pane'. The 'Pane' node itself also contains child elements like text fields and buttons of the Windows Calculator.

In this example the blind user has a TBD available. Therefor the appropriate output device with its display dimensions has to be selected from all available devices of the list in the framework (5). The simulated representation of a TBS is then displayed in the framework (9) according to the dimensions of the chosen output device.

In this example the assistant decided to use an existing design concept. Therefore the design concept template has to be loaded (10) (the design concept and its templates will be introduced more in detail in Sect. 4.2). Afterwards a new tree view for the braille output (6) is displayed in addition to the tree view of the filtered content (3). The tree view of the braille output contains all elements and properties of the content to be displayed on the output device.

Now the assistant can start designing the presentation of the application on the tactile output device. For this purpose the assistant arrange the e.g. buttons and text fields of the Windows Calculator for the braille output according to the personal desire of the blind user. The framework supports the assistant to select the elements to be displayed, there location to be set and there tactile design to be created. For example the button with the number '7' of the Windows Calculator is desired to be directly under the title bar. Therefore, the assistant marks the appropriate node of the button of the number '7' in the tree view (6) of the tactile representation. By marking the node:

- the corresponding node of the filtered tree view (3) is highlighted ('Button-7'),
- the properties of the highlighted node in the filtered tree are displayed (4),
- the element type and its predefined standard tactile widget representation is displayed (11),
- the button '7' is also highlighted on the calculator (1),
  the properties of the node of the tactile representation are displayed as tabular (7) next to the braille tree view and
- the element is highlighted on the simulated braille representation (9).

If the assistant wants to change properties of the element (Button '7') the appropriate property in the tabular has to be adapted. For example changing the position requires the customization of the x and y values of the 'boundingRectangle' (7). Consequently the position of the element on the simulated braille representation is updated.

If elements are not desired to be used (e.g. percent button), they should be deleted from the braille tree view (6). Deleted elements can be added again. Therefore the appropriate node has to be selected in the filtered tree view (3) and added to the braille view tree (6) by using the 'Add Node' button (11).

The assistant can store his customizing (included: filtered tree, braille tree, selected TBD and customized events) and load it again for updating it any time (12).

Thus, the presented framework offers simple adaption of various applications for blind users on different braille devices.

4 Architecture

4.1 Design Pattern of Architecture

The GRANT framework was developed with .Net 4.5 framework and is written in C#. One main goal of GRANT is that all components are (dynamically) interchangeable. For this reason, the strategy pattern was chosen as design model for the implementation, which can dynamically integrate algorithm over an interface during the runtime. Figure 4 shows an abstract representation of the used components. The *GrantDesigner* is responsible for displaying the User Interfaces of the wizard. The core of the application is the *GrantManager*. This is used to make settings (such as setting the desired strategy), basic functions (*BasicFunctions*), and forwarding the calls to the corresponding strategy. Forwarding to the corresponding strategy (lowest level of the figure) is done via the respective interfaces in *StrategyInterfaces*. For example, it is possible to dynamically change the filter library UI Automation against the Java Access Bridge during runtime.

UI Automation was implemented exemplary as a filter library. In order to generate the tactile output (*BrailleOutput*), a driver for the universal response of different output devices[6] was used as extension for the BrailleIO framework. This solution makes it possible to develop screen reader for different output device (e.g. braille display, braille line, etc.).

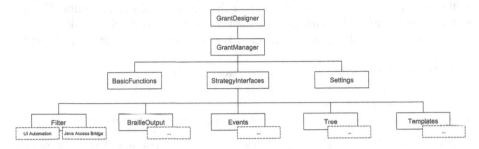

Fig. 4. Components of the framework.

4.2 Design Templates of Tactile Output

Blind people are accustomed to the GUI and memorize the positions and functions of the elements. If the GUI of the underlying application changes, blind (also elder or mentally disturbed) people face the challenge to re-discover the GUI. Therefor a design concept has been developed for two-dimensional tactile output devices within the HyperBraille project.

Based on this design concept the following views were developed [17, 18] to enable a standard tactile output design of the filtered application:

- operating view
  completely text-based braille display, comparable to braille lines
- outline view
  graphical representation of all structural elements using "boxes" without details
- symbol view
  tactile widgets with braille text
- layout view
  pixel-based representation of the original application

In addition to the different views following regions have also been created [12, 17]:

- *Header* shows general information of an application, e. g. the name of the currently selected application window.
- *Body* shows the content of the selected window.
- *Structure* shows further information e.g. for a text box the formatting of the text.
- *Detail* gives further information about the focused element or area. This output is similar to that on a Braille line.
- *Navigation bar* allowed to navigate simple to other views comparable with tabs in a web browser.

---

[6] http://download.metec-ag.de/MVBD/.

This design concept was taken into account and integrated in the GRANT framework as template to support the assistant in designing the tactile output. The framework allows to easily relate changes of the underlying application to a pre-defined output design. Furthermore, the same output design can be used for different applications of similar structure and behavior.

As part of the framework the layout view, symbol view and a simplified operating view (called text view) were focused and integrated until now. Figure 5 shows the Windows Calculator exemplary presented in the three different tactile views. The tactile views are automatically generated based on the filtered content (saved as tree structure) if the design concept is enabled and before any adjustments made by the assistant.

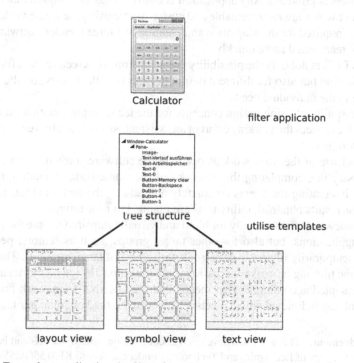

Fig. 5. Exemplary application, its filtered content as tactile views of the design concept.

From technical point of view, the symbol view represents the greatest challenge. On the one hand, all UI elements must be transferred automatically into a corresponding tactile representation. On the other hand, a sensible tactile arrangement must be determined, without knowledge of the concrete application. The prototypical implementation of this concept was therefore so far restricted to automatically arranging only the regions and most important UI elements of the filtered tree (e.g. buttons and menu bar) for the tactile representation.

In contrast to the *text view* the *symbol view* has to be completed for a suitable representation. The *text view* shows the complete content of the filtered application as a tree view. The *layout view* represents a screen shot of the application. Just like the text view a completion or adaption by the assistant is not required.

Depending on the output device an appropriate template is used in order to use the available dimensions of the hardware usefully and to receive a suitable result.

It is also possible to create new templates from scratch but using a template for adapted the output design to the needs of a blind person minimizes the effort of the assistant significantly.

5   Conclusion and Outlook

With the GRANT framework a solution to improving the inclusion of blind and visually impaired users is provided. Any application is easily accessible through individualized screen reader which are easy creatable and customizable using the framework. Since no developer is required for the adaptation and creation of a screen reader, software updates can also be reactivated more quickly.

GRANT offers not only the possibility create/customize screen readers for any software application but also for different output devices (braille display, braille line, etc.) depending to the individual needs.

The possibility of using design concepts for the tactile representation on the tactile output device reduces the working effort of an assistant but also enable creating a suitable standard design.

For a release of the framework as open source software some more extension are still necessary like completing the functions of the framework, expanding the design templates, integrating the events completely and adding the audio output. In order to evaluate the results obtained, utility tests are planned in near future.

The framework offers not only for blind and visually impaired people the possibility to adapt applications, but also for other target groups, such as seniors, people with dementia, temporarily ill people or persons with a lack of language skills. Therefore no change in the filtering process is necessary, only the output design on the desired device has to be adapted accordingly. That means that the GRANT framework provides the inclusion of any individual which meets a barrier in the field of computer technology.

Acknowledgement.   This work was developed in cooperation with Metec AG and is funded by the Federal Ministry of Economics and Technology under the license KF3155602SS4 as part of the support program 'Zentrales Innovationsprogramm Mittelstand' (ZIM).

References

1. Bundesministerium der Justiz und für Verbraucherschutz: Gesetz zur Gleichstellung behinderter Menschen (Behindertengleichstellungsgesetz - BGG) (2002)
2. Kerkmann, F.: Web accessibility. Informatik-Spektrum **36**(5), 455–460 (2013)
3. Völkel, T., Weber, G., Baumann, U.: Tactile graphics revised: the novel BrailleDis 9000 pin-matrix device with multitouch input. In: Miesenberger, K., Klaus, J., Zagler, W., Karshmer, A. (eds.) ICCHP 2008. LNCS, vol. 5105, pp. 835–842. Springer, Heidelberg (2008). doi: 10.1007/978-3-540-70540-6_124
4. Asakawa, C., Leporini, B.: Screen readers. In: Stephanidis, C. (ed.) The Universal Access Handbook, pp. 28.1–28.17. CRC Press, Boca Raton (2009)

5. Schmitz, B., Ertl, T.: Interactively displaying maps on a tactile graphics display. In: Graf, C., Giudice, N. A., Schmid, F. (eds.) Proceedings of 2012 Workshop on Spatial Knowledge Acquisition with Limited Information Displays, pp. 13–18 (2012)
6. Gutschmidt, R., Schiewe, M., Zinke, F., Jürgensen, H.: Haptic emulation of games: haptic sudoku for the blind. In: Makedon, F., Maglogiannis, I., Kapidakis, S. (eds.) 3rd International Conference on Pervasive Technologies Related to Assistive Environments (PETRA 2010), pp. 2:1–2:8. Samos. ACM, New York (2010)
7. Abascal, J., Azevedo, L., Cook, A.: Is universal accessibility on track? In: Antona, M., Stephanidis, C. (eds.) UAHCI 2016. LNCS, vol. 9737, pp. 135–143. Springer, Cham (2016). doi: 10.1007/978-3-319-40250-5_13
8. Humayoun, S.R., Dubinsky, Y., Catarci, T.: A three-fold integration framework to incorporate user–centered design into agile software development. In: Kurosu, M. (ed.) HCD 2011. LNCS, vol. 6776, pp. 55–64. Springer, Heidelberg (2011). doi:10.1007/978-3-642-21753-1_7
9. Kraus, M., Völkel, T., Weber, G.: An off-screen model for tactile graphical user interfaces. In: Miesenberger, K., Klaus, J., Zagler, W., Karshmer, A. (eds.) ICCHP 2008. LNCS, vol. 5105, pp. 865–872. Springer, Heidelberg (2008). doi:10.1007/978-3-540-70540-6_128
10. Spindler, M., Kraus, M., Weber, G.: A graphical tactile screen-explorer. In: Miesenberger, K., Klaus, J., Zagler, W., Karshmer, A. (eds.) ICCHP 2010. LNCS, vol. 6180, pp. 474–481. Springer, Heidelberg (2010). doi:10.1007/978-3-642-14100-3_71
11. Köhlmann, W., Zinke, F.: Einsatz von IKT an Hochschulen zur Unterstützung sehgeschädigter Studierender. In: Karl, W., Lucke, U., Tavangarian, D. (eds.) Tagungsband der INFORMATIK 2011, vol. P192 (2011)
12. Köhlmann, W.: Zugänglichkeit virtueller Klassenzimmer für Blinde. Dissertation, Potsdam, Universität Potsdam, Logos Verlag Berlin (2016)
13. Ivanchev, M., Zinke, F., Lucke, U.: Pre-journey visualization of travel routes for the blind on refreshable interactive tactile displays. In: Miesenberger, K., Fels, D., Archambault, D., Peňáz, P., Zagler, W. (eds.) ICCHP 2014. LNCS, vol. 8548, pp. 81–88. Springer, Cham (2014). doi: 10.1007/978-3-319-08599-9_13
14. Bornschein, J.: BrailleIO – a tactile display abstraction framework. In: Zeng, L., Weber, G. (eds.) This Proceedings of the International Workshop on Tactile/Haptic User Interfaces for Tabletops and Tablets. Dresden, Germany (2014)
15. Bala, R., Kaswan, K.: Strategy design pattern. Global J. Comput. Sci. Technol. 14(6), 35–38 (2014). Global Journals Inc. (USA), Online ISSN: 0975-4172, Print ISSN: 0975-4350
16. Köhlmann, W., Zinke, F., Schiewe, M., Jürgensen, H.: User-interface filter for two-dimensional haptic interaction. In: Miesenberger, K., Klaus, J., Zagler, W., Karshmer, A. (eds.) International Conference on Computers for Handicapped Persons, vol. 6180, pp. 498–505. Springer, Heidelberg (2010)
17. Schiewe, M., Köhlmann, W., Nadig, O., Weber, G.: What you feel is what you get: mapping guis on planar tactile displays. In: Stephandis, C. (ed.) International Conference on Universal Access in Human-Computer Interaction. Part II, vol. 5615, pp. 564–573. Springer, Berlin Heidelberg (2009)
18. Prescher, D., Weber, G., Spindler, M.: A tactile windowing system for blind users. In: Proceedings of the 12th International ACM SIGACCESS Conference on Computers and Accessibility (ASSETS 2010), pp. 91–98. ACM, New York (2010)

Gesture and Gaze-Based Interaction

Identifying the Usability Factors of Mid-Air Hand Gestures for 3D Virtual Model Manipulation

Li-Chieh Chen[1]($\boxtimes$), Yun-Maw Cheng[2], Po-Ying Chu[1], and Frode Eika Sandnes[3]

[1] Department of Industrial Design, Tatung University, Taipei, Taiwan
{lcchen, juby}@ttu.edu.tw
[2] Department of Computer Science and Engineering,
Graduate Institute of Design Science, Tatung University, Taipei, Taiwan
kevin@ttu.edu.tw
[3] Oslo and Akershus University College of Applied Sciences, Oslo, Norway
Frode-Eika.Sandnes@hioa.no

Abstract. Although manipulating 3D virtual models with mid-air hand gestures had the benefits of natural interactions and free from the sanitation problems of touch surfaces, many factors could influence the usability of such an interaction paradigm. In this research, the authors conducted experiments to study the vision-based mid-air hand gestures for scaling, translating, and rotating a 3D virtual car displayed on a large screen. An Intel RealSense 3D Camera was employed for hand gesture recognition. The two-hand gesture with grabbing then moving apart/close to each other was applied to enlarging/shrinking the 3D virtual car. The one-hand gesture with grabbing then moving was applied to translating a car component. The two-hand gesture with grabbing and moving relatively along the circumference of a horizontal circle was applied to rotating the car. Seventeen graduate students were invited to participate in the experiments and offer their evaluations and comments for gesture usability. The results indicated that the width and depth of detection ranges were the key usability factors for two-hand gestures with linear motions. For dynamic gestures with quick transitions and motions from open to close hand poses, ensuring gesture recognition robustness was extremely important. Furthermore, given a gesture with ergonomic postures, inappropriate control-response ratio could result in fatigue due to repetitive exertions of hand gestures for achieving the precise controls of 3D model manipulation tasks.

Keywords: Mid-air hand gesture · 3D virtual model manipulation · Scaling · Translation · Rotation

1 Introduction

Manipulating 3D digital contents through mid-air hand gestures is a new paradigm of Human Computer Interaction. In many applications, such as interactive and virtual product exhibition in public spaces and medical image displays in surgery rooms, the

© Springer International Publishing AG 2017
M. Antona and C. Stephanidis (Eds.): UAHCI 2017, Part II, LNCS 10278, pp. 393–402, 2017.
DOI: 10.1007/978-3-319-58703-5_29

tasks may include scaling, translation, and rotation of 3D components. In order to ensure the natural mapping between controls and displays, the selections of mid-air hand gestures for different tasks were based on the metaphors of physical object operations [1] or the gestures from user-elicitation studies [2]. Given a consensus hand gesture type for a specific task, the performance of gesture recognition and control could still be influenced by many factors, such as the moving speed and trajectory of hands, the occlusion of fingers due to hand pose changes and transitions, as well as the individual differences of performing a specific hand gesture. Since the characteristics of diverse gestures could result in different challenges, it is necessary to identify usability factors for specific gestures through experiments. Therefore, the objective of this research is to study the usability factors of hand gestures for 3D digital content manipulations.

2 Literature Review

With the benefits of natural and intuitive interactions, and free from sanitation problems in public spaces, the applications of mid-air hand gestures included interactive navigation systems in museum or virtual museum [3, 4], medical or surgical imaging system [5–8], large display interactions [9], interactive and public display [10], and 3D modelling [11–14]. Based on previous research, mid-air hand gestures could be analyzed in five gesture types: pointing, semaphoric, pantomimic, iconic, and manipulation [15]. Based on the number and trajectory of hands, mid-air gestures could be classified as one or two hands, linear or circular movements, and different degrees of freedom in path (1D, 2D, or 3D) [16]. Gesture vocabulary was dependent on the context [17, 18]. For example, the gestures for short-range human computer interaction [19] and TV controls [20] were reported to be different. For mid-air 3D object manipulation, natural gestures were necessary for accurate control tasks of scaling, translation, and rotation [21]. While choosing an appropriate mid-air hand gesture, it is necessary to consider the mental models of target users [22], reduce the workload [23], and increase gesture recognition robustness [24]. Although design principles could be derived from the literature, the factors that influence the perceived usability of gestures for specific tasks should be identified through experiments.

3 Experiment

In order to investigate the usability factors of mid-air hand gestures for manipulating 3D virtual models, an experimental system was constructed by modifying the sample programs of Intel RealSense 3D Camera with Unity 3D Toolkit (Fig. 1). In a laboratory with illumination control, the participant stood on the spot in front of a 100-inch projection screen, at a distance of 240 cm. During the experiments, the 3D virtual car model was projected on the screen. Each participant completed the tasks for scaling the

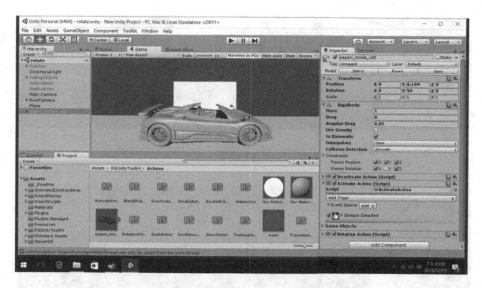

Fig. 1. A 3D Car model in the unity 3D system

car, translating the car seat, and rotating the car with respect to the vertical axis using designated hand gestures as follows.

Among the diverse gesture types, "grab and move" and bimanual "handle bar metaphor" were reported as the intuitive gestures for object manipulation tasks [1, 2, 25]. In addition, users often preferred using gestures resembling physical manipulation for wall-sized displays [26]. Therefore, the two-hand gesture with grabbing while moving apart/close to each other was applied to enlarging/shrinking the 3D virtual car (Fig. 2). The one-hand gesture with grabbing while moving up/down, left/right, or forward/ backward was applied to translating a car seat (Fig. 3). The two-hand gesture with grabbing while moving relatively along the circumference of a horizontal circle, a handlebar metaphor, was applied to rotating the car (Fig. 4). The characteristics of these gestures and referenced literature were summarized in Table 1.

Fig. 2. Enlarging/shrinking the 3D virtual car

Fig. 3. Translating the car seat to the target position

Fig. 4. Rotating the car with respect to the vertical axis

Table 1. Designated hand gestures for experiment tasks

Tasks	No. of hands	Hand pose	Hand orientation	Hand motion and trajectory	Referenced literature
Scaling	Two hands	Starting from open palm then grab (while moving)	Facing to each other	Moving apart/close to each other	[1, 25]
Translation	One hand		Facing to the target	Moving up/down, left/right, or forward/backward	[2, 25]
Rotation	Two hands		Facing down	Moving relatively along the circumference of a horizontal circle	handle bar metaphor [1, 25]

In the experiment, an Intel RealSense 3D Camera (F200) was used to extract the positions and movements of 22 joints on each hand skeleton. With the Intel RealSense SDK, basic gestures, such as spread fingers and fist could be recognized (Fig. 5). Spread fingers and fist were the static gestures of opening palm and grabbing, respectively. Therefore, it was expected to discriminate the transitions from opening palm to grabbing, and vice versa.

The camera was placed between the participant and the screen. The distance to the participant was adjusted with respect to the arm length. The height was adjusted to the elbow height of each participant.

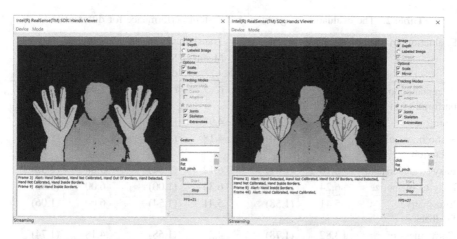

Fig. 5. The spread-fingers and fist gestures identified by the intel realsense SDK

4   Results and Discussions

Seventeen students, 7 female and 10 male, were invited to participate in the experiment. They studied in either the Ph.D. program of Design Science or the Master program of Industrial Design, with the age range from 22 to 37 (mean: 26.12, standard deviation: 4.65). All participants had the experiences of using 3D modelling software and smartphones with touch gestures. In the experiment, they were asked to apply gestures to carry out scaling, translation, and rotation tasks.

After completing each task, they were asked to evaluate the gesture using a 7-point Likert scale, indicating the degree of agreement, from the perspectives of acceptance to performing in public, comfort, smoothness of operation, easy to understand, easy to remember, informative feedback, correctness of system response, appropriate control-response ratio, and overall satisfaction (Table 2). The result of ANOVA indicated that there were significant differences in user evaluation among these usability criteria. The gesture for scaling was considered as the one needed to be improved in smoothness of operation, correctness of system response, control-response ratio, and overall satisfaction. The gesture for translation yielded the lowest score in the smoothness of operation. The gesture for rotation yielded the lowest score in appropriate control-response ratio.

Tables 3, 5, and 7 listed the reported usability problems with respect to scaling, translation, and rotation tasks, respectively. Two-hand gestures for scaling and rotation tasks caused more usability problems in failure of gesture recognition, lag in system response, gesture detection range, control-response ratio, and fatigue. Based on the original comments from participants, quick movements or rapid pose changes of two hands were the major causes of system failures. Evidently, the original detection range was not wide or deep enough for the natural and linear motions of both hands. The default control-response ratio needed to be adaptive for precise controls.

In addition, the participants were encouraged to offer user-defined gestures for each task. The alternative gestures were listed in Tables 4, 6, and 8. The alternative gestures

Table 2. The evaluation of gestures and system performance for different tasks

Evaluation criteria	Scaling		Translation		Rotation	
	Mean	Standard deviation	Mean	Standard deviation	Mean	Standard deviation
Acceptance to performing in public	5.41	(1.12)	6.12	(1.11)	4.94	(2.05)
Comfort	4.53	(1.59)	4.94	(1.60)	4.18	(1.55)
Smoothness of operation	3.12	(1.80)	4.18	(1.78)	4.18	(1.67)
Easy to understand	6.18	(1.01)	6.12	(1.54)	5.88	(1.32)
Easy to memorize	6.24	(0.83)	6.35	(1.00)	6.00	(1.46)
Informative feedback	5.41	(1.58)	5.41	(1.54)	6.00	(1.06)
Correctness of system response	3.82	(1.78)	4.24	(1.68)	4.18	(1.74)
Appropriate control-response ratio	3.65	(1.58)	4.24	(1.35)	4.12	(1.27)
Overall Satisfaction	3.82	(1.47)	4.59	(1.42)	4.41	(1.42)

Table 3. The usability problems of two-hand grabbing while moving apart/close for scaling

Problem types	Original comments from participants
Failure of gesture recognition	After enlarging or shrinking, the interactive mode could not be released through opening palm
	Sometimes, open palm or fist were not recognized by the system
	Sometimes, the grabbing gesture for initializing scaling was not detected
	If two hands were too close to each other, the switch between enlarge and shrink become unstable
Lag in system response	The scaling was lagged or discontinued while two hands were moving quickly
	The detection of hand movements was discontinued at some time
Gesture detection range	The detection area was too narrow. Sometimes, it was easy to move out of the range
Control-Response ratio	It was difficult to reach desired size
	Sometimes, it was not easy to control the size while scaling up
	The mapping between the distance of two hands and the scaling factor of enlarging or shrinking was not clear

for scaling (Table 4) included using one hand with posture change (from open palm to grab or pinch) or using two hands to form two corners of a rectangle boundary and slightly adjust the boundary size (Fig. 6). These gestures featured the benefit of requiring less movement range. The alternative gesture for translation was to employ pinching, instead of grabbing (Table 6). The alternative gestures for rotation ranged

Table 4. Alternative gestures for scaling

No. of Hands	Hand Pose	Hand orientation	Hand motion and trajectory
One hand	Open palm for scaling up; Grab for scaling down;	Facing toward the object	Staying still
One hand	Open palm for scaling up; Pinch for scaling down;	Facing toward the object	Staying still
Two hands	Both in L handshape (ASL); forming two corners of a rectangle boundary	One facing forward; the other facing backward	Moving apart for scaling up; Moving close for scaling down;

Table 5. The usability problems of one-hand grabbing while moving for translation

Problem types	Original comments from participants
Gesture discrimination	The gesture was too similar to the gestures of other operations in previous experiences, such as grabbing and moving forward/backward for zoom out/in of a 2D image
Control-response ratio	High gain of xyz movements made positioning difficult
	It was difficult to move to precise position
	The depth movement was not easy to control

Table 6. Alternative gestures for translation

No. of Hands	Hand pose	Hand orientation	Hand motion and trajectory
One hand	Pinch while moving; Open palm for releasing and stop moving	Facing toward the object	Moving from the original position to the target position

Table 7. The usability problems of two-hand grabbing while moving relatively on a circumference of a horizontal circle for rotation

Problem types	Original comments from participants
Failure of gesture recognition	The direction of rotation was inconsistent while two hands were crossing to each other in front of the body
	Sometimes, the gesture was not detected
Lag in system response	The rotation was not smooth
Gesture detection range	The system was too sensitive to the height of both hands
Control-Response ratio	It was difficult to rotate to the desired angle. Sometimes overshoot
Fatigue	Fatigue while operating repetitively to reach a desired angle

Fig. 6. Alternative gestures for two-hand scaling (enlarging/shrinking)

Table 8. Alternative gestures for rotation

No. of hands	Hand pose	Hand orientation	Hand motion and trajectory
One hand	Open palm	Facing down	Moving along the circumference of a horizontal circle
Two hands	Holding a virtual steering wheel	Facing to each other	Moving relatively with a constant distance along the circumference of a horizontal circle
Two hands	First hand fist; Second hand fist for rotating, open palm for stop rotation	Facing to each other	First hand staying still in front of the body and serving as a rotation axis; Second hand moving along the circumference of a horizontal circle with respect to the first hand;

from steering wheel metaphor, one-hand circular movement, or a more complicated gesture with the first hand staying still as a rotation axis and the second hand moving circularly with respect to the first hand (Table 8).

5   Conclusion

In this research, the usability factors of mid-air hand gestures for 3D virtual model manipulations were identified. The results indicated that the width and depth of detection ranges were the key factors for two-hand gestures with linear motions. For dynamic gestures with quick transitions and motions from open to close hand poses, ensuring gesture recognition robustness was extremely important. Furthermore, given a gesture with ergonomic postures, inappropriate control-response ratio could result in fatigue due to repetitive exertions of hand gestures for achieving the precise controls of 3D model manipulation tasks. These results could be used to inform the development team of vision-based mid-air hand gestures and serve as the checking lists for gesture evalation.

Acknowledgement. The authors would like to express our gratitude to the Ministry of Science and Technology of the Republic of China for financially supporting this research under Grant No. MOST 105-2221-E-036-009.

References

1. Song, P., Goh, W.B., Hutama, W., Fu, C., Liu, X.: A handle bar metaphor for virtual object manipulation with mid-air interaction. In: Proceedings of the 2012 ACM Annual Conference on Human Factors in Computing Systems - CHI 2012 (2012). doi:10.1145/2207676. 2208585
2. Groenewald, C., Anslow, C., Islam, J., Rooney, C., Passmore, P., Wong, W.: Understanding 3D mid-air hand gestures with interactive surfaces and displays: a systematic literature review. In: Proceedings of the 30th International BCS Human Computer Interaction Conference (BCS HCI 2016), 11-15 July 2016. Bournemouth University, Poole doi:10. 14236/ewic/hci2016.43
3. Hsu, F., Lin, W.: A multimedia presentation system using a 3D gesture interface in museums. Multimed. Tools Appl. **69**(1), 53–77 (2012). doi:10.1007/s11042-012-1205-y
4. Caputo, F.M., Ciortan, I.M., Corsi, D., De Stefani, M., Giachetti, A.: Gestural interaction and navigation techniques for virtual museum experiences. Zenodo (2016). http://doi.org/10. 5281/zenodo.59882
5. O'Hara, K., Gonzalez, G., Sellen, A., Penney, G., Varnavas, A., Mentis, H., Criminisi, A., Corish, R., Rouncefield, M., Dastur, N., Carrell, T.: Touchless interaction in surgery. Commun. ACM **57**(1), 70–77 (2014)
6. Rosa, G.M., Elizondo, M.L.: Use of a gesture user interface as a touchless image navigation system in dental surgery: case series report. Imaging Sci. Dentistry **44**(2), 155 (2014). doi:10.5624/isd.2014.44.2.155
7. Rossol, N., Cheng, I., Shen, R., Basu, A.: Touchfree medical interfaces. In: 2014 36th Annual International Conference of the IEEE Engineering in Medicine and Biology Society (2014). doi:10.1109/embc.2014.6945140
8. Hettig, J., Mewes, A., Riabikin, O., Skalej, M., Preim, B., Hansen, C.: Exploration of 3D medical image data for interventional radiology using myoelectric gesture control. In: Eurographics Workshop on Visual Computing for Biology and Medicine (2015)
9. Chattopadhyay, D., Bolchini, D.: Understanding visual feedback in large-display touchless Interactions: an exploratory study. [Research Report] IUPUI Scholar Works, Indiana University (2014)
10. Ackad, C., Clayphan, A., Tomitsch, M., Kay, J.: An in-the-wild study of learning mid-air gestures to browse hierarchical information at a large interactive public display. In: Ubicomp 2015, 7-11 September 2015, Osaka, Japan (2015)
11. Vinayak, Ramani, K.: A gesture-free geometric approach for mid-air expression of design intent in 3D virtual pottery. Comput. Aided Des. **69**, 11–24 (2015). doi:10.1016/j.cad.2015. 06.006
12. Vinayak, Ramani, K.: Extracting hand grasp and motion for intent expression in mid-air shape deformation: a concrete and iterative exploration through a virtual pottery application. Comput. Graph. **55**, 143–156 (2016). doi:10.1016/j.cag.2015.10.012
13. Cui, J., Fellner, Dieter W., Kuijper, A., Sourin, A.: Mid-air gestures for virtual modeling with leap motion. In: Streitz, N., Markopoulos, P. (eds.) DAPI 2016. LNCS, vol. 9749, pp. 221–230. Springer, Cham (2016). doi:10.1007/978-3-319-39862-4_21
14. Nakazato, K., Nishino, H., Kodama, T.: A desktop 3D modeling system controllable by mid-air interactions. In: 2016 10th International Conference on Complex, Intelligent, and Software Intensive Systems (CISIS) (2016). doi:10.1109/cisis.2016.80

15. Aigner, R., Wigdor, D., Benko, H., Haller, M., Lindlbauer, D., Ion, A., Zhao, S., Koh, J.: Understanding mid-air hand gestures: a study of human preferences in usage of gesture types for HCI. Microsoft Research Technical report MSR-TR-2012-111 (2012). http://research. microsoft.com/apps/pubs/default.aspx?id=175454

16. Nancel, M., Wagner, J., Pietriga, E., Chapuis, O., Mackay, W.: Mid-air pan-and-zoom on wall-sized displays. In: Proceedings of the 2011 Annual Conference on Human Factors in Computing Systems - CHI 2011 (2011). doi:10.1145/1978942.1978969

17. LaViola, Jr., J.J.: 3D gestural interaction: the state of the field. ISRN Artif. Intell., Article ID 514641 (2013)

18. Pisharady, P.K., Saerbeck, M.: Recent methods and databases in vision-based hand gesture recognition: a review. Comput. Vis. Image Underst. **141**, 152–165 (2015). Pose & Gesture

19. Pereira, A., Wachs, J.P., Park, K., Rempel, D.: A user-developed 3-d hand gesture set for human-computer interaction. Hum. Factors **57**(4), 607–621 (2015). doi:10.1177/0018720814559307

20. Choi, E., Kim, H., Chung, M.K.: A taxonomy and notation method for three-dimensional hand gestures. Int. J. Ind. Ergon. **44**(1), 171–188 (2014). doi:10.1016/j.ergon.2013.10.011

21. Mendes, D., Relvas, F., Ferreira, A., Jorge, J.: The benefits of DOF separation in mid-air 3D object manipulation. In: Proceedings of the 22nd ACM Conference on Virtual Reality Software and Technology - VRST 2016 (2016). doi:10.1145/2993369.2993396

22. Cui, J., Kuijper, A., Fellner, D.W., Sourin, A.: Understanding people's mental models of mid-air interaction for virtual assembly and shape modeling. In: Proceedings of the 29th International Conference on Computer Animation and Social Agents - CASA 2016 (2016). doi:10.1145/2915926.2919330

23. Nunnari, F., Bachynskyi, M., Heloir, A.: Introducing postural variability improves the distribution of muscular loads during mid-air gestural interaction. In: Proceedings of the 9th International Conference on Motion in Games - MIG 2016 (2016). doi:10.1145/2994258.2994278

24. Smedt, Q.D., Wannous, H., Vandeborre, J.: Skeleton-based dynamic hand gesture recognition. In: 2016 IEEE Conference on Computer Vision and Pattern Recognition Workshops (CVPRW) (2016). doi:10.1109/cvprw.2016.153

25. Fonseca, F., Ferreira, A., Mendes, D., Jorge, J., Araújo, B.: 3D mid-air manipulation techniques above stereoscopic tabletops. In: ISIS3D Workshop in Conjunction with ITS 2013, 6 October 2013, Scotland, UK (2013)

26. Wittorf, M.L., Jakobsen, M.R.: Eliciting mid-air gestures for wall-display interaction. In: Proceedings of the 9th Nordic Conference on Human-Computer Interaction - NordiCHI 2016 (2016). doi:10.1145/2971485.2971503

FittsFace: Exploring Navigation and Selection Methods for Facial Tracking

Justin Cuaresma and I. Scott MacKenzie[✉]

Department of Electrical Engineering and Computer Science, York University,
Toronto, ON, Canada
justincuaresma@gmail.com, mack@cse.yorku.ca

Abstract. An experimental application called *FittsFace* was designed according to ISO 9241-9 to compare and evaluate facial tracking and camera-based input on mobile devices for accessible computing. A user study with 12 participants employed a Google *Nexus 7* tablet to test two facial navigation methods (positional, rotational) and three selection methods (dwell, smile, blink). Positional navigation was superior, with a mean throughput of 0.58 bits/second (bps), roughly 1.5× the value observed for rotational navigation. Blink selection was the least accurate selection method, with a 28.7% error rate. The optimal combination was positional+smile, with a mean throughput of 0.60 bps and the lowest tracking drop rate.

Keywords: Camera input · Facial tracking · Blink selection · Smile selection · Fitts' law · ISO 9241-9 · Qualcomm Snapdragon · Accessible input techniques

1 Background

Smartphones and tablets are now an integral component of our daily lives, as new technologies emerging regularly. Current devices include a media player, a camera, and sophisticated communications electronics. More specifically, buttons have given way to smooth touchscreen surfaces. Not surprisingly, this impacts user interaction. Touchscreen surfaces allow input via touch gestures such as taps and swipes. Additional sensors, such as gyroscopes and accelerometers, enable other forms of interaction (e.g., tilt) to enhance the user experience.

One common sensor on smartphones and tablets that is rarely employed for user input is the front-facing camera. Although mostly used as a novelty, it is possible to adopt the front-facing camera to perform facial tracking. The front-facing camera is sometimes used in picture-taking applications to enhance or alter one's facial features. An app called *Reframe* on the App Store, shown in Fig. 1 illustrates a typical example. The app places a pair of user-selected glasses on the user's face, allowing him/her to virtually try on a pair to see how they look.

Besides novelty apps, there are additional ways to use facial tracking. For games, facial tracking is presently used to maneuver in-game elements [1]. Accessible computing is another candidate. Android and iOS already integrate accessible functionalities via voice I/O (e.g., *Siri*); however, there is still no comprehensive mobile solution

© Springer International Publishing AG 2017
M. Antona and C. Stephanidis (Eds.): UAHCI 2017, Part II, LNCS 10278, pp. 403–416, 2017.
DOI: 10.1007/978-3-319-58703-5_30

Fig. 1. Using the front-facing camera, *Reframe* lets a user try on eyeglasses and sunglasses.

for people with motor disabilities. Thus, a potential application for facial tracking is for users with deficient motor control in the hands or arms but with full motor control of the head, neck, and face. The starting point, however, is to determine if facial tracking can be used for simple interactions such as selecting on-screen targets.

FittsFace was designed as an ISO-conforming Fitts' law tool to study facial input methods for traditional point-select operations on mobile devices. Before detailing the operation of *FittsFace*, we review related work using facial tracking in a desktop environment.

2   Related Work

Most work on facial tracking is directed at desktop or laptop systems with a webcam. The literature generally focuses on computer vision algorithms rather than on usability. The following review is limited to the use of facial tracking for target selection and empirical evaluations of such.

Perini et al. used computer vision techniques and a webcam to develop *FaceMouse* [9]. The application was text-entry for tetraplegic users; thus, the targets were keys on a soft keyboard. Dwell-time selection was combined with a letter-prediction scheme. The text entry rate was 13 chars/min.

Varona et al. built a desktop-webcam facial tracking system that used nose position to detect face gestures [13]. A grid of 25 circular targets (radius = 15 pixels) was positioned on the display. Users selected the targets by moving their head (i.e., nose) and selected targets by dwelling or winking. Although selection time was not reported, accuracy was 85.9% for untrained users and 97.3% for trained users.

Javanovic and MacKenzie developed *MarkerMouse* using a laptop webcam and a head-mounted tracker [4]. Using a Fitts-type ISO 9241-9 experiment, they compared a conventional mouse with a head-mounted tracker using position control and velocity control. Position control was superior and considered more intuitive, yielding a throughput of 1.61 bits/second (bps). Not surprisingly, the mouse performed best with a throughput of 4.42 bps, which is consistent with other ISO 9241-9 evaluations [12].

Gizatdinova et al. presented a hands-free text entry system using facial tracking, gesture detection, and an on-screen keyboard [2]. They reported that single-row layouts achieved better results, especially when consecutive targets are far apart. They used eyebrow movement for selection, reporting that brow-up movements outperformed brow-down movements due to asymmetry in muscle control.

3   Performance Evaluation

To evaluate facial tracking as an input method in the mobile context, we used the methodology in the ISO 9241-9 standard for non-keyboard input devices [3]. *FittsFace* was modelled after *FittsTouch*, a touch-based Android application following the ISO standard [5]. The main difference is that *FittsFace* receives input from a facial tracking subsystem rather than from touch events. Details are provided below in the Method section.

The most common ISO 9241-9 evaluation procedure uses a two-dimensional task with targets of width W arranged in a circle. Selections proceed in a sequence moving across and around the circle (Fig. 2). Each movement covers an amplitude A – the diameter of the layout circle. The movement time (MT, in seconds) is recorded for each trial and averaged over the sequence.

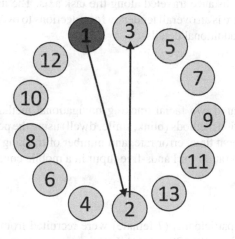

Fig. 2. Two-dimensional target selection task in ISO 9241-9 [3].

The difficulty of each trial is quantified using an index of difficulty (ID, in bits) and is calculated from A and W as follows:

$$ID = log_2\left(\frac{A}{W} + 1\right) \tag{1}$$

The main performance measure in ISO 9241-9 is throughput (TP, in bits/second or bps) which is calculated over a sequence of trials as the ID-MT ratio:

$$TP = \frac{ID_e}{MT} \tag{2}$$

The standard specifies calculating throughput using the *effective index of difficulty* (ID_e). The calculation includes an adjustment for accuracy to reflect what participants actually did, rather than what they were asked to do:

$$ID_e = \log_2\left(\frac{Ae}{We} + 1\right) \tag{3}$$

with

$$W_e = 4.133 \times SD_x \tag{4}$$

The term SD_x is the standard deviation in the selection coordinates computed over a sequence of trials. For the two-dimensional task, selections are projected onto the task axis, yielding a single normalized x-coordinate for each trial. For $x = 0$, the selection was on a line orthogonal to the task axis that intersects the center of the target. x is $-$ve for selections on the near side of the target centre and $+$ve for selections on the far side. The factor 4.133 adjusts the target width for a nominal error rate of 4% under the assumption that the selection coordinates are normally distributed. The effective amplitude (A_e) is the actual distance traveled along the task axis. The use of A_e instead of A is only necessary if there is an overall tendency for selections to overshoot or undershoot the target (see [5] for additional details).

4   Method

Our user study compared two facial tracking navigational methods (rotational, positional) and three selection methods (blink, smile, dwell) using the performance measures of throughput, movement time, error rate, and number of tracking drops. The goal was to find a viable configuration for hands-free input in a mobile context.

4.1   Participants

Twelve non-disabled participants (7 female) were recruited from the local university campus. Ages ranged from 19 to 29 years. All participants were casual smartphone users. Participants receive a nominal fee ($10).

4.2   Apparatus (Hardware and Software)

The hardware was a Google *Nexus 7* tablet running Android 5.0.2 (Fig. 3a). The device had a 7″ display (1920 × 1200 px, 323 px/inch). *FittsFace* was developed in Java using the Android SDK, with special focus on the Qualcomm Snapdragon Facial Recognition API (Fig. 3b) [10].

<p>**(a)**   **(b)**</p>

Fig. 3. (a) *Nexus 7* (b) Facial recognition SDK demonstration.

FittsFace implements the two-dimensional ISO task described earlier (Fig. 2). After entering setup parameters (Fig. 4a) a test condition appears with 9 targets (see Fig. 4b and c for examples). The participant navigates a white dot (cursor) around the display by moving his/her head. To avoid inadvertent selections, a sequence of trials started only after the participant selected a green circle in the center of the display. Data collection began when the first target circle (red) was selected. The goal was to place the cursor in the target circle via the current navigation method and select it via the current selection method. If a selection occurred with the cursor outside the target, an error was logged and the next target was highlighted.

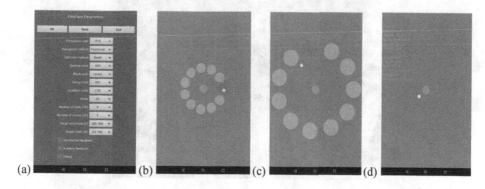

(a)   (b)   (c)   (d)

Fig. 4. FittsFace (a) setup activity (b) $A = 250$, $W = 60$ (c) $A = 500$, $W = 100$ (d) results after completing a sequence. (Color figure online)

A "pop" was heard on a correct selection, a "beep" for an error. After all 9 targets were selected, a results dialog appeared (see Fig. 4d).

Six configurations were tested to accommodate two navigation methods (positional, rotational) and three selection methods (smile, blink, dwell), as now described.

Positional navigation tracked the nose and its offset from the center of the display. The offset from the center was multiplied by a scaling factor to achieve efficient head movement. Through pilot testing, we settled on a scaling factor of 3.8.

Rotational navigation determines the pitch and yaw of one's face. More specifically, a z-plane point coordinate is derived with $x =$ arcsin(pitch)/(scaling factor) and $y =$ arcsin(yaw)/(scaling factor). We used a scaling factor of 1500.

Smile selection utilized the Qualcomm Snapdragon's smile detection API. A "select" was triggered when the smile value exceeded 65. Although the best way to select was a wide open smile, a big closed-mouth smile also worked.

Blink selection utilized the blink detection API with selection occurring when the blink value exceed 55 for 550 ms.

Dwell selection was triggered by maintaining the cursor within the target for 2500 ms. This rather high value was deemed necessary through pilot testing due to the overall slow pace of movements and selections with the facial processing API. If the cursor entered the target but the participant failed to complete a selection within a 60-second timeout, an error was registered and the next target was highlighted.

4.3 Procedure

Participants were tested in a controlled environment that provided adequate lighting for the front-facing camera. The test device was placed on a table using a laptop as a stand (Fig. 5). Before starting, participants were introduced to the objectives of the experiment and to the operation of *FittsFace*.

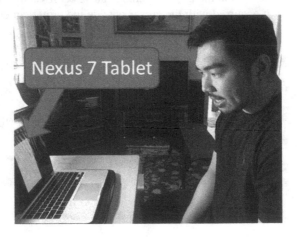

Fig. 5. Participant performing trials using smile as a selection method.

Each navigation and selection mode was briefly demonstrated. No practice trials were given. Participants took about 45 min to complete the experiment. After testing, participants were given a questionnaire to solicit qualitative feedback.

4.4 Design

The experiment was a 2 × 3 within-subjects design. The main independent variables and levels were

- Navigation method (positional, rotational)
- Selection method (smile, blink, dwell)

Two additional independent variables were target amplitude (250, 500) and target width (60, 100). These were included to ensure the tasks covered a range of difficulties. Using Eq. 1, the difficulties ranged from $ID = \log_2(250/100 + 1) = 1.81$ bits to $ID = \log_2(500/60 + 1) = 3.22$ bits. For each A-W condition, participants performed 9 target selections in a sequence.

The dependent variables were throughput, movement time, error rate, number of tracking drops, and timeouts (dwell only).

Participants were divided into six groups to counterbalance the six input conditions and thereby offset learning effects.

The total number of trials was 2592 (12 participants $\times$ 2 navigation methods $\times$ 3 selection methods $\times$ 2 widths $\times$ 2 amplitudes $\times$ 9 selections/sequence).

5 Results and Discussion

5.1 Throughput

The grand mean for throughput was 0.47 bps. Here, we see empirical evidence of the challenges in facial tracking. For a similar task in a desktop-mouse environment, throughput is typically 4–5 bps – about 10× greater [12]. However, other pointing devices, such as a touchpad or joystick, often yield low throughputs – under 2 bps. Given that an application for facial tracking is accessible computing, achieving high values for throughput is perhaps not so important. Furthermore, this user study was mostly concerned with examining various interaction possibilities for facial tracking, rather than directly comparing facial tracking to other input methods.

Throughput by condition is seen in Fig. 6. Rotational navigation produced a mean throughput of 0.36 bps. Positional, on the other hand, yielded a higher mean throughput of 0.58 bps, or 59% higher. The effect of navigation method on throughput was statistically significant ($F_{1,11} = 47.1$, $p < .0001$).

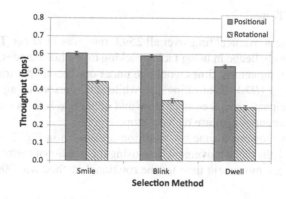

Fig. 6. Throughput (bps) by navigation method and selection method. Error bars show ± 1 SE.

By selection method, throughput was 0.47 bps (blink), 0.42 bps (dwell), and 0.53 bps (smile). Comparing the best to worst, throughput was 26% higher for smile selection than for dwell selection. The effect of selection method on throughput was statistically significant ($F_{2,22} = 8.83, p < .01$).

We examined different combinations of navigation and selection methods and their effects on throughput. Positional+smile performed best with a throughput of 0.60 bps. Positional+blink was similar with a throughput of 0.59 bps. At 0.53 bps, positional +dwell produced the lowest throughput among the positional combinations.

Rotational combinations resulted in lower throughputs. The highest among rotational combinations was rotational+smile, with a mean throughput of 0.45 bps. Rotational +blink produced a mean of 0.34 bps. The combination with the least throughput overall was the rotational+dwell combination, with a mean throughput of only 0.30 bps, a value 50% lower than for the positional+smile combination.

As observed, positional navigation was superior, producing higher throughputs than rotational navigation. Key factors that impact the throughput of both navigation methods were the stability and precision in the tracking system. Participants noted that positional tracking was more stable than rotational tracking. The values derived from the rotational data (pitch and yaw) were noisier than the values gathered from positional tracking of the nose. Although a running average algorithm was implemented to smooth the values, the effect of noise still impacted the stability of the cursor movement when using rotational tracking. More complex filter algorithms may achieve better results [7, 8, 14]. A common observation was a cursor drift or jump which caused additional movement time and, therefore, a lower throughput.

As observed, smile selection yielded the highest throughput. Our original assumption hypothesized that blink would have the highest throughput. The result can be justified by analyzing the implementation of the selection types. Smile selection did not use a timer, unlike dwell and blink. Hence, participants triggered selection as soon as they flashed their smile. With the blink and dwell selection methods, the timer-based trigger added to the overall movement time (and, hence, lowered throughput).

It follows from our analysis that positional+smile is the optimal combination due to its stability, more precise tracking, and the apparently instant triggering mechanism.

5.2   Movement Time

The grand mean for movement time over all 2592 trials was 7139 ms. This result is yet another sign of the challenge in using facial tracking on mobile devices. For a desktop-mouse experiment, movement times would be under one second per trial using similar index of difficulties (*ID*s). Controlling the white dot (cursor) using facial tracking required the participants to make rather slow and deliberate actions – quite unlike the rapid, facile movement of a mouse on a desktop.

The means for movement time by condition are shown in Fig. 7. Looking first at navigation method, the mean movement time using the positional method was 5180 ms. In contrast, the mean movement time for the rotational method was 9097 ms, or about

1.8× longer. Not surprisingly, the difference between the two input methods was statistically significant ($F_{1,11} = 8.56, p < .05$). The results suggest that rotational navigation was inferior to positional navigation when it comes to movement time.

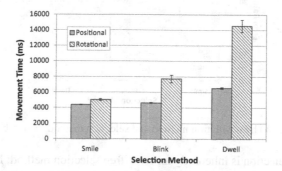

Fig. 7. Movement time (ms) by navigation method and selection method. Errors bars show ± 1 *SE*.

In terms of selection method, smile yielded the best movement time resulting in a mean of 4708 ms. Blink came second with a mean of 6171 ms, 1.3× more than smile. Lastly, dwell resulted in a mean of 10538 ms, roughly 2.2× more than smile. Hence, it is evident that smile is the superior selection method when considering movement time. The effect of selection method on movement time was statically significant ($F_{2,22} = 14.5$, $p < .0005$).

We examined different combinations of navigation methods paired with selection methods. Rotational+dwell produced the longest mean movement time, 14539 ms (see Fig. 7). The combination with the least movement time was positional+smile, having a mean movement time of 4383 ms, roughly one third the value for rotational+dwell. The next fastest combination was positional+blink, yielding a mean of 4621 ms. Considering all selection methods, those using rotational navigation produced longer mean movement times than those using positional navigation.

5.3 Error Rate

Error rate was observed as a percentage of missed selections. See Fig. 8. The grand mean for error rate was 16.6%. Positional navigation produced a mean of 7.6% compared to rotational navigation at 25.7%. Rotational navigation was about 3.3× more error prone and was, on average, missing a quarter of the targets. This result, however, is directly related to the issue of stability during rotational tracking, as discussed in the previous section. The effect of navigation method on error rate was statistically significant ($F_{1,11} = 52.6, p < .0001$).

Blink selection produced a mean error rate of 28.7% and was the most error prone among the selection methods. Smile had a mean error rate of 19.9%. Lastly, dwell had the least error rate at 1.4%. The effect of selection method on error rate was statistically significant ($F_{2,22} = 38.9, p < .0001$).

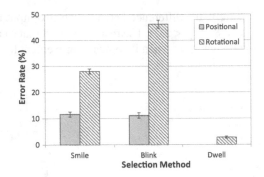

Fig. 8. Error rate (%) by navigation method and selection method. Errors bars show ± 1 *SE*.

Dwell-time selection is inherently an error-free selection method; however an error was logged if a timeout occurred (60 s without staying within the target for the prescribed dwell-time interval). No such events were logged for the positional+dwell condition. For the rotational+dwell condition, 2.8% of the trials were errors due to a timeout.

The blink timer had an impact on error rate. It was observed that participants some-times shifted the cursor out of the target before the timeout. This resulted in a missed selection.

The results of navigation and selection combinations, however, indicate a slightly different result. Other than dwell combinations, positional+blink produced the lowest error rate, 11.1%. Positional+smile had a slightly higher error rate at 11.6%. In some cases, the instantaneous triggering of smile selection was disadvantageous as natural reactions such as the opening of the mouth and speaking triggered a selection. For example, there were a few instances where a participant left his/her mouth slightly opened after flashing a smile, and this would inadvertently trigger a premature selection on the next target [9].

The rotational+blink combination was the least accurate with a mean error rate of 46.3%. This result is significant as this implies participants missed almost half the targets. Further investigation revealed that the rotational tracking system may have tracked the rotation of individual facial features as well [9]. This is evident in the error rates produced by the rotational+blink and rotational+smile.

Comparing blink and smile combined with rotational navigation suggests that the tracker is much more dependent on the eyes of the participant. This may be due to the large surface area occupied by one's mouth which makes it easier to track. Not surprisingly, the interaction effect of navigation method by selection method was statistically significant ($F_{2,22} = 13.5, p < .001$).

5.4 Tracking Drops

Another dependent variable was the number of times tracking was lost or dropped in a sequence of 9 target selections. This dependent variable is important as it bears on the efficiency and precision of a facial tracking system.

The grand mean for tracking drops was 1.4 per sequence (Fig. 9). Positional navigation averaged 0.4 drops/sequence. On the other hand, rotational navigation averaged 2.3 drops/sequence, roughly 500% more than with positional tracking. Our results are consistent with previous studies, which showed that the nose was the optimal facial feature to track [13, 14]. Blink selection had the highest mean number of drops in the context of selection methods, averaging 1.5 drops/sequence. Smile, lowest, averaged 1.2 drops/sequence, consistent with our observations on error rate: Smile is easier to track.

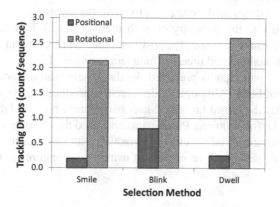

Fig. 9. Tracking drops per sequence by navigation method and selection method.

The optimal combination which yielded the least tracking drops was, again, positional+smile, with 0.19 drops/sequence. Positional+blink had 0.79 drops/sequence which further enforces that facial tracking is highly dependent on one's facial structure. However, rotational+dwell was highest at 2.27 drops/sequence.

It was observed that with rotational navigation participants rotated past a threshold where tracking holds (i.e., some facial features were occluded). Participants would tilt their head up to grab a target near the top of the display. Over tilting caused tracking drops due to the distorted perspective of the facial image. Although positional navigation suffers from a similar issue, tracking a single facial feature does not cause as many tracking drops since moving (versus just rotating) one's head adds to the movement of the cursor. The same effect was noted in previous studies [2, 4, 6, 11], where selection problems increased as target distance from the origin increased.

5.5 Participant Feedback

Based on the questionnaire given at the end of testing, participants praised the idea of integrating facial tracking as an assistive feature on mobile devices. Ten of the twelve participants preferred the positional navigation method to rotational. One participant expressed a preference thus:

The positional tracking was significantly easier to control and target the cursor accuracy compared to rotational. The direction and distance travelled by the cursor was predictable and expected.

One participant described a preference of rotational over positional:

I did not have to move my upper body to get the cursor to go to my desired direction. I stayed more relaxed and focused instead of figuring out how to position my shoulders, etc.

Overall, participants praised positional navigation for stability, smoothness, and controllability. The rotational navigation method was criticized for its occasional jitters, unexpected tracking drops, and extra effort to move the cursor.

When asked to rate the difficulty of each method on a Likert scale from 1 (not difficult) to 10 (extremely difficult), the positional method received an average rating of 2.9 while the rotational method received an average rating of 7.2.

Seven of the 12 participants preferred the dwell selection method; four preferred smile; one preferred blink. Although smile selection produced the highest throughput, it wasn't necessarily the crowd favorite. Many participants preferred dwell selection as there was no added effort required. Participants criticized the effort required for blinking and smiling. It seems the initial novelty of interacting with facial gestures wore off: After the experiment, they described the process of using facial gestures as more error prone and fatiguing.

6 Conclusion

Facial tracking radiates with potential to become an accessibility feature on modern mobile devices, allowing access to people with deficient motor control in the hands and arms but with full motor control of the head, neck, and face. Our study showed that facial tracking, given supporting hardware, has potential as an input method relying on position, rotation, and facial gestures to simulate touch gestures. The combination of positional tracking and smile selection performed best on the dependent variables throughput (0.60 bps) and movement time (4383 ms). The positional+smile combination also yielded the lowest number of tracking drops (0.19 per sequence of 9 trials). For error rates, positional+smile and positional+blink were similar (11.6% and 11.1%, respectively).

Participants overall expressed as preference for positional tracking over rotational tracking. Seven of 12 participants preferred dwell selection. Despite taking longer, dwell selecting was considered less fatiguing than smile or blink selection.

FittsFace was developed as an ISO-conforming tool to study the multidimensionality of facial tracking, observing different attributes and parameters that make an efficient and user-friendly experience. The potential to use facial tracking as a form of assistive technology using pre-installed front facing cameras is not far off. *FittsFace* allows us to step back and examine the different elements and characteristics of what constitutes a facial tracking input method that works well with users.

6.1 Future Work

Our research is open to future work. One idea is to use facial gestures as conventional touch-based events. As an example, a scroll event, normally triggered by a swipe touch gesture, could be implemented using facial tracking by closing one eye and flicking the head downward or upward. We aim to further extend our research by running the *Fitts-Face* experiment on users with motor disabilities. The project will be open sourced to encourage other similar HCI research and projects using facial tracking on mobile devices.

References

1. Cuaresma, J., MacKenzie, I.S.: A comparison between tilt-input and facial tracking as input methods for mobile games. In: Proceedings of the IEEE-GEM 2014, pp. 70–76. IEEE, New York (2014)
2. Gizatdinova, Y., Špakov, O., Surakka, V.: Face typing: vision-based perceptual interface for hands-free text entry with a scrollable virtual keyboard. In: IEEE WACV 2012, pp. 81–87. IEEE, New York (2012)
3. ISO, Ergonomic Requirements for Office Work with Visual Display Terminals (VDTs) - Part 9: Requirements for Non-keyboard Input Devices (ISO 9241-9), International Organisation for Standardisation Report Number ISO/TC 159/SC4/WG3 N147 (2000)
4. Javanovic, R., MacKenzie, I.S.: MarkerMouse: mouse cursor control using a head-mounted marker. In: Miesenberger, K., Klaus, J., Zagler, W., Karshmer, A. (eds.) ICCHP 2010. LNCS, vol. 6180, pp. 49–56. Springer, Heidelberg (2010). doi:10.1007/978-3-642-14100-3_9
5. Scott MacKenzie, I.: Fitts' throughput and the remarkable case of touch-based target selection. In: Kurosu, M. (ed.) HCI 2015. LNCS, vol. 9170, pp. 238–249. Springer, Cham (2015). doi: 10.1007/978-3-319-20916-6_23
6. Magee, J.J., Wu, Z., Chennamanemi, H., Epstein, S., Theriault, D.H., Betke, M.: Towards a multi-camera mouse-replacement interface. In: PRIS 2010, 10 p. (2010)
7. Manresa-Yee, C., Ponsa, P., Varona, J., Perales, F.J.: User experience to improve the usability of a vision-based interface. Interact. Comput. **22**, 594–605 (2010)
8. Manresa-Yee, C., Varona, J., Perales, F.J., Salinas, I.: Design recommendations for camera-based head-controlled interfaces that replace the mouse for motion-impaired users. UAIS **13**, 471–482 (2014)
9. Perini, E., Soria, S., Prati, A., Cucchiara, R.: FaceMouse: a human-computer interface for tetraplegic people. In: Huang, T.S., Sebe, N., Lew, M.S., Pavlović, V., Kölsch, M., Galata, A., Kisačanin, B. (eds.) Computer Vision in Human-Computer Interaction, pp. 99–108. Springer, Berlin (2006)
10. Qualcomm, Snapdragon SDK for Android. https://developer.qualcomm.com/mobile-development/add-advanced-features/snapdragon-sdk-android. Accessed 28 Mar 2016
11. Roig-Maimó, M.F., Manresa-Yee, C., Varona, J., MacKenzie, I.Scott: Evaluation of a mobile head-tracker interface for accessibility. In: Miesenberger, K., Bühler, C., Penaz, P. (eds.) ICCHP 2016. LNCS, vol. 9759, pp. 449–456. Springer, Cham (2016). doi:10.1007/978-3-319-41267-2_63
12. Soukoreff, R.W., MacKenzie, I.S.: Towards a standard for pointing device evaluation: perspectives on 27 years of Fitts' law research in HCI. Int. J. Hum. Comput. Stud. **61**, 751–789 (2004)

13. Varona, J., Manresa-Yee, C., Perales, F.J.: Hands-free vision-based interface for computer accessibility. J. Net. Comp. Appl. **31**, 357–374 (2008)
14. Villaroman, N.H., Rowe, D.C.: Improving accuracy in face tracking user interfaces using consumer devices. In: Proceedings of the RIIT 2012, pp. 57–62. ACM, New York (2012)

Comparing Pointing Performance of Mouse and Eye-Gaze Input System

Wenbin Guo[✉] and Jung Hyup Kim

Department of Industrial and Manufacturing Systems Engineering,
University of Missouri, Columbia, USA
wgk95@mail.missouri.edu, kijung@missouri.edu

Abstract. The purpose of this study is to identify strengths and weaknesses of an eye-gaze input system. The pointing performance of an eye-gaze input, such as reaction time and accuracy, were compared to the performance of a mouse input. Operator's sensitivity (d'), bias (β) and NASA-TLX were used as metrics for performance assessment during a gauge monitoring task. The results indicated that there was a significant difference in reaction time between a mouse input and eye-gaze input system. The participants who used a mouse as their input device showed more miss responses. However, the eye-gaze device users had more false-alarm responses. For workload, there was no significant difference between the eye-gaze input system and the mouse input system. The findings from this study showed that an eye-gaze system is favorable to the operations requiring fast human reactions and less sensitivity on false. The study provided deeper insight into user behavior regarding an eye-gaze input system.

Keywords: Eye-gaze input system · Visual search task · Human-in-the-loop simulation · Human performance · And workload

1 Introduction

There are numerous input systems, such as a mouse, multi-touch, and voice, in human-computer interaction (Bai et al. 2014). Among them, an eye-gaze system is one of the advanced systems (Chandra et al. 2015) and become more natural and non-intrusive recently (Chen and Ji 2015). One of the benefits of using an eye-gaze input system is that the system can quickly reflect human cognitive processes. For that reason, many researchers have studied an eye-gaze input system and found the impacts on pointing performance using eye-gaze input system (Jacob and Karn 2003; Murata et al. 2014; Murata et al. 2012; Sibert et al. 2001). However, they have not considered the practical usability of the eye-gaze input system. For example, reaction time, accuracy and mental workload in a dynamic control environment have not yet been examined until now.

In this study, the pointing performance of an eye-gaze input system was compared to a mouse input system. The time window-based human-in-the-loop (TWHITL) simulation (Kim et al. 2014) was used as a tool to collect accurate participant responses corresponding to the simulation events. Operator bias β and sensitivity d' (Lynn and Barrett 2014; Maniscalco and Lau 2012) were calculated by using the participant's

© Springer International Publishing AG 2017
M. Antona and C. Stephanidis (Eds.): UAHCI 2017, Part II, LNCS 10278, pp. 417–429, 2017.
DOI: 10.1007/978-3-319-58703-5_31

outcomes to compare accuracy between an eye-gaze input and mouse input system. During the experiment, the participants' mental workload was also measured by NASA-TLX. It is one of the well-known metrics for the mental workload in a dynamic task environment (Bodala et al. 2014; De la Torre et al. 2014).

The key research question for this study was: "how do the participants perform the TWHITL simulation differently when they use an eye-gaze input system compared to a mouse input system?"

We hypothesized that there was no difference in reaction time between a mouse input and an eye-gaze input. The response times from both input systems were expected to be similar when the participants experienced same stimuli during the task. Second, there was no significant difference in accuracy between a mouse input and an eye-gaze input. Finally, there was a significant difference in mental workload between a mouse input and eye-gaze input system. The mental workload of using an eye-gaze input system is expected to be higher than the workload of using a mouse input system.

2   Method

2.1   Apparatus

For the experiment, we selected a desk-mounted eye tracker Tobii EyeX Dev Kit (see Fig. 1). There were three synced infrared sensors in the Tobii EyeX sensor. Based on the angle and glint of the operator's eye, Tobii Eye X device calculated where he or she is looking at during the experiment.

Fig. 1.   Tobii EyeX Dev Kit

During the experiment, the visual image of flow, level, pressure, and temperature gauge shapes from the Visual Thesaurus as the underlying design of the gauge (Noah et al. 2014; Tharanathan et al. 2010). The participants were asked to acknowledge changes in the current state of all gauges by clicking the button corresponding to the gauge. Table 1 shows the more details of flow, level, pressure, and temperature gauge shape.

Table 1. Gauge shape and region

Event	Flow	Level	Pressure	Temperature
NORMAL				
ABNORMAL				
ALARM				

2.2 Participants

A total of twenty-four participants were recruited from the University of Missouri. Participants' age ranged from 18 to 28 (Mean = 21.4, SD = 1.92). First of all, participants were required to fill out a consent form and a demographic questionnaire. 90% of participants were right-handed, which mean that the majority of the participants used their right hand to use a mouse or keyboard. The participants were asked to use their input device to point and click alternately between the two presented target gauges as rapidly and accurately as they could.

2.3 Experimental Setup

There were two groups in this experiment (Group A: mouse input system and Group B: eye-gaze input system). For both groups, the subjects were seated roughly 60 cm in front of a 21.5" LCD monitor screen with a resolution of 1024 × 768. The experimental setup is illustrated in Fig. 2.

The participants took a pre-test before the experiment to determine their computer experience level and verify their eyesight. After that, a nine-points calibration was performed for the participants who assigned in the Group B. So that, they could control the eye-gaze input system sit without discomfort. During the calibration, they should not move their head. After the calibration, they can move their heads gently. This process is good for the accuracy of the gaze and fixation.

Fig. 2. Experimental setup

2.4   Study Design

The TWHITL gauge monitoring simulation is an interactive, real-time system (Kim et al. 2014). During the test, if a gauge value went beyond the normal range, the user needed to respond the change by clicking the button corresponding to the gauge. For the Group A, they could click the button as same as when they used a normal mouse device. For the Group B, however, the participants must look at the gauge first and click "Alt" button on the keyboard. The green box (see Fig. 3) represented the current location of the eye-gaze cursor. The simulation began with a normal condition for all 44 gauges, which include 11 flow gauges, 11 level gauges, 11 temperature gauges and 11 pressure gauges. The width of each gauge was 200 pixels, and the amplitude between abnormal gauges was different based on the given scenario conditions. Multiple events were scheduled in each scenario. Each event was designed based on the index of difficulty (ID) ranges from 1.0 to 4.0. By using the simulation, we collected the reaction time, task performance and cognitive workload of both groups. The data was used to evaluate the participants' ability to detect abnormal events in a continuous monitoring task.

As seen in Fig. 4, if a participant detected the abnormal condition gauge within the event duration time, the participant action would change the status of the gauge from an abnormal condition to a normal condition. This action was recorded as "Hit." If a participant failed to detect the abnormal status of this gauge, it would move to the alarm condition. If the participant also failed to detect the alarm condition within the full event duration time, then this one would be recorded as "Miss."

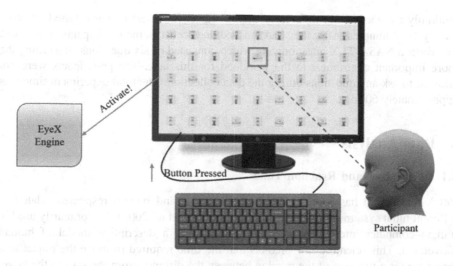

Fig. 3. Eye-gaze input human-in-the-loop simulation

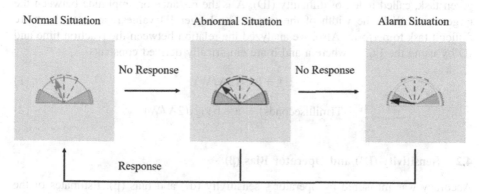

Fig. 4. Participant response

3 Procedure

The experiment began with a briefing on the TWHITL simulation. The purpose of this presentation was to explain the primary interface to the participants. During the presentation, which lasted approximately 10 min, they were allowed to ask any questions. Then, the participants performed a practice session. The training course was designed to teach participants how to respond to abnormal or alarm events. For the Group B, the participants needed to be trained how to control the eye-gaze input system.

The primary goal of this task was to compare the ability to detect abnormal situation between a mouse and eye-gaze input system and understand how participants used the two systems differently. The participants were free to ask questions throughout the practice tests. This training session lasted five minutes. The final step of the experiment was data collection. Each participant engaged in six scenarios. All participants were randomly assigned to six different scenario orders. Each test scenario lasted approximately eight minutes. After they had finished one scenario, the participants were asked to answer a NASA-TLX questionnaire which consisted of six questions concerning the more important contributor to the workload for this task. The participants were not allowed to ask any questions during the data collection. The total experiment time was approximately 60 min.

4 Data Analysis

4.1 Fitts' Law and Reaction Time

Fitts' law (1954) has been used widely to understand human responses related to different input systems (Burstyn et al. 2016; Forlines et al. 2007). It is primarily used in human–computer interaction and human factors as a descriptive model of human movement. This scientific law predicts that the time required to move the object to a target area is a function of the relation between the distance from the start to the target and the width of the target. The Eq. 1 shows how to calculate a difficulty level of a given task, called index of difficulty (ID). A is the distance or amplitude between the targets, and W is the width of the target. The bigger ID value represents the more difficult task to perform. Also, we analyzed the relation between the reaction time and ID by using the Eq. 2, where a and b are empirically derived constants.

$$ID = \log_2(2A/W) \tag{1}$$

$$T(\text{milliseconds}) = a + b \log_2(2A/W) \tag{2}$$

4.2 Sensitivity (D') and Operator Bias (β)

Accuracy was measured by operator's sensitivity (d') and bias (β). Estimates of the operator's sensitivity and bias were collected for the participant performance during the TWHITL simulation (Kim et al. 2015). The sensitivity refers to how well the operator discriminates the signal from the noise (Lerman et al. 2010). Thus, d' was calculated by subtracting the z-score that corresponds to the false alarm rate from the z-score that corresponds to the hit rate (Macmillan 1993).

$$\text{Sensitivity}(d') = |Z(\text{Hit}) - Z(\text{False Alarm})| \tag{3}$$

The operator's bias is the likelihood ratio of human response related to the presence of a signal. Z (Hit) is the z-score which corresponds to a hit rate, whereas Z (False Alarm) is the score which corresponds to a false alarm rate (Stanislaw and Todorov 1999).

$$\text{Bias}(\beta) = P(\text{ordinate of Hit})/P(\text{ordinate of false alarms}) \tag{4}$$

4.3   Mental Workload

NASA-TLX is a six-dimensional scale designed to obtain mental workload during a task or immediately afterward (Hart 2006). It has been applied within numerous domains, including civil and military aviation, driving, nuclear, power plant control room operation and air traffic control (Caldwell 2005; Erzberger 2005; Hwang et al. 2008; Kim et al. 2016; Lauer et al. 2007; Palinko et al. 2010; Wiegmann and Shappell 2001). Over the past 30 years, the research has revealed the NASA-TLX approach to be a tool which is easy to use and reliable for experimental manipulations.

5   Results

Figure 5 showed the reaction time comparisons between a mouse input and an eye-gaze input system. The horizontal axis displays two input systems and each index of difficulty (ID). Seven levels of ID were tested during the experiment (ID = {1.0, 1.5, 2.0, 2.5, 3.0, 3.5, 4.0}). The vertical axis presents the reaction time. Reaction time was charted as a function of different input systems and index of difficulty based on Fitts' law model.

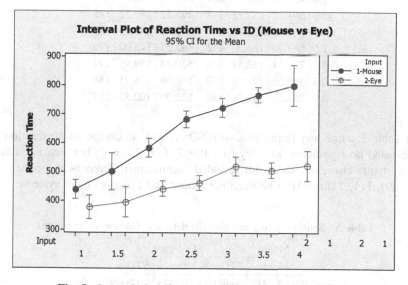

Fig. 5. Interval plot of reaction time vs ID (Mouse vs Eye)

Mouse input system:

$$RT = 327.4 + 130.1\,ID\ \left(R^2 = 40.2\%\ P < 0.001\right) \tag{5}$$

Eye-gaze input system:

$$RT = 325.2 + 55.86\,ID\,(R^2 = 9.4\%\,P < 0.001) \tag{6}$$

A two-way ANOVA general linear model was used (factor A: input systems, factor B: index of difficulty), which revealed that there were significant differences for reaction times between the input systems ($F(1,11) = 10.11$, $p = 0.002$), and index of difficulty ($F(6,66) = 5.89$, $p < 0.001$).

In Table 2, the mean reaction time is illustrated as a function of different IDs for the mouse and eye-gaze input systems, respectively. The smallest reaction times (ID 1.0) were 284 ms (milliseconds) and 152 ms for the mouse and eye-gaze input system, respectively. Additionally, the smallest reaction times (ID 4.0) were 579 ms and 267 ms for the mouse and eye-gaze input system, respectively. The average reaction time difference between the mouse and eye-gaze input systems is 193.76 ms.

Table 2. Reaction time (milliseconds) vs index of difficulty (Mouse vs Eye-gaze)

ID	Mouse			Eye-gaze		
	Mean	STD	MIN	Mean	STD	MIN
1.0	438.88	108.14	284	376.92	176.29	152
1.5	501.32	132.73	317	395.22	159.22	175
2.0	584.36	137.31	341	441.41	140.35	187
2.5	683.93	136.20	452	462.55	145.00	170
3.0	723.14	138.57	478	520.44	149.95	171
3.5	769.05	121.24	510	506.98	128.71	188
4.0	881.53	168.21	579	522.35	102.88	267

In Table 3, a one-way (input system) ANOVA was conducted on the reaction time and revealed no significant accuracy ($p = 0.992$, $F(1, 23) = 0$) between the different input systems. However, the result revealed significant differences in operator bias ($p < 0.001$, $F(1, 23) = 40.69$) between the mouse and eye-gaze input systems.

Table 3. Sensitivity (d') and bias (β) detection (Mouse vs Eye-gazc)

	Mouse		Eye-gaze	
	Mean	STD	Mean	STD
d'	3.3922	0.6366	3.3943	0.7009
β	69.67	29.38	21.13	22.94

In Table 4, a one-way (input system) ANOVA was conducted on the different input systems' mental workload and no significant differences ($F(1, 23) = 0.30$, $p = 0.587$) in the mental workload index between mouse and eye-gaze input systems were detected. The mean of the mental workload indices are 38.64 and 35.43 for mouse and eye-gaze input systems, respectively.

Table 4. Mental workload rating (Mouse vs Eye-gaze)

Group	Index	STD	F Value	P Value
Mouse	38.64	20.85	$F_{(1, 23)} = 0.30$	0.587
Eye-gaze	35.43	19.82		

6 Discussion

The objective of this study was to compare the pointing performance between a mouse input and an eye-gaze input. By using reaction time (millisecond), sensitivity (d'), operator's bias (β), and NASA-TLX, we were able to analyze participants' ability to detect abnormal events during the experiment.

6.1 Reaction Time

The results (see Fig. 5) showed that the index of difficulty (ID) influenced the reaction time of both input systems. However, according to the regression analysis, the model from the eye-gaze system was significantly different than the model from the mouse input. The Fitts' law could explain the regression model of the mouse input. The reaction time increased proportionally as ID increased. However, the model from the eye-gaze system was not. The influence caused by ID was compared to the mouse input. We also compared the reaction time difference between the mouse and eye-gaze system times for each ID level in Table 2. The results showed that the reaction time of the eye-gaze system was always faster than the mouse input system. The average reaction time difference from the easiest event (ID = 1.0) to the hardest event (ID =4.0) was only 146 ms for the eye-gaze system. All results pointed out that there was a significant difference between the eye-gaze input and traditional mouse input system in reaction time. Thus, one of our hypotheses: there is no significant difference in reaction time between mouse and eye-gaze systems should be rejected.

6.2 Accuracy

The results (see Table 3) showed that there was no significant difference in sensitivity between the mouse and eye-gaze system. Thus, the another hypothesis: there is no difference in accuracy between the mouse and eye-gaze system is proven. However, the results also revealed different operator biases between the mouse and eye-gaze system. The high β average represents that participants allowed more misses to avoid false alarms. This means that the mouse input system has more miss responses in comparison to the eye-gaze system, and the participants were more conservative when they experienced abnormal events. However, the users of the eye-gaze system made false alarm responses more often compared to the mouse input system, which means that the participants were more liberal when they made decisions about the abnormal events.

As illustrated in Fig. 6, the process concerning a stimulus response was faster, and the user response path was relatively short for the eye-gaze input system compared to

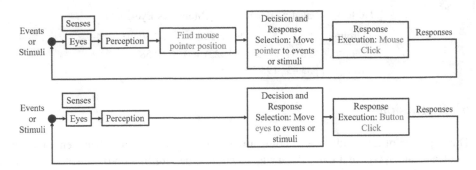

Fig. 6. Different responses procedure (Mouse vs Eye-gaze)

the mouse input system. The findings indicated that participants in the Group B did not need to navigate the input device to perform the given task. They only needed to pay attention to the abnormal gauges to reach out the targets and click them. However, the participants in the Group A needed to find the current position of the mouse after they discovered the abnormal gauges on the screen, and moved to the target location. Therefore, the probability of judging the stimulus as a signal was high when the participants used the eye-gaze input system.

6.3   Mental Workload

Although we hypothesized that the eye-gaze system would increase the user's mental workload compared to the mouse input system, it turned out that there was no workload significance between the mouse and eye-gaze system (see Table 4). Hence, our hypothesis regarding the workload should be rejected.

7   Conclusion and Future Work

7.1   Conclusion

In this research, we verified and confirmed the following three hypotheses. Firstly, there was a significant difference in reaction time between mouse and eye-gaze input system. The reaction time of the eye-gaze input system was faster than that of the mouse input, and was less influenced by the ID. According to the regression model, the mouse input system was more predictable as a linear pattern, but the eye-gaze input system was not. Secondly, there was no difference in accuracy between the mouse system and the eye-gaze system. The participants in both groups had a similar ability to detect the abnormal events during the experiment. It means that the eye-gaze input system could perform faster at the same accuracy level. Moreover, the probability of judging the stimulus as a signal was high for the eye-gaze input system, and its operator bias β values were lower than the mouse input system. This means that the eye tracking system users might be more liberal to make their decision compared to the mouse system users. However, the eye-gaze input system was easier to make false alarm responses. Thus, the findings recommend us to use either input system based on the cost of human errors: miss and false alarm. Finally, there was no significant difference in mental workload between the mouse and eye-gaze input system based on NASA-TLX results. The workload caused by using the eye-gaze system was not different than the mouse input system.

In conclusion, the eye-gaze input system can be regarded as a better input method for human computer interactions. It is confirmed that the eye-gaze system users' performance accuracy and mental workload were similar to the traditional mouse input system. However, the eye-gaze input system was better than the mouse input system with regard to the reaction time. Therefore, the eye-gaze system is favorable to the tasks, which require fast human responses and charge lower false alarm cost compared to the cost of miss.

7.2 Future Work

For future research, it is beneficial to explore how exactly the index of difficulty (ID) influences the response of the eye-gaze input system. Developing a generalized and extended model which can describe the relationship between reaction time and the ID for the eye-gaze system. Furthermore, it is necessary to study how to reduce the false alarm rate when the users use the eye-gaze system. Finally, for mental workload, different methods, such as pupil dilation, electroencephalogram, and functional magnetic resonance imaging, could be used as tools to measure the workload caused by various input systems.

References

Bai, H., Lee, G., Billinghurst, M.: Using 3d hand gestures and touch input for wearable ar interaction. Paper Presented at the CHI 2014 Extended Abstracts on Human Factors in Computing Systems (2014)

Bodala, I.P., Ke, Y., Mir, H., Thakor, N.V., Al-Nashash, H.: Cognitive workload estimation due to vague visual stimuli using saccadic eye movements. Paper Presented at the 2014 36th Annual International Conference of the IEEE Engineering in Medicine and Biology Society (2014)

Burstyn, J., Carrascal, J.P., Vertegaal, R.: Fitts' law and the effects of input mapping and stiffness on flexible display interactions. Paper Presented at the Proceedings of the 2016 CHI Conference on Human Factors in Computing Systems (2016)

Caldwell, J.A.: Fatigue in aviation. Travel Med. Infect. Dis. 3(2), 85–96 (2005)

Chandra, S., Sharma, G., Malhotra, S., Jha, D., Mittal, A.P.: Eye tracking based human computer interaction: applications and their uses. Paper Presented at the 2015 International Conference on Man and Machine Interfacing (MAMI) (2015)

Chen, J., Ji, Q.: A probabilistic approach to online eye gaze tracking without explicit personal calibration. IEEE Trans. Image Process. 24(3), 1076–1086 (2015)

De la Torre, V., Hernandez, J.L., García, J.L., Mejia, G.I.: Workload Assessment in Industrial Settings: A Proposal Applying the Analytic Hierarchy Process (2014)

Erzberger, H.: Automated conflict resolution for air traffic control (2005)

Fitts, P.M.: The information capacity of the human motor system in controlling the amplitude of movement. J. Exp. Psychol. **47**(6), 381 (1954)

Forlines, C., Wigdor, D., Shen, C., Balakrishnan, R.: Direct-touch vs. mouse input for tabletop displays. Paper Presented at the Proceedings of the SIGCHI Conference on Human Factors in Computing Systems (2007)

Hart, S.G.: NASA-task load index (NASA-TLX); 20 years later. Paper Presented at the Proceedings of the Human Factors and Ergonomics Society Annual Meeting (2006)

Hwang, S.-L., Lin, J.-T., Liang, G.-F., Yau, Y.-J., Yenn, T.-C., Hsu, C.-C.: Application control chart concepts of designing a pre-alarm system in the nuclear power plant control room. Nucl. Eng. Des. **238**(12), 3522–3527 (2008)

Jacob, R., Karn, K.S.: Eye tracking in human-computer interaction and usability research: ready to deliver the promises. Mind **2**(3), 4 (2003)

Kim, J.H., Rothrock, L., Laberge, J.: Using Signal Detection Theory and Time Window-based Human-In-The-Loop simulation as a tool for assessing the effectiveness of different qualitative shapes in continuous monitoring tasks. Appl. Ergon. **45**(3), 693–705 (2014)

Kim, J.H., Rothrock, L., Laberge, J.: Arousal and performance in a process monitoring task using signal detection theory. Paper Presented at the Proceedings of the Human Factors and Ergonomics Society Annual Meeting (2015)

Kim, J.H., Yang, X., Putri, M.: Multitasking performance and workload during a continuous monitoring task. Paper Presented at the Proceedings of the Human Factors and Ergonomics Society Annual Meeting (2016)

Lauer, T.R., Faber, S., Richstone, D., Gebhardt, K., Tremaine, S., Postman, M., Green, R.: The Masses of Nuclear Black Holes in Luminous Elliptical Galaxies and Implications for the Space Density of the Most Massive Black HolesBased on observations made with the NASA/ESA Hubble Space Telescope, obtained at the Space Telescope Science Institute, which is operated by the Association of Universities for Research in Astronomy, Inc., under NASA contract NAS 5-26555. These observations are associated with GO and GTO proposals 5236, 5446, 5454, 5512, 5943, 5990, 5999, 6099, 6386, 6554, 6587, 6633, 7468, 8683, and 91. Astrophys. J. **662**(2), 808 (2007)

Lerman, D.C., Tetreault, A., Hovanetz, A., Bellaci, E., Miller, J., Karp, H., Keyl, A.: Applying signal-detection theory to the study of observer accuracy and bias in behavioral assessment. J. Appl. Behav. Anal. **43**(2), 195–213 (2010)

Lynn, S.K., Barrett, L.F.: "Utilizing" signal detection theory. Psychol. Sci. **25**(9), 1663–1673 (2014)

Macmillan, N.A.: Signal detection theory as data analysis method and psychological decision model (1993)

Maniscalco, B., Lau, H.: A signal detection theoretic approach for estimating metacognitive sensitivity from confidence ratings. Conscious. Cogn. **21**(1), 422–430 (2012)

Murata, A., Uetsugi, R., Fukunaga, D.: Effects of target shape and display location on pointing performance by eye-gaze input system. In: 2014 Proceedings of the Paper Presented at the SICE Annual Conference (SICE) (2014)

Murata, A., Uetsugi, R., Hayami, T.: Study on cursor shape suitable for eye-gaze input system. In: 2012 Proceedings of the Paper Presented at the SICE Annual Conference (SICE) (2012)

Noah, B., Kim, J.-H., Rothrock, L., Tharanathan, A.: Evaluating alternate visualization techniques for overview displays in process control. IIE Trans. Occup. Ergon. Hum. Factors **2**(3–4), 152–168 (2014)

Palinko, O., Kun, A.L., Shyrokov, A., Heeman, P.: Estimating cognitive load using remote eye tracking in a driving simulator. Paper Presented at the Proceedings of the 2010 Symposium on Eye-Tracking Research & Applications (2010)

Sibert, L.E., Templeman, J.N., Jacob, R.J.: Evaluation and analysis of eye gaze interaction (2001). Accessed

Stanislaw, H., Todorov, N.: Calculation of signal detection theory measures. Behav. Res. Methods Instrum. Comput. **31**(1), 137–149 (1999)

Tharanathan, A., Laberge, J., Bullemer, P., Reising, D.V., McLain, R.: Functional versus schematic overview displays: Impact on operator situation awareness in process monitoring. Paper Presented at the Proceedings of the Human Factors and Ergonomics Society Annual Meeting (2010)

Wiegmann, D.A., Shappell, S.A.: Human error analysis of commercial aviation accidents: Application of the Human Factors Analysis and Classification System (HFACS). Aviat. Space Environ. Med. **72**(11), 1006–1016 (2001)

A Visuospatial Memory Game for the Elderly Using Gestural Interface

André Luiz Satoshi Kawamoto[1(✉)] and Valéria Farinazzo Martins[2]

[1] Computing Department, Federal University of Technology,
Campo Mourão, Brazil
kawamoto@utfpr.edu.br
[2] Computing and Informatics Program,
Mackenzie Prebisterian University, Sao Paulo, SP, Brazil
valeria.farinazzo@mackenzie.br

Abstract. This work presents a visuospatial game designed for the elderly that uses gesture based interaction. The game is a computer version of the Simon Memory Game (known in Brazil as "Genius"), which was quite popular in the 80s. All the development phases are presented, since the requirements elicitation to the tests with potential users. The elderly population characteristics were taken into account for the game development. Details on the usability tests results with 10 users are given and also the analysis of this data.

Keywords: Usability · Games · Serious games · Gestual interface · Kinect

1 Introduction

According to the World Population Aging Report of the United Nations (UN), the number of people considered elderly, aged over 60 years, is growing faster than any other age group. As a result, the share of elderly in the population is increasing virtually everywhere. In the year of 2050, it is expected that this population will reach 2.1 billion people [1]. Factors related to medical and technological advances, sanitation improvements, prevention, control and cure of diseases that once were considered fatal are crucial to reducing mortality and increasing life expectancy, even in countries under development, which led to an increase in the elderly population rate.

On the other hand, several areas of Medicine have been faced problems arising from the loss or decrease of memory, due to the aging process [2]. In fact, according to Souza and Chaves [3], a considerable part of the elderly population complains about the difficulty of storing and rescuing information, such as forgetting to take medicines, locating objects and naming known people, affecting your well-being.

The literature suggests that, in healthy aging, there is the possibility of (at least partial) compensation of cognitive deficits [4–6]. Research on cognitive and memory training indicates that the healthy elderly are able to approximate their current performance to their maximum possible performance, revealing cognitive plasticity [7]. In fact, the studies conducted by [3, 8, 9] point out that the exercise of memory stimulation in healthy elderly considerably improves this cognitive aspect.

© Springer International Publishing AG 2017
M. Antona and C. Stephanidis (Eds.): UAHCI 2017, Part II, LNCS 10278, pp. 430–443, 2017.
DOI: 10.1007/978-3-319-58703-5_32

In addition, according to Boot et al. [10], research shows that playing video games, even for a relatively short period of time, improves the performance of a series of tasks that measure visual and attention skills. These studies prove that playing, even for only 10 h, can improve performance in laboratory tasks differently from those who did not play.

Gestures have been used in human-computer interfaces to create more natural interfaces in new three-dimensional computing environments, leveraging the user experience as the basic movements of the domain, for example, raising a hand, walking or shaking his/her head [11]. The use of natural interfaces can reduce the degree of learning of the devices, especially important for the elderly population.

Although non-conventional devices, such as Microsoft Kinect [12], offer a good opportunity to motivate the physical and memory characteristics of the elderly by using gesture-based interfaces, the games available on the market may eventually cause danger, especially for the elderly population [13]. Therefore, it is necessary to develop these games taking into consideration usability issues, such as effort management and design concerning the age and simple configuration routines [14].

This paper aims to present the development of a computer memory game for the elderly, called Genius, using Kinect. Guidelines for the development of games for the elderly with natural interfaces are presented, such as the use of appropriate frequency sounds for the user class, the use of more vibrant cores, and the application to be run more slowly.

The current work is organized as follows: in Sect. 2, we present a series of Guidelines for the development of applications for the elderly; the Sect. 3 introduces a brief explanation on the types of memory and how ageing affects them; related works are presented in Sect. 4; in the Sect. 5 the development aspects are presented; in Sects. 6 and 7 we present the evaluation methodology used as well as the results obtained; and, finally, in Sect. 8 the discussion and future work.

2 Guidelines Addressed to Develop Serious Game for Elderly

The development of games for the elderly should take into account intrinsic requirements that this class of users has, such as physical limitations, memory, speed of movement, among others. As pointed out by [15, 16], to design an application taking into account the physical and mental limitations for the elderly, one must look at four sets:

- Stimulating elders to engage and play:
  - games must be playful, in other words, people should enjoy spending the time playing it;
  - games must involve another gamers, if possible. The reason is that playing with others tend to be more attractive than playing alone; this also explains the next guideline, which is the players shall be encouraged to use collaboration and competition;
  - games shall be developed according to the gender of the players, because men and women may have different themes topics of interest.

- Mitigating the memory decline:
  - games must avoid the use of prior information, such as RPG games;
  - games must use simple interactions;
  - quick and complex interactions as well as quick and parallel actions must be avoided;
  - learning time should be greater;
  - games should embed familiar metaphors;
  - during the period of the game, additional and more detailed information should be provided;
  - complex screen must be avoided;
  - redundant information through multiple modalities should be provided;
  - load on memory and cognitive processing should be kept to a minimum;
  - avoid contradictions and inconsistencies of information arrangement, because they may confuse the users;
  - in gestural interfaces, it is advisable to use a set of few and easy movements.
- Preserving the senses:
  - use appropriate size of objects and source text, as well as higher contrast;
  - avoid synthetic speech, because it may be hard to be understood by older people;
  - for non-speech audio signals, prefer lower frequency tones (in the 500–1000 Hz range), which are easier for elderly users to hear than higher pitched sounds;
  - avoid small targets and moving interface elements, and use appropriated colors;
  - use appropriate illumination and try creating intuitiveness.
- Working with impairments in motor skills:
  - create slower response times;
  - avoid continuous and flexible movements;
  - avoid a great variability in movement;
  - take into account motor disabilities;
  - try including Health stuff.

To summarize, the group of guidelines specific for designing applications for older adults addresses all the disabilities related, and is intended to provide hints to game developers to build more suitable interfaces this audience.

3 Types of Memory

In the Human-Computer Interface area, studies attempt to guide software designers in the construction of interfaces adapted to the characteristics of human memory, eliminating the need of memorization skills beyond the necessary and feasible from the typical user of certain systems.

Shneiderman [17] addresses three types of memory (Fig. 1) and the process of entry of information, as well as the search for this information:

1. Quick or Short-Term Memory: receives the input information captured by the sight, hearing, smell, taste and touch and passes them to the cognitive system. It is also where the output information are deposited, i.e. the information that is expressed by speech, movements and actions. The storage in this memory is of the order of 10 s

and its capacity is also quite limited. According to Miller [20], the amount of information stored is 7 ± 2, that is, by capturing a certain number of information by one of the perception senses, the short term memory is capable of storing an average of 7 of this information, with an average variation of 2, that is, between 5 and 9.

2. Work or Temporary Memory: where the information coming from the short-term memory is worked, concatenated, and then sent to the permanent memory. It is therefore a temporary memory, and the information contained therein can be retained for a much longer time than the short-term memory, but not permanently.

3. Permanent or Long-Term Memory: has large storage capacity in a long time. For example, events that occurred long ago and that a senior is able to count on many details.

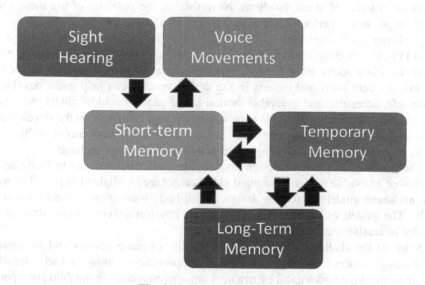

Fig. 1. Memory scheme [17]

Access to information is done not only by the working memory, but exceptionally directly by the fast memory. This information that "take shortcuts" does not need any mechanism for its recovery. For example, if we ask a person his/her name, address, telephone number, etc., this information comes immediately, since many of them are already brought up since one learns to speak, to understand, at a young age. However, when changing the phone number, or the car license plate, it will initially be necessary to use the working memory, using some mechanism to remember.

Often an elderly person has permanent memory intact, but forgets about recent events that would be in the short and medium term memory.

In this work, the short-term memory, which is capable of storing and reproducing visual and auditory stimuli specific to Genius, will be investigated.

4 Related Works

Several works have been carried out aiming the to develop applications to stimulate and enhance the elderly wellbeing. This section introduces a short survey on applications to the elderly audience and their intrinsic characteristics.

First, in [18], serious games for the older citizens are classified according to their specific goal and key design elements for improving the physical health of the target audience. This work shows that projects tend to take into consideration elder user needs in gaming design for health purposes, but little effort has been made to take into account the limitations of the aged cohort along the entire design process. It also points out that testing phases and usability evaluation are needed, and, finally, it claims that the use of modern input devices has allowed specialists to determine the patient performance in terms of motor functions. Nevertheless, the potential of use these capabilities to accurately perform medical assessment as a tool to guarantee effectiveness is not yet being totally exploited.

In [19], the challenges and opportunities of a new approach in motion-based game design for older adults are discussed. The importance of identifying core challenges and involve both users and experts in the design process can help game developers create safe, accessible and enjoyable motion-based games for older adults. As a conclusion, the authors argue that this approach could also contribute to the development of games for other user groups that consist of members with heterogeneous abilities and needs, fostering the creation of enjoyable games for vulnerable audiences.

The limitations of current design philosophies, and opportunities to facilitate the creation of accessible motion-controlled video games are highlighted in [14]. The work presents seven guidelines for the design of full-body interaction in games for older adults. The guidelines are designed to foster safe physical activity among older adults, thereby increasing their quality of life.

Some of the challenges to increase the quality of game designs and to improve game design processes, along with possible approaches, aiming to fuel intensified exchange about methodological experiences among researchers in the field are reported and classified in [20]. The authors suggest that, in order to obtain reliable results when evaluating exergames, it is necessary to provide methods which reduce the cognitive load of participants instead of overwhelming them by presenting too many new challenges at the same time. Small adjustments to the evaluation environment, accomplished with providing simple, specifically designed questionnaires, reading them out as structured interviews and keeping the session duration as short as possible helped reduce the cognitive load of participants experiencing age-related changes. It is also said that it is crucial to gain insights into long-term effects and detailed physical effects, which requires research methods that go far beyond those designed to examine exergames usability and accessibility.

In [21], an overview of common age-related changes, followed by a summary of game design considerations for senior audiences are presented. The impact of age on game design is discussed based on an analysis of the most important structural elements of games. The analysis shows that age-related changes in the cognitive and physical user abilities affect the use of games on multiple levels, making the complexity of games and interrelations between different game mechanics a crucial factor when designing for older adults.

5 Game Development

For the development of this game, a psychologist specialized in memory issues was consulted at the Neuroscience Laboratory of one of the Universities involved. The professional already uses some tests, such as the Corsi Block-Tapping Test [22] to analyze the amount of stored information dealing with visuospatial memory. The evaluation of the professional considered the game Genius based on the same principles of the Corsi Test and, thus, this game can be used with the same intention.

The interface of the electronic version of Genius is presented in Fig. 2a, and consists basically of four colored buttons: red, green, yellow and blue, associated to four different sounds. The player must memorize and reproduce sequences of sounds-colors in the same order they are presented. The first sequence has only one sound, and its size is increased by one every round. Advanced levels may reach 34-color sequences.

During an interview with the psychologist in the elicitation phase of the requirements for the virtual game, some functional and non-functional requirements were established. The functional requirements are presented below: (1) the electronic version must faithfully simulate the physical game; (2) one of the four buttons must be randomly selected incrementally; (3) in case of error, the user must be warned, by means of a characteristic sound accompanied by the finalization of the game; (4) the complete sequence of correct buttons should be recorded so that it can be analyzed by the psychologist.

In addition, it was defined that the non-functional requirements of this application would be: (1) the user must use the right or left hand to select an object (button); (2) each button has a distinctive sound; (3) the system should remain inactive for as long as the user does not press a button; (4) the game shall be single-player; (5) the user must use one hand at a time.

Developers followed the guidelines for game development for seniors presented in Sect. 3 of this article. Thus, it was taken into account that: (1) the game should allow slower movements than the original; (2) the test applicator shall provide explanations and demonstrations of how to use the game, considering that the majority of the public is not accustomed to using electronic games; (3) the buttons for the interaction should be large and with contrasting colors; (4) Depending on the person, an interview may replace or complement a post-test questionnaire; (4) the button, when selected, should provide visual feedback, such as resizing, brighter or changing color; (5) the game interface should adopt colors and sounds at appropriate frequencies.

There are several technologies available for the development of applications for the Kinect platforms different from the XBox 360 - OpenNI, OpenKinect, Microsoft SDK [12, 23, 24]. The game was implemented with the Microsoft Kinect SDK, which is Microsoft's solution for creating applications for the Windows operating system. The Microsoft Kinect SDK supports the C#, C++, and Visual Basic programming languages and requires Windows 7 (or higher). It allows you to use various features, for

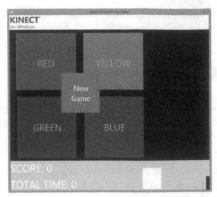

Fig. 2. (a) Genius by Estrela (Estrela [25]) (b) Genius Application Interface using Kinect

example, face tracking, voice commands, skeleton tracking, and others. The application interface is shown in Fig. 2b.

6 Evaluation Methodology

A preliminary usability evaluation of Genius game was carried out with 10 people from both genders, between 60 and 75 years old. Figure 3(a) and (b) show people using the game.

The physical environments used for the tests had no controlled conditions. The tests took place in two locations: a university room and also the home of some users.

Evaluations were performed through questionnaires and also interviews. Three questionnaires were designed: Profile, Expectations and Post-Test (Tables 1, 2 and 3). The Profile questionnaire contained multiple choice questions addressing gender, age, use of computer games, physical activities and knowledge in using Kinect; This questionnaire was based on and adapted from Mitchell [26].

The Expectation questionnaire used the 5-point Likert scale [27] and requested information related to the user's impression of the game to be interesting, easy, motivating and if the user liked to try out new technologies (based and adapted from [28]). The Post-Test questionnaire used the 5-point Likert scale and was based on and adapted from [29] and the Web Usability Questionnaire [30].

The Post-Test questionnaire addressed, through 20 questions, usability issues, pointed out by Nielsen [31], like feedback and cognitive load; as well as satisfaction, efficiency and effectiveness identified by the ISO 9241-11 [32], and the guidelines proposed by Gerling [13, 14].

The materials used in the evaluation (camera, questionnaires, computer with the game and Microsoft Kinect installed) were tested. Pilot tests indicated that an average of 30 min would be required for each test: 3 min for explanation/demonstration on the test; 3 min for filling in the profile and expectations questionnaires, 15 min for novice users to use the game for the first time and to adapt to the interaction form, 6 min for the test itself and finally 3 min for filling the Post-Test questionnaire.

Table 1. Pre-Test questionnaire (Profile)

1.Gender: () Female () Male	5.Age Group:
2.Workplace:	() under 45
() Company/homeoffice	() between 45 and 54
() University	() between 55 and 65
() home (housewife)	() between 65 and 74
() retired	() 74 or more
() undergraduate/graduate student	6.How often do you use the
() unemployed	computer in the week?
3.Do you practice any physical activity (running, gym,	() everyday
water aerobics, sports) regularly?	() 3 times/week
() Yes	() once a week
() No	() never/almost never
If yes, how many times per week	7.How often do you use computer
() once a week	games to have fun??
() 3 times/week	() everyday
() everyday	() every week
4.Have you ever used Kinect?	() every month
() Yes	() rarely/do not use
() No	

Table 2. Expectation questionnaire

Questions	Strongly Agree	Agree	Neither Agree nor Disagree	Disagree	Strongly Disagree
I believe this game will be very interesting					
I believe it will be easy to use this game					
I feel quite motivated to play					
I really like new technologies					

Table 3. Post-Test questionnaire

Questions	Strongly Agree	Agree	Neither Agree nor Disagree	Disagree	Strongly Disagree
1. Whenever I pointed the hand to the application, I was able to "click"					
2. The application warned me when I committed an error					

(*continued*)

Table 3. (*continued*)

Questions	Strongly Agree	Agree	Neither Agree nor Disagree	Disagree	Strongly Disagree
3. The application did not cause any muscular fatigue					
4. The application is quite enjoyable to use					
5. The Kinect movements are more precise than using a mouse					
6. My movements are faster using the Kinect than the mouse					
7. Kinect located my position and my hand easily					
8. I feel efficient while I'm playing the application					
9. I quickly understood the interaction mechanism of the game					
10. The application is very intuitive and easy to understand					
11. I would definitely use the application again					
12. Even at the first time, it can be assumed that this application is easy to use					
13. I did not feel stressed by this game in any situation					
14. It is quite easy to remember how to use this application					
15. My time was very well spent using the application					
16. Everything in the application is easy to understand					
17. The size of the buttons were suitable for playing. They did not hinder me.					
18. I could play for a long time, even standing					
19. The position I assume when I play is not uncomfortable and does not force me to stop					
20. The colors of the buttoms are easily identified when selected					

Fig. 3. Tests with people using the game

7 Results

From the answers obtained in the profile questionnaire, it was verified that, of the total users participating in the evaluation, 4 were female and 6 were male; no one had been in contact with Kinect; 7 people never or almost never use games to have fun, 1 uses weekly while 2 of them use monthly. Regarding the daily practice of physical exercises, 4 people never practice physical exercises.

In the responses to the expectations questionnaire, 2 participants fully agreed that the game would be very interesting, while the other 8 only agreed. Regarding the ease of use, the expectation was that it would be very easy (only 1 person indicated "totally agree"), 2 agreed and 7 disagreed. Regarding the motivational aspect of the game, 3 people totally agreed, 3 agreed, 3 became undecided and 1 disagreed. 5 evaluators agreed totally on the issue of very liking new technologies, 1 was undecided, 2 disagreed and 2 disagreed totally (Fig. 4).

The following charts 1 and 2 show the results from the compilation of responses from 10 users on the post-test questionnaire (Fig. 5).

The observation of the graphs allows to conclude, for this sample:

- Questions 1, 5, 6, 12 and 13 make it clear that the target audience finds it more difficult to use Kinect than using a mouse, nevertheless, they consider the use of the game to be safe (question 4);
- Users consider the feedback appropriate when they made a mistake in the game (question 2);
- the game was considered easy to understand and to learn and easy to memorize (questions 9, 10 and 14);
- not being able to use Kinect deftly on their first use caused a lot of frustration (question 8);
- Regarding physical limitations, the game did not cause muscle fatigue (question 3), but 40% of users were undecided or disagree as to whether they could play for a reasonable time because they would have to play standing (question 18). 40% were undecided if their position to play made them uncomfortable, while 10% said they were annoyed (question 19);

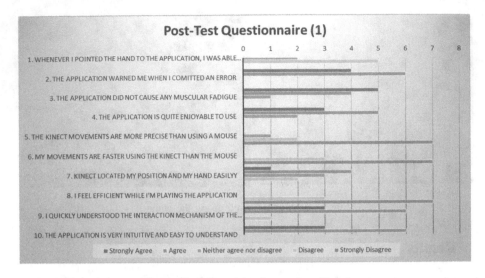

Fig. 4. Post-Questionnaire results – Part 1

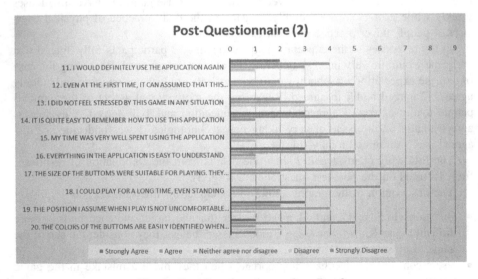

Fig. 5. Post-Questionnaire results – Part 2

- Questions 17 and 20, referring to the interface part, show that although most did not consider the size of the buttons a problem (question 17), the perception that the button was selected (change in brightness) was not as evident to the target public (question 20).

Through the interviews, it was noticed that the biggest complaint from the target audience was not having full control over the click movement and navigation, using the hands instead of the mouse. Several times, a hand icon (representing the mouse) disappeared, causing distress. Some people thought that the problem would be with them for not knowing how to use the device.

8 Conclusions

This paper presents the development of a memory computer game for the elderly using Kinect. The main focus is on the usability assessment, since not many papers are found in the literature addressing this topic, which was detailed enough in this article.

In order to develop applications for this target audience, it should be noted that directives, as pointed out by [13, 14], must be followed in order not to cause inconvenience or danger and still have a good usability for This population. It is also necessary to point out that in order to build computational applications for the elderly, it is necessary to have a multidisciplinary team, which certainly involves a health professional with the skills to do so. These professionals are able to guide the development and focus of the games, as well as can provide real testing environments and conditions with this target audience.

It was possible to verify, through the results of the evaluation questionnaires, that those users who do not have much frequency in the use of games nor of Kinect felt an initial difficulty in the handling of the equipment, but considered its use challenging. The data from this analysis will serve as feedback to the development team so that improvements can be incorporated into the game.

As future works, there is the possibility of performing visuospatial memory tests in the Neuroscience laboratory of the University (in a properly controlled environment); To verify if the use of this game, for training, can actually improve the storage capacity of the visuospatial memory of the elderly; And also, after improvements and interface adjustments required, provide a version of the game for free download.

References

1. United Nations, World Population Ageing Report 2015, New York, USA (2015)
2. Souza R.R.: Alterações anatômicas do sistema nervoso central associadas ao envelhecimento. In: Jacob Filho, W., Carvalho Filho, E.T. (eds.) Envelhecimento do sistema nervoso e a dor no idoso - monografias em geriatria III. São Paulo: FMUSP (1996)
3. de Souza, J.N., Chaves, E.C.: O efeito do exercício de estimulação da memória em idosos saudáveis. Rev. Esc. Enferm. USP **39**(1), 13–19 (2005)
4. Backman, L.: Varieties of memory compensation by older adults in episodic remembering. In: Poon, L.W., Rubin, D.C., Wilson, B.C. (eds.) Everyday Cognition in Adulthood and Late Life, pp. 509–544. Cambridge University Press, Cambridge (1989)
5. Baltes, P.B., Baltes, M.M.: Psychological perspectives on successful aging: the model of selective optimization with compensation. Successful Aging: Perspect. Behav. Sci. **1**, 1–34 (1990)
6. Dunlosky, J., Hertzog, C.: Training programs to improve learning in later adulthood: Helping older adults educate themselves. In: Hacker, D.J., Dunlosky, J., Graesser, A.C. (eds.) Metacognition in Educational Theory and Practice. The Educational Psychology Series, pp. 249–275. Lawrence Erlbaum Associates Publishers, Mahwah (1998). xiv, 407 pp

7. Verhaeghen, P.: The interplay of growth and decline: Theoretical and empirical aspects of plasticity of intellectual and memory performance in normal old age. In: Hill, R.D., Backman, L., Stigsdotter Neely, A. (eds.) Cognitive Rehabilitation in Old Age, pp. 3–22. Oxford University Press, New York (2000)

8. Yassuda, M.S., et al.: Treino de memória no idoso saudável: benefícios e mecanismos. Psicologia: reflexão e crítica **19**(3), 470–481 (2006)

9. Irigaray, T.Q., Schneider, R.H., Gomes, I.: Efeitos de um treino cognitivo na qualidade de vida e no bem-estar psicológico de idosos. Psicol. Reflex. Crit. **24**(4), 810–818 (2011)

10. Boot, W.R., et al.: The effects of video game playing on attention, memory, and executive control. Acta Physiol. (Oxf) **129**(3), 387 (2008)

11. Kwon, D.Y.: A design framework for 3D spatial gesture interfaces, Doctoral and Habilitation, Theses, Publisher: Eidgenössische Technische Hochschule ETH Zürich (2008)

12. Microsoft: Microsoft Kinect SDK Documentation, April 2013. http://www.microsoft.com/en-us/kinectforwindows/develop/resources.aspx

13. Gerling, K.M., Schild, J., Masuch, M.: Exergame Design for Elderly Users: The Case Study of SilverBalance. In: Proceedings of ACE 2010, Taipei, Taiwan (2010)

14. Gerling, K.M., Livingston, I.J., Nacke, L., Mandryk, R.L.: Full-body motion-based game interaction for older adults. In: CHI 2012, pp. 1873–1882 (2012)

15. Kawamoto, A.L.S., Martins, V.F., da Silva, F.S.C.: Converging Natural User Interfaces guidelines and the design of applications for older adults. In: 2014 IEEE International Conference on Systems, Man, and Cybernetics (SMC), pp. 2328–2334. IEEE, October 2014

16. Kawamoto, A.L.S., Martins, V.F.: Application designed for the elderly using gestural interface. Revista Brasileira de Computação Aplicada **5**(2), 96–109 (2013)

17. Shneiderman, B.: Designing the User Interface: Strategies for Effective Human-Computer Interaction. Addison-Wesley Publ. Co, Menlo Park (1992)

18. Marin, J.G., Karla Felix Navarro, E.L.: Serious games to improve the physical health of the elderly: a categorization scheme. In: Proceedings of The Fourth International Conference on Advances in Human-oriented and Personalized Mechanisms, Technologies, and Services - CENTRIC 2011. pp. 64–71. IARIA, October 2011, ISBN: 978-1-61208-167-0

19. Gerling, K., Smeddinck, J.: Involving users and experts in motion-based game design for older adults. In: CHI Workshop on Game User Research: Practice, Methods, and Applications, Paris, France (2013)

20. Smeddinck, J., Herrlich, M., Krause, M., Gerling, K., Malaka, R.: Did they really like the game? - challenges in evaluating exergames with older adults. In: CHI Workshop on Game User Research: Exploring Methodologies. Austin, Texas, USA (2012)

21. Gerling, K.M., Schulte, F.P., Smeddinck, J., Masuch, M.: Game design for older adults: effects of age-related changes on structural elements of digital games. In: Herrlich, M., Malaka, R., Masuch, M. (eds.) ICEC 2012. LNCS, vol. 7522, pp. 235–242. Springer, Heidelberg (2012). doi:10.1007/978-3-642-33542-6_20

22. LONGONI, A.: Memória (A). Edições Loyola (2003). http://books.google.com.br/books?id=6aadhRihfugC

23. OpenNI organization: OpenNI User Guide, November 2010. http://www.openni.org/documentation

24. OpenKinect: OpenKinect Documentation, April 2013. http://openkinect.org/wiki/Documentation

25. Estrela. Disponível em: http://www.estrela.com.br/. Acesso em: 15 de maio de 2016

26. Mitchell, P.P.: A Step-by-Step Guide to Usability Testing. iUniverse, Inc. (2007)

27. Likert, R.: A technique for the measurement of attitudes. Arch. Psychol. **22**(140), 1–55 (1932)

28. Hartikainen, M., Salonen, E.P., Turunen, M.: Subjective evaluation of spoken dialogue systems using SERVQUAL method. In: Proceedings of ICSLP, vol. 4 (2004)
29. Martins, V.F., Corrêa, A.G.D., Kawamoto, A.L.S., Guimarães, M.P.: Usability evaluation of television based gestures and voice control. In: Proceedings of LatinDisplay 2012/IDRC 2012 (2012)
30. Website Analysis and MeasureMent Inventory: Web Usability Questionnaire. http://www.wammi.com
31. Nielsen, J.: Ten usability heuristics. Website (2005). http://www.useit.com/papers/heuristic/heuristiclist.html
32. ISO, W. 9241-11. Ergonomic requirements for office work with visual display terminals (VDTs). Guidance on usability (1998)

The Application of Dynamic Analysis
to Hand Gestures

Toshiya Naka[1,2(✉)]

[1] Kyoto University, Yoshida Honmachi Sakyo-ku, Kyoto 608-8501, Japan
[2] Panasonic Corporation, Kadoma City, Osaka 571-8501, Japan
naka.tosiya@jp.panasonic.com

Abstract. In designing new user interfaces for the latest mobile devices, such as tablets and smartphones, intuitiveness and simplicity are very important factors. Interacting with hand-gestures is one of the best choices for enabling the ease of use of such products. However, there are several disadvantages to this kind of intuitive interface: one of the chief problems with gesture-based interaction is that it is difficult to distinguish reliably between unconscious and intentional gestures. To resolve this ambiguity, the authors have proposed a quantitative analysis method of human gestures using dynamics. We discovered a close correlation between intended gestures and the torque applied to each joint; however, our previous model was designed for the quantitative analysis of gesture interaction mechanisms in full-body motions. In this paper, we expand our dynamic motion analysis to finger gestures, and reveal that our proposed method is applicable to dynamic motion analysis of basic finger operations.

Keywords: Hand · Gesture · Dynamics · Easy-to-use · Human interaction

1 Introduction

In human communication, it is well known that gestures can be a richer channel of communication than language; we frequently use hand-gestures unconsciously, such as waving to say goodbye or beckoning with the hand. In designing new user interfaces for the latest mobile devices, interaction with hand-gestures is widely adopted for reasons of ease of use. The latest hand-gesture recognition technologies include *PrimeSense* (2010), which uses an infrared projector, camera and a special microchip to track the movement of our body in three dimensions [1]. The *Microsoft Kinect* (2015) adopted this technology in the *XBox* with gesture operation [2]. *Leap Motion* (2015) is a device specifically targeted for hand-gesture recognition that provides a limited set of relevant points [3], and *Google's Soli* (2015) is a major new gesture technology which uses miniature radar with high positional accuracy to pick up slight movements without the need to touch the device itself [4]. Unlike full-body gestures analysis, accurate motion tracking systems will be required to measure finger movement precisely. The most recently developed technology in this field, *Perception Neuron* (2014), employs a capture system which uses up to 32 inertial measurement units (*IMU*s) to track full-body motions. These *IMU*s have a gyroscope, accelerometer, and magnetometer, and can measure finger movements simply and accurately [5]. Using these latest

© Springer International Publishing AG 2017
M. Antona and C. Stephanidis (Eds.): UAHCI 2017, Part II, LNCS 10278, pp. 444–454, 2017.
DOI: 10.1007/978-3-319-58703-5_33

motion capture devices has made it possible to capture and analyze human gestures relatively inexpensively.

On the other hand, a great deal of research has been carried out in the field of hand gesture analysis. Rautaray and Agrawal (2015) briefly discussed the use of hand gestures as a natural interface for gesture taxonomies, their representations and recognition techniques, software platforms and frameworks [6]. Panwar (2012) presented a real-time system for hand gesture recognition that relies on the detection of meaningful shapes, based on features like orientation, center of mass, status of fingers and thumb in terms of raised or folded fingers, and their respective locations in images [7]. Meng et al. (2012) have proposed a new approach to hand gesture recognition, which is accomplished by dominant points-based hand finger counting using skin color extraction [8], and Dominguez et al. (2006) suggested a unique vision-based robust finger tracking algorithm in which they used to segment out objects by encircling them with the user's pointing fingertip to be robust to changes in the environment and user's movements [9]. In the new perspective of researchers' studies, the authors tried to clarify the dynamic mechanisms of certain characteristic behaviors, and revealed that some special gestures were quantified by the torque values of elements of the human skeletal model (Naka et al. 2016 [10]). Their basic idea was that human tend to apply greater forces than normal to the relevant portion of our arms or body to emphasize a particular action; it is therefore possible to quantify the dynamic effects in terms of the torque applied to each joint. By selecting hundreds of characteristic gestures and applying them to the proposed model, the authors found that it is possible to represent the degree of exaggeration in a quantitative manner, and found out that their model was applicable to the speaker's emphasized movements for attracting the audience's attention during speeches or presentations, too (rhetorical emphasis). There was a close correlation between the intended gesture and the applied torque.

In this paper, we will expand our proposed dynamic gesture analysis model to finger gestures by defining the hierarchical structure of the hand. Generally, there are structural differences such that the *DOF* (degree of freedom) of each joint is one or two, with the exception of the thumb joint. The total values derived from dynamic analysis of the fingers are much smaller than for the body, so to address these problems, the authors had to analyze the effects of twisting torques more precisely, and needed to consider how to improve the *SNR* (signal-to-noise ratio) for smaller torque values. We will describe our dynamic gesture analysis of finger movement in detail in the following sections.

2 Hand Gesture Analysis Model

In this section, a basic dynamic model and algorithm will be defined and verified to be able to accurately analyze finger gestures. In general, finger gestures can be expressed in the form of a hierarchical structure. Each parameter of the link model is shown in Fig. 1. The human body is typically built as a series of nested joints, each of which may have a link associated with it and facing in the +z direction with +y up and +x to the left (b). In the following experiments, we set the first target operation with fingers to the most popular touch panel (a). The latest touch devices are usually equipped with a mechanism for detecting the pressure of the fingers. It is also one of the most suitable applications for analyzing these mechanisms by using dynamic analysis (e.g., the correlation between pressure and torque). In Fig. 1, *DIP*, *PIP* and *MP* represent the distal interphalangeal, proximal interphalangeal and metacarpophalangeal joint, respectively.

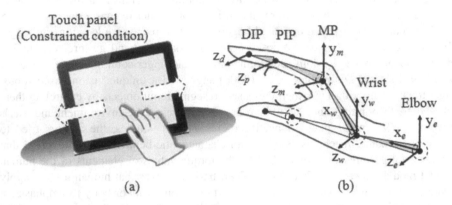

Fig. 1. (a) Finger gesture operation of touch panel (constrained conditions). (b) Hierarchical structure and definition of right hand. The reference (root) position in the dynamic analysis is set to the position of the elbow joints.

Once the structure of the human finger is defined using this hierarchical structure, any finger gestures can be quantitatively expressed as the rotational angles of the time-series around the x, y and z axes (local coordinate system) of each joint, such as the *DIP*, *PIP* and *MP*, and dynamical torque τ which is generated at each joint can be obtained using motion Eq. 1, employing joint angle θ. In this equation, θ is each joint's rotational angle in a time-series data set. $(\theta_w, \theta_m, \cdots \theta_d)$, M is the inertia matrix, C is the *Coriolis force*, g is the *gravity* term and $d\theta/dt$ and $d^2\theta/dt^2$ respectively represent the angular velocity and angular acceleration of each joint. See Naka et al. (2016) for more details [10].

$$\tau = M(\theta)\frac{d^2\theta}{dt^2} + C(\theta, \frac{d\theta}{dt})\frac{d\theta}{dt} + g(\theta) \tag{1}$$

As previously mentioned, it should be noted that in the dynamic analysis of finger movements, these values are noisy besides very small compared with the magnitudes of body values. Highly accurate measurement of angular change θ, noise removal and more precise motion prediction is therefore the key to these analyses.

3 Experiments and Results

To investigate what degree of accuracy is necessary in the analysis of finger movements, we conducted some preliminary experiments. The authors first measured the dynamical torque of each finger while operating the touch panel shown in Fig. 1(a). In this series of operational tasks, users usually employ only the index finger, and will move the *DIP*, *PIP*, *MP* and wrist joints only as required. Normally, this operation is carried out on the two-dimensionally constrained surface of a touch panel. The authors term this finger gesture operation as under "constrained conditions."

3.1 Experimental Conditions

In the following experiments, a data glove was used for motion tracking to measure finger gestures precisely. The main specifications of this system were listed in Table 1. Subjects were instructed to wear a data glove on the dominant hand and each motion was converted to each joint rotational angle θ in time-series data (60 fps). The latency of calculation was order of 10 to 20 ms and the data was translated from Hub to Computer by using wired USB (in a few ms). The conversion from angle θ to torque τ was executed about 5 ms on PC by using Eq. 1 (See Appendix for more detail sequences [10]). In general, each finger gestures θ is noisy and the total values derived from dynamic analysis of the fingers are much smaller than for the body, so to address these problems, we had to remove the noise by the low pass filter and adaptive cutoff frequency of the filter was selected a hundred to two hundred Hz to improve the *SNR* (signal-to-noise ratio) for smaller torque values. As for the motion prediction, we used the *three dimensional spline function* to estimate to track smooth the motion of finger gestures.

Table 1. Main specifications of data glove

Main specifications	
Number of sensors	5 to 18 (Repeatability: 3°) two sensors per finger
Sensor resolution	<1.0°
Sensor data rate	30/60 fps
Sensor linearity	0.6% maximum nonlinearity over full range

Twelve adults in their twenties (nine men and three women) were selected as subjects, and each subject was instructed to manipulate the graphical user interface (*GUI*) by using only their index finger gestures on the constrained touch panel. The main tasks of these basic experiments were the simple operation of scrolling a page up and down or to the left and right with the index finger.

3.2   Results 1

Figure 2 shows some typical analysis results of torque values of finger gesture operations. In this figure, (a) shows the operation of turning a GUI page left and (b) upwards with their index finger. In these results, τ_{mp-y} is the joint torque of the MP joint around the y-axis, τ_{mp-z} is the torque of the MP around the z-axis and τ_{mp-x} shows the torque of the wrist joint around the x-axis. The results of a series of preliminary experiments such as these showed that the required accuracy for analyzing finger operation could be obtained in the system environment shown in Table 1. However, there was also a need to create certain prediction methods and apply low-pass filtering to remove noise during each motion (Dominguez et al., 2006 [9]). With these tasks under "constrained" conditions, it should be possible to operate a GUI in parallel too, but slightly distant from the touch panel surface. The dynamic analysis results under "constrained" conditions showed only a small value for τ_{mp-x} and τ_{mp-z} the change in twisting torque around the wrist joint, as shown in Fig. 2.

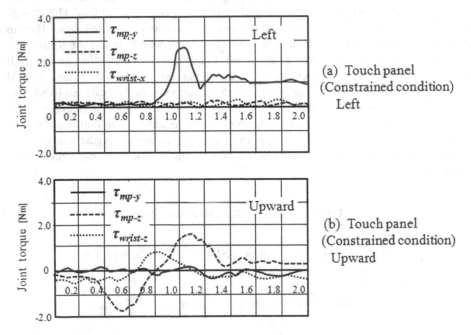

Fig. 2. Typical experimental results for torque values of finger gestures: (a) turning a page to the left and (b) upwards with the index finger. In this figures, τ_{pip-z} is the joint torque of the PIP around the z-axis, both τ_{mp-y} and τ_{mp-z} are the torque of the MP around the y-axis and z-axis, $\tau_{wrist-z}$ is the torque of the wrist around the z-axis, also $\tau_{wrist-x}$ and $\tau_{wrist-z}$ show the torque of the wrist joint around the x-axis and z-axis.

In the next experiment, we attempted to apply dynamic analysis to another typical finger gesture, which in this case was the natural and unconstrained motion shown in Fig. 3. Users often want to control displays with gestures at a distance from them, particularly if not able to touch the display directly due to having wet or dirty hands. These "constraint-free operations" are frequently reported as feeling natural, but in fact they tend to be difficult for inexperienced users because of too many degrees of freedom. To verify these facts mathematically, we attempted to analyze these types of finger gestures dynamically.

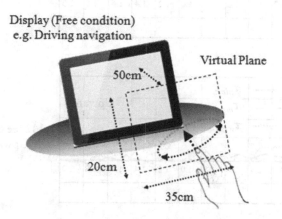

Fig. 3. Typical finger gesture operation under "free" conditions e.g. driving navigation. Usually this is necessary when operating a display using gestures at a distance from the screen. "Virtual plane" placed a transparent plane that was thin and transparent plastic plate (20 cm in length and 35 cm in width)" in 50 cm front of the display

3.3   Result 2

Figure 4 shows typical torque values in the time domain of finger gestures. In these experimental results, τ_{mp-y} is the joint torque of the MP around the y-axis, τ_{mp-z} is the torque of the MP around the z-axis, τ_{pip-z} is the torque of the PIP around the z-axis, and $\tau_{wrist-x}$ shows the torque of the wrist joint around the x-axis. All the subjects noted this to be more difficult than under the "constrained" conditions shown in Fig. 1. Qualitatively, rotational movement around the wrist joint was dominant due to the wrist position as the base not being fixed in this unconstrained situation. Figure 4 shows the typical dynamic analysis results describing such feelings. A comparison of the results in Figs. 2 and 4 suggest that the twisting torques of the wrist joint were observed to dominate during "free condition" operation. Most subjects usually operated the *GUI* using the *MP* joint around the y-axis for (a) moving left and (b) around the z-axis for moving upwards. It appears from the results of analysis that the higher the values of the torque around the wrist joint, the more unstable the operations tend to become.

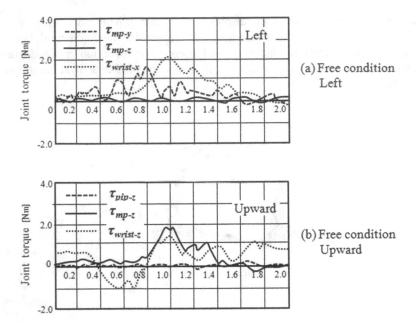

Fig. 4. Typical experimental results of torque value of finger gestures: (a) turning a page to the left. (b) upwards with the index finger ("free" condition). In these figures, τ_{pip-z} is the joint torque of the PIP around the z-axis; both τ_{mp-y} and τ_{mp-z} are the torque of the MP around the y-axis and z-axis, $\tau_{wrist-z}$ is the torque of the wrist around the z-axis, also $\tau_{wrist-x}$ and $\tau_{wrist-z}$ show the torque of the wrist joint around the x-axis and z-axis respectively.

4 Hypothesis and Verification

The authors propose the following hypothesis as a method of overcoming the difficulty faced due to completely free operation with no restraints: they tried to imagine the existence of a restraining surface above the actual surface, as shown in Fig. 3. Under these "pseudo-constrained" conditions, the task feels easier due to a perceived reduction in DOF. As a verification experiment, we placed a transparent plane that we term a "virtual plane (Thin and transparent plastic plate 20 cm in length and 35 cm in width)" in front of the display and asked the subjects to complete the same tasks as in Fig. 1. When asked about how easy they felt the task was, the same twelve subjects answered that it was considerably improved. The results of careful dynamic analysis of the finger gestures during these operations showed that almost all the results were uniformly very similar to the torque changes under the restrained conditions shown in Fig. 2. In other word, the torque values around their wrists had been uniformly suppressed.

4.1 Proposal for a New Improved Ease of Operability

In a completely free operating as shown in Fig. 3, there is potential to improve ease of use by suppressing the torque of the wrist joint around the x-axis. In general, to improve the reliability of the gesture operation, it appears that some tactile feedback would be effective. Electrical stimulation and air pressure have been proposed as a way of providing non-contact tactile feedback (Hachisu et al., 2014 [11]). With these mechanisms, it is likely that tactile feedback will improve if its effect is to counteract the change in torque curve in time series around the wrist $\tau_{wrist-x}$ as shown Fig. 4(a).

5 Conclusion

In this paper, the authors proposed an expanding dynamic motion analysis method for finger gestures. There are some structural differences with the original proposition that was designed for the whole body, such as the degree of freedom (DOF) of each joint, and the cumulative values of dynamic analysis of fingers are much smaller than for the whole body (Naka et al. 2016 [10]). To address these problems, we constructed a high-accuracy measurement system for finger movements and a noise removal method. As the first step, we focused on finger operation of touch panels, which are widely used in mobile phones and tablets, and compared the dynamic mechanisms of a basic gesture under both constrained and free conditions. We obtained the following results from the series of experiments carried out to verify the mechanism quantitatively.

1. The required accuracy for analyzing finger operations could be guaranteed by the system environment shown in Table 1. However, several prediction methods and a low-pass filtering process to remove noise from each motion were needed. With the tasks under "constrained" conditions, we would operate GUI with parallel direction on the touch panel surface, and the dynamic analysis results under "constrained" conditions showed only a small value for $\tau_{wrist-x}$, the change in twisting torque around the wrist joint, as shown in Fig. 2.

2. We also attempted to apply dynamic analysis to another typical finger gesture, this time without constraint, as shown in Fig. 3. These constraint-free operations were usually reported as feeling natural, but in fact that they were often difficult for inexperienced users due to their being too many degrees of freedom. A comparison of these dynamical experimental results showed that twisting torques around the wrist joint tended to dominate in "free condition" operations. Most subjects usually operated the GUI by using the MP joint around the y-axis to indicate movement to the left (a) and around the z-axis for upward movement (b), so it appears that the higher the values of the torque around the wrist joint, the less reliable the operations were.

3. The authors propose the following hypothesis as a method of overcoming the difficulty associated with completely free operation with no restraints: we attempted to intentionally place a restraint surface in the space as shown in Fig. 3. Under these "pseudo-constrained" conditions, the operation felt a good deal easier because of fewer DOF. We placed a transparent plane called a "virtual plane" in front of the display and asked the subjects to engage in the same tasks on it. Dynamic analysis of these tasks showed almost all the measurements to indicate very similar torque changes to those under restrained conditions. In other words, the torque values around their wrists was uniformly suppressed. To improve the difficulty of

completely free operation with no restraints, it would be suggested to cancel the twisting torque curve change around the wrist $\tau_{wrist-x}$ by using tactile feedback.

The experiments shown in this paper indicate that this approach can be effectively adapted to several basic finger gestures. In future studies, it will be necessary to verify further potential for improvement of this model in terms of accuracy or analysis of more complex finger movements. In addition, we would like to work on a method to more accurately capture and analyze finger gestures.

The authors wish to express their special thanks to Panasonic Corporation's PK-project, which supported this research.

Appendix

As mentioned in the Sect. 2, each dynamical torque τ which is generated at each joint can be obtained using motion Eq. 1, employing joint angle θ which is each joint's rotational angle in a time-series data set $(\theta_w, \theta_m, \cdots \theta_d)$. Since this equation is the general formula of the dynamic model, we have to calculate the torque τ using *Lagrange functions* in the following steps.

1. Step-1: We define the joints' rotational angles by the generalized coordinate system θ_i $(i = 0 \sim n)$ and physical parameters of the approximate finger model as shown Fig. 5.

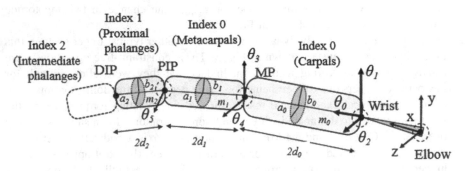

Fig. 5. Generalized finger model for dynamical analysis and definition of joints' rotational angles θi (i = 0 $\sim$ n) and physical parameters. (In case of index finger)

In addition, we used the physical parameter values such as width, length and mass of this approximate finger model as shown in Table 2.

2. Step-2: In generally, *Lagrange function L* of each link structure is given by the following Eq. A.1.

Table 2. The value of each parameter of the approximate model used for calculation: width, length and mass.

Width [mm]		Length [mm]		Mass [g]	
a_0 and b_0	19.4	$2d_0$	100.2	m_0	315.3
a_1 and b_1	15.3	$2d_1$	23.2	m_1	13.5
a_2 and b_2	8.1	$2d_2$	21.4	m_2	2.2

$$L = \sum_{0 \le i \le n} \{(\text{Kinetic energy of link } i) - (\text{Potential energy of link } i)\} \qquad (\text{A.1})$$

3. Step-3: Furthermore *Lagrange equation* of motion Qi is given by the following Eq. A.2.

$$Q_i = \frac{d}{dt}\left(\frac{\partial L}{\partial \theta_i'}\right) - \frac{\partial L}{\partial \theta_i} \quad \text{where i} = 0 \text{ to n} \qquad (\text{A.2})$$

Moreover, the Equation of motion Qi can be written in the following non-linear ordinary differential Eq. A.3 (the general formula is given by Eq. 1).

$$Q_i = \left[\frac{\partial T_j}{\partial \theta_k} J_j \frac{\partial T_j}{\partial \theta_i}\right]\frac{d^2\theta_k}{dt^2} + \sum_{j=i}^{n}\sum_{k=0}^{j}\sum_{l=0}^{j} trace\left[\frac{\partial 2T_j}{\partial \theta_l \partial \theta_k} J_j \frac{\partial T_j}{\partial \theta_i}\right]\frac{d^2\theta_k}{dt^2}\frac{d^2\theta_l}{dt^2}$$
$$- \sum_{j=i}^{n} m_j g^T \frac{\partial T_j}{\partial \theta_i} S_j$$

$$\text{where i} = 0 \text{ to n} \qquad (\text{A.3})$$

In this equation, Qi represents the torque in case of rotational motion, the first term of the right side shows the term of angular velocity, the second term is the part of *Centrifugal force* and *Coriolis force* and the third term is part of *gravity*. θ_i is *i*-th joint's rotational angle and T_j is the coordinate transformation matrix to convert the j-th local coordinate system from the world coordinates. Moreover, J_i is the *Inertia tensor* of the link j, m_i is the mass of *i*-th link. g^T is the *gravity vector* and S_j denotes the *position vector* of center of mass of link j.

4. Step-4: We approximated by the elliptic cylinder of each link as J_i, the length of the ellipse was $2d_i$, and the widths are a_i and b_i respectively as shown in Fig. 5. Furthermore, it was assumed that the density distribution is constant, and the center of gravity was located at the origin of the length of elliptic cylinder. It has been verified that the generality of dynamic analysis is not lost even if approximated in this way. In this simplified case, *Tensor inertia* J_i of the link i can be approximated by the following Eq. A.4 below.

$$J_i = \begin{bmatrix} d_i^2 m_i/3 & 0 & 0 & d_i/2 \\ 0 & a_i^2 m_i/2 & 0 & 0 \\ 0 & 0 & b_i^2 m_i/2 & 0 \\ d_i/2 & 0 & 0 & 1 \end{bmatrix} \tag{A.4}$$

5. *Quasi-Newton method* was used to execute the calculation on the computer based on the above definition formulae. And the adaptive step width Δt of the iterative calculation was selected to 0.07.

References

1. PrimeSense (2010). http://www2.technologyreview.com/tr50/primesense/, Accessed 24 Oct 2015
2. The Microsoft Kinect (2015) https://dev.windows.com/en-us/kinect, Accessed 24 Oct 2015
3. Leap Motion (2015). https://www.leapmotion.com/, Accessed 24 Oct 2015
4. Soli, "Project Soli" (2015). https://www.google.com/atap/project-soli/, Accessed 24 Oct 2015
5. Perception Neuron, developed the cap (2014). https://www.neuronmocap.com/
6. Rautaray, S., Agrawal, A.: Vision based hand gesture recognition for human computer interaction: a survey. Artif. Intell. Rev. **43**(1), 1–54 (2015)
7. Panwar, M.: Hand gesture recognition based on shape parameters. In: Proceedings of the International Conference on Computing, Communication and Applications (ICCCA 2012), pp. 1–6 (2012)
8. Meng, Z., Pan, J., Tseng, K., Zheng, W.: Dominant points based hand finger counting for recognition under skin color extraction in hand gesture control system. In: Proceedings of the 6th International Conference on Genetic and Evolutionary Computing (ICGEC 2012), pp. 364–367 (2012)
9. Dominguez, M., Keaton, T., Sayed, H.: A robust finger tracking method for multimodal wearable computer interfacing. IEEE Trans. Multimedia **8**(5), 956–972 (2006)
10. Naka, T., Ishida, T.: Dynamic motion analysis of gesture interaction. In: Handbook of Research on Human-Computer Interfaces, Developments and Applications, pp. 35–42. IGI Global (2016)
11. Hachisu, T., Fukumoto, M.: Vacuum touch: attractive force feedback interface for haptic interactive surface using air suction. In: Proceedings of the SIGCHI, pp. 411–420 (2014)

Camera Mouse: Dwell vs. Computer Vision-Based Intentional Click Activation

Rafael Zuniga and John Magee[✉]

Math and Computer Science Department,
Clark University, 950 Main Street, Worcester, MA 01610, USA
jmagee@clarku.edu

Abstract. People with severe motion impairments may face challenges using assistive interface devices for common point-and-click tasks. A motion tracking interface, the Camera Mouse, allows users to control a mouse pointer with their head and click by dwelling the pointer over a target. Previous studies evaluated the use of an attached sensor (ClickerAID) as an alternative to the dwell-time clicking. However, the sensor's proprietary hardware is a barrier to adaptation. Here, we present a computer-vision based alternative that can be used to actuate mouse clicks. We conducted a preliminary evaluation of our interface and compare to previous results. Although quantitative evaluation did not achieve the same speed and acuracy as the other measures, the non-contact approach to intentional click activation demonstrates benefits compared to the other techniques.

Keywords: Mouse-replacement interfaces · Camera Mouse · Dwelling · Intentional muscle contractions

1 Introduction

The *Camera Mouse*[1,8] system has been developed to provide computer access for people with severe disabilities. The system tracks the computer users movements with a video camera and translates them into the movements of the mouse pointer on the screen. This system also provides a clicking feature with *dwell-time* selection. This involves hovering over a button for a certain period of time in order to generate a click. While this clicking approach is intuitive and easy to use for some people, it has several disadvantages for other users and for use in certain applications. Anytime the mouse stops moving, a click can be generated, potentially causing unintended selection of whatever happens to be under the link. It is hard to click small buttons or links because users have problems keeping the pointer on top of the button for the time required. Other clicking interfaces such as the *ClickerAID*[2,7] solve the problem of inadvertent clicking but do so with an attached sensor in order to detect a single intentional muscle

---

[1] The Camera Mouse is freely available as a download at http://www.cameramouse. org/.

© Springer International Publishing AG 2017
M. Antona and C. Stephanidis (Eds.): UAHCI 2017, Part II, LNCS 10278, pp. 455–464, 2017.
DOI: 10.1007/978-3-319-58703-5_34

contraction. We present a computer vision based approach to detect intentional muscle contractions such as an "eyebrow shrug" (as in [3,5]), an upward motion followed by a downward motion.

This paper is a follow-up to a previous study [7] that compared dwell-time selections against intentional muscle selections using an evaluation conforming to ISO 9241-9, conducted as an empirical investigation using 2D Fitts law. The method for click activation was a sensor worn in a headband by the users. In the prior study, dwell-time resulted in higher communication throughput, but intentional muscle selections were qualitatively preferred by the participants. The major downside of the intentional muscle selection was that it required specialized hardware, and that the device must be attached physically to the user, causing some discomfort. The contribution of the study now presented are (1) the development of a computer-vision based gesture clicker, and (2) an empirical investigation to compare the new computer-vision based clicker against the prior studys results.

2   Alternative Point and Click Interfaces

Users of mouse replacement interfaces perform two different tasks when using a graphical user interface. These tasks involve first positioning the mouse pointer ("pointing") followed by selecting the user interface element under the pointer ("clicking"). Here we investigate an alternative hardware-free mouse selection technique: muscle-shrug selection. We then compare it against two other selection techniques: Dwell-Time and a single intentional muscle contraction with an attached sensor.

Our investigation is targeted for selection techniques that can be used with the Camera Mouse. The Camera Mouse provides a time-based selection technique called Dwell-Time. This technique involves hovering the pointer over a user interface element for a specified period of time in order to actuate a click (Fig. 1). Because of the time-based nature of this selection technique, there exist several issues such as the "Midas Touch" [4] problem and selecting small user interface elements.

The "Midas Touch" problem refers to the unintentional selection of any user interface element. The dwell-time technique relies on checking whether the Camera Mouse should actuate a click or not at all times. This means that even if the user is merely reading text on screen without the intention of clicking, but happens to stay still while the pointer is on top of a button, the Camera Mouse will actuate an unwanted click.

Another common problem involves trying to click small user interface elements. For the dwell-time technique to be responsive a shorter dwell-time configuration should be chosen, one to two seconds is usually best. The problem is that users might have problems maintaining the pointer on top of a user interface element long enough to actuate a click. Therefore, there are drawbacks regardless of what dwell-time configuration the user chooses. If the dwell-time configuration is too long, there is less inadvertent clicking but harder to select

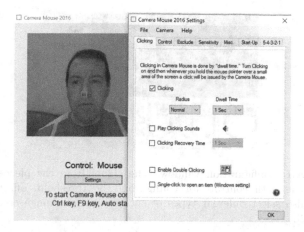

Fig. 1. Camera Mouse - tracking of a selected feature and menu system for dwell-time click configuration.

small user interface elements. If the dwell-time configuration is too short, the technique is more responsive but causes more inadvertent clicking. For other users with involuntary motions, holding the mouse still may be impossible for any period of time.

ClickerAID offers an alternative selection technique. It uses an attached sensor to detect intentional muscle contractions and actuates a mouse click when a contraction is recognized. This technique can be flexible because the user can decide what muscle group works best for him or her (e.g., eyebrow, jaw, forearm, ankle).

ClickerAID uses a Piezoelectric sensor in direct contact with the skin to measure small muscle movements. The user can choose any small muscle group that they can intentionally control. The sensor can be held in place with some elastic tape. The prior ClickAID studies tended to use a headband to hold the sensor over the brow muscle. Therefore, an eyebrow raise was used to control the clicking. The system is customizable by modifying a configurable threshold to determine when a mouse click should be simulated. The configuration screen is shown in Fig. 2. Since the system requires specialized hardware, accessibility is drastically reduced (i.e. the number of people who could easily adopt the interface).

In the next section we introduce the Muscle-Shrug selection technique that has capabilities similar to that of the ClickerAID but is completely software based.

3   Muscle-Shrug Technique

The Muscle-Shrug selection technique is a computer vision approach to a clicking in a mouse-replacement interface. This technique allows the user to select

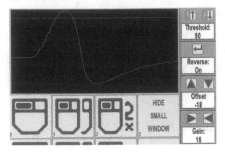

Fig. 2. ClickerAID configuration window. The signal from the piezoelectric sensor is displayed along with controls for configuring the threshold, offsets, and gains. The user can also select different types of clicking modes. Image credit Felzer and Rinderknecht [2].

two features (eyebrow, eye, jaw, chin, etc.) and actuate a click by making a "shrugging" motion with the muscle group that belongs to one of the features. Muscle-shrug selection also allows the same flexibility the ClickerAID does; the user can choose which ever pair of features work best for him or her. Furthermore, muscle-shrug selection can adapt to the user's range of movement and to the speed of the shrug and because of this it can also adapt to the user's distance from the camera.

Similar to the ClickerAID, the Muscle-Shrug selection technique solves the Midas Touch problem by actuating a click through an intentional muscle-gesture instead of a time based technique like dwell-time. Muscle-Shrug selection also has the advantage that performing double clicks is possible as compared against the dwell-time selection technique.

3.1   Computer Vision Clicking

Muscle-shrug selection takes advantage of the same tracking algorithm that the Camera Mouse implements, in order to keep track of the position of two features (eyebrow, eye, jaw, chin, etc.). We then define a shrug (a click actuation) as an increase in the distance between the two features followed by a decrease. This way we can detect the upward and downward motion of an eyebrow shrug or the downward and upward motion of opening and closing the users jaw. See Fig. 3.

With the users visual input, we calculate the change in distance between the two selected features across a specified number of frames. At every frame, our goal is to process N frames and calculate the average change in distance in terms of pixels of the two features being tracked across the first $N/2$ frames and the last $N/2$ frames. Where N is usually a number between eight to twenty depending on the framerate of the camera feed. If one of the features being tracked do a shrug type of motion (upward movement followed by a downward movement) then the average change of the first $N/2$ frames will be a positive number and the last $N/2$ frames will be a negative number. Then we compare these values to a positive and a negative threshold that can be adjusted to the user. If there is ever a frame where both thresholds are surpassed, a click is actuated.

A problem that we encountered was that depending on the speed of the shrug, more than one click can be actuated from a single shrug. That issue was easily solved by setting a small time delay after the first click recognition in order to not actuate any other recognized shrugs for a small period of time. Note that the delay is not long enough to affect the users ability to double click.

Muscle-Shrug selection gives us the flexibility to adapt to the user in two different ways. It can adapt to the users mobility by adjusting the thresholds either manually or through calibration. It can also adapt to the users movement speed by varying N, the number of frames we use to perform the calculations. A higher N being better to recognize slower shrugs and a lower N being better to recognize faster shrugs.

3.2 Failure Mode

Muscle-Shrug selection has some disadvantages though. Since our algorithm depends on the tracking algorithm of the camera mouse, if the tracking of any of the two features fails, the muscle-shrug selection will not be able to perform the calculations correctly until the features are assigned again. This means that moving out of the camera, moving too quickly, or anything that will hinder the tracking will also affect the muscle-shrug selection performance.

This failure mode is the *same* as that of the Camera Mouse: loss of tracking requires manual initialization. Prior experience with Camera Mouse users "in the wild" have shown that caregivers and assistants can easily understand a basic failure mode of: reset the tracking if it is lost.

4 Preliminary Evaluation

4.1 Participants and Apparatus

We performed an evaluation of the muscle-shrug selection technique using the Camera Mouse, replicating the evaluation conditions from the previous study comparing dwell-time selection versus ClickerAID selection [7]. This is a preliminary evaluation of dwell-time selection our proposed selection mechanism here. The pointing task is done with the Camera Mouse. Five participants, two female and three males, mean age 20, participated in this evaluation.

The interface test was conducted on a laptop screen viewed from a distance of approximately 2.5 ft. The integrated camera of the laptop, with a resolution of 1280×720, was used. The following Camera Mouse settings were used for all participants: medium horizontal and vertical gain, very low smoothing, and dwell-time click area was set to "Normal" and 1.0 s. Our click actuation selection was based on movements of the jaw.

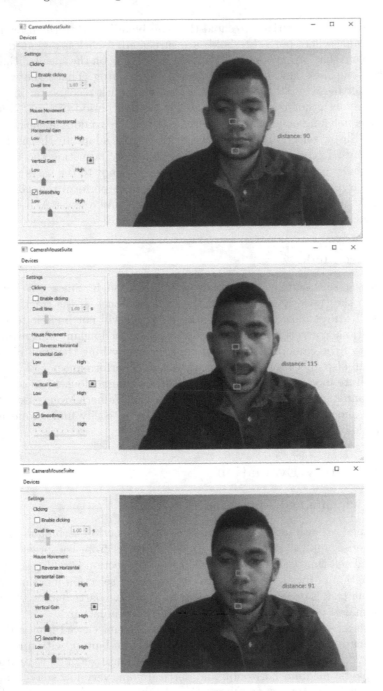

Fig. 3. Muscle-Shrug Detection - Two features are tracked with the Camera Mouse's computer vision tracking. The distance between the two features is monitored for an increase followed by a decrease. In the example above, the points start close together and move further apart as the jaw opens, then return closer together as the jaw closes. This sequence triggers a mouse click.

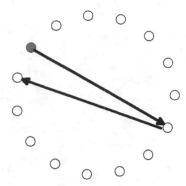

Fig. 4. FittsTaskTwo - Intended targets are highlighted in the a sequence as depicted by the overlaid arrows. Sizes and distances to targets are configurable. The software records and calculates movement time, throughput, error rates, and number of target re-entries. Trajectories of mouse movements are also recorded.

4.2 Procedure and Design

An interactive evaluation tool called FittsTaskTwo[2] [6] was used to perform the preliminary evaluation. Users performed repeated target selection tasks that involve first positioning the mouse pointer over a target and then selecting it with a click (Fig. 4). Log files from the tool were then analyzed to compare performance between the click modalities. Log files are also used to generate traces of mouse movements during the tests.

Each participant's session contained four sequences of thirteen targets at amplitudes 300 and 600 and widths 50 and 80 pixels. The main independent variable was input method with the following conditions:

- CM_DWELL – Camera Mouse with 1.0 s dwell time,
- CM_CA – Camera Mouse with ClickerAID,
- CM_MS – Camera Mouse with Muscle Shrug.

The dependent variables were movement time (speed), throughput (speed and accuracy – bits/s), error rate (%), and target re-entries.

4.3 Results and Discussion

We report our average measurements for the CM_MS condition and compare against CM_CA and CM_DWELL previously reported. The mean movement time for CM_MS was 4284 ms versus 2226 for CM_CA and 2609 for CM_DWELL.

For throughput (speed and accuracy), the CM_MS fared worse (0.67 bits/s) compared to CM_CA (1.43 bits/s) and CM_DWELL (1.28 bits/s).

---

[2] The software is freely available as a download at http://www.yorku.ca/mack/ HCIbook/.

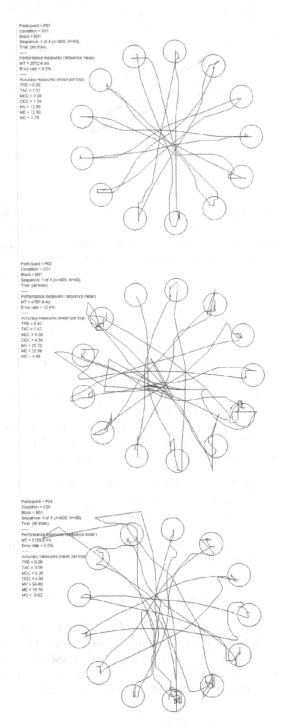

Fig. 5. Traces of mouse trajectories in target selection task.

Error rate demonstrated larger differences with means of 19.6% for CM_MS, 8.1% for CM_DWELL, and 10.8% for CM_CA.

Traces of mouse movements from three participants on the same target amplitude and width are shown in Fig. 5. The first user had more experience with the interface and his trace demonstrates more-or-less direct movements between targets and their selections. The other users were not as familiar with Camera Mouse or our selection interface - their traces show that the mouse pointer deviates significantly from the intended target trajectories. A longer study may show a learning effect and bring the performance of our system more in line with the other approaches.

In our subjective observation of the participants, we noted that many participants performed well for part of the experiment, but the tracking of one of the features drifting away from their original positions caused degraded performance. Sometimes the features would be lost completely and the tracking would have to be manually reset. This additional time was a factor in the averages reported above.

5   Conclusion and Future Direction

Our approach gives the user more control as to when the user wants to click, helping to address the Midas Touch problem. It is also more accessible for users because it does not require any hardware such as the sensor in the ClickerAID. Also, our algorithm is not limited to using nose and eyebrow. Nose and jaw actually seemed to perform better because the tracking algorithm worked better on them. Unfortunately, if the tracking algorithm fails, muscle-shrug selection will not work. At the same time though, this means that the performance of muscle-shrug selection will continue to improve as tracking algorithms get more accurate.

The muscle-shrug selection technique has room for improvements. A future direction can be to automatically recover the features being tracked if the user ever moves them out of the camera or moves too quickly.

References

1. Betke, M., Gips, J., Fleming, P.: The Camera Mouse: visual tracking of body features to provide computer access for people with severe disabilities. IEEE Trans. Neural Syst. Rehabil. Eng. **10**(1), 1–10 (2002)
2. Felzer, T., Rinderknecht, S.: ClickerAID: a tool for efficient clicking using intentional muscle contractions. In: Proceedings of ACM SIGACCESS Conference on Computers and Accessibility (ASSETS 2012), pp. 257–258. ACM (2012)
3. Grauman, K., Betke, M., Lombardi, J., Gips, J., Bradski, G.: Communication via eye blinks and eyebrow raises: video-based human-computer interfaces. UAIS **2**(4), 359–373 (2003)
4. Jacob, R.J.K.: What you look at is what you get: eye movement-based interaction techniques. In: Proceedings of SIGCHI Conference on Human Factors in Computing Systems (CHI 1990), pp. 11–18. ACM (1990)

5. Lombardi, J., Betke, M.: A camera-based eyebrow tracker for hands-free computer control via a binary switch. In: 7th ERCIM Workshop User Interfaces for All, UI4ALL 2002, pp. 199–200 (2002)
6. MacKenzie, I.S.: Human-Computer Interaction: An Empirical Research Perspective. Elsevier, New Delhi (2013)
7. Magee, J., Felzer, T., MacKenzie, I.S.: Camera mouse + ClickerAID: dwell vs. single-muscle click actuation in mouse-replacement interfaces. In: Antona, M., Stephanidis, C. (eds.) UAHCI 2015. LNCS, vol. 9175, pp. 74–84. Springer, Cham (2015). doi:10.1007/978-3-319-20678-3_8
8. Magee, J.J., Epstein, S., Missimer, E.S., Kwan, C., Betke, M.: Adaptive mouse-replacement interface control functions for users with disabilities. In: Stephanidis, C. (ed.) UAHCI 2011. LNCS, vol. 6766, pp. 332–341. Springer, Heidelberg (2011). doi:10.1007/978-3-642-21663-3_36

Author Index